ROYAL NAVY TRAWLERS
Part Two: Requisitioned Vessels

By Gerald Toghill

Dedication

To the men of the Royal Naval Patrol Service
Who went down to the sea in their little ships
To meet the foe.

CONTENTS

AUTHOR'S NOTES - VOL II

In this, the second part of *Trawlers of the Royal Navy*, the subject of Requisitioned Trawlers is considered. In modern parlance they would be referred to as STUFT – Ships Taken Up From Trade – a very apt description and they comprised the vast majority of Trawlers employed in both World Wars. This book is a record and, I hope, a recognition, of Britain's Fishing Fleet going to War.

Following the excellent reception of the first part of this work - *Admiralty Built Trawlers* - I acknowledge the numerous and vociferous demands for an Index and am delighted to report that the Index for both volumes is contained at the end of this book. All too well I know the feeling of utter frustration in picking up a book of reference only to find there is no Index and facing the prospect of hours of searching to find the snippet of information required. I sincerely hope that this, together with my apology, makes amends.

A second apology is in order for the inclusion on page 530 of the necessary Addenda to the First Part. There were a number of omissions in the book which readers were quick to point out. In the first place I had inadvertantly missed out two vessels, of the Isles Class - CAMPENIA and ST. KILDA - and a number of the Mersey Class. I have hastened to make amends. At the same time I have corrected the misplacing of the pictures of BASSETT/MASTIFF and these amendments are offered together with my humble apologies.

Once again the obtaining of photographs from between 50 and 90 years ago has been a massive headache and I am sincerely grateful to all those who assisted me in this enormous task, not least my Editor, Steve Bush of Maritime Books. In particular I feel the need to express my gratitude to Mr. Tom Gamble for permission to reproduce what is surely the most amazing picture of a Trawler, that of the PICTON CASTLE in her new role as a sailing vessel.

Abbreviations contained in this volume are the same as for Book One and a full list of them is contained on page 223 of that volume.

Finally may I draw the readers attention once more to page 226 of Book One where I have acknowledged the men of the Royal Naval Patrol Service and the many others who assisted me in these two volumes. My debt of gratitude is immense.

INTRODUCTION

The Requisitioning Programme

Six years before the outbreak of the First World War the Admiralty, in their search for a means to counteract the increasing menace of the sea-mine, had purchased into the Royal Navy two commercial Trawlers, ALGOMA and ANDES. These had been attached to the Naval establishment at Portland to carry out evaluation tests regarding their suitability for minesweeping tasks and then, suitability confirmed, to carry out experiments in minesweeping methods. Impressed with the capabilities of these vessels the Admiralty purchased several more of their kind, and set them to work on yet more trials. The next step was the formulation of plans for the requisitioning of commercial vessels from the fishing fleet should the need arise. Shortly after, in 1910, the first plans were laid for the recruitment or 'call-up' of men from the fishing industry to man such vessels, an organization which was to be known as the Royal Naval Patrol Service.

Within a few short years, in 1914, these plans were hastily activated when war was declared. The original estimate had allowed for the requisitioning of 150 vessels together with crews to man them, but the requirements of the war soon outstripped this very conservative estimate to the extent that by the end of the conflict in 1918, over 1,800 trawlers, and thousands of men to man them, had been employed in theatres of war around the world.

Britain's Fishing Fleet in 1914 and again in 1939 was vast. From Newlyn to Wick huge numbers of trawlers plied their trade in deep waters. Virtually every harbour in the Kingdom had at least a few vessels employed in deep-sea fishing whilst the major fishing ports, Grimsby, Hull, Aberdeen, Fleetwood, Lowestoft etc. could boast gigantic fleets. Often trawlers were owned by companies comprising just one person, or perhaps a family or friends, owning just one vessel. At the other end of the scale there were the giant companies like the Consolidated Fisheries and Sleight of Grimsby, Kingston STC, Pickering & Haldane, Jutland STC, Kelsall Bros. & Beeching, and Hudson SFC of Hull. In North Shields the Hastie Family and Irvin & Sons owned large numbers of trawlers, whilst in Cardiff Neale & West reigned supreme. Other prolific owners were spread around the country – Devlin of Leith, Inglis of Peebles and Wyre in Fleetwood to name but a few.

When it came to the Admiralty's requisitioning programme just about all trawlers were grist to the mill. None was too big or too small to avoid the demands of the Royal Navy in its quest for hulls to convert to Minesweepers, Anti Submarine vessels and the dozens of other jobs the Navy had in mind for them. Even the Royal National Mission to Deep Sea Fisherman were obliged to offer up their two missionary trawlers, *Alpha* and *Joseph and Sarah Miles* in 1915, whilst the big companies saw hundreds of their vessels sail away to war. The largest company at Grimsby, Consolidated Fisheries saw 63 of their vessels go in the 1914-18 War and 68 in 1939-45 and their near rivals in business, Sleight, surrendered 60 in the First World War and 30 in the Second. Across the water in Hull the Hellyer company supplied 37 and 18 respectively and Kelsall Bros. and

Beeching 34 in the first war but only 5 in the second. Strange to relate, the requisitioning of a vessel for war was neither let nor hindrance to the sale/purchase of trawlers. Thus a vessel requisitioned from one owner may well have been returned to a completely new owner at the end of its requisitioning, it having been sold on in the meantime.

There were many more trawlers requisitioned during the First World War than in the Second. Between 1914 and 1918 over 1,800 trawlers were taken up from trade compared to just over 1,100 between 1939 and 1945. Even allowing for the fact that the figure of 1,800 is bolstered by the 300 odd trawlers requisitioned in 1917 for the Fishery Reserve (*See Royal Navy Trawlers, Part One: Admiralty Built Trawlers, page 9*), there were still several hundred more taken up in that conflict. This is mainly explained by the Admiralty's building programme during the Second World War. As soon as the British building yards had become geared up in the early years of the war, escort vessels were one of the great priorities. The Flower Class corvettes began rolling off the building slips together with new frigates and destroyers. As soon as they were completed these ships were employed post haste on convoy duties so that the overworked and beaten-up trawlers could be relieved of their duties. At the same time a massive building programme for minesweepers got underway so that by as early as 1943 trawlers were being returned to the fishing fleet, and by the end of 1944 there was a veritable flood of vessels returning to the fishing ports, something which had not happened in the First World War when trawlers were still being requisitioned as late as 1917 and 1918.

Employment of Requisitioned Trawlers

As a general rule all the available vessels were graded by size, speed and general sea-worthiness. At the outbreak of the First World War anti-submarine warfare was in its infancy and the main weapons available were the 3.5-inch or 7.5-inch Bomb Thrower which fired a grenade type projectile. These were linked with Listening Hydrophones, a very basic and not very efficient piece of equipment, which could detect sound from underwater. The vast majority of vessels were, therefore, converted for much needed minesweeping. By the start of the next great conflict, however, huge advances had been made and Asdic and the Depth-charge had arrived. The newer, larger or faster trawlers were armed with these weapons and converted for Anti-Submarine service. They were formed into groups of 4/5 vessels and employed, in the main, on convoy escort duties. In the fullness of time a lot of these rugged little ships were to face the full fury of the Atlantic and Arctic as well as the violence of the enemy as they shepherded their charges through U-Boat infested waters. Indeed, in the early stages of the war the RN imposed heavy demands on them, particularly the A/S trawlers that carried out their duties as convoy escorts across the great oceans. Their extraordinary sea-keeping qualities became legend. In the full fury of the storm-lashed North Atlantic or Arctic, these game little ships stood to their tasks. That there were so many losses is not to be wondered at, but the fact that so few were lost to the elements alone is a massive vote of confidence in their designers and builders and to the skills and endurance of their commanders and crews.

Those trawlers of a slightly older vintage, or slower or smaller, were converted to Minesweepers and these comprised the vast majority in both World Wars. Although some were deployed overseas, they were, in the main, employed in home waters keeping the ports and sea-lanes of the UK clear. A reflection on the bravery of the men who manned these vessels is to be seen in the number of losses due to them falling prey to the very weapons they were employed to seek out. Large numbers of them were mined whilst sweeping.

Those vessels which were left after the A/S and M/Ss had taken their pick were converted for employment on a host of other tasks. The main group were Armed Patrol Vessels, but there were also the Boom Defence Vessels, Boom Gate Vessels, Examination Service, harbour service etc, all tasks which they carried out superbly.

In 1944 a number of trawlers were selected for an extremely important job. Freed up by the increasing flow of purpose built escort vessels and minesweepers from shipyards at home and abroad these trawlers were hastily converted to fuel-carrying and water-carrying duties. Those vessels converted for fuel carrying were given the generic name 'Essos'. Planning for the D-Day operations was well advanced and recognised that there would be a huge demand for fuel to support the landing troops and it was these vessels, and a host of others, which supplied them, criss-crossing the Channel countless times with the liquid gold which kept the tanks and vehicles of the invasion forces moving. With the advent of PLUTO, (Pipeline Under The Ocean), their services were, in the main, no longer required and they were mostly returned to the fishing fleet by the end of 1944.

A number of vessels were requisitioned only to be found unsuitable for conversion and were returned to their owners within a few weeks. In their own way they too contributed to the war effort by helping the Admiralty strike some sort of balance between those vessels requisitioned and those necessary for the much depleted fishing fleet to play its part in helping to feed the Nation. They had learned a sharp lesson on this subject in 1917 (See Vol 1 - page 9).

The requisitioning process in 1939 had not gone ahead without causing a few ripples in the fishing ports. In Grimsby, for example, it had been reported in the local press that the Admiralty had paid no less than £2,000,000, an unimaginable sum at that time, for the trawlers taken up from the port. All very well for the owners, but what of the fishermen? They were unemployed and unhappy. Bearing in mind that the Admiralty had not yet made overtures to these men to sign up to man the requisitioned vessels, it was looked upon in the light that the owners had made a packet out of a deal which had deprived them, the fishermen, of their livelihood. Local MPs took up the cry and assurances were quickly made that work would be found for the unemployed men. To assist this the Admiralty agreed that the conversion work for a number of trawlers should be carried out in Doig's Yard at Grimsby and in the Humber Graving Dock at Immingham, a promise which was quickly fulfilled as, in just a matter of days, the first ships, CRESTFLOWER, DALMATIA and WAVEFLOWER, arrived at Grimsby to be taken in hand at Doig's whilst others were sent to Hull.

As soon as they were fitted out and armed the trawlers went to war. Among their crews were large numbers of well-seasoned veterans of the First World War, but even these could have had little idea of just how ferocious this new conflict was to be. The Minesweepers and Anti-Submarine trawlers in particular were to be involved in a war so costly, so bloody, that even the most pessimistic could not have foreseen it. Nor could they have foreseen the incredible feats of endurance and bravery that these diminutive warships and their crews were to undertake. A good example of the Minesweeper's service is the gallant ROLLS ROYCE. Launched in 1906 as HERCULES she was requisitioned in 1914 and served as a Minesweeper throughout that conflict before returning to the fishing grounds. Changing ownership between the wars and renamed ROLLS ROYCE she was called-up again in 1940 and converted once more to a Minesweeper. Almost all her service was carried out on the East Coast during which she swept and destroyed an incredible 197 mines and despatched an enemy aircraft.

HMT ST. LOMAN was only three years old when she was called up in 1939 and there-fore qualified for conversion to Anti-Submarine warfare. When she left the fitting out yard in September of that year and headed north to Aberdeen to join the 15th A/S Group no-one aboard could have foreseen that before they were to lay down their arms again they would not only sail the grey inhospitable waters of the north, including Norway, but the Eastern Seaboard of the USA and the southern waters around the toe of the African continent. During that time they would be responsible for the destruction of no fewer than six enemy submarines, rescue a RAF pilot from the sea, and earn an extraordinary collection of awards. One DSC with a Bar for the CO, Lt. Colin Warwick, two further DSCs to her officers, nine DSMs, three Mentions-in-Despatches and two Bronze Medals of the Royal Humane Society. It's a wonder that it wasn't necessary to lighten ship to make way for the weight of the medals they earned through sheer bravery!

Losses

A brief trawl (no pun intended!) through the figures for both Wars reveals that approximately one in every six trawlers which went to war failed to survive. It also reveals some surprising statistics. In the two conflicts approximately 500 trawlers were lost. Perhaps not so surprising is the fact that nearly half of that total was by the dreaded sea-mine and that by far the most of those were the minesweepers themselves, which proves what a dangerous occupation it was.

The surprise comes when the figures for wrecks and collisions are studied. No fewer than 85 vessels are recorded as having foundered or been wrecked. Bearing in mind previous comments about their extraordinary sea-keeping qualities it is not surprising that only a very small part of this figure is attributable to foundering - less than a dozen - which means that more than 70 were wrecked. When, in conjunction with this figure, that for collisions is taken into account, the situation becomes even stranger. Throughout the two Wars 62 trawlers were lost in collisions, all but a very few in confined waters. These figures convey that very nearly one third of all trawler losses were due to these two phenomena. The obvious conclusion to draw from this fact is that trawlers were extreme-ly unhandy vessels, particularly in confined waters and, yet, when the old trawler hands are consulted on the matter they maintain that this was not the case and that, despite their being single-screwed they were reasonably handy vessels. It is not even the case that these collisions were confined to hostilities. The records show that even in peacetime when they went about their ordinary work they showed a great propensity for collision – often with each other. The records are littered with details of collisions. The hapless Grimsby trawler ATHENIAN, having safely completed her service as an Auxiliary Patrol Vessel before being converted to a minesweeper, returned to the fishing fleet to become involved in two collisions, one in the 1940s and another in the 1960s in which both the other trawlers were sunk. The question as to what drove so many of them to take the ground or to collide with such frequency remains a mystery.

In the First World War air power had made little impact on the war at sea but by the Second World War aircraft had been honed into a particularly vicious weapon, as evinced by the fact that 71 trawlers were destroyed by enemy air attack, mostly off the East Coast of the UK in the direct flight path of enemy aircraft attacking the mainland.

Another weapon of this war was the German equivalent of the MTB, the E-Boat, and 15 trawlers fell victim to their operations, again mostly off the East Coast involving attacks on convoys.

The Submarine was always a serious threat and they claimed a further 48. Of these 45 fell to U-Boats and the remaining three to Italian Submarines in the Mediterranean in the Second World War. Frequently they were torpedoed but on occasions they were captured, their crews taken prisoner, set adrift in the boats and the trawlers then despatched by gunfire. One remarkable surface action took place on the 11th July 1916. Three minesweeping trawlers, ERA, ONWARD and NELLIE NUTTEN had been detailed to escort a number of fishing trawlers to sea and when they were approximately 100 miles to the E. of Aberdeen they were confronted by no fewer than four German U-Boats, U-46, U-49, U-52 and U-69. There ensued a gun action in which all three escorting trawlers were sunk but there is no record of any of the fishing fleet having been destroyed. It appears that the three trawlers took on the four S/Ms allowing their charges to escape.

The remaining losses were attributable to surface action, seven, (including the extraordinary little JUNIPER taking on two German Battleships, a 10,000T cruiser and four destroyers) and 18 to other causes such as fire, explosion, destroyed on the stocks and several to unknown causes.

The high rate of loss of these game little vessels can do no other than to raise the highest sense of respect and gratitude for the men of the Royal Naval Patrol Service who manned them.

Groups

Groups in this instance refer not to operational groups such as minesweeping flotillas or A/S Groups, but to their nomenclature. Some owners became somewhat fanciful in naming their vessels whilst others became positively sporting. The Consolidated Fishing Co. of Grimsby had a large fleet named after football clubs, COVENTRY CITY, DERBY COUNTY etc., whilst the Crampin Co., also of Grimsby named a number of their fleet after cricketers, BRADMAN, HAMMOND etc. Sleight of Grimsby was even more fanci-ful with their fleet bearing names beginning with the letter R and ending with o, RALCO,

REBOUNDO, RECEPTO etc. In North Shields Irvin and Son named a number of their vessels with the prefix 'Ben' as in BEN HOLDEN, BEN IVER, BEN LOYAL etc. but this tended to be a little confusing as a number of other owners also used the prefix 'Ben'. H. Markham of Grimsby possessed a number of vessels bearing 'Shire' names, AYRESHIRE, FIFESHIRE, etc. but just to confuse matters each vessel was allotted its own company. The AYRESHIRE was registered, for example, as being owned by the Ayreshire Company and the FIFESHIRE by the Fifeshire Company and so on.

The conclusion

With the cessation of hostilities in 1918 and again in 1945 the requisitioned trawlers of the Royal Navy were gradually released from their duties and sent back to their owners. The minesweeping trawlers of 1918 had to wait a good deal longer as there were still massive amounts of mines both enemy and 'friendly' which had to be swept and so their release was delayed considerably, but in 1945, thanks to the Admiralty's minesweeper building programme the release was much swifter. The prolific numbers of minesweepers of the BYMS, MMS and Algerine Classes, together with the classes of Admiralty built trawlers, meant that within a short time all requisitioned trawlers were released from service. Trawler owners throughout the land welcomed their returning vessels and set them about earning their keep once again. Some ships were so beaten-up and worn out by their War service that they would never sail to the fishing grounds again but the gaps left by these and by those which had been lost in the conflicts were soon filled when the Admiralty-built trawlers were released (*See Royal Navy Trawlers - Part One: Admiralty Built Trawlers*). The Admiralty's foresight in initiating this building programme now bore fruit. Once more the fleets sailed to the fishing grounds near and far. Food was still rationed and scarce on shore and there were millions of hungry mouths to feed. For some a much more adventurous life lay ahead, particularly for those sold abroad many of which were to serve in other navies. An example of this is the CWG-built STALWART. Launched in 1914 she was 'called-up' as a minesweeper and returned home to Grimsby in 1919. She was sold to Spanish owners in 1921 and that led to her being commissioned into the Basque Navy in 1936. The Spanish Nationalist Navy captured her in 1937 and took her into their navy and there she remained until in 1985, at the grand old age of 71, she went to the breakers. During her life she sailed under five names: *Stalwart*, STALWART (RN), STALWART II (RN), *Santa Rosa* (Spanish), GAZ TIEZ (Basque Navy) and finally VIRGEN DEL CARMEN (Nationalist Navy).

During their service in 1939-45 requisitioned trawlers carried out a wide variety of tasks some of which were strange and unforeseen, like the 245T Aberdeen trawler GENERAL BOTHA which achieved stardom when she appeared in an Ealing film playing the part of a German ship. There were some notable first and lasts amongst them, too. As mentioned previously, the indefatigable ROLLS ROYCE was the first minesweeper to record 100 mines swept and by the end of her service was only a few short of 200. The last attack to be made on a U-Boat was carried out off Iceland by NORTHERN SKY on the penultimate day of the war, and the last Royal Navy warship to be sunk by a U-Boat was the hapless EBOR WYKE, again off Iceland, when, on 2nd May, she was torpedoed, and sank leaving only one survivor.

In two World Wars requisitioned trawlers had between them steamed countless thousands of miles and served in every theatre of war from the vast wastes of the Arctic to the Far East via the Mediterranean, South Africa, and the Eastern Seaboard of the United States. The ubiquitous trawlers were to be found sweeping, detecting, escorting, ferrying stores, water, fuel and personnel anywhere and everywhere. It is extremely doubtful if it will ever appreciated just how enormous is the debt of gratitude owed to them.

Post Second World War the Royal Naval Patrol Service that had manned the trawlers was disbanded and their base at Lowestoft was closed down. Little remains there now except the very excellent RNPS museum and an equally splendid War Memorial. The Admiralty, however, still maintains its Requisitioning Programme but the training of reserves now comes under the Royal Naval Reserve. No doubt the orders for the Programme are gathering dust somewhere in the MoD and it is to be fervently hoped that the necessity to sweep away that dust never again arises.

Part II
REQUISITIONED VESSELS

ABELARD   1914/16   Displacement: 187TG
                                                 Armament: 1 x 6pdr
                                                 Admty No: 151
                                                 Port Reg: M. 17
1909: Launched. 1914: Requisitioned in August and converted to a M/S. 1916: LOST. Wrecked off Plymouth Breakwater on 24th December.

ABERDEEN   1914/19   Displacement: 163TG 69TN
                                                  Engines: 45HP
                                                 Armament: 1 x 6pdr
                                                 Admty No: 639
                                                 Port Reg: GY. 129
1896: Launched. Built at Govan. Owned by Consolidated Fisheries of Grimsby. 1914: Requisitioned in August. 1919: Returned to owners.

ABERGELDIE   1915/19   Displacement: 200TG 86TN
                                                  Engines: 76HP
                                                 Armament: 1 x 6pdr
                                                 Admty No: 1508
                                                 Port Reg: A. 391
1915: Launched. Built at Aberdeen. Owned by M.J & J. Ellison of Aberdeen. Requisitioned in July. 1919: Returned to owners. 1938: Owned by Irvine & Sons of North Shields.

ABOYNE   1914/19   Displacement: 233TG 86TN
                                                  Engines: 68HP
                                                 Armament: 1 x 6pdrAA
                                                 Admty No: 65
                                                 Port Reg: A. 183.
1908: Launched. Built at Aberdeen. Owned by A. Robb of Torry. 1914: Requisitioned in August and converted to a M/S. 1919: Returned to owners.

ABRONIA   1914/19 1939/40 Displacement: 242TG 21TN
                                                 Engines: 63HP
                                                 Armament: 1 x 12pdr
                                                 Admty No: 704
                                                 Port Reg: GY. 112
                                                 P.No: WWII: FY. 734
1906: Launched Built at Selby by Cochrane. Owned by the North Eastern SFC of Grimsby. 1914: Requisitioned in November and converted to a M/S. 1919: Returned to owners. 1938: Owned by T.C.& F. Moss of Grimsby. 1939: Requisitioned in November

and converted to a M/S. 1940: LOST. Foundered in the Thames on 7th September. 1941: Raised. 1947: BU.

ACHILLES	1915/18	Displacement: 225TG
		Armament: 1 x 6pdr
		Admty No: 293
		Port Reg: GY. 182

1906: Launched. 1915: Requisitioned in August. Renamed ACHILLES II in September. 1918: LOST. Mined off the Shipwash LV on 26th June.

| ACHILLES II | | See under ACHILLES above |

ACHROITE	1939/45	Displacement: 314TG 138TN
		Engines: 89HP = 11.4K
		Armament: 1 x 12pdr
		Port Reg: H. 81
		P.No: FY. 914

1934: Launched. Built at Beverley by CWG. Owned by Kingston STC of Hull. 1939: Requisitioned in August and converted to a M/S. Joined the 19th M/S Group based at Grimsby. 1945: Returned to owners. 1963: Sold to BU in Ireland. Developing engine trouble whilst being delivered to the breakers, she ran aground and was re-sold to BU in situ.

ACTIVE	1915/18	Displacement: 185TG 75TN
		Engines: 50HP
		Armament: 1 x 6pdr
		Admty No: 2768
		Port Reg: PD. 361

1899: Launched. Built at Irvine. Owned by the Peterhead TC of Peterhead. 1915: Requisitioned in August and renamed ACTIVE IV. 1918: Returned to owners in November. 1938: Owned by Robertson of Aberdeen. PR: A. 897.

| ACTIVE IV | 1915/18 | See under ACTIVE above |

ACUBA	1914/19	Displacement: 211TG
		Armament: 1 x 3pdr
		Port Reg: GY.117

1914: Requisitioned in December and converted to a BDV. 1919: Returned to owners.

| ADASTRAL | | See under WILLIAM GILLETT |
| | | (Vol 1 p192) |

| ADAM | | See under THOMAS MALONEY |
| | | (See Addenda p532) |

ADELE   See under KINGFISHER 1915

ADMIRAL CRADOCK   1917/19   Displacement: 295TG 123TN
                                         Engines: 93HP
                                         Port Reg: FD. 11
1914: Launched. Built at Selby by Cochrane. Owned by Endeavour Trawlers of
Fleetwood. 1917: Requisitioned for the Fishery Reserve. 1919: Returned to owners.
1920: Acquired by Pickering & Haldane's STC of Hull. PR: H. 103.

ADMIRAL SIR JOHN LAWFORD   1939/46 Displacement: 338TG 127TN
                                         Engines: 99HP
                                         Armament: 1 x 12pdr
                                         Port Reg: LO. 42
                                         P.Nos: FY. 533 (M/S) 4. 415 (WDV)
1930: Launched. Built at Stockton-on-Tees. Owned by Iago Trawlers of Fleetwood.
1939: Requisitioned in August and converted to a M/S. 1944: Converted to a WDV in
May. 1946: Returned to owners in January.

ADONIS   See under NORDHAV I

ADRIAN   1914/18   Displacement: 199TG
                                         Armament: 1 x 6pdr
                                         Admty No: 820
                                         Port Reg: GY. 1185
1900: Launched. Built at Beverley. Owned by the Allen SFC of Grimsby. 1914:
Requisitioned in December and converted to a M/S. 1918: LOST. Sunk in collision off
Harwich on 3rd March.

ADRIAN   1940   See under CORMORANT IV

ADVANCE   1917/19   Displacement: 62TG 42TN
                                         Engines: 45HP
                                         Port Reg: LT. 570
1905: Launched. Built at Lowestoft. Owned by DJ Ayers of Lowestoft. 1917:
Requisitioned into the Fishery Reserve. 1919: Returned to owners.

ADVENTURE II   1914/18   Displacement: 184TG 71TN
                                         Engines: 70HP
                                         Armament: 1 x 6pdrAA
                                         Admty No: 2771
                                         Port Reg: FD. 154
1906: Launched. Built at Aberdeen. Owned by AG Brown of Granton. 1914:
Requisitioned in June and converted to a M/S. 1918: Returned to owners.

AFRICAN PRINCE   1917/19   Displacement: 125TG 48TN
                                         Engines: 50HP
                                         Port Reg: A. 114
1896: Launched. Built at South Shields. Owned by A. Walker of Aberdeen. 1917:
Requisitioned for the Fishery Reserve. 1919: Returned to owners.

AFRICANA   1939/47   SAN
                                         Displacement: 313TG
                                         Armament: 1 x 3-inch
                                         Port Reg: S. African
                                         P. No: T. 0
1930: Launched. South African fishing vessel. 1939: Requisitioned in September for the
SAN and converted to a M/S. 1947: Returned to owners on 10th April.

AGAMEMNON   1914/15   Displacement: 225TG
                                         Admty No: 19
                                         Port Reg: GY. 187
1907: Launched.   1914: Requisitioned in August and converted to a M/S.   1915:
Renamed AGAMEMNON II in February. LOST. Mined off the Shipwash LV on 15th July.

AGAMEMNON II   1915/15   See under AGAMEMNON

AGAMI   1917/19   Displacement: 186TG 76TN
                                         Engines: 50HP
                                         Port Reg: GY.143
1899: Launched. Built at Selby by Cochrane. Owned by JL Green of Grimsby. 1917:
Requisitioned for the Fishery Reserve. 1919: Returned to owners. 1938: Owned by
Grimsby Trawler Owners of Grimsby.

AGATE   1915/18   Displacement: 248TG
                                         Armament: 1 x 6pdr
                                         Admty No: 1635
                                         Port Reg: H. 2
1914: Launched. 1915: Requisitioned in May and converted to a M/S. 1918: LOST.
Mined off the Royal Sovereign LV on 14th March.

AGATHA II   1914/19   Displacement: 137TG 56TN
                                         Engines: 40HP
                                         Armament: 1 x 3pdr
                                         Admty No: 803
                                         Port Reg: GY.107
1896: Launched.   Built at Beverley. Owned by W. Grant of Grimsby.   1914:
Requisitioned in November and converted to a M/S. 1919: Returned to owners.

AGILE   1914/17   Displacement: 246TG 100TN
Engines: 63HP = 10.5K
Admty No: 697
Port Reg: GY. 263

1907: Launched. Built at Beverley by CWG. Owned by W. Grant of Grimsby. 1914: Requisitioned in December and Converted to a M/S. 1917: LOST. Mined off the Sunk LV. on 27th April.

AGNES H. HASTIE   1914/19   Displacement: 210TG 81TN
Engines: 62HP
Armament: 1 x 6pdr
Admty No: 105
Port Reg: SN.187

1912: Launched. Built at South Shields. Owned by Hastie of North Shields. 1914: Requisitioned in August and converted to a M/S. 1919: Returned to owners.

AGNES H. WETHERLY   1917/19 1940/45 Displacement: 229TG 89TN
Engines: 71HP
Armament: 1 x 6pdrAA
Admty No: 3041
Port Reg: A. 743
P.No: WWII: 4. 279

1917: Launched. Built at Aberdeen. Owned by Wetherley SFC of Aberdeen. Requisitioned in May and converted to a M/S. 1919: Returned to owners. Acquired by the North Eastern SFC of Aberdeen. Same PR. 1940: Requisitioned in June and converted to an APV. 1945: Returned to owners in December. *Notes*: When she was requisitioned in 1940 the initial letter H was dropped.

AGNES NUTTEN   1915/20 1940/46 Displacement: 183TG 79TN
Engines: 67HP
Port Reg: A. 295
P.No: WWII: 4. 274

1915: Launched. Built at Aberdeen. Owned by W. Robbens & Son of Lowestoft. Requisitioned in June and converted to a BDV. 1920: Returned to owners. 1938: Owned by J. Walker of Aberdeen. 1940: Requisitioned in June and converted to an APV. 1946: Returned to owner in January.

AGNES WICKFIELD   1914/19 1939/45 Ex-*Solva*
Displacement: 219TG 85TN
Engines: 72HP
Armament: 1 x 6pdr
Admty No: 125
Port Reg: FD. 32
P.No: WWII: FY. 727

1909: Launched. Built at North Shields. Owned by the New Docks SFC of Fleetwood. 1914: Requisitioned in August and converted to a M/S. 1919: Returned to owners. 1939: Requisitioned in November and converted to a M/S. 1945: Returned to owners in December.

AIGLE	1917/19	Displacement: 305TG

1898: Launched. 1917: Requisitioned. 1919: Returned to owners.

AIGLON	1940/46	Displacement: 305TG
		Port Reg: Boulogne
		P.No: FY.1841

1907: Launched. French fishing vessel. 1940: French APV seized at Plymouth on 3rd July in Operation Grab. Converted to a M/S and deployed to the Med. 1941: Returned to the UK. Joined the 152nd M/S Group based at Grimsby. 1945: Converted for the Examination Service. 1946: Returned to France in July.

AISNE	1917/19	Displacement: 316TG 126TN
		Engines: 84HP
		Port Reg: H. 243

1915: Launched. Built at Selby by Cochrane. Owned by The East Riding SFC of Hull. 1917: Requisitioned for the Fishery Reserve. 1919: Returned to owners.

AKITA	1939/45	Displacement: 314TG 116TN
		Engines: 125HP
		Armament: 1 x 12pdr
		Port Reg: CF. 4
		P.No: FY. 610

1939: Launched. Built at Selby by Cochrane. Owned by Neale & West of Cardiff. Requisitioned direct from the builders and completed as a M/S. 1945: Returned to owners in October. 1958: Sold to Newfoundland owners. 1962: Mercantile Loss.

AKRANES	1915/19	Displacement:184TG
		Port Reg: FD.133

1899: Launched. Built at North Shields. 1915: Requisitioned and converted to a BDV. 1919: Returned to owners. 1920: Acquired by ED. Baxter of Grimsby. PR: GY.1219.

AKRANES	1939/41	Displacement: 358TG 153TN
		Engines: 103HP
		Port Reg: GY.155
		P.No: FY.513

1929: Launched. Built at Selby by Cochrane. Owned by Consolidated Fisheries of Grimsby. 1939: Requisitioned in August and converted to a M/S. Joined the 40th M/S Group based at Grimsby. 1941: LOST. Sunk by a/c attack in Bridlington Bay on 4th July.

ALAFOSS   1939/46   Displacement: 357T 153TN
                                            Engines: 103HP
                                            Armament: 1 x 12pdr
                                            Port Reg: GY.160
                                            P.No: FY. 715
1929: Launched. Built at Selby by Cochrane. Owned by Consolidated Fisheries of
Grimsby. 1939: Requisitioned in August and converted to a M/S. Subsequently
purchased into the RN. 1940: Based at Grimsby (ungrouped). 1941: 16th M/S Group
based at Grimsby. 1943: 179th M/S Group based at Grimsby. 1946: Sold to Mercantile
in January. Retained the same name. Acquired by original owners. PR: GY. 307.

ALASKA   1914/19   Displacement: 135TG 52TN
                                            Engines: 30HP
                                            Armament: 1 x 6pdr
                                            Admty No: 728
                                            Port Reg: LT.1031
1898: Launched. Built at North Shields. Iron construction. Owned by H. Colville of
Lowestoft. 1914: Requisitioned in December and converted to a M/S. 1919: Returned to
owners.

ALASKA II   1918/19   Displacement: 52TN
                                            Engines: 30HP
                                            Port Reg: GY. 477
1898: Launched. Built at North Shields. Constructed of Iron. Owned by J & G Alward of
Grimsby. 1918: Requisitioned. 1919: Returned to owners.

ALBATROSS   1914/19   Displacement: 220TG 88TN
                                            Engines: 65HP
                                            Armament: 1 x 6pdr
                                            Admty No: 919
                                            Port Reg: PH. 17
1906: Launched. Built at Aberdeen. Owned by J. Chant & T. Padden of South Brent,
Devon. 1914: Requisitioned in November and converted to a M/S. 1915: Renamed
ALBATROSS II in February. 1919: Returned to owners.

ALBATROSS II   1915/19   See under ALBATROSS above

ALBATROSS III   1914/18   Displacement: 151TG 65TN
                                            Engines: 45HP = 10K
                                            Armament: 1 x 12pdr
                                            Admty No: 772
                                            Port Reg: H. 277
1895: Launched. Built at Hull by CWG. Iron construction. Owned by Pickering &
Haldane STC of Hull. 1914: Requisitioned in December, renamed ALBATROSS III and

converted to a M/S. 1917: Acquired by JS Ellis of Scarborough. 1918: Returned to owners in September and reverted to original name. 1926: Sold to Spanish mercantile and renamed *Punta Paloma*. 1969: BU in Spain.

ALBATROSS V	1918/19	Displacement: 88TN
		Engines: 65HP
		Port Reg: FD. 353

1906: Launched. Built at Aberdeen. Owned by Swan Trawlers of Fleetwood. 1918: Requisitioned. 1919: Returned to owners.

ALBERIA	1914/19 1940/41	Displacement: 286TG 112TN
		Engines: 91HP
		Armament:1 x 12pdr
		Admty No: 768
		Port Reg: GY. 588

1910: Launched. Built at Selby by Cochrane. Owned by the Crown SFC of Grimsby. 1914: Requisitioned in December and converted to a M/S. 1919: Returned to owners. Acquired by the Alberic SFC of Fleetwood. 1940: Requisitioned in April. Renamed ALBERIC. Converted to a M/S. 1941: LOST. Sunk in a collision off Scapa Flow in 3rd May.

| ALBERIC | 1940/41 | See under ALBERIA above |

ALBERTA	1914/16	Displacement: 209TG
		Admty No: 7
		Port Reg: GY. 212

1907: Launched. 1914: Requisitioned in August and converted to a M/S. 1916: LOST. Mined off Grimsby on 14th April.

ALBION	1914/16	Displacement: 240TG
		Admty No: 139
		Port Reg: M. 219

1907: Launched. 1914: Requisitioned in August. 1915: Renamed ALBION II in February. 1916: LOST. Mined off St. Catherine's Point on 13th January.

| ALBION II | 1915/16 | See under ALBION above |

ALCMARIA	1939/46	Displacement: 148TG 64TN
		Engines: 250HP
		Port Reg: LT. 48
		P.No: FY. 1525

1916: Launched. Built in Holland. Owned by Bowden Ramster of Fleetwood. 1939: Purchased in November and converted to a M/S. 1940: Commissioned with a Norwegian crew in October. Remained Norwegian manned throughout WWII. 1945: Paid Off and reduced to the Reserve. Placed on the Disposal List. 1946: Sold to the mercantile.

ALERT IV   1917/19   Displacement: 150TN
Port Reg: CF. 22
1896: Launched. 1917: Requisitioned for the Fishery Reserve. 1919: Returned to owners.

ALEXANDRA   1914/19   Displacement: 182TG 69TN
Engines: 51HP
Armament: 1 x 6pdr
Admty No: 316
Port Reg: SN. 81
1904: Launched. Built at North Shields. Owned by the Purdy SFC of North Shields.
1914: Requisitioned in August and converted to a M/S. 1919: Returned to owners.

ALEXANDRITE   1939/45   Displacement: 313TG 139TN
Engines: 89HP = 11.3K
Port Reg: H. 7
P.No: FY. 560
1933: Launched. Built at Beverley by CWG. Owned by Kingston STC of Hull. 1939:
Requisitioned in September and converted to a M/S. 1940: 46th M/S Group based at
Grimsby. 1945: Returned to owners in November. 1963: BU at Grangemouth.

ALEX HASTIE   1915/19   Displacement: 206TG 91TN
Engines: 82HP
Armament: 1 x 6pdr
Admty No: 1457
Port Reg: SN. 56
1914: Launched. Built at Willington Quay. Owned by Hastie of South Shields. 1915:
Requisitioned in April and converted to a M/S. 1919: Returned to owners. 1939:
Requisitioned in October for conversion to an APV. Returned in December. *Notes*:
Sister-ships also requisitioned: MARY HASTIE, MARJORIE HASTIE, ROBERT HASTIE
and WILLIAM HASTIE.

ALFIE CAM   1940/44   RAN   Ex-*Asama*
Displacement: 282TG 110TN
Engines: 85HP = 10.5K
Port Reg: Australian
P.No: FY. 97
1919: Launched as *Asama*. Built at Beverley by CWG. Owned by Neale & West of
Cardiff. PR: CF. 62. 1929: Acquired by Cam & Sons of Sydney, NSW and renamed *Alfie
Cam*. 1940: Requisitioned in July for the RAN and converted to a M/S. 1943:
Purchased into the RAN. 1944: Resold to original owners in September. 1953:
Mercantile Loss. Wrecked in July near Eden, NSW.

ALFRED EDITH   1917/19   Displacement: 262TG 141TN
Engines: 63HP = 10.5K

Port Reg: O. 35

1908: Launched. Built at Beverley by CWG. Belgian fishing vessel owned by AT Golder of Ostend. 1917: Requisitioned into the Fishery Reserve with the permission of her owners. 1919: Returned to Belgium. 1933: Acquired by Dobson Ship Repair Co of Grimsby and renamed *Lucerne* PR: GY.510. 1937: BU.

ALFREDIAN	1939/46	See under WALDORF

ALGIE	1939/39	RCN
		Displacement: 146TG

1929: Launched. 1939: Requisitioned for the RCN in September. Returned to owners in November.

ALGOA BAY	1939/40	SAN See under TR.46 (Vol 1 p.82)

ALGOMA	1908/19	Displacement: 66TN
		Engines: 45HP
		Port Reg: GY. 6

1899: Launched. Built at North Shields. 1908: Purchased into the RN for M/S trials. Based at Portland carrying out trials as an Auxiliary M/S ICW ANDES. 1917: Transferred to the Fishery Reserve. 1919: Sold to mercantile. Acquired by The Spurn SFC of Grimsby. PR: GY.6.

ALIDA	1915/19 1940/45	Displacement: 270TG 105TN
		Engines: 88HP
		Armament: 1 x 6pdr
		Admty No: 1977
		Port Reg: FD. 192
		P.No: WWII: Z. 152

1915: Launched. Built at Dundee. Owned by The Lancashire SFC of Fleetwood. Requisitioned in December and converted to a M/S. 1919: Returned to owners. 1938: Owned by Marr & Sons of Fleetwood. 1940: Requisitioned in January and converted to a BDV. 1945: Returned to owners.

ALKANET	1941/46	Ex-*Anemone*.
		Displacement: 296TG

1936: Launched. 1941: Requisitioned in November and converted to a M/S. 1946: Returned to owners in March.

ALLAN RAMSAY	1915/19	Displacement: 210TG 78TN
		Engines: 56HP
		Port Reg: A. 356

1911: Launched. Built at Aberdeen. Owned by the F.M.& O Co. of Aberdeen. 1915: Requisitioned in June and converted to a BDV. 1919: Returned to owners.

ALL HALLOWS   See under JAMAICA

ALMA   See under TROOPER 1915
(Vol 1 p.154)

ALMANDINE   1939/45   Displacement: 295TG 135TN
Engines: 89HP = 11K
Port Reg: H. 415
P.No: FY. 645

1932: Launched. Built at Beverley by CWG. Owned by Kingston STC of Hull. 1939: Requisitioned in August and converted to a M/S. 1940: 40th M/S Group based at Grimsby. 1945: Returned to owners in December. 1963: BU at Troon.

ALNMOUTH   1914/19   Displacement: 236TG 92TN
Engines: 66HP
Armament: 1 x 6pdrAA
Admty No: 12

1912: Launched. Built at Selby by Cochrane. 1914: Purchased in July and converted to a M/S. 1919: Sold to mercantile and retained same name. Acquired by The Vulcan STC of Fleetwood. PR: FD. 335.

ALONZO   1917/19   Displacement: 172TG 66TN
Engines: 36HP
Port Reg: H. 887

1906: Launched. Built at Govan. Owned by E. Headspith of Hull. 1917: Requisitioned for the Fishery Reserve. 1919: Returned to owners. 1938: Owned by Brand of Milford Haven. *Notes*: Listed in Mercantile lists as *Alonso*.

ALOUETTE   1939/42   Ex-*Esquimaux*
Displacement: 520T 191TN
Engines: 99HP
Armament: 1 x 4-inch
Port Reg: H. 29
P.No: FY. 101

1939: Launched. Built at Southbank-on-Tees by Smiths Dock. Owned by Hull Northern FCL of Hull. 1939: Requisitioned in August, renamed and converted to A/S. 1942: LOST. Sunk by U-552 off Portugal on 19th September.

ALPHA   1915/20   Displacement: 274TG 108TN
Engines: 70HP
Armament: 1 x 12pdr
Admty No: 1131
Port Reg: LO. 24

1900: Launched. Built at Leith. Owned by the Royal National Mission to Deep Sea

Fishermen, London. 1915: Requisitioned in March and converted to a M/S. 1920: Returned to owners.

ALPHA II   1915/19   Displacement: 200TG
                                             Armament: 1 x 3pdr
1915: Requisitioned and converted to a M/S. 1919: Returned to owners.

ALSATION   1914/16 1918/19 Displacement: 191TG
1899: Launched. 1914: Requisitioned. Renamed ALSATION MINOR. 1916: Returned to owners and reverted to original name. 1918: Requisitioned as ALSATION for the Fishery Reserve. 1919: Returned to owners.

ALSATION MINOR   1914/16   See under ALSATION above

ALSEY   1940/45   Displacement: 416TG 153TN
                                             Engines: 99HP
                                           Port Reg: GY. 460
                                           P.No: M. 51
1932: Launched. Built at Selby by Cochrane. Owned by Alsey SFC of Grimsby. 1940: Requisitioned in February and converted to a M/L. 1945: Based at Grimsby. Returned to owners in June.

ALVIS   See under PETER HALL (Vol 1 p.70)

AMADAVAT   1914/15   Displacement: 171TG 68TN
                                             Engines: 55HP
                                           Armament: 1 x 6pdr
                                           Admty No: 922
                                           Port Reg: PH. 8
1899: Launched Built at Greenock. Owned by W. Walker of North Shields. 1914: Requisitioned in November. 1915: Returned to the Fishing Fleet. 1917: Mercantile Loss. Probably mined off the East Coast of Shetland with the loss of 9 men.

AMBASSADOR   1917/19   Displacement: 149TG 57TN
                                             Engines: 52HP
                                           Port Reg: DE. 3
1899: Launched. Built at Aberdeen. Owned by AC. Cameron & W. McFarlane of Dundee. 1917: Requisitioned for the Fishery Reserve. 1919: Returned to owners. 1938: Owned by The Don SFC of Dundee.

AMBER   1917/19   Displacement: 172TG 67TN
                                             Engines: 55HP
                                           Port Reg:H. 398
1898: Launched. Built at Govan. Owned by Kingston STC of Hull. 1917: Requisitioned

for the Fishery Reserve. 1919: Returned to owners.

AMBITION   1944/45   ex-*Thrush*
                                                  Displacement: 166 TG
                                                  Armament: None
1902: Launched. 1944: Requisitioned in March and converted to an Esso. 1945: Returned to owners.

AMBROSE PARE   1940/46   Displacement: 326TG
                                                  Armament: 3 x 100mm (French)
                                                  Port Reg: French
                                                  P.No: FY. 346
1906: Launched. French fishing vessel. 1940: French APV AMBROISE PARE. Escaped from France at the time of Dunkirk. Seized at Plymouth in Operation Grab on 3rd July and converted to an A/S vessel at Devonport in August. Fitted with DCTs. Commissioned at Devonport with a mixed French/RN crew and RNR CO. Employed on A/S patrols in the Channel. 1946: Returned to France in March.

AMEER   1914/16   Displacement: 216TG
                                                  Armament: 1 x 6pdr
                                                Admty No: 38
                                                Port Reg: GY. 397
1908: Launched. Owned by Sleight of Grimsby. 1914: Requisitioned in August and converted to a M/S. 1916: LOST. Mined off Felixstowe on 18th March.

AMENITY   1917/19   Displacement: 212TG 77TN
                                                  Engines: 59HP
                                                Port Reg: GY. 481
1908: Launched. Built at Nantes, France. Owned by WG Alnutt of Grimsby. 1917: Requisitioned into the Fishery Reserve. 1919: Returned to owners.

AMETHYST   1915/15 1917/19 Displacement: 172TG 67TN
                                                  Engines: 55HP
                                                Armament: 1 x 3pdr
                                                Admty No: 1214
                                                Port Reg: H. 401
1898: Launched. Built at Govan. Owned by The Kingston STC of Hull. 1915: Requisitioned in January and converted to a M/S. Renamed AMETHYST II in February. Returned to the Fishing Fleet in October. 1917: Requisitioned for the Fishery Reserve. 1919: Returned to owners.

AMOS   See under KALMIA

AMPERE   1917/19   Displacement: 154TG 63TN
Engines: 50HP
Port Reg:H. 169
1891: Launched. Built at Beverley. 1917: Requisitioned into the Fishery Reserve. 1919: Returned to owners. 1920: Owned by F & T. Ross of Hull. PR: H.169. 1938: Owned by Consolidated Fisheries of Grimsby.

AMPLIFY   1916/17   Displacement: 342TG
Armament: 1 x 6pdr
Admty No:1982
Port Reg: GY. 789
1916: Launched. Requisitioned in February and converted to a M/S. 1917: LOST. Wrecked at Skeirascape on 17th January.

AMROTH CASTLE   1915/19 1940/45 Displacement: 255TG 100TN
Engines: 85HP
Armament: WWI: 1 x 6pdr
WWII: 1 x 12pdr
Admty No: 2665
Port Reg: SA. 8
P.No: WWII: 4. 120
1913: Launched. Built at Middlesborough by Smith's Dock. Owned by Consolidated Fisheries of Grimsby. 1915: Requisitioned in May and converted to a M/S. 1919: Returned to owners. 1940: Requisitioned in May and converted to an APV. 1941: Converted to a M/S in January. Based at Grimsby. 1945: Returned to owners.

AMSTERDAM   1940/46   Displacement: 241TG
Port Reg: Dutch
P.No: FY. 1921
1913: Launched. Dutch fishing vessel. 1940: Hired in June from Dutch owners and converted to a M/S. Commissioned with a Dutch crew. 1941: Renamed ANDYK. 1943: Commissioned with RN crew. 1946: Returned to Holland.

AMY   1914/17   Displacement: 223TG
Admty No: 334
Port Reg: FD. 39
1905: Launched. 1914: Requisitioned in August and converted to a M/S. 1917: LOST. Mined off Le Havre on 11th April.

ANDANES   1917/19   Displacement: 169TG
1899: Launched. 1917: Requisitioned. 1919: Returned to owners.

ANDANES   1940/45   See under WIMPOLE

ANDES   1908/19   Displacement: 66TN
                   Engines: 45HP
1899: Launched. Built at North Shields. 1908: Purchased into the Royal Navy for M/S trials. Based at Portland carrying out trials as an Auxiliary M/S ICW ALGOMA. 1917: Transferred to the Fishery Reserve. 1919: Sold to mercantile and retained the same name. Acquired by The Spurn SFC of Grimsby. PR: GY. 5.

ANDRADITE   1939/46   Displacement: 313TG 139TN
                   Engines: 89HP = 11.4K
                   Armament: 1 x 12pdr
                   Port Reg: H. 26
                   P.No: FY. 559
1934: Launched. Built at Beverley by CWG. Owned by Kingston STC of Hull. 1939: Requisitioned in August and converted to a M/S. 1940: 46th M/S Group based at Grimsby. 1946: Returned to owners in January. 1957: Mercantile Loss. Wrecked in Castle Bay, Outer Hebrides on 7th March. No loss of life.

ANDRE-LOUIS   1940/45   Displacement: 284TG
                   Port Reg: French
                   P.No: FY. 1798
1907: Launched. French fishing vessel. 1940: French M/S seized at Plymouth in Operation Grab on 3rd July. Commissioned into the RN as a M/S. 1945: Returned to France on 3rd April.

ANDRE MONIQUE   1940/45   Displacement: 152TG
                   Armament: 1 x 6pdr; 3 x HG (3x1)
                   Port Reg: Belgian
1937: Launched. Belgian fishing vessel. 1940: Hired from Belgian owners and converted to an APV. 1945: Returned to Belgium.

ANDREW MARVEL   1915/19   Displacement: 285TG 114TN
                   Engines: 64HP
                   Armament: 1 x 12pdr
                   Admty No: 1180
                   Port Reg: H. 466
1912: Launched. Built at Selby by Cochrane. Owned by The Jutland STC of Hull. 1915: Requisitioned in February and converted to a M/S. 1919: Returned to owners.

ANDROMEDA   1917/19   Displacement: 149TG 51TN
                   Engines: 47HP
                   Port Reg: SD. 9
1898: Launched. Built at South Shields. Owned by Vedra SFC of Sunderland. 1917: Requisitioned for the Fishery Reserve. 1919: Returned to owners.

ANDYK	1941/46	See under AMSTERDAM

ANGELE-MARIE   1940/46   Displacement: 238TG
                                       Port Reg: French
                                       P.No: FY. 1708
1929: Launched. French fishing vessel. 1940: French M/S seized at Southampton in
Operation Grab on 3rd July. Commissioned into the RN in August as a M/S. 1946:
Returned to France in January.

ANGELUS   1915/16   Displacement: 304TG
                                       Armament: 1 x 12pdr
                                       Admty No: 1629
                                       Port Reg: GY. 19
1914: Launched. 1915: Requisitioned in May and converted to a M/S. 1916: LOST.
Mined off Dover on 28th February.

ANGERTON   1914/19   Displacement: 186TG
                                       Armament: 1 x 6pdr
                                       Admty No: 526
                                       Port Reg: BN. 92
1901: Launched. 1914: Requisitioned in November and converted to a M/S. 1919:
Returned to owners.

ANGLE   1915/19   Displacement: 222TG 86TN
                                       Engines: 68HP
                                       Armament: 1 x 12pdr
                                       Admty No: 1367
                                       Port Reg: FD. 57
1908: Launched. Built at Lowestoft. Owned by Croston STC of Fleetwood. 1915:
Requisitioned in April and converted to a M/S. 1919: Returned to owners.

ANGLE   1939/45   Displacement: 531TG 195TN
                                       Engines: 99HP.
                                       Port Reg: H. 307
                                       P.No: FY. 201
1936: Launched. Built at Southbank-on-Tees by Smith's Dock. Owned by Hull Northern
FC. 1939: Requisitioned in September and converted to A/S. Joined the 16th A/S
Striking Force. Based at Aberdeen for operations around Northern Scotland. 1940: TPI
the Norwegian Campaign in April/May. 1945: Returned to owners in October.

ANGLIA   1917/19   Displacement: 196TG
                                       Port Reg: LO. 186
1904: Launched. 1917: Requisitioned for the Fishery Reserve. 1919: Returned to owners.

ANGOLIAN   See under TEUTON

ANGUS   1914/   Displacement: 179TG
1906: Launched. 1914: Requisitioned. NFI.

ANIDA   1917/19   Displacement: 270TG 105TN
                                         Engines: 88HP
                                         Armament: 1 x 12pdr
                                         Admty No: 3059
                                         Port Reg: FD. 299
1917: Launched. Built at Dundee. Owned by Marr of Fleetwood. Requisitioned in September and converted to a M/S. Fitted with Listening Hydrophones. 1919: Returned to owners.

ANN FORD MELVILLE   1915/19 1944/44 Displacement: 212TG 81TN
                                         Engines: 66HP
                                         Armament: 1 x 6pdr
                                         Admty No: 1347
                                         Port Reg: A. 365
1911: Launched. Built at Aberdeen. Owned by Melville of Aberdeen. 1915: Requisitioned in April and converted to a M/S. 1919: Returned to owners. 1938: Owned by D. Wood & J. Flett of Aberdeen. 1944: Requisitioned in March as SHIELBURN. Returned to owners in October.

ANN LEWIS   1916/19 1940/45 Displacement: 216TG 83TN
                                         Engines: 80HP
                                         Armament: 1 x 6pdrAA
                                         Admty No: 2985
                                         Port Reg: WWI: A. 62; WWII: A. 174
                                         P.No: WWII: FY. 1677
1916: Launched. Built at Selby by Cochrane. Owned by RW. Lewis of Aberdeen. Requisitioned in December and converted to a M/S. 1919: Returned to owners. Acquired by Stephen FC of Aberdeen and renamed *Jean Edmonds*. 1940: Requisitioned in January as JEAN EDMUNDS and converted to a M/S. 1945: Returned to owners in September.

ANN MELVILLE   1915/19 1940/44 Displacement: 201TG 77TN
                                         Engines: 66HP
                                         Armament: 1 x 6pdr
                                         Admty No: 1596
                                         Port Reg: A . 254
                                         P.No: WWII: FY. 1945
1909: Launched. Built at Aberdeen. Owned by Harley & Miller of Liverpool. 1915: Requisitioned in June and converted to a M/S. 1919: Returned to owners. 1938: Owned by John Craig of Aberdeen AO. 1940: Requisitioned in February and converted to a M/S. 1944: Converted to an Esso. Returned to owners in October.

ANNABELLE   See under GEORGE BORTHWICK
(Vol 1 p.170)

ANNIE MELLING   1915/18   Displacement: 221TG 85TN
                                        Engines: 65HP
                                        Armament: 1 x 6pdr
                                        Admty No: 1593
                                        Port Reg: PN. 61
1906: Launched. Built at North Shields. Owned by J. Melling STC of Fleetwood. 1915: Requisitioned in April and converted to a M/S. 1918: Returned to owners. *Notes*: Sister-ships also requisitioned: LENA MELLING, LILY MELLING, and LIZZIE MELLING.

ANNIE WALKER   1917/19   Displacement: 123TG 50TN
                                          Engines: 50HP
                                        Port Reg: LH.195
1890: Launched. Built at Aberdeen. Owned by W. Flockhart of Port Sedon, Cockenzie. 1917: Requisitioned for the Fishery Reserve. 1919: Returned to owners.

ANSON   1915/20 1939/46 Displacement: 211TG 83TN
                                          Engines: 65HP = 10K
                                        Armament: 1 x 6pdr
                                        Admty No: 1090
                                        Port Reg: GY. 47
1905: Launched. Built at Beverley by CWG. Owned by William Grant of Grimsby. 1915: Requisitioned in February and converted to a M/S. 1917: Renamed ANSON II in March. 1920: Returned to owners and reverted to original name. 1931: Acquired by C.Dobson of Grimsby. 1939: Requisitioned in October and converted to an APV. 1940: Converted to a D/L in May. 1941: Renamed COCKADE and based at Grimsby. 1944: Converted to a Water Carrier. Renamed STOCKADE. 1945: Acquired by Wembley SFC of Grimsby. 1946: Returned to owners and reverted to original name. Laid up at Grimsby prior to BU. 1949: BU by King of Gateshead.

ANSON II   1917/20   See under ANSON above

ANT   1915/19   Displacement: 158TG
1891: Launched. 1915: Requisitioned. 1919: Returned to owners.

ANTHONY HOPE   1915/16   Displacement: 288TG
                                          Armament: 1 x 3pdr
                                        Admty No: 1380
                                        Port Reg: H. 1006
1913: Launched. 1915: Requisitioned in April. 1916: LOST. Mined off Le Havre on 16th November.

ANTIC   1918/18   See under AUK of 1903

ANTIOCH II   1940/46   See under JAMES CEPELL
                                      (Vol 1 p.56)

ANTONIO   1917/19   Displacement: 210TG 82TN
                                      Engines: 47HP
                                      Port Reg: H. 990
1908: Launched. Built at Hull. Owned by Hellyer SFC of Hull. 1917: Requisitioned for
the Fishery Reserve. 1919: Returned to owners.

ANWOTH   1915/19   Displacement: 211TG 92TN
                                      Engines: 74HP
                                      Armament: 1 x 6pdr
                                      Admty No: 1158
                                      Port Reg: GN. 29
1915: Launched. Built at Leith. Requisitioned in February and converted to a M/S.
Fitted with Listening Hydrophones. 1919: Returned to owners. Acquired by H. Scales
of Lowestoft. PR: LH. 2.

ANZAC   1916/19   Displacement: 317TG 127TN
                                      Engines: 74HP
                                      Armament: 1 x 6pdr; 1 x 7.5-inch
                                      Bomb Thrower (A/S Howitzer)
                                      Admty No: 3305
                                      Port Reg: H. 487
1916: Launched. Built at Selby by Cochrane. Owned by The East Riding SFC of Hull.
Requisitioned in August and converted to a M/S. 1917: Renamed ANZAC II in March.
1919: Returned to owners.

ANZAC II   1917/19   See under ANZAC above

APLEY   1914/17   Displacement: 222TG
                                      Armament: 1 x 3pdr
                                      Admty No: 143
                                      Port Reg: M. 226
1908: Launched. 1914: Requisitioned in August and converted to a M/S. 1917: LOST.
Mined off Worthing on 6th December.

AQUAMARINE   1915/19   Displacement: 333TG 134TN
                                      Engines: 82HP
                                      Armament: 1 x 6pdr; 1 x 7.5-inch Bomb
                                      Thrower (A/S Howitzer)
                                      Admty No:1843

Port Reg: H. 356

1911: Launched. Built at Selby by Cochrane. Owned by The Kingston STC of Hull. 1915: Requisitioned in August and converted to a M/S. 1919: Returned to owners.

AQUAMARINE   1939/443   Displacement: 357TG 146TN
Engines: 96HP = 11K
Port Reg: H. 388
P.No: 4. 00

1927: Launched. Built at Beverley by CWG. Owned by Kingston STC of Hull. 1939: Requisitioned in August and converted to an APV. Converted to A/S and joined the Northern Patrol. 1944: Returned to owners in September. 1945: Acquired by Grimsby Motor Trawlers and renamed *Hargood* PR: GY. 97. 1948: Acquired by Llewellin of Milford Haven and renamed *Westhaze*. 1955: BU at Gateshead by King.

AQUARIUS   1915/15 1917/19 Displacement: 187TG 73TN
Engines: 50HP
Port Reg: GY. 76

1905: Launched. Built at North Shields. Owned by Lindsey SFC of Grimsby. 1915: Requisitioned in June. Returned to the fishing fleet in August. 1917: Requisitioned into the Fishery Reserve. 1919: Returned to owners.

ARAB   1939/45   Displacement: 531TG 195TN
Engines: 99HP
Dimensions: 70ft x 28ft
Port Reg: H. 293
P.No: FY. 202

1936: Launched. Built at Southbank-on-Tees by Smith's Dock. Owned by Hellyer Bros. of Hull. 1939: Requisitioned in September and converted to A/S. Joined the 16th A/S Strike Force based at Aberdeen for operations around the North of Scotland. 1940: TPI the Norwegian Campaign in April/May. Went alongside the blazing pier at Namsen Fjord on 28th April. The pier was crammed with stores and ammunition and she lay alongside for over 2 hours attempting to save it. An a/c attack by 16 Stukas finally made her give up and seek shelter under overhanging cliffs. Took off survivors from the bombed BITTERN on 30th April. Set up an AA position ashore as the surrounding mountains screened attacking a/c from radar. TPI in the evacuation of troops and returned to the UK. Her tally of awards from this operation was: 1 x VC (Captain) 1 x DSC (1st Lt.) 2 x DSMs and 1 x MiD. 1941: Based at Londonderry for Atlantic Convoy duties. 1945: Sustained severe damage in May when she attacked a U-Boat off the Minches. One of her depth-charges went off on the surface and caused considerable damage to her engine-room. By the time she was repaired the war in Europe was over. Returned to owners in November.

ARABESQUE   1943/44   See under HENRY FLIGHT
(Vol 1 p.172)

ARABIAN   1915/19   Displacement: 180TG 70TN
Engines: 57HP
Armament: 1 x 3pdr
Port Reg: A. 209

1899: Launched. Built at Aberdeen. 1915: Requisitioned in June and converted to a M/S. 191?: Converted to a BDV. 1919: Returned to owners. Acquired by N. Ashworth AO of Fleetwood. PR: FD. 325.

ARACARI 1914/19 1939/40 1943/43 Displacement: 245TG 113TN
Engines: 76HP = 10.5K
Armament: 1 x 12pdr; 1 x 6pdrAA
Admty No: 514
Port Reg: WWI: GY. 355
WWII: M. 101
P.No: WWII: Y7. 2 (Esso)

1908: Launched. Built at Beverley by CWG Laid Down as *Seagull*. Owned by Cleethorpes STC of Grimsby. 1914: Requisitioned in September and converted to a M/S. 1919: Returned to owners. 1920: Acquired by The Talbot STC of Fleetwood. PR: FD. 21. 1938: Acquired by Pettit & Younds of Milford Haven. PR: M. 101. 1939: Requisitioned and designated as a M/S. 1940: Returned to owners. 1943: Requisitioned in January and converted to an Esso. Deployed to the Med. LOST. Took the ground on Filicudi Island, Northern Sicily, on 13th October. TCL.

ARAGONITE   1939/39   Displacement: 315TG 138TN
Engines: 89HP = 11.3K
Port Reg: H. 79

1934: Launched. Built at Beverley by CWG. Owned by Kingston STC of Hull. 1939: Requisitioned in August and converted to a M/S. Based at Dover. LOST. Mined off Deal on 22nd November. Broke in two and sank.

ARALIA   1917/19   Displacement: 229TG 113TN
Engines: 59HP
Port Reg: GY. 371

1899: Launched. Built at Grimsby. Owned by The North Eastern SFC of Grimsby. 1917: Requisitioned into the Fishery Reserve. 1919: Returned to owners.

ARCTIC EXPLORER 1939/45   Displacement: 501TG 189TN
Engines: 132HP
Armament: 1 x 4-inch
Port Reg: H. 445
P.No: FY. 162

1937: Launched. Built at Selby by Cochrane. Owned by Boyds of Hull. 1939: Requisitioned in August and converted to A/S. Purchased into the RN in October. 1942: Temporary loan, with crew, to the USN for A/S duties. 1943: Transferred to the

S. Africa station and based at Durban for convoy duties. 1945: Sold to Mercantile.

ARCTIC HUNTER   1939/45   Ex-*Capel*
Displacement: 356TG 145TN
Engines: 96HP = 10.9K
Armament: 1 x 12pdr; 2 x 0.5-inchAA
(1x2); 2 x MG (2x1)
Port Reg: H. 17
P.No: FY. 1614

1929: Launched. Built at Beverley by CWG as *Capel*. Owned by F & T Ross of Hull.
1939: Acquired by Boyd Line of Hull and renamed *Arctic Hunter*. Requisitioned in August
and converted to a M/S. 1945: Returned to owners in May. 1950: Acquired by Lord Line
of Hull and renamed *Lord Foyle*. 1952: BU at Sunderland by T. Young Ltd.

ARCTIC PIONEER   1939/42   Displacement: 501TG 189TN
Engines: 132HP
Armament: 1 x 4-inch
Port Reg: H. 462
P.No: FY. 164

1929: Launched. Built at Selby by Cochrane. Owned by Boyds of Hull. 1939:
Requisitioned in August and converted to an APV. 1940: TPI the Norwegian Campaign
in Apr/May. 1942: LOST. Sunk in the Cowes Roads by a Stuka dive-bomber on 27th
May. Only 18 survivors. 17 of those lost were buried at the RNH, Haslar. 1947:
Salvaged. Sold to mercantile and renamed *Arctic Venturer*. 1961: Mercantile Loss.
Sank with all hands off Flamborough Head on 18th October.

ARCTIC PRINCE   1915/19 1939/46 Displacement: 194TG 86TN
Engines: 80HP
Armament: 1 x 12pdr
Admty No: 1470
Port Reg: SN. 169
P.No: WWII: FY. 67

1915: Launched. Built at Willington Quay. Owned by Prince FC of North Shields.
Requisitioned in April. 1919: Returned to owners. Acquired by T & CF Moss of Grimsby
and renamed *Clifton*. 1939: Requisitioned in November as CLIFTON and converted to
a M/S. 1946: Returned to owners in March.

ARCTIC RANGER   1939/46   Displacement: 493TG 189TN
Engines: 132HP
Port Reg: H. 251
P.No: FY. 186

1937: Launched. Built at Selby by Cochrane. Owned by Boyds of Hull. 1939: Purchased
into the RN in August and converted to an A/S. 1941: Based at Gibraltar. 1946: Sold to
mercantile and retained the same name. Acquired by the original owners. Same PR.

ARCTIC TRAPPER   1940/41   Displacement: 493TG 145TN.
                                          Engines: 96HP.
                                          Armament: 1 x 12pdr.
                                          Port Reg: GW. 217.

1928: Launched. Built at Selby by Cochrane. Owned by Shire Trawlers of London. 1940: Requisitioned in May and converted to an APV. Based at Grimsby. 1941: LOST. Sunk by a/c attack off Ramsgate on 3rd February.

ARDENT   1915/19   Displacement: 228TG 87TN
                                          Engines: 68HP
                                          Armament: 1 x 6pdr
                                          Port Reg: M. 222

1908: Launched. Built at Goole. Owned by the Pater SFC of Pembroke. 1915: Requisitioned in June. 1917: Renamed ARDENT II in March. 1919: Returned to owners.

ARDENT II   1917/19   See under ARDENT above

ARFON   1914/17   Displacement: 227TG
                                            Armament: 1 x 6pdrAA
                                          Admty No:134
                                          Port Reg: M. 223

1908: Launched. 1914: Requisitioned in August and converted to a M/S. 1917: LOST. Mined off St. Alban's Head on 30th April.

ARGO   1917/19   Displacement: 174TG 68TN
                                          Engines: 46HP
                                          Port Reg: A. 554

1903: Launched. Built at North Shields. Owned by G. Pearce AO of Grimsby. 1917: Requisitioned into the Fishery Reserve. 1919: Returned to owners.

ARGON   1915/19   Displacement: 226TG 87TN
                                          Engines: 71HP
                                          Armament: 1 x 6pdrAA
                                          Admty No: 1540
                                          Port Reg: SA. 48

1907: Launched. Built at Goole by Goole SB. Owned by F. Langley of Kingston-on-Hull. 1915: Requisitioned in June and converted to a M/S. 1917: Renamed ARGON II in May. 1919: Returned to owners.

ARGON II   1917/19   See under ARGON above

ARGYLLSHIRE   1939/40   Displacement: 540TG 198TN
                                          Engines: 99I IP
                                          Port Reg: GY. 528

1938: Launched in September. Built at Southbank-on-Tees by Smith's Dock. Owned by Banffshire SF (H.Markham), Grimsby. 1939: Requisitioned in September and converted to A/S. Joined the 11th A/S Striking Group. 1940: TPI the Norwegian Campaign in April/May. TPI in Operation Dynamo, the evacuation of Dunkirk. LOST. Torpedoed by E-Boat off Dunkirk on 1st June.

ARIADNE II	1914/18	Displacement: 225TG 106TN
		Engines: 67HP
		Armament: 1 x 6pdrAA
		Admty No: 349
		Port Reg: GY. 173

1906: Launched. Built at Selby by Cochrane. Owned by Consolidated SFC of Grimsby. 1914: Requisitioned in August. 1918: Returned to owners in November. 1938: Owned by Dobson of Grimsby.

ARIAN	1915/19	Displacement: 221TG 102TG
		Engines: 70HP
		Admty No: 1404
		Port Reg: GY. 584

1910: Launched. Built at Selby by Cochrane. 1915: Requisitioned in March and converted to a M/S. 1919: Returned to owners. Acquired by Taylor & Tomlinson Ltd of Fleetwood. PR: FD.130. 1938: Owned by Tudor ST of Fleetwood.

| ARIANA | 1917/18 | Displacement: 285TG |

1902: Launched. 1917: Requisitioned. 1918: Returned to owners.

ARIEL	1914/19	Displacement: 174TG 68TN
		Engines: 45HP = 9.5K
		Armament: 1 x 6pdrAA
		Admty No: 616
		Port Reg: H. 843

1905: Launched. Built at Beverley by CWG. Owned by Hellyers SFC of Hull. 1914: Requisitioned in September and converted to a M/S. 1915: Renamed ARIEL II in February. 1919: Returned to owners and reverted to original name. 1935: Acquired by Walkington of Fleetwood. 1945: Mercantile Loss. Sank after a collision with a merchant ship in the Irish Sea on 2nd August. No loss of life.

| ARIEL II | 1915/19 | See under ARIEL above |

ARIES	1914/19 1940/45	Displacement: 250TG 103TN
		Engines: 76HP
		Armament: 1 x 12pdr
		Admty No: 28
		Port Reg: WWI: GY.131

WWII: GY. 225
P.No: WWII: FY. 513

1906: Launched. Built at Selby by Cochrane. Owned by Ariesona SFC of Grimsby. 1914: Requisitioned in September and converted to a M/S. 1915: Renamed ARIES II in February. 1919: Returned to owners. Acquired by The Boston DSF & Ice Co of Fleetwood. PR: GY. 225. 1940: Requisitioned in October as SORANUS and converted to a M/S. 1945: Returned to owners in October.

ARIES II	1915/19	See under ARIES above

ARIES II   1917/19   Displacement: 159TG
Port Reg: A. 295
1899: Launched. 1917: Requisitioned into the Fishery Reserve. 1919: Returned to owners.

ARIES III   1918/19   Displacement: 159TG 59TN
Engines: 54HP
1899: Launched. Built at Leith. 1918: Requisitioned. 1919: Returned to owners. Acquired TG Hancock of Milford Haven. PR. MH.97.

ARISTEA   1940/44   SAN
Displacement: 261TG
Port Reg: S. African
P.No: T. 18
1935: Launched. South African fishing vessel. 1940: Requisitioned for the SAN in January. 1944: Returned to owners in December.

ARKWRIGHT   1940/45   Displacement: 370TG 149TN
Engines: 96HP = 10.4K
Armament: 1 x 12pdr
Port Reg: H. 314
P.No: FY. 653
1930: Launched. Built at Beverley by CWG. Owned by F & T Ross, Hull. 1940: Requisitioned in August and converted to a M/S. 1945: Based at Loch Ewe sweeping friendly minefields Cairnryan-Isle of Craig to Stornaway. Paid off at Hull in November. Returned to owners in December. 1946: Acquired by Iago STL of London and renamed *Red Charger*. PR: LO. 460. 1955: BU at Troon.

ARLETTE   1940/45   See under GEORGE FRENCH
(Vol 1 p.171)

ARLEY   1914/19 1939/45 Displacement: 304TG 122TN
Engines: 69HP
Armament: 1 x 12pdr; I x 6pdr; 1 x
7.5-inch Bomb Thrower (A/S Howitzer)

Admty No: 591
Port Reg: FD .44
P.No: WWII: FY. 620

1914: Launched. Built at Middlesborough by Smith's Dock. Owned by Wyre STC of Fleetwood. Requisitioned in October and converted to a M/S. 1919: Returned to owners. 1939: Requisitioned in August and converted to a M/S. 1943: 51st M/S Group based at Grimsby. 1945: LOST. Damaged by a mine in the North Sea and subsequently sank in tow on 3rd February.

ARMAGEDDON   1915/19 1940/45   Displacement: 323TG 129TN
Engines: 97HP
Armament: 1 x 6pdr
Admty No: 1748
Port Reg: WWI: H. 319; WWII: FD. 54
P.No: WWII: 4. 131

1915: Launched. Built at Selby by Cochrane. Requisitioned in September and converted to a M/S. 1919: Returned to owners. 1938: Owned by the Wyre STC. of Fleetwood. 1940: Requisitioned as DHOON in May and converted to a M/S. 1943: Renamed DHOON GLEN. 1945: Returned to owners in November.

ARMANA   1940/45   Displacement: 375TG 139TN
Engines: 97HP
Armament: 1 x 12pdr
Engines: 97HP
Port Reg: FD. 121
P.No: WWII: FY. 1809

1930: Launched. Built at Selby by Cochrane. Owned by J. Marr & Son Ltd. of Fleetwood. 1940: Requisitioned in June and converted to a M/S. 1945: Returned to owners in November.

ARNOLD BENNETT   1939/45   Displacement: 374T 147TG
Engines: 95HP
Armament: 1 x 12pdr
Port Reg: H. 259
P.No: FY. 1939

1930: Launched. Built at Selby by Cochrane. Owned by the Newington STC. of Hull. 1939: Requisitioned and converted to an APV. 1941: Converted to a M/S. 1945: Based at Gibraltar prior to return to UK in January. Based at Devonport prior to Paying Off. Transferred to Hull to de-store and de-ammunition. Paid Off at Hull on 12th March and laid up. Returned to owners in July.

A. ROSE   1940/45   Displacement: 208TG 100TN
Engines: 46HP
Port Reg: YH. 69

P.No: FY. 1692

1924: Launched. Built at Selby by Cochrane. Owned by Albert A. Hudson of Caister-on-Sea. 1940: Requisitioned and converted to a D/L. Converted to a M/S in December. Renamed SIESTA. 1944: Converted to an Esso in May. Renamed ADELPHI. 1945: Returned to owner. *Notes*: Aka ARTHUR ROSE.

ARREST	1941/45	See under BUZZARD

ARSENAL	1939/40	Football Group
		Displacement: 389TG 151TN
		Engines: 99HP
		Port Reg: GY. 505
		P.No:FY. 140

1933: Launched   Built at Middlesborough by Smith's Dock. Owned by Consolidated Fisheries of Grimsby. 1939: Requisitioned in August and converted to an A/S. 1940: LOST. Sunk in a collision with the Polish destroyer BURZA off the Clyde on 16th November.

ARTEGAL	1940/45	See under ROBERT HARDING
		(Vol 1 p.185)

ARUM	1940/44	SAN
		Displacement: 194TG
		P.No: T. 10

1926: Launched. 1940: Requisitioned for the SAN in January and converted to a M/S. 1944: Returned in October.

ASAMA	1917/17	Displacement: 284TG
		Port Reg: CF. 12

1914: Launched. 1917: Requisitioned in January and converted to a 'Q' Ship. LOST. Sunk by S/M 160 miles South West of Fastnet on 16th July.

ASAMA	1939/41	Displacement: 303TG 113TN
		Engines: 99HP
		Armament: 1 x 12pdr
		Port Reg: CF. 18

1929: Launched. Built at Southbank-on-Tees by Smith's Dock. Owned by Neale & West of Cardiff. 1939: Requisitioned in September and converted to a M/S. 1941: LOST. Sunk by enemy a/c off Plymouth on 23rd January.

ASHLYN	1914/19 1940/45	Displacement: 304TG 121TN
		Engines: 61HP
		Armament: 1 x 6pdr
		Admty No: 191
		Port Reg: WWII: FD. 1

1914: Launched. Built at Aberdeen. Owned by The Brooklyn FCL of Fleetwood. Requisitioned in November and converted to a M/S. 1919: Returned to owner. Acquired by French owners. 1940: Hired from French owners in July as BERNADETTE. Converted to a BDV. 1945: Returned to owners in December.

ASHTON	1914/18	Displacement: 144TG 54TN
		Engines: 30HP
		Armament: 1 x 3pdr
		Admty No: 640
		Port Reg: GY. 123

1896: Launched. Built at North Shields. Owned by Consolidated Fisheries of Grimsby. 1914: Requisitioned in October. 1918: Returned to owners in September.

ASIA	1914/17	Displacement: 309TG
		Armament: 1 x 3pdr
		Admty No: 653
		Port Reg: H. 829

1905: Launched. Owned by North Eastern SFC of Grimsby. 1914: Requisitioned in October and converted to a M/S. 1917: LOST. Mined off Bressay on 12th September.

ASIE	1940/46	Displacement: 551TG
		Port Reg: French
		P.No: FY. 370

1914: Launched. French fishing vessel. 1940: French APV seized at Plymouth in Operation Grab on 3rd July. Converted to A/S. 1946: Returned to France in April.

ASIE (1943) (MPL)

ASPASIA   1916/19   Displacement: 342TG 141TN
Engines: 89HP
Armament: 1 x 12pdr
Admty No: 1996
Port Reg: GY. 793

1916: Launched. Built at Southbank-on-Tees by Smith's Dock. Owned by AV Cole of Cleeve Hill, Glos. Requisitioned in April and converted to a M/S. 1919: Returned to owner.

A. SPENCE MACDONALD 1914/19   Displacement: 195TG 76TN
Engines: 78HP
Armament: 1 x 6pdrAA
Admty No: 113
Port Reg: A. 357

1911: Launched. Built at Aberdeen. Owned by The Gamecock STC of Scarborough. 1914: Requisitioned in August and converted to a M/S. 1919: Returned to owners.

ASTON VILLA   1939/40   Football Group
Displacement: 546TG 196TN
Engines: 99HP
Armament: 1 x 4-inch
Port Reg: GY. 428
P.No: FY. 261

1937: Launched. Built at Southbank-on-Tees by Smith's Dock. Owned by Consolidated Fisheries of Grimsby. 1939: Requisitioned and converted to A/S. Joined the 16th A/S Strike Force as Group Leader. Based at Aberdeen for operations around Northern Scotland. 1940: TPI the Norwegian Campaign in April/May. Whilst alongside with others of the Group having set up an AA post ashore, she came under heavy air attack. A bomb scored a direct hit and she caught fire. The fire was eventually extinguished and she was still able to steam at 6K. LOST. Sunk by enemy a/c off Norway on 3rd May.

ASTROS   1939/46   See under WILLIAM SPENCER
(Vol 1 p.89)

ATHELSTAN   1914/19 1939/40 Displacement: 202TG 90TN
Engines: 67HP = 10K
Armament: 1 x 6pdrAA
Admty No: 343
Port Reg: GY. 648

1911: Launched. Built at Beverley by CWG. Owned by Onward SFC of Grimsby. 1914: Requisitioned in August and converted to a M/S. 1919: Returned to owners. 1927: Acquired by Robinson of Grimsby. 1939: Requisitioned in November and designated as an APV. 1940: Conversion not undertaken and returned to owners in January. Mercantile Loss. Last seen on 27th April in the North Sea. Lost with all hands.

29

ATHENIAN   1939/46   Displacement: 218TG 97TN
                                   Engines: 67HP = 10K
                                   Port Reg: GY. 357
                                   P.Nos: FY. 757 (M/S) Y7.1 (Esso)
1919: Launched. Built at Beverley by CWG. Owned by Onward SF Co., Ltd., Grimsby.
1939: Requisitioned in November and converted to an APV. 1940: Converted to a M/S
in June. 1944: Converted to an Esso in March. 1946: Returned to owners in September.
1964: BU in Belgium. *Notes*: The last coal burning steam trawler in service, she had the
unenviable reputation of having sunk two other trawlers in collisions, the *Serapion* in
1946 and the *Zefyr* in 1960. Both were Grimsby trawlers.

ATLANTIC   1917/19   Displacement: 166TG 65TN
                                   Engines: 58HP
                                   Port Reg: DE. 126
1898: Launched. Built at Beverley. Iron construction. Owned by WJ.Allen AO of
Grimsby. 1917: Requisitioned into the Fishery Reserve. 1919: Returned to owners.
1937: Owned by Plymouth Trawlers Ltd., of Plymouth.

ATTENTIVE II   1918/19   See under SEAWARD HO

AUCKLAND   1914/19   Displacement: 155TG 61TN
                                   Engines: 35HP = 9K
                                   Armament: 1 x 6pdr
                                   Admty No: 648
                                   Port Reg: H. 441
1899: Launched. Built at Hull by CWG. Owned by Hull SF & Ice Co of Hull. 1914:
Requisitioned in October and converted to a M/S. 1919: Returned to owners. Acquired
by A. Gouldby of Lowestoft. PR: LT. 445. 1936: BU.

AUCUBA   1915/19   Displacement: 211TG 76TN
                                   Engines: 66HP = 10K
                                   Port Reg: GY. 117
1906: Launched. Built at Beverley by CWG. Owned by Grant & Robinson of Grimsby.
1915: Requisitioned and converted to a BDV. 1919: Returned to owners. 1951:
Mercantile Loss. Sank following a collision with the Italian *SS Maria Bibolini* off Robin
Hood's Bay, Yorkshire on 5th September. No loss of life.

AUDREY   1917/19   Displacement: 186TG 73TN
                                   Engines: 36HP
                                   Port Reg: A. 482
1906: Launched. Built at Aberdeen. Owned by The Silver City STC of Aberdeen. 1917:
Requisitioned into the Fishery Reserve. 1919: Returned to owners.

AUK	1914/18	Displacement: 168TG 64TN
		Engines: 45HP
		Armament: 1914: 1 x 12pdr; 1 x 6pdr
		1917: 1 x 12pdr; 1 x 7.5-inch Bomb
		Thrower (A/S Howitzer)
		Admty No: 422
		Port Reg: H. 755

1903: Launched. Built at Goole by Goole SB. Owned by Kelsall Bros. & Beeching of Hull. 1914: Requisitioned in November and converted to a M/S. 1917: Converted to a 'Q' ship and rearmed. 1918: Renamed ANTIC in April. Returned to owners in November. 1937: Owned by Brixham Trawlers Ltd., of Brixham. *Notes*: Operational names as a 'Q' Ship: *Ben Nevis, Claymore, Girdler, Glen; Afric, Hope, Lorne, St.Gothard* and *Spika*.

AUK	1915/19	Displacement: 183TG 69TN
		Engines: 61HP
		Armament: 1 x 3pdr
		Port Reg: A. 482

1901: Launched. Built at Aberdeen. Owned by The Silver City STC of Aberdeen. 1915: Requisitioned in June and converted to a BDV. 1919: Returned to owners.

AUREA	1917/20	Displacement: 270TG 105TN
		Engines: 89HP
		Armament: 1 x 12pdr; 1 x 3.5-inch
		Bomb Thrower (A/S Howitzer)
		Admty No: 3066
		Port Reg: FD. 300

1917: Launched. Built at Dundee. Owned by The Brooklyn FC of Fleetwood. Requisitioned in September and fitted with Listening Hydrophones. 1920: Returned to owners.

AURORA	1914/19	Displacement: 225TG 106TN
		Engines: 67HP
		Armament: 1 x 6pdrAA
		Admty No: 345
		Port Reg: GY. 172

1906: Launched. Built at Selby by Cochrane. Owned by Consolidated Fisheries of Grimsby. 1914: Requisitioned in August and converted to a M/S. 1915: Renamed AURORA II in February. 1919: Returned to owners. 1937: Owned by Charles Dobson of Grimsby.

AURORA II	1915/19	See under AURORA above

AUSTRALIA	1916/19	Displacement: 238TG 146TN
		Engines: 60HP
		Armament: 1 x 6pdrAA

Port Reg: H. 1328

1882: Launched. Built at Hull. Owned by Hull SF & Ice Co of Hull. 1916: Requisitioned in August and converted to a BDV. 1918: Renamed BENDIGO in April. 1919: Returned to owners.

AVACANORA   1917/19   Displacement: 147TG
1894: Launched. 1917: Requisitioned. 1919: Returned to owners.

AVALANCHE   1940/45   See under BALMORAL

AVALON   1940/41   See under NORDHAV 1

AVANTURINE   1939/45   Ex-*Mendip*
        Displacement: 412TG 158TN
        Engines: 106HP
        Port Reg: H. 114
        P.No: FY. 249

1934: Launched. Built at Selby by Cochrane. Owned by WB Wiley & Sons of Hull. 1939: Requisitioned in August and converted to A/S. Purchased into the RN in November. 1940: Renamed SPHENE in February. Based at Grimsby (ungrouped). 1945: Sold to Mercantile and reverted to original name *Mendip*. Acquired by Charleson-Smith Trawlers of Hull. PR: H. 202.

AVANTURINE   1940/43   Displacement: 296TG 130TN
        Engines: 89HP = 11K
        Armament: 1 x 12pdr
        Engines: 89HP
        Port Reg: H. 197
        P.No: FY. 1886

1930: Launched. Built at Beverley by CWG. Owned by Kingston STC of Hull. 1940: Requisitioned in February and converted to an APV. 1942: Converted to a M/S. 1943: LOST. Torpedoed by E-Boat off Beachy Head whilst in tow on 1st December with the loss of all hands.

AVOLA   1939/46   See under SASEBO of 1915

AVON   1914/19 1940/41 Displacement: 250TG 111TN
        Armament: 1 x 12pdr
        Engines: 70HP
        Admty No: 708
        Port Reg: GY. 340
        P.No: WWII: 4. 177

1907: Launched. Built at Selby by Cochrane. Owned by Jeff Bros. of Grimsby. 1914: Requisitioned in December and converted to a M/S. 1916: Renamed AVON II in July.

1919: Returned to owners. Purchased by Bantock of Hull. 1937: Owned by Dobson Ship Repairing Co. of Grimsby. 1940: Requisitioned in May and converted to an APV. 1941: Returned to owners in December. 1948: Acquired by Wembley SFC (Grimsby) Ltd., of Fleetwood.

| AVON II | 1916/19 | See under AVON above |

AVONDEE — See under THOMAS EVISON (Vol 1 p.188)

AVONGLEN — See under CAPTAIN POLLEN

AVONMOUTH 1915/19
Displacement: 139TG 50TN
Engines: 45HP
Armament: 1 x 3pdr
Admty No: 963
Port Reg: M. 54

1890: Launched. Built at Middlesborough by Smith's Dock. Owned by C. Graham of London. 1915: Requisitioned in January. Returned to the Fishing Fleet in April. 1917: Requisitioned into the Fishery Reserve. 1919: Returned to owners.

AVON STREAM 1939/45 See under EVA WALES

AVON WATER 1939/46
Displacement: 260TG 113TN
Engines: 74HP
Port Reg: A. 142
P.No: Z. 119

1930: Launched. Built at Aberdeen. Owned by North Star SFC of Aberdeen. 1939: Requisitioned in September and converted to a BDV. 1946: Returned to owners in May.

AYACANORA 1917/19
Displacement: 147TG
Port Reg: M. 54

1894: Launched. 1917: Requisitioned into the Fishery Reserve. 1919: Returned to owners.

AYRESHIRE 1939/45
Shire Group
Displacement: 540TG 215TN
Engines: 99HP
Dimensions: 175ft x 28ft
Armament: 1 x 4-inch; 2 x LG (2x1)
Port Reg: GY. 520
P.No: FY. 225

1938: Launched. Built at Southbank-on-Tees by Smith's Dock. Owned by Ayreshire SF (H. Markham) of Grimsby. 1939: Transferred to Hull base port in August. Requisitioned in September and converted to A/S. Joined the 11th A/S Striking Force based at Rosyth.

1940: On 20th February, ICW sister-ship FIFESHIRE, 70 miles E.of Copinsay in the Orkneys, they were attacked by 2 x Heinkel 111s. The FIFESHIRE succumbed to a bombing attack, but AYRESHIRE survived having managed to drive off the enemy a/c with only her secondary armament of Lewis guns. Her main armament of a 4-inch had not yet been mounted. 1941: Transferred to the Iceland Command in August for Russian Convoys. 1942: Part of the escort for the ill-fated PQ.17 Convoy to Russia. After the convoy was ordered to scatter, she found several stragglers and shepherded them up to the ice. Her CO then had the idea of painting all the ships white on the South facing sides and decks to hide them in the ice. They remained undiscovered and reached Russia in safety. 1945: Returned to owners in October. 1946: Acquired by Devon FC of Hull and renamed *Macbeth*. PR: H. 113.

BABIANA   1939/44   SAN   Displacement: 262TG
                                          P.No: T. 20
1935: Launched. 1939: Requisitioned for the SAN in September and converted to a M/S. 1944: Returned to owners.

BABS   1918/19   See under BARBADOS

BADEN POWELL II   1917/19   Displacement: 93TG 35TN
                                          Engines: 32HP
                                          Port Reg: SN. 268
1900: Launched. Built at Anstruther. Owned by The Warrior SFC of North Shields. 1917: Requisitioned into the Fishery Reserve. 1919: Returned to owners.

BADINAGE   1941/45   See under SABREUR

BALFOUR   1915/18   Displacement: 285TG
                                          Armament: 1 x 3pdr
                                          Admty No: 1228
                                          Port Reg: H. 432
1912: Launched. 1915: Requisitioned in February and converted to a M/S. 1918: LOST. Sunk in collision with the Royal Sovereign LV. on 13th May.

BALGOWNIE   1917/19   Displacement: 185TG 72HP
                                          Engines: 61HP
                                          Port Reg: GY. 934
1902: Launched. Built at Aberdeen. Owned by Dobson of Healing, Lincs. 1917: Requisitioned into the Fishery Reserve. 1919: Returned to owners.

BALISE   1942/46   See under VAILLANT

BALMEDIE   1914/15   Displacement: 205TG
                                          Admty No: 350
                                          Port Reg: A. 113
1906: Launched. 1914: Requisitioned in August and converted to a M/S. 1915: Deployed to the Med. LOST. Sunk in a collision in the Dardenelles on 27th April.

BALMORAL   1917/19 1939/45 Displacement: 222TG 97TN
                                          Engines: 66HP
                                          Armament: 1 x 6pdrAA
                                          Admty No: 3043
                                          Port Reg: GY. 1001

P.No: WWII: FY. 1895

1916: Launched. Built at Selby by Cochrane. Owned by The Queen SFC of Grimsby. 1917: Requisitioned in June and converted to a M/S. 1919: Returned to owners. 1939: Requisitioned in November and converted to an APV. 1940: Converted to a M/S in June and renamed AVALANCHE. Based at Grimsby (ungrouped). 1944: Converted to a BBV. 1945: Returned to owners in May.

BALTIC	1915/15	Displacement: 154TG
		Armament: 1 x 3pdr
		Admty No: 967
		Port Reg: GY. 186

1888: Launched. 1915: Requisitioned in January. Returned to owners in June.

BANDELERO	1939/40	Displacement: 440TG 168TN
		Engines: 99HP
		Port Reg: H. 149
		P.No: FY. 788

1935: Launched. Built at Southbank-on-Tees by Smith's Dock. Owned by Hull Northern FC of Hull. 1939: Purchased in August and converted to A/S. 1940: LOST. Sunk in collision with the destroyer WATERHEN off Sollum on 30th December.

BANYERS	1914/15	Ex-*The Banyers*
		Displacement: 448TG 281TN
		Engines: 89HP = 11K
		Admty No: 450
		Port Reg: GY. 128

1914: Launched. Built at Beverley by CWG. Owned by South Western FC of Grimsby. Requisitioned in August, converted to a M/S and renamed. 1915: LOST. Mined whilst sweeping in Cayton Bay near Scarborough on 6th January.

BARBADOS	1914/19 1939/45	Displacement: 211TG 83TN
		Engines: 60HP = 10K
		Port Reg: GY. 71

1905: Launched. Built at Beverley by CWG. Owned by Grant & Baker SFC of Grimsby. 1914: Requisitioned in October and converted to a BDV. 1918: Renamed BABS in April. 1919: Returned to owners and reverted to original name. 1928: Acquired by Robinson & Sons of Grimsby. 1939: Requisitioned and converted to an APV. 1940: Transferred to miscellaneous duties. 1944: Acquired by Dominion SFC of Grimsby. 1945: Returned to owners and renamed *Alsation*. 1955: BU at Charlestown.

BARBARA ROBB	1939/44	Displacement: 263TG 115TN
		Engines: 65HP
		Port Reg: A. 124
		P.No: Z. 155

1930: Launched. Built at Aberdeen. Owned by G. Robb & Sons of Aberdeen. 1939: Requisitioned in September and converted to a BDV. 1944: Returned to owner in December.

BARBARA ROBERTSON 1939/39 See under JAMES McDONALD
(Vol 1 p.138)

BARLE 1915/19 Displacement: 283TG 120TN
Engines: 87HP
Armament: 1 x 6pdrAA; 1 x 3.5-inch
Bomb Thrower (A/S Howitzer)
Admty No: 1862
Port Reg: GY. 78
1914: Launched. Built at Selby by Cochrane. Owned by GW & HB Jeffs of Grimsby. 1915: Requisitioned in September and converted to a M/S. 1919: Returned to owners.

BARNET 1933/45 See under JOHN MANN (Vol 1 p.142)

BARNSLEY 1914/15 Displacement: 144TG
1896: Launched. 1914: Requisitioned in October and converted to a M/S. 1915: Returned to owners in May. 1917: Mercantile Loss. Captured by a German S/M 13 miles North of Inishtrahull and then sunk by bombs. Skipper and Chief Engineer taken prisoner.

BARNSNESS 1940/44 See under CICERO

BARON RUZETTE 1917/19 Displacement: 214TG
Port Reg: Belgian
1910: Launched. Belgian fishing vessel. 1917: Requisitioned, with the Belgian owners permission, into the Fishery Reserve. 1919: Returned to owners.

BASSANIO 1914/19 Displacement: 270TG 108TN
Engines: 80HP = 10.5K
Armament: 1 x 12pdr
Admty No: 309
Port Reg: H. 372
1904: Launched. Built at Beverley by CWG. Owned by Hellyer SFC of Hull. 1913: Acquired by Imperial SFC of Hull. 1914: Requisitioned in August and converted to a M/S. 1919: Returned to owners. 1935: BU.

BASS ROCK 1914/19 Displacement: 169TG 67TN
Engines: 54HP
Admty No: 513
Port Reg: LH. 296

1907: Launched. Built at Leith. 1914: Requisitioned in September and converted to a M/S. 1919: Returned to owner. 1938: Owned by WH. East of Milford Haven. PR: A. 759.

BASTION	1917/19	See under BOSTONIAN

BASUTO	1940/46	Displacement: 388TG 151TN
		Engines: 101HP = 11.2K
		Port Reg: H. 401
		P. No: Z. 106

1932: Launched. Built at Beverley by CWG. Owned by Hellyer Bros. of Hull. 1940: Requisitioned in January and converted to a BDV. Based at Grimsby. 1945: Acquired by Lord Line of Hull. 1946: Returned to owners in January. 1947: Renamed *Lord Montgomery*. 1963: BU at Troon.

BAYARD	1917/18	Displacement: 231TG
		Port Reg: French

1908: Launched. French fishing vessel. 1917: Hired from French owners. 1918: Returned to France.

BEATHWOOD	1939/40	See under OSBORNE STROUD

BEATRICE	1914/18	Displacement: 173TG 68TN
		Engines: 45HP = 9.5K
		Armament: 1 x 12pdr
		Admty No: 621
		Port Reg: H. 922

1906: Launched. Built at Beverley by CWG. Owned by Hellyers of Hull. 1914: Requisitioned in September and converted to a M/S. 1917: Acquired by Curzon of Milford Haven. 1918: Returned to owners. 1936: BU.

BEATRICE II	1914/19	Displacement: 239TG 92TN
		Engines: 57HP
		Armament: 1 x 3pdr
		Admty No: 362
		Port Reg: M. 212

1907:Launched. Built at North Shields. 1914: Requisitioned in August and converted to a M/S. Renamed BEATRICE II in December. 1919: Returned to owners. Acquired by the Middleton STC of West Hartlepool. PR: HL.16.

BEAULNE VERNEUIL	1940/46	See under JOHN BRICE (Vol 1 p.61)

BEAUMARIS CASTLE	1940/45	See under JAMES BURGESS
		(Vol 1 p.56)

BEDFORDSHIRE	1939/42	Shire Group

Displacement: 900T 433TG
Engines: 99HP
Dimensions: 162ft oa x 27ft x 14ft
Armament: 1 x 4-inch
Complement: 34
Port Reg: GY. 196
P.No: FY. 141

1935: Launched in August. Built at Southbank-on-Tees by Smith's Dock. Owned by Bedfordshire SFC. (H. Markham) of Grimsby. Completed in August. 1939: Purchased into the RN in August and converted to A/S. Completed in December and joined the 17th A/S Group based at Swansea for A/S patrols in the Bristol Channel. 1942: Employed on convoy duties Bristol/English Channels. Loaned to the USN in March, together with her crew, for A/S duties. Escorted the damaged AMC QUEEN OF BERMUDA from Halifax to New York for repair. Employed on convoy duties off the East Coast of the USA and Canada. LOST. Sunk by U-558 off Cape Lookout, North Carolina, on 11th May. She was struck by 2 torpedoes and disintegrated. Out of the Ship's Company of 34, there was only one survivor.

BEDOUIN   1914/15   Displacement: 188TG
                                            Admty No: 353
                                            Port Reg: GN. 80

1902: Launched. 1914: Requisitioned in August and converted to a M/S. 1915: LOST. Mined off Tory Island on 13th February.

BEECHWOLD   1914/14   Displacement: 129TG
                                            Port Reg: GY. 779

1895: Launched. 1914: Requisitioned in August. Returned to owners in September. 1916: Mercantile Loss. Sunk by gunfire from a German S/M 40 miles SE x E from Spurn LV. on 23rd September.

BEGA   1914/17   Displacement: 318TG
                                            Armament: 1 x 12pdr
                                            Admty No: 923
                                            Port Reg: FD. 233

1914: Launched. Requisitioned in November. 1917: LOST. Sunk by German S/M 40 miles North of Muckle Flugga.

BELGAUM   1916/19   Displacement: 337TG
                                            Armament: 1 x 6pdrAA
                                            Admty No: 1985
                                            Port Reg: RE. 161

1916: Launched. Owned by Abunda Fishing Co. of Grimsby and registered in Iceland. Requisitioned in March and converted to a M/S. 1919: Returned to owners.

BELLDOCK	1939/40	See under LEAM

BELLEROPHON 1914/19 Displacement: 184TG 88TN
Engines: 57HP
Armament: 1 x 12pdr
Admty No: 5 and 168
Port Reg: GY. 335

1907: Launched. Built at Selby by Cochrane. Owned by Consolidated Fisheries of Grimsby. 1914: Requisitioned in August and converted to a M/S. 1915: Renamed BELLEROPHON II in February. 1919: Returned to owners.

BELLEROPHON II 1915/19 See under BELLEROPHON above

BELLONA 1914/19 1939/45 Displacement: 184TG 88TN
Engines: 57HP
Armament: 1 x 6pdr
Admty No: 23
Port Reg: GY. 336

1907: Launched. Built at Selby by Cochrane. Owned by Consolidated Fisheries of Grimsby. 1914: Requisitioned in August and converted to a M/S. 1915: Renamed BELLONA III in May. 1919: Returned to owners. 1939: Requisitioned in November and converted to an APV. 1940: Renamed EGERIA. Converted to a D/L. 1941: Converted back to a M/S in January. 1945: Returned to owners.

BELLONA III 1915/19 See under BELLONA above

BELLWORT 1915/19
1915: Requisitioned. 1919: Returned to owners.

BELMONT 1915/19 Displacement: 209TG 81TN
Engines: 66HP
Armament: 1 x 6pdrAA
Admty No: 3248
Port Reg: FD. 64

1906: Launched. Built at Bowling. Owned by W. Would of Grimsby. 1915: Requisitioned in June and converted to a M/S. 1919: Returned to owners.

BELTON 1940/45 See under THOMAS FOLEY
(Vol 1 p.188)

BEMPTON 1915/19 Displacement: 226TG 87TN
Engines: 50HP=11K
Armament: 1 x 12pdr
Admty No: 1369

Port Reg: H. 19

1914: Launched. Built at Beverley by CWG. Owned by Hull SF & Ice Co of Hull. 1915: Requisitioned in April and converted to a M/S. 1919: Returned to owners. 1958: BU in Germany.

BEN AGDALE   1915/19   Displacement: 197TG 76TN
                                     Engines: 78HP
                                     Port Reg: A. 473

1912: Launched. Built at Aberdeen. Owned by Irvin & Sons of North Shields. 1915: Requisitioned in June and converted to a BDV. 1919: Returned to owners.

BEN ALDER   1915/19   Displacement: 151TG 59TN
                                     Engines: 50HP
                                     Armament: 1 x 3pdr
                                     Port Reg: A. 16

1899: Launched. Built at Aberdeen. Owned by Holbech STC of Scarborough. 1915: Requisitioned in June and converted to a BDV. 1919: Returned to owners.

BEN ARDNA   1914/15   Displacement: 197TG
                                     Admty No: 289
                                     Port Reg: A. 517

1912: Launched. 1914: Requisitioned in August and converted to a M/S. 1915: LOST. Mined near the Elbow Buoy on 8th August.

BEN ARDNA   1939/45   See under JOHN BRADFORD
                                     (Vol 1 p.176)

BEN ATTOW   1916/19   Displacement: 156TG 61TN
                                     Engines: 50HP
                                     Port Reg: A. 168

1900: Launched. Built at Aberdeen. Owned by J. Craig Jnr of Aberdeen. 1916: Requisitioned in August and converted to a BDV. 1919: Returned to owners. 1938: Owned by H. Macfarlane of Dundee. PR: DE. 33.

BEN BARVAS   1915/19 1940/40 Displacement: 198TG 86TN
                                     Engines: 57HP
                                     Port Reg: A. 111

1914: Launched. Built at Aberdeen. Owned by Irvin & Sons of North Shields. 1915: Requisitioned in June and converted to a BDV. 1919: Returned to owners. 1940: Requisitioned in June and designated as an APV. Returned to owners in September.

BEN BEULAH   1939/45   See under THOMAS DOWDING
                                     (Vol 1 p.76)

BEN BHRACHIE 1916/19 1940/45 Displacement: 235TG 102TN
Engines: 78HP
Armament: 1 x 6pdrAA
Admty No: 2951
Port Reg: A. 704
P.No: WWII: FY. 997

1916: Launched. Built at Aberdeen. Owned by Irvin & Sons of North Shields. Requisitioned in March and converted to a M/S. 1919: Returned to owners. 1940: Requisitioned in March and converted to a M/S. 1945: Returned to owners in December

BEN BREAC 1916/19 1940/45 Displacement: 235TG 102TN
Engines: 78HP
Armament: 1 x 12pdr
Admty No: 2953
Port Reg: A. 705
P.No: WWII: FY. 336

1916: Launched. Built at Aberdeen. Owned by Irvin & Sons of North Shields. Requisitioned in August and converted to a M/S. 1919: Returned to owners. 1940: Requisitioned in June and converted to a M/S. 1945: Returned to owners in December

BEN CHOURN 1914/38 Displacement: 197TG 77TN
Engines: 78HP
Armament: 1 x 3pdr
Admty No: 83
Port Reg: A. 40

1914: Launched. Built at Aberdeen. Requisitioned in August and converted to a M/S. 1919: Returned to owners. 1938: Owned by Irvin & Sons of North Shields.

BEN EARN **(Steve Bush Collection)**

BEN DEARG   1918/20   See under BEN RINNES

BEN DEARG   1939/46   See under THOMAS ALEXANDER
                                          (Vol 1 p.74)

BEN DORAN   1915/20   Displacement: 155TG 60TN
                                         Engines: 50HP
                                         Port Reg: A. 178
1900: Launched. Built at Aberdeen. Owned by T. Davidson of Aberdeen. 1915:
Requisitioned in September and converted to a BDV. 1920: Returned to owners.

BEN EARN   1916/20 1940/46 Displacement: 235TG 102TN
                                    Engines: 78HP
                                    Armament: 1 x 12pdr; 1 x 7.5-inch
                                    Bomb Thrower (A/S Howitzer)
                                    Admty No: 3309
                                    Port Reg: SN. 312
                                    P.No: WWII: FY. 999
1916: Launched. Built at Aberdeen. Owned by Irvin & Sons of North Shields.
Requisitioned in October and converted to a M/S. 1920: Returned to owners. 1940:
Requisitioned in February and converted to a M/S. 1946: Returned to owners in February.

BEN GAIRN   1916/19 1940/41 Displacement: 204TG 102TN
                                    Engines: 78HP
                                    Armament: 1 x 12pdr; 1 x 7.5-inch
                                    Bomb Thrower (A/S Howitzer)
                                    Admty No: 3314
                                    Port Reg: A. 738
1916: Launched. Built at Aberdeen. Owned by Irvin & Sons of North Shields.
Requisitioned in November and converted to a M/S. 1919: Returned to owners. 1940:
Requisitioned in June and converted to a M/S. 1941: LOST. Sunk by a parachute mine
at Lowestoft on 4th May.

BEN GLAMAIR   1915/19   Displacement: 198TG 86TN
                                         Engines: 78HP
                                         Admty No: 1494
                                         Port Reg: SN. 110
1914: Launched. Built at Aberdeen. Owned by Irvin & Sons of North Shields. 1915:
Requisitioned in May and converted to a M/S. 1919: Returned to owners.

BEN GLAS   1917/19 1939/44 Displacement: 234TG 102TN
                                    Engines: 78HP
                                    Armament: 1 x 6pdrAA
                                    Admty No: 3039

Port Reg: SN. 336
P.No: WWII: FY. 808

1917: Launched. Built at Aberdeen. Owned by Irvin & Sons of North Shields. Requisitioned in May and converted to a M/S. 1919: Returned to owners. 1939: Requisitioned in November and converted to an APV. 1940: Converted to a M/S in June. 1944: Converted to an Esso. Returned to owners in October.

BEN GULVAIN   1914/19 1939/46 Displacement: 197TG 86TN
                                        Engines: 78HP
                                        Armament: 1 x 6pdrAA
                                        Admty No: 1344
                                        Port Reg: A. 118
                                        P.No: WWII: FY. 1680

1914: Launched. Built at Aberdeen. 1915: Requisitioned in March and converted to a M/S. 1919: Returned to owners. Owned by Irvin & Sons of North Shields. 1939: Requisitioned in August and converted to a M/S. 1946: Returned to owners in August.

BEN HEILEM   1914/17   Displacement: 196TG
                                        Armament: 1 x 12pdr; 1 x 6pdrAA

1912: Launched. 1914: Requisitioned in August and converted to a M/S. 1917: LOST. Wrecked off Berwick on 8th October.

BEN HEILEM   1939/46   Displacement: 224TG 98TN
                                        Engines: 78HP
                                        Port Reg: A. 242
                                        P. No: FY. 765

1919: Launched. Built at Aberdeen. Owned by Irvin & Sons of North Shields. 1939: Requisitioned in November and converted to an APV. 1941: Converted to a M/S. 1946: Returned to owners in April.

BEN HOLDEN   1914/19   Displacement: 197TG 77TN
                                        Engines: 78HP
                                        Armament: 1 x 3pdr
                                        Admty No: 84
                                        Port Reg: A. 38

1914: Launched. Built at Aberdeen. Owned by Irvin & Sons of North Shields. Requisitioned in August and converted to a M/S. 1919: Returned to owners.

BEN HOPE   1917/19   Displacement: 160TG 61TN
                                        Engines: 56HP
                                        Port Reg: LT. 352

1900: Launched. Built at Aberdeen. Owned by HW Barker of London. 1917: Requisitioned into the Fishery Reserve. 1919: Returned to owners.

BEN IDRIS   1939/45   Displacement: 232TG 101TN
                                     Engines: 65HP
                                     Port Reg: SN. 137
                                     P.No: FY. 1766
1931: Launched. Built at Aberdeen. Owned by Irvin & Sons of North Shields. 1939: Requisitioned in August and converted for the Exam Service. 1941: Converted to a M/S. 1945: Returned to owners in September.

BEN IVER   1914/19   Displacement: 197TG
                                     Armament: 1 x 6pdr
                                     Port Reg: A. 602
1914: Launched. Built at Aberdeen. Owned by Irvin & Sons of North Shields. Requisitioned and converted to a M/S. 1919: Returned to owners. 1938: Owned by J. Walker AO of Aberdeen. PR: A. 341.

BEN LAWYERS   1914/919   Displacement: 176TG 68TN
                                     Engines: 62HP
                                     Armament: 1 x 12pdr
                                     1 x 6pdrAA
                                     Admty No: 472
                                     Port Reg: A. 311
1900: Launched. Built at Aberdeen. Owned by J. Craig Snr. AO of Aberdeen. 1914: Requisitioned in November and converted to a M/S. 1919: Returned to owners.

BEN LEDI   1918/19   Displacement: 149TG 58TN
                                     Engines: 52HP
                                     Port Reg: A. 847
1898: Launched.   Built at Aberdeen. Owned by T. Davidson of Aberdeen. 1918: Requisitioned. 1919: Returned to owners.

BEN LORA   1914/19   Displacement: 197TG 76TN
                                     Engines: 78HP
                                     Armament: 1 x 6pdrAA
                                     Admty No: 303
                                     Port Reg: SN. 269
1913: Launched.   Built at Aberdeen. Owned by Irvin & Sons of North Shields. 1914: Requisitioned in August and converted to a M/S. 1919: Returned to owners.

BEN LOYAL   1914/19   Displacement: 183TG 71TN
                                     Engines: 62HP
                                     Armament: 1 x 3pdr
                                     Admty No: 279
                                     Port Reg: A. 500
1901: Launched.   Built at Aberdeen. Owned by Irvin & Sons of North Shields. 1914:

Requisitioned in August and converted to a M/S. 1919: Returned to owners. 1938: Owned by the Dundee FCL of Dundee. PR: DE. 105.

BEN LUI	1915/19	Displacement: 155TG 60TN
		Engines: 50HP
		Port Reg: A. 185

1900: Launched. Built at Aberdeen. Owned by J. Cormack of Aberdeen. 1915: Requisitioned in June and converted to a BDV. 1919: Returned to owners.

BEN MEIDIE	1917/19 1940/46	Displacement: 234TG 102TN
		Engines: 78HP
		Armament: 1 x 6pdr
		Admty No: 3036
		Port Reg: SN. 340
		P.No: WWII: FY. 1818

1917: Launched. Built at Aberdeen. Owned by Irvin & Sons of North Shields. Requisitioned in April and converted to a M/S. 1919: Returned to owners. 1940: Requisitioned in January and converted to a M/S. Joined the 110th M/S Group based at Grimsby. Operated in the area Cromer-Flamborough Head. 1941: 113th M/S Group based at Grimsby. 1943: 111th M/S Group based at Grimsby. 1946: Returned to owners in March.

BEN RINNES	1915/20	Displacement: 183TG 71TN
		Engines: 63HP
		Armament: 1 x 6pdr
		Port Reg: A.488

1901: Launched. Built at Aberdeen. Owned by T. Davidson AO of Aberdeen. 1915: Requisitioned in September and converted to a BDV. 1918: Renamed BEN DEARG in June. 1920: Returned to owners.

BEN ROSSAL	1939/46	Displacement: 260TG 114TN
		Engines: 63HP
		Port Reg: A. 65
		P. No: Z. 120

1929: Launched. Built at Aberdeen. Owned by Irvine & Sons of North Shields. 1939: Requisitioned in September and converted to a BDV. Based at Scapa Flow. 1946: Returned to owners in March.

BEN ROY	1940/45	Displacement: 260TG 114TN
		Engines: 63HP
		Port Reg: SN. 61
		P. No: FY. 1557

1929: Launched. Built at Aberdeen. Owned by Irvin & Sons of North Shields. 1940: Requisitioned in February and converted to a M/S. 1945: Returned to owners.

BEN SCREEL   1915/19   Displacement: 197TG 86TN
                                            Engines: 78HP
                                            Port Reg: A. 121
1914: Launched. Built at Aberdeen. Owned by Irvin & Sons of North Shields. 1915:
Requisitioned in June and converted to a BDV. 1919: Returned to owners.

BEN TARBERT   1915/19 1940/46 Displacement: 197TG 76TN
                                            Engines: 78HP
                                            Port Reg: WWI: A. 476. WWII: HL 21
                                            P. No: WWII: Z .212
1912: Launched. Built at Aberdeen. Owned by Irvin & Sons of North Shields. 1915:
Requisitioned in June and converted to a BDV. 1919: Returned to owners. Acquired by
The Friarage SFC of Hartlepool and retained the same name. 1940: Requisitioned in
May converted to an APV. Converted to a BDV in July. 1941: Converted to a M/S. 1944:
Converted to a Stores Carrier. 1946: Returned to owners.

BEN TORC   1917/19 1940/45 Displacement: 199TG 78TN
                                            Engines: 78HP
                                            Armament: 1 x 6pdrAA
                                            Admty No: 3325
                                            Port Reg: A. 604
                                            P. No: WWII: FY. 1569
1916: Launched. Built at Aberdeen. Owned by Irvin & Sons of Aberdeen. 1917:
Requisitioned in January and converted to a M/S. 1919: Returned to owner. 1940:
Requisitioned in February and converted to a M/S. 1945: Returned to owners in
December.

BEN VURIE   1915/19   Displacement: 200TG 78TN
                                            Engines: 78HP
                                            Admty No: 1497
                                            Port Reg: SN. 113
1914: Launched. Built at Aberdeen. Owned by Irvin & Sons of North Shields. 1915:
Requisitioned in May. 1919: Returned to owners.

BEN ZINNES   1915/19
1915: Requisitioned and converted to a BDV. 1919: Returned to owners.

BENDIGO   1918/19   See under AUSTRALIA

BENGAL   1915/19 1939/44 Displacement: 211TG 83TN
                                            Engines: 60HP = 10.5K
                                            Armament: 1 x 6pdrAA
                                            Admty No: 1150
                                            Port Reg: WWI: GY. 108

WWII: GY. 103

P.No: WWII: FY.1591

1905: Launched. Built at Beverley by CWG. Owned by Grant & Baker SFC of Grimsby. 1915: Requisitioned and converted to a M/S. 1919: Returned to owners. Acquired by Robinson & Son of Grimsby. 1939: Requisitioned in November and converted to an APV. 1940: Renamed STAUNCH and converted to a M/S. 1944: Converted to an Esso. Returned to owners in November and reverted to original name. 1955: BU at Charlestown.

BENGAL II   1915/19   Ex-*Bengal*

Displacement: 149TG 64TN

Engines: 35HP = 9.5K

Armament: 1 x 6pdr

Admty No: 1203

Port Reg: H. 287

1896: Launched. Built at Hull by CWG. Owned by Hull SF & Ice Co of Hull. 1915: Requisitioned in February and converted to a M/S. Renamed BENGAL II in March. 1919: Returned to owners. Acquired by A. Gouldby of Lowestoft. PR: LT. 575. 1923: Acquired by Dutch mercantile and renamed *Roode Zee*. 1937: BU in Holland.

BENGALI   1939/42   Displacement: 455TG 166TN

Engines: 99HP

Port Reg: H. 397

P.No: FY. 165

1937: Launched. Built at Southbank-on-Tees by Smith's Dock. Owned by Hellyer Bros. of Hull. 1939: Purchased into the RN in August and converted to an A/S. 1942: LOST. Destroyed by a petrol explosion at Lagos, Nigeria, on 5th December. *Notes*: See under KELT.

BENSTROME   1915/19   Displacement: 196TG 86TN

Engines: 78HP

Armament: 1 x 6pdr

Admty No: 2657

Port Reg: A. 109

1914: Launched. Built at Aberdeen. Owned by Irvin & Sons of North Shields. 1915: Requisitioned in April and converted to a M/S. 1919: Returned to owners. *Notes*: Mercantile Lists as *Ben Strom*.

BENTON CASTLE   1915/16   Displacement: 283TG

Armament: 1 x 6pdr

Admty No: 1972

Port Reg: SA. 1

1914: Launched. 1915: Requisitioned in September. 1916: LOST. Mined off Dartmouth on 10th November.

BENVOLIO   1939/40   Displacement: 352TG 139TN
                                   Engines: 96HP
                                   Port Reg: H. 347
                                   P.No: FY. 710
1930: Launched. Built at Selby by Cochrane . Owned by the Hull Northern FC. 1939: Requisitioned in September and converted to a M/S. 1940: LOST. Mined off the Humber on 23rd February.

BERENGA   1939/45   See under FEUGH

BERGEN   1940/45   Displacement: 236TG
                                   Port Reg: Norwegian
1907: Launched. Norwegian fishing vessel. 1940: Hired from Norwegian owners and converted to a M/S. Commissioned with a Norwegian Crew. 1943: Converted to a BGV. Manned with RN crew. 1945: Returned to owners.

BERKSHIRE   1914/15   Displacement: 133TG
                                   Admty No: 995
                                   Port Reg: GY. 398
1897: Launched. Owned by the Shire TC. of Grimsby. 1914: Requisitioned in December. 1915: LOST. Sunk in a collision in Red Bay on 15th May.

BERKSHIRE   1939/45   Shire Group
                                   Displacement: 466TG 168TN
                                   Engines: 99HP
                                   Port Reg: GY. 286
                                   P.No: FY. 183
1936: Launched. Built at Southbank-on-Tees by Smith's Dock. Owned by Berkshire SFC. (H. Markham) of Grimsby. 1939: Requisitioned in October and converted to A/S. Joined the 23rd A/S Group. 1940: TPI the Norwegian Campaign in April/May. 1945: Returned to owner in November. Acquired by the Newington STC of Hull. PR: H. 139. 1946: Transferred to Hull and renamed *Conan Doyle*.

BERMUDA   1914/20   Displacement: 211TG 83TN
                                   Engines: 60HP = 10K
                                   Armament: 1 x 6pdr
                                   Admty No: 712
                                   Port Reg: GY. 56
1905: Launched. Built at Beverley by CWG. Owned by Grant & Baker SFC of Grimsby. 1914: Requisitioned in December and converted to a M/S. 1920: Returned to owners. 1928: Acquired by Robinson of Grimsby and renamed *Thracian*. 1955: BU in Belgium.

BERNADETTE   1940/45   Displacement: 302TG
                                   Port Reg: French

P.No: Z. 175

1914: Launched. 1940: French M/S seized at Dover on 3rd July in Operation Grab. Converted to a BDV in November. 1945: Returned to France in December.

BERRYHEAD	1917/19	Displacement: 58TG 39TN
		Engines: 15HP
		Port Reg: YH. 285

1901: Launched. Built at Lowestoft by Chambers. Owned by HJ Eastick of Gt. Yarmouth. 1917: Requisitioned into the Fishery Reserve. 1919: Returned to owner.

BERU	1914/19 1939/39	Displacement: 195TG 87TN
		Engines: 67HP
		Armament: 1 x 3pdr
		Admty No: 30 and 50
		Port Reg: GY. 611

1911: Launched. Built at Selby by Cochrane. Owned by A. Grant & Son of Grimsby. 1914: Requisitioned in November and converted to a M/S. 1919: Returned to owner. 1939: Requisitioned in October and designated as an APV. Returned to owner in December.

BERVIE BRAES	1939/44	See under GEORGE BURTON
		(Vol 1 p.171)

BERYL	1914/19 1939/46	Displacement: 248TG 98TN
		Engines: 76HP
		Armament: 2 x 6pdrAA
		Port Reg: H. 31
		P.No: WWII: FY. 71 (M/S) Z. 101(BGV)

1914: Launched. Built at Selby by Cochrane. Owned by the Kingston STC of Hull. Requisitioned in December and converted to a M/S. 1915: Renamed BERYL II in March. 1919: Returned to owners. 1939: Requisitioned in September for the RAN and converted to a M/S. 1944: Converted to a BGV. 1946: Returned to owners.

BERYL II	1915/19	See under BERYL 1914

BETTY INGLIS	1917/19 1939/46	Displacement: 104TG 44TN
		Engines: 45HP
		Port Reg: BF. 349

1895: Launched. Built at Aberdeen. 1917: Requisitioned into the Fishery Reserve. 1919: Returned to owners. 1938: Owned by JF Wilson & A Reid of McDuff. 1939: Requisitioned in December and converted to a M/S. 1940: Paid Off and Laid Up. 1946: Returned to owners in March.

BIANCA	1914/19	Displacement: 174TG 68TN
		Engines: 45HP = 9.5K

Armament: 1 x 3pdr
Admty No: 600
Port Reg: H. 845

1905: Launched. Built at Beverley by CWG. Owned by Hellyer SFC of Hull. 1914: Requisitioned in September and converted to a M/S. 1917: Acquired by C. Dobson of Grimsby. PR: GY.686. 1919: Returned to owners. 1941: Mercantile Loss. Sank with the loss of 5 of her 9 crew when she trawled up a bomb or mine in the Irish Sea on 20th March.

| BILSDEAN | 1940/45 | See under SARRAIL |

BIRCH	1915/16	Displacement: 215TG 106TN
		Engines: 67HP = 10.5K
		Admty No: 1129
		Port Reg: GY. 677

1912: Launched. Built at Beverley by CWG. Owned by W. Grant of Grimsby. 1915: Requisitioned in February and converted to a M/S. 1916: LOST. Mined off Yarmouth in 23rd August by a mine laid by the German UC-1 three days previously.

BITTERN	1914/19	Displacement: 207TG 84TN
		Engines: 55HP
		Armament: 1 x 6pdr
		Admty No: 432
		Port Reg: GY. 1278

1903: Launched. Built at Hull. Owned by J. Holland & WH Johnston of Grimsby. 1914: Requisitioned in December. 1915: Renamed BITTERN II in February. 1919: Returned to owners.

| BITTERN II | 1915/19 | See under BITTERN above |

BLACKBURN ROVERS	1939/40	Football Group
		Displacement: 422TG 161TN
		Engines: 99HP =12K
		Fuel: Coal
		Port Reg: GY. 102

1934: Launched. Built at Southbank-on-Tees by Smith's Dock. Owned by Consolidated Fisheries Ltd., Grimsby. Completed in November. 1939: Requisitioned in August and converted to an A/S at Cammell Laird, Birkenhead. Commissioned in October and based at Dover. On 26th November she was on A/S patrol off the Goodwin Sands in heavy weather. A cable was washed off her foredeck and wrapped around the screws. Adrift and helpless in the gale she dropped her anchor, but it dragged and she drifted into the minefield. The Dover lifeboat coming to her aid managed to take off all the crew and secret equipment in the midst of the minefield. For this heroic feat, the Coxswain of the Lifeboat was subsequently awarded the silver medal for gallantry. The order was given by the Admiral Commanding at Dover for the Trawler to be scuttled as by this time she was well into the minefield and it was a race as to whether she was mined or wrecked on the Goodwins. The seacocks were opened, but something went wrong and two days later, some 30 miles from where she had been abandoned, she was found, still with her anchor down off the Kentish Knock Sand. 1940: LOST. ICW Trawlers WESTELLA and SAON on 2nd June, she detected a U-Boat by ASDIC. During the attack her CO, Cdr. English, took her into a known British minefield and she struck a mine and sank. Her DCs had been set ready for the attack and as she sank they exploded injuring a number of her survivors. WESTELLA, going to their rescue, also struck a mine and sank. The official records of these events show an anomaly. BLACKBURN ROVERS is shown as having been sunk in the North Sea whilst WESTELLA's state 'off Dunkirk'.

BLACKFLY   1939/46   Ex-*Barnett*
                                      Cricketer Group
                                      Displacement: 482TG 202TN
                                      Engines: 155HP = 12.5K
                                      Port Reg: GY. 454
                                      P.No: FY. 117
1937: Launched on 26th July. Built at Beverley by CWG as *Barnett*. Owned by Crampin SFC of Grimsby. 1939: Purchased into the RN in August and converted to A/S. Renamed as there was already a BARNET in the Fleet. Joined the 12th A/S Striking Force and employed in Northern waters. Based at Grimsby/Chatham. 1940: TPI the Norwegian Campaign in April/May. 1942: Employed on Arctic Convoys. 1944: Transferred to the MF. ICW the Gunboat KILMARNOCK sank U-731 off Tangier on 15th May. 1945: Returned to the UK. Paid Off and placed on the Disposal List. 1946: Sold back to her original owners in March. Reverted to her original Cricketer name and re-registered GY.200. 1960: BU in Belgium.
Notes: 1. Named after the England and Gloucestershire cricketer Charles Barnett.
           2. The prototype for the Admiralty-built Hills Class.

BLACKSTONE   1915/21   Displacement: 148TG
                                      Admty No: X.01 and X.09
1915: Launched. Purchased into the RN in October and converted to a Fuel Carrier. 1921: Sold to the mercantile. Acquired by MS. Hilton.

BLACKWATER   1920/46   See under WILLIAM INWOOD
                                      (Vol 1 p.149)

BLAKE   1915/15   Displacement: 207TG
                                      Admty No: 1044
                                      Port Reg: GY. 1162
1900: Launched. 1915: Requisitioned in January. Renamed BLAKEDOWN in February. LOST. Wrecked at Crudensgier on 19th February.

BLAKEDOWN   1915/15   See under BLAKE above

BLANCHE   1915/19   Displacement: 173TG 68TN
Engines: 45HP = 9.5K
Armament: 1 x 6pdr
Admty No: 1768
Port Reg: H. 982
1907: Launched. Built at Beverley by CWG. Owned by Hellyers SFC of Hull. 1915: Requisitioned in May and converted to a M/S. 1919: Returned to owners. 1952: BU.

BLIGHTY   1940/44   See under JOHN COTTERELL
(Vol 1 p.140)

BLOMVEI   1940/45   SAN
Displacement: 252TG
Port Reg: S. African
P.No: T. 17
1935: Launched. South African fishing vessel. 1940: Hired in March and converted to an A/S. 1945: Returned to owners in March.

BLOODHOUND   1915/19   Displacement: 150TG 59TN
Engines: 45HP = 10K
Armament: 1 x 3pdr
Port Reg: A. 533
1890: Launched. Built at Hull by CWG. Iron construction. Owned by Humber STC of Hull. PR: H. 89. 1912: Acquired by T. Lauder of Aberdeen. PR: A. 533. 1915: Requisitioned in June and converted to a BDV. 1919: Returned to owners. 1937: BU.

BLUEBELL   1914/19   Displacement: 169TG 67TN
Engines: 47HP
Armament: 1 x 6pdr
Admty Nos: 728 and 479
Port Reg: GW. 5
1904: Launched. Built at Govan. Owned by H. Alexander AO, Glasgow. 1914: Requisitioned in November. 1915: Renamed BLUEBELL III in August. 1919: Returned to owners. 1938: Owned by AG Brown of Granton.

BLUEBELL III   1915/19   See under BLUEBELL above

BLUFF   1939/44   SAN
Displacement: 262TG
Port Reg: S. African
P.No: T. 21
1935: Launched. South African fishing vessel. 1939: Hired into the SAN in September and converted to a M/S. 1944: Returned to owners in December.

BLUFF (MPL)

BOADICEA II 1919/20 See under HENRY FORD (Vol 1 p.136)

BOMBAY 1915/19 1939/40 Displacement: 229TG 116TN
Engines: 70HP
Armament: 1 x 12pdr; 1 x 3pdr
Admty No: 1890
Port Reg: GY. 247

1907: Launched. Built at Selby by Cochrane. Owned by Grant & Baker SFC of Grimsby.
1915: Requisitioned in September. 1919: Returned to owners. 1929: Sold to the
Diamond SFC Grimsby. Same PR. 1939: Requisitioned in October and converted to an
APV. 1940: Returned to owners in January. 1942: Mercantile Loss. Lost by unknown
cause approx. 62N 18W. Possibly torpedoed by U-605 on 3rd August.

BONA   1917/19 1944/44 Displacement: 186TG 73TN
Engines: 36HP
Port Reg: WWI: H. 855. WWII: A. 427

1906: Launched. Built at Govan by Govan SB. Owned by the Trident SFC of Hull. 1917: Requisitioned into the Fishery Reserve. 1919: Returned to owners. Acquired by A. Hay AO of Aberdeen. 1944: Requisitioned in April and converted to an Esso. Employed ferrying fuel to the Normandy beaches. Returned to owners in November.

BON ACCORD   1914/19   Displacement: 214TG 78TN
Engines: 76HP
Armament: 1 x 6pdr
Admty No: 510
Port Reg: A. 231

1908: Launched. Built at Aberdeen. Owned by the Friarage STC of Hartlepool. 1914: Requisitioned in September and converted to a M/S. 1919: Returned to owners. 1938: Owned by R. Irvin & Sons of North Shields.

BONA DEA   1915/19   Displacement: 322TG
Armament: 1 x 12pdr
Admty No: 458
Port Reg: GY. 429

1915: Launched. Requisitioned in February and converted to a M/S. Subsequently converted to an Escort. 1919: Returned to owners.

BONAR LAW   1915/15   Displacement: 285TG
Armament: 1 x 3pdr
Admty No: 1223
Port Reg: H. 437

1912: Launched. 1915: Requisitioned in February and converted to a M/S. LOST. Sunk in a collision off the South Goodwins on 27th October.

BONTHORPE   1940/46   RAN
Displacement: 273TG
Port Reg: Australian

1916: Launched. 1940: Hired on 5th February and converted to an A/S. 1941: Converted to a M/S. 1946: Returned to owners.

BORDER GLEN   1915/16   Displacement: 123TG
1901: Launched. 1915: Requisitioned. 1916: Returned to owners.

BOREAS   1914/19 1939/40 Displacement: 184TG 88TN
Engines: 57HP
Armament: 1 x 6pdr
Admty No: 165

Port Reg: WWI: GY. 338.
WWII: LT. 398

1907: Launched. Built at Selby by Cochrane. Owned by Consolidated Fisheries of Grimsby. 1914: Requisitioned in August and converted to a M/S. 1919: Returned to owners. 1939: Requisitioned and converted to an APV. 1940: Renamed CUCKOO. Returned to owners in February.

BORNEO   1914/17   Displacement: 211TG 76TN
                Engines: 60HP = 10K
                Armament: 1 x 6pdr
                Admty No: 1809
                Port Reg: GY. 115

1906: Launched. Built at Beverley by CWG. Owned by Grant & Robinson of Grimsby. 1914: Requisitioned in November and converted to a M/S. 1917: Rescued an a/c which had come down in the Channel on 1st February due to engine failure. Towed the a/c back to Portland. LOST. Mined off Beachy Head on 18th June by a mine laid that same day by the German S/M UC-17.

BORTIND   1940/46   See under MYNA

BOSCOBEL   1915/19   Displacement: 225TG 92TN
                Engines: 54HP
                Armament: 1 x 6pdr
                Admty No: 1761
                Port Reg: FD. 70

1906:Launched. Built at Aberdeen. Owned by the Active FC of Fleetwood. 1915: Requisitioned in May and converted to a M/S. 1919: Returned to owners.

BOSTONIAN   1914/18   Displacement: 192TG
                Armament: 1 x 6pdr
                Admty No: 670
                Port Reg: BN. 74

1900: Launched. 1914: Requisitioned in November and converted to a M/S. 1917: Renamed BASTION in August. 1918: Returned to owners.

BOTANIC   1939/42   Displacement: 348TG 138TN
                Engines: 95HP
                Port Reg: H. 463
                P.No: FY. 707

1928: Launched. Built at Selby by Cochrane. Owned by the City SFC of Hull. 1939: Requisitioned in August and converted to a M/S. 1942: LOST. Sunk by enemy a/c in the North Sea on 18th February.

BOVIC   1914/17   Displacement: 162TG
                  Armament: 1 x 3pdr
                  Admty No: 377
                  Port Reg: H. 51
1896: Launched. 1914: Requisitioned in November. 1917: LOST. Sunk in a collision off Souter Point in 5th August.

BOYNE   1920/46   See under WILLIAM JONES
                  (Vol 1 p.149)

BRABANT   1939/45   See under EMMANUEL CAMELAIRE
                  (Vol 1 p.52)

BRACKLYN   1914/17   Displacement: 303TG
                  Admty No: 667
                  Port Reg: FD. 2
1914: Launched. Requisitioned in December. 1917: LOST. Mined off Yarmouth on 11th May.

BRACONBURN 1944/44   See under RICHARD BRISCOLL
                  (Vol 1 p.184)

BRACONDALE 1914/19   Displacement: 189TG 74TN
                  Engines: 49HP
                  Armament: 1 x 3pdr
                  Port Reg: A. 631
1903: Launched. Built at South Shields. Owned by GE Killington of Kessingland. 1914: Requisitioned in September and converted to a BDV. 1919: Returned to owners. 1938: Owned by JW Morrice AO of Aberdeen.

BRACONDENE 1916/19 1939/46 Displacement: 235TG 89TN
                  Engines: 83HP
                  Armament: 1 x 6pdrAA
                  Admty No: 3261
                  Port Reg: A. 615
                  P. No: WWII: FY. 1812
1916: Launched. Built at Aberdeen. Owned by the Bracken STC (Aberdeen) Ltd. Requisitioned in February and converted to a M/S. 1919: Returned to owners. 1939: Requisitioned in November and converted to a M/S. 1940: SO of the 113th M/S Group based at Grimsby. 1946: Returned to owners in August.

BRACONMOOR 1939/46   See under SAMUEL BAKER
                  (Vol 1 p.185)

BRADFORD   1914/16   Displacement: 163TG
                                            Armament: 1 x 6pdr
                                            Admty No: 829
                                            Port Reg: GY. 132

1896: Launched. 1914: Requisitioned in November. 1916: LOST. Foundered near the Old Head of Kinsale on 28th October.

BRADMAN   1939/40   Cricketer Group
                                            Displacement: 452TG 190TN
                                            Engines: 133HP
                                            Armament: 1 x 4-inch
                                            Port Reg: GY. 358
                                            P.No: FY. 189

1937: Launched. Built at Selby by Cochrane. Owned by Crampin of Grimsby. 1939: Requisitioned in August and converted to an A/S. Joined the 22nd A/S Group. 1940: TPI the Norwegian Campaign in April. LOST. Sunk by enemy a/c off the W. Coast of Norway on 25th April. Salvaged by the German Navy, commissioned and renamed FREISE.

BRAEMAR   1914/19   Displacement: 197TG 78TN
                                            Engines: 50HP
                                            Armament: 1 x 12pdr
                                            Port Reg: FD. 215

1900: Launched. Built at Aberdeen. Owned by TF Kelsall of Aberdeen. 1914: Requisitioned in June and converted to a BDV. 1919: Returned to owners.

BRAEMAR   1940/42   Displacement: 212TG 93TN
                                            Engines: 56HP
                                            Port Reg: A. 252
                                            P.No: FY. 1634

1927: Launched. Built at Aberdeen. Owned by John Lewis of Aberdeen. 1940: Purchased into the RN in April and converted to a D/L. Renamed JENNIFER. Based at Grimsby. 1942: Laid Up. 1946: Sold to mercantile and reverted to *Braemar*. Acquired by Neale & West of Cardiff. PR: CF. 38.

BRAERIACH   1918/19   Displacement: 199TG 77TN
                                            Engines: 50HP
                                            Port Reg: A. 462

1902: Launched. Built at Aberdeen. Owned by W. Grieve of Murtle. 1918: Requisitioned into the Fishery Reserve. 1919: Returned to owners.

BRAES o' MAR   1915/19 1939/40 Displacement: 227TG 98TN
                                            Engines: 82HP
                                            Armament: 1 x 6pdrAA

Admty No: 104
Port Reg: A. 331
1915: Launched. Built at Leith. Owned by the Standard SFC of Aberdeen. Requisitioned in September and converted to a M/S. 1919: Returned to owner. 1939: Requisitioned and designated as an APV. 1940: Returned to owners.

BRAS d' OR	1939/40	RCN
		Displacement: 221TG
		Port Reg: Canadian

1901: Launched. 1939: Requisitioned in October and converted to a M/S. 1940: LOST. Foundered in the Gulf of St. Lawrence on 19th October.

BRAVO	1917/19	Displacement: 137TG 54TN
		Engines: 45HP
		Port Reg: A. 305

1896: Launched. Built at Hull. Owned by G. Wood AO of Torry. 1917: Requisitioned into the Fishery Reserve. 1919: Returned to owners.

BREADALBANE	1917/19	Displacement: 112TG 41TN
		Engines: 35HP
		Port Reg: GN. 32

1891: Launched. Built at Bowling. Owned by G. Devlin of Leith AO. 1917: Requisitioned into the Fishery Reserve. 1919: Returned to owners.

BRECON CASTLE	1916/19 1939/45	Displacement: 274TG 107TN
		Engines: 87HP
		Armament: 1 x 6pdrAA; 1 x 5-inch
		Bomb Thrower (A/S Howitzer)
		Admty No: 1989
		Port Reg: SA. 36
		P. No: WWII: FY. 507

1916: Launched. Built at Southbank-on-Tees by Smith's Dock. Owned by Consolidated Fisheries of Grimsby. Requisitioned in March and converted to a M/S. 1919: Returned to owners. 1939: Requisitioned in August and converted to a M/S. 1945: Returned to owners in December.

BRENT	1917/19	Displacement: 142TG 54TN
		Engines: 45HP
		Admty No: Not issued
		Port Reg: GY. 1087

1892: Launched. Built at Port Glasgow. Owned by G. Pearce of Grimsby. 1917: Requisitioned into the Fishery Reserve. 1919: Returned to owners.

BRETWALDA   1940/46   Ex-*Imperialist*
                                    Displacement: 488TG   226TN
                                    Engines: 99HP = 11K
                                    Armament: 2 x 20mmAA (2x1)
                                    Port Reg: French
                                    P.No: FY. 266
1925: Launched. Built at Beverley by CWG. Owned by Hellyer of Hull. PR: H. 143.
1938: Acquired by L'Armement St. Perrais of France and renamed *Administrateur de Bournat*. 1940: French ADMINISTRATEUR DE BOURNAT seized in Operation Grab in July. Converted to A/S and renamed ALASTOR. Purchased into the RN and renamed BRETWALDA. 1944: Involved in collision with the Dutch S/M 015 in the Clyde. TIH for repairs. 1946: Sold to mercantile in May. Acquired by St. Andrews SFC and renamed *White Nile* PR: H. 39. 1947: Acquired by the Polish Government Fleet and renamed *Jupiter.* 1960: BU.

BRIDLINGTON   1917/19   Displacement: 205TG 82TN
                                    Engines: 50HP
                                    Port Reg: LO. 194
1913: Launched.   Built at Selby by Cochrane. Owned by Hewett FCL.   1917: Requisitioned into the Fishery Reserve. 1919: Returned to owners. Acquired by the Hull SFC of Hull. PR: H.1009. 1956: BU.

BRILLIANT STAR   1918/19   Displacement: 125TG 49TN
                                    Engines: 45HP
                                    Port Reg: SH. 46
1896: Launched. Built at Aberdeen. Owned by T. Davidson of Aberdeen.   1918: Requisitioned into the Fishery Reserve. 1919: Returned to owners. 1939: Owned by AR Sutton of Hartlepool.

BRIMNES   1939/45   Displacement: 413TG 156TN
                                    Engines: 99HP
                                    Armament: 1 x 4-inch
                                    Port Reg: H. 9
                                    P.No: FY. 254
1933: Launched. Built at Southbank-on-Tees. Owned by Oddsson & Co of Hull. 1939: Requisitioned in September and converted to A/S. 1945: Returned to owners in July.

BRISBANE   1918/19   Displacement: 207TG 81TN.
                                    Engines: 60HP = 10.5K.
                                    Port Reg: GY.1281
1903: Launched. Built at Hull. Owned by W. Grant & HC Baker of Grimsby. 1918: Requisitioned into the Fishery Reserve. Acquired by A. Grant of Grimsby.   1919: Returned to owners. 1954: BU at Grimsby.

BRITANNIA   1915/15   Displacement: 138TG
                                      Armament: None
                                      Port Reg: GY. 410
1891: Launched. 1915: Requisitioned in January and converted to a Stores/Water
Carrier. Renamed BRITANNIA III in May. Returned to owners in September. Mercantile
Loss. Captured by German S/M 40 miles SE x E from Spurn LV. and sunk by gunfire on
23rd November.

BRITANNIA III   1915/15   See under BRITANNIA above.

BRITISH   1939/45   Ex-*Vinur*
                                      Displacement: 406TG 161TN
                                      Engines: 99HP = 10.9K
                                      Port Reg: GY. 249
                                      P.No: FY. 506
1930: Ordered by Little & Olgierrsson, and sold before completion. Launched. Built at
Beverley by CWG. Owned by The Vinur SFC of Grimsby. 1936: Renamed *British*.
1939: Requisitioned in August and fitted out at Woolwich as a M/S. Based at Grimsby
(ungrouped). 1943: Senior Officer of 21st M/S Group based at Grimsby. 1945: Returned
to owners in December. 1954: Acquired by Wyre STL of Fleetwood and renamed *Wyre
British*. 1957: BU at Ghent in Belgium.

BRITISH GUIANA   1939/46   Displacement: 146TG 53TN
                                      Engines: 91HP
                                      Port Reg: GY. 331
                                      P.No: FY. 271
1936: Launched. Built at Selby by Cochrane. Owned by Grimsby Motor Trawlers Ltd.
1939: Requisitioned in November and converted to A/S. 1946: Returned to owners in
March.

BRITISH HONDURAS   1939/46   Displacement: 147TG 55TN
                                      Engines 76HP
                                      Port Reg: GY. 513
                                      P.No: FY. 272
1937: Launched. Built at Selby. Owned by Grimsby Motor Trawlers Ltd. 1939:
Requisitioned in December and converted to A/S. 1946: Returned to owners in January.

BRITON   1915/15   Displacement: 196TG
                                      Admty No: 1170
                                      Port Reg: A. 101
1906: Launched. 1915: Requisitioned in February. LOST. Mined off The Longsands on
21st July.

BROCK   1914/19 1939/45 Displacement: 304TG 122TN
Engines: 69HP
Armament: WWI: 1 x 6pdr; WWII: 1 x
6pdr; 2 x 20mmAA (2x1)
Admty No: 927
Port Reg: FD. 47
P.No: WWII: FY. 621

1914: Launched. Built at Middlesborough by Smith's Dock. Owned by the Wyre STC of Fleetwood. Requisitioned in November. 1919: Returned to owners. 1939: Requisitioned in August and converted to a M/S. 1945: Returned to owners.

BROMELIA   1915/19   Displacement: 242TG 121TN
Engines: 63HP
Armament: 1 x 12pdr
Admty No: 3203
Port Reg: GY. 113

1906: Launched. Built at Selby by Cochrane. Owned by the North Eastern SFC of Grimsby. 1915: Requisitioned in June and converted to a M/S. Fitted with Listening Hydrophones. 1919: Returned to owners. 1942: Mercantile Loss. Lost with all hands off Iceland having been posted missing from 22nd June.

BRONTES   1939/45   Displacement: 424TG 159TN
Engines: 111HP = 11.7K
Port Reg: H. 41
P. No:: FY. 118

1934: Launched. Built at Beverley by CWG. Owned by Henriksen of Hull. 1939: Purchased into the RN in August and converted to A/S. 1945: Sold to Mercantile. Reacquired by original owners. Re-registered H. 236. 1959: BU at Ghent in Belgium.

BRUCE   1917/19   Displacement: 103TG 43TN
Engines: 42HP
Port Reg: GN. 10

1883: Launched. Built at Leith. Iron Construction. Owned by G. Devlin of Leith AO. 1917: Requisitioned into the Fishery Reserve. 1919: Returned to owners.

BRUCKLAY   1918/19   Displacement: 182TG 77TN
Engines: 59HP
Port Reg: GY. 1052

1900: Launched. Built at Aberdeen. Owned by Sleights of Grimsby. 1918: Requisitioned. 1919: Returned to owners.

BRUTUS   1914/19   Displacement: 311TG 124TN
Engines: 102HP
Armament: 1 x 3pdr

Admty No: 79
Port Reg: H. 893

1906: Launched. Built at Hull. Owned by Hellyer Bros. of Hull. 1914: Requisitioned in November and converted to a M/S. 1919: Returned to owners.

BUCCLEUCH	1917/19	Displacement: 146TG 53TN
		Engines: 57HP
		Port Reg: GN. 27

1903: Launched. Built at Leith. Owned by the General SFC of Edinburgh. 1917: Requisitioned into the Fishery Reserve. 1919: Returned to owners.

BUCENTAUR	1914/19 1939/40	Displacement: 184TG 88TN
		Engines: 57HP
		Armament: 1 x 6pdr
		Admty No: 297
		Port Reg: GY. 339

1907: Launched. Built at Selby by Cochrane. Owned by Consolidated Fisheries of Grimsby. 1914: Requisitioned in August and converted to a M/S. 1919: Returned to owners. 1939: Requisitioned in November and designated as an APV. 1940: Returned to owners in January.

| BUCEPHALUS | 1944/45 | See under VENTURE |

| BUCHANS II | 1940/46 | See under PAT CAHERTY |
| | | (Vol 1 p.183) |

BUCKINGHAM	1917/19	Displacement: 172TG 71TN
		Engines: 50HP
		Port Reg: GY. 1096

1899: Launched. Built at Beverley. Iron Construction. Owned by the Queen SFC of Grimsby. 1917: Requisitioned into the Fishery Reserve. 1919: Returned to owners.

BUCKINGHAM	1939/45	Displacement: 253TG 100TN
		Engines: 83HP
		Port Reg: GY. 296
		P.No: WWII: Z. 121

1930: Launched. Built at Selby by Cochrane. Owned by the Queen SFC of Grimsby. 1939: Requisitioned in August and converted to a M/S. 1940: Converted to a BDV in February. 1945: Returned to owners in December. 1957: Renamed *Ocean Vinca*. 1959: Renamed *Saxon Alfred*. 1962: Acquired by Danish mercantile.

BUFFALO	1915/19	Displacement: 230TG 92TN
		Engines: 65HP = 10K
		Armament: 1 x 6pdr

Admty No: 1597
Port Reg: GY. 52

1905: Launched. Built at Beverley by CWG. Owned by H. Morris & TE. Fisher of Grimsby. 1915: Requisitioned in July and converted to a M/S. Renamed BUFFALO II in December. 1919: Returned to owners and reverted to original name. 1937: BU at Thornaby.

BUFFALO II	1915/19	See under BUFFALO above

BUGLER	1919/20	See under BRIGADIER (Vol 1 p.152)

BULLDOG	1917/19	Displacement: 148TG 62TN
		Engines: 45HP = 10K
		Armament: None
		Port Reg: GY. 576

1892: Launched. Built at Hull by CWG. Owned by Humber STC of Hull. PR: H. 192. 1915: Acquired by WH. Beeley of Grimsby. PR: GY. 576. 1917: Requisitioned for the Fishery Reserve. 1919: Returned to owners. Acquired by N. Ashworth of Fleetwood. PR: FD. 328. 1924: BU.

BURKE	1939/46	Ex- *George Aunger*
		Displacement: 363TG 173TN
		Engines 91HP = 10.9K
		Port Reg: GY. 285
		P.No: FY. 605

1930: Launched. Built at Beverley by CWG. Owned by the Bunch SFC of Grimsby. 1935: Renamed *Sandham*. 1938: Acquired by Premier SFC of Grimsby and renamed *Burke*. 1939: Requisitioned in September and converted to a M/S. Served in the North Atlantic. 1944: Converted to a WDV. 1946: Returned to owners. 1955: BU in Belgium.

BURMAH	1914/14 1917/19.	Displacement: 168TG 63TN
		Engines: 60HP
		Port Reg: H. 86

1892: Launched. Built at North Shields. Owned by Kelsall Bros. & Beeching of Hull. 1914: Requisitioned in October and designated as a M/S. Returned to the Fishing Fleet in November. 1917: Requisitioned into the Fishery Reserve. 1919: Returned to owners.

BURNBANKS	1940/44	See under STRATHISLA

BURNLEY	1916/16.	Displacement: 276TG
		Armament: 1 x 12pdr
		Admty No: 3277
		Port Reg: FD. 242

1916: Requisitioned in May. LOST. Mined off Orford Ness on 25th November.

BUSH   1915/20 1940/44 Displacement: 221TG 85TN
               Engines: 66HP
               Armament: 1 x 12pdr
               Admty No: 2667
               Port Reg: WWI: M. 227. WWII: FD. 60

1908: Launched. Built at North Shields. 1915: Requisitioned in May. 1920: Returned to owners. Acquired by Scarisbrick STL of Fleetwood. 1940: Requisitioned and converted to an APV. 1944: Returned to owners.

BUZZARD   1914/20   Displacement: 199TG 73TN
               Engines: 55HP
               Armament: 1 x 6pdrAA
               Admty No: 549
               Port Reg: H. 971

1907: Launched. Built at Goole by Goole SB. Owned by Kelsall Bros. & Beeching of Hull. 1914: Requisitioned in October and converted to a M/S. 1920: Returned to owners.

BUZZARD II   1917/19 1940/45. Displacement: 181TG 74TN
               Engines: 50HP
               Port Reg: GY. 825
               P.No: WWII: Z. 246

1898: Launched. Built at Beverley. Iron construction. Owned by A. Bannister of Grimsby & W. Barton of Cleethorpes. 1917: Requisitioned into the Fishery Reserve. 1919: Returned to owners. 1940: Requisitioned and converted to a BGV. 1941: Renamed ARREST. Based at Grimsby. 1945: Returned to owners in July. Laid up at Grimsby prior to BU.

BY GEORGE   1914/17   Displacement: 225TG
               Armament: 1 x 3pdr
               Admty No: 253
               Port Reg: GY. 69

1914: Launched. Owned by North Western SFC of Grimsby. Requisitioned in August and converted to a M/S. 1915: Acquired by H. Croft Baker of Grimsby. 1917: LOST. Mined in the Gulf of Ruphani, in the Aegean Sea, on 7th September.

CADELLA   1939/46   See under PEARL of 1913

CADET   1917/19 1940/46   Displacement: 323TG 134TN
                                          Engines: 87HP = 10.5K
                                          Armament: WWI: None
                                          Admty No: Not issued
                                          P.No: WWII: FY. 176

1914: Launched. Built at Beverley by CWG. Owned by the Marine SFC of Hull. 1917: Requisitioned into the Fishery Reserve. 1919: Returned to owners. 1926: Acquired by Storr STC of Hull and renamed *Saiph*. 1929: Acquired by Trident SFC of Hull and renamed *Roseness*. 1938: Acquired by Jutland Amalgamated Trs. of Hull and renamed *Lady Estelle*. 1940: Requisitioned in June as LADY ESTELLE and converted to A/S. 1942: Acquired by Marr of Hull. 1943: Acquired by Thornton Trs. of Hull. 1945: Acquired by Parkholme Trs. of Grimsby. PR:GY. 52. Acquired by Trs. Grimsby. 1946: Returned to owners in September. 1947: Acquired by Dutch owners. 1955: BU.

CADORNA   1917/19 1940/45   Displacement: 255TG 101TN
                                          Engines: 82HP
                                          Armament: 1 x 12pdr
                                          Admty No: 3055
                                          Port Reg: WWI: GY. 1072
                                          WWII: A. 125
                                          P. No: WWII: FY. 1651

1917: Launched. Built at Aberdeen. Requisitioned in July. 1919: Returned to owners. Acquired by the Aberdeen Pioneer SFC. 1940: Requisitioned in May and converted to a M/S. 1945: Returned to owners.

CAERPHILLY CASTLE   1939/40   See under THOMAS GREEN
                                          (Vol 1 p.76)

CAESAR   1914/19   Displacement: 311TG
                                          Armament: 2 x 6pdrs
                                          Admty No: 539
                                          Port Reg: H. 874

1906: Launched. 1914: Requisitioned in October and converted to a M/S. 1915: Renamed CAESAR II in February. 1919: Returned to owners.

CAESAR II   1915/19   See under CAESAR above

CAIRNWELL   1918/19   Displacement:141TG 60TN
                                          Engines: 44HP

Admty No: Not issued
Port Reg: FD. 45

1895: Launched. Built at Beverley. Iron construction. Owned by Cairn STC of Liverpool. 1918: Requisitioned into the Fishery Reserve. 1919: Returned to owners.

CAIRO	1914/19	Displacement: 172TG 67TN
		Engines: 45HP = 10K
		Armament: 1 x 6pdr
		Admty No: 635
		Port Reg: H. 550

1902: Launched. Built at Beverley by CWG. Iron construction. Owned by the Hull SF & Ice Co. 1914: Requisitioned in October and converted to a base ship for Minesweepers. 1916: Converted to a M/S. 1919: Returned to owners. 1959: BU at Grays by Ward.

CALDY	1915/19 1939/40	Displacement: 222TG 85TN
		Engines: 68HP
		Armament: 1 x 12pdr
		Port Reg: WWI: M. 228. WWII: FD. 66

1908: Launched. Built at North Shields. 1915: Requisitioned in April and converted to a M/S. 1919: Returned to owners. Acquired by J. Uttley of Fleetwood. 1939: Requisitioned on 27th November and designated as an APV. 1940: Returned to owners on 22nd January.

CALEDONIA	1917/17	Displacement: 161TG
		Port Reg: GN.34

1906: Launched. 1917: Requisitioned in March and designated for Special Service. LOST. Sunk by a German S/M off Newton, Northumberland on 17th March whilst on passage to fit out.

CALEDONIA II	1917/19	Displacement: 148TG 55TN
		Engines: 50HP
		Admty No: Not issued
		Port Reg: A. 93

1898: Launched. Built at Aberdeen. Owned by J.Cormack AO of Aberdeen. 1917: Requisitioned into the Fishery Reserve. 1919: Returned to owners.

CALIBAN	1939/46	See under HENRY CORY (Vol 1 p.55)

CALIPH	1914/19	Displacement: 226TG 87TN
		Engines: 55HP
		Armament: 1 x 6pdrAA; 1 x 3.5-inch
		Bomb Thrower (A/S Howitzer)
		Admty No: 133

Port Reg: M. 197

1906: Launched. Built at North Shields. Owned by D. Pettit of Milford Haven. 1914: Requisitioned in August and converted to a M/S. Fitted with Listening Hydrophones. 1917: Based at Portland. ICW Tr. MARISTO engaged a U-Boat in the Channel. Dropped a depth charge when she saw a periscope on her starboard bow and claimed an unconfirmed kill. 1919: Returned to owners.

CALLIOPE   1914/16   Displacement: 240TG
                                           Armament: 1 x 3pdr
                                           Admty No: 367
                                           Port Reg: M. 214

1907: Launched. 1914: Requisitioned in August and converted to a M/S. 1915: Renamed CALLIOPE II in June. 1916: LOST. Sunk in a collision off the Butt of Lewis on 5th March.

CALLIOPE II   1915/16   See under CALLIOPE above

CALVI   1939/40   Ex-*Galleon*
                                             Displacement: 363TG 173TN
                                           Engines: 91HP = 11K
                                           Port Reg: GY. 269
                                           P. No: FY. 673

1930: Launched. Built at Beverley by CWG. Owned by the Perihelion SFC of Grimsby. 1938: Acquired by Premier SFC of Grimsby and renamed *Calvi*. 1939: Requisitioned in September and converted to a M/S. Based at Dover for Sweeping operations in the Channel. 1940: TPI Operation Dynamo, the evacuation of Dunkirk. LOST. Sunk by a/c whilst embarking troops at Dunkirk on 29th May.

CALVIA   1915/19   Displacement: 304TG 158TN
                                             Engines: 80HP
                                           Armament: 1 x 12pdr; 1 x 7.5-inch
                                           Bomb Thrower (A/S Howitzer)
                                           Admty No: 852
                                           Port Reg: GY. 476

1915: Launched. Built at Selby by Cochrane. Owned by JL. Green Ltd of Grimsby. Requisitioned in May and converted to a M/S. 1919: Returned to owners.

CALVINIA   1915/19 1940/45 Displacement: 191TG 94TN
                                             Armament: 1 x 6pdrAA
                                           Admty No: 734
                                           Port Reg: WWI: GY. 559; WWII: A .8
                                           P. No: WWII: FY. 1850

1901: Launched. Built at Hull. Iron construction. Owned by WHS. Doughty AO of Grimsby. 1915: Requisitioned in January and converted to a M/S. 1919: Returned to owners. Acquired by the Gorspen STC of Aberdeen. 1940: Requisitioned in January and converted to a M/S. 1943: Converted to a D/L. 1945: Returned to owners in January.

CALYPSO	1917/19	Displacement: 187TG 71TN
		Engines: 53HP
		Admty No: Not issued
		Port Reg: GY. 1083

1901: Launched. Built at Aberdeen. Owned by the Victorian SFC of Grimsby. 1917: Requisitioned into the Fishery Reserve. 1919: Returned to owners.

CAMBODIA	1915/19	Displacement: 284TG 115TN
		Engines: 78HP = 10.5K
		Armament: 1 x 6pdrAA; 1 x 3pdr
		Admty No: 1521
		Port Reg: GY. 597

1911: Launched. Built at Beverley by CWG. Owned by the Grimsby Alliance SFC of Grimsby. 1915: Requisitioned in May. 1918: Acquired by Savoy SFC of Grimsby. 1919: Returned to owners. 1928: Acquired by Forward SFC of Grimsby and renamed *Napier*. 1937: BU at Charlestown.

CAMBRIA	1914/19	Displacement: 206TG 78TN
		Engines: 54HP
		Armament: 1 x 12pdr
		Admty Nos: 154 and 1358
		Port Reg: M. 92

1905: Launched. Built at North Shields. Owned by East Garnham of Grimsby. 1914: Requisitioned in September and converted to a M/S. 1919: Returned to owners.

CAMBRIAN	1914/19	Displacement: 191TG 75TN
		Engines: 51HP
		Armament: 1 x 6pdrAA
		Admty No: 662
		Port Reg: BN. 75

1900: Launched. Built at North Shields. Owned by the Boston DSF & Ice Co. of Boston, Lincs. 1914: Requisitioned in November and converted to a M/S. 1915: Renamed CAMBRIAN II in February. 1919: Returned to owners.

CAMBRIAN II	1915/19	See under CAMBRIAN above

CAMBRIDGESHIRE	1939/45	Shire Group
		Displacement: 443TG 161TN
		Engines: 99HP
		Armament: 1 x 4-inch

Port Reg: GY. 180
P. No: FY. 142
1935: Launched in September. Built at Southbank-on-Tees by Smith's Dock. Owned by Cambridgeshire SF (H. Markham), of Grimsby. 1939: Requisitioned in August and converted to an A/S. 1940: Involved in the rescue of survivors from the *Lancastria* which was carrying over 1,000 troops when she was bombed off St. Nazaire on 17th June. The little trawler was crammed with survivors but, before she left the scene, she dropped all her own life-saving equipment. 1944: TPI Operation Neptune, the D-Day Landings in June. 1945: Returned to owners.

CAMEO   1915/19   Displacement: 172TG 67TN
                                          Engines: 55HP
                                          Armament: 1 x 12pdr
                                          Admty No: 1216
                                          Port Reg: H. 394
1898: Launched. Built at Govan. Owned by the Holliungwood STFC of Hull. 1915: Requisitioned in February and converted to a M/S. 1919: Returned to owners.

CAMPANIA II   1918/18   Displacement: 167TG
1895: Launched. 1918: Requisitioned for a short period and then returned to owners.

CANADA   1916/19   Displacement: 231TG
                                          Armament: 1 x 6pdrAA
                                          Port Reg: H. 1
1886: Launched. Owned by North Eastern SFC of Grimsby. 1916: Requisitioned in November and converted to a BDV. 1917: Renamed CANADA II. 1919: Returned.

CANADA II   1917/19   See under CANADA above

CANADIAN PRINCE   1939/39   Displacement: 455TG 166TN
                                          Engines: 99HP
                                          Armament: 1 x 4-inch
                                          Port Reg: H. 241
                                          P.No: FY.166
1937: Launched. Built at Southbank-on-Tess by Smith's Dock. Owned by the Prince FC of Hull. 1939: Purchased into the RN in August and converted to an A/S. Sold to the French Navy on 28th November and renamed BONOISE.

CANCER   1916/19 1940/46 Displacement: 230TG 107TN
                                          Engines: 76HP
                                          Armament: 1 x 6pdr
                                          Admty No: 2957
                                          Port Reg: WWI: GY .918
                                          WWII: GN. 49

P. No: WWII: FY. 1748

1916: Launched. Built at Beverley by CWG. Owned by Grimsby & North Sea SF Co. Requisitioned in August and converted to a M/S. 1919: Returned to owners. 1936: Transferred to Granton, Scotland and renamed *Invertay*. Acquired by GR Cook of Edinburgh. 1940: Requisitioned in August as INVERTAY. Converted to a M/S. 1946: Returned to owners in July. 1961: Mercantile Loss. Sunk in a collision in the North Sea on 10th March.

CANDIDATE	1914/19	Displacement: 161TG 61TN
		Engines: 66HP
		Armament: 1 x 6pdr
		Admty No: 91
		Port Reg: GN. 31

1906: Launched. Built at Aberdeen. Owned by G. Devlin of Leith AO. 1914: Requisitioned. 1919: Returned to owners.

CANTATRICE	1915/16	Displacement: 302TG 152TN
		Engines: 82HP = 10.5K
		Admty No: 3205
		Port Reg: GY. 469

1915: Launched. Built at Beverley by CWG. Owned by WJ Barrett of Grimsby. Requisitioned in July and converted to a M/S. Subsequently fitted to carry 2 x a/c and employed on North Sea anti-Zeppelin patrols. 1916: LOST. Mined off Great Yarmouth on 15th November.

CAP d' ANTIFER	1940/44	Ex-*Compass*
		Displacement: 294TG
		P. No: FY. 350

1920: Launched. 1940: Ex-Belgian trawler converted to a French M/S. Seized at Southampton in Operation Grab on 3rd July and converted to an APV. 1941: Converted to a M/S. Based on the Humber for sweeping operations. 1943: 19th M/S Group based at Grimsby. 1944: Sweeping off the Humber in January when she encountered a flotilla of 4 German E-Boats and successfully drove them off. LOST. Encountered another flotilla of E-Boats off the Humber on 13th February. This time she was not so lucky and succumbed to a torpedo.

CAPE ARGONA	1939/45	Displacement: 494TG 192TN
		Engines: 132HP
		Armament: 1 x 4-inch
		Port Reg: H. 265
		P. No: FY. 190

1936: Launched. Built at Selby by Cochrane. Owned by the Hudson Fishing Co. Hull. 1939: Purchased into the RN in August and converted to A/S. Joined the 12th A/S Strike Force at Belfast. 1940: TPI the Norwegian Campaign in April/May. 12th A/S Strike Force transferred to Grimsby. Transferred to the Western Approaches. Employed on Convoy Escort duties. TPI the rescue of survivors from the burning *Empress of Britain* approximately 300 miles W. of Ireland. 1945: Sold to mercantile.

CAPE BARRACOUTA   1939/39 1940/46 Ex-*Leonidas*
                                       Displacement: 390TG 159TN
                                       Engines: 99HP = 10.7K
                                       Armament: 1 x 12pdr
                                       Port Reg: H. 267
                                       P. No: 4. 122

1930: Launched. Built at Beverley by CWG. Owned by Christensen & Co. of Hull. 1938: Acquired by Hudson SFC of Hull and renamed *Cape Barracouta*. 1939: Requisitioned in August and designated as a M/S. Returned to owners on 30th October. 1940: Requisitioned once more in June and converted to an APV. 1941: Converted to a M/S. 1946: Returned to owners in August. 1948: Acquired by Heward Trs. of Fleetwood and renamed *New Prince*. PR: LO. 471. 1959: BU in Belgium.

CAPE CHELYUSKIN   1939/40   Displacement: 494TG 192TN
                                         Engines: 132HP
                                         Armament: 1 x 4-inch
                                         Port Reg: H. 248
                                         P.No: FY. 119

1936: Launched. Built at Selby by Cochrane. Owned by the Hudson Fishing Co. of Hull. 1939: Purchased into the RN in August and converted to A/S. Joined the 12th A/S Strike Force at Belfast. 1940: TPI the Norwegian Campaign in April. LOST. Sunk by air attack off the coast of Norway on 29th April.

CAPE COMORIN   1939/45   Displacement: 504TG 192TN
                                           Engines: 137HP = 12K
                                         Armament: 1 x 4-inch
                                         Port Reg: H. 291
                                         P.No: FY. 143

1936: Launched. Built at Beverley by CWG. Owned by the Hudson Bros. of Hull. 1939: Purchased into the RN on 14th August and converted to A/S. 1945: Sold to the original owners. PR: H. 139. Retained the same name. 1955: Acquired by Victoria FCL of Hull and renamed *Olvina*. 1960: Acquired by Irvin & Johnson of Capetown, South Africa and renamed *Lobelia*. 1968: Reduced to a hulk and then scuttled off Capetown to form an artificial reef.

CAPE FINESTERRE   1940/40   Displacement: 594TG 225TN
                                         Engines: 163HP
                                         Armament: 1 x 12pdr
                                       Port Reg: H. 178

1939: Launched. Built at Selby by Cochrane. Owned by the Hudson Fishing Co. of Hull.

1940: Requisitioned in February and converted to A/S. LOST. Attacked by a flight of 4 enemy a/c off Harwich on 2nd August. She shot down 1 and damaged the others before being overwhelmed.

CAPE MARIATO   1940/45   Displacement: 497TG 191TN
                                       Engines: 132HP
                                       Armament: 1 x 4-inch
                                       Port Reg: H
                                       P. No: 4. 172

1936: Launched. Built at Selby by Cochrane. Owned by the Hudson SFC of Hull. 1940: Requisitioned in June and converted to A/S. 1945: Employed as an escort on Iceland-UK Convoys. Returned to owners in December.

CAPE MELVILLE   1939/45   Displacement: 342TG 191TN
                                        Engines: 132
                                        Armament: 1 x 12pdr
                                        Port Reg: H. 364
                                        P. No: FY. 651

1929: Launched. Built at Selby by Cochrane. Owned by the Hudson FC. of Hull. 1939: Requisitioned in August and converted to a M/S. 1940: TPI Operations Quentin/Quidnunc/Quixote on 18th/19th May, the cutting of the telephone cables between Germany and the UK in the North Sea. 1945: Returned to owners in September.

CAPE NYEMETSKI   1939/46   Displacement: 422TG 165TN
                                         Engines: 102HP
                                         Armament: 1 x 4-inch
                                         Port Reg: H. 16
                                         P. No: FY. 670

1934: Launched. Built at Selby by Cochrane. Owned by the Hudson FC. of Hull. 1939: Requisitioned in August and converted to a M/S. 1946: Returned to owners in February.

CAPE PALLISER   1939/45   Displacement: 497TG 190TN
                                        Engines:132HP
                                        Armament: 1 x 4-inch
                                        Port Reg: H. 354
                                        P. No: FY. 256

1936: Launched. Built at Selby by Cochrane. Owned by the Hudson FC. of Hull. 1939: Requisitioned in August and converted to A/S. 1941: Joined the Iceland Command in August for Russian Convoys. 1942: Unit of the Escort for the ill-fated convoy PQ.17 in August. 1945: Returned to owners in September.

CAPE PASSARO   1939/40   Displacement: 590TG 225TN
                                       Engines: 163HP
                                       Armament:1 x 4-inch

Port Reg: H. 135
P.No: FY. 270

1939: Launched. Built at Selby by Cochrane. Owned by the Hudson Fishing Co. of Hull. Requisitioned in September and converted to A/S. Joined the 15th A/S Strike Force as Leader. Based at Aberdeen for operations off N. Scotland. 1940: Afforded the rare honour of being inspected by HM Queen Elizabeth whilst alongside at Aberdeen. TPI the Norwegian Campaign in April/May. LOST. Sunk by a/c attack off Narvik on 21st May.

CAPE PORTLAND   1939/45   Displacement: 497TG 189TN
Engines:163HP
Armament: 1 x 4-inch; 2 x 0.5-inchAA
(1x2); 2 x MG (2x1)
Port Reg: H. 357
P. No: FY. 246

1936: Launched. Built at Selby by Cochrane. Owned by the Hudson FC. of Hull. 1939: Purchased into the RN in September and converted to A/S. 1943: TIH at Liverpool for refitting in August. Transferred on loan to the Portuguese Navy from 8th October. Handed over in the Azores and renamed P.5. 1944: Returned to the RN on 6th August. 1945: Sold to mercantile.

CAPE SIRETOKO   1939/40   Displacement: 590TG 225TN
Engines: 163HP
Port Reg: H. 106
P. No: FY. 263

1939: Launched. Built at Selby by Cochrane. Owned by the Hudson Fishing Co. of Hull. Purchased into the RN in September and converted to A/S. Joined the 11th A/S Strike Force. 1940: TPI the Norwegian Campaign in April. LOST. Sunk by a/c attack off Norway on 29th April. Subsequently salvaged by the Germans and commissioned into the German Navy as GOTE. 1944: German Naval Loss. Sunk once again by a/c attack near Makkaur on 11th May.

CAPE SPARTEL   1939/42   Displacement: 346TG 137TN
Engines: 96HP
Armament: 1 x 12pdr
Port Reg: H. 23

1929: Launched. Built at Selby by Cochrane. Owned by the Hudson FC. of Hull. 1939: Requisitioned in August and converted to a M/S. 1941: Employed on 'Double-L Sweep' trials. 1942: LOST. Sunk by a/c attack off the Humber on 2nd February.

CAPETOWN II   1917/19 1939/40 Ex-*Capetown*
Displacement: 188TG 74TN
Engines: 50HP = 10K
Armament: WWI: None; WWII: None
Admty No: Not issued

Port Reg: H. 998

1908: Launched. Built at Beverley by CWG. Owned by Hull SF & Ice Co. 1917: Requisitioned into the Fishery Reserve and renamed. 1919: Returned to owners and reverted to original name. 1937: Acquired by RP Lewis of Milford Haven. Same PR. 1939: Requisitioned in December. Renamed STORMCOCK and designated as a M/S. 1940: Returned to owners in January and reverted to original name. 1948: Acquired by Cranbrook Shipping Co. of London and based at Lowestoft. 1956: BU at Bruges, Belgium.

CAPE TRAFALGAR   1940/47   Displacement: 326T

1917: Launched. 1940: Purchased into the RN and converted to an APV. 1941: Converted to a BDV in January. 1946: Sold to mercantile in January.

CAPE WARWICK   1939/46   Ex-*Compton*
                                     Ex-*Fighter*
                                     Displacement: 516TG 285TN
                                     Engines: 516HP
                                     Armament: 1 x 4-inch
                                     Port Reg: H. 272
                                     P. No: FY. 167

1937: Launched in May as *Fighter* GY. 421. Built at Selby by Cochrane. Owned by Earle SF of Grimsby. 1938: Sold to Hudson Bros. of Hull and renamed *Compton*. 1939: Purchased into the RN in August converted to A/S. 1940: Based at Iceland. 1942: Transferred on loan to the USN in March, together with crew. Returned to the RN in October. Transferred to the S. African Station. Employed on convoy escorts around S. Africa. 1943: Escorting a small convoy from Walvis Bay to Capetown when one of the ships carrying 300 passengers was torpedoed and sunk. 260 survivors were taken aboard and grossly over-laden she struggled on to Capetown. 1946: Sold to mercantile on 26th January. Acquired by Consolidated Fisheries of Grimsby and renamed *Lincoln City* PR: GY. 464. 1963: BU.

CAPRICORNUS   1917/19 1939/40 Displacement: 219TG 97TN
                                     Engines: 76HP
                                     Armament: 1 x 6pdrAA
                                     Admty No: 1264
                                     Port Reg: GY. 1022

1917: Launched. Built at Goole by Goole SB. Owned by the Grimsby & North Sea STC. Requisitioned in April and converted to a M/S. 1919: Returned to owners. 1939: Requisitioned in November and converted to an APV. 1940: Converted to a M/S. LOST. Mined off the SE Coast of England on 7th December.

CAPSTONE   1940/45   See under JAMES ROBERTSON
                                    (Vol 1 p.59)

CAPTAIN   1917/19   Displacement: 130TG 49TN
Engines: 50HP
Admty No: Not issued
Port Reg: GN. 50

1898: Launched. Built at Aberdeen. Owned by G. Devlin of Leith AO. 1917: Requisitioned into the Fishery Reserve. 1919: Returned to owners.

CAPTAIN POLLEN   1917/19 1940/46 Displacement: 275TG 109TN
Engines: 82HP
Armament: 1 x 12pdr
Admty No: 1656
Port Reg: WWI: GY.1108
WWII: A. 383
P.No: WWII: 4. 432

1917: Launched. Built at Aberdeen. Owned by AV. Cole of Cheltenham. Requisitioned in December and converted to a M/S. 1919: Returned to owners. Acquired by the North Star SFC of Aberdeen and renamed *Avonglen*. 1940: Requisitioned in August as AVONGLEN and converted for the Examination Service. 1942: Converted to a Hospital Tender. 1946: Returned to owners in August.

CARBILL   1917/19 1939/45 Displacement: 242TG 94TN
Engines: 74HP
Armament: 1 x 12pdr; 1 x 6pdrAA
Admty No: 1648
Port Reg: GY. 1100
P.No: FY. 557

1917: Launched. Built at Selby by Cochrane. Owned by H. Smethurst of Grimsby. Requisitioned in August and converted to a M/S. 1919: Returned to owners. 1939: Requisitioned in September as HOVERLEY and converted to a M/S. 1945: Returned to owners on 15th January.

CARDIFF CASTLE   1914/19   Displacement: 255TG 98TN
Engines: 70HP
Armament: 1 x 12pdr; 1 x 7.5-inch
Bomb Thrower (A/S Howitzer)
Admty No: 638
Port Reg: SA. 44

1907: Launched. Built at North Shields. Owned by the Consolidated Fisheries of Grimsby. 1914: Requisitioned in November and converted to a M/S. 1919: Returned to owners.

CARDIFF CASTLE   1939/46   See under EDWARD GALLAGHER
(Vol 1 p.52)

CARDINAL   1915/20   Displacement: 309TG 133TN
                                   Engines: 80HP = 10.5K
                                   Armament: 1 x 12pdr
                                   Admty No: 1576
                                   Port Reg: H. 584
1912: Launched. Built at Beverley by CWG. Owned by the Marine SFC of Hull. 1915: Requisitioned in May and converted to a M/S. 1920: Returned to owners. 1925: Mercantile Loss. Wrecked near Injoy, Rolvsoeyhavn, Norway. No loss of life.

CARENCY   1916/19 1939/46 Displacement: 233TG 108TN
                                   Engines: 70HP = 10.25K
                                   Armament: 1 x 6pdrAA
                                   Admty No: 2984
                                   Port Reg: GY. 956
                                   P. No: WWII: FY. 295
1916: Launched. Built at Beverley by CWG. Owned by the Earl SFC of Hull. Requisitioned in December and converted to a M/S. 1916: Acquired by Beacon SFC of Grimsby. 1918: Acquired by Great Northern SFC of Hull. PR: H. 611. 1919: Returned to owners. 1939: Requisitioned and converted for the Examination Service. 1946: Returned to owners in March. 1947: Acquired by W. Wood of Aberdeen. PR: A.129. 1957: Mercantile Loss. Stranded at Greenigoe, North of Wick and subsequently sank.

CAREW CASTLE   1915/17   Displacement: 256TG
                                   Armament: 1 x 12pdr
                                   Admty No: 2671
                                   Port Reg: SA. 106
1912: Launched. 1915: Requisitioned in May and converted to a M/S. 1917: LOST. Mined off Hartland Point on 12th June.

CARIEDA   1915/19 1940/40 Displacement: 225TG 112TN
                                   Engines: 66HP = 10K
                                   Armament: 1 x 12pdr
                                   Admty No: 1751
                                   Port Reg: GY. 908
1913: Launched. Built at Beverley by CWG. Owned by Pelham SFC of Grimsby. 1915: Requisitioned in April and converted to a M/S. Acquired by Rushworth SFC of Grimsby. 1918: Acquired by Yarborough SFC of Grimsby. 1919: Returned to owners. 1940: Requisitioned in April and designated as a BBV. Returned to owners in the same month. 1958: BU in Holland.

CARILON   1915/15   Displacement: 226TG 109TN
                                   Engines: 75HP = 9K
                                   Armament: 1 x 3pdr
                                   Admty No: 21

Port Reg: GY. 692

1915: Launched. Built at Beverley by CWG. Owned by Marshall Line SFC of Grimsby. Requisitioned in November and converted to a M/S. LOST. Mined off Margate on 24th December.

CARISBROOKE	1939/46	Displacement: 230TG 90TN
		Engines: 83HP
		Armament: 1 x 12pdr
		Port Reg: GY. 472
		P. No: FY. 583

1928: Launched. Built at Selby by Cochrane. Owned by the Queen SFC of Grimsby. 1939: Requisitioned in August and converted to a M/S. Subsequently purchased into the RN. 1946: Sold to mercantile.

CARLTON	1915/16	Displacement: 267TG
		Armament: 1 x 3pdr
		Admty No: 1965
		Port Reg: GY. 270

1907: Launched. 1915: Requisitioned in December and converted to a M/S. 1916: LOST. Mined off Folkestone on 21st February.

CARMANIA II	1915/19	Displacement: 250TG 107TN
		Engines: 76HP
		Armament: 1 x 6pdrAA; 24 mines
		Admty No: 3221
		Port Reg: GY. 268
		P. No: N.1A

1907: Launched. Built at Grimsby. Owned by the Strand SFC of Grimsby. 1915: Requisitioned in May and converted to a M/L. 1919: Returned to owners. *Notes:* Reported by some sources as having been converted to a M/S later in the War.

CAROLINE	1940/41	Displacement: 253TG
		Port Reg: Dutch
		P. No: FY. 1729

1930: Launched. 1940: Hired from Dutch owners and converted to a M/S. Commissioned with a Dutch Crew. 1941: LOST. Mined off Milford Haven on 28th April.

CARYSFORT II	1915/19	Displacement: 243TG 105TN
		Engines: 75HP
		Armament: 1 x 6pdrAA; 7.5-inch
		Bomb Thrower (A/S Howitzer)
		Admty No: 1533
		Port Reg: M. 32

1915: Launched. Built at Selby by Cochrane. Owned by D. Pettit of Milford Haven. Requisitioned in June and converted to a M/S. 1919: Returned to owners.

CASORIA   1914/19   Displacement: 185TG 72TN
Engines: 55HP
Armament: 1 x 6pdrAA
Admty No: 808
Port Reg: GY. 567
1897: Launched. Built at Hull. Owned by JL. Green AO of Grimsby. 1914: Requisitioned in November and converted to a M/S. 1919: Returned.

CASPIAN   1918/19   Displacement: 150TG 56TN
Engines: 45HP
Admty No: Not issued
Port Reg: GY. 755
1895: Launched. Built at North Shields. Owned by the Economy SFC of Grimsby. 1918: Requisitioned into the Fishery Reserve. 1919: Returned to owners.

CASSANDRA   1915/19   Displacement: 174TG 68TN
Engines: 45HP = 9.5K
Armament: 1 x 3pdr
Admty No: 1767
Port Reg: H. 848
1905: Launched. Built at Beverley by CWG. Owned by Hellyer SFC of Hull. 1915: Requisitioned in May and converted to a M/S. 1917: Renamed CASSANDRA II in July. 1919: Returned to owners and reverted to original name. 1935: Mercantile Loss. Foundered in the North Sea on 26th August E.N.E. of Aberdeen.

CASSANDRA II   1917/19   See under CASSANDRA above

CASSOWARY   1914/19   Displacement: 222TG 89TN
Engines: 60HP
Armament: 1 x 6pdr
Admty No: 806
Port Reg: GY. 634
1898: Launched. Built at Beverley. Iron construction. Owned by T Baskcomb Ltd. of Grimsby. 1914: Requisitioned in November and converted to a M/S. 1919: Returned to owners.

CASTELNAU   1940/46   See under JOHN JACOBS
(Vol 1 p.141)

CASTLEROCK   1940/45   Displacement: 259TG
1904: Launched. 1940: Requisitioned on 13th May and converted to an APV. 1945: Returned to owners in September.

CASTLETON	1916/19	See under EARL GRANARD

CASTOR 1917/19 Displacement: 209TG 91TN
Engines: 51HP
Armament: 1 x 12pdr
Admty No: 2960
Port Reg: GY. 963

1916: Launched. Built at Selby by Cochrane. Owned by the Grimsby & North Sea STC. Requisitioned in September and converted to a M/S. 1917: Renamed CASTOR II in March. 1919: Returned to owners. Acquired by the Lindsey SFC of Grimsby. 1946: Sold to Poland.

CASTOR II 1917/19 See under CASTOR above

CASWELL 1917/19 1940/46 Displacement: 276TG 107TN
Engines: 88HP
Armament: 1 x 6pdrAA
Admty No: 3323
Port Reg: SA. 70
P. No: WWII: FY. 500

1917: Launched. Built at Southbank-on-Tees by Smith's Dock. Owned by the Rhondda FC of Swansea. Requisitioned in January and converted to a M/S. 1919: Returned to owners. 1940: Requisitioned in February and converted to a M/S. 1946: Returned to owners in July.

CAULONIA 1915/19 1940/43 Displacement: 296TG 130TN
Engines: 79HP
Armament: 1 x 6pdrAA; 1 x 7.5-inch
Bomb Thrower (A/S Howitzer)
Admty No: 3201
Port Reg: GY. 792
P.No: WWII: 4. 163

1912: Launched. Built at Selby by Cochrane. Owned by the Strand SFC of Grimsby. 1915: Requisitioned in May and converted to a M/S. 1919: Returned to owners. 1940: Requisitioned and converted to an APV. 1942: Converted to a M/S. 1943: LOST. Took the ground in Rye Bay on 31st March and foundered.

CAVALCADE 1945/46 See under COURSER

CAVE 1914/19 Displacement: 247TG 99TN
Engines: 70HP
Armament: 1 x 12pdr; 1 x 6pdrAA
Admty No: 389
Port Reg: H. 643

1902: Launched. Built at Selby by Cochrane. Owned by JH. Collinson of Hull. 1914: Requisitioned in November and converted to a M/S. 1919: Returned to owners.

CAYRIAN   1917/19 1939/45 Displacement: 216TG 85TN
                                           Engines: 7HP
                                           Admty No: 645
                                           Port Reg: GY. 645
                                           P.No: WWII: FY. 791
1911: Launched. Built at Selby by Cochrane. Owned by JW. Smethurst of Grimsby. 1917: Requisitioned in November and converted to a BDV. 1919: Returned to owners. 1939: Requisitioned in November and converted to a M/S. Joined the 112th M/S Group based at Grimsby. 1945: Returned to owners in December.

CAYTON WYKE   1939/40   Displacement: 373TG 142TN
                                         Engines: 96HP
                                         Armament: 1 x 12pdr
                                         Port Reg: H. 440
                                         P.No: FY. 191
1932: Launched. Built at Selby by Cochrane. Owned by the West Dock SFC of Hull. 1939: Purchased into the RN in August and converted to A/S. Based at Dover ICW PUFFIN and SAON. Group attacked U-16 on 23rd October and forced her onto the Goodwin Sands where she was eventually destroyed. 1940: LOST. Torpedoed by E-Boat off Dover on 8th July.

CECIL COOMBES   1919/20   See under GEORGE AIKEN
                                         (Vol 1 p.53)

CECIL RHODES   1918/19   Displacement: 112TG 47TN
                                         Engines: 44HP
                                         Admty No: Not issued
                                         Port Reg: A. 667
1891: Launched. Built at Hull. Iron construction. Owned by G. Craig AO of Aberdeen. 1918: Requisitioned into the Fishery Reserve. 1919: Returned to owners.

CEDAR   1915/19   Displacement: 219TG 106TN.
                                         Engines: 69HP = 10.25K
                                         Armament: 1 x 6pdrAA
                                         Admty No: 1229
                                         Port Reg: GY. 480
1909: Launched. Built at Beverley by CWG. Owned by W. Grant of Grimsby. 1915: Requisitioned in March and converted to a M/S. 1919: Returned to owners. 1924: Acquired by Spanish owners and renamed *Nere Fedea*. 1969: BU in Spain.

CEDAR LEAF   1914/19   Displacement: 176TG 31TN
                                         Engines: 24HP

Port Reg: BF.253
1910: Launched. Built at Macduff. Owned by C. Thomson AO of Macduff. 1914: Requisitioned in November. 1919: Returned to owners.

CEDRIC   1939/44   See under LORD GEORGE

CELTIA 1917/19   1939/40   Displacement: 239TG 93TN
                                     Engines: 68HP
                                     Admty No: Not issued
                                     Port Reg: M. 216
1907: Launched. Built at North Shields. Owned by Harley & Miller Ltd. of Liverpool. 1917: Requisitioned into the Fishery Reserve. 1919: Returned to owners. 1939: Requisitioned in November and designated as an APV. 1940: Returned to owners in January.

CENTURION   1915/19   Displacement: 156TG 60TN
                                     Engines: 58 HP
                                     Armament: 1 x 3pdr
                                     Port Reg: GN. 6
1904: Launched. Built at Aberdeen. Owned by G. Devlin of Leith AO. 1915: Requisitioned in October and converted to a BDV. 1919: Returned to owners.

CEPHEUS   1917/19   Displacement: 155TG 64TN
                                     Engines: 58HP
                                     Admty No: Not issued
                                     Port Reg: A. 656
1891: Launched. Built at Glasgow. Owned by G. Craig AO of Aberdeen. 1917: Requisitioned into the Fishery Reserve. 1919: Returned to owners.

CERBERUS   1915/15   Displacement: 155TG
1891: Launched. Owned by North Sea SFC of Grimsby. 1915: Requisitioned for a short period before being returned to owners.

CEREALIA   1914/19   Displacement: 220TG 115TN
                                     Engines: 60HP
                                     Armament: 1 x 3pdr
                                     Admty No: 674
                                     Port Reg: GY. 549
1905: Launched. Built at Selby by Cochrane. 1914: Requisitioned in December. 1919: Returned to owners. 1920: Owned by N. Ashworth AO of Fleetwood. PR: FD.165.

CERESIA   1914/19 1940/42 Displacement: 284TG 112TN
                                     Engines: 85HP
                                     Armament: 1 x 12pdr; 1 x 7.5-inch

Bomb Thrower (A/S Howitzer)
Admty No:194
Port Reg: FD. 26
P.No: Z. 153

1914: Launched. Built at Middlesborough by Smith's Dock. Owned by the Palatine SFC of Fleetwood. Requisitioned in November and converted to a M/S. 1919: Returned to owners. Acquired by Ora Trs. of Fleetwood. Same PR. 1940: Requisitioned in January as CHORLEY and converted to a BDV. 1942: LOST. Foundered off Start Point on 25th April.

CERISIO	1939/45	See under RUSHCOE

CETUS	1918/19	Displacement: 139TG 56TN
		Engines: 40HP
		Admty No: Not issued
		Port Reg: GY. 548

1893: Launched. Built at Govan. Owned by J. Mengel of Grimsby. 1918: Requisitioned into the Fishery Reserve. 1919: Returned to owners.

CEVIC	1918/19	Displacement: 151TG
		Admty No: Not issued
		Port Reg: FD. 186

1895: Launched. Built at North Shields. Iron construction. Owned by E. Taylor & N. Ashworth of Fleetwood. 1918: Requisitioned into the Fishery Reserve. 1919: Returned to owners.

CEVIC	1943/44	See under PELICAN

CEYLONITE	1940/46	See under THOMAS BUCKLEY
		(Vol 1 p.187)

CHALCEDONY	1914/19	Displacement: 333TG 134TN
		Engines: 82HP
		Armament: 1 x 6pdr
		Admty No: 346
		Port Reg: H. 341

1911: Launched. Built at Selby by Cochrane. Owned by Colebrook & Knight Ltd., of London. 1914: Requisitioned in August and converted to a M/S. 1919: Returned to owners.

CHALCEDONY	1939/46	Displacement: 357TG 146TN
		Engines: 96HP = 11.2K
		Armament: 1 x 12pdr
		Port Reg: H. 392
		P.No: 4. 124

1928: Launched. Built at Beverley by CWG. Owned by the Kingston STC of Hull. 1939: Requisitioned in August and converted to an APV. 1941: Converted to a M/S. 1943: 19th M/S based at Grimsby. 1945: Acquired by Parkholme Trs. of Grimsby and renamed *Laforey*. PR: GY.109. 1946: Returned to owners in May. 1949: Acquired by Wyre STC of Fleetwood and renamed *Wyre Mariner* PR: FD. 34. 1954: BU at Haulbowline, S. Ireland.

CHALLENGER	1917/19	Displacement: 160TG 54TN
		Engines: 50HP
		Armament: None
		Admty No: Not issued
		Port Reg: GN. 49

1897: Launched. Built at Aberdeen. Owned by G. Devlin of Leith AO. 1917: Requisitioned into the Fishery Reserve. 1919: Returned to owners.

CHAMBERLAIN	1917/19	Displacement: 161TG 61TN
		Engines: 66HP
		Armament: 1 x 6pdrAA
		Admty No: 3336
		Port Reg: GN.19

1905: Launched. Built at Aberdeen. Owned by G. Devlin of Leith AO. 1917: Requisitioned in March and converted to a M/S. 1919: Returned to owners. Acquired by A. King of Aberdeen and renamed *River Ythan*. PR: A.188. 1940: Listed as RIVER YTHAN to be requisitioned but not taken up.

CHAMPION	1915/19	Displacement: 150TG 63TN
		Engines: 45HP = 10K
		Armament: 1 x 3pdr
		Port Reg: A. 367

1894: Launched. Built at Hull by CWG. Owned by R. Simpson of Hull. 1899: Acquired by London & Yorkshire ST & Fish Carrying Co. of Hull. 1904: Acquired by Neale & West of Cardiff. PR: CF. 6. 1913: Acquired by RW Lewis of Aberdeen. 1915: Requisitioned in May and converted to a BDV. 1919: Returned to owners. 1920: Acquired by RW. Crawford of Scarborough. PR: SH. 350. 1931: BU.

CHANCELLOR	1915/19	Displacement: 186TG 60TN
		Engines: 53HP
		Armament: None
		Port Reg: GN. 7

1904: Launched. Built at Aberdeen. Owned by J. Inglis of Peebles. 1915: Requisitioned in June and converted to an Accommodation Ship. 1919: Returned to owners.

CHANCELLOR	1917/19	Displacement: 156TN 64TN
		Engines: 53HP
		Armament: None

Admty No: Not issued
Port Reg: FD. 339
1904: Launched. Built at Aberdeen. Owned by E. Taylor & N. Ashworth of Fleetwood. 1917: Requisitioned into the Fishery Reserve. 1919: Returned to owners.

| CHANDBALI | 1939/43 | RIN |
| | | Displacement: 362TG |

1919: Launched. 1939: Requisitioned and converted to an APV. Commissioned into the RIN. 1943: Returned to owners.

| CHANDOS | 1939/40 | See under THOMAS GOODCHILD |
| | | (Vol 1 p.188) |

CHANTICLEER	1914/18	Displacement: 150TG 62TN
		Engines: 45HP = 10K
		Armament: 1 x 6pdr
		Admty No: 921
		Port Reg: PH. 402

1894: Launched. Built at Hull by CWG. Owned by ST White, AO of Hull. 1898: Acquired by J. Chant and MJ Paddon of Plymouth. PR: PH. 402. 1914: Requisitioned in November and converted to a M/S. 1918: Returned to owners in November. 1926: Acquired by French owners and renamed *Henriville*. 1938: BU.

CHARLES VAILLANT	1940/46	Displacement: 224TG
		Port Reg: French
		P. No: FY.1804

1916: Launched. French fishing vessel. 1940: French M/S seized at Southampton in Operation Grab on 3rd July. Commissioned into the RN as a M/S. 1946: Returned to France in June.

CHARMOUTH	1914/19	Displacement: 195TG 116TN
		Engines: 85HP
		Armament: 1 x 6pdrAA
		Admty No: 366
		Port Reg: BL.14

1910: Launched. Built at Aberdeen. Owned by the Western STC of Bristol. 1914: Requisitioned in August and converted to a M/S. 1919: Returned to owners.

CHASSE MARIE	1940/45	Displacement: 251TG
		Port Reg: French
		P.No: FY.1793

1920: Launched. French fishing vessel. 1940: French M/S seized at Southampton in Operation Grab on 3rd July. Commissioned into the RN as a M/S. 1944: Converted to an Esso in January. 1945: Returned to France.

CHASSIRON 1939/45 Displacement: 258TG 116TN
Engines: 85HP
Port Reg: A. 435
P.No: FY. 1857
1913: Launched. Built at Middlesborough by Smith's Dock. 1938: Owned by J. Mackie
& A. Robertson of Aberdeen. 1939: Requisitioned in September and converted to a M/S.
1945: Returned to owners in August.

CHERWELL 1920/46 See under JAMES JONES (Vol 1 p.137)

CHESTER 1915/16 Displacement: 143TG
Armament: 1 x 3pdr
Admty No: 629
Port Reg: GY. 148
1896: Launched. 1915: Requisitioned in October and converted to a M/S. Renamed
CHESTER II. 1916: LOST. Sunk in a collision in the Firth of Forth on 29th February.

CHESTER II 1915/16 See under CHESTER above

CHIEFTAN 1915/19 Displacement: 278TG 112TN
Engines: 70HP = 10.5K
Armament: 1 x 12pdr; 1 x 7.5-inch
Bomb Thrower (A/S Howitzer).
Admty No: 945
Port Reg: H. 847
1905: Launched. Built at Beverley by CWG. Owned by Marine SFC of Hull. 1915:
Requisitioned in January and converted to a M/S. 1918: Acquired by East Riding SFC
of Hull. 1919: Returned to owners. 1936: BU.

CHIEFTAN II 1917/19 Displacement: 149TG 50TN
Engines: 76HP
Armament: 1 x 12pdr
Admty No: Not issued
Port Reg: A. 237
1899: Launched. Built at Leith. Owned by A. Buthlay AO of Aberdeen. 1917:
Requisitioned into the Fishery Reserve and armed. 1919: Returned to owners.

CHIKARA 1914/19 Displacement: 250TG 98TN
Engines: 76HP
Armament: 1 x 12pdr
Admty No: 67
Port Reg: GY. 364
1908: Launched. Built at Grimsby. Owned by H. Morris AO of Grimsby. 1914:
Requisitioned in October and converted to a M/S. 1919: Returned to owners.

| CHILTERN | 1940/45 | See under JOHN CORMACK |
| | | (Vol 1 p.140) |

CHINA	1915/19	Displacement: 190TG 93TN
		Engines: 50HP
		Armament: 1 x 6pdrAA
		Admty No: 946
		Port Reg: GY. 557

1893: Launched. Built at Beverley. Owned by the North Eastern SFC of Grimsby. 1915: Requisitioned in January and converted to a M/S. 1919: Returned to owners.

CHOICE	1914/19	Displacement: 165TG 66TN
		Engines: 61HP
		Armament: 1 x 6pdr
		Admty No: 476
		Port Reg: GN.16

1905: Launched. Built at Beverley. Owned by DJ. Ayres of Lowestoft. 1914: Requisitioned in November and converted to a M/S. 1919: Returned to owners.

| CHOICE | 1944/44 | See under STALKER |

| CHORLEY | 1940/42 | See under CERESIA |

| CHRISTANIA T. PURDY | 1939/46 | See under JOHN ABBOTT |
| | | (Vol 1 p.176) |

CHRISTOPHER	1915/17	Displacement: 316TG 135TN
		Engines: 93HP = 11K
		Armament: 1 x 12pdr
		Admty No: 1502
		Port Reg: H. 207

1911: Launched. Built at Beverley. Owned by Pickering & Haldane STC of Hull. 1915: Requisitioned and converted to a M/S. Fitted to carry 1 a/c on a platform aft. 1916: Employed on North Sea anti-Zeppelin patrols. 1917: LOST. Mined off Southwold on 30 March.

CHRYSEA	1914/19 1940/45	Displacement: 210TG 81TN
		Engines: 78HP
		Armament: 1 x 6pdr
		Admty No: 626
		Port Reg: GY. 745

1912: Launched. Built at Middlesborough by Smith's Dock. Owned by Sleight SFC of Grimsby. 1914: Requisitioned in September and converted to a M/S. 1919: Returned to owners. 1940: Requisitioned in April and converted to a BBV. 1945: Returned to owners in January.

CHRYSOLITE   1916/19 1940/46 Displacement: 251TG 98TN
                                        Engines: 76HP
                                        Armament: 1 x 6pdr
                                        Admty No: 2982
                                        Port Reg: WWI: H. 513; WWII: GY. 260
                                        P. No: WWII: FY. 1827
1916: Launched. Built at Selby by Cochrane. Owned by R. Noble & Co Ltd & AD Buchan
of Aberdeen. Requisitioned in December and converted to a M/S. 1919: Returned to
owners. Acquired by Beely & Sleight of Grimsby. 1940: Requisitioned in August and
converted to a M/S. 1946: Returned to owners in January.

CICERO   1914/19 1940/44 Displacement: 173TG 68TN
                                        Engines: 45HP = 9.5K
                                        Armament: 1 x 12pdr
                                        Admty No: 149
                                        Port Reg: WWI: H. 931; WWII: A.146
                                        P.No: WWII: 4. 443
1906: Launched. Built at Beverley by CWG. Owned by Hellyer SFC of Hull. 1914:
Requisitioned in September and converted to a M/S. 1917: Acquired by C. Curzon of
Milford Haven. Renamed CICERO II in November. 1919: Returned to owners and
reverted to original name. 1929: Acquired by Trident SFC of Hull and renamed
Barnsness. 1940: Acquired by G. Robb & Sons of Aberdeen. Requisitioned in February
as BARNSNESS and converted to a BBV. 1944: Converted to an Esso. Returned to
owners in December. 1952: BU at Bo'ness.

CICERO II   1917/19   See under CICERO above

CINCERIA   1919/19   See under COOMASIN (Vol 1 p.214)

CITY OF ABERDEEN   1917/19 1939/40 Displacement: 194TG 75TN
                                        Engines: 63HP
                                        Admty No: Not issued
                                        Port Reg: H. 383
1898: Launched. Built at Aberdeen. Owned by Consolidated Fisheries of Grimsby. 1917:
Requisitioned into the Fishery Reserve. 1919: Returned to owners. 1939: Requisitioned
on 4th December and designated as an APV. 1940: Returned to owners on 18th January.

CITY OF CARLISLE   1915/19   Displacement: 208TG 82TN
                                        Engines: 70HP
                                        Armament: 1 x 6pdr
                                        Admty No: 1205
                                        Port Reg: H. 58
1899: Launched. Built at Greenock. Owned by GS. Bowman of Hull. 1915:
Requisitioned in January and converted to a M/S. 1919: Returned to owners.

CITY OF DUNDEE   1914/15   Displacement: 269TG
                                        Admty No: 678
                                        Port Reg: FD. 4
1914: Launched. Requisitioned in November and converted to a M/S. 1915: LOST.
Sunk in a collision off Folkestone on 14th September.

CITY OF EDINBURGH   1914/19   Displacement: 300TG 115TN
                                        Engines: 80HP
                                        Armament: 1 x 6pdrAA
                                        Admty No: 338
                                        Port Reg: FD. 185
1908: Launched. Built at Dundee. Owned by F. Kelsall & Co of Fleetwood. 1914:
Requisitioned in August and converted to a M/S. 1919: Returned to owners.

CITY OF HULL   1918/18   Displacement: 181T
1898: Launched. 1918: Requisitioned for a short period and then returned to owners.

CITY OF LIVERPOOL   1915/18   Displacement: 179TG 69TN
                                        Engines: 52HP
                                        Port Reg: FD. 197
1900: Launched. Built at North Shields. Owned by N. Ashworth & E Tomlinson of
Fleetwood. 1915: Requisitioned in June and converted to a BDV. 1918: Returned to
owners in August.

CITY OF LONDON   1917/19   Displacement: 195TG 76TN
                                        Engines: 55HP = 10K
                                        Admty No: Not issued
                                        Port Reg: FD. 201
1901: Launched. Built at Hull BY by CWG. Owned by F. Kelsall of Fleetwood. 1917:
Requisitioned into the Fishery Reserve. 1919: Returned to owners. 1926: Acquired by
Regent FC of Aberdeen and renamed *Danurie II*. PR: A. 113. 1937: BU.

CITY OF MANCHESTER 1915/18   Displacement: 189TG 75TN
                                        Engines: 52HP
                                        Port Reg: FD. 193
1900: Launched. Built at North Shields. Owned by N. Ashworth & E. Tomlinson of
Fleetwood. 1915: Requisitioned in June and converted to a BDV. 1918: Returned to
owners in August.

CITY OF PERTH   1919/22   See under WILLIAM ASHTON
                                        (Vol 1 p.189)

CITY OF SELBY   1914/19 1940/47 Displacement: 284TG 112TN
                                        Engines: 85HP

89

Armament: 1 x 12pdr
Admty No: 193
Port Reg: FD 8
P.No: WWII: Z.154

1914: Launched. Built at Middlesborough by Smith's Dock. Owned by F. Kelsall & Co. of Fleetwood. Requisitioned in November and converted to a M/S. 1917: Converted to an Escort. 1919: Returned to owners. Acquired by T. Cardwell and R.H Bagshaw of Fleetwood and renamed *Westlyn*. 1940: Purchased into the RN in February as WESTLYN and converted to a BDV. 1947: Sold to mercantile on 2nd May.

CITY OF YORK   1915/20   Displacement: 202TG 79TN
                                       Engines: 52HP
                                       Armament: 1 x 12pdr
                                       Port Reg: FD. 16

1904: Launched. Built at Goole by Goole SB. Owned by F. Kelsall & Co of Fleetwood. 1915: Requisitioned in June and converted to a BDV. 1920: Returned to owners

CLAESJE   1940/45   Displacement: 229TG
                                       Port Reg: Dutch
                                       P.No: FY. 1716

1933: Launched. Dutch fishing vessel. 1940: Dutch M/S commissioned into the RN when Holland was overrun. 1945: Returned to Holland.

CLAIRE   1915/19 1939/40 Displacement: 219TG 112TN
                                       Engines: 67HP = 10K
                                       Armament: 1 x 6pdr
                                       Admty No: 1466
                                       Port Reg: GY. 318

1907: Launched. Built at Beverley by CWG. Owned by W. Grant AO of Grimsby. 1915: Requisitioned in April and converted to a M/S. 1919: Returned to owners. 1927: Acquired by A. Grant of Grimsby. 1939: Requisitioned in November and converted to a M/S. 1940: Returned to owners in February. 1958: BU in Belgium in August.

CLARIBELLE   1941/45   See under WILLIAM BARROW
                                       (Vol 1 p.190)

CLARINET   1940/46   Ex-*Bardolf*
                                       Displacement: 257T
                                       P.No: Z.132

1911: Launched. 1939: Requisitioned in December and converted to a BDV. 1943: Purchased into the RN in November. 1946: Sold to mercantile.

CLAVERTON   1939/40   See under LOROONE

CLEMENTINA II   1915/19   Displacement: 200TG 76TN
Engines: 60HP
Armament: 1 x 6pdr
Admty No: 1175
Port Reg: A. 900

1903: Launched. Built at Aberdeen. Owned by G. Robb Snr. & G. Robb Jnr. of Aberdeen. 1915: Requisitioned in March and converted to a M/S. 1919: Returned to owners.

CLEON   1915/18   Displacement: 266TG
Armament: 1 x 3pdr
Admty No: 1514
Port Reg: GY. 240

1907: Launched. 1915: Requisitioned in May and converted to a M/S. 1918: LOST. Mined off Folkestone on 1st February.

CLEOPATRA   1914/19 1940/40 Displacement: 240TG 91TN
Engines: 68HP
Armament: 1 x 6pdr
Admty No: 140
Port Reg: M. 213

1907: Launched. Built at North Shields. Owned by D. Pettit of Milford Haven. 1914: Requisitioned in August and converted to a M/S. Renamed CLEOPATRA II in December. 1919: Returned to owners. Retained the name *Cleopatra II*. 1939: Requisitioned in August and designated as an APV. 1940: Renamed TEAZER in February. Returned to owners in the same month.

CLEOPATRA   1914/19   Displacement: 311TG
Armament: 1 x 12pdr; 1 x 7.5-inch
Bomb Thrower (A/S Howitzer)
Admty No: 657
Port Reg: H. 860

1906: Launched. 1914: Requisitioned in October and converted to a M/S. 1915: Renamed CLEOPATRA III in April. 1919: Returned to owners.

CLEOPATRA II   1914/19   See under CLEOPATRA 1907

CLEOPATRA III   1915/19   See under CLEOPATRA 1906

CLEVELA   1939/45   Displacement: 387TG 167TN
Engines: 97HP
Armament: 1 x 12pdr
Port Reg: FD. 94
P.No: FY. 678

1930: Launched. Built at Selby by Cochrane. Owned by Marr & Son of Fleetwood. 1939: Requisitioned in September and converted to a M/S. Joined the 19th M/S Group based at Grimsby. 1945: 134th M/S Group based at Grimsby. 1946: Returned to owners in May. *Notes*: aka CLEVELLA.

CLIFTON   1914/17   Displacement: 242TG
                                          Armament: 1 x 12pdr
                                          Admty No: 954
                                          Port Reg: GY. 116
1906: Launched. 1914: Requisitioned in December. 1917: LOST. Mined off the Daunt LV. on 18th February.

CLIO   1915/16   Displacement: 144TG
1896: Launched. 1915: Requisitioned. 1916: Returned to owners.

CLOTILDE   1914/19 1940/45 Displacement: 289TG 114TN
                                          Engines: 84HP
                                          Armament: 1 x 6pdr
                                          Admty No: 924
                                          Port Reg: FD. 232
                                          P.No: WWII: FY. 534
1913: Launched. Built at Selby by Cochrane. Owned by the Active FC of Fleetwood. 1914: Requisitioned in November and converted to a M/S. 1919: Returned to owners. 1940: Requisitioned in February and converted to a M/S. 1945: Returned to owners in December.

CLOUGHSTONE   1940/45   Displacement: 233TG 114TN
                                          Engines: 67HP
                                          Port Reg: A. 257
                                          P.No: 4. 446
1907: Launched. Built at Selby by Cochrane. 1938: Owned by JC. Douglas of Aberdeen. 1940: Requisitioned in December and converted to a BBV. 1944: Converted to an Esso. 1945: Returned to owners in April.

CLOUGHTON WYKE   1940/42   See under JOHN JOHNSON
                                          (Vol 1 p.142)

CLYDE   1915/17   Displacement: 146TG
                                          Armament: 1 x 3pdr
                                          Admty No: 971
                                          Port Reg: GY. 317
1891: Launched. 1915: Requisitioned in February and converted to a M/S. 1917: LOST. Sunk in a collision off Sidmouth on 14th October.

CLYNE CASTLE	1914/19	Displacement: 252TG
		Armament: 1 x 6pdr
		Admty No: 137
		Port Reg: SA. 43

1907: Launched. 1914: Requisitioned in September and converted to a M/S. 1919: Returned to owners.

CLYNE CASTLE	1939/45	Displacement: 307TG 117TN
		Engines: 91HP
		Armament: 1 x 12pdr
		Port Reg: SA. 1
		P.No: FY. 508

1929: Launched. Built at Selby by Cochrane. Owned by Consolidated Fisheries of Grimsby. 1939: Requisitioned in August and converted to a M/S. 1944: Converted to a WDV. 1945: Returned to owners in November.

| CLYTHNESS | 1939/46 | See under DANIEL DICK |
| | | (Vol 1 p.150) |

COADJUTOR	1915/19	Displacement: 207TG 90TN
		Engines: 57HP
		Armament: 1 x 6pdr
		Admty No: 1415
		Port Reg: GN. 41

1915: Launched. Built at Leith. Owned by J .Inglis of Peebles. Requisitioned in March and converted to a M/S. 1919: Returned to owners.

| COBBERS | 1940/41 | See under WILLIAM KNIGHT |
| | | (Vol 1 p.188) |

| COCKADE | 1940/41 | See under ANSON 1915 |

COCKATRICE	1914/15	Displacement: 115TG
		Admty No: 802
		Port Reg: GY. 610

1894: Launched. 1914: Requisitioned in November and converted to a M/S. 1915: Renamed COCKATRICE II in February. Returned to the Fishing Fleet in June. 1916: Mercantile Loss. Captured by a German S/M 40 miles SE x E from the Spurn LV. and sunk by gunfire. No loss of life.

| COCKATRICE II | 1915/15 | See under COCKATRICE above |

| COLLEAGUE | 1915/19 | Displacement: 207TG 190TN |
| | | Engines: 74HP |

Armament: 1 x 6pdrAA
Admty No: 1631
Port Reg: GN. 53

1915: Launched. Built at Leith. Owned by J. Inglis of Peebles. Requisitioned in May and converted to a M/S. 1919: Returned to owners.

COLLENA   1915/19 1940/45   Displacement: 293TG 116TN
Engines: 84HP
Armament: 1 x 6pdrAA
Admty No: 1585
Port Reg: FD. 115
P.No: WWII: Z. 151

1915: Launched. Built at Selby by Cochrane. Owned by Marr of Fleetwood. Requisitioned in May and converted to a M/S. 1919: Returned to owners. 1940: Purchased into the RN in January and converted to a BDV. 1945: Sold to mercantile in July.

COLLINGWOOD   1917/19 1940/45   Displacement: 179TG 69TN
Engines: 55HP = 9.5K
Armament: WWI: None
Admty No: Not issued
Port Reg: GY. 1229

1902: Launched. Built at Beverley by CWG. Owned by W. Grant & HC Baker of Grimsby. 1917: Requisitioned into the Fishery Reserve. 1919: Returned to owners. 1931: Acquired by C. Dobson of Grimsby. 1940: Requisitioned and converted to a BDV. Renamed FIELDGATE in October. 1945: Returned to owners. Acquired by Wembley SFC, Grimsby. 1949: BU by Pounds of Portsmouth.

COLNE   1920/46   See under ISAAC CHANT
(Vol 1 p.136)

COLTMAN   1914/19   Displacement: 312TG 128TN
Engines: 89
Armament: 1 x 12pdr
Admty No: 344
Port Reg: H. 973

1907: Launched. Built at Hull. Owned by the City SFC of Hull. 1914: Requisitioned in August and converted to a M/S. Fitted with Listening Hydrophones. 1919: Returned to owners.

COLUMBA   1916/18   Displacement: 138TG
Armament: 1 x 3pdr
Port Reg: GN. 43

1893: Launched. 1916: Requisitioned in May and converted to a BDV. 1918: LOST. Mined off May Island on 10th March.

COLUMBIA   1914/15   Displacement: 266TG
                                            Admty No: 200
                                            Port Reg: H. 42
1886: Launched. 1914: Requisitioned in September and converted to an APV. 1915:
LOST. Sunk by German TB off Thornton Ridge, Foreness, on 1st May.

COMBER   1940/40   Displacement: 306TG
1916: Launched. American fishing vessel. 1940: Designated by USN for Lend/Lease.
Cancelled.

COMET   1939/40   Ex-*Tamura*
                                            Displacement: 301TG 113TN
                                            Engines: 99HP
                                            Port Reg: LO. 63
1924: Launched. Built at Southbank-on-Tees by Smith's Dock. Owned by T. Jenkerson
of Milford Haven. 1939: Requisitioned in September and converted to a Decoy Vessel.
1940: LOST. Mined off Falmouth on 30th September.

COMITATUS   1939/45   See under JOHN GULIPSTER
                                            (Vol 1 p.64)

COMMANDANT   1915/16   Displacement: 207TG
                                            Admty No: 1440
                                            Port Reg: GN. 36
1915: Launched. Requisitioned in April and converted to a M/S. 1916: LOST. Mined off
the Sunk LV. on 2nd April.

COMMANDER EVANS   1939/45   Displacement: 344TG 142TN
                                            Engines: 93HP
                                            Armament: 1 x 12pdr
                                            Port Reg: H. 20
                                            P. No: FY. 113
1924: Launched. Built at Selby by Cochrane. Owned by the Hudson SFC of Hull. 1939:
Requisitioned in November and converted to an APV. 1944: Converted to a D/L. 1945:
Returned to owners in August.

COMMANDER FULLERTON   1915/15 Displacement: 227TG 89HP
                                            Engines: 60HP
                                            Admty No: 3063
                                            Port Reg: H. 286
1915: Launched. Built at Goole by the Goole SB Co. Owned by Hellyer SFC of Hull.
Requisitioned in September. LOST. Sunk by SMS EMDEN and Destroyers of the
German Third Half-Flotilla on 12th December.   ICW Destroyers PELLEW and
PARTRIDGE together with Trs. LIVINGSTONE, LORD ALVERSTONE and TOKIO she

was escorting a Scandinavian convoy when attacked by the Germans. The Skipper, J.W. Whelan, was killed and all the ships in the convoy were sunk as were all the escorts with the exception of PELLEW.

COMMANDER HOLBROOK 1917/19 1940/45 Displacement: 227TG 93TN
Engines: 60HP
Armament: 1 x 6pdr
Port Reg: H. 223
P.No: FY. 111

1915: Launched. Built at Goole by the Goole SB Co. Owned by the Hellyer SFC of Hull. Requisitioned in January. 1917: Reduced to the Fishery Reserve. 1919: Returned to owners. Acquired by the Eastern SFC (1923) of Hull. 1940: Requisitioned in June and converted to an A/S. 1942: Converted to a M/S. 1945: Returned to owners in November.

COMMANDER HORTON 1917/19 1940/40 Displacement: 227TG 89TN
Engines: 60HP
Admty No: Not issued
Port Reg: H. 233

1915: Launched. Built at Goole by the Goole SB Co. Owned by the Hellyer SFC of Hull. 1917: Requisitioned into the Fishery Reserve. 1919: Returned to owners. Acquired by the Eastern FC (1923) of Hull. 1940: Requisitioned in June and designated as an APV. Returned to owners in October.

COMMANDER NASMITH 1915/19 Displacement: 243TG 96TN
Engines: 80HP = 10.5K
Admty No: 1968
Port Reg: H. 385
P.No: WWII: FY. 516

1915: Launched. Built at Beverley by CWG. Owned by Hellyer SFC of Hull. Requisitioned in September and converted to a M/S. 1919: Returned to owners. 1923: Acquired by the Eastern FC (1923) of Hull. 1940: Requisitioned in January and converted to an APV. 1942: Converted to a M/S. 1944: Converted to an Esso. 1945: Returned to owners in May. 1951: Acquired by J. Mowatt of Aberdeen and renamed *Elmo*. 1953: BU at Granton.

COMMILES 1939/45 See under MATTHEW FLYNN
(Vol 1 p.68)

COMMISSIONER 1917/19 Displacement: 161TG 61TN
Engines: 66HP
Armament: 2 x 12pdrs; 1 x 3pdr; 1 x
7.5-inch Bomb Thrower (A/S Howitzer);
As a 'Q' Ship: 1 x 12pdr; 1 x 6pdr
Admty No: 1690

Port Reg: GN. 18
1905: Launched. Built at Aberdeen. Owned by J. Inglis of Peebles. 1917: Requisitioned in March and converted to an APV. 1918: Converted to a 'Q' Ship and rearmed. 1919: Returned to owners. *Notes*: 'Q' Ship aliases: *Champion*, *Recorder* and *Roller*.

COMMODATOR   1939/45   See under RICHARD BACON 1917
                                     (Vol 1 p.68)

COMMODORE   1917/19   Displacement: 137TG
                                     Port Reg: GN. 33
1891: Launched.   1917: Requisitioned into the Fishery Reserve.   1919: Returned to owners.

COMPANION   1917/19   Displacement: 163TG 65TN
                                     Engines: 65HP
                                     Armament: 1 x 6pdrAA
                                     Admty No: 3012
                                     Port Reg: GN. 23
1903: Launched. Built at Aberdeen. Owned by J. Inglis of Peebles. 1917: Requisitioned in March and converted to a Training vessel. Based at Portland attached to the A/S School for sea instruction. 1919: Returned to owners.

COMPT HORACE Van der BURGH 1917/19 Displacement: 200TG
                                     Port Reg: Belgian.
1905: Launched. Belgian fishing vessel. 1917: Requisitioned into the Fishery Reserve with the permission of her Belgian owners. 1919: Returned to owners.

COMPUTATOR   1939/45   See under EGILIAS AKERMAN
                                     (Vol 1 p.52)

COMRADE   1915/19   Displacement: 161TG 61TN
                                     Engines: 66HP
                                     Armament: 1 x 12pdr
                                     Admty No: 1500
                                     Port Reg: GN. 30
1906: Launched. Built at Aberdeen. Owned by J.Inglis of Peebles. 1915: Requisitioned in May. 1919: Returned to owners.

CONAN DOYLE   1917/19   Displacement: 314TG 26TN
                                     Engines: 86HP
                                     Admty No: Not issued
                                     Port Reg: H. 240
1915: Launched. Built at Selby by Cochrane. Owned by the Newington ST Co. Ltd. of Hull. 1917: Requisitioned into the Fishery Reserve. 1919: Returned to owners.

CONCERTATOR   1939/46   See under JOHN THORLING
(Vol 1 p.65)

CONCORD   1914/19   Displacement: 235TG 95TN
Engines: 63HP
Armament: 1 x 12pdr
Admty No: 722
Port Reg: GY. 95

1905: Launched. Built at Selby by Cochrane. Owned by GW. White & JW. Willows of Grimsby. 1914: Requisitioned in December and converted to a M/S. 1915: Renamed CONCORD III in December. 1919: Returned to owners.

CONCORD III   1915/19   See under CONCORD above

CONDOR II   1914/14   Displacement: 227TG 95TN
Engines: 63HP = 10.5K
Armament: 1 x 6pdr
Port Reg: GY. 85

1905: Launched. Built at Beverley by CWG. Owned by T. Baskcomb of Grimsby. 1914: Requisitioned in November. LOST. Wrecked off Lowestoft on 22nd November.

CONDUCTOR   1915/19   Displacement: 163TG 65TN
Engines: 65HP
Port Reg: GN. 21

1903: Launched. Built at Aberdeen. Owned by J. Inglis of Peebles. 1915: Requisitioned in October and converted to a BDV. 1919: Returned to owners.

CONFEDERATE   1914/19   Displacement: 202TG 77TN
Engines: 57HP
Armament: 1 x 6pdr
Admty No: 317
Port Reg: GN. 81

1913: Launched. Built at Aberdeen. Owned by J. Inglis of Peebles. 1914: Requisitioned in August and converted to a M/S. 1919: Returned to owners.

CONGO   1914/19   Displacement: 152TG 63TN
Engines: 45HP = 10K
Armament: 1 x 3pdr
Admty No: 822
Port Reg: GY. 274

1897: Launched. Built at Hull by CWG. Iron construction. Owned by the Ocean STC of Grimsby. 1914: Requisitioned in November and converted to a M/S. 1917: Reduced to the Fishery Reserve in January. 1919: Returned to owners. 1937: BU at Bo'ness.

CONGRE 1940/46 See under JOHN GEOGHAN
(Vol 1 p.63)

CONINGSBY 1914/19 Displacement: 257TG 106TN
Engines: 70HP
Armament: 1 x 6pdr
Admty No: 34
Port Reg: BN. 119
1906: Launched. Built at North Shields. Owned by Thelma Ltd of Aberdeen. 1914: Requisitioned in September and converted to a M/S. 1919: Returned to owners.

CONISTON 1939/40 See under INGOMAR

CONNIE 1915/19 Displacement: 198TG 78TN
Engines: 52HP
Port Reg: FD. 194
1900: Launched. Built at Hull. Owned by the Fleetwood SFC of Fleetwood. 1915: Requisitioned in June and converted to a BDV. 1919: Returned to owners.

CONQUEROR II 1917/19 Displacement: 148TG
Port Reg: A. 360
1899: Launched. 1917: Requisitioned into the Fishery Reserve. 1919: Returned to owners.

CONQUISTADOR 1939/40 Displacement: 224TG 100TN
Engines: 83HP
Port Reg: GY. 244
1915: Launched. Built at Aberdeen. Owned by TL Devlin of Leith. 1939: Requisitioned in November and converted to an APV. 1940: Converted to a M/S in June. LOST. Sunk in a collision in the Thames Estuary on 25th November.

CONSBRO 1940/45 Displacement: 350TG 157TN
Engines: 91HP
Port Reg: GY. 244
P. No: Z. 107
1930: Launched. Built at Selby by Cochrane. Owned by the Champion SFC of Grimsby. 1940: Requisitioned in January and converted to a BDV. 1945: Returned in September.

CONSORT 1915/19 Displacement: 181TG 80TN
Engines: 60HP = 10K
Armament: 1 x 12pdr
Admty No: 1612
Port Reg: GY. 498
1909: Launched. Built at Beverley by CWG. Owned by the Queen SFC of Grimsby.

1915: Requisitioned in April and converted to a M/S. 1919: Returned to owners. 1954: BU at Antwerp.

CONSTANCE   1917/19   Displacement: 166TG
                                              Port Reg: LH
1902: Launched. 1917: Requisitioned into the Fishery Reserve. 1919: Returned to owners.

CONTENDER   1940/45   Displacement: 236TG 101TN
                                              Engines: 64HP
                                              Armament: 1 x 12pdr; 2 x LMG (2x1)
                                                Port Reg: GN.22
                                              P.No: FY. 543
1930: Launched. Built at Aberdeen. Owned by TL Devlin of Leith. 1940: Requisitioned in February and converted to a M/S. Fitted with Oropesa gear. Operated in the North Sea from Lowestoft to Sheringham Shoal. 1945: Returned to owners.

CONTROLLER   1914/19 1940/44 Displacement: 201TG 76TN
                                              Engines: 57HP
                                            Armament: 1 x 3pdr
                                            Admty No: 298
                                            Port Reg: GN. 79
1913: Launched. Built at Aberdeen. Owned by J. Inglis of Peebles. 1914: Requisitioned in August and converted to a M/S. 1919: Returned to owners. 1940: Requisitioned in January and converted to a D/L. 1942: Converted to a BBV. 1944: Converted to an Esso in April. Returned to owners in September.

CONWAY   1915/19 1939/40 Displacement: 228TG 105TN
                                              Engines: 58HP
                                            Armament: 1 x 6pdrAA
                                            Admty No: 1532
                                            Port Reg: GY. 1288
1904: Launched. Built at Selby by Cochrane. Owned by TC & F. Moss of Grimsby. 1915: Requisitioned in June and converted to a M/S. 1919: Returned to owner. 1939: Requisitioned in November and converted to an APV. 1940: Returned to owners.

CONWAY CASTLE   1916/19 1939/45 Displacement: 274TG 107TN
                                              Engines: 87HP
                                            Armament: 1 x 6pdrAA
                                            Admty No: 1987
                                            Port Reg: SA. 35
                                            P.No: WWII: FY 509
1916: Launched. Built at Southbank-on-Tees by Smith's Dock. Owned by Consolidated Fisheries of Grimsby. Requisitioned in March and converted to a M/S. 1919: Returned

to owners. 1939: Requisitioned in August and converted to a M/S. 1945: Returned to owners.

COOT	1914/20	Displacement: 172TG 65TN
		Engines: 60HP
		Armament: 1 x 12pdr; 1 x 7.5-inch
		Bomb Thrower (A/S Howitzer)
		As a 'Q' Ship: 2 x 12pdr; 1 x 6pdr
		Admty No: 420
		Port Reg: H. 897

1906: Launched. Built at Goole by Goole SB. Owned by Kelsall Bros. & Beeching of Hull. 1914: Requisitioned in November and converted to a M/S. 1917: Converted to a 'Q' Ship. 1920: Returned to owners. *Notes*: 'Q' Ship aliases: *Burmah, Dora, Kia Ora,* and *Lorne.*

COQUET	1915/19	Displacement: 174TG 67TN
		Engines: 52HP
		Port Reg: A. 390

1901: Launched. Built at North Shields. 1915: Requisitioned in June and converted to a BDV. 1919: Returned to owners. Acquired by Stringer's SF & Ice Co. of Boston, Lincs.

CORCYRA	1914/19	Displacement: 225TG 112TN
		Engines: 68HP = 9.5K
		Admty No: 278
		Port Reg: WWI: GY.1021; WWII: D.120
		P.No: WWII: FY. 293

1914: Launched. Built at Beverley by CWG. Owned by South Western SFC of Grimsby. Requisitioned in August and converted to a M/S. 1915: Stranded off Bacton on 20th February. 1916: Salvaged and returned to owners. 1917: Requisitioned into the Fishery Reserve. 1919: Returned to owners. 1938: Acquired by McCabe & Curtis of Dublin. 1940: Purchased into the RN in November and converted to an APV. 1941: Based at Grimsby. 1943: Converted to a Water Carrier in May. 1946: Sold to mercantile on 27th August. Acquired by Earl SFC of Grimsby. PR: GY. 281. 1961: BU in Holland.

CORDELA	1939/46	Displacement: 355TG 139TN
		Engines: 97HP
		Armament: 1 x 12pdr
		Port Reg: FD. 120
		P. No: FY.713

1930: Launched. Built at Selby by Cochrane. Owned by the Active SFC of Fleetwood. 1939: Purchased into the RN in August and converted to a M/S. 1946: Sold to mercantile

| CORELLA | 1914/19 | Ex-*Renown* |
| | | Displacement: 243TG 95TN |

Engines: 70HP = 10.5K
Armament: 1 x 3pdr
Admty No: 952
Port Reg: GY. 281

1907: Launched. Built at Beverley by CWG as *Renown*. Owned by Marshall Line SFC of Grimsby. 1911: Acquired by T.Baskcomb of Grimsby and renamed *Corella*. 1914: Requisitioned in December and converted to a M/S. 1919: Returned to owners. Mercantile Loss. Lost with all hands on 22nd September. Cause unknown.

CORENA   1939/46   Ex-*Andalusite*
                                       Displacement: 352TG 144TN
                                       Engines: 99HP = 11K
                                       Armament: 1 x 12pdr
                                       Port Reg: FD.195
                                       P. No: FY. 709

1924: Launched. Built at Beverley by CWG. Owned by Kingston STC of Hull. PR: H. 90. 1933: Acquired by J.Marr of Fleetwood and renamed *Corena*. 1934: Acquired by City SFC of Hull. 1937: Operating out of Fleetwood. PR: FD. 195. 1939: Requisitioned in August and converted to a M/S. 1946: Returned to owners. Acquired by J.Craig of Aberdeen. PR: A. 198. 1948: Mercantile Loss. Wrecked off Frederikshaab, Greenland, of 24th August. No loss of life, all hands being rescued by Eskimos from Frederikshaab.

CORIENTES   1915/17   Displacement: 280TG 119TN
                                       Engines: 80HP = 10.25K
                                       Armament: 1 x 6pdr
                                       Admty No: 1149
                                       Port Reg: GY. 552

1910: Launched. Built at Beverley by CWG. Owned by T.Baskcomb of Grimsby. 1915: Requisitioned in February and converted to a M/S. 1917: LOST. Mined off Malin Head on 23rd June.

CORIOLANUS   1940/44   Displacement: 226TG 87TN
                                       Engines: 71HP
                                       Port Reg: GN. 40
                                       P. No: FY. 1946

1917: Launched. Built at Aberdeen. Owned by TL Devlin of Leith. 1940: Requisitioned in August and converted to a M/S. Renamed CRAFTSMAN in December. 1944: Returned to owners in October.

CORMORANT II   1915/19   Displacement: 154TG

1891: Launched. 1915: Requisitioned. 1919: Returned to owners.

CORMORANT IV   1914/19   Displacement: 162TG 69TN
                                       Engines: 45HP

Armament: 1 x 6pdrAA.
As a 'Q' Ship: 1 x 6pdr
Admty No: 831
Port Reg: GY. 345

1897: Launched. Built at Beverley. Owned by the Savoy SFC of Grimsby. 1914: Requisitioned in November and converted to a M/S. 1917: Converted to a 'Q' Ship. 1919: Returned to owners. Acquired by the Roulette SDT & F of North Shields. 1940: Reportedly served in the RN as ADRIAN. NFI. (*Adrian* LT. 114 owned by Consolidated of Grimsby).

| CORNCRAKE | 1942/43 | See under MACKEREL (Vol 1 p.99) |

| CORNELIAN | 1917/19 | Displacement: 262TG 104TN |

Engines: 76HP
Armament: 1 x 12pdr
Admty No: 3067
Port Reg: H. 575
P.No: WWII: 4. 243

1917: Launched. Built at Selby by Cochrane. Owned by the Kingston SFC of Hull. Requisitioned in September and converted to a M/S 1919: Returned to owners. 1940: Requisitioned in January, converted to an APV and renamed FORFEIT. 1946: Returned to owners in June and reverted to original name.

| CORNET | 1917/19 | Displacement: 191TG 75TN |

Engines: 55HP
Admty No: Not issued
Port Reg: GY. 1006

1899: Launched. Built at Selby Cochrane. Owned by Sleight of Grimsby. 1917: Requisitioned into the Fishery Reserve. 1919: Returned to owners.

| CORONA | 1915/16 | Displacement: 212TG |

Armament: 1 x 6pdr 1 x 2pdr
Admty No: 1137
Port Reg: GY .684

1912: Launched. 1915: Requisitioned in February. 1916: LOST. Mined near Ramsgate on 23rd March.

| CORONATIA | 1914/19 1939/46 | Displacement: 185TG 74TN |

Engines: 45HP
Armament: 1 x 12pdr
Admty No: 323
Port Reg: SN. 337
P.No: WWII: Z. 204

1902: Launched. Built at North Shields. 1914: Requisitioned in August and converted to a M/S. 1919: Returned to owners. Acquired by B. Levinson of Grimsby. PR: GY. 1224. Acquired by Trawlers (White Sea & Grimsby). 1939: Requisitioned in December and converted to a BGV. 1946: Returned to owners.

CORONET   1933/46   See under ROBERT CLOUGHTON
(Vol 1 p.72)

CORRY ROY   1915/19   Displacement: 327TG 171TN
Engines: 90HP
Armament: 1 x 12pdr; 1 x 7.5-inch
Bomb Thrower (A/S Howitzer)
Admty No: 3218
Port Reg: GY. 635
1915: Launched. Built at Selby. Owned by the Orient SFC of Grimsby. Requisitioned in November. 1919: Returned to owners. Notes: Mercantile Lists *Corrie Roy.*

CORTINA   1915/19 1939/40 Displacement: 213TG 80TN
Engines: 66HP = 10K
Armament: 1 x 6pdr
Admty No: 1621
Port Reg: GY. 862
1913: Launched. Built at Beverley by CWG. Owned by N. Green of Grimsby. 1915: Requisitioned in April and converted to a M/S. 1919: Returned to owners. 1920: Acquired by Trawlers (White Sea & Grimsby). 1939: Requisitioned in November and converted to an APV. Fitted out at Hull. Based at Grimsby. 1940: Converted to a M/S in June. Joined the 111th M/S Group based at Grimsby. LOST. Sunk in a collision off the Humber on 7th December.

CORVUS   1917/19   Displacement: 140TG 56TN
Engines: 40HP
Admty No: Not issued
Port Reg: GY. 550
1893: Launched. Built at Govan. Iron construction. Owned by H. Bennett AO of Grimsby. 1917: Requisitioned into the Fishery Reserve. 1919: Returned to owners.

CORYPHENE   1944/45   See under SILURIA

CORYTHAIX   1915/19   Displacement: 280TG 119TN
Engines: 80HP = 10.25K
Admty No: 456
Port Reg: GY. 553
1910: Launched. Built at Beverley by CWG. Owned by T.Baskcombe of Grimsby. 1915: Requisitioned in February and converted to a M/S. 191?: Converted to a BDV. 1919: Returned to owners. 1920: Acquired by Spanish mercantile. Renamed *Jose Maria.* 1970: BU in Spain.

COTSMUIR   1915/17   Displacement: 243TG
                                           Armament: 1 x 6pdrAA
                                           Admty No:1537
                                           Port Reg: M. 15
1915: Launched. Requisitioned in June and converted to a M/S. 1917: LOST.
Disappeared whilst on passage from the Tyne to the Humber on 2nd February.

COTSMUIR   1940/45   See under THOMAS GOBLE
                                           (Vol 1 p.76)

COUNCILLOR   1917/19   Displacement: 116TG 43TN
                                           Engines: 40HP
                                           Admty No: Not issued
                                           Port Reg: GN. 17
1885: Launched. Built at Leith. Owned by J. Inglis of Peebles. 1917: Requisitioned into
the Fishery Reserve. 1919: Returned to owners.

COUNT   1940/45   Displacement: 410TG 140TN
                                           Engines: 99HP
                                           Port Reg: FD. 89
                                           P. No: Z. 109
1929: Launched. Built at Wivenhoe by Rennie Forrestt. Owned by the Adam STC of
Fleetwood. 1940: Purchased into the RN and converted to a BDV. Based at Grimsby.
1945: Sold to mercantile and renamed *Guttaberg*.

COUNTY OF FIFE   1917/19   Displacement: 114TG 43TN
                                           Engines: 34HP
                                           Port Reg: YH. 514
1896: Launched. Built at Leith. Owned by JTC. Salmon & J. Wright of Great Yarmouth.
1917: Requisitioned. 1919: Returned to owners.

COURSER   1916/19 1940/46 Displacement: 227TG 95TN
                                           Engines: 63HP = 10.5K
                                           Port Reg: GY. 79
                                           P.No: WWII: FY. 1823
1905: Launched. Built at Beverley by CWG. Owned by T. Baskcomb of Grimsby. 1916:
Acquired by H. Croft Baker of Grimsby in February. Acquired by S & T. Wood of Grimsby.
Requisitioned in October and converted to a BDV. 1919: Returned to owners. 1924:
Acquired by C. Dobson of Grimsby. 1940: Acquired by Consolidated Fisheries of
Grimsby. Requisitioned in September and converted to a M/S. 1942: Acquired by J.
Bennett of Grimsby. 1943: SO. of the 72nd M/S Group based at Grimsby. 1945:
Renamed CAVALCADE in April. 1946: Returned to owners on 31st December. 1952:
BU at Granton.

COURTIER   1915/16   Displacement: 181TG 80TN
Engines: 55HP = 10K
Admty No: 449
Port Reg: GY. 564

1910: Launched. Built at Beverley by CWG. Owned by Queen SFC of Grimsby. 1915: Requisitioned in January and converted to a M/S. 1916: LOST. Mined off Kilnsea, Yorkshire, on 6th January.

COURTIER   1939/45   Displacement: 225TG 100TN
Engines: 83HP
Armament: 1 x 12pdr
Port Reg: GY. 115
P. No: FY. 592

1929: Launched. Built at Selby by Cochrane. Owned by the Queen SFC of Grimsby. 1939: Requisitioned in August and converted to a M/S. 1945: Returned to owners in July.

COVENTRY CITY   1939/46   Football Group
Displacement: 546TG 196TN
Engines: 99HP
Armament: 1 x 4-inch
Port Reg: GY. 422
P.No: FY. 267

1937: Launched. Built at Southbank-on-Tees by Smith's Dock. Owned by Consolidated Fisheries of Grimsby. 1939: Requisitioned in September and converted to an A/S. 1942: Temporary loan to the USN in March, together with crew, for A/S duties. Returned to the RN in October. Transferred directly to the S. African Station. 1945: Returned to the UK. 1946: Returned to owners in June.

CRAFTSMAN   1940/44   See under CORIOLANUS 1940

CRAIG COILLEACH   1940/46   Displacement: 233TG 91TN
Engines: 78HP
Port Reg: A. 860
P.No: FY. 1770

1917: Launched. Built at Aberdeen. Owned by R. Irvin of North Shields. Acquired by G. Leiper AO of Aberdeen. 1940: Requisitioned in August and converted to a M/S. 1946: Returned to owners.

CRAIGELLACHIE   1917/19   Displacement: 112TG 45TN
Engines: 45HP
Admty No: Not issued
Port Reg: SN. 266

1896: Launched. Built at Aberdeen. Owned by RJ. Balls Jnr of Tynemouth. 1917: Requisitioned into the Fishery Reserve. 1919: Returned to owners.

CRAIGENDARROCH 1915/19 Ex-*John C. Meikle*
Displacement: 198TG 77TN
Engines: 77HP
Port Reg: A. 51
1910: Launched. Built at Aberdeen. Owned by W. Walker of South Shields. 1915: Requisitioned in June and converted to a BDV. 1919: Returned to owners.

CRAIG EWAN 1914/19 Displacement: 204TG 78TN
Engines: 75HP
Armament: 1 x 12pdr
Admty No: 88
Port Reg: PD. 551
1910: Launched. Built at Aberdeen. Owned by the Peterhead TCL of Peterhead. 1914: Requisitioned in August and converted to a M/S. 1919: Returned to owners.

CRAIG GOWAN 1918/19 Displacement: 126TG
Port Reg: A. 820
1897: Launched. 1918: Requisitioned into the Fishery Reserve. 1919: Returned to owners.

CRAIGIEVAR 1917/19 Displacement: 112TG 44TN
Engines: 45HP
Admty No: Not issued
Port Reg: A. 762
1896: Launched. Built at Aberdeen. Owned by J. Main AO of Aberdeen. 1917: Requisitioned into the Fishery Reserve. 1919: Returned to owners.

CRAIG ISLAND 1939/45 See under MARTHE

CRAIG MILLAR 1917/19 Displacement: 112TG 44TN
Engines: 45HP
Armament: 1 x 6pdrAA
Admty No: 1647
Port Reg: A. 860
1896: Launched. Built at Aberdeen. 1917: Requisitioned in August and converted to a M/S. 1919: Returned to owners. Acquired by G. Robb of Aberdeen. PR: A. 783.

CRAIGMORE 1916/19 Displacement: 210TG 91TN
Engines: 78HP
Admty No: 3294
Port Reg: HL. 83
1916: Launched. Built at Aberdeen. Owned by RH. Davidson of Hartlepool. Requisitioned in June and converted to a M/S. 1919: Returned to owners.

CRAIK 1915/19 1939/44 Displacement: 219TG 85TN

Engines: 77HP
Armament: 1 x 12pdr
Admty No: 1471
Port Reg: FD. 134

1915: Launched. Built at Middlesborough by Smith's Dock. Owned by the Wyre STC of Fleetwood. Requisitioned in April. 1919: Returned to owners. Acquired by RC. Kelman & A. Robertson of Aberdeen. PR: A. 300. 1939: Requisitioned in August and converted for the Examination Service. 1944: Returned to owners in November.

CRAITHIE	1914/14	Displacement: 210TG
		Admty No: 106
		Port Reg: A. 350

1911: Launched. 1914: Requisitioned in August and designated as a M/S. LOST. Mined off the Tyne on 27th August.

CRAITHIE	1916/16	Displacement: 225TG
		Armament: 1 x 6pdrAA
		Admty No: 2980
		Port Reg: A. 713

1916: Launched. Requisitioned in November and converted to a M/S. LOST. Wrecked on Nizam Point, Barra Head, on 16th December.

CRAMMOND ISLAND	1915/19 1939/41	Displacement: 180TG 70TN
		Engines: 70HP
		Armament: 1 x 12pdr; 1 x 6pdrAA
		Admty No: 1495
		Port Reg: LH. 114

1910: Launched. Built at Govan. Owned by the Leith SFC of Leith. 1915: Requisitioned in May and converted to a M/S. 1919: Returned to owners. Acquired by TH. Scales of Newhaven. Same PR. 1939: Requisitioned in November and converted to a BDV. 1941: LOST. Sunk by a/c attack off St.Abbs Head, E. Scotland on 2nd April.

| CRANEFLY | 1939/46 | See under GEORGE ANDREW |
| | | (Vol 1 p.134) |

CRASSULA	1940/46	SAN
		Displacement: 261TG
		P.No: T. 19

1935: Launched. 1940: Requisitioned for the SAN in June and converted to a M/S. 1946: Returned to owners in December.

CRATER	1917/19	Displacement: 132TG 54TN
		Engines: 45HP
		Admty No: Not issued

Port Reg: FD. 330
1896: Launched. Built at Govan. Owned by E. Taylor & N. Ashworth of Fleetwood.
1917: Requisitioned into the Fishery Reserve. 1919: Returned to owners.

CRESCENT II   1915/18   Displacement: 200TG
1910: Launched. 1915: Requisitioned. 1918: Returned to owners.

CRESTFLOWER   1939/40   Displacement: 367TG 142TN
                                        Engines: 96HP
                                        Armament: 1 x 12pdr
                                        Port Reg: H. 239
1930: Launched. Built at Selby. Owned by the Yorkshire SFC of Hull. 1939: Purchased into the RN in August. TIH at Doig's Yard, Grimsby and converted to a M/S. 1940: LOST. Sunk by enemy a/c off Portsmouth on 19th July.

CREVETTE   1939/40 1944/44 See under THOMAS HENRIX
                                        (Vol 1 p.189)

CROTON   1914/19   Displacement: 149TG 58TN
                                        Engines: 41HP
                                        Armament: 1 x 12pdr; 1 x 6pdr
                                        Admty No: 709
                                        Port Reg: GY. 49
1898: Launched. Built at Govan. Owned by the Orient SFC of Grimsby. 1914: Requisitioned in November and converted to a M/S. 1919: Returned to owners.

CROUPIER   1914/19   Displacement: 302TG 159TN
                                          Engines: 84HP
                                        Armament: 1 x 12pdrAA
                                        Admty No: 27
                                        Port Reg: GY. 271
1914: Launched. Built at Selby by Cochrane. Owned by the Anchor SFC of Grimsby. Requisitioned in September and converted to a M/S. 1919: Returned to owners.

CROXBY   1915/19   Displacement: 215TG 104TN
                                          Engines: 67HP = 10.5K
                                        Armament: 1 x 6pdrAA
                                        Admty No: 1632
                                        Port Reg: GY. 642
1911: Launched. Built at Beverley by CWG. Owned by W. Grant of Grimsby. 1915: Requisitioned in May and converted to a M/S. 1919: Returned to owners. 1935: Sank in a collision with the Grimsby Trawler *Ebor Belle* on 7th March off Aberdeen. Subsequently salvaged. 1960: BU in Holland.

CRYSTAL   1917/19   Displacement: 149TG
                                          Port Reg: H. 303
1895: Launched. 1917: Requisitioned into the Fishery Reserve. 1919: Returned to owners.

CUCKOO   1917/19   Displacement: 135TG
                                          Admty No: Not issued
                                          Port Reg: LT. 689
1894: Launched. 1917: Requisitioned into the Fishery Reserve. 1919: Returned to owners.

CUCKOO   1940/40   See under BOREAS

CUIRASS   1915/19 1939/45 Displacement: 321TG 139TN
                                          Engines: 91HP
                                          Armament: 1 x 6pdrAA
                                          Admty No: 851
                                          Port Reg: GY. 436
                                          P. No: WWII: Z. 150
1915: Launched. Built at Selby by Cochrane. Owned by the Crown SFC of Grimsby. Requisitioned in May and converted to a M/S. 1919: Returned to owners. Acquired by GEJ. Moody AO of Grimsby. 1939: Purchased into the RN in September and converted to a BDV. 1945: Sold to mercantile.

CULBLEAN   1914/19   Displacement: 110TG 78TN
                                          Engines: 86HP
                                          Armament: 1 x 6pdrAA
                                          Admty No: 108
                                          Port Reg: A. 339
1911: Launched. Built at Aberdeen. Owned by Grampian FC of Aberdeen. 1914: Requisitioned in August and converted to a M/S. 1919: Returned to owners.

CURLEW   1917/19   Displacement: 125TG 45TN
                                          Engines: 45HP
                                          Port Reg: A. 906
1897: Launched. Built at Dundee. Owned by AW. King of Torry. 1917: Requisitioned. 1919: Returned to owners.

CURTANA   1939/45   Ex-*Lady Enid*
                                          Displacement: 354TG 149TN
                                          Engines: 96HP = 11K
                                          Armament: 1 x 12pdr
                                          Port Reg: GY. 369
                                          P. No: FY. 674
1929: Launched. Built at Beverley by CWG as *Lady Enid*. Owned by the Jutland Amalgamated Trs. of Hull. PR: H.172. 1937: Acquired by Standard SFC of Grimsby and

renamed *Curtana*. 1939: Requisitioned in August and converted to a M/S. 1945: Returned to owners in October. 1953: Acquired by Marr of Hull and Laid Up at Grimsby. 1954: BU at Grimsby.

CYELSE   1915/19 1940/46   Displacement: 237TG 93TG
      Engines: 58HP
      Armament: 1 x 12pdr; 1 x 7.5-inch
      Bomb Thrower (A/S Howitzer)
      Admty No: 975
      Port Reg: M. 139
      P. No: WWII: Y7. 8

1912: Launched. Built at Selby by Cochrane. Owned by D. Pettitt of Milford Haven. 1915: Requisitioned in February and converted to a M/S. 1919: Returned to owners. 1940: Requisitioned in August and converted to a Water Carrier. 1946: Returned to owners in March.

CYGNET   1915/19   Displacement: 300TG 117TN
      Engines: 75HP
      Armament: 1 x 6pdr
      Admty No: 126
      Port Reg: FD. 110

1907: Launched. Built at North Shields. Owned by the Cygnet SFC of Fleetwood. 1915: Requisitioned in August and converted to a M/S. 1917: Renamed CYGNET II in March. 1919: Returned to owners.

CYGNET II   1917/19   See under CYGNET above

CYGNET III   1917/19   Displacement: 138TG 59TN
      Engines: 35HP
      Admty No: Not issued
      Port Reg: YH. 127

1893: Launched. Built at Govan. Owned by JTC Salmon AO of Great Yarmouth. 1917: Requisitioned into the Fishery Reserve. 1919: Returned to owner. 1927: BU in December.

CYNTHIA   1917/19   Ex-*Lord Selborne*
      Ex-*Sargon*
      Displacement: 167TG 68TN
      Engines: 50HP = 9.5K
      Admty No: Not Issued
      Port Reg: GY. 392

1897: Launched. Built at Hull by CWG as *Sargon*. Owned by the Standard SFC of Grimsby. PR: GY.305. 1912: Acquired by Port of Blyth SFC and renamed *Lord Selborne*. PR: BH. 91. 1914: Acquired by Beacon SFC of Grimsby. PR: GY. 392. 1916:

Acquired by Allen SFC of Grimsby and renamed *Cynthia*. 1917: Requisitioned into the Fishery Reserve. 1919: Returned to owners. 1953: BU at Granton.

CYRANO   1915/19   Displacement: 214TG
                                           Armament: 1 x 12pdr
                                           Admty No: 1528
                                           Port Reg: GY. 80
1905: Launched. 1915: Requisitioned in June and converted to a M/S. 1919: Returned to owners.

DAGNY   1942/45   Displacement: 138TG
                                      Port Reg: Icelandic
1904: Launched. 1942: Hired from Icelandic owners and converted to a Boom Tender.
1945: Returned to owners.

DAGON   1915/16   Displacement: 250TG
                                      Armament: 1 x 12pdr
                                      Admty No: 3202
                                      Port Reg: GY. 957
1914: Launched. 1915: Requisitioned in June. 1916: LOST. Mined off the Royal
Sovereign LV on 8th December.

DAGON   1939/39   Displacement: 282TG 142TN
                                      Engines: 85HP = 10.5K
                                      Port Reg: Y. 438
1919: Launched. Built at Beverley by CWG. Owned by Neale & West of Cardiff. PR:
CF. 61.   1927:   Acquired by Consolidated Fisheries and renamed *Dagon*.   1939:
Requisitioned in August and designated as a M/S. Returned to owners in October.
1952: Acquired by Devanha FCL of Aberdeen and renamed *Casimar* PR: A. 710. 1955:
BU at Charlestown.

DAHLIA   1915/18   Displacement: 154TG 91TN
                                      Engines: 50HP
                                      Armament: 1 x 6pdrAA
                                      Admty No: 731
                                      Port Reg: GY. 223
1889: Launched. Built at Beverley. Owned by North Eastern SFC of Grimsby. 1915:
Requisitioned in January. Renamed DAHLIA II in October. 1918: Returned to owners in
July. Retained the name *Dahlia II.*

DAHLIA II   1915/18   See under DAHLIA above

DAIMLER   1914/19   Ex-*S.L. Haldane*
                                      Displacement: 257TG 105TN
                                      Engines: 75HP
                                      Admty No: 260
                                      Port Reg: H.167
1910: Launched. Built at Selby by Cochrane. Owned by JW Smethurst of Grimsby.
1914: Requisitioned in August and converted to a M/S. 1919: Returned to owners.

DAISY II   1939/45   Displacement: 248TG
1912: Launched. 1939: Requisitioned in September and employed on Harbour Service.
1945: Returned to owners in November.

DALE   1915/17   Displacement: 198TG
                                             Admty No: 823
1900: Launched. 1914: Requisitioned in December and converted to an APV. 1915:
Returned to the Fishing Fleet. 1917: Mercantile Loss. Captured by German S/M 42
miles S x E & a quarter E from Ronaldshay on 12th February. Blown up and the Skipper
taken prisoner.

DALE CASTLE   1915/19 1940/46 Displacement: 246TG
                                         Armament: 1 x 3pdr; WWII: 2 x MGs
                                         Admty No: 976
                                         Port Reg: SA. 99
                                         P.No: WWII: 4. 156
1909: Launched. 1915: Requisitioned in February and converted to a M/S. 1919:
Returned to owners. 1940: Requisitioned in May and converted to an APV. 1944:
Converted for Target Towing. 1946: Returned to owners in March.

DALMATIA   1939/46   Ex-*Lady Rosemary*
                                            Displacement: 357TG 153TN
                                            Engines: 96HP = 11K
                                            Armament: 1 x 12pdr
                                            Port Reg: GY. 374
                                            P. No: FY. 844
1928: Launched. Built at Beverley by CWG as *Lady Rosemary*. Owned by Jutland
Amalgamated of Hull. PR: H. 422. 1937: Acquired by Gt. Grimsby & East Coast SFC
and renamed *Dalmatia*. 1939: Purchased into the RN in September. TIH at Doig's Yard
at Grimsby and converted to a M/S. 1944: Converted to a D/L. TPI in Operation
Neptune, the D-Day Landings attached to the 9th M/S Flotilla off Juno Beach. 1946:
Sold to mercantile and renamed *Westhawk*. Acquired by JC Llewellyn of Milford Haven.
PR: H. 474. 1952: BU at Gateshead.

DALMATIAN   1914/16   Displacement: 357TG
                                            Admty No: 656
                                            Port Reg: BN. 83
1900: Launched. 1914: Requisitioned and converted to an APV. 1916: Returned to the
Fishing Fleet in February. 1917: Mercantile Loss. Captured by a German S/M in the
North Sea on 15th April. Blown up with the loss of 9 crew.

DAMITO   1939/46   See under OLIVER PICKIN
                                            (Vol 1 p.69)

DANDINI	1917/19	Displacement: 212TG
		Armament: 1 x 6pdr
		Admty No: 1265
		Port Reg: GY. 1032

1917: Launched. Requisitioned in April and converted to a M/S. 1919: Returned to owners.

DANDOLO	1944/44	See under HORACE STROUD

DANE	1915/15	Displacement: 265TG
		Admty No: 1446
		Port Reg: GY. 947

1913: Launched. 1915: Requisitioned in April and converted to an APV. LOST. Mined off Aldeburgh on 28th August.

DANE	1915/19 1940/46	Displacement: 346TG 135TN
		Engines: 87HP = 11K
		Armament: 1 x 6pdrAA
		Admty No: 1370
		Port Reg: H. 227
		P. No: FY. 554

1911: Launched. Built at Beverley by CWG. Owned by Imperial SFC of Hull. 1915: Requisitioned in April and converted to a M/S. Renamed DANE II in June. 1919: Returned to owners and reverted to original name. 1939: Acquired by Prince FCL of Fleetwood. 1940: Requisitioned in January and converted to a M/S. 1943: Acquired by H. Markham Cook of Grimsby. 1946: Returned to owners in January and re-registered. GY. 417. 1947: Acquired by Drum FCL of Granton and renamed *Drumskeugh*. PR: GN. 37. 1954: BU at Granton.

DANE II	1915/19	See under DANE

DANEMAN	1939/43	Displacement: 516TG
		Armament: 1 x 4-inch
		Port Reg: GY. 426
		P. No: FY. 123

1937: Launched. Built at Selby by Cochrane. Owned by the Earl SF of Grimsby. 1939: Purchased into the RN in August and converted to an A/S. Joined the 21st A/S Striking Force. Employed on Atlantic Convoys. 1940: TPI the Norwegian Campaign in April/May. 1942: TPI as escort to Convoy PQ.18 from Iceland to Russia in September. Ran out of fuel approx. 20 miles from Archangel and drifted, after the anchor cable parted, until she took the ground, on 21st September, off Mudyugski Island in heavy weather. The ship was abandoned but after spending some time ashore with shortage of food etc. the crew returned to the ship and remained there through the gales until they were rescued and refloated on 19th October. TIH at Murmansk and docked down for temporary repairs. Completed repairs and sailed from Russia on 30th December escorting a convoy to

Iceland. 1943: Arrived at Iceland on 5th January and despatched to Belfast for major repairs. Completed repairs in April and employed on Atlantic convoys. LOST. Collided with ice in the N. Atlantic. Taken in tow but sank when the tow was abandoned on 8th May.

DANESTON   1915/18   Displacement: 239TG
                                                 Port Reg: A. 245
1915: Launched. Requisitioned in June and converted to a BDV. 1919: Returned to owners.

DANIA   1917/19   Displacement: 196TG
                                                 Admty No: Not issued
                                                 Port Reg: LO. 187
1904: Launched. 1917: Requisitioned into the Fishery Reserve. 1919: Returned to owners.

DANIEL STROUD   1914/19 1939/43 Displacement: 209TG 78TN
                                                 Engines: 66HP
                                                 Armament: 1 x 12pdr
                                                 Admty No: 163
                                                 Port Reg: WWII: A. 438
                                                 P.No: WWII: FY. 896
1912: Launched. Built at Aberdeen by Hall. 1914: Purchased into the RN in July and converted to a M/S. 1919: Sold to mercantile and renamed *Loch Esk*. Owned by IB Wood of Aberdeen AO. 1939: Requisitioned in November as LOCH ESK and converted to a M/S. 1943: Returned to owners.

DARGLE   1917/18   Displacement: 351TG
1914: Launched. 1917: Requisitioned and converted to a 'Q' Ship. 1918: Returned to owners.

DARNET NESS   1939/45   See under THOMAS BOUDIGE
                                                 (Vol 1 p.75)

DAROGAH   1915/20 1939/41 Displacement: 221TG
                                                 Armament: 1 x 6pdrAA
                                                 Admty No: 1491
                                                 Port Reg: GY. 191
1914: Launched. 1915: Requisitioned in May and converted to a M/S. 1920: Returned to owners. 1939: Requisitioned in December and converted to an APV. 1940: Converted to a M/S in February. 1941: LOST. Mined in the Thames Estuary on 27th January.

DARRACQ   1914/19   Ex-*H.A.L. Russell*
                                                 Displacement: 256TG
                                                 Armament: 1 x 4-inch; 1 x 6pdrAA

Admty No: 770
Port Reg: H. 138
1914: Requisitioned in December and converted to a M/S. 1919: Returned to owners.

DARTHEMA 1939/45 Ex-*Larwood*
Displacement: 373TG 161TN
Engines: 91HP = 12K
Armament: 1 x 12pdr;
2 x 20mmAA (3x1)
Port Reg: H. 214
P.No: FY. 676

1929: Launched. Built at Selby by Cochrane as *Larwood* and owned by Crampin of Grimsby. Acquired by Alliance SFC of Hull and renamed. 1939: Requisitioned in October and converted to a M/S. Employed in UK Waters throughout WWII. 1944: TPI Operation Neptune, the D-Day Landings in June. Towed one of the midget S/Ms from Portsmouth to La Havre area and then brought her back after the invasion had started. To Harwich to collect and tow a section of Mulberry Harbour to the Normandy beaches. Paid off at North Shields in December and Laid Up. 1945: Returned to owners in December. *Notes*: One of the original Cricketer Group of Crampins of Grimsby.

DARTMOUTH 1917/19 Displacement: 139TG 56TN
Engines: 40HP
Admty No: Not issued
Port Reg: M. 80

1890: Launched. Built at Middlesborough. Owned by S. Bell of Lowestoft. 1917: Requisitioned into the Fishery Reserve. 1919: Returned to owners.

DARWEN 1939/46 See under LANERCOST

DASHER 1939/40 See under VENTURE

DAVARA 1914/19 Displacement: 291TG 116TN
Engines: 89HP
Armament: 1 x 6pdrAA
Admty No: 523
Port Reg: FD. 152

1912: Launched. Built at Selby by Cochrane. Owned by The Mount SFC of Fleetwood. 1914: Requisitioned in November and converted to a M/S. 1919: Returned to owners.

DAVID HAIGH 1939/46 See under TR.60 (Vol 1 p.83)

DAVY 1939/45 Displacement: 450TG 171TN
Engines: 114HP = 11.9K
Port Reg: H. 322

P. No: FY.147

1936: Launched. Built at Beverley by CWG. Owned by F.& T. Ross of Hull. 1939: Purchased into the RN in August and converted to an A/S. 1945: Sold to mercantile. Re-acquired by F & T Ross. PR: H. 213. 1951: Acquired by Hudson Bros. of Hull and renamed *Cape Barfleur*. 1954: Acquired by Iago STL of London and renamed *Red Falcon*. 1959: Mercantile Loss. Lost off Skerryvore, Scotland with the loss of all 19 hands.

DEAN SWIFT	1917/19	Ex-*City of Hull*
		Displacement: 181TG 65TN
		Engines: 58HP = 10K
		Armament: None
		Admty No: Not issued
		Port Reg: D. 335

1898: Launched. Built at Hull by CWG as *City of Hull*. Owned by City SFC of Hull. PR: H. 396. 1907: Acquired by Dublin STC of Dublin and renamed *Dean Swift*. PR: D. 335. 1917: Requisitioned into the Fishery Reserve. 1919: Returned to owners. 1959: BU at Dublin. *Notes*: Entered in some RN Lists as CITY OF HULL.

DEBENEY	1918/19	See under DERBY

DEE	1917/19	Displacement: 151TG 61TN
		Engines: 45HP
		Admty No: Not issued
		Port Reg: GY. 513

1893: Launched. Built at Hull. Iron construction. 1917: Requisitioned into the Fishery Reserve. 1919: Returned to owners. 1920: Owned by W. Gould of Grimsby.

DEE	1920/46	See under BATTLEAXE (Vol 1 p.31)

DEFENDER	1917/19	Displacement: 128TG 50TN
		Engines: 57HP
		Admty No: Not Issued
		Port Reg: SD. 176

1899: Launched. Built at Dundee. Owned by Newton of Sunderland. 1917: Requisitioned into the Fishery Reserve. 1919: Returned to owners.

De La POLE	1915/16	Displacement: 255TG 107TN
		Engines: 72HP = 10.5K
		Armament: 1 x 47mm
		Admty No: 1636
		Port Reg: H. 377

1911: Launched. Built at Beverley by CWG. Owned by National SFC of Hull. 1915: Requisitioned in May and converted to a M/S. 1916: LOST. Wrecked on the Goodwin Sands on 4th February.

DELHI   1917/19   Displacement: 171TG   57TN
                                              Engines: 45HP = 10K
                                              Admty No: Not issued
                                              Port Reg: H. 742

1903: Launched.   Built at Beverley by CWG. Owned by Hull SFC & Ice Co of Hull.
1917: Requisitioned into the Fishery Reserve. 1919: Returned to owners. 1957: BU at
Milford Haven.

DELILA   1940/46   See under JOHN HUNTER
                                              (Vol 1 p.180)

DELPHIN II   1940/46   Displacement: 253TG
                                              Port Reg: Polish
                                              P.No: 4. 244

1938: Launched.   1940: Hired from Polish owners and converted for Examination
Service. Commissioned with a Polish Crew. 1946: Returned to owners in January.

DELPHINE   1915/19   Displacement: 250TG   97TN
                                              Engines: 85HP
                                              Armament: 1 x 6pdrAA
                                              Admty No: 1619
                                              Port Reg: GY. 958

1914: Launched. Built at Middlesborough by Smith's Dock. Owned by Consolidated
Fisheries of Grimsby.   1915: Requisitioned in May and converted to a M/S.   1919:
Returned to owners.

DELPHINUS   1914/19   Ex-*Amelia*
                                              Displacement: 257TG
                                              Armament: WWI: 1 x 12pdr;
                                              1 x 6pdrAA
                                              WWII: 1 x 12pdrAA;
                                              2 x 0.5-inchAA (1x2); 2 x MG (2x1)
                                              P. No: WWII: FY. 846

1906: Launched. 1914: Requisitioned in September and converted to a M/S. 1919:
Returned to owners. Acquired by Trawlers (White Sea & Grimsby) of Grimsby. PR: GY.
981. 1939: Purchased into the RN in November and converted to a M/S. 1945: Sold to
mercantile.

DELTA   1917/19   Displacement: 241TG
                                              Admty No: Not issued
                                              Port Reg: O.170

1908: Launched. Belgian fishing vessel. 1917: Requisitioned into the Fishery Reserve
with permission of Belgian owners. 1919: Returned to owners.

DENTARIA   1914/20   Displacement: 259TG 103TN
                                   Engines: 86HP
                                   Armament: 1 x 12pdr; 1 x 7.5-inch
                                   Bomb Thrower (A/S Howitzer)
                                   Admty No: 610
                                   Port Reg: GY. 344
1908: Launched.   Built at Grimsby.   Owned by T. Baskcomb of Grimsby.   1914:
Requisitioned in September and converted to a M/S. 1920: Returned to owners.

DERBY   1915/19   Displacement: 144TG 54TN
                                   Engines: 45HP
                                   Armament: 1 x 6pdr
                                   Admty No: 1779
                                   Port Reg: GY. 153
1896: Launched. Built at North Shields. Owned by Consolidated Fisheries of Grimsby.
1915: Requisitioned in May and converted to a M/S.   1918: Renamed DEBENEY in
October. 1919: Returned to owners and reverted to original name.

DERBY COUNTY   1939/45   Football Group
                                   Displacement: 399TG 151TN
                                   Engines: 99HP
                                   Armament: 1 x 4-inch
                                   Port Reg: GY. 194
                                   P.No: FY. 171
1938: Launched. Built at Southbank-on-Tees by Smith's Dock. Owned by Consolidated
Fisheries of Grimsby. 1939: Purchased into the RN in August and converted to an A/S.
Joined the 17th A/S Group based at Swansea. 1943: Based at Milford Haven. A/S
Group with sister-ships GRIMSBY TOWN, HUDDERSFIELD TOWN, LEEDS UNITED
and YORK CITY. Remained with the Group for the remainder of the war. Employed on
Western Approaches convoys. Group transferred to the MF escorting a convoy of
Landing Craft to Gibraltar on the way. Employed on Med. convoys. Returned to UK at
the end of the year and based once more at Milford Haven for Western Approaches
convoys. 1944: TPI Operation Neptune, the D-Day Landings in June as A/S Escort.
1945: Sold to mercantile. Re-acquired by Consolidated Fisheries. 1964: BU in Belgium.

DERVISH   1940/40   See under NORMAN

DERWENT   1917/19   Displacement: 151TG
                                   Admty No: Not issued
                                   Port Reg: GY. 525
1893: Launched. 1917: Requisitioned into the Fishery Reserve. 1919: Returned to
owners.

DERWENT   1920/23   See under JOHN BRICE (Vol 1 p.61)

DESIREE   1914/19 1939/41 Displacement: 213TG 88TN
                         Engines: 58HP = 10K
                         Armament: 1 x 6pdr
                         Admty No: 251
                         Port Reg: GY. 788
1912: Launched. Built at Beverley by CWG. Owned by Pelham SFC of Grimsby. 1914: Requisitioned in August and converted to a M/S. 1919: Returned to owners. 1920: Acquired by Trawlers (White Sea & Grimsby) of Grimsby. 1939: Requisitioned in November and converted to a M/S. 1941: LOST. Mined in the Thames Estuary on 16th January.

DESTINN   1914/19 1940/46 Displacement: 226TG 113TN
                         Engines: 74HP = 10K
                         Armament: 1 x 6pdr
                         Admty No: 1587
                         Port Reg: WWI: GY. 307; WWII: D. 124
                         P.No: WWII: FY. 1719
1914: Launched. Built at Beverley by CWG. Owned by Marshall Line SFC of Grimsby. Requisitioned in May and converted to a M/S. 1919: Returned to owners. 1938: Acquired by McCabe and Curtis of Dublin. 1940: Purchased into the RN in January and converted to an APV. 1946: Transferred to the War Dept. 1947: BU by Wards at Preston.

DEVANHA   1915/19   Displacement: 196TG 77TN
                         Engines: 52HP
                         Armament: 1 x 6pdr
                         Admty No: 129
                         Port Reg: A. 458
1901: Launched. Built at Aberdeen.   Owned by A. Walker of Aberdeen.   1915: Requisitioned in August and converted to a BDV. 1919: Returned to owners.

DEVERON   1914/19   Displacement: 233TG 102TN
                         Engines: 68HP
                         Armament: 1 x 6pdrAA; 1 x 7.5-inch
                         Bomb Thrower (A/S Howitzer)
                         Port Reg: GY. 96
1905: Launched. Built at Hull. Owned by D. Lines SFC of Grimsby. 1914: Requisitioned in November and converted to a M/S. 1919: Returned to owners.

DEWSLAND   1915/19   Displacement: 236TG 93TN
                         Engines: 72HP
                         Armament: 1 x 12pdr
                         Admty No: 2664
                         Port Reg: M. 220
1907: Launched. Built at Selby by Cochrane. Owned by W. Wilkins & G. Moreland of Manchester. 1915: Requisitioned in May and converted to a M/S. 1919: Returned to owners.

DHOON   1916/16   Displacement: 275TG
              Armament: 1 x 3pdr
              Admty No: 2959
              Port Reg: FD. 244

1916: Launched. Requisitioned in September and converted to a M/S. LOST. Mined near the Newarp LV. on 24th November.

DHOON   1940/43   See under ARMAGEDDON

DHOON GLEN 1943/45   See under ARMAGEDDON

DIADEM   1917/19   Displacement: 55TG
              Admty No: Not issued
              Port Reg: LT. 274

1901: Launched. 1917: Requisitioned into the Fishery Reserve. 1919: Returned to owners.

DIAMOND   1915/19   Displacement: 289TG
              Armament: 1 x 6pdrAA
              Admty No:1376
              Port Reg: H. 665

1913: Launched. 1915: Requisitioned in April and converted to a M/S. Renamed DIAMOND II in June. 1919: Returned to owners.

DIAMOND II 1915/19   See under DIAMOND above

DIAMOND III 1918/19   Displacement: 150TG 63TN
              Engines: 45HP
              Admty No: Not Issued
              Port Reg: GY. 603

1894: Launched. Built at Beverley. Owned by TC & F. Moss of Grimsby. 1918: Requisitioned into the Fishery Reserve. 1919: Returned to owners.

DIANA   1915/20   Displacement: 172TG 67TN
              Engines: 50HP
              Armament: 2 x 12pdrs
              Port Reg: FD. 135

1899: Launched. Built at Govan. 1915: Requisitioned in June and converted to a BDV. 191?: Reported converted to a Collier. 1920: Returned to owners. Acquired by J. Walker & RA. Morrice of Aberdeen. PR: A.148.

DIANA II.   1916/19
1916: Requisitioned. 1919: Returned to owners.

DIGIT 1940/46 Ex-*Tilsitt*
Displacement: 422TG
1919: Launched. 1940: Purchased into the RN and converted to a BDV. 1946: Sold to mercantile and renamed *Erik Jall.*

DINAS 1914/19 Displacement: 219TG 85TN
Engines: 72HP
Armament: 1 x 6pdrAA
Admty No: 155
Port Reg: M. 19
1909: Launched. Built at North Shields. 1914: Requisitioned in August and converted to a M/S. 1919: Returned to owners. Acquired by Dinas STC of Fleetwood. PR: FD. 63.

DINORAH 1914/19 Ex-*Picton Castle*
Displacement: 192TG 72TN
Armament: 1 x 3pdr
Admty No: 288
Port Reg: A. 505
1903: Launched. Built at North Shields. 1914: Requisitioned in August and converted to a M/S. 1919: Returned to owners. Acquired by Bowerings SFC of Grimsby. PR: GY. 1107.

DIRK 1917/18 Displacement: 181TG
Armament: 1 x 12pdr; 1 x 6pdr
1909: Launched. 1917: Requisitioned. 1918: LOST. Sunk by U-Boat off Flamborough Head on 28th May.

DIRKJE 1940/45 Displacement: 234TG
Port Reg: Dutch
P.No: FY.1745
1934: Launched. 1940: Hired from Dutch owners and converted to a M/S. Commissioned with a Dutch crew. 1945: Returned to owners.

DISA 1939/40 SAN
Displacement: 197TG
Port Reg: S. African
1924: Launched. . 1939: Requisitioned on 19th September, converted to a M/S and Commissioned into the SAN. 1940: Returned to owners on 16th May.

DIVER 1917/18 Displacement: 207TG
Admty No: 594
Port Reg: GY. 1205
1900: Launched. Owned by Baskcombe of Grimsby. 1917: Requisitioned into the Fishery Reserve. 1918: Returned to owners.

DIXON   1916/19
1916: Requisitioned. 1919: Returned to owners.

DOCTOR LEE   1915/19 1939/44 Displacement: 307TG 124TN
                                      Engines: 93HP
                                      Armament: 1 x 12pdr
                                      Admty No: 1582
                                      Port Reg: H. 50
                                      P.No: WWII: Z. 133
1914: Launched. Built at Selby by Cochrane. 1915: Requisitioned in May. 1919:
Returned to owners. Acquired by Dinas ST of Fleetwood. 1939: Requisitioned in
December and converted to a BDV. 1944: Returned to owners in November.

DOGGER BANK   1915/20   Displacement: 274TG 117TN
                                        Engines: 100HP
                                        Port Reg: H. 673
1913: Launched. Built at Selby by Cochrane. Owned by Hull SF & Ice Co of Hull. 1915:
Requisitioned in June and converted to a BDV. 1920: Returned to owners.

DOLFIJN   1940/45   Displacement: 168T
                                       Port Reg: Dutch
                                       P.No: FY. 1761
1920: Launched. 1940: Hired from Dutch owners and converted to a M/S.
Commissioned with a Dutch Crew. 1942: Renamed GOEREE. 1944: Converted to an
Esso. Commissioned with a RN crew. 1945: Returned to owners.

DOLORES   1940/46   See under RAINBOW

DON   1915/19   Displacement: 168TG 65TN
                                        Engines: 40HP
                                        Armament: 2 x 3pdrs
                                        Port Reg: A. 443
1898: Launched. Built at Irvine. 1915: Requisitioned in June and converted to a BDV.
1919: Returned to owners.

DONALDA   1915/19   Displacement: 226TG 113TN
                                        Engines: 68HP = 9.5K
                                        Armament: 1 x 6pdr
                                        Admty No: 1760
                                        Port Reg: GY. 149
1914: Launched. Built at Beverley by CWG. Owned by A. Black of Grimsby. 1915:
Requisitioned in May and converted to a M/S. 1919: Returned to owners. 1957: BU at
Gateshead.

DONALD & DORIS   1942/44   Displacement: 149TG
1897: Launched. 1942: Requisitioned and converted to a BDV. 1944: Returned.

DONNA NOOK   1916/19 1939/43 Displacement: 307TG 150TN
                                      Armament: WWI: 1 x 12pdr; 1 x 3pdr
                                      AA; 1 x 7.5-inch Bomb Thrower
                                      (A/S Howitzer)
                                      WWII: 1 x 12pdr
                                      Admty No: 1981
                                      Port Reg: GY. 237
                                      P.No: 4. 132 (APV) FY. 1559 (M/S)
1915: Launched. Built at Selby by Cochrane. 1916: Requisitioned in February and
converted to a M/S. 1919: Returned to owners. Acquired by Mount SFC of Fleetwood.
PR: FD. 237. 1939: Requisitioned. Converted to an APV. 1941: Converted to a M/S.
1943: LOST. Sunk in a collision with STELLA RIGEL off Harwich on 25th September.
The two Trawlers were in company when they were attacked by E-Boats. Both took
evasive action but they were too close to each other with the result that STELLA RIGEL
rammed DONNA NOOK amidships, rolled her onto her beam ends and she sank.

DONSIDE   1914/17   Displacement: 182TG
                                   Admty No: 268
                                   Port Reg: A. 155
1900: Launched. 1914: Requisitioned in August and converted to a M/S. 1917: LOST.
Mined off Lowestoft on 7th January.

DOON   1917/19   Displacement: 199TG
                                   Port Reg: GY. 1132
1899: Launched. 1917: Requisitioned into the Fishery Reserve. 1919: Returned to owners.

DOON   1920/46   See under FRASER EAVES
                                   (Vol 1 p.134)

DOONIE BRAES   1940/45   Displacement: 213TG 84TN
                                   Engines: 57HP
                                   Armament: 1 x 3pdr
                                   Port Reg: A. 881
                                   P.No: 4. 235
1918: Launched. Built at Aberdeen. Owned by HW Lewis of Pitfodels. Acquired by A.
King AO of Aberdeen. 1940: Requisitioned in May and converted to a D/L. 1942:
Converted to a M/S. 1945: Returned to owners in January.

DORA   1915/16   Displacement: 295TG
1900: Launched. 1915: Requisitioned. 1916: Returned to the Fishing Fleet.

DORANDO   1914/18   Displacement: 139TG 56TN
                                            Engines: 45HP
                                            Armament: 1 x 6pdrAA
                                            Admty No: 824
                                            Port Reg: GY. 844
1894: Launched. Built at Govan. Owned by Trawlers (White Sea & Grimsby) of
Grimsby. 1914: Requisitioned in December and converted to a M/S. 1918: Returned to
owners in July.

DORCAS   1917/19   Displacement: 173TG 53TN
                                            Engines: 45HP = 9.5K
                                            Armament: 1 x 6pdr
                                            Admty No: 14
                                            Port Reg: H. 925
1906: Launched. Built at Beverley by CWG. Owned by Hellyer SFC of Hull. 1914:
Requisitioned in August and converted to a M/S. 1917: Acquired by C. Curzon of Milford
Haven. 1919: Returned to owners. 1920: Acquired by Spanish owners and renamed
Donostia. 1973: BU in Spain.

DOREEN   1916/19   Displacement: 194TG
                                            Port Reg: SD.130
1903: Launched. 1916: Requisitioned in May and converted to a BDV. 1917: Converted
to a Training Ship. 1919: Returned to owners.

DORILEEN   1940/46   See under WILLIAM BARLOW
                                            (Vol 1 p.189)

DORINDA   1917/19 1939/45 Displacement: 270TG 105TN
                                            Engines: 87HP
                                            Armament: 1 x 2pdr
                                            Admty No: 3003
                                            Port Reg: FD. 198
                                            P. No: WWII: FY. 623
1917: Launched. Built at Dundee. Owned by Active FCL of Fleetwood. Requisitioned in
February and converted to an Escort Vessel. 1919: Returned to owners. 1939:
Requisitioned in August and converted to a M/S. 1945: Returned to owners in November.

DORIS   1917/19   Displacement: 174TG 73TN
                                            Engines: 58HP
                                            Admty No: Not issued
                                            Port Reg: H. 364
1897: Launched. Built at Beverley. Owned by East Hull STC of Hull. 1917:
Requisitioned into the Fishery Reserve. 1919: Returned to owners.

DORIS   1918/19   Displacement: 122TG
1902: Launched. 1918: Requisitioned. 1919: Returned to owners.

DOROTHY F   1915/19
1915: Requisitioned. 1919: Returned to owners.

DOROTHY GRAY   1914/19 1940/44 Displacement: 199TG 76TN
                                           Engines: 75HP
                                           Armament: 1 x 6pdr
                                           Admty No: 96
                                           Port Reg: PD. 533
                                           P.No: WWII: 4. 222
1908: Launched. Built at Aberdeen. Owned by Peterhead Trawling Co of Peterhead.
1914: Requisitioned in August and converted to a M/S. 1919: Returned to owners.
Acquired by Irvine & Sons of North Shields. 1940: Requisitioned in July and converted
to an APV. 1944: Returned to owners in December.

DOROTHY LAMBERT   1940/46   Displacement: 299TG 114TN
                                          Engines: 99HP
                                          Port Reg: FD. 122
                                          P.No: FY. 558
1923: Launched. Built at Southbank-on-Tees by Smiths Dock. Owned by Clifton STL of
Fleetwood.   1940: Requisitioned in February and converted to a M/S.   1944: TPI
Operation Neptune, the D-Day Landings in June as a D/L attached to the 15th M/S Flot.
off Sword Beach. 1946: Returned to owners in February.

DOURO   1917/19   Displacement: 299T 150TN
                                          Engines: 45HP = 10K
                                          Armament: None
                                          Admty No: Not issued
                                          Port Reg: GY. 310
1897: Launched. Built at Hull by CWG. Owned by Ocean STC of Grimsby. 1917:
Requisitioned into the Fishery Reserve. 1919: Returned to owners. 1937: BU at Bo'ness.

DOVE   1914/19   Displacement: 168TG 66TN
                                          Engines: 41HP
                                          Armament: 1 x 3pdr
                                          Admty No: 390
                                          Port Reg: H. 279
1897: Launched. Built at North Shields. Owned by Kelsall Bros. & Beeching of Hull.
1914: Requisitioned in November and converted to a M/S. 1915: Renamed DOVE II in
February. 1919: Returned to owners and reverted to original name.

DOVE II   1915/19   See under DOVE above

DOVER   1914/18   Displacement: 163TG 69TN
Engines: 45HP
Armament: 1 x 3pdr
Admty No: 630
Port Reg: GY. 142

1896: Launched. Built at Govan. 1914: Requisitioned in October and converted to a M/S. 1918: Returned to owners. Acquired by G. Wardell of Hartlepool. PR: HL. 38.

DOWNIEHILLS   1917/19   Displacement: 227TG 98TN
Engines: 83HP
Armament: 1 x 6pdrAA
Admty No: 3040
Port Reg: PD. 277

1916: Launched. Built at Leith. Owned by Peterhead TCL of Peterhead. 1917: Requisitioned in May. 1919: Returned to owners.

DRACO   1915/19   Displacement: 139TG 56TN
Engines: 45HP
Port Reg: GY. 842

1895: Launched. Built at Govan. 1915: Requisitioned in January and converted to a BDV. 1919: Returned to owners. Acquired by Boston DSF & Ice of Boston, Lincs. PR: BN. 167.

DRAGON   1914/19   Displacement: 214TG 99TN
Engines: 52HP
Armament: 1 x 6pdr
Admty No: 428
Port Reg: GY. 201

1906: Launched. Built at North Shields. Owned by JR, FW & JH. Mackrill of Grimsby. 1914: Requisitioned in November and converted to a M/S. 1917: Renamed DRAGON II in March. 1919: Returned to owners and reverted to original name.

DRAGON II   1917/19   See under DRAGON above

DRAKE   1914/17   Displacement: 207TG
Armament: 1 x 3pdr
Admty No: 817
Port Reg: GY. 1163

1900: Launched. Owned by W. Grant AO of Grimsby. 1914: Requisitioned In November. 1915: Renamed DRAKE II in February. 1917: LOST. Wrecked in the Kenmare River, Ireland, on 3rd July.

DRAKE II   1915/17   See under DRAKE above

DRANGEY   1939/46   Displacement: 343TG 237TN
              Engines: 110HP
              Port Reg: GY. 126

1935: Launched. Built at Selby by Cochrane. Owned by Rinovia SF Co. of Grimsby. 1939: Purchased into the RN in August and converted to an A/S. 1946: Sold to mercantile.

DREADNOUGHT II 1917/19   Displacement: 150TG 61TN
              Engines: 61HP
              Armament: 1 x 6pdrAA
              Admty No: 2992
              Port Reg: A. 144

1907: Launched. Built at Aberdeen. 1917: Requisitioned in February. 1919: Returned to owners. Acquired by Monkshaven FCL of Whitby.

DRIVER   1910/20   Displacement: 207TG
              Armament: 1 x 6pdr AA
              Admty No: 57

1910: Launched. Built at Aberdeen by Duthie. Purchased into the RN. Employed on A/S trials. 1914: Based at Devonport as M/S Training Ship for Trawler Reserve Crews. 1919: Renamed NAIRN in June. 1920: Sold to mercantile and retained the same name.

DROMIO   1939/39   Displacement: 195TG 143TN
              Engines: 99HP = 10.8K
              Armament: 1 x 12pdr
              Port Reg: H. 94

1929: Launched. Built at Beverley by CWG. Owned by the Hull Northern FCL of Hull. 1939: Requisitioned in August and converted to a M/S. Based at Sheerness. LOST. Sunk in a collision to the N. of Whitby on 22nd December.

DRUMBLADE   1914/19   Displacement: 195TG 78TN
              Engines: 58HP
              Admty No: 467
              Port Reg: A. 133

1900: Launched. Built at Montrose. Owned by North of Scotland SFC of Aberdeen. 1914: Requisitioned in September. Designated as a M/S but converted to an APV. 1919: Returned to owners.

DRUMBLAIR   1918/19   Displacement: 196TG 79TN
              Engines: 58HP
              Admty No: Not issued
              Port Reg: A. 130

1900: Launched. Built at Montrose by Montrose SB. Owned by North of Scotland SFC of Aberdeen. 1918: Requisitioned into the Fishery Reserve. 1919: Returned to owners.

DRUMMER BOY   1916/19 1939/45 Displacement: 209TG 91TN
                                      Engines: 51HP
                                      Armament: 1 x 12pdr
                                      Admty No: 2969
                                      Port Reg: WWI: GY. 964
                                      WWII: GY. 442
                                      P.No: WWII: FY. 851

1916: Launched. Built at Selby by Cochrane. Requisitioned in September and converted
to a M/S. 1919: Returned to owners. 1939: Requisitioned in November and converted to
a M/S. Acquired by Stringer's SFC of Boston, Lincs. PR: BN. 141. Acquired by Robinson
& Son of Grimsby. PR: GY. 447. 1945: Returned to owners in August.

DRUMOAK   1914/14   Displacement: 208TG
                                      Admty No: 342
                                      Port Reg: A. 516

1902: Launched. 1914: Requisitioned in August and converted to a M/S. LOST. Mined
off the Belgian Coast on 5th October.

DRUMTOCHTY   1915/18   Displacement: 211TG
                                      Armament: 1 x 3pdr
                                      Admty No: 357
                                      Port Reg: A. 408

1915: Launched. Requisitioned in October and converted to a M/S. 1918: LOST. Mined
off Dover on 29th January.

DRUSILLA   1915/19   Displacement: 250TG 97TN
                                      Engines: 85HP
                                      Armament: 1 x 12pdr
                                      Admty No: 36
                                      Port Reg: GY. 951

1914: Launched. Built at Middlesborough by Smith's Dock. Owned by Consolidated
Fisheries of Grimsby. 1915: Requisitioned in May and converted to a M/S. 1919:
Returned to owners.

DRYPOOL   1915/19   Displacement: 331TG 132TN
                                      Engines: 94HP
                                      Armament: 1 x 12pdr
                                      Admty No: 1753
                                      Port Reg: H. 375

1911: Launched. Built at Selby by Cochrane. Owned by City SFC of Hull. 1915:
Requisitioned in April. 1919: Returned to owners.

DUCHESSE de BRABANT 1940/45   Displacement: 338TG
                                      Port Reg: Belgian

1924: Launched. 1940: Hired from Belgian owners in July and converted to an APV. 1945: Returned to owners.

DULCIBELLE	1939/45	See under BARNARD BOYLE
		(Vol 1 p.168)

DUNGENESS	1940/40	See under SEA RANGER

DUNLEATH   1939/46   Displacement: 292TG

1896: Launched. 1939: Requisitioned in September and converted to a Stores Hulk. 1946: Returned to owners in February.

DUNNETT   1917/19   Displacement: 205TG 79TN
Engines: 49HP
Armament: 1 x 6pdrAA
Admty No: 3004
Port Reg: H. 77

1914: Launched. Built at Selby by Cochrane. Owned by Hull SF & Ice Co of Hull. 1917: Requisitioned in February and converted to a M/S. 1919: Returned to owners.

DUNRAVEN CASTLE   1917/19 1940/45 Displacement: 276TG 107TN
Engines: 87HP
Armament: 1 x 12pdr; 1 x 3.5-inch
Bomb Thrower (A/S Howitzer)
Admty No: 3045
Port Reg: SA. 69
P. No: WWII: FY. 570

1917: Launched. Built at Southbank-on-Tees by Smith's Dock. Owned by Consolidated Fisheries of Grimsby. Requisitioned in June and converted to a M/S. 1919: Returned to owners. 1940: Requisitioned in March and converted to a M/S. 1945: Returned to owners in September.

DURAWEEN   1914/17   RAN. See under TR.20 (Vol 1 p.79)

DURBAN   1914/15 1917/19 Displacement: 152TG 60TN
Engines: 35HP = 9.5K
Admty No: 1209
Port Reg: H. 378

1897: Launched. Built at Hull by CWG. Owned by Hull SF & Ice Co of Hull. 1914: Requisitioned in December and converted to an APV. 1915: Returned to the Fishing Fleet in October. 1917: Requisitioned into the Fishery Reserve. 1919: Returned to owners. Mercantile Loss. Presumed mined in the North Sea in March with the loss of all hands.

DURGA   1914/19   Displacement: 216TG 83TN
Engines; 76HP
Armament: 1 x 6pdrAA
Admty No: 300
Port Reg: GY. 612
1911: Launched. Built at Middlesborough by Smith's Dock. Owned by Sleight of Grimsby. 1914: Requisitioned in August and converted to a M/S. 1919: Returned to owners.

DUSK   1942/46   See under ESTRELLA do MAR

DUSTER   1914/17   Displacement: 192TG
Armament: 1 x 6pdrAA
Admty No: 421
Port Reg: H. 267
1911: Launched. 1914: Requisitioned in November and converted to a M/S. 1917: LOST. Wrecked near Portreath, Cornwall on 17th December.

D.W.FITZGERALD   1916/19 1940/45 Displacement: 235TG 102TN
Engines: 78HP
Armament: 1 x 6pdrAA
Admty No: 863
Port Reg: A. 629
P. No: WWII: FY. 1820
1916: Launched. Built at Aberdeen. Owned by Irvin & Sons of North Shields. Requisitioned in April and converted to a M/S. 1919: Returned to owners. 1940: Requisitioned in August and converted to a M/S. Fitted with LL and Acoustic Hammer. Joined the 110th M/S Group based at Grimsby sweeping Cromer-Flamborough Head. 1944: Transferred to Portsmouth in June for Channel sweeping. Returned to Grimsby in December and Paid Off. 1945: Returned to owners in January.

DYNEVOR CASTLE   1917/19   Displacement: 283TG
Admty No: Not issued
Port Reg: SA. 3
1914: Launched. Built at Middlesborough by Smith's Dock. Owned by Consolidated Fisheries of Grimsby. 1917: Requisitioned into the Fishery Reserve. 1919: Returned to owners.

E & F   1940/40   See under JAMES GREEN (Vol 1 p.58)

EAGLE   1914/18   Displacement: 168TG 66TN
                                            Engines: 40HP
                                            Armament: 1 x 6pdr
                                            Admty No: 393
                                            Port Reg: H. 454

1899: Launched. Built at Govan. 1914: Requisitioned in December and converted to a M/S. 1916: Renamed EAGLET in February. 1918: Returned to owners. Acquired by J.L. Green of Grimsby. Retained the name *Eaglet* PR: GY. 1263.

EAGLE   1917/19   Displacement: 146TG 70TN
                                            Engines: 45HP
                                            Admty No: Not issued
                                            Port Reg: GY. 378

1891: Launched. Built at Beverley. Iron Construction. Owned by HL Taylor AO of Grimsby. 1917: Requisitioned into the Fishery Reserve. 1919: Returned to owners.

EAGLET   1916/18   See under EAGLE 1914

EARL ESSEX   1914/19 1939/46   Displacement: 225TG 112TN
                                            Engines: 68HP = 9.5K
                                            Armament: 1 x 12pdr
                                            Admty No: 292
                                            Port Reg: GY. 48
                                            P. No: WWII: FY. 852

1914: Launched. Built at Beverley by CWG. Owned by Earl SFC of Grimsby. Requisitioned in August and converted to a M/S. 1919: Returned to owners. 1937: Acquired by Robinson & Sons of Grimsby. 1939: Requisitioned in November and converted to a M/S. 1946: Returned to owners. Mercantile Loss. Trawled up a mine in the North Sea on 24th April. The mine exploded sinking the vessel. One survivor, ten lost.

EARL GRANARD   1915/19 1939/40   Ex-*Pauline*
                                            Ex-*Grotius*
                                            Ex-*Courtland*
                                            Displacement: 211TG 76TN
                                            Engines: 65HP = 10K
                                            Armament: 1 x 6pdrAA
                                            Admty No: 2653
                                            Port Reg: GY. 449

1904: Launched. Built at Beverley by CWG as *Courtland*. Owned by A. Black of Grimsby. 1908: Acquired by Dutch owners and renamed *Grotius*. 1910: Acquired by Faroese owners and renamed *Pauline*. 1915: Acquired by Earl SFC of Grimsby and renamed *Earl Granard*. PR: GY. 449. Requisitioned in April and converted to a M/S. Acquired by Rushworth SFC of Grimsby. 1918: Acquired by I. Bunch of Grimsby. 1919: Returned to owner. 1930: Acquired by TC & F Moss of Grimsby . 1931: Renamed *Castleton*. 1939: Requisitioned in November as CASTLETON and designated as an APV. 1940: Returned to owners in January. Mercantile loss. Disappeared near the Orkneys on 28th June. Cause unknown but thought to have been torpedoed by the German U-62. All 10 hands were lost.

EARL KITCHENER	1915/19 1939/46	Displacement: 348TG 162TN
		Engines: 87HP = 10.5K
		Armament: 1 x 12pdr
		Admty No: 1907
		Port Reg: H. 345
		P.No: WWII: FY. 1633

1915: Launched. Built at Beverley by CWG. Owned by the Imperial SFC of Hull. Requisitioned in October and converted to a M/S. 1919: Returned to owners. Acquired by Hellyer Bros. of Hull. 1939: Requisitioned in August and converted to a M/S. 1946: Returned to owners in April. 1953: BU at Thornaby-on-Tees.

EARL LENNOX	1914/17	Displacement: 226TG 113TN
		Engines: 75HP = 10K
		Armament: 1 x 6pdr
		Admty No: 1441
		Port Reg: GY. 367

1914: Launched. Built at Beverley by CWG. Owned by Earl SFC of Grimsby. 1915: Acquired by Strand SFC of Grimsby. Requisitioned in April and converted to a M/S. 1917: LOST. Mined off the Sound of Islay on 23rd October.

EARL OF BUCHAN	1916/19	Displacement: 227TG 98TN
		Engines: 82HP
		Armament: 1 x 6pdrAA
		Admty No: 3292
		Port Reg: PD. 242

1916: Launched. Built at Leith. Owned by the Peterhead TCL of Peterhead. Requisitioned in June and converted to a M/S. 1919: Returned to owners.

EARL OF WARWICK	1915/19	Displacement: 208TG 82TN
		Engines: 60HP = 10K
		Armament: 1 x 12pdr
		Admty No: 2652
		Port Reg: GY. 446

1905: Launched. Built at Beverley by CWG. Owned by Earl SFC of Grimsby. PR: GY. 77. 1909: Acquired by Faroese owners and renamed *Thora*. 1915: Re-acquired by Earl SFC of Grimsby and renamed *Earl Warwick*. Requisitioned in March and converted to a M/S. Acquired by Rushworth SFC of Grimsby in September. 1918: Acquired by Yarborough SFC of Grimsby. 1919: Returned to owners. 1930: Acquired by TC & F Moss of Grimsby and renamed *Clacton*. 1954: BU at Bruges, Belgium. *Notes*: Entered in Mercantile Lists as *Earl Warwick*.

EASTBOURNE 1917/19 Displacement: 163TG 69TN
Engines: 45HP
Admty No: Not issued
Port Reg: GY. 155
1896: Launched. Built at Govan. Owned by E. Taylor & N. Ashworth of Fleetwood. 1917: Requisitioned into the Fishery Reserve. 1919: Returned to owners.

EAST COAST 1944/45 See under HORACE STROUD

EASTCOATES 1939/45 See under JOHN GRAHAM
(Vol 1 p.63)

EASTELLA 1915/19 Displacement: 183TG 72TN
Engines: 48HP
Armament: 1 x 3pdr
Admty No: 1766
Port Reg: H. 765
1903: Launched. Built at Govan. Owned by the Great Northern SFC of Hull. 1915: Requisitioned in May and converted to a M/S. 1919: Returned to owners.

EASTWARD HO 1915/18 Displacement: 162TG 63TN
Engines: 55HP = 10K
Armament: 1 x 3pdr
Admty No: 1217
Port Reg: H. 415
1898: Launched. Built at Hull by CWG. Owned by ST. White of Hull. 1915: Requisitioned in February and converted to a M/S. 1918: Returned to owners in December. 1936: BU.

EBOR 1917/19 Displacement: 165TG 64TN
Engines: 45HP
Admty No: Not issued
Port Reg: H. 360
1897: Launched. Built at Govan. Owned by the British TCL of Bootle. 1917: Requisitioned into the Fishery Reserve. 1919: Returned to owners.

EBOR ABBEY   1940/46   See under NELLIE DODDS

EBOR WYKE   1939/45   Displacement: 348TG 138TN
                                    Engines: 96HP
                                    Armament: 1 x 12pdr
                                    Port Reg: H. 78
                                    P. No: FY. 1601

1929: Launched. Built at Selby by Cochrane. Owned by the West Dock SFC of Hull.
1939: Requisitioned in August and converted to a M/S. 1940: Based at Iceland.
1943: 134th M/S Group based at Grimsby. 1945: LOST. Attacked by U-Boat and
torpedoed whilst on patrol off Iceland on 2nd May. Only 1 survivor. *Notes*: Earned
the dubious distinction of being the last British warship to be sunk by a U-Boat.

EBRO   1914/18   Displacement: 175TG 71TN
                              Engines: 45HP
                              Armament: 1 x 3pdr
                              Admty No: 998
                              Port Reg: GY. 743

1898: Launched. Built at Beverley. Owned by the Economy SFC of Grimsby. 1914:
Requisitioned in December. 1915: Renamed EBRO II in June. 1918: Returned to
owners and reverted to original name.

EBRO II   1915/18   See under EBRO above

ECCLESHILL   1917/19 1940/45 Displacement: 226TG 87TN
                                    Engines: 51HP
                                    Armament: 1 x 6pdr; 1 x 3.5-inch Bomb
                                    Thrower (A/S Howitzer)
                                    Admty No: 3334
                                    Port Reg: H. 376

1911: Launched. Built at Selby by Cochrane. Owned by the Great Northern SFC of Hull.
1917: Requisitioned in March and converted to a M/S. 1919: Returned to owners. 1940:
Requisitioned in February and converted to a BDV. 1945: Returned to owners.

ECHO   1915/19   Displacement: 185TG
                              Port Reg: H.367

1897: Launched. 1915: Requisitioned in September and converted to a BDV. 1919:
Returned to owners.

ECLIPSE   1917/17   Displacement: 185TG
                                 Admty No: Not issued
                                 Port Reg: PD. 36

1899: Launched. 1917: Requisitioned into the Fishery Reserve. LOST. Captured by a
U-Boat and sunk by gunfire 100 miles N x W of the Orkneys on 1st July.

EDDYSTONE   1917/19   Displacement: 165TG 64TN
Engines: 45HP
Port Reg: H. 368
1897: Launched. Built at Govan. Owned by E. Taylor of Fleetwood. 1917:
Requisitioned into the Fishery Reserve. 1919: Returned to owners.

EDEN   1934/39   See under THOMAS JOHNS
(See Addenda)

EDINBURGH CASTLE   1915/19   Displacement: 241TG 94TN
Engines: 80HP
Port Reg: GY. 1285
1899: Launched. Built at Dundee. Owned by A. Bannister & W. Barton of Grimsby.
1915: Requisitioned in June and converted to a BDV. 1919: Returned to owners.

EDISON   1914/15   Displacement: 196TG
Admty No: 395
Port Reg: H. 430
1898: Launched. 1914: Requisitioned in September and converted to a M/S. 1915:
LOST. Wrecked on the Isle of Lewis on 6th July.

EDITH M. PURDY   1940/45   See under JOHN FRANCOIS
(Vol 1 p.179)

EDITOR   1914/18   Displacement: 169TG 67TN
Engines: 40HP
Armament: 1 x 12pdr
Admty No: 398
Port Reg: H. 442
1899: Launched. Built at Govan. 1914: Requisitioned in December and converted
to a M/S. 1917: Reduced to the Fishery Reserve. 1918: Returned to owners.
Acquired by N. Bull of Cardiff. PR: GY. 1218.

EDUARD van VLAENDEREN   1940/41 Displacement: 324TG
Port Reg: Belgian
P.No: FY. 1832
1925: Launched. Belgian fishing vessel. 1940: Hired from Belgian owners in June
and converted to an APV. 1941: LOST. Wrecked off the Faroes on 22nd January.
Notes: Aka *Edouard van Vlaenderen*.

EDWARD VII   1917/19   Displacement: 231TG 88TN
Engines: 75HP
Armament: 1 x 6pdrAA
Admty No: 22

Port Reg: M. 196

1906: Launched. Built at North Shields. Owned by WM. Beesley AO of Grimsby.
1914: Requisitioned in August and converted to a M/S. 1917: Converted to a Cable
Repair Vessel. 1919: Returned to owners.

EDWARDIAN	1915/19	Displacement: 295TG 121TN
		Engines: 89HP = 10.5K
		Armament: 1 x 12pdr; 1 x 7.5-inch
		Bomb Thrower (A/S Howitzer)
		Admty No: 1453
		Port Reg: GY. 704

1912: Launched. Built at Beverley by CWG. Owned by the Loyal SFC of Grimsby.
1915: Requisitioned in April and converted to a M/S. 1919: Returned to owners.
1930: Mercantile Loss. Stranded near Myrar Dyra Fjiord, N. Iceland on 21st March
with the loss of 1 life.

EDWARDIAN	1939/46	Displacement: 348TG 148TN
		Engines: 96HP = 10.5K
		Armament: 1 x 12pdr
		Port Reg: GY. 328
		P. No: FY. 691

1931: Launched. Built at Beverley by CWG. Owned by the Loyal SFC of Grimsby.
1939: Requisitioned in September and converted to a M/S. 1946: Returned to
owners in January. 1948: Acquired by Devon FCL of Hull and renamed *Ophelia*.
PR: H. 576. 1955: BU at Gateshead.

EDWINA	1915/19 1941/45	Displacement: 267TG 104TN
		Engines: 84HP
		Armament: 1 x 12pdr
		Admty No: 1919
		Port Reg: FD .205
		P. No: WWII: 4. 314

1915: Launched. Built at Dundee. Owned by J. Marr of Fleetwood. Requisitioned
in October and converted to a M/S. 1919: Returned to owners. 1940: Requisitioned
in May and converted to an APV. 1945: Returned to owners in May.

EGERIA	1939/45	Ex-*Bellona*
		Displacement: 184TG 88TN
		Engines: 57HP
		Port Reg: GY. 336

1907: Launched. Built at Selby by Cochrane. Owned by Consolidated Fisheries of
Grimsby. 1939: Requisitioned in November and converted to an APV. 1940:
Converted to a D/L in August. 1941: Converted to a M/S in January. 1945: Returned
to owners in January.

EGRET 1917/19 Displacement: 224TG 91TN
Engines: 60HP
Port Reg: GY. 1084
1899: Launched. Built at Beverley. Iron construction. Owned by T. Baskcomb of Grimsby. 1918: Requisitioned into the Fishery Reserve. 1919: Returned to owners.

EIDER 1914/19 Displacement: 168TG
Armament: 1 x 6pdrAA
Admty No: 8 & 404
Port Reg: H. 459
1899: Launched. 1914: Requisitioned in August and converted to a M/S. 1919: Returned to owners.

EIDER II 1917/19 Displacement: 142TG 54TN
Engines: 45HP
Admty No: Not issued
Port Reg: GY. 1056
1892: Launched. Built at Port Glasgow. Owned by JW. Smethurst of Grimsby. 1917: Requisitioned into the Fishery Reserve. 1919: Returned to owners.

EILEEN DUNCAN 1914/19 1940/41 Displacement: 223TG 86TN
Engines: 67HP
Armament: 1 x 6pdrAA
Admty No: 508
Port Reg: WWI: LL. 36; WWII: A. 413.
1910: Launched. Built at Selby by Cochrane. Owned by J & WA. Duncan of Liverpool. 1915: Requisitioned in January and converted to a M/S. 1919: Returned to owners. Acquired by W. & GR. Wood of Aberdeen. PR: A. 413. 1940: Requisitioned in January and converted to a M/S. 1941: LOST. Sunk by enemy a/c off North Shields on 30th September.

ELBE 1917/19 Displacement: 165TG 64TN
Engines: 45HP
Admty No: Not issued
Port Reg: H. 358
1897: Launched. Built at Govan. Owned by the Great Northern SFC of Hull. 1918: Requisitioned into the Fishery Reserve. 1919: Returned to owners.

ELBURY 1939/45 Ex-*Pict*
Displacement: 394TG 174TN
Engines: 99HP = 11K
Port Reg: H. 250
P.No: FY. 656
1923: Launched. Built at Beverley as *Pict*. Owned by Hellyer Bros. of Hull. 1935:

Acquired by Devon FCL of Hull and renamed *Elbury*. 1939: Requisitioned in September and converted to a M/S. 20th M/S Group based at Grimsby. 1943: Acquired by Pickering & Haldane STC of Hull. 1945: Returned to owners in July. Acquired by Lord Line of Hull and renamed *Lord Gort*. 1947: Acquired by Wyre STC of Fleetwood and renamed *Wyre General* PR: FD. 258. 1956: BU at Boom in Belgium.

ELCHO   1914/19   Displacement: 155TG 59TN
                                            Engines: 53HP
                                            Armament: 1 x 3pdr
                                            Admty No: 622
                                            Port Reg: GN. 68
1908: Launched. Built at Leith. Owned by the General SFC of Edinburgh. 1914: Requisitioned in September and converted to a M/S. 1919: Returned to owners.

ELDORADO   1917/19 1940/45 Displacement: 180TG 70TN
                                            Engines: 48HP
                                            Port Reg: WWI: H. 710; WWII: A. 51
                                            P. No: WWII: FY. 571
1902: Launched. Built at Govan. Owned by T. Crimlick of Filey & B. Simpson Jr. of Scarborough. 1917: Requisitioned into the Fishery Reserve. 1919: Returned to owners. Acquired by G. Cormacj & A. Robertson of Aberdeen. PR: A. 51. 1940: Requisitioned in February and converted to a D/L. Converted to a M/S in August. 1945: Returned to owners in December.

ELEANOR   1915/18   Displacement: 193TG
1914: Launched. 1915: Requisitioned. 1918: Returned to owners.

ELEAZOR   1917/17   Displacement: 111TG
                                            Admty No: Not issued
                                            Port Reg: WY. 105
1895: Launched. 1917: Requisitioned into the Fishery Reserve. LOST. Captured by U- Boat on 12th August and sunk by gunfire.

ELECTOR   1917/19   Displacement: 169TG 67TN
                                            Engines: 45HP
                                            Admty No: Not issued
                                            Port Reg: H. 438
1898: Launched. Built at Govan. Owned by A. Gouldby AO of Lowestoft. 1917: Requisitioned for the Fishery Reserve. 1919: Returned to owners.

ELECTRA   1915/19 1940/46 Displacement: 269TG 109TN
                                            Engines: 70HP = 10.5K
                                            Armament: 1 x 6pdrAA

Admty No: 1743
Port Reg: WWI: H. 661; WWII: Belgian
P.No: WWII: 4. 159

1904: Launched. Built at Beverley by CWG. Owned by F & T. Ross of Hull. 1915: Requisitioned in July and converted to a M/S. Renamed ELECTRA II in August. 1919: Returned to owners and retained the name *Electra II*. Acquired by H. Elliot & Sons of Fleetwood. 1940: Hired from Belgian owners in May as ELECTRA II and converted to an APV. 1942: Acquired by Alfred FCL of Fleetwood. 1944: Converted to a BGV. 1946: Returned to owners in February. Laid up in the Alexandra Dock, Grimsby prior to BU. BU in November at Paull.

ELECTRA II	1915/19 1940/46	See under ELECTRA

ELECTRIC	1918/19	Displacement: 79TN
		Engines: 55HP
		Admty No: Not issued
		Port Reg: GY. 286

1890: Launched. Built at Hull. Owned by R. White of Grimsby. 1917: Requisitioned into the Fishery Reserve. 1919: Returned to owners.

ELENA	1940/45	See under VIOLA

ELF	1917/19	Displacement: 165TG 64TN
		Engines: 45HP
		Admty No: Not issued
		Port Reg: 362

1897: Launched. Built at Govan. Owned by the Hesketh STL of Fleetwood. 1917: Requisitioned into the Fishery Reserve. 1919: Returned to owners.

ELF KING	1917/19	Displacement: 289TG 115TN
		Engines: 79HP
		Armament: 1 x 12pdr; 1 x 7.5-inch
		Bomb Thrower (A/S Howitzer)
		Admty No: 3019
		Port Reg: H. 1012

1913: Launched. Built at Selby by Cochrane. 1917: Requisitioned in February. 1919: Returned to owners. Acquired by Grant & Baker SFC of Grimsby. PR: GY. 1247.

ELISE	1915/18	Displacement: 239TG
		Armament: 1 x 6pdr
		Admty No: 1622
		Port Reg: PD. 164

1907: Launched. 1915: Requisitioned in June and converted to a M/S. 1917:

Employed on convoy escort duties in northern waters. Part of the escort for a Scandinavian convoy sailing from Lerwick on 15th October. Rescued the CO and 44 other survivors from the stricken STRONGBOW which had been attacked by German surface ships. 1918: LOST. Blown up 2 miles NE of St. Mary's Lighthouse, Blyth, on 22nd September. Presumed to have been torpedoed.

ELITE   1914/19   Displacement: 180TG 70TN
                 Engines: 48HP
                 Armament: 1 x 6pdr
                 Admty No: 150
                 Port Reg: H. 714

1902: Launched. Built at Govan. 1914: Requisitioned in September and converted to a M/S. 1919: Returned to owners. Acquired by C. Dobson of Grimsby. PR: GY. 100.

ELIZABETH ANGELA 1939/40   Displacement: 253TG 98TN
                 Engines: 84HP
                 Armament: 1 x 12pdr
                 Port Reg: A. 322
                 P.No: FY. 767

1928: Launched. Built at Dalmuir. Owned by Boston DSF & Ice Co of Fleetwood. 1939: Requisitioned in November and converted to a M/S. 1940: LOST. Sunk by enemy a/c in the Downs on 13th August.

ELK   1915/19 1939/40 Displacement: 181TG 70TN
                 Engines: 62HP = 10K
                 Armament: 1 x 3pdr
                 Admty No: 706
                 Port Reg: WI: GY. 1235; WWII: M. 36
                 P. No: WWII: 4. 24

1902: Launched. Built at Beverley by CWG. Owned by Morris & Fisher of Grimsby. 1914: Requisitioned in December and converted to a M/S. 1917: Reduced to the Fishery Reserve. 1918: Renamed ELK II. Acquired by Victoria SFC of Grimsby. 1919: Returned to owners in July. 1938: Acquired by WHE Nichols of Milford Haven. 1939: Requisitioned in October and converted to a D/L. 1940: LOST. Mined off East Cornwall on 27th November. No loss of life.

ELK   1917/19   Displacement: 67TN
                 Engines: 40HP
                 Port Reg: GY. 1287

1898: Launched. Built at Govan. Owned by C. Dobson of Grimsby. 1917: Requisitioned. 1919: Returned to owners.

ELK II 1914/19 Displacement: 169TG
Armament: 1 x 6pdrAA
Admty No: 380
Port Reg: H 440
1898: Launched. 1914: Requisitioned in November and converted to a M/S. 1919: Returned to owners.

ELLESMERE 1916/19 1939/40 Displacement: 183TG 72TN
Engines: 48HP
Armament: 1 x 6pdrAA
Admty No: 1275
Port Reg: H. 767
1903: Launched. Built at Govan. Owned by the Great Northern SFC of Hull. 1916: Requisitioned in March and converted to a M/S. 1919: Returned to owners. Acquired by Crescent TCL of Milford Haven. 1939: Requisitioned in December and designated as a M/S. Renamed HYAENA. (1940: Conversion not carried out and returned to owners on 10th February).

ELLIE 1917/19 Displacement: 87TN
Engines: 43HP
Port Reg: BN. 63
1919: Launched. Built at Wivenhoe. Owned by Stringers SFC of Boston, Lincs. 1917: Requisitioned. 1919: Returned to owners.

ELM 1914/20 Displacement: 168TG 66TN
Engines: 40HP
Armament: 1 x 12pdr
Admty No: 397
Port Reg: H. 23
1899: Launched. Built at Govan. Owned by the Great Northern SFC of Hull. 1914: Requisitioned in December and converted to a M/S. 1920: Returned to owners.

EL MENZALA 1940/46 Displacement: 308TG
P.No: FY. 1740
1917: Launched. 1940: Purchased into the RN in April and converted to a M/S. Renamed TORNADO in July. 1943: Renamed TORNADO II in August. Converted to a Water Carrier. 1946: Sold to mercantile.

ELMIRA 1915/19 Displacement: 197TG 76TN
Engines: 68HP
Armament: 1 x 6pdrAA
Admty No: 1603
Port Reg: GY. 969
1914: Launched. Built at Middlesborough by Smith's Dock. Owned by Consolidated

143

Fisheries of Grimsby. 1915: Requisitioned in March and converted to a M/S. 1919: Returned to owners.

ELSE RYKENS   1939/45   Displacement: 250TG 113TN
                                      Engines: 525HP
                                      Port Reg: A. 314
                                      P.No: FY. 1646
1935: Launched. Built at Bremmerhaven, Germany. Owned by the Aberdeen ST & F Co. Ltd., Aberdeen. 1939: Requisitioned in December and converted to A/S. 1945: Returned to owners. *Notes*: Sister-ship PAUL RYKENS.

ELSIE   1916/19   Displacement: 184TG 79TN
                                      Engines: 60HP
                                      Armament: 1 x 6pdr
                                      Admty No: 944
                                      Port Reg: H. 320
1896: Launched. Built at Beverley. Owned by the Ellis STC of Scarborough. 1915: Requisitioned in January and converted to a M/S. 1917: Reduced to the Fishery Reserve. 1919: Returned to owners.

ELSIE CAM   1940/46   *Ex-Sophie Busse*
                                      Displacement: 250TG
                                      P.No: FY. 1646
1922: Launched. 1940: Requisitioned in February and converted to a M/S. 1946: Returned to owners in January.

ELSWICK   1915/19   Displacement: 215TG 83TN
                                      Engines: 66HP
                                      Armament: 1 x 6pdr
                                      Admty No: 1535
                                      Port Reg: FD. 78
1906: Launched. Built at Bowling by Scott. 1915: Requisitioned in July and converted to a M/S. 1919: Returned to owners.

ELVINA   1915/19   Displacement: 210TG 78TN
                                      Engines: 68HP
                                      Armament: 1 x 12pdr; 1 x 7.5-inch
                                      Bomb Thrower (A/S Howitzer)
                                      Port Reg: GY. 238
1914: Launched. Built at Middlesborough by Smith's Dock. Owned by Consolidated Fisheries of Grimsby. Requisitioned in November and converted to a M/S. 1919: Returned to owners.

ELY   1915/19   Displacement: 183TG 72TN
                                      Engines: 45HP
                                      Armament: 1 x 3pdr
                                      Admty No: 1777
                                      Port Reg: H. 770
1903: Launched. Built at Govan. Owned by the Great Northern SFC of Hull. 1915:
Requisitioned in May and converted to a M/S. 1919: Returned to owners.

ELYSIAN   1915/19   Displacement: 214TG 83TN
                                      Engines: 70HP
                                      Armament: 1 x 6pdrAA
                                      Admty No: 3206
                                      Port Reg: GY. 661
1912: Launched. Built at Selby by Cochrane. Owned by the Wilberforce SFC of
Scarborough. 1915: Requisitioned in January and converted to a M/S. 1919:
Returned to owners. *Notes*: Reported as requisitioned for WWII as P & Y. NFI.

EMERALD   1915/19 1939/40 Displacement: 289TG 115TN
                                      Engines: 83HP
                                      Armament: 1 x 12pdr
                                      Admty No: 1579
                                      Port Reg: WWI: GY. 214; WWII: H. 910
                                      P. No: WWII: 4. 153
1913: Launched. Built at Selby by Cochrane. Owned by the Amaranth FCL of
Grimsby. 1914: Requisitioned in November and converted to a M/S. 1919:
Returned in owners. 1939: Requisitioned in September and converted to an APV.
1940: LOST. Mined off Holyhead on 22nd July.

EMERALD II   1917/19   Displacement: 150TG 63TN
                                      Engines: 45HP
                                      Port Reg: GY. 613
1894: Launched. Built at Beverley. Owned by TC. Moss of Grimsby. 1917:
Requisitioned. 1919: Returned to owner.

EMERALD III   1917/19   Displacement: 150TG
                                      Admty No: Not issued
                                      Port Reg: GY. 613
1917: Requisitioned into the Fishery Reserve. 1919: Returned to owners.

EMILIA PRIMEIRO   1940/40   Displacement: 421TG
                                      Port Reg: Portuguese
                                      P.No: Z. 203
1919: Launched. Portuguese fishing vessel. 1940: Purchased into the RN from
Portuguese owners on 8th June and converted to a BDV. Renamed SUNRISE.

1946: Sold to mercantile on 17th May.

EMILION   1915/19 1939/41 Displacement: 201TG 78TN
                                      Engines: 45HP
                                      Armament: 1 x 12pdr
                                      Admty No: 1613
                                      Port Reg: GY. 243
                                      P. No: WWII: FY. 853

1914: Launched. Built at Middlesborough by Smith's Dock. Owned by Consolidated
Fisheries of Grimsby. 1915: Requisitioned in April and converted to a M/S. 1919:
Returned to owners. 1939: Requisitioned in November and converted to a M/S.
Based at Grimsby (ungrouped). 1941: LOST. Mined in the Thames Estuary in 24th
October.

EMLEY   1914/18   Displacement: 223TG
                                       Armament: 1 x 12pdr
                                       Admty No: 665
                                       Port Reg: H. 384

1911: Launched. 1914: Requisitioned in October and converted to a M/S. 1918: LOST.
Mined off May Island on 28th April.

EMPEROR   1914/19   Displacement: 181TG 71TN
                                       Engines: 46HP = 10K
                                       Admty No: 552
                                       Port Reg: H. 741

1903: Launched. Built at Beverley by CWG. Owned by Hull SF & Ice Co of Hull.
1914: Requisitioned in September and converted to a M/S. 1917: Transferred to the
Fishery Reserve in February. 1918: Acquired by RF Scotter & R Cammish of
Scarborough. 1919: Returned to owners. 1937: BU.

EMPYREAN   1914/19 1939/45. Displacement: 215TG 98TN
                                       Engines: 76HP
                                       Armament: 1 x 6pdrAA; 1 x 7.5-inch
                                       Bomb Thrower (A/S Howitzer)
                                       Admty No: 9
                                       Port Reg: GY. 209
                                       P.No: WWII: FY. 873 (M/S);
                                       Y. 7.10 (Store Carrier)

1914: Launched. Built at Goole by Goole SB. Owned by the Grimsby & North Sea
STC of Grimsby. Requisitioned in September and converted to a M/S. 1920:
Returned to owners. Acquired by the Lindsay SFC of Grimsby. Same PR. 1939:
Requisitioned in November and converted to an APV. 1940: Converted to a M/S in
April. 1945: Converted to an Esso in January. 1946: Returned to owners in July.

EMU   1915/19   Displacement: 164TG 57TN
                                     Engines: 40HP = 10K
                                     Armament: 1 x 3pdr
                                     Admty No: 1765
                                     Port Reg: H. 516
1900: Launched. Built at Hull by CWG. Owned by Great Northern Steam Ship FCL
of Hull. 1915: Requisitioned in May and converted to an APV. Converted to a BDV.
1918: Acquired by H. Croft Baker of Grimsby. PR: GY.1227. 1919: Returned to
owners. Acquired by Tena Blau & H. Wood of Grimsby and renamed *Our Tena*.
1937: BU.

EMU   1917/19   Displacement: 154TG 65TN
                                     Engines: 50HP
                                     Port Reg: GY. 1
1895: Launched. Built at Beverley. Owned by HL. Taylor Ltd. of Grimsby. 1917:
Requisitioned into the Fishery Reserve. 1919: Returned to owners.

EMULATOR   1917/19 1941/42 Displacement: 168TG 66TN
                                     Engines: 40HP
                                     Port Reg: H.468
1899: Launched. Built at Govan. Owned by the Great Northern SFC of Hull. 1917:
Requisitioned into the Fishery Reserve. 1919: Returned to owners. Acquired by the
Filey USTC of Scarborough. Same PR. 1941: Requisitioned and employed on
Harbour Service. 1942: Returned to owners.

EN AVANT   1940/45   Displacement: 264TG
                                     Port Reg: Dutch
1911: Launched. Dutch fishing vessel. 1940: Hired from Dutch owners in June and
converted to a M/S. Commissioned with a Dutch Crew. 1944: Commissioned with
a RN Crew. 1945: Returned to Holland in November.

ENCORE   1917/19   Displacement: 164TG 65TN
                                     Engines: 40HP = 10K
                                     Armament: None
                                     Admty No: Not issued
                                     Port Reg: H. 523
1900: Launched. Built at Hull by CWG. Iron construction. Owned by Great Northern
Steam Ship FCL of Hull. 1917: Requisitioned into the Fishery Reserve. 1919: Returned
to owners. 1936: BU.

ENDEAVOUR   1915/18   Displacement: 156TG
                                     Port Reg: A. 403
1915: Requisitioned in June and converted to a BDV. 1918: LOST. Sunk in a collision
off Kirkwall on 18th March.

ENDON   1915/19   Displacement: 235TG   235TN
Engines: 51HP
Armament: 1 x 6pdrAA
Admty No: 1371
Port Reg: H. 161

1914: Launched. Built at Middlesborough by Smith's Dock. Owned by the Hull SF & Ice Co of Hull. 1915: Requisitioned in April and converted to a M/S. 1919: Returned to owners.

ENDYMION   1917/19   Displacement: 164TG   65TN
Engines: 40HP = 10K
Port Reg: H. 519

1900: Launched. Built at Hull by CWG. Iron construction. Owned by Great Northern Steam Ship FCL of Hull. 1917: Requisitioned into the Fishery Reserve. 1918: Acquired by Alliance SFC of Hull. Acquired by R. Scotter & R. Cammish of Hull. 1919: Returned to owners. 1934: BU.

ENGLISH ROSE   1914/19   Displacement: 188TG   82TN
Engines: 25HP
Armament: 1 x 6pdrAA
Admty No: 229
Port Reg: YH. 80

1914: Launched. Built at Selby by Cochrane. Owned by R. Sutton of Gt. Yarmouth. Requisitioned in September and converted to a M/S. 1919: Returned to owners.

ENNERDALE   1917/19   Displacement: 183TG
Admty No: Not issued
Port Reg: H. 769

1903: Launched. 1917: Requisitioned into the Fishery Reserve. 1919: Returned to owners.

ENVOY   1918/19   Displacement: 150TG   63TN
Engines: 45HP
Port Reg: FD. 23

1895: Launched. Built at Govan. Owned by Scarisbrick ST (Fleetwood) Ltd. 1918: Requisitioned. 1919: Returned to owners.

EPINE   1939/46   Ex-*Solway Firth*
Displacement: 358TG   154TN
Engines: 96HP = 10.8K
Port Reg: GY. 7
P.No: FY. 682

1929: Launched. Built at Beverley by CWG. Owned by J. Stewart TCL of Hull. PR: H.107. 1931: Acquired by Firth STC of Hull in January. Acquired by HW Hall of Hull

in June. 1939: Acquired by Premier SFC of Grimsby in January. Renamed *Epine*.
PR: GY. 7. Requisitioned in September and converted to a M/S. 1946: Returned to
owners in January. 1948: Mercantile Loss. Wrecked on the W. Coast of Iceland with
the loss of 14 lives and 5 saved.

EPWORTH	1914/17	Displacement: 223TG 88TN
		Engines: 51HP
		Armament: 1 x 3pdr
		Admty No: 379
		Port Reg: H. 386

1912: Launched. Built at Selby by Cochrane. Owned by the Great Northern SFC of Hull.
1914: Requisitioned in November and converted to a M/S. 1917: LOST. Sunk in a
collision off the E. Coast on 22nd May.

EQUATOR	1915/19	Displacement: 168TG 66TN
		Engines: 40HP
		Armament: 1 x 6pdr
		Admty No: 836
		Port Reg: H. 463

1899: Launched. Built at Govan. 1914: Requisitioned in December and converted to a
M/S. 1918: Returned to owners in November. Acquired by H. Wood of Grimsby. PR:
GY. 1260.

EQUERRY	1939/45	Ex-*Lady Eleanor*
		Displacement: 369TG 179TN
		Engines: 96HP = 10.8K
		Port Reg: GY. 375
		P.No: FY. 668

1929: Launched. Built at Beverley by CWG as *Lady Eleanor*. Owned by Jutland
Amalgamated Trs of Hull. PR: H.50. 1937: Acquired by Loyal SFC of Grimsby and
renamed *Equerry*. PR: GY. 375. 1939: Requisitioned in August and converted to a
M/S. 1943: SO of the 34th M/S Group based at Grimsby. 1945: Returned to
owners in October. 1957: BU on the Tyne by CW Dorkin.

EQUINOX	1915/16	Ex-*Catulus*
		Displacement: 198TG
		Armament: 1 x 3pdr
		Admty No: 3353
		Port Reg: GY. 461

1899: Launched. 1915: Requisitioned in June. Returned to the Fishing Fleet in
August. 1916: Mercantile Loss. Mined 39 miles SE x E from the Humber LV on 25th
August.

EQUITY   1917/19   Displacement: 158TG   63TN
                                           Engines: 45HP
                                           Port Reg: H. 315
1896: Launched. Built at Govan. Iron construction. Owned by the Icelandic Fisheries
Ltd. of Grimsby. 1917: Requisitioned into the Fishery Reserve. 1919: Returned to
owners.

ERA   1914/16   Displacement: 168TG
                                           Armament: 1 x 3pdr
                                           Admty No: 406
                                           Port Reg: H. 461
1899: Launched. 1914: Requisitioned in October and converted to a M/S. 1916:
LOST. Sunk by gunfire from German S/Ms U-46, U-49, U-52 and U-69 100 miles E.
of Aberdeen on 11th July. She, ICW Trs NELLIE NUTTEN and ONWARD, were
escorting a Fishing Fleet when they were attacked by the S/Ms and all three escorts
were sunk.

ERIC STROUD   1915/19   Displacement: 213TG   79TN
                                           Engines: 57HP
                                           Armament: 1 x 6pdr; 1 x 7.5-inch Bomb
                                           Thrower (A/S Howitzer)
                                           Admty No: 1184
                                           Port Reg: A. 90
1914: Launched. Built at Aberdeen. Owned by Strouds SFC of Aberdeen. 1915:
Requisitioned in March and converted to a M/S. 1919: Returned to owners.

ERIDANUS   1944/44   See under PELICAN II

ERILLUS   1915/19 1939/40 Displacement: 201TG   78TN
                                           Engines: 68HP
                                           Armament: 1 x 6pdr
                                           Admty No: 1403
                                           Port Reg: GY. 234
1914: Launched. Built at Middlesborough by Smith's Dock. Owned by Consolidated
Fisheries of Grimsby. 1915: Requisitioned in March and converted to a M/S. 1919:
Returned to owners. 1939: Requisitioned in November and designated as an APV.
1940: Returned to owners in January.

ERIMO   1939/45   Displacement: 265TG   104TN
                                           Engines: 84HP
                                           Armament: 1 x 12pdr
                                           Port Reg: GY. 288
                                           P.No: FY. 569
1930: Launched. Built at Selby by Cochrane. Owned by the Diamonds SFC of Grimsby.

1939: Requisitioned in August and converted to a M/S. 1945: Returned to owners in August.

ERIN   1914/15   Displacement: 181TG 62TN
                                             Engines: 46HP = 10K
                                             Admty No: 381
                                             Port Reg: H. 757
1903: Launched. Built at Beverley by CWG. Owned by Great Northern SFC of Hull.
1914: Requisitioned in September and converted to a M/S. 1915: Renamed ERIN
II in February. LOST. Mined off the Nab on 19th October with the loss of 7 lives.

ERIN   1940/42   Ex-*Sheffield Wednesday*
                                             Football Group
                                             Displacement: 394TG
1933: Launched.   Owned by Consolidated Fisheries of Grimsby.   1940:
Requisitioned, renamed and converted to A/S. Joined the 7th A/S Group based at
Gibraltar. 1942: LOST. Sunk at Gibraltar on 11th January. Whilst alongside, the
middle of three trawlers, she blew up. The inboard vessel, HONJO, was destroyed
and the outboard one, IMPERIALIST, was badly damaged. Speculation put the
cause of the explosion on either Italian Frogmen or a bomb planted in her depth
charges by a Spanish saboteur.

ERIN II   1914/15   See under ERIN of 1914

ERITH   1940/45   See under THOMAS ATKINSON
                                             (See Addenda p.530)

ERMINE   1915/19   Displacement: 181TG 71TN
                                             Engines: 46HP = 10K
                                             Armament: 1 x 3pdr
                                             Admty No: 1776
                                             Port Reg: H. 753
1903: Launched. Built at Beverley by CWG. Owned by the Great Northern Steam Ship
FCL of Hull. 1915: Requisitioned in May. 1918: Acquired by Hull SF & Ice of Hull. 1919:
Returned to owners. 1952: BU at Grays.

ERNA   1915/19 1940/46 Displacement: 330TG 135TN
                                             Engines: 94HP
                                             Armament: 1 x 6pdrAA; 24 mines (As a
                                             M/L)
                                             Admty No: 1586
                                             Port Reg: FD. 158
                                             P.No: WWII: Z. 112
1915: Launched. Built at Aberdeen. Owned by the New Docks STC of Fleetwood.

Requisitioned in May and converted to a M/L. Subsequently converted to a M/S. 1920: Returned to owners. Acquired by Clifton STL of Fleetwood. 1940: Requisitioned in May and converted to a BDV. 1946: Returned to owners.

ERNE   1914/18   Displacement: 168TG 66TN
Engines: 40HP
Armament: 1 x 3pdr
Admty No: 405
Port Reg: H. 465

1899: Built at Govan. 1914: Requisitioned in October and converted to a M/S. 1918: Returned to owners in November. Acquired by H. Wood of Grimsby. PR: GY.1237.

ERNE   1920/22   See under JOHN CHIVERS
(Vol 1 p.62)

EROICAN   1915/19 1940/45 Displacement: 225TG 112TN
Engines: 68HP = 9.5K
Armament: 1 x 3pdr
Admty No: 294
Port Reg: GY. 35
P. No: WWII: FY. 518 (M/S)
Y. 144(Esso)

1914: Launched. Built at Beverley by CWG. Owned by North Western SFC of Grimsby. Requisitioned in August and converted to a M/S. 1920: Returned to owners . 1937: Acquired by Dominion SFC of Grimsby. 1940: Requisitioned in April and converted to a D/L. 1941: Based at Grimsby. 1942: Converted to a M/S. 1944: Converted to an Esso. 1945: Returned to owners in February. 1961: BU in Holland.

EROS   1914/17   Displacement: 286TG 122TN
Engines: 70HP = 11K
Admty No: 698
Port Reg: GY. 284

1907: Launched. Built at Beverley by CWG. Owned by Roberts & Ruthven of Grimsby. 1914: Requisitioned in December and converted to a M/S. 1917: LOST. Mined off Felixstowe on 5th September.

EROS   1917/18   Displacement: 181TG 62TN
Engines: 46HP = 10K
Armament: None
Admty No: Not Issued
Port Reg: H. 768

1903: Launched. Built at Beverley by CWG. Owned by Great Northern Steam Ship FCL of Hull. 1917: Requisitioned into the Fishery Reserve. 1918: LOST. Mined in the North Sea on 8th June with the loss of 6 lives.

ESCALLONIA 1914/19 Displacement: 285TG 123TN
Engines: 80HP = 10.5K
Armament: 1 x 12pdr
Admty No: 43
Port Reg: GY. 631

1911: Launched. Built at Beverley by CWG. Owned by the North Eastern SFC of Grimsby. 1914: Requisitioned in March and converted to a M/S. 1919: Returned to owners. 1938: BU.

ESCORT 1915/20 Displacement: 165TG
Port Reg: H. 33

1897: Launched. 1915: Purchased into the RN in September and converted to a BDV. 1920: Sold to mercantile.

ESHER 1915/19 Displacement: 235TG 92TN
Engines: 70HP
Armament: 1 x 3pdr
Admty No: 1754
Port Reg: H. 163

1914: Launched. Built at Middlesborough by Smith's Dock. Owned by the Great Northern SFC of Hull. 1915: Requisitioned and converted to a M/S. 1919: Returned to owners.

ESKE 1916/19 Displacement: 290TG 119TN
Engines: 70HP
Armament: 1 x 6pdrAA; 1 x 7.5-inch
Bomb Thrower (A/S Howitzer)
Admty No: 1225
Port Reg: H. 859

1906: Launched. Built at Selby by Cochrane. Owned by JH. Collinson of Hull. 1915: Requisitioned in February and converted to a M/S. 1919: Returned to owners.

ESMERALDA 1918/19 Displacement: 181TG 71TN
Engines: 46HP = 10K
Armament: None
Admty No: Not Issued
Port Reg: H. 747

1903: Launched. Built at Beverley by CWG. Owned by Great Northern Steam Ship FCL of Hull. 1918: Requisitioned into the Fishery Reserve. 1919: Returned to owners. 1937: BU.

ESSEX 1914/19 Displacement: 220TG 105TN
Engines: 54HP

Armament: 1 x 6pdrAA
Admty No: 142
Port Reg: M. 193

1906: Launched. Built at North Shields. Owned by W. Wolfe AO of Milford Haven. 1914: Requisitioned in August and converted to a M/S. 1915: Renamed ESSEX II in February. 1919: Returned to owners.

ESSEX	1918/19	Displacement: 180TG 72TN
		Engines: 48HP
		Armament: 1 x 6pdrAA
		Admty No: 3329
		Port Reg: H. 762

1903: Launched. Built at Govan. 1918: Requisitioned in March and converted to a M/S. Renamed ESSEX III in April. 1919: Returned to owners. Acquired by C. Dobson of Grimsby. PR: GY.130.

| ESSEX II | 1914/19 | See under ESSEX 1906 |

| ESSEX III | 1918/19 | See under ESSEX 1903 |

| ESTRELLA d'ALVA | 1940/42 | See under SIR JAMES RECKITT |

ESTRELLA do MAR	1940/46	Displacement: 327TG
		Armament: 1 x 12pdr
		Port Reg: Portuguese
		P. No: FY. 1916

1914: Launched. Portuguese fishing vessel. 1940: Purchased into the RN from Portuguese owners and converted to a M/S. 1942: Renamed DUSK. 1946: Sold to mercantile and renamed *Akbari*.

| ESTRELLA do NORTE | 1940/42 | See under DANIEL MUNRO |
| | | (Vol 1 p.133) |

ETHEL	1915/19	Displacement: 278TG 109TN
		Engines: 76HP
		Armament: 1 x 6pdr
		Admty No: 1595
		Port Reg: FD. 173

1907: Launched. Built at Goole by Goole SB. Owned by the Active SFC of Fleetwood. 1915: Requisitioned in June and converted to a M/S. 1919: Returned to owners.

| ETHEL NUTTEN | 1917/19 | Displacement: 182TG 70TN |
| | | Engines: 67HP |

Armament: 1 x 6pdrAA
Admty No: 3333
Port Reg: GN. 59

1906: Launched. Built at Aberdeen. Owned by J. Inglis of Peebles. 1917: Requisitioned in March and converted to a M/S. 1919: Returned to owners.

ETHEL TAYLOR   1940/40   See under JAMES HUNNIFORD
(Vol 1 p.58)

ETHELWULF   1914/15   Displacement: 185TG
Admty No: 286
Port Reg: SN. 344

1903: Launched. 1914: Requisitioned in August and converted to a M/S. 1915: Returned to the Fishing Fleet in January. 1918: Mercantile Loss on 1st December.

ETNA   1917/18   Displacement: 189TG 74TN
Engines: 56HP
Armament: 1 x 6pdr
Admty No: 1276
Port Reg: H. 940

1907: Launched. Built at Govan. Owned by the Great Northern Steam Ship SFC of Hull. 1917: Requisitioned in March. 1918: Returned to owners in December.

ETOILE POLAIRE   1915/15   Displacement: 278TG
Armament: 1 x 3pdr
Admty No: 1402
Port Reg: French

?: Launched. French fishing vessel. 1915: Hired in March. LOST. Mined off the South Goodwin LV. on 3rd December.

ETON   1915/19   Displacement: 165TG 95TN
Engines: 45HP
Armament: 1 x 6pdr
Port Reg: H. 380

1897: Launched. Built at Govan. 1915: Requisitioned in September and converted to a BDV. 1919: Returned to owners. Acquired by W. Brown of Leith. PR: GN. 88.

ETRURIA   1940/46   Ex-*Lady Elsa*
Displacement: 376TG 158TN
Engines: 96HP = 11K
Port Reg: GY. 365
P.No: Z. 187 (BDV)

1930: Launched. Built at Beverley by CWG as *Lady Elsa*. Owned by Jutland

Amalgamated Trs. of Hull. PR: H. 287. 1937: Acquired by Great Grimsby & East Coast SFC of Grimsby and renamed *Etruria*. PR: GY. 365. 1939: Suffered damage from enemy a/c bombs to the SE of Duncansby Head, Scotland. 1940: Requisitioned in May and converted to an APV. 1941: Converted to a BDV in November. 1946: Returned to owners. 1953: BU at Antwerp, Belgium.

ETRURIAN   1914/19   Displacement: 186TG 75TN
                                     Engines: 52HP
                                     Armament: 1 x 6pdr
                                     Admty No: 669
                                     Port Reg: BN. 85

1900: Launched. Built at North Shields. Owned by the Boston DSF & Ice Co of Boston, Lincs. 1914: Requisitioned in November and converted to a M/S. 1919: Returned to owners.

ETRUSCAN   1915/19 1939/44 Displacement: 202TG 90TN
                                     Engines: 67HP = 10K
                                     Armament: 1 x 6pdr
                                     Admty No: 1882
                                     Port Reg: GY. 939
                                     P. No: WWII: FY. 584

1913: Launched. Built at Beverley by CWG Owned by T. Robinson of Grimsby. 1915: Requisitioned in September and converted to a M/S. 1919: Returned to owners. 1939: Requisitioned in November and converted to an APV. Based at Grimsby. 1940: Converted to a M/S in June. 1944: Converted to an Esso in April. Returned to owners in November. 1945: Mercantile Loss. Posted missing in December with 11 crew.

ETTRICK   1920/26   See under SAMUEL JAMESON
                                     (Vol 1 p.147)

EUCLASE   1940/46   Displacement: 295TG 131TN
                                     Engines: 89HP = 11.2HP
                                     Armament: 1 x 12pdr
                                     Port Reg: H. 384
                                     P.No: FY. 1636

1931: Launched. Built at Beverley. Owned by the Kingston STC of Hull. 1940: Requisitioned in February and converted to a M/S. 1946: Returned to owners in April. 1953: Mercantile Loss. Wrecked on 22nd September near Duncansby Head, Scotland.

EUDOCIA   1918/19   Displacement: 147TG 62TN
                                     Engines: 45HP = 10K
                                     Armament: None

Admty No: Not Issued
Port Reg: A. 205

1891: Launched. Built at Hull by CWG. Owned by C. Hellyer of Hull. PR: H.130.
1914: Acquired by T. Lauder of Aberdeen. PR: A. 205. 1917: Requisitioned into the
Fishery Reserve. Acquired by H. Smethurst of Grimsby. PR: GY. 1049. 1919:
Returned to owners. 1950: BU by Wards at Preston.

EUREKA	1915/22	Displacement: 165TG
		Armament: 1 x 6pdrAA
		Port Reg: H. 373

1897: Launched. 1915: Requisitioned in September and converted to a BDV. 1916:
Purchased into the RN. 1922: Sold to mercantile.

EURIPEDES	1915/19	Displacement: 307TG 120TN
		Engines: 84HP
		Armament: 2 x 6pdrs
		Admty No: 1740
		Port Reg: H. 959

1907: Launched. Built at Govan. Owned by the City SFC of Hull. 1915:
Requisitioned in July and converted to an Escort vessel. 1919: Returned to owners.

EUSTON	1915/17	Displacement: 209TG
		Armament: 1 x 3pdr
		Admty No: 1589
		Port Reg: FD. 67

1906: Launched. 1915: Requisitioned in June and converted to a M/S. 1917: LOST.
Mined off Hartlepool on 12th February.

EUTHAMIA	1917/18	Displacement: 142TG
		Admty No: Not issued
		Port Reg: GY. 285

1890: Launched. Owned by North Eastern SFC of Grimsby. 1917: Requisitioned
into the Fishery Reserve. 1918: LOST. Mined 65 miles E x N from the Humber LV
on 22nd September.

EVADNE	1915/17	Displacement: 189TG 74TN
		Engines: 56HP
		Armament: 1 x 3pdr
		Admty No: 148
		Port Reg: H. 945

1907: Launched. Built at Govan. Owned by the Great Northern SFC of Hull. 1914:
Requisitioned in September and converted to a M/S. 1917: LOST. Mined off the
Owens LV. on 27th February.

EVANGEL   1916/17   Displacement: 197TG
                                         Armament: 1 x 6pdr
                                         Admty No: 1408
                                         Port Reg: GY. 970
1914: Launched. 1915: Requisitioned in March and converted to a M/S. 1917: LOST.
Mined off Milford Haven on 25th March.

EVA WALES   1915/19 1939/45 Displacement: 251TG 101TN
                                         Engines: 77HP
                                         Armament: 1 x 12pdr
                                         Admty No: 966
                                         Port Reg: WWI: FD. 85; WWII: A. 327
                                         P. No: WWII: FY. 1529
1915: Launched. Built at Goole by Goole SB. Owned by the Red Rose STL of
Fleetwood. Requisitioned in January and converted to a M/S. Fitted with Listening
Hydrophones. 1919: Returned to owners. Acquired by the North Star SFC of
Aberdeen. 1939: Requisitioned in September as AVONSTREAM and converted to
a M/S. 1945: Returned to owners in July.

EVILINA   1939/39   See under JOHN HOWARD
                                         (Vol 1 p.180)

EVELINE   1940/42   Displacement: 206TG
                                         Port Reg: Dutch
                                         P.No: FY. 756
1912: Launched. Dutch fishing vessel. 1940: Hired from Dutch owners in July and
converted to a M/S. Commissioned with a Dutch Crew. 1942: LOST. Sunk in a
collision off Milford Haven on 27th January.

EVELINE NUTTEN   1915/19   Displacement: 183TG 78TN
                                         Engines: 67HP
                                         Armament: 1 x 6pdrAA
                                         Admty No: 1581
                                         Port Reg: A. 286
1915: Launched. Built at Aberdeen. Owned by EC. Nutten of Aberdeen. Requisitioned
in May and converted to a M/S. 1919: Returned to owners.

EVELYN   1914/19   Displacement: 235TG 92TN
                                         Engines: 56HP
                                         Armament: 1 x 6pdrAA
                                         Admty No: 121
                                         Port Reg: FD. 59
1906: Launched. Built at Goole by Goole SB. Owned by J. Marr & Sons of Fleetwood.
1914: Requisitioned in August and converted to a M/S. 1919: Returned to owners.

EVELYN ROSE   1939/45   See under WILLIAM JACKSON
                                      (Vol 1 p.149)

EVEREST   1914/19   Displacement: 189TG 74TN
                                      Engines: 56HP
                                      Armament: 1 x 6pdr; 1 x 7.5-inch Bomb
                                      Thrower (A/S Howitzer)
                                      Admty No: 43, 656 & 385
                                      Port Reg: H. 942
1907: Launched. Built at Govan. Owned by Hull SF & Ice Co. 1914: Requisitioned
in September. 1919: Returned to owners.

EVERGREEN   1917/19   Displacement: 180TG 70TN
                                      Engines: 48HP
                                      Port Reg: H. 718
1902: Launched. Built at Govan. Owned by T. Crimlick of Filey & B. Simpson Jnr.
of Scarborough. 1917: Requisitioned into the Fishery Reserve. 1919: Returned to
owners.

EVERTON   1915/19 1939/46 Displacement: 239TG 90TN
                                      Engines: 51HP
                                      Armament: 1 x 6pdrAA
                                      Admty No: 1515
                                      Port Reg: WWI: H. 297; WWII: LO. 188
                                      P. No: WWII: FY. 1645
1915: Launched. Built at Selby by Cochrane. Owned by the Great Northern Steam
Ship SFC of Hull. Requisitioned in May and converted to a M/S. 1919: Returned to
owners. Acquired by Heward Trs. of London. PR: LO. 188. 1939: Requisitioned in
December and converted to an APV. Based at Grimsby. 1946: Returned to owners
in March.

EVESHAM   1915/19 1939/41. Displacement: 239TG 90TN
                                      Engines: 51HP
                                      Armament: 1 x 6pdrAA
                                      Admty No: 1544
                                      Port Reg: H. 306
1915: Launched. Built at Selby by Cochrane. Owned by the Hull SF & Ice Co.
Requisitioned in June. 1919: Returned to owners. 1939: Requisitioned in
December and converted to an APV. 1941: LOST. Sunk by enemy a/c off Gt.
Yarmouth on 27th May. Wreck subsequently salvaged. 1946: BU at Troon in April.

EWALD   1940/45   Displacement: 209TG
                                      Port Reg: Dutch
                                      P.No: FY. 1733

1913: Launched. Dutch fishing vessel. 1940: Hired from Dutch owners and converted to a M/S. Commissioned with a Dutch Crew. 1945: Returned to Holland.

EXCEL II   1915/17   Displacement: 157TG
1895: Launched. 1915: Requisitioned. 1917: Returned to owners.

EXCELLENT   1915/19   Displacement: 103TG
1907: Launched. 1915: Requisitioned and converted to a BDV. 1919: Returned to owners.

EXE   1920/26   See under THOMAS JARVIS
                                                 (See Addenda p.531)

EXETER   1917/19   Displacement: 165TG 64TN
                                                 Engines: 45HP
                                                 Admty No: Not issued
                                                 Port Reg: GY. 426
1897: Launched. Built at Govan. Owned by Consolidated Fisheries of Grimsby. 1917: Requisitioned into the Fishery Reserve. 1919: Returned to owners.

EXMOUTH   1914/19   Displacement: 236TG
                                                 Armamont: 1 x 3pdr
                                                 Admty No: 146
                                                 Port Reg: BL. 16
1912: Launched. 1914: Requisitioned in August and converted to a M/S. 1915: Renamed EXMOUTH II in February. Employed as a M/S Training Ship. 1919: Returned to owners.

EXMOUTH II   1915/19   See under EXMOUTH above

EXPERT   1914/19   Displacement: 156TG 64TN
                                                 Engines: 45HP
                                                 Port Reg: A. 521
1894: Launched. Built at Porthleven by Kitto Iron construction. Owned by RF. Scotter & R. Cammish of Filey. 1914: Requisitioned in September and converted to a BDV. 1919: Returned to owners.

EXYAHNE   1915/19 1939/45 Displacement: 226TG 113TN
                                                 Engines: 68HP = 9.5K
                                                 Armament: 1 x 12pdr
                                                 Admty No: 264
                                                 Port Reg: GY. 150
                                                 P.No: WWII: FY. 878
1914: Launched. Built at Beverley by CWG. Owned by Marshall Line SFC of Grimsby.

1915: Requisitioned in September and converted to a M/S. Acquired by Savoy SFC of Grimsby. 1919: Returned to owners. 1937: Acquired by T. Robinson & Sons of Grimsby. 1939: Requisitioned in November and converted to a M/S. 1945: Returned to owners in December. 1961: BU in Holland.

FAIR ISLE   1914/14   1917/20   Displacement: 192TG
                                           Armament: 1914: 1 x 6pdr;
                                           1917: 1 x 6pdrAA
                                           Admty No: 263
                                           Port Reg: 1914: GN. 70   1917: GN. 94

1909: Launched. Built at Aberdeen. Owned by R. Bell of Newhaven. 1914: Requisitioned in August and converted to a M/S. LOST. Wrecked in Sinclair Bay on 26th December. 1917: Salvaged and reacquired in April. Re-armed and re-registered as above and fitted out as a M/S. Renamed FAIR ISLE II in May. 1920: Returned to owners.

FAIR ISLE II   1917/20   See under FAIR ISLE above

FAIRVIEW   1914/19   Displacement: 187TG   71TN
                                           Engines: 68HP
                                           Armament: 2 x 6pdrs
                                           Admty No: 266
                                           Port Reg: GN. 71

1909: Launched. Built at Aberdeen. Owned by John Inglis of Peebles. 1914: Requisitioned in August and converted to a M/S. 1919: Returned to owners.

FAIRWAY   1940/46   See under RICHARD JEWELL
                                           (Vol 1 p.146)

FAITH   1917/19   Displacement: 135TG   56TN
                                             Engines: 50HP
                                           Admty No: Not Issued
                                           Port Reg: A. 55

1891: Launched. Built at Kinghorn. Owned by JR. Ditchburn of Whitby AO. 1918: Requisitioned into the Fishery Reserve. 1919: Returned to owners.

FALCON   1917/19   Displacement: 154TG   65TN
                                             Engines: 50HP
                                             Admty No: Not issued
                                             Port Reg: GY. 798

1895: Launched. Built at Beverley. Owned by HL. Taylor of Grimsby. 1917: Requisitioned into the Fishery Reserve. 1919: Returned to owners.

FALMOUTH   1914/15   Displacement: 187TG
                                             Admty No: 152
                                             Port Reg: BL.12

1909: Launched. 1914: Requisitioned in August and converted to a M/S. 1915: Renamed FALMOUTH III in April. LOST. Mined off Deal on 19th November.

FALMOUTH	1914/19	Displacement: 165TG 64TN
		Engines: 45HP
		Armament: 1 x 6pdr
		Admty No: 769
		Port Reg: GY.428

1897: Launched. Built at Govan. Owned by Consolidated Fisheries of Grimsby. 1914: Requisitioned in December. 1915: Renamed FALMOUTH II in February. 1919: Returned to owners.

| FALMOUTH II | 1915/19 | See under FALMOUTH of 1897 |

| FALMOUTH III | 1915/15 | See under FALMOUTH of 1909 |

FALSTAFF	1915/19	Displacement: 173TG 68TN
		Engines: 45HP
		Armament: 1 x 3pdr
		Admty No: 1795
		Port Reg: H. 917

1906: Launched. Built at Beverley. Owned by Hellyers SFC of Hull. 1915: Requisitioned in October and converted to a M/S. 1919: Returned to owners.

FANCY	1917/19	Displacement: 53TG 27TN
		Admty No: Not issued
		Port Reg: YH. 376

1899: Launched. Built at Lowestoft by Chambers. Owned by RJ Ball of Gt. Yarmouth. 1917: Requisitioned into the Fishery Reserve. 1919: Returned to owners. *Notes*: Also listed in some mercantile registers as a drifter.

FANE	1914/19	Displacement: 269TG 108TN
		Engines: 85HP
		Armament: 1 x 6pdrAA
		Admty No: 132
		Port Reg: FD. 94

1907: Launched. Built at South Shields. 1914: Requisitioned in August and converted to a M/S. 1919: Returned to owners. Acquired by G. Craig of Aberdeen. PR: A.184.

FANE	1939/45	Displacement: 310TG 119TN
		Engines: 85HP
		Port Reg: GY. 539
		P.No: FY. 575

1930: Launched. Built at Southbank-on-Tees by Smith's Dock. Owned by the Earl SFC of Grimsby. 1939: Requisitioned in August and converted to a M/S. Renamed SNAKEFLY in October. 1945: Returned to owners in October.

FARADAY 1917/19 1939/41 Displacement: 322TG 131TN
 Engines: 86HP
 Armament: WWI: 1 x 12pdr;
 WWII: 1 x 6pdr
 Admty No: 3312
 Port Reg: H. 490

1916: Launched. Built at Selby by Cochrane. Owned by F&T Ross of Hull. Requisitioned in November and converted to a M/S. 1919: Returned to owners. 1939: Requisitioned in December and converted to an APV. 1941: Renamed FRANCOLIN. LOST. Sunk by enemy a/c off Cromer on 12th November.

FASTNET 1933/42 See under BENJAMIN HAWKINS
 (Vol 1 p.131)

FAVORITA 1917/19 Displacement: 314TG 162TN
 Engines: 87HP
 Armament: 1 x 12pdr
 Admty No: 1655
 Port Reg: GY. 1039

1916: Launched. Built at Selby by Cochrane. Owned by Consolidated Fisheries of Grimsby. 1917: Requisitioned in December and converted to a M/S. 1919: Returned to owners.

FAWN 1917/19 Displacement: 210TG 88TN
 Engines: 50HP
 Admty No: Not issued
 Port Reg: GY.1008

1898: Launched. Built at Hull. Iron construction. Owned by JL. Green of Grimsby. 1918: Requisitioned into the Fishery Reserve. 1919: Returned to owners.

FELICIA 1917/19 Displacement: 75TG
 Admty No: Not issued
 Port Reg: SN. 73

1908: Launched. 1917: Requisitioned into the Fishery Reserve. 1919: Returned to owners.

FENTONIAN 1914/19 1939/45 Displacement: 221TG 99TN
 Engines: 70HP
 Armament: 1 x 6pdrAA
 Admty No: 448
 Port Reg: GY. 804
 P. No: WWII: FY. 868 (M/S);
 Y. 7.11 (Esso)

1913: Launched. Built at Selby by Cochrane. Owned by HC. Baker of Cleethorpes.

1915: Requisitioned in March and converted to a M/S. 1919: Returned to owners. Acquired by Robinson & Sons of Grimsby. 1939: Requisitioned in November and converted to an APV. 1940: Converted to a M/S in July. 1944: Converted to an Esso in March. 1945: Returned to owners in February.

FERMO   1917/19   Displacement: 175TG
                                           Admty No: Not issued
                                           Port Reg: GY0. 773
1898: Launched. 1918: Requisitioned into the Fishery Reserve. 1919: Returned to owners.

FERRIBY   1915/19 1940/42 Displacement: 324TG 128TN
                                           Engines: 84HP
                                           Armament: 1 x 12pdr
                                           Port Reg: H. 629
1913: Launched. Built at Goole. Owned by JH. Collinson of Hull. 1915: Requisitioned in May and converted to a M/S. 1919: Returned to owners. 1940: Requisitioned for the RNZN in August and converted to a M/S. 1942: LOST. Sunk in collision with *Warhine* on 19th December.

FEUGH   1917/19 1939/45 Displacement: 227TG 88TN
                                           Engines: 80HP
                                           Armament: 1 x 12pdr

FERRIBY (1915)   **(MPL)**

Admty No: 1278
Port Reg: WWI: A. 706; WWII: GY. 366
P.No: WWII: FY. 774

1916: Launched. Built at Selby by Cochrane. Owned by RW. Lewis of Aberdeen. 1917: Requisitioned in June and converted to a M/S. 1919: Returned to owners. Acquired by the Trawlers (White Sea & Grimsby) Ltd. and renamed *Berenga*. 1939: Requisitioned in November as BERENGA and converted to an APV. 1942: Converted to a BDV in June. 1945: Returned to owners in September.

FEZENTA   1915/19 1939/45 Displacement: 228TG 95TN
                                   Engines: 68HP
                                   Armament: 1 x 6pdrAA
                                   Admty No: 1362
                                   Port Reg: GY. 444
                                   P. No: WWII: FY. 587

1914: Launched. Built at Beverley by CWG. Owned by JL. Greene Ltd. of Grimsby. 1915: Requisitioned in March and converted to a M/S. 1919: Returned to owners. Acquired by the Onward SFC of Grimsby. Same PR. 1939: Requisitioned in November and converted to a M/S. 112th M/S Group. based at Grimsby. 1945: Returned to owners in November.

FIAT   1918/19   Displacement. 314TG 162TN
                                   Engines: 87HP
                                   Armament: 1 x 12pdr
                                   Admty No: 1650
                                   Port Reg: GY. 1040

1916: Launched. Built at Selby by Cochrane. Owned by Consolidated Fisheries of Grimsby. 1918: Requisitioned in January and converted to a M/S. 1919: Returned to owners.

FIDELIA   1917/19 1940/41 Displacement: 147TG 161TN
                                   Engines: 50HP
                                   Admty No: Not issued
                                   Port Reg: WWI: H. 177; WWII: LT. 187

1891: Launched. Built at Hull. Iron construction. Owned by F&T Ross of Hull. 1918: Requisitioned into the Fishery Reserve. 1919: Returned to owners. Acquired by Consolidated Fisheries of Grimsby. 1940: Purchased into the RN on 15th May and converted to a BDV. 1941: LOST. Sunk by enemy a/c at Lowestoft on 5th May.

FIELDGATE   1940/45   See under COLLINGWOOD

FIFESHIRE   1939/40   Shire Group
                                   Displacement: 540TG 198TN
                                   Engines: 99HP

166

Armament: 2 x LG (See below)
Port Reg: GY. 524

1938: Launched. Built at Southbank-on-Tees by Smith's Dock. Owned by Fifeshire SF (H. Markham) of Grimsby. 1939: Requisitioned in September and converted to A/S. Joined the 11th A/S Striking Force based at Rosyth. 1940: LOST. ICW sister-ship AYRESHIRE 70 miles E. of Copinsay on 20th February they were attacked by 2 x Heinkel 111s. She had not received her designated 4-inch gun and had only her two insignificant Lewis guns. In the first pass by the a/c she was struck by 2 bombs and rapidly sank leaving only 1 survivor. Her more heavily armed sister-ship survived the attack.

FIFENELLA   1917/19   Displacement: 314TG 161TN
                                    Engines: 87HP
                                    Armament: 1 x 6pdr
                                    Admty No: 1279
                                    Port Reg: GY. 1038

1916: Launched. Built at Selby by Cochrane. Owned by Consolidated Fisheries of Grimsby. 1917: Requisitioned in July and converted to a M/S. 1919: Returned to owners.

FILEY   1915/16 1917/20 Displacement: 226TG 87TN
                                Engines: 94HP = 11K
                                Armament: 1 x 12pdr
                                Admty No: 1915: 1363; 1917: 3826
                                Port Reg: H. 8

1913: Launched. Built at Beverley by CWG. Owned by Hull SF & Ice Co of Hull. 1915: Purchased into the RN in March. 1916: LOST. Wrecked in Camusmore Bay, Tory Island, on 2nd October. 1917: Salvaged in July and reacquired. 1920: Acquired by the original owners and re-registered H.191. 1936: Acquired by Heward Trs. Ltd. of London. PR: LO. 189. 1959: BU at Antwerp, Belgium.

FILEY BAY   1939/45   Ex-*Ross*
                                    Displacement: 370TG 152TN
                                    Engines: 96HP =10.7K
                                    Armament: 1 x 12pdr
                                    Port Reg: H. 27
                                    P.No: FY. 679

1931: Launched. Built at Beverley by CWG as Ross. Owned by Rugby SFC of Grimsby. PR: GY. 329. 1934: Acquired by Marine SFC of Hull and renamed *Filey Bay* PR: H. 27. 1939: Requisitioned in August and converted to a M/S. 19th M/S Group. based at Grimsby. 1945: Returned to owners in March. Acquired by Trawlers Grimsby Ltd. of Grimsby. PR: GY. 135. 1956: BU at Ghent, Belgium.

FINESSE   1942/46   See under TREVO TERCEIRO

FINLANDE	1940/46	Displacement: 344TG
		Armament: Unarmed
		Port Reg: French

1937: Launched. French fishing vessel. 1940: Seized off Newfoundland on 25th September. Designated for use by the Free French but laid up instead. 1941: Brought forward and transferred to the MWT in April. 1947: Struck from the Navy List.

FINTRAY	1940/45	See under NORTH QUEEN

FIREFLY	1939/45	Ex-*St.Just*
		Displacement: 394TG 176TN
		Engines: 96HP = 11.2K
		Port Reg: H. 320
		P. No: FY. 673

1930: Launched. Built at Beverley by CWG as *St. Just*. Owned by the St. Andrews SFC of Hull. 1939: Requisitioned in September, converted to a M/S and renamed FIREFLY. Fitted out at Harland & Wolff at Glasgow. Based at Belfast for sweeping off N. Ireland /N. Scotland. 1940: Detailed to sail from Leith to recover a floating mine off shore. She rolled heavily as the mine was at the derrick head and it struck the ship and exploded. 16 men were killed and everything above deck level was flattened but she remained afloat and was repaired. 1945: Returned to owners and reverted to original name. 1961: BU in Southern Ireland.

FISHERGATE	1915/19	Displacement: 205TG 77TN
		Engines: 52HP
		Armament: 1 x 6pdrAA
		Admty No: 969
		Port Reg: LO. 209

1905: Launched. Built at North Shields. Owned by the Phoenix TC of London. 1915: Requisitioned in February and converted to a M/S. 1919: Returned to owners.

FISHTOFT	1914/19	Displacement: 188TG 76TN
		Engines: 52HP
		Armament: 1 x 6pdr
		Admty No: 522
		Port Reg: BN. 94

1901: Launched. Built at North Shields. Owned by the Boston DSF & Ice Co of Boston, Lincs. 1914: Requisitioned in November and converted to a M/S. 1919: Returned to owners.

FLANDERS	1939/45	See under CHARLES ANTRIM
		(Vol 1 p.49)

FLANDRE   1915/19 1940/45 Displacement: 226TG 109TN
                                            Engines: 70HP
                                            Armament: 1 x 6pdr
                                            Admty No: 853
                                            Port Reg: GY. 589
                                            P. No: WWII: FY. 1715
1915: Launched. Built at Beverley by CWG. Owned by the Rushworth SFC of Grimsby.
Requisitioned in September and converted to a M/S. 1918: Returned to owners in
December. 1940: Requisitioned in June and converted to an APV. 1942: Converted to
a M/S in January. 1945: Returned to owners in March.

FLEETWING II   1917/19   Displacement: 119TG 51TN
                                            Engines: 40HP
                                            Admty No: Not issued
                                            Port Reg: A. 419
1896: Launched.   Built at Govan.   Owned by T. Davidson of Aberdeen.   1917:
Requisitioned into the Fishery Reserve. 1919: Returned to owners.

FLEETWOOD   1917/19   Displacement: 163TG
                                            Admty No: Not issued
                                            Port Reg: GY. 166
1896: Launched. 1917: Requisitioned into the Fishery Reserve. 1919: Returned to
owners.

FLEMING   1939/40   Displacement: 356TG 145TN
                                            Engines: 96HP
                                            Armament: 1 x 12pdr
                                            Port Reg: H. 3
1929: Launched. Built at Beverley by CWG. Owned by F&T. Ross of Hull. 1939:
Requisitioned in August and converted to a M/S. 1940: LOST. Sunk by enemy a/c in
the Thames Estuary on 24th June.

FLICKER   1915/16   Displacement: 192TG
                                            Armament: 1 x 3pdr
                                            Admty No: 413
                                            Port Reg: H. 334
1911: Launched. 1914: Requisitioned in November. 1916: LOST. Mined off Dover on
4th March.

FLINT CASTLE   1916/19   Displacement: 275TG 107TN
                                            Engines: 87HP
                                            Armament: 1 x 6pdrAA
                                            Admty No: 3315
                                            Port Reg: SA. 66

1916: Launched. Built at Southbank-on-Tees by Smith's Dock. Owned by Consolidated Fisheries of Grimsby. Requisitioned in December and converted to a M/S. 1919: Returned to owners.

FLINTSHIRE	1916/26	1939/45	Displacement: 215TG 100TN
			Engines: 87HP
			Armament: 1 x 6pdrAA; 1 x 7.5-inch
			Bomb Thrower (A/S Howitzer)
			Admty No: 3287
			Port Reg: WWI: GY. 875; WWII: GY. 389
			P. No: WWII: FY. 787

1919: Launched. Built at Selby by Cochrane. Owned by the North Lincolnshire SFC of Grimsby. Purchased into the RN in April and converted to a M/S. 1919: Employed on Mine Clearance in the North Sea. 1926: Sold to mercantile on 5th January. Purchased by the Diamond SF Co of Grimsby and renamed *Taipo*. 1939: Requisitioned in November as TAIPO. Converted to an APV. 1940: Converted to a M/S in May. Based at Grimsby (ungrouped). 1944: Converted to an Esso in April. Returned to owners in November. 1961: BU in Holland.

FLIXTON	1939/46	See under WILLIAM HARVEY (Vol 1 p.193)

FLORENCE BRIERLEY	1940/46	See under JOHN DUNN (Vol 1 p.140)

FLORENCE DOMBEY	1917/19	Ex-*Wyre*
		Displacement: 182TG 182TN
		Engines: 52HP
		Admty No: Not issued
		Port Reg: FD. 196

1900: Launched. Built at North Shields. Owned by R. Milne of Aberdeen. 1917: Requisitioned into the Fishery Reserve. 1918: Returned to owners in September.

FLORIO	1917/19	1939/45	Displacement: 314TG 162TN
			Engines: 87HP
			Armament: 1 x 12pdr
			Admty No: 1653
			Port Reg: GY. 1042
			P.No: WWII: FY. 988

1916: Launched. Built at Selby. Owned by Consolidated Fisheries of Grimsby. 1917: Requisitioned in October and converted to a M/S. 1919: Returned to owners. 1939: Requisitioned in August and converted to a M/S. 1945: Returned to owners in April.

FLY	1917/19	Displacement: 158TG 60TN
		Engines: 45HP

Admty No: Not issued
Port Reg: FD. 166

1890: Launched. Built at Beverley by CWG. Iron construction. Owned by the Active FCL of Fleetwood. 1917: Requisitioned into the Fishery Reserve. 1919: Returned to owners.

FLYING ADMIRAL	1940/41	See under JOHN BULLOCK (Vol 1 p.61)

FLYING WING	1915/19 1939/46	Displacement: 226TG 109TN
		Engines: 70HP
		Armament: 1 x 6pdrAA
		Admty No: 1958
		Port Reg: GY. 690
		P. No: WWII: FY. 880

1915: Launched. Built at Beverley by CWG. Owned by W. Baynton & W. Jagger of Grimsby. Requisitioned in November and converted to a M/S. 1919: Returned to owners. 1939: Requisitioned in November and converted to A/S. Subsequently purchased. 1941: Converted to a M/S in May. 1946: Sold to mercantile.

FOAMCREST	1939/46	See under TR.47 (Vol 1 p.82)

FONTENOY	1940/40	See under SIAM DUFFY (Vol 1 p.73)

FORCE	1940/41	See under JAMES BUCHANAN (Vol 1 p.136)

FORFEIT	1940/46	See under CORNELIAN of 1917

FORT ALBERT	1914/19	Displacement: 193TG 74TN
		Engines: 68HP
		Armament: 1 x 6pdrAA
		Admty No: 273
		Port Reg: A. 71

1906: Launched. Built at Aberdeen. 1914: Requisitioned in August and converted to a M/S. 1919: Returned to owners. Acquired by the County FCL of Lowestoft. PR: LT. 357. Acquired by T. Stephen of Aberdeen. PR: A. 932.

FORT EDWARD	1915/19	Displacement: 208TG 80TN
		Engines: 66HP
		Armament: 1 x 6pdr
		Admty No: 2654
		Port Reg: A. 180

1908: Launched. Built at Aberdeen. 1915: Requisitioned in April and converted to a M/S. 1919: Returned to owners. Acquired by Arthur Edwards Fisheries of Lowestoft.

FORT GEORGE	1917/19	Displacement: 180TG 69TN
		Engines: 62HP
		Armament: 1 x 6pdr
		Port Reg: GN. 77

1902: Launched. Built at Aberdeen. Owned by W. Lyle of Leith. 1917: Requisitioned in March and converted to a 'Q' Ship. Operated under the name of *Robina*. Reduced to the Fishery Reserve. 1919: Returned to owners in November.

| FORT ROBERT | 1939/45 | See under JAMES BENTOLE |
| | | (Vol 1 p.174) |

| FORT ROSE | 1940/45 | See under MATTHEW CROOKE |
| | | (Vol 1 p.182) |

FORT ROYAL	1939/40	Displacement: 351TG
		Armament: 1 x 12pdr
		P. No: FY. 711

1931: Launched. 1939: Requisitioned in August and converted to a M/S. Subsequently purchased into the RN. Formed a M/S Group ICW OHM, ROBERT BOWEN and THOMAS ALTOFT based at Aberdeen for sweeping off the N E. Coast of Scotland. 1940: LOST. The Group was sweeping approx. 20 miles NE of Aberdeen on 9th February when they were attacked by 2 x Heinkel 111s. In the second strike she was struck simultaneously by two bombs and sank in just three minutes.

FORT RYAN	1939/44	Displacement: 255TG 111TN
		Engines: 68HP
		Port Reg: A. 190
		P. No: Z. 156

1932: Launched. Built at Aberdeen. Owned by J. Lewis of Aberdeen. 1939: Requisitioned in September and converted to a BDV. 1944: Returned to owners in December.

FORTUNA	1917/19 1940/41	Displacement: 259TG 111TN
		Engines: 68HP
		Armament: WWI: 1 x 3pdr;
		WWII: 1 x 6pdr
		Admty No: Not issued
		Port Reg: WWI: GY. 1048; WWII: GY. 140

1906: Launched. Built at Beverley by CWG. Owned by Sleight of Grimsby. 1917: Requisitioned into the Fishery Reserve. 1919: Returned to owners. Acquired by Dobson Ship Repairing of Grimsby. 1940: Requisitioned in June and converted to an APV. 1941: LOST. Sunk by enemy a/c off St. Abbs Head on 3rd April.

| FORT WILLIAM | 1917/19 | Displacement: 188TG 69TN |
| | | Engines: 62HP |

Admty No: Not issued
Port Reg: GY. 712

1903: Launched.   Built at Aberdeen.   Owned by JL. Green of Grimsby.   1917: Requisitioned into the Fishery Reserve.   1919: Returned to owners.

FORWARD   1915/19   Displacement: 250TG 105TN
                                            Engines: 70HP
                                            Armament: 1 x 6pdr
                                            Admty No: 1409
                                            Port Reg: GY. 98

1906: Launched. Built at Selby by Cochrane. Owned by JG. Smith & AW. Green of Grimsby. 1915: Requisitioned in April and converted to a M/S. Renamed FORWARD II in May. 1919: Returned to owners. Retained the name of *Forward II*.

FORWARD II   1915/19   See under FORWARD

FORWARD HO   1915/19   Displacement: 269TG 107TN
                                            Engines: 78HP
                                            Armament: 1 x 6pdr
                                            Admty No: 1560
                                            Port Reg: H. 331

1915: Launched.   Built at North Shields.   Owned by ST. White & Co of Hull. Requisitioned in July and converted to a M/S. 1919: Returned to owners.

FOSDYKE   1914/19   Displacement: 245TG 95TN
                                            Engines: 88HP
                                            Armament: 1 x 6pdrAA
                                            Admty No: 35
                                            Port Reg: BN. 149

1908: Launched. Built at North Shields. Owned by the Boston DSF & Ice Co. of Boston, Lincs. 1914: Requisitioned in August and converted to a M/S. 1919: Returned to owners.

FOSS   1916/19 1940/46 Displacement: 275TG 108TN
                                            Engines: 88HP
                                            Armament: 1 x 12pdr
                                            Admty No: 3278
                                            Port Reg: FD. 243
                                            P.No: WWII: Z. 144

1916: Launched. Built at Southbank-on-Tees by Smith's Dock. Owned by the Wyre STC of Fleetwood. Requisitioned in May and converted to a M/S. 1919: Returned to owners. 1940: Requisitioned in January and converted to a BDV. 1946: Returned to owners in July.

FOYLE   1920/46   See under JOHN EDMUND
                                            (Vol 1 p.141)

FRANCOLIN   1941/41   See under FARADAY of 1917

FRANC TIREUR   1916/19 1940/43 Displacement: 314TG 162TN
                                        Engines: 87HP
                                        Armament: WWI: 1 x 6pdr:
                                        WWII: 1 x 12pdr
                                        Port Reg: GY. 1041
                                        P. No: WWII: 4. 70(APV);
                                        FY. 1560 (M/S)

1916: Launched. Built at Selby by Cochrane. Owned by Consolidated Fisheries of Grimsby. 1917: Requisitioned in June and converted to a M/S. 1919: Returned to owners. 1940: Requisitioned in May and converted to an APV. Based at Grimsby. 1941: Converted to a M/S. Joined the Harwich M/S Groups. 1943: LOST. Torpedoed by a German E-Boat whilst sweeping off Harwich on 29th September with the loss of 16 of her crew.

FRASCATI   1914/19   Displacement: 220TG 98TN
                                          Engines: 70HP
                                        Armament: 1 x 12pdr
                                        Admty No: 49
                                        Port Reg: GY. 315

1914: Launched. Built at Selby by Cochrane. Owned by the Strand SFC of Grimsby. Requisitioned in November and converted to a M/S. 1919: Returned to owners.

FRASER   1915/17   Displacement: 310TG 125TN
                                          Engines: 84HP
                                        Armament: 1 x 3pdr
                                        Admty No: 1379
                                        Port Reg: H. 951

1907: Launched. Built at Beverley by CWG. Owned by the Neptune of Hull. 1915: Requisitioned in April and converted to a M/S. 1917: LOST. Mined near Boulogne on 17th April.

FREESIA   1914/19   Displacement: 285TG 123TN
                                          Engines: 80HP
                                        Armament: 1 x 12pdr; 1 x 7.5-inch
                                        Bomb Thrower (A/S Howitzer)
                                        Admty No: 716
                                        Port Reg: GY. 633

1911: Launched. Built at Beverley by CWG. Owned by the North Eastern SFC of Grimsby. 1914: Requisitioned in December and converted to a M/S. 1919: Returned to owners.

FREYA   1914/19
1904: Launched. Owned by the Scottish Fisheries Board. 1914: Requisitioned in August and fitted out for the Examination Service. 1919: Returned to the Fisheries Board.

FRIARAGE   1940/45   Displacement: 210TG 94TN
                                           Engines: 69HP
                                           Armament: 1 x 6pdr
                                           Port Reg: HL.18
                                           P. No: FY. 904

1930: Launched. Built at Aberdeen. Owned by the Friargate SFC of Hartlepool. 1939: Requisitioned in September and converted for the Examination Service. Subsequently converted to an APV. 1945: Returned to owners in December.

FRIGATE BIRD II   1917/19   Displacement: 99TG
                                           Admty No: Not issued
                                           Port Reg: A. 769

1895: Launched. 1917: Requisitioned into the Fishery Reserve. 1919: Returned to owners.

FRIESLAND   1915/19   Displacement: 268TG 121TN
                                           Engines: 80HP
                                           Armament: 1 x 12pdr
                                           Port Reg: GY. 459

1899: Launched. Built at Dundee. Owned by the Zaree SFC of Grimsby. 1914: Requisitioned in December and converted to a M/S. 1919: Returned to owners.

FRIESLAND   1940/46   Displacement: 247TG
                                           Port Reg: German
                                           P.No: FY.1663

1921: Launched. German fishing vessel built in Germany. 1940: Captured in the North Sea in April. Added to the Navy List and converted to a M/S. Based at Belfast for operations in the Western Approaches. 1942: Placed in Quarantine at Belfast when typhoid broke out on board. The vessel was over-run by rats which had to be exterminated and the whole Company was landed for 24hrs whilst this operation was carried out. 1946: Sold to mercantile.

FUJI   1915/19 1940/45 Displacement: 255TG 100TN
                                           Engines: 82HP
                                           Armament: 1 x 12pdr
                                           Admty No: 2661
                                           Port Reg: CF. 40
                                           P.No: WWII: FY. 1779

1912: Launched. Built at Middlesborough by Smith's Dock. Owned by Neale & West of Cardiff. 1915: Requisitioned in May and converted to a M/S. 1919: Returned to owners. 1940: Hired from Dutch owners as GERBERDINA JOHANNA and converted to a M/S. 1945: Returned to owners.

FULMAR   1915/16   Displacement: 231TG
                                       Armament: 1 x 3pdr
                                       Admty No: 1756
                                       Port Reg: GY. 470

1899: Launched. 1915: Requisitioned in May. 1916: LOST. Mined in the Gulf of Sollum on 17th January.

FUTURIST   1940/45   RNZN
                                       Displacement: 234TG
                                       Port Reg: New Zealand

1920: Launched. 1940: Requisitioned in August and converted to a M/S. Commissioned into the RNZN. 1945: Returned to owners.

FYLDEA   1939/45   Displacement: 377TG 149TN
                                       Engines: 97HP
                                       Armament: 1 x 12pdr; 2 x MG (2x1)
                                       Port Reg: FD. 72
                                       P.No: FY. 666

1930: Launched. Built at Selby by Cochrane. Owned by J. Marr of Fleetwood. 1939: Requisitioned in September and converted to a M/S. 1945: Returned to owners in December.

CHAPTER 7 - GABIR to GWMAHO

GABIR   1916/18   Displacement: 219TG
      Admty No: 1486
      Port Reg: GY. 497

1909: Launched. Owned by A. Grant of Grimsby. 1915: Requisitioned in May and converted to a M/S. 1918: LOST. Mined off Lowestoft on 24th May.

GABY   1917/19   Displacement: 210TG
      Port Reg: O. 182

1909: Launched. 1917: Requisitioned into the Fishery Reserve with the permission of her Belgian owners. 1919: Returned to owners.

GADFLY   1939/45   See under DOMINICK ADDISON
      (Vol 1 p.51)

GADRA   1915/19 1939/40   Displacement: 219TG
      Armament: 1 x 6pdr
      Admty No: 1467
      Port Reg: GY. 484

1909: Launched. Owned by HC Baker & W. Grant of Grimsby. 1915: Requisitioned in April and converted to a M/S. 1919: Returned to owners. 1939: Requisitioned in November and designated as an APV. 1940: Returned to owners in January. 1941: Mercantile Loss. Mined 1.5 miles off Myling Head, Faroes, on 6th January.

GAELIC   1917/19   Displacement: 159TG
      Port Reg: GY. 245

1890: Launched. 1917: Requisitioned into Fishery Reserve. 1919: Returned to owners.

GALLINULE   1915/19 1939/40   Displacement: 238TG
      Armament: 1 x 6pdrAA
      Admty No: 908
      Port Reg: LL. 116

1907: Launched. 1915: Requisitioned in January and converted to a M/S. 1919: Returned to owners. 1939: Requisitioned in November and designated as an APV. 1940: Returned to owners in January.

GALVANI   1940/45   Displacement: 353TG
      Armament: 1 x 12pdr
      Port Reg: H
      P. No: 4. 71

1929: Launched. 1940: Requisitioned in June and converted to an APV. 1941: Converted to a M/S. Based at Lowestoft for sweeping off Cromer. 1945: Returned to owners in August.

GAMBRI   1917/18   Displacement: 274TG
                                       Armament: 1 x 6pdr
                                       Admty No: 1263
                                       Port Reg: GY. 992
1916: Launched. 1917: Requisitioned in April and converted to a M/S. 1918: LOST.
Mined off the Sovereign LV. on 18th January.

GAMECOCK   1914/19   Displacement: 171TG
                                       Armament: 1 x 6pdr
                                       Admty No: 419
                                       Port Reg: H. 810
1905: Launched. 1914: Requisitioned in November and converted to a M/S. 1919:
Returned to owners.

GANTON   1915/19   Displacement: 330TG
                                       Armament: 1 x 12pdr
                                       Admty No: 1524
                                       Port Reg: H. 110
1905: Launched. 1915: Requisitioned in May and converted to a M/S. 1919: Returned
to owners.

GARDENIA   1915/18   Displacement: 146TG
                                       Armament. 1 x 6pdrAA
                                       Admty No: 723
                                       Port Reg: GY. 402
1891: Launched. Owned by North Eastern SFC of Grimsby. 1914: Requisitioned in
December and converted to a M/S. 1919: Returned to owners in November.

GARMO   1914/14   Displacement: 203TG
                                       Admty No: 810
                                       Port Reg: GY. 1165
1900: Launched. 1914: Requisitioned in November and converted to an APV. LOST.
Mined off Scarborough on 20th December.

GARNET   1916/19 1940/46 Displacement: 251TG
                                       Armament: 1 x 6pdrAA
                                       Admty No: 3001
                                       Port Reg: H. 495
                                       P. No: WWII: FY. 1917
1916: Launched. 1917: Requisitioned in February and converted to a M/S. 1919:
Returned to owners. 1940: Hired from French owners in July as LOUISE et MARIE and
converted to a M/S. 1946: Returned to owners in January.

GAROLA   1914/19   1939/46   Displacement: 249TG   135TN
Engines: 75HP
Armament: WWI: 1 x 6pdr; WWII: 1 x
2pdr; 2 x 20mmAA; 2 x Browning MGs
Admty No: 457
Port Reg: GY. 679
P.No: FY. 865 (M/S); Y7. 4 (Esso)

1912: Launched. Built at Selby by Cochrane. Owned by Taylor SF Co. of Grimsby. 1915: Requisitioned in February and converted to a M/S. 1919: Returned to owners in December. 1939: Requisitioned in November and converted to an APV. 1940: Converted to a M/S in June. 1942: Based at N. Shields ICW Whalers SOUTHERN FIELD and SOUTHERN FOAM for sweeping off the NE Coast. Credited with having shot down a German Heinkel a/c. 1943: Paid Off at Hull in October and TIH for conversion to an Esso. 1944: Conversion completed. On completion of Esso duties transferred to target-towing. 1946: Returned to owners in May.

GARRY   1920/46   See under GOLDAXE (Vol 1 p.31)

GARU   1915/19   Displacement: 215TG
Armament: 1 x 3pdr
Admty No: 1601
Port Reg: GY. 644

1911: Launched. Owned by HC Baker & W Grant of Grimsby. 1915: Requisitioned in March and converted to a M/S. 1919: Returned to owners.

GAUL   1915/19   Displacement: 270TG
Armament: 1 x 12pdr; 1 x 7.5-inch
Bomb Thrower (A/S Howitzer)
Admty No: 733
Port Reg: H. 761

1905: Launched. 1915: Requisitioned in February and converted to a M/S. 1920: Returned to owners.

GAUL   1939/40   Displacement: 531TG   195TN
Engines: 99HP
Armament: 1 x 4-inch
Port Reg: H. 292

1936: Launched. Built at Southbank-on-Tees by Smith's Dock. Owned by Hellyer Bros. of Hull. 1939: Purchased into the RN and converted to an A/S. Joined the 16th A/S Strike Force based at Aberdeen for operations around the N. of Scotland. 1940: TPI the Norwegian Campaign April/May. LOST. Sunk by enemy a/c off Norway on 3rd May.

GAVA   1939/46   Displacement: 256TG   100TN
Engines: 93HP

Armament: 1 x 12pdr
Port Reg: FD. 380
P.No: 4.14 (WWII)

1920: Launched. Built at Aberdeen. Owned by New Docks STC of Fleetwood. 1939: Requisitioned in November and converted to an APV. 1942: Converted to a M/S in May. Transferred to target-towing duties from September. 1946: Returned to owners in June.

GAVINA	1916/19	Displacement: 289TG
		Armament: 1 x 12pdr

1915: Launched. 1916: Requisitioned. 1919: Returned to owners.

GELSINA	1916/17	Displacement: 226TG
		Armament: 1 x 3pdrAA
		Admty No: 3258
		Port Reg: GY. 869

1915: Launched. 1916: Requisitioned in February and converted to a M/S. 1917: LOST. Mined off Girdle Ness on 25th June.

GEMMA	1940/49	Displacement: 271TG
		Armament: 1 x 12pdr
		Port Reg: American

1918: Launched. 1940: Purchased into the RN from American owners. Converted to an APV. Served on the WI Station throughout. 1949: Sold to mercantile at Trinidad.

GENERAL	1917/19	Displacement: 191TG
		Admty No: Not issued
		Port Reg: A. 173

1898: Launched. 1917: Requisitioned into the Fishery Reserve. 1919: Returned to owners.

GENERAL BIRDWOOD	1939/46	See under JAMES McLAUGHLIN (Vol 1 p.138)

GENERAL BOTHA	1916/19	1940/45	Displacement: 245TG 92TN
			Engines: 83HP
			Armament: 1 x 6pdrAA
			Admty No: 3316
			Port Reg: A. 709
			P. No: FY. 599

1916: Launched. Built at Selby by Cochrane. Requisitioned in December and converted to a M/S. 1919: Returned to owners. 1940: Owned by John Lewis Ltd. of Aberdeen. Requisitioned in July and converted to a M/S. Based at N. Shields for sweeping in the North Sea. 1943: Employed as a film star. Played the part of a German ship in an Ealing film. 1945: Returned to owners.

GENERAL FOCH   1942/47   Displacement: 248TG
                                    Armament: Unarmed
                                    Port Reg: French
1916: Launched. 1942: Hired from French owners and employed on Harbour Service.
1947: Returned to owners.

GENERAL GORDON   1917/19   Displacement: 267TG
                                    Armament: 1 x 6pdr
                                    Admty No: 3331
                                    Port Reg: H. 844
1905: Launched. 1917: Requisitioned in March and converted to a M/S. 1920: Returned
to owners

GENERAL JOFFRE   1916/19   Displacement: 194TG   86TN
                                    Engines: 79HP
                                    Armament: 1 x 6pdr
                                    Admty No: 1455
                                    Port Reg: SN. 123
1914: Launched. Built at Willington Quay. 1915: Requisitioned in April and converted to
a M/S. 1919: Returned to owners.

GEORGE D. IRVIN   1914/19 1940/45 Displacement: 194TG   75TN
                                    Engines: 78HP
                                    Armament: 1 x 6pdrAA
                                    Admty No: 116
                                    Port Reg: A. 387; WWII: HL. 20
                                    P.No: WWII: Z. 249
1911: Launched. Built at Aberdeen. 1914: Requisitioned in August and converted to a
M/S. 1919: Returned to owners. 1938: Owned by the Friarage SFC. Ltd of Hartlepool.
1940: Requisitioned in May and converted to a BDV. 1941: Converted to a M/S in
January. 1944: Converted to a Stores Carrier. 1945: Returned to owners in July.

GEORGE DIXON   1919/21   See under JOHN CAMPBELL
                                    (Vol 1 p.62)

GEORGE H. HASTIE   1916/19   Displacement: 229TG   89TN
                                    Engines: 83HP
                                    Armament: 1 x 6pdrAA
                                    Admty No: 2952
                                    Port Reg: SN. 274
1916: Launched. Built at Aberdeen. Owned by R. Hastie and Sons Ltd. of North Shields.
Requisitioned in August and converted to a M/S. 1919: Returned to owners.

GEORGE MILBURN   1916/17   Displacement: 235TG
                                       Armament: 1 x 6pdrAA
                                       Admty No: 3301
                                       Port Reg: A. 634
1916: Launched. Requisitioned in July and converted to a M/S. 1917: LOST. Mined off Dunmore on 12th July.

GEORGE ROBB   1939/46   Displacement: 217TG
                                       Armament: 1 x 12pdr
                                       P.No: FY. 685
1930: Launched. 1939: Requisitioned in August and converted to a M/S. Subsequently purchased into the RN. 1946: Sold to mercantile in January.

GEORGE R. PURDY   1940/44   See under ISRAEL ALDCROFT
                                       (Vol 1 p.173)

GEORGE SCOTT   1916/20   Displacement: 209TG
                                       Armament: 1 x 6pdrAA
                                       Admty No: 3262
                                       Port Reg: SN. 270
1916: Launched. Requisitioned in March and converted to a M/S. 1919: Returned to owners.

GEORGE STROUD   1914/19   Ex-*Loch Earn*
                                       Displacement: 202TG
                                       Armament: 1 x 6pdr
                                       Admty No: 359
                                       Port Reg: A. 64
1906: Launched. 1914: Requisitioned in August and converted to a M/S. 1919: Returned to owners.

GEORGETTE   1939/46   See under JAMES HARTWELL
                                       (Vol 1 p.175)

GERBERDINA JOHANNA 1915/20   See under FUJI

GERTRUDE CAPPLEMAN 1915/20   Displacement: 195TG
                                       Port Reg: HL. 74
1915: Launched. Requisitioned in June and converted to a BDV. 1920: Returned to owners.

GILDEROY   1917/19   Displacement: 153TG
                                       Port Reg: GY. 1120
1899: Launched. 1917: Requisitioned into the Fishery Reserve. 1919: Returned to owners.

GILLIAN 1939/45 See under JOHN KENNEDY
(Vol 1 p.181)

GILLYGATE 1915/19 Displacement: 207TG
Armament: 1 x 12pdr
Admty No: 968
Port Reg: LO. 231
1915: Launched. 1915: Requisitioned in February. 1919: Returned to owners.

GIRARD 1940/47 See under EDWARD DRUCE
(Vol 1 p.133)

GLACIER 1940/44 Ex-*Magnolia*
Displacement: 260TG
P. No: 4. 257
1909: Launched. 1940: Requisitioned in May and converted to an APV. 1944: Returned
to owners in June.

GLADYS 1939/46 See under JOHN ARTHUR
(Vol 1 p.139)

GLAMIS CASTLE 1915/19 Displacement: 203TG
Armament: 1 x 12pdr
Admty No: 482
Port Reg: GW. 12
1902: Launched. 1914: Requisitioned in December and converted to a M/S. 1919:
Returned to owners.

GLATIAN 1914/19 1939/45 Displacement: 220TG
Armament: 1 x 6pdr
Admty No: 821
Port Reg: GY. 866
P. No: WWII: FY. 881
1913: Launched. 1914: Requisitioned in November and converted to a M/S. 1919:
Returned to owners. 1939: Requisitioned in November and converted to an APV. 1945:
Returned to owners.

GLEN BERVIE 1916/19 1939/40 Displacement: 224TG
Armament: 1 x 12pdr
Admty No: 438
Port Reg: GW. 14
1915: Launched. Requisitioned in November and converted to a M/S. 1919: Returned to
owners. 1939: Requisitioned in November as CONQUISTADOR. Converted to an APV. 1940:
Converted to a M/S in June. LOST. Sunk in a collision in the Thames on 25th November.

GLEN BOYNE   1915/19   Displacement: 224TG
Armament: 1 x 6pdr
Admty No: 289
Port Reg: GW. 10

1915: Launched. Requisitioned in September and converted to a M/S. 1919: LOST. Mined off the N. Foreland on 4th January.

GLEN COVA   1917/19   Displacement: 161TG
Admty No: Not issued
Port Reg: GW. 13

1894: Launched. 1917: Requisitioned into the Fishery Reserve. 1919: Returned to owners.

GLEN ESK   1914/19   Displacement: 226TG
Armament: 1 x 6pdrAA
Admty No: 301
Port Reg: GW. 18

1907: Launched. 1914: Requisitioned in August and converted to a M/S. 1919: Returned to owners.

GLEN KIDSTONE   1939/45   Displacement: 360TG
Armament: 1 x 12pdr
P. No: 4. 77

1930: Launched. 1939: Requisitioned in August and converted to a M/S. 1940: Converted to an APV in June. 1941: Re-converted to a M/S. 1945: Returned to owners in July.

GLENOGIL   1914/16   Displacement: 203TG
Port Reg: GW

1902: Launched. 1915: Requisitioned in August and converted to a BDV. 1919: Returned to owners.

GLENOGIL   1915/19   Displacement: 203TG
Port Reg: GW. 8

1902: Launched. 1915: Requisitioned in August and converted to a BDV. 1919: Returned to owners.

GLEN PROSEN   1914/16   Displacement: 224TG
Admty No: 315
Port Reg: GW. 20

1907: Launched. 1914: Requisitioned in August and converted to a M/S. 1916: LOST. Mined off the Cross Sand LV. on 3rd November. *Notes*: Also listed as GLEN PROSEEN.

GLENROY   1916/19   Displacement: 137TG
                                         Armament: 1 x 6pdr
                                         Admty No: 595
                                         Port Reg: GY. 817

1895: Launched. 1914: Requisitioned in December and converted to a M/S. 1919: Returned to owners.

GLORIA   1914/19 1940/44 Displacement: 187TG
                                         Armament: 1 x 6pdr
                                         Admty No: 275
                                         Port Reg: A. 135

1907: Launched. 1914: Requisitioned in August and converted to a M/S. 1915: Renamed GLORIA II in July. 1919: Returned to owners. 1940: Requisitioned in February and converted to a BBV. 1945: Returned to owners in February.

GLORIA   1915/19   Displacement: 264TG
                                         Armament: 1 x 6pdr
                                       Admty No: 2673
                                       Port Reg: M. 215

1907: Launched. 1915: Requisitioned in June. 1919: Returned to owners.

GLORIA II   1915/19   See under GLORIA above

G. M.   1915/19   Displacement: 225TG
                                         Armament: 1 x 6pdr
                                       Admty No: 308
                                       Port Reg: M. 47

1910: Launched. 1914: Requisitioned in August and converted to a M/S. 1919: Returned to owners.

GOELAND II   1915/19 1939/45 Displacement: 245TG
                                         Armament: 1 x 6pdr
                                       Admty No: 1194
                                       Port Reg: LL. 2
                                       P. Nos: WWII: FY. 760 (M/S)
                                       Y7. 21 (Esso)

1915: Launched. Requisitioned in March and converted to a M/S. 1919: Returned to owners. 1939: Requisitioned in November as NEW COMET and converted to an APV. 1940: Converted to a M/S in May. 1943: Converted to an Esso in December. 1945: Returned to owners in December.

GOEREE   1942/45   See under DOLFIJN 1940

GOLDEN GLEAM   1917/19   Displacement: 191TG
                                       Admty No: Not issued
                                       Port Reg: GY. 871
1895: Launched. 1917: Requisitioned into the Fishery Reserve. 1919: Returned to owners.

GONZALO   1915/19   Displacement: 173TG
                                       Armament: 1 x 3pdr
                                       Admty No: 2578
                                       Port Reg: H. 892
1906: Launched. 1915: Requisitioned in June and converted to a M/S. 1919: Returned
to owners.

GOOD HOPE II   1914/21   Displacement: 256TG   93TN
                                       Engines: 75HP = 11K
                                       Armament: 1 x 12pdr
                                       Admty No: 355
                                       Port Reg: H. 722
1903: Launched. Built at Beverley by CWG. Owned by Cargill STC of Hull. 1914:
Requisitioned and converted to a M/S. 1918: Acquired by JRE Mardaunt of Grimsby.
PR: GY. 1187. 1919: Acquired by WH Rachkind of Grimsby. Returned to owner. 1927:
Acquired by Canadian owners of Halifax, NS. 1929: Mercantile Loss. Sank in a collision
at Halifax.

GOOD LUCK   1915/19 1940/42 Displacement: 294TG
                                       Armament: 1 x 12pdr
                                       Admty No: 1342
                                       Port Reg: H. 497
                                       P.No: WWII: FY. 920
1912: Launched. 1915: Requisitioned in April and converted to a M/S. 1917: Converted
to an Escort. 1919: Returned to owners. 1940: Requisitioned in April as TRANQUIL.
1942: LOST. Sunk in a collision off Deal on 16th June.

GOOLGWAI   1939/47   RAN. See under TR.19 (Vol 1 p.79)

GOONAMBEE   1940/44   RAN
                                       Displacement: 222TG
                                       Port Reg: Australian
                                       P. No: FY. 94
1919: Launched. 1940: Requisitioned in July and converted to a M/S. Commissioned
into the RAN. 1944: Returned to owners in October.

GOORANGAI   1939/40   RAN
                                       Displacement: 223TG
                                       Port Reg: Australian

1919: Launched. 1939: Requisitioned in October and converted to a M/S. Commissioned into the RAN. 1940: LOST. Sank off Port Phillip, Victoria, in a collision with *Dunroon* on 20th November.

GOOSANDER 1914/19 1939/40 1943/46 Displacement: 238TG
Armament: 1 x 6pdr
Admty No: 910
Port Reg: LL. 118
P. No: WWII: Y7. 20

1908: Launched. 1914: Requisitioned in January and converted to a M/S. 1919: Returned to owners. 1939: Requisitioned in November and converted to an APV. 1940: Returned to owners. 1943: Purchased into the RN in February and converted to an Esso. 1946: Sold to mercantile in February.

GOSHAWK 1914/19 Displacement: 208TG
Armament: 1 x 6pdr
Admty No: 430
Port Reg: GY. 1194

1900: Launched. Owned by Baskcombe of Grimsby. 1914: Requisitioned in December and converted to a M/S. 1915: Renamed GOSHAWK II in May. 1919: Returned to owners.

GOSHAWK II 1915/19 See under GOSHAWK above

GOTH 1939/45 Displacement: 394TG
Armament: 1 x 12pdr
P. No: FY.640

1925: Launched. 1939: Purchased into the RN in August and converted to a M/S. 1945: Sold to mercantile in November.

GOWAN 1915/19 Displacement: 173TG
Armament: 1 x 12pdr
Admty No: 477
Port Reg: GW. 9

1905: Launched. 1914: Requisitioned in December and converted to a M/S. 1920: Returned to owners.

GOZO 1914/19 Displacement: 172TG
Armament: 1 x 6pdrAA
Admty No: 644
Port Reg: H. 545

1902: Launched. 1914: Requisitioned in October and converted to a M/S. 1919: Returned to owners.

GRACE WETHERLEY   1917/19   Displacement: 270TG
                                     Armament: 1 x 6pdrAA
                                     Admty No: 3337

1917: Launched. Requisitioned in March and converted to a M/S. 1919: Returned to owners.

GRACKLE   1915/19   Displacement: 191TG
                                     Armament: 1 x 6pdr
                                     Admty No: 1218
                                     Port Reg: H. 224

1915: Launched. Requisitioned in January and converted to a M/S. 1919: Returned to owners.

GRAMPIAN   1939/46   Ex-*Kopanes*
                                     Displacement: 409T 397TG 151TN
                                     Engines: 99HP = 10.7K
                                     Armament: 1 x 12pdr
                                     Port Reg: H.502
                                     P.No: FY. 546

1930: Launched. Built at Beverley by CWG. Owned by Oddsson of Hull. 1933: Acquired by WB Willey of Hull and renamed *Grampian*. 1939: Requisitioned in August and converted to a M/S. 1940: Acquired by Hudson Bros. of Hull. TPI Operations Quenton/Quixote/Quidnunc, the cutting of the telephone cable between Germany and the UK in the North Sea on 18 /19th May. 1946: Returned to owners in March and renamed *Cape Pembroke*. Acquired by Ocean STC in December and renamed *Frobisher*. 1957: BU at Ghent, Belgium.

GRAND DUKE   1915/19 1940/47 Displacement: 327TG
                                     Armament: 1 x 12pdr
                                     Admty No: 2512
                                     Port Reg: GY. 683
                                     P. No: WWII: Z. 113

1915: Launched. Requisitioned in November and converted to a M/S. 1919: Returned to owners. 1940: Purchased into the RN in January as NIGHT RIDER. Converted to a BDV. 1946: Paid Off and Laid Up. Placed on the Disposal List. 1947: Sold to mercantile in February.

GRANTON N.B.   1914/19 1940/46 Displacement: 180TG
                                     Armament: 1 x 6pdr
                                     Admty No: 290
                                     Port Reg: GN. 78
                                     P. No: WWII: Z. 215

1912: Launched. 1914: Requisitioned in August and converted to a M/S. 1919: Returned to owners. 1940: Requisitioned in January as PANORAMA (ex-*Curlew*). Converted to a BDV. 1946: Returned to owners in March.

GRANUWEAL   1914/19   Displacement: 174TG
                                               Armament: 1 x 6pdr
                                               Admty No: 474
                                               Port Reg: A. 265

1909: Launched. 1914: Requisitioned in November and converted to a M/S. 1919: Returned to owners.

GREAT ADMIRAL   1917/19 1940/45 Displacement: 284TG 117TN
                                               Engines: 32HP
                                               Admty No: Not issued
                                               Port Reg: GY. 733
                                               P. No: 4. 146

1909: Launched. Built at Beverley by CWG. Owned by the Arctic SFC Ltd of Grimsby. 1917: Requisitioned into the Fishery Reserve. 1919: Returned to owners. 1940: Requisitioned in May and converted to an APV. 1945: Returned to owners in June.

GREBE   1917/19   Displacement: 265TG 108TN
                                               Engines: 70HP = 11K
                                               Port Reg: GY. 219

1907: Launched. Built at Beverley by CWG. Owned by Baskcombe of Grimsby. 1917: Requisitioned into the Fishery Reserve. 1919: Returned to owners. 1933: Acquired by Amalgamated SFC of Grimsby. 1935: BU in Holland.

GRECIAN   1915/15   Displacement: 119TG
                                               Armament: 1 x 3pdr
                                               Admty No: 1208
                                               Port Reg: GY. 15

1896: Launched. 1915: Requisitioned in January. Returned to the Fishing Fleet in July. 1917: Mercantile Loss. Captured by a German S/M 22 miles NE x E from Longstone and sunk by bomb. No loss of life. *Notes*: The armament probably refers to a designated armament. It is likely that she was employed on harbour service for her short spell in the RN.

GRECIAN EMPIRE   1915/19   Displacement: 195TG
                                               Armament: 1 x 12pdr
                                               Admty No: 792
                                               Port Reg: H. 479

1899: Launched. 1915: Requisitioned in January and converted to a M/S. 1919: Returned to owners.

GRECIAN PRINCE   1917/18   Displacement: 126TG
                                               Port Reg: SN. 4

1899: Launched. 1917: Requisitioned into the Fishery Reserve. 1918: LOST. Mined on 15th December.

GREENFLY 1939/45 Ex-*Quantock*
Displacement: 441TG 171TN
Engines: 114HP
Armament: 1 x 4-inch
Port Reg: H. 321
P.No: FY. 156

1936: Launched. Built at Selby by Cochrane. Owned by W.B. Willey & Sons of Hull. 1939: Purchased into the RN in September and converted to an A/S. Joined the 19th A/S Group at Harwich for E. Coast convoys. 1945: Sold to mercantile and assumed her original name *Quantock*.

GREEN HOWARD 1939/46 Displacement: 349T 151TN
Engines: 82HP
Armament: 1 x 12pdr
Port Reg: GY. 433
P. No: FY. 632

1927: Launched. Built at Selby by Cochrane. Owned by Consolidated Fisheries of Grimsby. 1939: Requisitioned in August and converted to a M/S. 1944: TPI Operation Neptune, the D-Day Landings in June as a D/L attached to the 31st (Canadian) M/S Flot in Force O. 1946: Returned to owners in March.

GREGNESS 1917/19 Displacement: 240TG
Armament: 1 x 6pdrAA; 1 x 7.5-inch
Bomb Thrower (A/S Howitzer)
Admty No: 3035
Port Reg: A. 730

1917: Launched. Requisitioned in April and converted to a M/S. 1919: Returned to owners.

GREGORY 1939/45 Ex-*Malmata*
Displacement: 355TG 169TN
Engines: 91HP = 11.2K
Armament: 1 x 12pdr
Port Reg: GY. 199
P. No: FY. 1875

1930: Launched. Built at Beverley by CWG as *Malmata*. Owned by the Malmata FCL of Grimsby. 1936: Acquired by Dalmatia FC of Grimsby and renamed *Gregory*. 1939: Requisitioned in August and converted to an APV. Acquired by Crampin SFC in December. 1941: Converted to a M/S. 1945: Returned to owners in July. 1956: BU at Ghent, Belgium.

GRENADA 1914/19 Displacement: 220TG 112TN
Engines: 67HP
Armament: 1 x 6pdrAA
Admty No: 714

Port Reg: GY. 323
1907: Launched. Built at Beverley by CWG. Owned by Grant & Baker SFC of Grimsby.
1914: Requisitioned in October, converted to a M/S and renamed GRENADIER. 1919:
Returned to owners and reverted to original name. 1938: Owned by James Porter of
Aberdeen PR: H. 947. 1951: BU at Charlestown in April.

GRENADIER 1914/19 See under GRENADA above

GRETA 1914/19 Displacement: 273TG
Armament: 1 x 6pdr
Admty No: 119
Port Reg: FD. 79
1906: Launched. 1914: Requisitioned in August and converted to a M/S. 1915:
Renamed GRETA II in May. 1919: Returned to owners.

GRETA II 1915/19 See under GRETA above

GRETA III 1914/19 Displacement: 168TG
1913: Launched. 1914: Requisitioned . 1919: Returned to owners.

GRIFFIN 1917/19 Displacement: 183TG
Admty No: Not issued
Port Reg: GY. 1240
1903: Launched. 1917: Requisitioned into the Fishery Reserve. 1919: Returned to
owners.

GRIMENCO 1917/19 Displacement: 153TG
Port Reg: GY 9
1899: Launched. 1917: Requisitioned in April and converted to a BDV. 1919: Returned
to owners.

GRIMSBY 1914/18 Displacement: 163TG
Armament: 1 x 3pdr
Admty No: 951
Port Reg: GY. 168
1896: Launched. 1915: Requisitioned in January. 1918: Returned to owners in July.

GRIMSBY TOWN 1939/45 Football Group
Displacement: 422TG 159TN
Engines: 99HP
Port Reg: GY. 81
P.No: FY. 125
1934: Launched. Built at Southbank-on-Tees by Smiths Dock. Owned by Consolidated
Fisheries of Grimsby. 1939: Requisitioned in August and converted to an A/S. 1943: A/S

Group ICW sister-ships DERBY COUNTY, HUDDERSFIELD TOWN, LEEDS UNITED and YORK CITY based at Milford Haven. Remained with this Group throughout the remainder of the War. Employed on Escort duties in the Western Approaches. Group transferred to the MF escorting a convoy of Landing Craft to Gibraltar enroute. Employed on Med. Convoys escorts. Returned to the UK at the end of the year and based again at Milford Haven for Western Approaches. 1944: The Group TPI Operation Neptune, the D-Day Landings in June as A/S Escorts. 1945: Returned to owners in November. 1946: Mercantile loss. Took the Ground off Iceland.

GRIMSBY TOWN   **(Steve Bush Collection)**

GROENLAND   1940/41   Displacement: 1,179TG
                                            Port Reg: French
1930: Launched. French fishing vessel. 1940: French fishing vessel seized at Plymouth in operation Grab on 3rd July. Laid up. 1941: Brought forward and transferred to the MWT on 30th March. *Notes*: Extremely large for a trawler of her era which was probably the reason for her not being employed in the Fleet.

GROSBEAK   1914/19   Displacement: 192TG   71TN
                                            Engines: 55HP
                                            Armament: 1 x 12pdr
                                            Admty No: 660
                                            Port Reg: H. 108
1910: Launched. Built at Goole by Goole SB. 1914: Requisitioned in August and converted to a M/S. 1919: Returned to owners. 1938: Owned by Kelsall Bros. & Beeching Ltd of Hull.

GROSMONT CASTLE   1940/46   See under JOHN POLLARD
                                          (Vol 1 p.65)

GROUSE   1914/19   Displacement: 167TG
                                          Armament: 1 x 12pdr
                                          Admty No: 371
                                          Port Reg: H. 100
1897: Launched.   1914: Requisitioned in October and converted to a M/S.   1919:
Returned to owners.

GRUNA   1941/41   See under EARRAID (Vol 1 p.110)

GUAVA   1939/45   Ex-*British Columbia*
                                          Displacement: 134TG 50TN
                                          Engines: 310HP
                                          Fuel: Diesel
                                          Armament: 1 x 6pdr; 1 x MG
                                          Port Reg: GY. 153
1935: Launched. Built at Lowestoft. Owned by Grimsby Motor Trs. Ltd of Grimsby.
1939: Purchased into the RN and converted to A/S.   1945: Sold to mercantile and
reverted to original name.

GUILLEMOT   1914/19   Displacement: 208TG
                                          Armament: 1 x 6pdr
                                          Admty No: 730
                                          Port Reg: GY. 1198
1900: Launched. Owned by Baskcombe of Grimsby. 1914: Requisitioned in December
and converted to a M/S. 1919: Returned to owners.

GUILLEMOT   **(IWM Neg No: SP885)**

GULL   1914/19   Displacement: 166TG
                                         Armament: 1 x 3pdr
                                         Admty No: 409
                                         Port Reg: H. 241

1897: Launched.   1914: Requisitioned in October and converted to a M/S.   1919:
Returned to owners.

GULFOSS   1939/41   Displacement: 358TG 153TN
                                         Engines: 103HP
                                         Armament: 1 x 12pdr
                                         Port Reg: GY. 146
                                         P.No: FY. 710

1929: Launched. Built at Selby by Cochrane. Owned by Consolidated Fisheries of
Grimsby. 1939: Requisitioned in August and converted to a M/S. 1941: LOST. Mined
in the Channel on 9th March. Notes: Built to Cochrane's own design which in turn
became the basic design for the Fish Class.

GUNNER   1939/46   Displacement: 350TG 151TN
                                         Engines: 82HP
                                         Armament: 1 x 12pdr;
                                         4 x 0.303-inch LG (2 x 2)
                                         Port Reg: GY. 434
                                         P. No: FY. 568

1927: Launched. Built at Selby by Cochrane. Owned by Consolidated Fisheries of
Grimsby. 1939: Requisitioned in September and converted to a M/S. 1940: Joined the
41st M/S Group based at Aberdeen. Transferred to Ardrossan in December. 1944: TPI
Operation Neptune, the D-Day Landings in June as a D/L attached to the 31st
(Canadian) M/S Flot. in Force O. 1946: Returned to owners in February.

GURTH   1915/19   Displacement: 226TG 91TN
                                         Engines: 60HP
                                         Armament: 1 x 12pdr
                                         Admty No: 663
                                         Port Reg: GY. 39

1905: Launched. Built at Selby by Cochrane. Owned by the United SF Co. Ltd. of
Grimsby. 1914: Requisitioned in October and converted to a M/S. 1919: Returned to
owners.

GWEAL   1942/46   See under BRORERAY (Vol 1 p.107)

GWENLLAIN   1914/19 1939/46 Displacement: 220TG 85TN
                                         Engines: 76HP
                                         Armament: 1 x 3pdr
                                         Admty No: 354

Port Reg: M. 7; WWII: FD. 102
P. No: WWII: FY. 544

1911: Launched. Built at Middlesborough by Smith's Dock. 1914: Requisitioned in August and converted to a M/S. 1919: Returned to owners. 1938: Owned by the New Docks STC Ltd. of Fleetwood. 1939: Requisitioned in November and converted to an APV. 1940: Converted to a M/S in September. 1946: Returned to owners in January.

GWMAHO   1939/46   See under THOMAS CROFTON
                                               (Vol 1 p.75)

HAARLEM   1940/46   Displacement: 431TG
                                              Port Reg: Dutch
                                              P.No: FY. 306

1938: Launched. Dutch fishing vessel. 1940: Hired from Dutch owners in June and converted to A/S. 1946: Returned to owners in May.

HALCYON II   1917/19   Displacement: 190TG
                                              Port Reg: A. 514

1898: Launched. 1917: Requisitioned into the Fishery Reserve. 1919: Returned to owners.

HALIFAX   1917/19   Displacement: 165TG 64TN
                                              Engines: 45HP
                                              Admty No: Not issued
                                              Port Reg: GY. 442

1897: Launched. Built at Govan. Owned by Consolidated Fisheries of Grimsby. 1917: Requisitioned into the Fishery Reserve. 1919: Returned to owners.

HAMLET   1914/19   Displacement: 311TG 124TN
                                              Engines: 102HP
                                              Armament: 1 x 6pdr
                                              Admty No: 80
                                              Port Reg: H. 867

1906: Launched. Built at Hull. Owned by Hellyers SFC of Hull. 1914: Requisitioned in November and converted to a M/S. 1919: Returned to owners.

HAMMOND   1939/40   Cricketer Group
                                              Displacement: 452TG 191TN
                                              Engines: 133HP
                                              Armament: 1 x 4-inch
                                              Port Reg: GY. 284
                                              P. No: FY. 149

1936: Launched. Built at Selby by Cochrane and completed in February. Owned by Crampins of Grimsby. 1939: Requisitioned in August and converted to A/S. Joined the 22nd A/S Group. 1940: TPI the Norwegian Campaign in April. LOST. Sunk by enemy a/c at Aandalsnes, Norway, on 25th April. 1941: Salvaged by the German Navy. 1942: Commissioned into the German Navy in February. 1945: Sold to mercantile. Acquired by Faroese owners and renamed *Vesturskin*. Subsequently acquired by Norwegian owners and renamed *Sletnes*.

HAMPSHIRE   1939/39   Shire Group
                                              Displacement: 425TG 160TN

Engines: 99HP
Armament: 1 x 4-inch
Port Reg: GY. 85
P. No: FY. 173

1934: Launched in September. Built at Southbank-on-Tees by Smith's Dock. Owned by the Hampshire SF Co. Ltd. (H. Markham) of Grimsby. 1939: Purchased into the RN in September and converted to A/S. Sold to the French Navy on 28th November and renamed La TOULONNAISE.

HARLECH CASTLE	1916/19 1940/45	Displacement: 275TG 108TN
		Engines: 87HP
		Armament: 1 x 6pdr
		Admty No: 1990
		Port Reg: SA.42
		P. No: WWII: FY. 741

1916: Launched. Built at Southbank-on-Tees . Owned by Consolidated Fisheries of Grimsby. Requisitioned in April and converted to a M/S. Also employed on Escort duties. 1919: Returned to owners. 1940: Requisitioned in February and converted to a M/S. 1944: Joined the 47/48th M/S Flots. employed off the N. of Scotland. 1945: Took the surrender of German U-1009 off the N. of Scotland on 8th May. A second U-Boat surrendered to them shortly afterwards. Paid Off and returned to owners in July.

HARRY ROSS	1914/19	Displacement: 183TG 71TN
		Engines: 62HP
		Port Reg: A. 453

1901: Launched. Built at Aberdeen. Owned by Ross STFC of Aberdeen. 1915: Requisitioned in June and converted to a BDV. 1919: Returned to owners.

HATANO	1916/19	Displacement: 255TG 100TN
		Engines: 82HP
		Armament: 1 x 6pdrAA
		Admty No: 2662
		Port Reg: CF. 39

1912: Launched. Built at Middlesborough by Smith's Dock. Owned by Neale & West of Cardiff. 1915: Requisitioned in May and converted to a M/S. 1919: Returned to owners.

HATANO	1939/46	Displacement: 297TG 110TN
		Engines: 99HP
		Armament: 1 x 12pdr
		Port Reg: LO. 177
		P. No: FY. 662

1925: Launched. Built at Southbank-on-Tees by Smith's Dock. Owned by T. Jenkerson AO of Milford Haven. 1939: Requisitioned in September and converted to a M/S. 1946: Returned to owners in May.

HATSUSE   1939/45   Displacement: 295TG 108TN
                                                Engines: 99HP
                                                Armament: 1 x 12pdr
                                                Port Reg: CF 21
                                                P. No: FY. 1749
1927: Launched. Built at Southbank-on-Tees by Smith's Dock. Owned by Neale & West
of Cardiff. 1939: Requisitioned in August and converted to a M/S. 1945: Returned to
owners in August.

HAWK   1914/17   Displacement: 243TG 96TN
                                                Engines: 70HP
                                                Armament: 2 x 3pdrs
                                                Admty No: 690
                                                Port Reg: H. 23
1897: Launched. Built at Howden-on-Tees. Owned by Kelsall Bros. & Beeching Of Hull.
1914: Requisitioned in November and converted to a M/S. 1917: MF. LOST. Mined off
Malta on 17th February.

HAWTHORN II   1917/19   Displacement: 180TG 69TN
                                                Engines: 55HP
                                                Admty No: Not issued
                                                Port Reg: GY. 1228
1902: Launched. Built at Hull. Owned by Hawthorn Fishing Co. Ltd of Milford Haven.
1917: Requisitioned into the Fishery Reserve. 1919: Returned to owners.

HAYBURN WYKE   1940/45   See under ROBERT BARTON
                                                (Vol 1 p.146)

HEATHER   1917/19   Displacement: 169TG 67TN
                                                Engines: 47HP
                                                Port Reg: FD. 101
1904: Launched. Built at Govan. Owned by AG Brown of Granton Harbour. 1917:
Requisitioned into the Fishery Reserve. 1919: Returned to owners.

HEKLA   1940/46   Displacement: 354TG 151TN
                                                Engines: 103HP
                                                Armament: 1 x 12pdr
                                                Port Reg: GY. 118
                                                P. No: FY. 1650
1929: Launched. Built at Selby by Cochrane. Owned by Consolidated Fisheries of
Grimsby. 1940: Requisitioned in May and converted to an APV. Based at Grimsby for
Fishery Patrols. 1942: Converted to a M/S in January. 1946: Returned to owners in May.

HELCIA   1914/19   Displacement: 230TG
                                 Armament: 1 x 6pdr
                                 Admty No: 958
                                 Port Reg: GY. 152
1906: Launched. 1915: Requisitioned in January. 1919: Returned to owners.

HELGIAN   1915/15   Displacement: 220TG
                                 Armament: 1 x 3pdr
                                 Admty No: 696
                                 Port Reg: GY. 965
1914: Launched. Requisitioned in November and converted to a M/S. 1917: LOST. Mined in the Gulf of Ruphania, Aegean, on 6th September.

HELIOS   1917/19   Displacement: 201TG 78TN
                                 Engines: 55HP
                                 Admty No: 953
                                 Port Reg: GY. 784
1903: Launched. Built at Hull. Owned by Roberts & Ruthven of Grimsby. 1917: Requisitioned into the Fishery Reserve. 1919: Returned to owners. 1938: Owned by Sir Thomas Robinson & Son, Ltd. of Grimsby.

HELVETIA   1917/19 1940/46 Displacement: 261TG 102TN
                                 Engines: 75HP = 9.5K
                                 Armament: 1 x 12pdr
                                 Admty No: 1266
                                 Port Reg: GY. 1026
                                 P. No: WWII: 4. 86
1917: Launched. Built at Beverley by CWG. Owned by Gt. Grimsby & E. Coast SFC of Grimsby. Requisitioned in April and converted to a M/S. Fitted with Listening Hydrophones. 1919: Returned to owners. 1940: Acquired by Black of Grimsby. Requisitioned in June and converted to an APV. Based at Grimsby for Fishery Protection. 1942: Converted to a M/S. 1946: Returned to owners in September. 1958: BU at Bruges, Belgium.

HENE CASTLE   1915/19   Displacement: 274TG
                                 Armament: 1 x 2pdr
                                 Admty No: 1975
                                 Port Reg: SA. 33
1915: Launched. Requisitioned in December and converted to a M/S. Fitted with Listening Hydrophones. 1919: Returned to owners.

HENRIETTE   1939/40   See under ROBERT HARDING
                                 (Vol 1 p.185)

HENRIETTE   1940/41   Displacement: 261TG
                                        Port Reg: French

1906: Launched. French fishing vessel. 1940: French M/S seized at Southampton in Operation Grab on 3rd July. Commissioned with a Free French Crew in September. 1941: LOST. Mined off the Humber on 26th December.

HENRY GRATTON   1915/19   Ex-*Diadem*
                                          Displacement: 212TG 84TN
                                          Engines: 60HP
                                          Armament: 1 x 12pdr
                                          Port Reg: D. 86

1903: Launched. Built at Hull. Owned by the Dublin STC of Dublin. 1915: Requisitioned in June and converted to a BDV. 1919: Returned to owners.

HEORTNESSE   1914/19   Displacement: 165TG
                                          Engines: 75HP
                                          Armament: 1 x 6pdrAA
                                          Admty No: 63
                                          Port Reg: HL. 57

1911: Launched. Built at Aberdeen. Owned by The Hartness SF Co. Ltd. of Hartlepool. 1914: Requisitioned in September and converted to a M/S. 1919: Returned to owners.

HERCULES   1940/46   Displacement: 255TG
                                          Port Reg: Dutch
                                          P. No: FY. 1731

1905: Launched. 1940: Hired from Dutch owners in June and converted to a M/S. 1946: Returned to owners in January.

HERCULES II   1914/19   Displacement: 165TG   65TN
                                          Engines: 45HP
                                          Armament: 1 x 6pdrAA
                                          Admty No: 431
                                          Port Reg: GY. 811

1898: Launched. Built at North Shields. Owned by Trawlers (White Sea & Grimsby) Ltd. of Grimsby. 1914: Requisitioned in December. 1919: Returned to owners.

HERCULES III   1914/19 1940/46 Displacement: 238TG
                                          Engines: 70HP
                                          Armament: WWI: 1 x 6pdr; WWII: 1 x
                                          12pdr; 1 x 20mmAA; 2 x LG (2x1); 4 x
                                          0.303-inch Browning MGs
                                          Admty No: 8
                                          Port Reg: WWI: A. 562
                                          WWII: GY.1045

1906: Launched. Built at Selby by Cochrane. 1914: Requisitioned in December and converted to a M/S. 1915: Renamed HERCULES III in March. 1919: Returned to owners. Sold to Grimsby owners and renamed *Woodbury*. Acquired by the Woodbury SFC of Grimsby. PR. GY.1045. 1924: Acquired by Alfred Bannister of Cleethorpes AO. Renamed *Rolls Royce* Same PR. 1940: Requisitioned in July as ROLLS ROYCE and converted to a M/S. Fitted with LL Sweep and Acoustic Hammer. Joined the 110th M/S Group, Grimsby as Leader sweeping the area from Cromer - Flamborough Head. 1941: The first Tr. M/S to sweep 100 mines, a feat she achieved on 24th December. 1943: Rearmed. 2 x LGs removed and replaced with 4 x Browning MGs. Senior Officer of the111th M/S Group based at Grimsby. 1944: Transferred to Portsmouth for sweeping in the Channel. Returned to Grimsby in December. 1945: Transferred back to Portsmouth in June. 197th mine swept in July. Channel sweeping and towing empty barges from Portsmouth to Tilbury. TIH at Portsmouth in December for engine repairs. 1946: Paid Off at Sheerness in April and returned to owners. Laid up at Grimsby awaiting disposal. 1949: BU. *Notes*: One of the most famous of the WWII Trawlers with the remarkable record of 197 mines swept and 1 x enemy a/c shot down.

HERCULES IV	1915/19	Displacement: 261TG 103TN
		Engines: 70HP
		Armament: 1 x 12pdr
		Admty No: 1361
		Port Reg: FD. 172

1903: Launched. Built at Beverley by CWG. Owned by the Lancashire SFC of Fleetwood. 1915: Requisitioned in March and converted to a M/S. 1919: Returned to owners.

HERMIA	1915/19	Displacement: 216TG 83TN
		Engines: 61HP
		Armament: 1 x 6pdrAA
		Admty No: 156
		Port Reg: GY. 1153

1900: Launched. Built at Inverkeithing. 1915: Requisitioned in June and converted to a M/S. 1919: Returned to owners. Acquired by The Mersey STL of Fleetwood. PR: FD. 92.

HERO	1914/20 1940/44	Displacement: 217TG
		Armament: WWI: 1 x 6pdr; WWII: 1 x 6pdrAA; 24 mines (As a M/L)
		Admty No: 156
		Port Reg: M. 219
		P. No: WWII: FY. 1866

1906: Launched. 1914: Requisitioned in August and converted to a M/L. 1917: Converted to a M/S. 1920: Returned to owners. 1940: Requisitioned in June as HEROINE and converted to a M/L. 1944: Converted to an Esso in April. Returned to owners in November.

HERO II   1915/19   Displacement: 173TG 85TN
Engines: 71HP
Port Reg: FD. 227

1906: Launched. Built at Dundee. Owned by Clifton STL of Fleetwood. 1915: Requisitioned. 1919: Returned to owners.

HEROINE   1940/44   See under HERO above

HERON   1914/19 1939/40 Displacement: 233TG 95TN
Engines: 60HP
Armament: 1 x 12pdr
Admty No: 715
Port Reg: GY. 1230

1902: Launched. Built at Hull. Owned by T. Bascombe of Grimsby. 1914: Requisitioned in December and converted to a M/S. 1919: Returned to owners. 1939: Requisitioned in November and designated as an APV. 1940: Returned to owner in January. 1942: Mercantile Loss. Thought to have been mined off the Faroes on 12th July.

HERTFORDSHIRE   1939/45   Shire Group
Displacement: 458TG 164TN
Engines: 99HP
Armament: 1 x 4-inch
Port Reg: GY. 332
P.No: FY. 176

1936: Launched in September. Built at Southbank-on-Tees by Smith's Dock. Owned by The Rutlandshire SF Co. Ltd. (H. Markham) of Grimsby. 1939: Requisitioned and converted to A/S. 1940: TIH at Portland for refitting. She was in the Floating Dock in the harbour when the Dock was damaged in an air-raid, but she was floated out without damage. 1942: Temporary Loan to the USN in March, together with her crew, for A/S duties. Returned to the RN in October. Transferred direct to the S. Africa Station. 1945: Returned to the UK. Paid Off and returned to owners. 1951: Acquired by Northern Trawlers of Hull and renamed *Northern Gift*.

H.E.STROUD   1915/19   Displacement: 214TG 79TN
Engines: 69HP
Armament: 1 x 6pdr
Admty No: 1346
Port Reg: A. 270

1915: Launched. Built at Aberdeen. Owned by H.E. Stroud of Aberdeen. Requisitioned in April and converted to a M/S. 1919: Returned to owners.

HEUGH   1915/19   Displacement: 200TG 78TN
Engines: 78HP
Armament: 1 x 6pdr; 1 x 6pdrAA

Admty No: 1480
Port Reg: HL. 64

1914: Launched. Built at Aberdeen. Owned by Heugh ST Co. Ltd. of Hartlepool. 1915: Requisitioned in May and converted to a M/S. 1919: Returned to owners.

HIBERNIA II	1914/19	Displacement: 216TG 82TN
		Engines: 52HP
		Armament: 1 x 6pdrAA
		Admty No: 141
		Port Reg: LO. 266

1907: Launched. Built at North Shields. Owned by the Hewett Fishing Co. London. 1914: Requisitioned in August and converted to a M/S. 1915: Renamed HIBERNIA II in May. 1919: Returned to owners.

HILARIA	1917/19	Displacement: 207TG 90TN
		Engines: 57HP
		Port Reg: GY. 698

1898: Launched. Built at Dundee. Owned by I. Burch & R. Payne of Grimsby. 1918: Requisitioned into the Fishery Reserve. 1919: Returned to owners.

HILDINA	1939/46	See under WILLIAM LEEK (Vol 1 p.88)

HIROSE	1915/16	Displacement: 274TG
		Armament: 1 x 3pdr
		Admty No: 3280
		Port Reg: CF. 44

1915: Launched. 1916: Requisitioned in June. LOST. Mined off Aldborough Napes on 29th June.

HOBART	1915/19	Displacement: 172TG 67TN
		Engines: 45HP
		Port Reg: H. 555

1902: Launched. Built at Beverley by CWG. Owned by the Hull SF & Ice Co. Ltd. 1915: Requisitioned in September and converted to a BDV. 1919: Returned to owners.

HOLDENE	1915/17	Displacement: 174TG
		Armament: 1 x 3pdr; 1 x 3pdrAA
		Port Reg; FD. 161

1915: Launched. Requisitioned in September. 1917: LOST. Mined off Orford Ness on 2nd February.

HOLYROOD	1915/19 1939/40	Displacement: 210TG 96TN
		Engines: 66HP
		Armament: 1 x 12pdr

Admty No: 1438
Port Reg: WWII: GY. 90

1914: Launched. Built at Selby by Cochrane. Owned by the Queen SF Co. Ltd of Grimsby. 1915: Requisitioned in April and converted to a M/S. 1919: Returned to owners. 1939: Requisitioned in December and designated as an APV. 1940: Returned to owners in January.

HONDO	1914/19	Displacement: 229TG 118TN
		Engines: 66HP
		Armament: 1 x 6pdrAA
		Admty No: 16
		Port Reg: GY. 701

1912: Launched. Built at Selby by Cochrane. Owned by Diamond SF Co. Ltd. of Grimsby. 1914: Requisitioned in August. 1919: Returned to owners.

HONJO	1918/18	Displacement: 275TG
		Armament: 1 x 12pdr (Designated)
		Port Reg: CF. 48

1917: Launched. Owned by Neale & West of Cardiff. 1918: Requisitioned in January and designated as a M/S. Returned to owners in the same month.

HONJO	1939/42	Displacement: 308TG 116TN
		Engines: 99HP
		Armament: 1 x 12pdr
		Port Reg: CF. 26
		P. No: FY. 661

1928: Launched. Built at Southbank-on-Tees by Smith's Dock. Owned by Neale and West of Cardiff. 1939: Requisitioned in October and converted to a M/S. 1942: LOST. Alongside ERIN at Gibraltar when that ship blew up. HONJO caught fire and was destroyed. *Notes*: See under ERIN for more details on destruction.

HONNINGSVAAG	1940/45	Ex-MALANGEN
		Displacement: 487TG

1940: Launched. Built in Germany for the German Navy as MALANGEN. Captured in Norway by Norwegian Forces during the Norwegian Campaign in April. Brought to the UK by Norwegians and converted to an APV. Commissioned in June with a Norwegian crew. 1945: Sold.

HORACE STROUD	1914/19 1944/45	Displacement: 207TG 74TN
		Engines: 68HP
		Armament: 1 x 6pdr
		Admty No: 280
		Port Reg: WWI: A. 324; WWII: A. 935

1907: Launched. Built at Aberdeen. 1914: Purchased into the RN in August and converted to a M/S. 1919: Sold to Mercantile. Acquired by DD. Noble & Mrs. J. Noble of Aberdeen. Renamed *East Coast*. 1944: Requisitioned as EAST COAST and converted to an Esso. 1945: Returned to owners.

HORATIO   1914/19   Displacement: 174TG   67TN
                                          Engines: 45HP
                                          Armament: 1 x 12pdr
                                          Admty No: 615
                                          Port Reg: H. 877

1906: Launched. Built at Govan. 1914: Requisitioned in September and converted to a M/S. 1919: Returned to owners. Subsequently acquired by CH. Brand of Milford Haven. PR: H. 904.

HORNSEA   1914/19?   Displacement: 305TG   126TN
                                          Engines: 85HP
                                          Port Reg: H. 485

1900: Launched. Built at Hull. Iron construction. Owned by Hull SF & Ice Co of Hull. 1914: Requisitioned and converted to a BGV. 1919: Returned (?)

HORTENSIA   1915/19 1940/45 Ex-*Conquest*
                                          Displacement: 305TG   118TN
                                          Engines: 76HP
                                          Port Reg: GY. 292
                                          P. No: WWII: FY. 1795

1907:Launched. Built at Dundee. Owned by J. Coombes of Grimsby. 1916: Requisitioned in August and converted to a BGV. 1919: Returned to owners in October. 1938: Owned by Charles Dobson of Grimsby. 1940: Requisitioned in July and converted to a M/S. 1945: Returned to owner in November.

HOUBARA   1915/19   Displacement: 293TG   128TN
                                          Engines: 80HP
                                          Armament: 1 x 12pdr
                                          Admty No: 1618
                                          Port Reg: GY. 650

1911: Launched. Built at Beverley by CWG. Owned by T. Baskcombe of Grimsby. 1915: Requisitioned in April and converted to a M/S. 1919: Returned to owners.

HOVERFLY   1939/45   Ex-*Euryalus*
                                          Displacement: 242TG   94TN
                                          Engines: 75HP
                                          Port Reg: A. 309
                                          P. No: FY. 557

1917: Launched. Built at Selby by Cochrane. 1938: Owned by David Wood AO of Aberdeen. 1939: Requisitioned in September and converted to a M/S. 1945: Returned to owners on 15th January.

HOWE 1914/18 Displacement: 134TG
Armament: 1 x 6pdr
Admty No: 724
Port Reg: GY. 26

1896: Launched. 1914: Requisitioned in December. 1917: Renamed HOWE II in March. 1918: Returned to owners in July.

HUDDERSFIELD TOWN 1939/45 Football Group
Displacement: 399TG 151TN
Engines: 99HP
Port Reg: GY. 521
P. No: FY. 197

1933: Launched. Built at Southbank-on-Tees by Smiths Dock. Owned by Consolidated Fisheries of Grimsby. 1939: Purchased into the RN in September and converted to A/S. 1943: Based at Milford Haven. Convoy escort Group ICW sister-ships GRIMSBY TOWN, DERBY COUNTY, LEEDS UNITED and YORK CITY. Group transferred to the MF and escorted a convoy of Landing Craft enroute. Employed on Med. Convoys. Returned to the UK at the end of the year. 1944: TPI Operation Neptune, the D-Day Landings in June, as A/S Escort. 1945: Paid Off at Newport in March and de-stored prior to sale. Sold to original owners. 1962: Renamed *Leeds United*. 1963: BU in Holland.

HUGH WALPOLE 1939/46 Displacement: 498TG 193TN
Engines: 129HP
Armament: 1 x 4-inch
Port Reg: H. 409
P.No: FY. 102

1937: Launched. Built at Selby by Cochrane. Owned by the Newington SFC of Hull. 1939: Purchased into the RN in August and converted to A/S. 1944: TPI Operation Neptune, the D-Day Landings in June, as an A/S Escort. 1946: Sold to mercantile in April. Acquired by Newington ST Co. Ltd of Hull.

HULL CITY WWII
Reported in some lists some as serving, but was probably a misrepresentation of CITY OF HULL.

HUMPHREY 1939/44 See under ROBERT FAIRCLOTH
(Vol 1 p.185)

HUNGARIAN 1914/19 Displacement: 186TG
Armament: 1 x 6pdr
Admty No: 525
Port Reg: BN. 89

1900: Launched. 1914: Requisitioned in November and converted to a M/S. 1919: Returned to owners.

HUNTER	1914/19	Displacement: 185TG 72TN
		Engines: 71HP
		Admty No: 90
		Port Reg: GN. 74

1903: Launched. Built at Aberdeen. 1914: Requisitioned in August and converted to a M/S. 1919: Returned to owners. 1938: Owned by James W. Morrice AO of Aberdeen.

HUXLEY	1915/19	Ex-*Khedive*
		Displacement: 191TG 74TN
		Engines: 52HP
		Armament: 1 x 6pdrAA
		Admty No: 1531
		Port Reg: GY. 536

1899: Launched. Built at North Shields. Owned by WJ Allen of Grimsby. 1915: Requisitioned in June and converted to a M/S. 1919: Returned to owners.

| HYAENA | 1939/40 | See under ELLESMERE |

HYDRA	1915/19	Displacement: 214TG 99TN
		Engines: 52HP
		Armament: 1 x 6pdrAA; 1 x 7.5-inch
		Bomb Thrower (A/S Howitzer)
		Admty No: 1918
		Port Reg: GY. 196

1906: Launched. Built at North Shields. Owned by JR Mackrill AO of Grimsby. 1915: Requisitioned in October and converted to a M/S. 1916: Renamed HYDRA II in July. 1919: Returned to owners.

| HYDRA II | 1915/19 | See under HYDRA above |

IAGO   1915/19   Displacement: 206TG 75TN
Engines: 50HP
Armament: 1 x 3pdr
Admty No: 1364
Port Reg: H. 963

1907: Launched. Built at Beverley by CWG. Owned by Iago STC of Milford Haven.
1915: Requisitioned in March and converted to a M/S. 1919: Returned to owners. 1938:
Owned by AER Dexter of Brixham.

IBIS   1914/19   Displacement: 168TG 75TN
Engines: 50HP
Armament: 1 x 12pdr; 1 x 6pdrAA
Admty No: 410
Port Reg: H. 764

1903: Launched. Built at Goole by Goole SB. Owned by Kelsall Bros. & Beeching of
Hull. 1914: Requisitioned in October and converted to a M/S. 1919: Returned to
owners. 1938: Owned by Brixham Trs. Ltd. of Brixham.

IBIS V   1917/19   Displacement: 196TG
Admty No: Not issued
Port Reg: O. 75

1908: Launched. Belgian fishing vessel. 1917: Requisitioned into the Fishery Reserve
with the permission of her Belgian owners. 1919: Returned to owners.

ICELAND   1916/18   Displacement: 312TG
Armament: 1 x 6pdrAA
Admty No: 3308

1916: Launched. Requisitioned in October and converted to a M/S. 1917: Converted to
an Escort. 1918: Returned to owners.

IDA ADAMS   1915/19   Displacement: 275TG 109TN
Engines: 83HP
Armament: 1 x 4-inch; 1 x 7.5-inch
Bomb Thrower (A/S Howitzer)
Admty No: 252
Port Reg: GY. 58

1907: Launched. Built at Selby. Owned by N. Ashworth & E. Tomlinson of Fleetwood.
1914: Requisitioned in August and converted to a M/S. 1919: Returned to owners.

IDENA   1917/18   Displacement: 270TG
Armament: 1 x 12pdr

Admty No: 3332
Port Reg: FD. 288

1917: Launched. Requisitioned in March and converted to a M/S. 1918: LOST. Scuttled and abandoned and then finally sunk by gunfire off Tromso, Norway, on 5th February.

IJUIN	1939/46	See under JAMES BAIRD (Vol 1 p.56)

ILFRACOMBE	1917/19	Displacement: 165TG 64TN
		Engines: 45HP
		Port Reg: GY. 450

1897: Launched. Built at Govan. Owned by Consolidated Fisheries of Grimsby. 1917: Requisitioned into the Fishery Reserve. 1919: Returned to owners.

ILUSTRA	1914/19	Displacement: 448TG 281TN
		Engines: 89HP
		Armament: 1 x 4-inch; 1 x 6pdr
		Admty No: 53 & 1221
		Port Reg: GY. 127

1914: Launched. Built at Beverley. Owned by South Western Fishing Co of Grimsby. Requisitioned in August and converted to a M/S. 1919: Returned to owners. Acquired by T.Baskcomb of Grimsby. Same PR. 1920: Mercantile Loss. Wrecked at Paroe Bay, Iceland, on 21st January.

IMELDA	1914/19 1939/46	Displacement: 252TG 97TN
		Engines: 80HP
		Armament: 1 x 6pdrAA
		Admty No: 519
		Port Reg: FD. 13
		P. No: WWII: Z. 136

1914: Launched. Built at Dundee. Owned by The Lancashire SFC of Fleetwood. Requisitioned in September and converted to a M/S. 1919: Returned to owners. 1938: Owned by J. Marr & Son Ltd. of Fleetwood. 1939: Requisitioned in December and converted to a BDV. 1946: Returned to owners in January.

IMMORTELLE	1921/34	SAN. See under THOMAS JOHNS
		(See Addenda p.531)

IMPERIA	1914/19 1939/45	Displacement: 213TG 88TN
		Engines: 58HP
		Armament: 1 x 6pdrAA
		Admty No: 620
		Port Reg: GY. 758
		P.No: FY. 813

1912: Launched. Built at Beverley by CWG. Owned by Pelham SFC of Grimsby. 1913:

Acquired by North Western SFC of Grimsby. Same PR. 1914: Requisitioned in September and converted to an APV. 1919: Returned to owners. 1921: Acquired by Grimsby & North Sea STC of Grimsby. Same PR. 1939: Requisitioned in November and converted to an APV. 1940: Converted to a BGV. 1945: Returned to owners in November. 1946: Acquired by TC & F. Moss of Grimsby. 1957: BU at Charlestown.

IMPERIALIST	1939/45	Displacement: 520TG 193TN
		Engines: 99HP
		Armament: 1 x 4-inch; 1 x 40mmAA;
		2 x 20mmAA (2x1); 2 x 0.5-inch MGs;
		DCs
		Port Reg: H. 2
		P. No: FY. 126

1939: Launched. Built at Southbank-on-Tees by Smith's Dock. Owned by Northern Fishing Co. of Hull. Requisitioned in August and converted to A/S. 1942: Gibraltar Trawler Force. Sustained serious damage in January when she caught fire alongside ERIN at Gibraltar when that ship blew up. TIH at Gibraltar for repair. 1943: Attacked the German U-732 in the Straits on 31st December. She damaged the S/M so severely that when she surfaced later that night she was unable to dive again and was sunk by the Destroyer DOUGLAS. 1945: Returned to the UK and Paid Off. Returned to owners in October.

IMPERIALIST   **(Ben Warlow Collection)**

IMPERIAL PRINCE	1917/19	Displacement: 128TG 50TN
		Engines: 47HP
		Admty No: Not issued
		Port Reg: A. 146

1899: Launched. Built at South Shields. Owned by A. Walker of Aberdeen. 1917: Requisitioned into the Fishery Reserve. 1919: Returned to owners.

IMPERIAL QUEEN   1916/19   Displacement: 246TG 96TN
                                        Engines: 76HP
                                        Armament: 1 x 12pdr; 1 x 7.5-inch
                                        Bomb Thrower (A/S Howitzer)
                                        Admty No: 1348
                                        Port Reg: H. 193

1914: Launched. Built at Dundee. Owned by the Great Northern SFC of Hull. 1915:
Requisitioned in May and converted to a M/S. Fitted with Listening Hydrophones. 1919:
Returned to owners.

INA WILLIAMS   1916/17   Displacement: 337TG
                                        Armament: 1 x 12pdr
                                        Admty No: 2658
                                        Port Reg: GY. 872

1913: Launched. 1915: Requisitioned in April and converted to a M/S. 1917: LOST.
Mined off Bull Point, Berehaven, on 30th May.

INCHGARTH   1917/19 1939/46 Displacement: 226TG 87TN
                                        Engines: 71HP
                                        Armament: 1 x 6pdrAA
                                        Admty No: 3338
                                        Port Reg: WWI: A. 755; WWII: A. 110
                                        P. No: WWII: T. 42

1917: Launched. Built at Aberdeen. Owned by Garth STC of Fleetwood. Requisitioned
in March and converted to a M/S. 1919: Returned to owners. Acquired by Walker STFC

IMPERIAL QUEEN   **(MPL)**

of Aberdeen and renamed *Star of Freedom*. 1939: Requisitioned in December as STAR OF FREEDOM. Converted to a Store Carrier. Subsequently purchased into the RN. Based at Longhope in the Orkneys. 1943: Employed running small mines to Lerwick for use by the Norwegian Resistance. 1946: Sold to mercantile in July.

INCHGOWER	1939/46	See under JOHN JACKSON (Vol 1 p.180)

INCHKEITH	1915/19	Displacement: 174TG 69TN Engines: 44HP Armament: 1 x 6pdr Admty No: 481 Port Reg: LH. 106

1906: Launched. Built at Govan. Owned by Leith SFC of Leith. 1914: Requisitioned in December and converted to a M/S. 1919: Returned to owners.

INDIA	1915/19	Displacement: 215TG

1906: Launched. 1915: Requisitioned. 1919: Returned to owners.

INDIA	1917/19	Displacement: 190TG 93TN Engines: 50HP Admty No: Not issued Port Reg: GY.570

1894: Launched. Built at Beverley by CWG. Owned by North Eastern SFC of Grimsby. 1917: Requisitioned into the Fishery Reserve. 1919: Returned to owners.

INDIAN EMPIRE	1914/19	Displacement: 289TG 116TN Engines: 85HP Armament: 1 x 12pdr; 1 x 7.5-inch Bomb Thrower (A/S Howitzer) Admty No: 798 Port Reg: H. 957

1907: Launched. Built at Selby by Cochrane. Owned by M. Wilkins of Manchester. 1914: Requisitioned in November and converted to a M/S. 1919: Returned to owners.

INGOMAR	1917/19 1939/40	Displacement: 217TG 87TN Engines: 60HP Armament: 1 x 6pdr Admty No: Not issued Port Reg: GY. 32 P. No: FY. 833

1904: Launched. Built at Selby by Cochrane. Owned by TC & F. Moss Ltd of Grimsby. 1917: Requisitioned into the Fishery Reserve. 1919: Returned to owners. 1939: Requisitioned in November and designated as an APV. 1940: Returned to owners.

INVERCAULD	1940/45	See under SAPLER
INVERCLYDE	1939/42	See under PERIHELIAN
INVERFORTH	1939/45	See under JACINTH
INVERTAY	1940/46	See under CANCER

IONA   1917/19   Displacement: 187TG   73TN
                               Engines: 45TN = 10K
                               Admty No: Not issued
                               Port Reg: H. 709

1904: Launched. Built at Beverley by CWG. Owned by the Hull SF & Ice Co. Ltd. 1917: Requisitioned into the Fishery Reserve. 1919: Returned to owners. 1936: BU at Charlestown.

IONIC   1917/19   Displacement: 159TG 64TN
                                Engines: 55HP
                                Port Reg: GY. 256

1890: Launched. Built at Hull. Owned by Grimsby SFC of Grimsby. 1917: Requisitioned into the Fishery Reserve. 1919: Returned to owners.

IPSWICH   1914/19   Displacement: 161TG   63TN
                                  Engines: 45TN
                                  Armament: 1 x 6pdrAA
                                  Admty No: 429
                                  Port Reg: GY. 178

1896: Launched. Built at Govan. Owned by Consolidated Fisheries of Grimsby. 1914: Requisitioned in December and converted to a M/S. 1919: Returned to owners. 1938: PR: LT.128.

IRANIAN   1915/19 1939/40 Displacement: 202TG   89TN
                                  Engines: 67HP = 10K
                                  Armament: 1 x 6pdr
                                  Admty No: 1604
                                  Port Reg: GY. 728

1911: Launched. Built at Beverley by CWG. Owned by T & FW Robinson of Cleethorpes. 1915: Requisitioned in March and converted to a M/S. 1919: Returned to owners. 1927: Acquired by T. Robinson & Sons of Grimsby. 1939: Requisitioned in November and designated as an APV. 1940: Returned to owners in January. 1944: Mercantile Loss. Lost with all 12 hands in January. Probably mined.

IRAWADI   1915/16   Ex-*Hector*
                                  Displacement: 238TG   91TN

Engines: 70HP
Admty No: 270
Port Reg: H. 941

1906: Launched. Built at Selby by Cochrane. Owned by East Riding SFC of Hull. 1914: Requisitioned in August and converted to a M/S. 1916: LOST. Wrecked on the Tigani Rocks in the E. Med.

IRENE WRAY	1915/19 1940/46	Displacement: 216TG 82TN
		Engines: 78HP
		Armament: 1 x 6pdrAA
		Admty No: 1456
		Port Reg: WWI: HL. 73; WWII: Dutch
		P.No: FY. 1785

1914: Launched. Built at Southbank-on-Tees by Smith's Dock. Owned by W. Wray of Hartlepool. 1915: Requisitioned in May and converted to a M/S. 1919: Returned to Owners. 1940: Hired from Dutch owners as MARIA R. OMMERING and converted to a M/S. 1946: Returned to owners in February.

| IRVANA | 1940/42 | See under ARTHUR LESSIMORE |
| | | (Vol 1 p.48) |

IRWELL	1917/19 1939/40	Displacement: 197TG 79TN
		Engines: 55HP
		Admty No: Not issued
		Port Reg: GY. 1176

1900: Launched. Built at Montrose. Owned by HB & GW Jeffs of Grimsby. 1918: Requisitioned into the Fishery Reserve. 1919: Returned to owners. 1938: Owned by East Anglia SF Co of Grimsby. 1939: Requisitioned in November and designated as an APV. 1940: Returned to owners in January.

| ISA | 1917/19 | Displacement: 217TG |
| | | Port Reg: O. 81 |

1912: Launched. Belgian Fishing vessel. 1917: Requisitioned into the Fishery Reserve with the permission of her Belgian owners. 1919: Returned to owners.

ISABEL	1917/19 1940/45	Displacement: 166TG 67TN
		Engines: 45HP
		Port Reg: WWI: H. 878; WWII: Dutch
		P. No: WWII: FY. 896

1906: Launched. Built at Govan. Owned by J. Storr of Hull. 1917: Requisitioned into the Fishery Reserve. 1919: Returned to owners. 1940: Hired from Dutch owners and converted to a M/S. Commissioned with a Dutch crew. 1944: Converted to an Esso and RN manned. 1945: Returned to owners.

ISABELLA FOWLIE 1916/19   Displacement: 196TG 76TN
                  Engines: 78HP
                  Armament: 1 x 12pdr; 1 x 6pdrAA
                  Admty No: 473
                  Port Reg: A. 418

1911: Launched. Built at Aberdeen. Owned by Hartness SFC of Hartlepool. 1915: Requisitioned in July and converted to a M/S. 1920: Returned to owners.

ISERNIA   1915/19   Displacement: 198TG 79TN
                  Engines: 50HP = 10K
                  Armament: 1 x 6pdrAA; 1 x 7.5-inch
                  Bomb Thrower (A/S Howitzer)
                  Admty No: 1746
                  Port Reg: GY.164

1899: Launched. Built at Hull by CWG. Owned by Great Grimsby & East Coast SFC of Grimsby. 1914: Acquired by Strand SFC of Grimsby. 1915: Requisitioned in July and converted to a M/S. 1920: Returned to owners. 1938: BU.

ISIS   1915/16   Displacement: 168TG
1899: Launched. 1915: Requisitioned. 1916: Returned to the Fishing Fleet.

ISIS   1917/19   Displacement: 175TG 65TN
                  Engines: 50HP = 9.5K
                  Admty No: Not issued
                  Port Reg: GY. 75

1899: Launched. Built at Hull by CWG. Owned by Roberts & Ruthven of Grimsby. 1917: Requisitioned into the Fishery Reserve. 1919: Returned to owners. 1920: Acquired by G. Pearce of Grimsby. 1925: BU.

ISLAND PRINCE   1914/19   Displacement: 205TG 80TN
                  Engines: 74HP
                  Armament: 1 x 6pdrAA
                  Admty No: 62
                  Port Reg: SN. 148

1911: Launched. Built at South Shields. Owned by R. Boyle & W. Rayner of North Shields. 1914: Requisitioned in August and converted to a M/S. 1919: Returned to owners.

ISLAND PRINCE   1919/19   See under GENERAL BOTHA.

ISLE OF MAN   1914/19   Displacement: 176TG 69TN
                  Engines: 45HP
                  Armament: 1 x 12pdr
                  Admty No: 651

Port Reg: H. 826

1905: Launched. Built at Hull. Owned by the Hull SF & Ice Co. 1914: Requisitioned in October and converted to a M/S. 1919: Returned to owners.

ISLE OF WIGHT	1914/19	Displacement: 176TG 69TN
		Engines: 45HP
		Armament: 1 x 6pdr; 1 x 7.5-inch Bomb Thrower (A/S Howitzer)
		Admty No: 543
		Port Reg: H. 852

1905: Launched. Built at Hull. Owned by the Hull SF & Ice Co. 1914: Requisitioned in October and converted to a M/S. 1919: Returned to owners.

ISTRIA	1939/46	Displacement: 409TG 162TN
		Engines: 111HP = 11.6K
		Armament: 1 x 4-inch
		Port Reg: GY. 41
		P. No: FY. 150

1935: Launched. Built at Beverley by CWG. Owned by Hellyer Bros. of Hull. PR: H. 521. 1939: Acquired Great Grimsby & East Coast SFC of Grimsby and renamed *Istria*. PR: GY. 41. 1939: Requisitioned in August and converted to an A/S. 1946: Returned to owners. 1947: Acquired by T. Hamling of Hull and renamed *St. Arcadius*. PR: H. 363. Acquired by Eton FCL of Hull and renamed *Reptonian*. 1959: BU at Preston.

ITALY	1914/16	Displacement: 145TG
		Armament: 1 x 6pdr
		Admty No: 720
		Port Reg: GY. 92

1896: Launched. 1914: Requisitioned in December. 1916: LOST. Sunk on 3rd September in a collision off Sunderland.

ITCHEN	1920/26	See under THOMAS HAGGERTY (Vol 1 p.189)

ITONIAN	1915/19	Displacement: 288TG 150TN
		Engines: 80HP
		Armament: 1 x 6pdr; 1 x 7.5-inch Bomb Thrower (A/S Howitzer)
		Admty No: 1980
		Port Reg: GY. 108

1914: Launched. Built at Selby by Cochrane. Owned by Consolidated Fisheries of Grimsby. 1916: Requisitioned in January and converted to a M/S. 1919: Returned to owners.

IVANHOE   1914/14   Displacement: 190TG
                                              Admty No: 664
                                              Port Reg: GY. 902

1898: Launched. 1914: Requisitioned in October and converted to an APV. LOST. Wrecked in the Firth of Forth on 3rd November.

IZAAC WALTON   1914/19   Displacement: 252TG 96TN
                                              Engines: 68HP
                                              Armament: 1 x 6pdrAA
                                              Admty No: 661
                                              Port Reg: SA. 47

1907: Launched. Built at North Shields. Owned by the Izaac Walton FCL of Swansea. 1914: Requisitioned in November and converted to a M/S. 1919: Returned to owners.

JABOO II   1915/19   Displacement: 236TG 102TN
Engines: 88HP
Armament: 1 x 6pdrAA
Admty No: 1592
Port Reg: LL. 3

1915: Launched. Built at Aberdeen. Requisitioned in May and converted to a M/S.
1919: Returned to owners. Acquired by Port St Mary F & CC of London.

J. BAELS MAURICX   1917/19   Displacement: 211TG
Port Reg: H. 406

1906: Launched. 1917: Requisitioned into the Fishery Reserve. 1919: Returned to
owners.

JACAMAR   1915/17   Displacement: 293TG 128TN
Engines: 80HP = 10.5K
Armament: 1 x 12pdr
Admty No: 1207
Port Reg: GY. 649

1911: Launched. Built at Beverley by CWG. Owned by T. Baskcomb of Grimsby. 1915:
Requisitioned in May and converted to a M/S. 1917: LOST. Sunk on 28th January in a
collision off the Southgate LV, Folkestone.

JACINTA   1915/19 1940/46 Displacement: 288TG 115TN
Engines: 84HP
Armament: WWI: 1 x 6pdr; 1 x 7.5-inch
Bomb Thrower (A/S Howitzer)
WWII: 1 x 12pdr
Admty No: 1976
Port Reg: FD. 235
P.No: 4. 138

1915: Launched. Built at Selby by Cochrane. Owned by J. Marr & Son of Fleetwood.
Requisitioned in December and converted to a M/S. 1919: Returned to owners. 1940:
Requisitioned in May and converted to an APV. Subsequently purchased into the RN.
1942: Converted to a M/S in March. 1944: Converted to a WDV in January. 1946: Sold
to mercantile in May. Acquired by H.B. Ingram of Fleetwood.

JACINTH   1916/19 1939/45 Displacement: 248TG 98TN
Engines: 76HP
Armament: 1 x 12pdr; 1 x 6pdrAA
Admty No: 1226
Port Reg: WWI: H. 33; WWII: GN. 52

1913: Launched. Built at Selby by Cochrane. Owned by Kingston STC of Hull. 1916: Requisitioned in February and converted to a M/S. 1919: Returned to owners. Subsequently renamed *Inverforth*. Acquired by D. Dryburgh of Edinburgh. 1939: Requisitioned in November as INVERFORTH. Converted to an APV. 1940: Converted to a M/S in April. 1945: Returned to owner in July.

JACKDAW	1914/18	Displacement: 250TG 107TN
		Engines: 67HP
		Armament: 1 x 12pdr
		Admty No: 372
		Port Reg: H. 727

1903: Launched. Built at Goole by Goole SB. Owned by Kelsall Bros. & Beeching of Hull. 1914: Purchased into the RN in October and converted to a M/S. 1917: Renamed EXCELLENT in February. 1919: Reverted to JACDAW in February. Sold to mercantile.

JACQUELINE CLASINE	1940/46	Displacement: 206TG
		Port Reg: Dutch
		P. No: FY. 1783

1906: Launched. Dutch fishing vessel. 1940: Hired from Dutch owners and converted to a M/S. Commissioned with a Dutch crew. 1944: Converted to an Esso. 1946: Returned to Holland.

JAMAICA	1917/19 1944/45	Displacement: 205TG 77TN
		Engines: 55HP
		Admty No: 1666
		Port Reg: WWI: H. 216; WWII: LO. 186

1914: Launched. Built at Selby by Cochrane. Owned by the Hull F. & Ice Co. of Hull. 1917: Requisitioned in February and converted to a Hydrophone Tender. 1919: Returned to owners. 1938: Acquired by Heward Trawlers of London and renamed *All Hallows*. 1944: Requisitioned as ALL HALLOWS and converted to an Esso. 1945: Returned to owners.

JAMES BARRIE	1940/45	Displacement: 338TG 132TN
		Engines: 96HP
		Port Reg: H. 460
		P. No: Z. 110

1928: Launched. Built at Selby by Cochrane. Owned by Newington SF Co. Ltd. of Hull. 1940: Requisitioned in April and converted to a BDV. 1945: Returned to owners in November.

JAMES B. GRAHAM	1914/19	Displacement: 198TG 78TN
		Engines: 78HP
		Armament: 1 x 3pdr

Admty No: 64
Port Reg: HL. 9

1914: Launched. Built at Aberdeen. Owned by the Hartness SFC of Hartlepool. Requisitioned in September and converted to a M/S. 1919: Returned to owners.

JAMES PITCHERS   1914/19   Displacement: 197TG 75TN
                                         Engines: 78HP
                                         Armament: 1 x 3pdr
                                         Admty No: 85
                                         Port Reg: SN. 172

1911: Launched. Built at Aberdeen. Owned by Irvin & Son of North Shields. 1914: Requisitioned in August and converted to a M/S. 1919: Returned to owners.

JAMES S. MELVILLE   1914/19   Displacement: 211TG 81TN
                                         Engines: 66HP
                                         Armament: 1 x 12pdr; 1 x 7.5-inch
                                         Bomb Thrower (A/S Howitzer)
                                         Port Reg: A. 392

1911: Launched. Built at Aberdeen. Owned by AG Brown of Granton Harbour. 1914: Requisitioned in September and converted to a M/S. 1919: Returned to owners.

JAN de WAELE   1940/45   Displacement: 324TG
                                         Port Reg: Belgian
                                         P. No: Z. 231

1925: Launched. Belgian fishing vessel. 1940: Hired from Belgian owners in September and converted to an APV. 1945: Returned to Belgium in December.

JANE ROSS   1915/19   Displacement: 184TG 69TN
                                        Engines: 56HP
                                        Armament: 1 x 12pdr
                                        Admty No: 3351
                                        Port Reg: A. 454

1901: Launched. Built at Aberdeen. Owned by Ross STC of Aberdeen. 1915: Requisitioned in June and converted to a M/S. 1919: Returned to owners.

JANUS   1914/20   Displacement: 243TG 93TN
                                        Engines: 86HP
                                        Armament: 1 x 12pdr
                                        Admty No: 167
                                        Port Reg: GY. 1138

1911: Launched. Built at Goole by Goole SB. 1914: Purchased into the RN in May and converted to a M/S. 1919: Renamed KILDA. 1920: Sold to mercantile and renamed *Tubal Cain*. Acquired by D. Gault AO of Lossiemouth.

JANUS II	1914/20	Displacement: 240TG 98TN
		Engines: 70HP
		Armament: 1 x 3pdr
		Admty No: 325
		Port Reg: GY. 64

1905: Launched. Built at Selby by Cochrane. Owned by Orient SFC of Grimsby. 1914: Requisitioned in August and converted to a M/S. Renamed JANUS II in December. 1920: Returned to owners.

JAPAN	1915/15	Displacement: 205TG
		Admty No: 42
		Port Reg: GY. 28

1904: Launched. 1915: Requisitioned in August and converted to a M/S. LOST. Mined off the Shipwash on 16th August.

JARDINE	1939/40	Cricketer Group
		Displacement: 191TN
		Engines: 133HP
		Armament: 1 x 4-inch
		Port Reg: GY. 301
		P. No: FY. 169

1936: Launched. Built at Selby by Cochrane. Owned by Crampins of Grimsby. 1939: Purchased into the RN in August and converted to A/S. Joined the 22nd A/S Group. 1940: TPI the Norwegian Campaign in April. LOST. Scuttled off the W. Coast of Norway on 30th April having sustained heavy damage in an air attack. Subsequently salvaged, repaired and commissioned into the German Navy as CHERUSKER. 1942: German Loss. Mined on 6th December.

JASON	1914/19	Displacement: 176TG
		Admty No: 10
		Port Reg: SN. 76

1898: Launched. 1914: Requisitioned in August. Designated as a M/S but deemed unsuitable. Returned to owners in September. 1915: Mercantile Loss. Captured and sunk by a German S/M 40 miles off the Tyne on 1st April.

JASPER	1914/15	Ex-*Rayvernol*
		Displacement: 221TG
		Admty No: 1

1912: Launched. Built at Southbank-on-Tees by Smiths Dock. 1914: Purchased into the RN and converted to a M/S. 1915: LOST. Mined in the Moray Firth on 26th August.

| JASPER | 1917/19 | Displacement: 156TG |
| | | Port Reg: H. 176 |

1917: Requisitioned into the Fishery Reserve. 1919: Returned to owners.

JAVELIN   1914/15   Ex-*Braconlea*
                                          Displacement: 205TG
                                          Admty No: 21
1913: Launched. Built at Aberdeen by Hall. 1914: Purchased into the RN and converted
to a M/S. 1915: LOST. Mined off the Longsands on 17th October.

JAY   1914/17   Displacement: 144TG
                                          Armament: 1 x 6pdrAA
                                          Admty No: 375
                                          Port Reg: H. 534
1897: Launched. 1914: Requisitioned in October and converted to a M/S. 1917: LOST.
Torpedoed off Southwold on 11th August.

JAY   1940/44   Ex-*Kingston Pearl*
                                          Ex-*Nautilus*
                                          Displacement: 352TG 147TN
                                          Engines: 96HP = 11K
                                          Port Reg: Belgian O. 160
                                          P. No: M. 06
1926: Launched. Built at Beverley by CWG. Owned by Kingston SFC of Hull. PR:
H.296 1939: Acquired by Belgian mercantile and renamed *Nautilus* PR: O.160. 1940:
Fled from Belgium during the German invasion and arrived at Fleetwood in May. Hired
from Belgian Owners and converted to a M/L. 1944: Renamed SANDMARTIN in
December. 1946: Returned to owners and reverted to original name. 1950: Acquired by
Polish mercantile and renamed *Perseus*. 1952: Mercantile loss. Struck a wreck and
sank on 3rd June off Szezecin, Poland.

JEAN EDMUNDS   1940/45   Displacement: 216TG   83TN
                                          Engines: 80HP
                                          Port Reg: A. 174
                                          P. No: FY. 1677
1916: Launched. Built at Selby by Cochrane. Owned by the Stephen Fishing Co of
Aberdeen. 1940: Requisitioned in January and converted to a M/S. 1945: Returned to
owners in September.

JEAN FREDERICK   1940/41   See under JAMES HULBERT
                                          (Vol 1 p.137)

JEANIE STEWART   1916/19   Displacement: 210TG 91TN
                                          Engines: 78HP
                                          Armament: 1 x 6pdrAA; 1 x 3.5-inch
                                          Bomb Thrower (A/S Howitzer)
                                          Admty No: 3282
                                          Port Reg: SN. 18

1916: Launched. Built at Aberdeen. Owned by R. Irvine & Sons of S. Shields. Requisitioned in June and converted to a M/S. Fitted with Listening Hydrophones. 1919: Returned to owners.

JELLICOE   1915/19 1939/45   Displacement: 338TG   189TN
                                             Engines: 88HP = 10K
                                             Armament: 1 x 4-inch; 1 x 12pdr;
                                             1 x 3pdr
                                             Admty No: 1546
                                             Port Reg: WWI: GY. 522
                                             WWII: H. 447
                                             P. No: WWII: FY. 534

1915: Launched. Built at Beverley by CWG. Owned by Earl SFC of Grimsby. Requisitioned in July and renamed RUSHCOE. 1917: Acquired (on paper) by N. Green of Grimsby with the designated name of *Ceriesio*. 1919: Returned to owners and reverted to original name. 1920: Acquired by H. Bacon of Grimsby. Acquired by Trawlers, White Sea & Grimsby. 1922: Acquired by Hellyer Bros. of Hull. PR: H. 447. 1939: Requisitioned in September as CERESIO and converted to a M/S. 1983: Stores Hulk at Port of Spain, Trinidad.

JENNET   1939/46   Ex-*Bunsen*
                                             Displacement: 358TG   141TN
                                             Engines: 96HP = 10.7K
                                             Port Reg: H. 269
                                             P. No: Z. 21

1926: Launched. Built at Beverley by CWG. Owned by F & T Ross Ltd of Hull. 1939: Purchased into the RN in April, fitted out as a Boom Trawler and renamed JENNET. Served in the Clyde throughout the War. 1946: Sold to mercantile in January and retained the same name. Acquired by JC Llewllyn of Hull and renamed *Westheron*. PR: H. 465. 1950: Acquired by Lord Line of Hull and renamed *Lord Bann*. 1951: Acquired by Belgian owners as a stores hulk. BU in Belgium.

JENNIFER   1940/42   See under BRAEMAR of 1940

JERIA   1916/19   Displacement: 344TG   138TN
                                               Engines: 89HP = 10K
                                             Armament: 1 x 6pdr
                                             Admty No: 3319
                                             Port Reg: GY. 985

1916: Launched. Built at Beverley by CWG. Owned by Great Grimsby & East Coast SFC of Grimsby. Requisitioned in December and converted to a M/S. 1917: Returned in December. 1929: Mercantile Loss. Took the ground in thick fog on St. John's Head, Hoy, Orkneys.

JERICHO   1915/19 1940/41 Ex-*Sir John Jellicoe*
                                             Displacement: 351TG 165TN
                                             Engines: 100HP = 11K
                                             Armament: 1 x 12pdr
                                             Admty No: 1577
                                             Port Reg: WWI: H. 310
                                             WWII: GY. 1170

1914: Launched. Built at Beverley by CWG. Owned by Imperial SFC of Hull. 1915:
Requisitioned in May and renamed JERICHO. Fitted to carry 2 a/c and employed on
Anti-Zeppelin patrols in the North Sea. 1918: Acquired by D Line SFC of Grimsby whilst still
in Admiralty service. 1920: Returned to owners and renamed *Dargle* PR: GY.1170. 1933:
Acquired by Kopanes SFC of Grimsby and renamed *Kopanes* 1940: Requisitioned as
KOPANES and converted to an APV. 1941: LOST. Sunk by air attack off the Tyne on 19 April.

JESSICA   1914/19   Displacement: 173TG 68TN
                                             Engines: 45HP = 9.5K
                                             Armament: 1 x 6pdrAA
                                             Admty No: 13
                                             Port Reg: H .870

1906: Launched. Built at Beverley by CWG. 1914: Requisitioned in August and
converted to a M/S. 1917: Acquired by Curzon of Milford Haven whilst in Admiralty
Service. 1919: Returned to owners. Acquired by Dobson SFC of Grimsby. PR: GY. 674.
1923: Acquired by Kelsall Bros. & Beeching of Hull. PR: H. 895. 1936: BU.

JESSIE NUTTEN   1914/16   Displacement: 187TG
                                             Admty No: 312
                                             Port Reg: A. 243

1908: Launched. 1914: Requisitioned in August and converted to a M/S. 1916: LOST.
Mined off Lowestoft on 4th September.

JOHANNESBURG   1915/19   Displacement: 181TG 65TN
                                             Engines: 45HP = 10K
                                             Armament: 1 x 3pdr
                                             Admty No: 1796
                                             Port Reg: H. 711

1903: Launched. Built at Beverley by CWG. Owned by Hull SF & Ice Co of Hull. 1915:
Requisitioned in October and converted to a M/S. 1919: Returned to owners. 1922:
Acquired by W. Normandale of Scarborough and renamed *Nordale*. PR: SH. 89. 1938:
Acquired by Torbay Trawlers of Scarborough. 1942: Mercantile Loss. Wrecked on the
Mull of Kintyre, Scotland on 15th January.

JOHN   1917/19   Displacement: 221TG
                                             Admty No: Not issued
                                             Port Reg: O. 131

1910: Launched. Belgian fishing vessel. 1917: Requisitioned into the Fishery Reserve with the permission of her Belgian owners. 1919: Returned to owners.

JOHN C. MEIKLE	1914/19	Displacement: 194TG 86TN
		Engines: 80HP
		Port Reg: SN. 70

1914: Launched. Built at Willington Quay. Owned by R. Irvin & Son of North Shields. Requisitioned. 1919: Returned to owners.

JOHN DONOVAN	1914/19	Displacement: 206TG 78TN
		Engines: 82HP
		Armament: 1 x 3pdr
		Admty No: 435
		Port Reg: SN. 52

1914: Launched. Built at Willington Quay. Owned by R. Hastie of N. Shields. Requisitioned in December and converted to a M/S. 1919: Returned to owners.

JOHN E. LEWIS	1914/18	Displacement: 253TG
		Armament: 1 x 3pdr
		Admty No: 321
		Port Reg: A. 354

1911: Launched. 1914: Requisitioned in August and converted to a M/S. 1918: LOST. Mined off the Cork LV. Harwich.

JOHN G. WATSON	1914/15	Displacement: 196TG
		Armament: 1 x 6pdr
		Admty No: 427
		Port Reg: A. 327

1910: Launched. 1914: Requisitioned in November and converted to a M/S. 1915: LOST. Sunk on 31st October in a collision near Stornaway.

JOHN G. WATSON	1916/19	Displacement: 235TG
		Armament: 1 x 6pdrAA
		Admty No: 3322
		Port Reg: SN. 305

1916: Launched. Requisitioned in January and converted to a M/S. Converted to an Escort. 1919: Returned to owners.

JOHN HIGH	1916/16	Displacement: 228TG
		Armament: 1 x 6pdrAA
		Admty No: 3252
		Port Reg: SN. 233

1915: Launched. 1916: Requisitioned in January and converted to a M/S. LOST. Mined on 7th August off Mount Sozonova in the White Sea.

JOHN H. IRVIN   1915/19   Displacement: 199TG   77TN
                                            Engines: 78HP
                                            Port Reg: A. 593
1913: Launched.   Built at Aberdeen.   Owned by Irvine of North Shields.   1915:
Requisitioned in June and converted to a BDV. 1919: Returned to owners. Acquired by
Reliable SFC of Scarborough.

JOHN MASON   1920/21   See under JOHN ABBOTT
                                            (Vol 1 p.176)

JOHN SHERBURN   1915/15   Displacement: 244TG   97TN
                                            Engines: 63NHP = 10K
                                            Admty No: 815
                                            Port Reg: H. 644
1902: Launched.   Built at Hull by CWG.   Owned by Humber STC of Hull.   1915:
Requisitioned and converted to an APV. LOST. Wrecked near Dover on 6th March.

JOHN T. GRAHAM   1914/19   Displacement: 198TG   77TN
                                            Engines: 76HP
                                            Armament: 1 x 6pdr AA
                                            Admty No: 467
                                            Port Reg: HL. 69
1912: Launched.   Built at Aberdeen.   Owned by Fairy ST Co of Hartlepool.   1914:
Requisitioned in October and converted to a M/S. 1919: Returned to owners. Acquired
by JB Graham AO of Milford Haven. PR: LO. 430.

JONQUIL   1917/19   Displacement: 143TG   54TN
                                            Engines: 45HP
                                            Port Reg: GY. 391
1891: Launched.   Built at London.   Owned by North Eastern SFC of Grimsby.   1917:
Requisitioned into the Fishery Reserve. 1919: Returned to owners. Acquired by TW.
Bascombe of Grimsby. PR: GY. 391. Acquired by Consolidated Fisheries of Grimsby.

JOSEPH & SARAH MILES 1915/19   Displacement: 272TG   100TN
                                            Engines: 65HP
                                            Armament: 1 x 12pdr
                                            Admty No: 1132
                                            Port Reg: LO. 175
1902: Launched.   Built at Leith.   Owned by the Royal National Mission to Deep Sea
Fisherman. 1915: Requisitioned in April and converted to a M/S. 1920: Returned to
owners.   1938: Still in the ownership of The Royal National Mission to Deep Sea
Fishermen.

JOSEPH DUHAMEL   1940/41   Displacement: 928TG
                                         Port Reg: French
1929: Launched. 1940: French fishing vessel seized in the Atlantic on 26th December.
1941: Designated as A/S and commenced fitting out but transferred to the MWT in April
before completion.

JOSEPHINE I   1919/20   See under SPARROW

JULIET   1914/19   Displacement: 173TG   53TN
                                         Engines: 45HP = 9.5K
                                         Armament: 1 x 6pdrAA
                                         Admty No: 45
                                         Port Reg: H. 880
1906: Launched. Built at Beverley by CWG. Owned by Hellyer SFC of Hull. 1914:
Requisitioned in September and converted to a M/S. 1917: Acquired by Lady
Beardmore (C. Curzon) of Milford Haven whilst still in Service. 1919: Returned to
owners. Acquired by Kelsall Bros. & Beeching of Hull. PR: H. 902. 1936: Acquired by
Crescent TCL of Hull. 1941: Mercantile Loss. Sunk by enemy a/c 30 miles S. of Old
Head of Kinsal. No loss of life.

JUNCO   1917/19 1940/46   Displacement: 191TG   72TN
                                         Engines: 55HP
                                         Armament: 1 x 12pdr
                                         Admty No: 1657
                                         Port Reg: WWII: H. 587
                                         P. No: WWII: FY. 1830
1917: Launched. Built at Goole by Goole SB. Owned by Kelsall Bros. & Beeching of
Hull. 1918: Requisitioned in January and converted to a M/S. 1919: Returned to
owners. 1940: Requisitioned in October and converted to a HDPC. 1944: Employed on
Target-towing. 1946: Returned to owners in May.

KALMIA   1915/18   Displacement: 189TG 93TN
                                     Engines: 50HP
                                     Armament: 1 x 6pdr
                                     Admty No: 1778
                                     Port Reg: GY. 572

1894: Launched. Iron construction. Owned by North Eastern SFC of Grimsby. 1915: Requisitioned in May. 1918: Severely damaged by fire at Stavros on 7th October. Repaired and returned to owners. Notes: Reported in some lists as requisitioned in WWII as AMOS. NFI.

KALMIA II   1916/19   Displacement: 194TG 73TN
                                     Engines: 61HP
                                     Armament: 1 x 6pdrAA
                                     Admty No: 791
                                     Port Reg: M. 142

1898: Launched. Built at Aberdeen. Owned by Rainbow SFC of Milford Haven. 1915: Requisitioned in January and converted to a M/S. Renamed KALMIA II in August. 1919: Returned to owners.

KALSO   1917/19   Displacement: 179TG 70TN
                                     Engines: 52HP
                                     Admty No: Not issued
                                     Port Reg: GY .725

1899: Launched. Built at North Shields. Owned by the Spurn SFC of Grimsby. 1917: Requisitioned into the Fishery Reserve. 1919: Returned to owners.

KAPHREDA   1914/16   Displacement: 245TG
                                     Admty No: 364
                                     Port Reg: FD. 188

1911: Launched. 1914: Requisitioned in August and converted to a M/S. 1916: LOST. Mined near the Corton LV on 8th June.

KASTORIA   1917/19 1940/46 Displacement: 307TG 121TN
                                     Engines: 89HP = 10K
                                     Armament: 1 x 12pdr
                                     Admty No: 3324
                                     Port Reg: GY. 1017
                                     P. No: WWII: 4. 148

1916: Launched. Built at Beverley by CWG. Owned by Gt. Grimsby & E. Coast SFC of Grimsby. 1917: Requisitioned in January and converted to a M/S. 1918: Converted to an Escort. 1919: Returned to owners. 1940: Requisitioned in May and converted to A/S.

1941: Converted to a M/S in May. 1942: Acquired by Boston Deep Sea Fishing Co. of Grimsby. 1946: Returned to owners in May. 1947: Acquired by Polish owners. 1959: BU in Poland.

KATE LEWIS   1916/39   Displacement: 207TG 79TN
                                     Engines: 80HP
                                     Armament: 1 x 6pdrAA; 24 mines
                                     Admty No: 2975
                                     Port Reg: A .260
1916: Launched. Built at Selby by Cochrane. Owned by RW Lewis of Aberdeen. Purchased into the RN in August and converted to a M/L. 1919: Attached as a tender to HMS VERNON, Portsmouth, as a tender for M/L trials. 1939: Sold.

KATHLEEN BURTON   1916/19   Displacement: 197TG 86TN
                                     Engines: 57HP
                                     Admty No: 1469
                                     Port Reg: HL. 30
1914: Launched. Built at Aberdeen. Owned by the Doris Burton STC of Hartlepool. 1916: Requisitioned in May and converted to a M/S. 1919: Returned to owners.

KELT   1939/45   Displacement: 455TG
                                     Armament: 1 x 4-inch
                                     P. No: FY. 112
1937: Launched. 1939: Purchased into the RN in August and converted to an A/S. 1942: Operating off W. Africa employed on Escort duties. Severely damaged alongside in Lagos in December. A tanker *Athelvictor* which she had just escorted from the Gold Coast accidentally discharged 60T of petrol into the Harbour which then ignited. Her bow was blown off, her foredeck collapsed and her bridge was buckled. Three other Trs. alongside her were destroyed, (BENGALI, CANNA and SPANIARD). TIH for repairs. 1945: Sold to mercantile and renamed *Camilla*.

KELVIN   1915/17   Displacement: 322TG
                                     Armament: 1 x 6pdrAA
                                     Admty No: 1974
                                     Port Reg: H. 357
1915: Launched. Requisitioned in November and converted to a M/S. 1917: LOST. Mined off Harwich on 7th July.

KENNET   1915/19   Displacement: 167TG 66TN
                                     Engines: 45HP
                                     Port Reg: A. 332
1899: Launched. Built at Irvine. 1915: Requisitioned in June and converted to a BDV. 1919: Returned to owners. Acquired by GB Musson of Grimsby AO.

KENNET   1920/46   See under ICEAXE (Vol 1 p.32)

KENNYMORE   1915/19 1939/40 Displacement: 225TG 112TN
                                        Engines: 67HP = 10K
                                        Armament: 1 x 12pdr; 1 x 7.5-inch
                                        Bomb Thrower (A/S Howitzer)
                                        Admty No: 1373
                                        Port Reg: GY. 38
                                        P. No: WWII: FY. 857
1914: Launched. Built at Beverley by CWG. Owned by South Western SFC of Grimsby.
1915: Requisitioned in April and converted to a M/S. Acquired by TW Baskcomb of
Grimsby. 1919: Returned to owners. 1935: Acquired by Dobson Ship Repair of Grimsby.
1939: Requisitioned in November and converted to a M/S. 1940: LOST. Mined in the
Thames Estuary on 25th November.

KENSINGTON   1914/19   Displacement: 172TG   67TN
                                       Engines: 57HP
                                       Armament: 1 x 3pdr; 1 x 2pdr
                                       Admty No: 687
                                       Port Reg: GY. 1156
1900: Launched. Built at Beverley. Owned by the Queen SFC of Grimsby. 1914:
Requisitioned in November. 1919: Returned to owners. 1938: Owned by A.W. Clark of
Milford Haven. Port Reg: M. 208.

KERNEVAL   1944/44   Displacement: 172TG 65TN
                                       Engines: 57HP
                                       Port Reg: SD. 36
1906: Launched. Built at Aberdeen. Owned by the Sunderland Ice Co of Sunderland.
1944: Requisitioned in April and converted to an Esso. Returned to owners in
November.

KERYADO   1940/41   Displacement: 252TG
                                       Port Reg: French
1920: Launched. French fishing vessel. 1940: French M/S seized in Operation Grab on
3rd July. Added to the Navy List as a M/S. 1941: LOST. Mined in the Channel on 6th
March.

KESTREL II   1914/19 (?)   Displacement: 181TG
1898: Launched. 1914: Requisitioned. 1919: Returned to owners (?).

KIDWELLY CASTLE   1914/19   Displacement: 259TG 100TN
                                       Engines: 54HP
                                       Armament: 1 x 6pdrAA
                                       Admty No: 541

Port Reg: SA. 40

1907: Launched. Built at Maryport. Owned by Consolidated Fisheries of Grimsby. 1915: Requisitioned in April and converted to a M/S. 1919: Returned to owners.

KIELDER CASTLE 1917/19 Displacement: 129TG 50TN
Engines: 50HP
Admty No: Not issued
Port Reg: FD. 40

1900: Launched. Built at Willington Quay. Owned by Garth STC of Fleetwood. 1917: Requisitioned into the Fishery Reserve. 1919: Returned to owners.

KILLDEER 1914/19 Displacement: 192TG 73TN
Engines: 55HP
Armament: 1 x 6pdrAA
Admty No: 387
Port Reg: H. 1014

1913: Launched. Built at Goole. Owned by Kelsall Bros. & Beeching of Hull. 1914: Requisitioned in November and converted to a M/S. 1919: Returned to owners. *Notes*: Mercantile Lists as *Kildier*.

KIMBERLEY 1914/19 1939/40 Displacement: 190TG 74TN
Engines: 55HP
Armament: 1 x 12pdr
Admty No: 11
Port Reg: GY. 167

1902: Launched. Built at Selby by Cochrane. Owned by Taylor & Staff of Grimsby. 1914: Requisitioned in August and converted to a M/S. 1919: Returned to owners. Acquired by Diamonds SFC of Grimsby. 1939: Requisitioned in November and converted to an APV. Renamed MANLY in December. 1940: Returned to owners.

KIMBERLEY 1915/19 Displacement: 102TG 39TN
Engines: 38HP
Armament: 1 x 3pdr
Port Reg: BF. 965

1907: Launched. Built at Aberdeen. Owned by J. Falconer of Portknockie & J. Mitchell of Peterhead. 1915: Requisitioned. 1919: Returned to owners.

KIMBERLEY II 1915/19 Displacement: 181TG 71TN
Engines: 45HP = 10K
Port Reg: H. 707

1902: Launched. Built at Beverley by CWG as *Kimberley*. Owned by the Hull SF & Ice Co. of Hull. 1915: Requisitioned in October, converted to a M/S and renamed KIMBERLEY II. 1919: Returned to owners and reverted to original name. 1936: BU at Charlestown.

KIMBERLEY IV   1917/19   Displacement: 102TG
                                       Port Reg: BF. 965
1907: Launched. 1917: Requisitioned into the Fishery Reserve. 1919: Returned to owners.

KINALDIE   1915/19   Displacement: 197TG 86TN
                                       Engines: 78HP
                                       Armament: 1 x 6pdr
                                       Admty No: 805
                                       Port Reg: A. 83
1914: Launched. Built at Aberdeen. Owned by GJ & W Leiper of Aberdeen. 1915: Requisitioned in November and converted to a M/S. 1919: Returned to owners.

KINCORTH   1917/18   Displacement: 148TG 57TN
                                       Engines: 46HP
                                       Port Reg: A. 263
1909: Launched. Built at Aberdeen. Owned by G. Leiper AO of Aberdeen. 1917: Requisitioned in February and fitted out for Special Mine Service. 1920: Returned to owners. Acquired by R. Irvin & Sons of North Shields.

KINELLAR   1917/19   Displacement: 216TG 84TN
                                       Engines: 78HP
                                       Armament: 1 x 6pdr
                                       Admty No: 3042
                                       Port Reg: A. 813
1917: Launched. Built at Aberdeen. Owned by G. Leiper of Aberdeen & Irvin & Sons of North Shields. Requisitioned in June and converted to a M/S. 1919: Returned to owners. 1938: Owned by R. Irvin & Sons of N. Shields. Port Reg: A. 839.

KING ARTHUR   1915/19   Displacement: 159TG 70TN
                                       Engines: 40HP
                                       Armament: 1 x 3pdr
                                       Admty No: 3354
                                       Port Reg: GY. 11
1899: Launched. Built at Aberdeen. Owned by Consolidated Fisheries of Grimsby. 1915: Requisitioned in June and converted to a M/S. 1920: Returned to owners.

KING CANUTE   1917/19   Displacement: 195TG 98TN
                                       Engines: 40HP
                                       Port Reg: GY. 1124
1899: Launched. Built at Grimsby. Owned by W. Smith of Grimsby. 1917: Requisitioned into the Fishery Reserve. 1919: Returned to owners.

KING EDWARD   1915/19   Displacement: 163TG 73TN
                                       Engines: 40HP
                                       Armament: 1 x 6pdr
                                       Port Reg: GY. 1195
1900: Launched. Built at Grimsby. Owned by Consolidated Fisheries of Grimsby. 1915:
Requisitioned in January and converted to a BDV. 1919: Returned to owners.

KING EGBERT   1915/20   Displacement: 159TG 66TN
                                       Engines: 40HP
                                       Armament: 1 x 3pdr
                                       Admty No: 2576
                                       Port Reg: GY. 97
1899: Launched. Built at Grimsby. Owned by Consolidated Fisheries of Grimsby. 1915:
Requisitioned in June and converted to a M/S. 1920: Returned to owners.

KING EMPEROR   1915/19 1940/46 Displacement: 246TG 96TN
                                       Engines: 76HP
                                       Armament: WWI: 1 x 6pdr; 24 Mines
                                       WWII: 1 x 6pdr
                                       Admty No: 3220
                                       Port Reg: WWI: H. 202; WWII: LH. 130
                                       P. No: WWI: N. 5A (M/L); N. 66 (M/S)
                                       WWII: FY. 730 (M/L); Y7. 14 (Esso)
1914: Launched. Built at Dundee. Owned by Mills SS Co. of London. 1915:
Requisitioned in May and converted to a M/L. 1918: Converted to a M/S. 1919:
Returned to owners. Acquired by Consolidated Fisheries of Grimsby. 1940:
Requisitioned in February and converted to a M/S. 1943: Converted to an Esso. 1946:
Returned to owners in January.

KING ERIK   1915/19   Displacement: 228TG 90TN
                                       Engines: 54HP
                                       Armament: 1 x 3pdr
                                       Admty No: 1368
                                       Port Reg: GY. 474
1899: Launched. Built at Selby by Cochrane. Owned by F. Barrett of Grimsby. 1915:
Requisitioned in April and converted to a M/S. 1919: Returned to owners. 1941:
Mercantile Loss. Lost with all hands off Iceland on 5th September. Believed torpedoed
by U-141.

KING FREDERICK   1915/19 1940/44 Ex-*King Frederick III*
                                       Displacement: 260TG 103TN
                                       Engines: 76HP = 11K
                                       Armament: 1 x 3pdr
                                       Admty No: 2659

Port Reg: GY. 482

P. No: WWII: 4. 257

1909: Launched. Built at Beverley by CWG as *King Frederick III*. Owned by GE Forum of Esbjerg, Denmark. PR: F.145. 1915: Acquired by F. Barrett of Grimsby. PR: GY.482. 1915: Requisitioned in May and converted to a M/S. 1919: Returned to owners. 1922: Acquired by TW Baskcomb of Grimsby. 1928: Renamed *Magnolia*. 1935: Acquired by H. Franklin of Grimsby. 1940: Requisitioned in May, converted to an APV and renamed GLACIER. 1944: Returned to owners in June and reverted to *Magnolia*. 1952: Mercantile Loss. Foundered whilst in tow in the North Sea on 20th August. Having sprung a leak, she was taken in tow by another trawler, *Rose of England* but after 19 hours in tow she finally sank with the loss of three lives.

KINGFISHER   1915/19   Ex-*Alcyon*
                                     Displacement: 322TG
                                     Armament: 1 x 12pdr; 1 x 6pdr; 1 x a/c
                                     Admty No: 1498 (KINGFISHER),
                                     1499 (ADELE)

1915: Launched. Purchased into the RN in April and converted to an APV. Fitted with Listening Hydrophones and to carry 1 x a/c. Employed on anti-Zeppelin patrols in the North Sea 1918: Renamed ADELE in June having exchanged Name and No. with the Drifter of that name. 1919: Sold to mercantile and renamed *Alcyon*.

KING GEORGE   1917/19   Displacement: 164TG 73TN
                                     Engines: 40HP
                                     Port Reg: GY. 1214

1901: Launched. Built at Grimsby. Owned by F. Barrett of Grimsby. 1917: Requisitioned into the Fishery Reserve. 1919: Returned to owner.

KING HAROLD   1917/19   Displacement: 227TG 93TN
                                     Engines: 55HP
                                     Admty No: Not issued
                                     Port Reg: GY. 479

1899: Launched. Built at Selby by Cochrane. Owned by F. Barrett of Grimsby. 1917: Requisitioned into the Fishery Reserve. 1919: Returned to owners.

KING HENRY   1917/19 1940/4   Displacement: 162TG 72TN
                                     Engines: 45HP
                                     Port Reg: WWI: GY. 1169
                                     WWII: LT. 355

1900: Launched. Built at Grimsby. 1917: Requisitioned into the Fishery Reserve. 1919: Returned to owners. 1938: Owned by Consolidated Fisheries of Grimsby. 1940: Requisitioned in May and converted to a BGV. 1941: Converted to an APV. LOST. Sunk by enemy a/c off Lowestoft on 13th June.

KING LEAR   1914/19   Displacement: 311TG 124TN
                                          Engines: 102HP
                                          Armament: 1 x 12pdr; 1 x 7.5-inch
                                          Bomb Thrower (A/S Howitzer)
                                          Admty No: 78
                                          Port Reg: H. 871
1906: Launched. Built at Hull. Owned by Hellyers SFC of Hull. 1914: Requisitioned in November and converted to a M/S. 1917: Converted to a 'Q' Ship in May. 1918: Returned to General Service in April. 1919: Returned to owners. *Notes*: 'Q' Ship operational names: *Diana, Enid* and *Kib.*

KING RICHARD   1915/19   Displacement: 162TG 74TN
                                          Engines: 45HP
                                          Armament: 1 x 3pdr
                                          Admty No: 1775
                                          Port Reg: GY. 1181
1900: Launched. Built at Grimsby. Owned by Consolidated Fisheries of Grimsby. 1915: Requisitioned in October and converted to a M/S. 1920: Returned to owners. 1938: Reregistered. LT. 161.

KINGSCOURT   1939/45   See under WILLIAM BIGGS
                                          (Vol 1 p.190)

KINGS GREY   1915/19 1939/46 Displacement: 338TG 189TN
                                          Engines: 92HP = 11K
                                          Armament: WWI: 1 x 6pdr;
                                          WWII: 1 x 12pdr
                                          Admty No: 1628
                                          Port Reg: WWI: GY .486; WWII: H. 402
                                          P. No: WWII: 4. 87 (APV)
                                          FY. 502 (M/S)
1915: Launched. Built at Beverley by CWG. Owned by the Earl SFC of Grimsby. Requisitioned in May and converted to a M/S. 1919: Returned to owners. 1920: Acquired by South Western SFC of Grimsby. Acquired by Black of Grimsby. 1922: Acquired by Hellyer Bros. of Hull. 1939: Requisitioned in August and converted to an APV. Returned to owners in October. 1940: Requisitioned in May and converted to a M/S. Based at Devonport for sweeping in the Channel. 1944: TPI Operation Neptune, the D-Day Landings in June, as a D/L attached to the 16th M/S Flot. in Force U. 1946: Returned to owners in September. 1950: Renamed *Arctic Rover*. 1952: Renamed *Swanland*. 1954: BU in Belgium.

KING SOL   1939/45   Displacement: 486TG 238TN
                                          Engines: 129HP
                                          Port Reg: GY. 338

P.No: FY. 235

1936: Launched. Built at Selby by Cochrane. Owned by Rinovia SF Co. Ltd. of Grimsby. 1939: Requisitioned in September and converted to A/S. 1942: Employed on convoy duties UK-Iceland. 1943: Transferred to the Med. sailing from Milford Haven to Gibraltar in February. Subject of suspected sabotage later in the year. Whilst she was as sea it was discovered that she was taking water very rapidly. The pumps were unable to cope and baling by hand was employed using a bucket chain for two days and nights until she eventually made Bone. It was discovered that a sea-cock had been opened and the culprit was thought to be one of the Spanish workers who had been onboard during coaling at Gibraltar. 1945: Returned to owners in December. 1961: BU.

KING STEPHEN	1915/16	Displacement: 162TG
		Armament: 1 x 6pdr QF Hotchkiss
		Port Reg: GY. 1174

1900: Launched. Owned by the Consolidated Fishing Co of Grimsby. 1916: Requisitioned in February and converted to a 'Q' Ship. Involved in an incident which led to the crew being branded war criminals. See Notes below. LOST. Sunk by German S/M in the North Sea on 25th April. No loss of life, but the crew all taken prisoner. *Notes*: Operated under the name of *Ledger No.778* as well as her own name as a 'Q' Ship. The incident in February 1916 occurred when she came across a 'downed' German Zeppelin L.19 in the North Sea. There were 19 German aircrew in the Zeppelin and Skipper William Martin refused to rescue them on the grounds that it would have been 'tempting fate' to take onboard 19 armed enemy when he had a crew of only 9. All L.19's crew perished and the German High Command branded the trawler's crew War Criminals. When she was sunk just two months later there was a new crew and Skipper aboard. Even so the Skipper was put through an interrogation about the incident with the L.19, but no evidence against him was found.

KINGSTON	1915/19	Displacement: 161TG 63TN
		Engines: 45HP
		Armament: 1 x 3pdr
		Admty No: 2575
		Port Reg: GY. 206

1897: Launched. Built at Govan. Owned by Consolidated Fisheries of Grimsby. 1915: Requisitioned in June. 1919: Returned to owners.

KINGSTON AGATE	1939/45	Displacement: 464TG 168TN
		Engines: 155HP = 12.5K
		Armament: 1 x 4-inch; 2 x MGs; 2 x
		0.5-inch MGs; DCs
		Complement: 52
		Port Reg: H. 489
		P. No: FY. 212

1937: Launched. Built at Beverley by CWG. Owned by Kingston STC of Hull. 1939:

Requisitioned in September and converted to A/S. 1940: ICW VASCAMA, NORTHERN FOAM and NORTHERN GIFT based at Kirkwall for contraband patrols between Norway and Greenland. 1941: TPI the operation to rescue the German S/M U-570 which had been captured by RAF a/c off Ireland on 27th August. The U-Boat, which subsequently became HMS/M GRAPH, gave up her Cypher Machine intact. 1942: Based at Portsmouth employed on Needles/IOW patrols and S/M escorts. 1943: TIH at Grimsby for refitting. On completion transferred to the Northern Patrol. 1946: Returned to owners in January. 1963: BU in Belgium.

KINGSTON ALALITE   1939/40   Displacement: 412TG 166TN
                                           Engines: 111HP = 11.8K
                                           Port Reg: H. 538
                                           P. No: FY. 136
1933: Launched. Built at Beverley by CWG. Owned by Kingston STC of Hull. 1939: Requisitioned in August and converted to A/S. Joined the 9th A/S Group based at Devonport. 1940: LOST. Mined off Plymouth Breakwater on 10th November.

KINGSTON AMBER   1939/46   Displacement: 467TG 170TN
                                         Engines: 99HP
                                         Armament: 1 x 4-inch; 2 x 0.5-inchAA
                                         (1x2); 2 x MG (2x1)
                                         Port Reg: H. 471
                                         P. No: FY. 211
1937: Launched. Built at Southbank-on-Tees by Smith's Dock. Owned by Kingston ST Co. of Hull. 1939: Requisitioned in September and converted to A/S. Formed an Escort Group ICW STELLA CARINA, LADY HOGARTH and LORD NUFFIELD. Remained with the Group throughout WWII. Employed on Atlantic/Med convoys. 1942: Transferred to the

KINGSTON AMBER   **(WSPL)**

Med. and based at Gibraltar for N. African convoys. Transferred to Malta. Transferred to Alexandria. 1943: TPI Operation Husky, the Landings in Sicily in July/August. TPI the Salerno Landings in September/October. Based at Tripoli for Corsica-Salerno convoys. 1945: Group returned to the UK. 1946: Returned to owners in February.

KINGSTON ANDALUSITE 1939/45

Displacement: 415TG 168TN
Engines: 111HP = 11.8K
Port Reg: H. 15
P. No: FY. 160

1934: Launched. Built at Beverley by CWG. Owned by Kingston STC of Hull. 1939: Purchased into the RN in August and converted to A/S. 1944: TPI Operation Neptune, the D-Day Landings in June, as an A/S Escort. 1945: Sold to mercantile and retained the same name. Acquired by original owners. PR: H. 133. 1948: Renamed *Milyna*. 1956: BU in Belgium.

KINGSTON BERYL   1939/43

Displacement: 356TG 150TN
Engines: 96HP = 11.4K
Port Reg: H. 499
P. No: 4. 03

1928: Launched. Built at Beverley by CWG. Owned by Kingston STC of Hull. 1939: Requisitioned in September and converted to an ABV. 1941: Converted to A/S in March. 1943: LOST. Mined to the SW of Skerrymore on Xmas Day. Whilst 'buttoning' a small convoy she ran onto 'friendly' floating mines which had broken free from a British minefield and was lost with all 28 hands.

KINGSTON CAIRNGORM 1939/40

Displacement: 448TG 174TN
Engines: 112HP = 12.2K
Armament: 1 x 4-inch
Port Reg: H. 175

1935: Launched. Built at Beverley by CWG. Owned by Kingston STC of Hull. 1939: Requisitioned in September and converted to A/S. Joined the 27th A/S Group based at Portsmouth. 1940: Damaged in a grounding in June and TIH at Portsmouth for repairs. LOST. Mined in the Channel on 18th October.

KINGSTON CEYLONITE   1939/42

Displacement: 448TG 174TN
Engines: 117HP = 12.3K
Armament: 1 x 4-inch
Port Reg: H. 173
P. No: FY. 214

1935: Launched. Built at Beverley by CWG. Owned by Kingston STC of Hull. 1939: Requisitioned in September and converted to A/S. Purchased into the RN in November. 1942: Temporary Loan to the USN in March, together with Crew, for A/S duties. LOST. Mined in Chesapeake Bay on 15th June with the loss of 18 of her 32 crew. Three US ships, a destroyer and two tankers were lost in the minefield at the same time.

KINGSTON CHRYSOBERYL   1939/46 Displacement: 448TG 174TN
                                       Engines: 117NHP = 12.2K
                                       Armament: 1 x 4-inch
                                       Port Reg: H. 177
                                       P. No: FY. 236

1935: Launched. Built at Beverley by CWG. Owned by Kingston STC of Hull. 1939: Requisitioned in September and converted to A/S. 1944: TPI Operation Neptune, the D-Day Landings in June, as an A/S Escort. 1946: Returned to owners in March. 1955: BU in Belgium.

KINGSTON CHRYSOLITE 1939/45   Displacement: 448TG 174TN
                                       Engines: 117NHP = 12.3K
                                       Port Reg: H. 169
                                       P. No: FY. 184

1935: Launched. Built at Beverley by CWG. Owned by Kingston STC of Hull. 1939: Purchased into the RN in August and converted to A/S. 1945: Sold to mercantile and retained the same name. Acquired by the original owners. H. 205. 1956: BU at Dunston.

KINGSTON CORAL   1939/46   Displacement: 433TG 166TN
                                       Engines: 117NHP = 12.5K
                                       Armament: 1 x 4-inch
                                       Port Reg: H. 241
                                       P. No: FY. 215

1936: Launched. Built at Beverley by CWG. Owned by Kingston STC of Hull. 1939: Requisitioned in September and converted to A/S. 1942: Transferred to the MF. 1946: Returned to owners in August. Reregistered H. 242. 1956: BU at Dunston.

KINGSTON CORNELIAN 1939/40   Displacement: 449TG 174TN
                                       Engines: 117NHP = 11.6K
                                       Port Reg: H. 75
                                       P. No: FY. 121

1934: Launched. Built at Beverley by CWG. Owned by Kingston STC of Hull. 1939: Purchased into the RN in August and converted to an A/S. Joined the 7th A/S Group based at Gibraltar. 1940: LOST. Sunk in a collision with the French liner *Cheila* to the E. of Gibraltar on 5th January. Her DCs exploded as she sank and all hands were lost.

KINGSTON CRYSTAL   1939/46   Displacement: 433TG 166TN
                                       Engines: 117HP = 12.5K
                                       Port Reg: H. 281
                                       P. No: FY. 217

1936: Launched. Built at Beverley by CWG. Owned by Kingston STC of Hull. 1939: Requisitioned in September and converted to A/S. 1942: Joined the MF. 1946: Returned to the UK in January. Returned to owners in March. 1958: BU in Belgium.

KINGSTON CYANITE   1939/46   Displacement: 433TG 166TN
                                       Engines: 117HP = 12.3K
                                       Port Reg: H. 237
                                       P. No: FY. 217

1936: Launched. Built at Beverley by CWG. Owned by Kingston STC of Hull. 1939: Requisitioned in September and converted to A/S. 1941: Joined the MF. 1945: Returned to the UK in September. 1946: Returned to owners in May. Re-registered as H. 237. 1957: BU in Belgium.

KINGSTON GALENA   1939/40   Displacement: 415TG 168TN
                                       Engines: 111HP = 11.9K
                                       Armament: 1 x 4-inch
                                       Port Reg: H. 31
                                       P. No: FY. 145

1934: Launched. Built at Beverley by CWG. Owned by Kingston STC of Hull. 1939: Purchased into the RN in August and converted to A/S. Joined the 9th A/S Group based at Dover. 1940: LOST. Sunk by enemy a/c off Dover on 24th July.

KINGSTON JACINTH   1939/40   Displacement: 352TG 149TN
                                       Engines: 96HP = 10.7K
                                       Port Reg: H. 44
                                       P. No: 4. 45

1929: Launched. Built at Beverley by CWG. Owned by Kingston STC of Hull. 1939: Requisitioned in August and converted to an ABV. 1940: Converted to A/S in October. 1943: LOST. Mined off Portsmouth on 12th January.

KINGSTON OLIVINE   1939/45   Displacement: 378TG 148TN
                                       Engines: 96HP = 11K
                                       Armament: 1 x 4-inch; 3 x 20mmAA
                                       (3x1); 1 x 0.5-inch MG 1 x Holman
                                       Projector
                                       Port Reg: H .209
                                       P. No: FY. 193

1930: Launched. Built at Beverley by CWG. Owned by Kingston STC of Hull. 1939: Purchased into the RN in August and converted to an A/S. Joined the 19th A/S Group based at Harwich. Employed on E. Coast convoys. 1942: Converted to a M/S in July. 1945: Sold to mercantile. 1947: Renamed *Langland Bay* PR: SA. 72. 1954: Renamed *Masona* PR: FD.16. 1956: BU at Troon.

KINGSTON ONYX   1939/44   Displacement: 357TG 146TN
                                       Engines: 96HP = 10.8K
                                       Armament: 1 x 4-inch; 1 x 20mmAA;
                                       DCs
                                       Port Reg: H. 365

P. No: 4. 54

1927: Launched. Built at Beverley by CWG. Owned by Kingston STC of Hull. 1939: Requisitioned in August and converted to an ABV. 1941: Converted to A/S in April and joined the Northern Patrol. 1944: Returned to owners in September. 1945: Renamed *Moorsom* PR: GY.119. 1947: Renamed *Westhope* PR: H.590. 1956: BU at Dunston.

KINGSTON PERIDOT   1939/45   Displacement: 356TG 152TN
                                      Engines: 96HP = 11.1K
                                      Port Reg: H. 55
                                      P. No: 4. 69

1929: Launched. Built at Beverley by CWG. Owned by Kingston STC of Hull. 1939: Requisitioned in August and converted to an ABV. Joined the Northern Patrol. 1940: Involved in a diplomatic incident in June when she towed the damaged Swedish destroyer PUKE from off the Faroe Islands to Scapa Flow. 1941: Converted to A/S in April. 1945: Returned to owners in December. 1946: Renamed *Stockham* in September. PR: GY. 89. 1948: Renamed *Wyre Monitor* PR: FD. 304. 1954: BU in Ireland.

KINGSTON SAPPHIRE   1939/41   Displacement: 356TG   150TN
                                       Engines: 96HP = 10.9K
                                       Port Reg: H. 39
                                       P.No: 4. 81

1929: Launched. Built at Beverley by CWG. Owned by Kingston STC of Hull. 1939: Purchased in September and converted to an ABV. Based at Gibraltar. 1941: LOST. Sunk by the Italian S/M NANI off Gibraltar on 5th October with the loss of 13 lives. The other 28 survived for 15days in the lifeboat before being rescued by a Spanish tanker.

KINGSTON TOPAZ   1939/45   Displacement: 357TG 146TN
                                      Engines: 96HP = 11K
                                      Port Reg: H. 352
                                      P. No: 4. 31

1927: Launched. Built at Beverley by CWG. Owned by Kingston STC of Hull. 1939: Requisitioned in August and converted to an ABV. 1945: Returned to owners in November. Acquired by Grimsby Motor Trs. Ltd. of Grimsby and renamed *Hawkins* PR: GY. 93. 1956: BU at Gateshead.

KINGSTON TURQUOISE   1939/45   Displacement: 356TG 150TN
                                      Engines: 96HP = 10.9K
                                      Port Reg: H. 45
                                      P. No: 4. 91

1929: Launched. Built at Beverley by CWG. Owned by Kingston STC of Hull. 1939: Requisitioned in August and converted to an ABV. 1940: Converted to an A/S in October. 1945: Returned to owners in November. 1946: Renamed *Cunningham* PR: GY. 86. 1957: BU in Belgium.

KINGSWAY   1915/19 1939/40   Displacement: 211TG 83TN
                                            Engines: 65HP = 10K
                                            Armament: 1 x 3pdr
                                            Port Reg: GY. 37

1905: Launched. Built at Beverley by CWG. Owned by A. Black of Grimsby. 1914: Requisitioned in December and converted to a BDV. 1919: Returned to owners. 1929: Acquired by S. Chapman & Sons of Grimsby. 1931: Acquired by C. Dobson of Grimsby. 1939: Requisitioned in November and converted to an APV. 1940: Returned to owner in January. 1954: BU at Gateshead.

KIRKELLA   1939/46   Displacement: 436TG 170TN
                                              Engines: 116HP
                                              Armament: 1 x 4-inch
                                              Port Reg: H. 319
                                              P.No: FY. 174

1936: Launched. Built at Selby by Cochrane. Owned by J. Marr & Son of Fleetwood. 1939: Purchased into the RN in August and converted to A/S. Joined the 17th A/S Group based at Swansea. 1946: Sold to mercantile and retained the same name. Acquired by the original owners. PR: H.155.

KIRKLAND   1915/17   Displacement: 224TG
                                              Admty No: 360
                                              Port Reg: LO. 262

1914: Requisitioned in August and converted to a M/S. 1917: LOST. Mined off Fugla Skerry, Papastour, Shetland on 20th August.

KIRKLINTON   1916/19   Displacement: 227TG 87TN
                                              Engines: 80HP
                                              Armament: 1 x 6pdrAA
                                              Admty No: 3272
                                              Port Reg: SN. 236

1916: Launched. Built at Southbank-on-Tees. Requisitioned in April. 1919: Returned to owners. Acquired by Wyre STC of Fleetwood. PR: FD. 293.

KIRTON   1916/19   Displacement: 168TG 55TN
                                              Engines: 35HP
                                              Armament: 1 x 3pdr
                                              Port Reg: GN. 42

1886: Launched. Built at Beverley. Iron construction. Owned by J. Inglis of Peebles. 1916: Requisitioned in May and converted to a BDV. 1919: Returned to owners.

KITE   1914/15   Displacement: 168TG 63TN
                                              Engines: 45HP
                                              Armament: 1 x 6pdrAA

Admty No: 415
Port Reg: H. 773

1903: Launched. Built at Goole by Goole SB. Owned by Kelsall Bros. & Beeching of Hull. 1914: Requisitioned in November as KITE and converted to a M/S. 1915: Renamed KITE II in February. 1919: Returned to owners. 1938: Owned by Brixham Trs. Ltd. of Brixham.

KITE II	1915/19	See under KITE above

KITTIWAKE   1917/19   Displacement: 153TG 63TN
                                         Engines: 45HP
                                         Port Reg: A. 469

1891: Launched. Built at Beverley. Iron construction. Owned by WL Mullender AO of Lowestoft. 1917: Requisitioned into the Fishery Reserve. 1919: Returned to owners.

KITTY   1917/19   Displacement: 191TG 49TN
                                         Engines: 50HP
                                         Port Reg: A. 819

1898: Launched. Built at Aberdeen. Owned by JH. Waite of Great Yarmouth. 1917: Requisitioned into the Fishery Reserve. 1919: Returned to owners.

KLONDIKE   1915/16   Displacement: 155TG 155TN
                                         Engines: 50NHP = 9K
                                         Admty No: 647
                                         Port Reg: H. 420

1898: Launched. Built at Hull by CWG. Owned by Hull SF & Ice Co. 1914: Requisitioned in October and converted to a M/S. 1916: LOST. Sunk in a collision near the Owers LV. on 14th June.

KNOT   1915/16   Displacement: 168TG
                                         Armament: 1 x 3pdr
                                         Admty No: 683
                                         Port Reg: H. 784

1903: Launched. 1914: Requisitioned in November and converted to a M/S. 1916: LOST. Wrecked on the North Caer Rock on 5th November.

KODAMA   1915/19   Displacement: 257TG 103TN
                                         Engines: 79HP
                                         Armament: 1 x 12pdr
                                         Admty No: 2668
                                         Port Reg: CF. 34

1911: Launched. Built at Middlesborough by Smith's Dock. Owned by Neale & West of Cardiff. 1915: Requisitioned. 1919: Returned to owners. 1938: Owned by The Croston ST Co. of Fleetwood. Port Reg: FD. 36.

KOORAH	1914/19	Displacement: 227TG 86TN
		Engines: 76HP
		Armament: 1 x 3pdr
		Admty No: 324
		Port Reg: M. 120

1912: Launched. Built at Aberdeen. 1914: Requisitioned in August and converted to a M/S. 1919: Returned to owners. Acquired by EE Cox of Grimsby. PR: GY.122. 1938: Owned by P. & G.M. Liston of Edinburgh.

KOPANES	1940/41	Displacement: 351TG 165TN
		Engines: 100HP
		Armament: 1 x 12pdr
		Port Reg: GY. 1170

1914: Launched. Built at Beverley. Owned by Kopanes SFC of Grimsby. 1940: Requisitioned in June and converted to an APV. Based at Grimsby for Fishery Protection. 1941: LOST. Sunk by enemy a/c off the Tyne on 19th April.

KORAB I	1940/46	Displacement: 263TG
		Port Reg: Polish
		P. No: 4. 297

1938: Launched. Polish fishing vessel. 1940: Hired from Polish owners in October and fitted out for the Examination Service. 1946: Returned to owners.

| KOROWA | 1939/45 | RAN. See under EDWARD McGUIRE |
| | | (Vol 1 p.134) |

KOSMOS	1916/19	Displacement: 231TG 89TN
		Engines: 71HP
		Armament: 1 x 6pdrAA
		Admty No: 3273
		Port Reg: A. 617

1916: Launched. Built at Aberdeen. Owned by East Coast SFC (Aberdeen) Ltd. Requisitioned in April and converted to a M/S. 1919: Returned to owners.

KUDOS	1915/19	Displacement: 207TG 77TN
		Engines: 75HP
		Armament: 1 x 6pdr
		Admty No: 1343
		Port Reg: A. 374

1911: Launched. Built at Aberdeen. 1915: Requisitioned in April and converted to a M/S. 1919: Returned to owners. 1920: Acquired by the Friarage FC of Hartlepool. PR: HL. 93.

| KUMU | 1914/19 | Displacement: 315TG 129TN |
| | | Engines: 69HP |

Armament: 1 x 6pdr
Port Reg: FD. 176

1913: Launched. Built at Aberdeen. Owned by Clifton STL of Fleetwood. 1914: Requisitioned. 1919: Returned to owners.

KUNISHI	1917/19	Displacement: 268TG 111TN
		Engines: 85HP
		Armament: 1 x 12pdr
		Port Reg: CF. 46

1917: Launched. Built at Selby by Cochrane. Owned by Neale & West of Cardiff. Requisitioned. 1919: Returned to owners.

KUNISHI	1939/46	Displacement: 303TG 144TN
		Engines: 99HP
		Armament: 1 x 12pdr
		Port Reg: CF. 20
		P. No: FY. 892

1927: Launched. Built at Southbank-on-Tees by Smith's Dock. Owned by Neale & West of Cardiff. 1939: Purchased into the RN in August as NORINA and converted to a M/S. 1946: Sold to mercantile in April.

KURD	1939/45	Displacement: 352TG 138TN
		Engines: 96HP
		Armament: 1 x 12pdr
		Port Reg: H. 344
		P. No: FY. 639

1930: Launched. Built at Selby by Cochrane. Owned by Hellyer Bros. of Hull. 1939: Requisitioned and converted to a M/S. Based at Grimsby. 1940: 17th M/S Group based at Grimsby. 1943: 40th M/S Group based at Grimsby. 1945: LOST. Mined off the Lizard on 10th July.

KUROKI	1915/19 1940/45	Displacement: 248TG 95TN
		Engines: 81HP
		Armament: 1 x 6pdr
		Port Reg: CF. 8
		P.No: WWII: Z. 137

1909: Launched. Built at N. Shields . Owned by Neale & West of Cardiff. 1915: Requisitioned. 1919: Returned to owners. 1938: Owned by Huddleston AO of Milford Haven. 1940: Requisitioned in January and converted to a BDV. 1945: Returned to owners in July.

KUVERA	1940/45	Displacement: 202TG 97TN
		Engines: 74HP
		Armament: 1 x 6pdr

1919: Launched. Built at Hook by Ouse SB. Owned by F. Pearce of Cleethorpes & JH. Healy of Grimsby. 1938: Owned by R. Baxter AO of Aberdeen. PR: A.384. 1940: Requisitioned in July and converted to an APV. 1945: Returned to owners in September.

KYMERIC   1916/19   Displacement: 126TG 51TN
                                                      Engines: 45HP
                                                      Armament: 1 x 6pdr
                                                      Port Reg: GY. 421

1891: Launched. Built at Hull. Owned by Grimsby SFC. 1916: Requisitioned. 1919: Returned to owners.

CHAPTER 12 - LABORE ET HONORE to LYSANDER III

LABORE ET HONORE   1917/19   Displacement: 150TG   58TN
Engines: 45HP = 10K
Admty No: Not Issued
Port Reg: SA. 110

1893: Launched. Built at Hull by CWG. Owned by R. Simpson of Hull. PR: H. 217. 1904: Acquired by Neale & West of Cardiff. PR: CF. 5. 1911: Acquired by G. Shoulder of Swansea. PR: SA. 110. 1913: Acquired by ME Newman of Swansea. 1917: Requisitioned into the Fishery Reserve. 1919: Returned to owners. 1926: BU.

LACENNIA   1939/46   Displacement: 348TG   148TN
Engines: 96HP = 10.5K
Armament: 1 x 12pdr
Port Reg: GY. 345
P.No: FY. 712

1931: Launched. Built at Beverley by CWG. Owned by The Gt. Grimsby & E. Coast SF Co. of Grimsby. 1939: Requisitioned in October and converted to a M/S. 1943: 134th M/S Group based at Grimsby. 1946: Returned to owners. 1954: BU at Antwerp.

LACERTA   1914/19 1940/46   Displacement: 270TG   121TN
Engines: 71HP
Armament: 1 x 12pdr
Admty No: 625
Port Reg: GY 641
P. No: 4. 07

1911: Launched. Built at Selby by Cochrane. Owned by the Lindsay SF Co. of Grimsby. 1914: Requisitioned in September and converted to a M/S. 1919: Returned to owners. 1940: Requisitioned in June and converted to an APV. Subsequently purchased into the RN. 1946: Sold to mercantile in February and retained the same name. Acquired by the original owners and with original PR.

LADAS   1917/19   Displacement: 172TG   69TN
Engines: 52HP
Admty No: Not issued
Port Reg: GY. 282

1898: Launched. Built at North Shields. Owned by Orient SFC of Grimsby. 1917: Requisitioned into the Fishery Reserve. 1919: Returned to owners. Acquired by TW Baskcomb of Grimsby.

LADY BERYL   1939/45   Displacement: 417TG   157TN
Engines: 117HP = 12.4K
Armament: 1 x 4-inch
Port Reg: H. 222

P.No: FY. 100

1935: Launched. Built at Beverley by CWG. Owned by Jutland Amalgamated Trs. of Hull. 1939: Purchased into the RN in September and converted to A/S. 1945: Sold to mercantile. Re-acquired by original owners and re-registered H. 151. 1948: Acquired by Newington Trs. of Hull and renamed *Warwick Deeping*. 1959: BU at Ghent, Belgium.

LADY ELEANOR	1940/47	See under THOMAS JAGO (See Addenda p.531)

LADY ELSA	1939/46	Ex-*Italia Caesar* Displacement: 518TG 283TN Engines: 135HP = 12.8K Port Reg: H. 532 P. No: FY. 124

1937: Launched. Built at Beverley by CWG as *Italia Caesar*. Owned by Earl SFC of Grimsby. PR: GY. 442. 1938: Acquired by Jutland Amalgamated Trawlers of Hull and renamed *Lady Elsa*. PR: H. 532. 1939: Purchased into the RN in August and converted to A/S. Joined the 21st A/S Strike Force. 1940: TPI the Norwegian Campaign in April/May. 1941: Sustained damage to her bow when she was in collision with a Norwegian S/M off Cambletown, W. Scotland on 25th March. 1942: Temporary Loan to the USN from March, together with crew, for A/S duties. Returned to the RN in October and transferred to the S. Africa Station. 1945: Returned to the UK. 1946: Sold to mercantile in January. Acquired by original owners and re-registered H. 286. 1950: Acquired by Associated FTC of Hull and renamed *Lord Tay*. 1953: Acquired by Lord Line of Hull and converted to fuel oil. 1964: Damaged by fire in her engine room whilst alongside at Hull in September. BU at Grays by T. Ward in November.

LADY ENID	1939/45	See under JOHN JEFFERSON (Vol 1 p.142)

LADY ESTELLE	1940/46	Displacement: 323TG Armament: 1 x 6pdr Port Reg: H. 210 P.No: FY. 176

1915: Launched. Built at Beverley. Owned by Jutland Amalgamated TCL of Hull. 1940: Requisitioned and converted to an APV. Owned by Jutland Amalgamated Trs. of Hull. 1942: Converted to a M/S in January. 1946: Returned to owners in September.

LADY HOGARTH	1939/46	Displacement: 472TG 177TN Engines: 120NHP = 12.3K Armament: 1 x 12pdr Port Reg: H. 479 P. No: 4. 89

1937: Launched. Built at Beverley by CWG. Owned by Jutland Amalgamated Trs of Hull.

1939: Requisitioned in October and converted to an APV. 1940: Converted to A/S in December. ICW STELLA CARINA, LORD NUFFIELD and KINGSTON AMBER formed an escort Group employed on Atlantic and Med. convoys. Remained with the Group for the remainder of WWII. 1941: Transferred to the Med. Based at Gibraltar for N. African convoys. Towed the LADY SHIRLEY into neutral Madeira for engine repairs in September. Transferred to Malta and then to Alexandria. 1942: Acquired by Kingston STC. 1944: TPI Operation Husky, the Landings in Sicily in July/April. TPI the Salerno Landings in September/October. Transferred to Tripoli for Corsica-Salerno convoys. 1945: Returned to the UK. 1946: Returned to owners in May. Renamed *Kingston Emerald*. 1951: Renamed *Staxton Wyke*. 1959: Mercantile Loss. Sank in a collision with a bulk carrier with the loss of five lives.

LADY LILIAN	1940/41	Displacement: 581TG 214TN
		Engines: 165NHP = 12.8K
		Armament: 1 x 4-inch
		Port Reg: H. 229

1939: Launched. Built at Beverley by CWG. Owned by Jutland Amalgamated TCL of Hull. 1940: Requisitioned in January and converted to A/S. Joined the A/S Force based at Belfast. 1941: LOST. Sunk by enemy a/c to the W. of Ireland on 16th March.

| LADYLOVE | 1940/40 | See under OPHIR III |

LADY MADELEINE	1940/46	Displacement: 581TG 214TN
		Engines: 165HP = 12.8K
		Armament: 1 x 4-inch
		Port Reg: H. 229
		P. No: FY. 283

1934: Launched. Built at Beverley by CWG. Owned by Jutland Amalgamated Trs of Hull. 1940: Requisitioned in February and converted to an A/S. Based at Grimsby. 1941: Joined the Iceland Command in August. 1942: TPI Convoy PQ.16 to Russia. Acquired by Kingston STC of Hull. 1946: Returned to owners in February. Renamed *Kingston Diamond* in April. 1965: BU at Glasson Dock.

LADY PHILOMENA	1939/45	Displacement: 417TG 157TN
		Engines: 105HP = 12.4K
		Armament: 1 x 4-inch
		Port Reg: H. 230
		P. No: FY. 148

1936: Built at Beverley by CWG. Owned by Jutland Amalgamated Trs. of Hull. 1939: Requisitioned in August and converted to A/S. Joined the 19th A/S Group based at Harwich for E. Coast convoys. 1941: Escorting a convoy off Dover when she shot down a German Ju.87b which had just attacked and sunk the TOURMALINE. She then picked up survivors. 1945: Returned to owners in October. Re-registered PR: H. 167. 1946: Renamed *St. Attalus*. 1948: Renamed *Onslow*. 1960: BU at Preston by TW. Ward.

LADY ROSEMARY   1940/46   Displacement: 472TG 177TN
                                    Engines: 120HP = 12.3K
                                    Port Reg: H. 442
                                    P.No: FY. 253

1937: Launched. Built at Beverley by CWG. Owned by Jutland Amalgamated Trs of
Hull. 1940: Requisitioned in May and converted to an A/S. 1942: Temporary Loan to the
USN from March, together with crew, for A/S duties. Returned to the RN in October and
transferred to the S. African Station. Acquired by Kingston STC of Hull in November.
1945: Returned to the UK. Paid Off and Laid up. 1946: Returned to owners in May and
renamed *Kingston Ruby*. PR: H. 477. 1963: BU at Ghent, Belgium.

LADY SHIRLEY   1940/41   Displacement: 472TG 177TN
                                    Engines: 120 NHP =10K
                                    Armament: 1 x 2pdr
                                    Port Reg: H. 464

1937: Launched. Built at Beverley by CWG. Owned by Jutland Amalgamated Trs of
Hull. 1940: Requisitioned in May and converted to an APV. 1941: Converted to A/S in
January. Work-up at Tobermory.   Joined the 31st A/S Group based at Gibraltar.
Suffered engine trouble at sea in September. Towed into neutral Madeira by LADY
HOGARTH for repairs which lasted 3 days. Sank the German U-111 off Teneriffe on 4th
October rescuing 45 of her survivors which she landed at Gibraltar on 8th October The
C.O. was awarded the DSO, the 1st Lt. and S .Lt. the DSCs, one seaman the CGM and
5 others the DSM. LOST.   Torpedoed by U-374 off Gibraltar on 11th December. Lost
with all 33 hands.

LADYSMITH   1915/20   Displacement: 254TG 109TN
                                    Engines: 69HP
                                    Armament: 1 x 12pdrAA
                                    Admty No: 4
                                    Port Reg: GY. 183

1906: Launched. Built at Selby by Cochrane. Owned by Taylor & Staff of Grimsby.
1914: Requisitioned in August. 1920: Returned to owners.

LADY STANLEY   1940/45   Displacement: 276TG 107TN
                                    Engines: 513HP
                                    Armament: 1 x 12pdr
                                    Port Reg: FD. 125
                                    P. No: 4. 233

1917: Launched. Built at South Shields. Owned by St. Andrews SFCL of Hull. 1940:
Requisitioned in June and converted to an APV. 1941: Converted to a M/S in May. 1945:
Returned to owners in September.

La NANTISE   1940/45   See under ST. ARCADIUS

LANCER II   1917/18   See under LANCER 1914

LANERCOST   1916/19 1939/46 Displacement: 227TG 87TN
                                          Engines: 80HP
                                          Armament: 1 x 12pdr
                                          Admty No: 3254
                                          Port Reg: FD. 292
                                          P. No: WWII: FY. 1895
1916: Launched. Built at Southbank-on-Tees by Smith's Dock. Owned by Palatine STC
of Fleetwood. Requisitioned in January and converted to a M/S. 1919: Returned to
owners. Acquired by TM. Reed of Tynemouth and renamed *Darwen*. 1939:
Requisitioned in November as DARWEN and converted to an APV. 1940: Converted to
a M/S in June. 1946: Returned to owners in February.

LAPAGERIA   1916/19 1940/46 Displacement: 274TG 120TN
                                          Engines: 79HP = 10.5K
                                          Armament: 1 x 12pdr
                                          Admty No: 3311
                                          Port Reg: GY. 890
                                          P. No: WWII: 4 .315
1916: Launched. Built at Beverley by CWG. Requisitioned in October and converted to a M/S.
1919: Returned to owners. 1924: Acquired by H & FD Robinson of Grimsby. 1940:
Requisitioned in September and converted to an APV. 1942: Converted to an Esso in January
and transferred to the MF. 1943: Unit of the Supply Group known colloquially as "Walt Disney's
Navy" ferrying stores to the invasion forces throughout the Med. 1946: Returned to owners in
February. 1951: Renamed *Mary Croan*. PR: LH. 99. 1957: BU at Granton.

LAPWING   1939/40   See under LAPWING II

LAPWING II   1915/19 1939/40 Displacement: 217TG 87TN
                                          Engines: 60HP
                                          Armament: 1 x 6pdrAA
                                          Admty No: 1206
                                          Port Reg: GY. 24
1904: Launched. Built at Selby by Cochrane. Owned by Lindsay SFC of Grimsby.
1915: Requisitioned in January and converted to a M/S. Renamed LAPWING II in
February. 1918: Returned to owners in October. 1939: Requisitioned in November as
LAPWING and converted to an APV. 1940: Returned to owners in January.

LAPWING III   1915/19   Displacement: 217TG
                                         Armament: 1 x 6pdrAA
                                         Admty No: 39
1903: Launched. 1915: Requisitioned in August, converted to a M/S and renamed
LAPWING III. 1919: Returned to owners.

LAPWING V   1917/19   Displacement: 152TG 64TN
Engines: 45HP
Port Reg: H. 258

1894: Launched. Built at Beverley. Iron construction. Owned by Ellis STC of Scarborough. 1917: Requisitioned into the Fishery Reserve. 1919: Returned to owners.

LARCHWOLD   1917/19   Displacement: 129TG 53TN
Engines: 35HP
Port Reg: GY. 68

1896: Launched. Built at Beverley. Iron construction. Owned by Northwold SFC of Grimsby. 1917: Requisitioned into the Fishery Reserve. 1919: Returned to owners.

LARK   1914/15   See under LARK II

LARK II   1915/19   Displacement: 280TG 123TN
Engines: 88HP
Armament: 1 x 12pdr; 1 x 6pdrAA
Admty No: 480
Port Reg: GY. 322

1907: Launched. Built at Hull. Owned by Grimsby SFC. 1914: Requisitioned in December and converted to a M/S. 1915: Renamed LARK II in February. 1919: Returned to owners. Retained the name *Lark II*.

LARWOOD   1939/40 1945/47 Cricketer Group
Displacement: 452TG 191TN
Engines: 133HP
Armament: 1 x 4-inch
Port Reg: GY. 255
P. No: FY. 172

1936: Launched. Built at Selby by Cochrane. Owned by Crampins of Grimsby. 1939: Requisitioned in August and converted to A/S. Joined the 22nd A/S Group. 1940: TPI the Norwegian Campaign in April. LOST. Sunk by enemy a/c off Norway on 25th April. Salvaged by the Germans and TIH for repair. Commissioned into the German Navy on 30th May as VPG 111 FRANKE. 1945: Recovered by the RN and Laid Up. 1947: Sold to mercantile in April.

L'ATALANTIQUE   1940/46   Displacement: 659T
Armament: 3 x 100mm; DCs
Port Reg: French

1920: Launched. French fishing vessel. 1940: French APV which escaped from France at the time of Dunkirk. Seized at Plymouth in Operation Grab on 3rd July. TIH at Devonport for conversion to A/S and fitted with DCs. Commissioned with a mixed Free French/RN crew and RNR CO. Employed on A/S patrols in the Channel. 1946: Returned to French owners in April.

LAURA	1917/19	Displacement: 280TG 110TN
		Engines: 65HP
		Admty No: Not issued
		Port Reg: FD. 29

1905: Launched. Built at Hull. Owned by Fleetwood SFC. 1917: Requisitioned into the Fishery Reserve. 1919: Returned to owners.

LAUREATE	1917/19	Displacement: 194TG 77TN
		Engines: 65HP
		Port Reg: SN. 237

1898: Launched. Built at Aberdeen. Owned by Hesketh STC of Fleetwood. 1917: Requisitioned into the Fishery Reserve. 1919: Returned to owners. 1938: Owned by Albert E. Marchant AO of Milford Haven. PR: M. 29.

LAUREL II	1914/19	Displacement: 138TG 56TN
		Engines: 40HP
		Armament: 1 x 3pdr
		Admty No: 708
		Port Reg: GY. 275

1897: Launched. Built at Beverley. Iron Construction. Owned by W. Grant of Grimsby. 1914: Requisitioned in November. 1915: Renamed LAUREL II in February. 1917: Reduced to the Fishery Reserve. 1918: Returned to owners in November.

LAVEROCK	1939/46	See under JAMES GREEN
		(Vol 1 p.58)

LAVINIA	1915/19	Displacement: 198TG 83TN
		Engines: 55HP
		Armament: 1 x 3pdr
		Admty No: 1797
		Port Reg: GY. 1117

1900: Launched. Built at Selby by Cochrane. Owned by Lindsey SF Co. of Grimsby. 1915: Requisitioned in May and converted to a BDV. 1919: Returned to owners.

LAWRENNY CASTLE	1916/19	Displacement: 256TG 101TN
		Engines: 80HP
		Armament: 1 x 12pdr
		Admty No: 1357
		Port Reg: SA. 52

1908: Launched. Built at North Shields. Owned by Consolidated Fisheries of Grimsby. 1915: Requisitioned in March and converted to a M/S. 1919: Returned to owners.

LAXMI	1940/46 RIN	See under GEORGE HARRIS
		(Vol 1 p.54)

LEAM   1917/19 1939/40 Displacement: 236TG 90TN
                                          Engines: 78HP
                                          Admty No: 2995
                                          Port Reg: WWI: FD .20; WWII: SN. 11
1917: Launched. Built at Southbank-on-Tees by Smith's Dock. Owned by the Wyre STC
of Fleetwood. Requisitioned in January and converted to an APV. 1919: Returned to
owners. Acquired by The Shields Eng. & DD Co of N. Shields and renamed *Belldock*.
1939: Requisitioned in November as BELLDOCK and designated as an APV. 1940:
Returned to owners.

LEANDER   1914/15   Displacement: 276TG
                                          Admty No: 18
                                          Port Reg: GY. 260
1907: Launched. 1914: Requisitioned in August and converted to a M/S. 1915:
Renamed LEANDROS in February. LOST. Mined off North Knock on 6th August.

LEANDROS   1915/15   See under LEANDER

LEEDS   1917/19   Displacement: 162TG 63TN
                                          Engines: 45HP
                                          Port Reg: GY. 207
1897: Launched. Built at Govan. Owned by Consolidated Fisheries of Grimsby. 1917:
Requisitioned into the Fishery Reserve. 1919: Returned to owners.

LEEDS UNITED   1939/45   Football Group
                                          Displacement: 405TG 151TN
                                          Engines: 99HP
                                          Port Reg: GY. 62
                                          P. No: FY. 196
1933: Launched. Built at Southbank-on-Tees by Smith's Dock. Owned by Consolidated
Fisheries of Grimsby. 1939: Requisitioned in October and converted to A/S. 1943:
Formed an Escort Group with sister-ships DERBY COUNTY, GRIMSBY TOWN,
HUDDERSFIELD TOWN and YORK CITY and based at Milford Haven for Western
Approaches convoys. Remained with the Group throughout WWII. Transferred to the
Med. Escorted a convoy of Landing Craft to Gibraltar enroute. Employed on Med.
Convoys. Group returned to Western Approaches at Milford Haven at the end of the
year. 1945: Returned to owners.

LEICESTER CITY   1939/46   Football Group
                                          Displacement: 422TG 151TN
                                          Engines: 99HP
                                          Port Reg: GY. 62
                                          P. No: FY. 223
1934: Launched. Built at Southbank-on-Tees by Smith's Dock. Owned by Consolidated

Fisheries of Grimsby. 1939: Requisitioned in September and converted to A/S. 1946: Returned to owners.

LEITH N.B. 1914/19 Displacement: 203TG 87TN
Engines: 76 HP
Armament: 1 x 12pdr
Admty No: 469
Port Reg: GN. 374

1914: Launched. Built at Aberdeen. 1915: Requisitioned in July. 1919: Returned to owners in July. Acquired by E. Taylor & N. Ashworth of Fleetwood. PR: F. 323. 1938: Owned by A. King of Aberdeen. PR: A. 389.

LEMBERG 1915/18 Displacement: 275TG 147TN
Engines: 79HP
Armament: 1 x 12pdr
Admty No: 1547
Port Reg: GY. 372

1914: Launched. Built at Selby by Cochrane. Owned by Lemberg Ltd. of Halifax, N. Scotia. 1915: Requisitioned in July. 1919: Returned to owners.

LENA MELLING 1915/16 Displacement: 274TG
Armament: 1 x 3pdr
Admty No: 3223
Port Reg: FD. 189

1915: Launched. Requisitioned in November and converted to a M/S. Owned by Mellings Ltd. of Fleetwood. 1916: LOST. Mined near the Elbow Light Buoy off Broadstairs on 23rd April. *Notes*: Sister-ships: LILY MELLING and LIZZIE MELLING.

LEO 1917/19 1939/40 Displacement: 181TG 69TN
Engines: 45HP
Port Reg: GY. 36

1904: Launched. Built at Selby by Cochrane. Owned by The Lindsay SF Co. of Grimsby. 1917: Requisitioned into the Fishery Reserve. 1919: Returned to owners. 1939: Requisitioned in November and designated as an APV. 1940: Returned to owners in February.

LEONATO 1917/19 Displacement: 213TG 78TN
Engines: 45NHP = 10K
Port Reg: H. 41

1909: Launched. Built at Beverley by CWG. Owned by Hellyer SFC of Hull. 1917: Requisitioned into the Fishery Reserve. 1919: Returned to owners. 1955: BU at Charlestown.

LEONORA   1914/19   1939/41   Displacement: 217TG 87TN
Engines: 60HP
Armament: 1 x 6pdrAA
Admty No: 37
Port Reg: GY. 20

1904: Launched. Built at Selby by Cochrane. Owned by the Lindsay SF Co. of Grimsby. 1914: Requisitioned in August and converted to a M/S. 1920: Returned to owners. 1939: Requisitioned in November and converted to an APV. 1941: Transferred to the Air Ministry in January.

LEPHRETO   1939/44   See under WILLIAM SYMONS
(Vol 1 p.89)

Le TIGER   1939/45   Displacement: 516TG 258TN
Engines: 156HP
Dimensions: 188ft oa 173ft pp
Armament: 1 x 4-inch
Port Reg: GY. 398
P. No: FY. 243

1937: Launched. in April. Built at Selby by Cochrane. Owned by Earl SF Co of Grimsby. 1939: Purchased in to the RN in December and converted to A/S. 1940: Employed on Convoy escort duties in Home waters. Rescued survivors from the mined Tr. AMETHYST in the Thames Estuary on 24th October. 1942: Temporary Loan to the USN from March, together with her crew, for A/S duties. Employed on convoy escorts on the E. Coast of the USA. Sank the German U-215 off New York on 3rd July. Returned to the RN in October and resumed convoy escorts. 1943: Transferred to the S. Africa Station in February and employed on convoy escorts around the S. African Coast for the remainder of WWII. 1945: Returned to the UK. Paid Off and placed on the Disposal List. Sold to mercantile in October and retained the same name. Acquired by The Hull Ice Co. 1947: Renamed *Regal* in July. 1948: Renamed *Othello* in September. 1963: BU. *Notes*: To commemorate the building of what, at that time, was considered to be an exceptional vessel, each man at the Builder's yard was presented with a shilling by the proud owners.

LEUKOS   1915/19   Displacement: 216TG 83TN
Engines: 70HP
Port Reg: A.103

1914: Launched. Built at Aberdeen. Owned by AR Tucker & JC Tippett of Cardiff. 1915: Requisitioned in June and converted to a BDV. 1919: Returned to owners.

LEVEN   1915/19   Displacement: 168TG 67TN
Engines: 45HP
Port Reg: A. 447

1900: Launched. Built at Govan. Owned by L. Brown of South Shields. 1915: Requisitioned in June and converted to a BDV. 1919: Returned to owners.

LEYLAND 1917/19 Displacement: 236TG 90TN
Engines: 78HP
Armament: 1 x 6pdrAA
Admty No: 3026
Port Reg: FD. 291
1917: Launched. Built at Southbank-on-Tees by Smith's Dock. Owned by Palatine STC of Fleetwood. Requisitioned in March and converted to a M/S. 1919: Returned to owners.

LEYLAND 1939/42 Displacement: 452TG 191TN
Engines: 133HP
Armament: 1 x 4-inch
Port Reg: GY. 254
P. No: FY. 103
1936: Launched. Built at Selby by Cochrane. Owned by The Bunch SF Co. of Grimsby. 1939: Purchased into the RN in September and converted to A/S. Employed on convoy escorts. 1942: LOST. Sunk in collision with a merchantman off Gibraltar on 25th November.

LEYS 1916/19 Displacement: 222TG 97TN
Engines: 66HP
Armament: 1 x 6pdrAA
Admty No: 3330
Port Reg: GY. 1023
1916: Launched. Built at Selby by Cochrane. Owned by CA. Osborne AO of Grimsby. 1917: Requisitioned in March and converted to a M/S. 1919: Returned to owners. 1938: Owned by Queen SF of Grimsby. 1957: BU.

LIBERATOR 1940/46 See under HEKLA

LIBERIA 1914/19 1940/46 Displacement: 250TG 101TN
Engines: 69HP
Armament: WWI: 1 x 3pdr; WWII: 1 x 1pdrAA; 2 x 0.5-inchAA (1x2); 2 x MG (2x1)
Admty No: 26
Port Reg: GY. 159
P. No: WWII: FY. 1826
1906: Launched. Built at Selby by Cochrane. Owned by Lindsay SFC of Grimsby. 1914: Requisitioned in August. 1919: Returned to owners. 1938: Owned by Lindsay SFC of Grimsby. 1940: Requisitioned in August and converted to a M/S. 1945: Returned to owners in July.

LIBRA 1914/19 1939/45 Displacement: 211TG 82TN
Engines: 56HP

Armament: 1 x 3pdr
Admty No: 29
Port Reg: GY. 687
P. No: WWII: FY. 593

1912: Launched. Built at Dundee. Owned by Grimsby & North Sea STC of Grimsby. 1914: Requisitioned in September and converted to a M/S. 1919: Returned to owners. Acquired by Trawlers (White Sea & Grimsby) of Grimsby. Same PR. 1939: Requisitioned in November and converted to an APV. 1940: Converted to a M/S in June. Renamed TOCSIN in December. 1944: Converted to an Esso in April. 1945: Returned to owners in September.

LIBRA	1940/45	Displacement: 221TG
		Port Reg: Dutch

1908: Launched. Dutch fishing vessel. 1940: Hired from Dutch owners and converted to a M/S. Commissioned with a Dutch crew. 1943: Commissioned with a RN crew. 1945: Returned to owners.

LIBYAN	1915/19 1939/46	Displacement: 202TG 90TN
		Engines: 67HP
		Armament: 1 x 6pdr
		Admty No. 1127
		Port Reg: GY. 938
		P. No: WWII: FY. 1800 (M/S)
		Y7. 18 (Esso)

1913: Launched. Built at Beverley by CWG. Owned by Onward SF Co of Grimsby. 1915: Requisitioned in February and converted to a M/S. 1919: Returned to owners. 1939: Requisitioned in November and converted to an APV. 1940: Converted to a M/S in June. 1944: Converted to an Esso on March. Employed on Target-towing. 1946: Returned to owners in August.

LIDDOCH	1939/41	See under ISAAC DOBSON
		(Vol 1 p.173)
LIFFEY	1920/47	See under STONEAXE (Vol 1 p.33)
LIGNY	1940/45	See under HENRY CHEVALLIER
		(Vol 1 p.55)
LILY MELLING	1914/19	Displacement: 246TG 96TN
		Engines: 85HP
		Armament: 1 x 6pdr
		Admty No: 400
		Port Reg: FD. 222

1908: Launched. Built at North Shields. Owned by Mellings STC of Fleetwood. 1914:

Requisitioned in December and converted to a M/S. 1919: Returned to owners. *Notes*: Sister-ships: LENA MELLING and LIZZIE MELLING.

LIMEWOLD   1914/19   Ex-*Derwent*
                                           Displacement: 189TG 76TN
                                           Engines: 50HP
                                           Armament: 1 x 6pdr
                                           Admty No: 777
                                           Port Reg: GY. 1125

1898: Launched. Built at Beverley. Iron construction. Owned by Northwold SFC of Grimsby. 1914: Requisitioned in December and converted to a M/S. 1919: Returned to owners.

LINCOLN CITY   1939/41   Football Group
                                           Displacement: 398TG 198TN
                                           Engines: 104HP
                                           Port Reg: GY. 464

1933: Launched. Built at Selby by Cochrane. Owned by Consolidated Fisheries of Grimsby. 1939: Requisitioned in September and converted to A/S. 1941: LOST. Sunk by enemy a/c off the Faroes on 21st February.

LINCOLNIA   1917/19   Displacement: 138TG 52TN
                                           Engines: 42HP
                                           Port Reg: FD. 118

1896: Launched. Built at Middlesborough by Smith's Dock. Owned by W. Olney of Thornton, Lancs. 1917: Requisitioned into the Fishery Reserve. 1919: Returned to owners.

LINCOLNSHIRE   1939/45   Displacement: 432TG 157TN
                                           Engines: 99HP
                                           Armament: 1 x 4-inch
                                           Port Reg: H. 164
                                           P. No: FY. 222

1936: Launched.   Built at Southbank-on-Tees by Smith's Dock.   Owned by Lincolnshire Fishing Co of Grimsby. PR: GY. 251. 1938: Acquired by Boyd Line of Hull. PR: H.164. 1939: Requisitioned in September and converted to A/S. 1944: TPI Operation Neptune, the D-Day Landings in June, as A/S Escort. 1945: Returned to owners in September.

LINNET   1914/19   Displacement: 142TG 58TN
                                           Engines: 50HP

1891: Launched. Built at Middlesborough by Smith's Dock. Owned by Overseas SFC of Grimsby. 1914: Requisitioned in September and converted to a BDV. 1919: Returned to owners.

LINNET   1917/19   Ex-*Her Majesty*
Displacement: 142TG 59TN
Engines: 45HP
Port Reg: A. 43

1887: Launched. Built at Hull. Owned by J. Lewis Ltd of Aberdeen. 1918: Requisitioned into the Fishery Reserve in June. 1919: Returned to owners.

LINN o' DEE   1915/19 1939/44 Displacement: 227TG 98TN
Engines: 82HP
Armament: WWI: 1 x 6pdr;
WWII: 1 x 12pdr; 1 x 20mmAA;
2 x HMG (2x1)
Admty No: 513
Port Reg: WWI: A. 338; WWII: LH. 78
P.No: WWII: 4. 364

1915: Launched. Built at Leith. Owned by The Standard FC (Aberdeen) Ltd. Requisitioned in November and converted to a M/S. 1919: Returned to owners. Acquired by J. Lockhart of Edinburgh and renamed *Ocean Brine*. 1939: Requisitioned in November as OCEAN BRINE and converted to an APV. 1944: Returned to owners.

LITTLE EMMA   1917/19   Displacement: 167TG
Admty No: Not issued
Port Reg: GY. 703

1890: Launched. 1917: Requisitioned into the Fishery Reserve. 1919: Returned to owners.

LIVINGSTONE   1914/17   Displacement: 213TG 71TN
Engines: 60NHP = 10K
Armament: 1 x 3pdr
Admty No: 256
Port Reg: H. 496

1900: Launched. Built at Hull by CWG. Owned by Nation STC of Hull. 1914: Requisitioned in August and converted to a M/S. 1917: Acquired by East Riding SFC of Hull. Employed as escort for Scandinavian convoys. LOST. Sunk by SMS EMDEN and Destroyers of the German 3rd Half-Flotilla on 12th December whilst escorting a Scandinavian convoy with destroyers PELLEW and PARTRIDGE and Trs. COMMANDER FULLERTON, LORD ALVERSTONE and TOKIO. All the ships in the convoy were sunk as were the escort vessels with the exception of PELLEW.

LIZZIE   1914/19   Displacement: 278TG
Armament: 1 x 12pdr
Admty No: 332
Port Reg: H. 496

1900: Launched. 1914: Requisitioned in August and converted to a M/S. 1920: Returned to owners.

LIZZIE MELLING   1915/19   Displacement: 207TG 79TN
                                         Engines: 62HP
                                         Armament: 1 x 6pdr
                                         Admty No: 2511
                                         Port Reg: PN. 45
1904: Launched. Built at N. Shields. Owned by Mellings STC of Fleetwood. 1915: Requisitioned in June and converted to a M/S. 1919: Returned to owners. *Notes*: Sister-ships: LENA MELLING and LILY MELLING.

LOBELIA   1914/17   Displacement: 184TG
                                         Armament: 1 x 3pdr
                                         Admty No: 974
                                         Port Reg: M. 147
1898: Launched. 1915: Requisitioned in April. Renamed LOBELIA II in December. 1917: LOST. Mined off Fanad Point, Lough Swilly, on 19th April.

LOCH ALSH   1939/42   Ex-*Lady Madeleine*
                                         Ex-*Cameron*
                                         Displacement: 358TG 153TN
                                         Engines: 96HP = 11K
                                         Armament: 1 x 12pdr
                                         Port Reg: H. 73
1926: Launched. Built at Beverley as Lady Madeleine. Owned by Jutland Amalgamated Trawlers of Hull. PR: H. 278. 1934: Acquired by Clan SFC of Grimsby and renamed Cameron PR: GY. 65. 1939: Acquired by Loch FCL of Hull and renamed *Loch Alsh*, PR: H. 73. Requisitioned in December and converted to a M/S. 1940: 17th M/S Group based at Grimsby. 1942: LOST. Damaged by enemy a/c off the Humber on 30th January. Taken in tow but sank NE of Skegness.

LOCH ARD   1914/17   Displacement: 225TG
                                         Admty No: 330
                                         Port Reg: A. 503
1912: Launched. 1914: Requisitioned in August and converted to a M/S. 1917: LOST. Mined off Lowestoft on 10th October.

LOCH ASSATER   1915/19 1940/40 Displacement: 210TG 79TN
                                         Engines: 56HP
                                         Armament: 1 x 3pdr
                                         Admty No: 1198
                                         Port Reg: A. 321
1910: Launched. Built at Aberdeen. Owned by Empire SFC of Aberdeen. 1915:

Requisitioned in April and converted to a M/S. 1919: Returned to owners. Acquired by Stephen Fishing Co. & T Stephen of Aberdeen. 1940: Purchased into the RN on 24th February and converted to an APV. LOST. Sunk by a 'friendly' RN mine off the E. Coast of Scotland on 22nd March.

LOCH AWE	1915/19	Displacement: 216TG 82TN
		Engines: 76
		Armament: 1 x 6pdr
		Admty No: 1341
		Port Reg: A. 274

1909: Launched. Built at Aberdeen. Owned by Loch Line of Aberdeen. 1915: Requisitioned in April and converted to a M/S. 1919: Returned to owners. 1936: Owned by Alexander A. Davidson of Aberdeen.

| LOCH BLAIR | 1940/46 | See under JAMES BEAGAN |
| | | (Vol 1 p.174) |

LOCH BROOM	1914/19	Displacement: 197TG 75TN
		Engines: 60HP
		Armament: 1 x 3pdr
		Admty No: 26
		Port Reg: A. 141

1907: Launched. Built at Aberdeen. 1914: Requisitioned in August and converted to a M/S. Fitted with Listening Hydrophones. 1919: Returned to owners. 1920: Acquired by Resolute SFC of Lowestoft. PR: LT. 327.

LOCH BUIE	1916/19	Displacement: 221TG 85TN
		Engines: 70HP
		Armament: 1 x 12pdr
		Admty No: 3263
		Port Reg: A. 761

1915: Launched. Built at Aberdeen. Owned by Bonaccord SFC of Aberdeen. 1916: Requisitioned in March and converted to a M/S. 1919: Returned to owners.

| LOCH BUIE | 1939/46 | See under ISAAC ARTHAN (Vol 1 p.55) |

LOCH DOON	1914/19	Displacement: 198TG 76TN
		Engines: 69HP
		Armament: 1 x 6pdrAA
		Admty No: 271
		Port Reg: A. 161

1907: Launched. Built at Aberdeen. 1914: Requisitioned in August and converted to a M/S. 1919: Returned to owners. 1920: Acquired by The Montrose SFC of Montrose. PR: ME. 248.

LOCH DOON   1939/39   Displacement: 534TG 198TN
Engines: 98HP
Armament: 1 x 4-inch
Port Reg: H. 435

1937: Launched. Built at Southbank-on-Tees by Smith's Dock. Owned by Loch FC of Hull. 1939: Requisitioned in August and converted to A/S. LOST. Believed mined off Blyth on 25th December with the loss of 15 lives.

LOCH ERIBOL   1939/45   Ex-BEVERLAC
Displacement: 352TG 150TN
Engines: 96HP = 11.1K
Armament: 3 x 0.5-inch MG (3x1)
Port Reg: H. 72
P. No: FY. 704

1929: Launched. Built at Beverley by CWG as *Beverlec*. Owned by WA Massey of Hull. 1938: Acquired by Loch FCL of Hull and renamed *Loch Eriboll*. 1939: Purchased into the RN in August and converted to a M/S. 1940: 16th M/S Group. Based at Grimsby. 1943: 179th M/S Group based at Grimsby. 1945: SO of 136th M/S Group based at Grimsby. LOST. Sunk in a collision with the American merchantman *Sydney Sharman* off Start Point, South Devon on 12th October.

LOCH ESK   1914/19   Displacement: 215TG 80TN
Engines: 76HP
Armament: 1 x 3pdr
Admty No: 340
Port Reg: A. 241

1908: Launched. Built at Aberdeen. Owned by The Empire SFC of Aberdeen. 1914: Requisitioned in August and converted to a M/S. 1920: Returned to owners.

LOCH ESK   1939/40   See under DANIEL STROUD

LOCH EYE   1916/17   Displacement: 225TG
Armament: 1 x 6pdr
Admty No: 2965
Port Reg; A. 693

1916: Launched. Requisitioned in September and converted to a M/S. 1917: LOST. Mined off Dunmore on 20th April.

LOCH GARRY   1915/16   Displacement: 176TG
Port Reg: HL. 32

1906: Launched. 1916: Requisitioned in January and converted to an APV. LOST. Foundered off Kirkwall on 14th September.

LOCH HOPE   1939/45   See under PRINCESS MARIE JOSE

LOCH HOURNE   1915/19   Displacement: 209TG 79TN
                                      Engines: 71HP
                                      Armament: 1 x 12pdr
                                      Admty No: 1173
                                      Port Reg: A .502
1912: Launched. Built at Aberdeen. Owned by Loch Line SFC of Aberdeen. 1915:
Requisitioned in February and converted to a M/S. Fitted with Listening Hydrophones.
1919: Returned to owners. 1936: Owned by D. Wood & R. Main of Aberdeen. Port Reg:
A. 933.

LOCHIEL   1917/19   Displacement: 241TG
                                      Armament: 1 x 6pdr
1908: Launched. 1917: Requisitioned. 1918: LOST. Mined or torpedoed off Whitby on
24th July.

LOCH INVER   1939/40   Displacement: 356TG 151TN
                                      Engines: 96HP = 10.8K
                                      Armament: 1 x 12pdr
                                      Port Reg: H. 195
1930: Launched. Built at Beverley by CWG. Owned by A & M Smith of Aberdeen. 1930:
Acquired by Hellyer Bros. of Hull. 1935: Acquired by Caledonian FC of Hull. 1939:
Requisitioned in October and converted to an APV. Based at Harwich. 1940: LOST.
Mined off Harwich on 24th September. No survivors.

LOCH KILDONIAN   1914/19   Displacement: 211TG 80TN
                                      Engines: 69HP
                                      Armament: 1 x 3pdr
                                      Admty No: 107
                                      Port Reg: A. 163
1907: Launched. Built at Aberdeen. 1914: Requisitioned in August and converted to a
M/S. 1919: Returned to owners. 1920: Acquired by Montrose FCL of Montrose. PR:
ME. 249.

LOCH LAGGAN   1939/45   Displacement: 255TG 110TN
                                      Engines: 68HP
                                      Port Reg: A. 82
1930: Launched. Built at Aberdeen. Owned by Bon Accord SF Co of Aberdeen. 1939:
Requisitioned in September and converted to a BDV. 1945: Returned to owners in June.

LOCH LEE   1915/19   Displacement: 210TG 79TN
                                      Engines: 56HP
                                      Armament: 1 x 6pdr
                                      Admty No: 1190
                                      Port Reg: A. 325

1910: Launched. Built at Aberdeen. Owned by Bon Accord SF Co of Aberdeen. 1915: Requisitioned in March. 1919: Returned to owners.

LOCH LEVEN	1939/46	Displacement: 357TG 154TN
		Engines: 96HP = 10.6K
		Armament: 1 x 12pdr; 2 x 20mmAA
		(2x1)
		Port Reg: H. 186
		P. No: FY. 642

1928: Launched. Built at Beverley by CWG. Owned by Loch Line STC of Aberdeen. 1930: Acquired by Hellyer Bros. of Hull. PR: H.186. 1939: Acquired by Caledonian FCL of Hull. Requisitioned in August and converted to a M/S. 16th M/S Group based at Grimsby for sweeping from Flamborough Head to Cromer. 1943: 179th M/S Group based at Grimsby. 1946: Returned to owners in February.

LOCH LOMOND	1917/19	Displacement: 145TG 55TN
		Engines: 52HP
		Port Reg: A. 857

1898: Launched. Built at Aberdeen. 1917: Requisitioned into the Fishery Reserve. 1919: Returned to owners.

| LOCH LONG | 1940/46 | See under TIMOTHY CRAWLEY |
| | | (See Addenda p.532) |

LOCH LOYAL	1914/19	Displacement: 196TG 121TN
		Engines: 68HP
		Armament: 1 x 3pdr
		Port Reg: A. 733

1907: Launched. Built at Aberdeen. 1914: Requisitioned. 1919: Returned to owners. 1920: Acquired by A. Evans of Lowestoft. PR: LT. 347.

LOCH LYON	1916/19	Displacement: 225TG 84TN
		Engines: 69HP
		Armament: 1 x 12pdr
		Admty No: 3298
		Port Reg: A. 649

1916: Launched. Built at Aberdeen. Owned by Loch Line Tr. & Fishing Co. of Aberdeen. Requisitioned in July and converted to a M/S. 1919: Returned to owners.

LOCH MAREE	1915/19	Displacement: 215TG 80TN
		Engines: 76HP
		Armament: 1 x 6pdr
		Admty No: 1339
		Port Reg: A .312

1910: Launched. Built at Aberdeen. Owned by White Star SFC of Aberdeen. 1915: Requisitioned in April and converted to a M/S. 1919: Returned to owners.

LOCH MELFORT   1939/46   Displacement: 440TG 164TN
                                       Engines: 99HP
                                       Port Reg: H. 111
1934: Launched. Built at Southbank-on-Tees by Smith's Dock. Owned by Loch Fishing Co. of Hull. 1939: Purchased into the RN in August and converted to A/S. 1946: Sold to mercantile in February.

LOCH MOIDART   1940/46   See under JAMES WRIGHT
                                       (Vol 1 P.139)

LOCH MONTIETH   1939/45   Displacement: 531TG 195TN
                                       Engines: 99HP
                                       Armament: 1 x 4-inch
                                       Port Reg: H. 305
1936: Launched. Built at Southbank -on-Tees by Smith's Dock. Owned by Loch Fishing Co of Hull. 1939: Requisitioned in September and converted to A/S. 1940: Based at Portland. Sustained damage and casualties on 24th September when, whilst on Anti-invasion Patrol off Portland, she was attacked by a German bomber a/c. Her bows were damaged and 6 men killed. TIH for repairs. 1941: Employed as S/M escort for the remainder of the war. 1945: Returned to owners in November.

LOCH MORAR   1914/19   Displacement: 228TG 113TN
                                       Engines: 61HP
                                       Armament: 1 x 6pdr
                                       Admty No: 272
                                       Port Reg: A. 361
1912: Launched. Built at Ayr. Owned by White Star SF Co. of Aberdeen. 1914: Requisitioned in August and converted to a M/S. 1919: Returned to owners. 1920: Acquired by United SFC of Aberdeen. PR: A. 501.

LOCH NAVER   1915/18   Displacement: 216TG
                                       Armament: 1 x 6pdr
                                       Admty No: 1179
                                       Port Reg: A. 45
1906: Launched. 1915: Requisitioned in February. 1918: LOST. Mined in the Aegean on 13th May.

LOCH NAVER   1939/40   See under EDWARD CATTELLY
                                       (Vol 1 p.51)

LOCH OSKAIG   1939/45   Displacement: 534TG 198TN
                                          Engines: 99HP
                                          Armament: 1 x 4-inch
                                          Port Reg: H. 431

1937: Launched. Built at Southbank-on-Tees by Smith's Dock. Owned by The Caledonian Fishing Co. of Aberdeen. 1939: Requisitioned in August and converted to A/S. 1941: Converted to an ABV. 1943: Joined the Gibraltar Trawler Force. 1945: Returned to the UK. Returned to owners in November.

LOCH RANNOCH   1915/19 1940/44 Displacement: 178TG 68TN
                                            Engines: 62HP
                                          Port Reg: A. 475

1901: Launched. Built at Aberdeen. Owned by T. Davidson AO of Aberdeen. 1916: Requisitioned in September and converted to a BDV. 1919: Returned to owners. 1938: Owned by William Brebner AO of Aberdeen. 1940: Requisitioned in January and converted to a M/S. 1944: Returned to owners in January.

LOCH SHIEL   1916/16   Displacement: 216TG
                                            Armament: 1 x 3pdr
                                          Admty No: 1572
                                          Port Reg: A .273

1909: Launched. 1916: Requisitioned in April. LOST. Mined off Milford Haven on 26th September.

LOCH SHIN   1939/40   Displacement: 255TG 110TN
                                            Engines: 68HP
                                          Port Reg: A. 78

1930: Launched. Built at Aberdeen by Lewis. Owned by Empire SF Co. of Aberdeen. 1939: Requisitioned in September and converted to a BDV. 1940: TPI the Norwegian Campaign in April/May. LOST. Suffered bomb damage off Harstadt, Lofoton Islands, and finally capsized and sank on 26th May.

LOCH STROM   1917/19   Displacement: 176TG 67TN
                                            Engines: 62HP
                                          Admty No: Not issued
                                          Port Reg: GY. 867

1903: Built at Aberdeen. Owned by H. Wood & Co (Grimsby) Ltd. 1917: Requisitioned into the Fishery Reserve . 1919: Returned to owners.

LOCH TULLA   1939/46   Displacement: 423TG 163TN
                                            Engines: 99HP
                                          Armament: 1 x 4-inch
                                          Complement: 45
                                          Port Reg: H. 225

1934: Launched. Built at Southbank-on-Tees by Smith's Dock. Owned by Loch Fishing Co of Hull. 1939: Requisitioned in August and converted to A/S. 1944: Based at Wallasey Dock, Birkenhead and employed on escort duties for coastal and Atlantic convoys as far as Iceland. 1946: Returned to owners in January.

LOCH TUMMEL	1916/18	Displacement: 228TG
		Armament: 1 x 6pdr
		Admty No: 1178
		Port Reg: A. 494

1912: Launched. Built at Aberdeen. Owned by the White Star SFC of Aberdeen. 1915: Requisitioned in April. 1918: LOST. Foundered in the Med. at Lat. 33 degrees 35' N 21 degrees 45' E from an unknown cause on 14th July.

LOCH WASDALE	1916/19	Displacement: 210TG 81TN
		Engines: 70HP
		Armament: 1 x 12pdrAA
		Admty No: 3222
		Port Reg: A. 457

1915: Launched. Built at Abedeen. Owned by the White Star SFC of Aberdeen. Requisitioned in October and converted to a M/S. 1919: Returned to owners.

LOIS	1915/19	Displacement: 310TG 125TN
		Engines: 91HP
		Armament: 1 x 12pdr
		Admty No: 961
		Port Reg: FD. 113

1910: Launched. Built at Selby by Cochrane. Owned by The Forward STC of Fleetwood. 1915: Requisitioned in January and converted to a M/S. 1919: Returned to owners.

LOIS	1940/44	See under JOHN APPLEBY
		(Vol 1 p.139)

LOLIST	1917/19	Displacement: 180TG
		Port Reg: LT. 427

1914: Launched. 1917: Requisitioned into the Fishery Reserve. 1919: Returned to owners.

LOMBARD	1916/20 1940/45	Displacement: 272TG 122TN
		Engines: 71HP
		Armament: 1 x 12pdr
		Admty No: 1611
		Port Reg: GY. 478
		P.No: WWII: 4. 169

1909: Launched. Built at Beverley by CWG. Owned by Lindsay SF Co of Grimsby.

1915: Requisitioned in April and converted to a M/S. 1917: Converted to an Escort. 1920: Returned to owners. 1940: Requisitioned in May and converted to an APV. 1942: Converted to a M/S in March. 1945: Returned to owners in December. 1958: BU.

LONGSCAR   1939/45   Displacement: 215TG 94TN
                                       Engines: 69HP
                                       Port Reg: HL. 16

1930: Launched. Built at Aberdeen. Owned by Heugh ST Co. of Hartlepool. 1939: Requisitioned in August and fitted out for the Examination Service. 1945: Returned to owners.

LONGSET   1915/17   Displacement: 275TG
                                       Armament: 1 x 6pdr
                                       Admty No: 1503
                                       Port Reg: GY. 376

1914: Launched. 1915: Requisitioned in May. 1917: LOST. Mined off Wells Point on 6th February.

LOON   1914/19 1940/45 Displacement: 191TG 73TN
                                       Engines: 55HP
                                       Armament: 1 x 12pdr
                                       Admty No: 406
                                       Port Reg: H. 119

1914: Launched. Built at Goole by Goole SB. Owned by Kelsall Bros. & Beeching of Hull. Requisitioned in October and converted to a M/S. 1919: Returned to owners. 1940: Requisitioned in March and converted to a BBV. 1943: Converted to a Water Carrier. 1945: Returned to owners in December.

L'ORAGE   1940/42   Displacement: 580TG
                                           Port Reg: French

1921: Launched. 1940: French fishing vessel seized in the Atlantic on 24th November. 1941: Employed on Special Service from July. 1942: Transferred to the MWT.

LORD AIREDALE   1915/16   Displacement: 215TG
                                         Armament: 1 x 3pdr
                                       Admty No: 847
                                       Port Reg: GY. 910

1911: Launched. Owned by Consolidated Fisheries of Grimsby. 1915: Requisitioned in February. 1916: LOST. Mined off the Sunk LV. on 29th November. *Notes*: Sister-ships: LORDs: ALLENDALE, ASHBY, DE RAMSAY, DURHAM, GREY, PERCY, RIDLEY, WIMBORNE and WOLMER.

LORD ALLENDALE   1915/19   Displacement: 215TG 84TN
                                         Engines: 76HP

Armament: 1 x 12pdr
Admty No: 1351
Port Reg: GY. 891

1911: Launched. Built at Middlesborough by Smith's Dock. Owned by Consolidated Fisheries of Grimsby. 1915: Requisitioned in February and converted to a M/S. 1919: Returned to owners. *Notes*: See under LORD AIREDALE.

LORD ALVERSTONE   1916/17   Displacement: 247TG 98TN
Engines: 69NHP = 10K
Dimensions: 117ft x 22ft x 12ft 6ins
Armament: 1 x 6pdrAA
Admty No: 3047
Port Reg: GY. 1059

1917: Launched in June. Built at Beverley by CWG. Owned by North Western SFC of Grimsby. Acquired by Beacon SFC of Grimsby. Requisitioned in June and converted to a M/S. LOST. Sunk by German forces on 12th December. See notes under LIVINGSTONE.

LORD ASHBY   1915/19   Displacement: 215TG 84TN
Engines: 75HP
Armament: 1 x 3pdr
Admty No: 1234
Port Reg: GY. 909

1911: Launched. Built at Middlesborough by Smith's Dock. Owned by Consolidated Fisheries of Grimsby. 1915: Requisitioned in March and converted to a M/S. 1919: Returned to owners. *Notes*: See under LORD AIREDALE.

LORD ASHFIELD   1939/45   Displacement: 346TG 135TN
Engines: 96HP
Armament: 1 x 12pdr
Port Reg: H. 53

1929: Launched. Built at Selby by Cochrane. Owned by Pickering & Haldane ST Co of Hull. 1939: Requisitioned in September and converted to a M/S. 1940: Joined the 41st M/S Flot based at Aberdeen. 1941: Based at Ardrossan. 1944: TPI Operation Neptune, the D-Day Landings in June, as a D/L attached to the 1st M/S Flot. in Force S. 1945: Returned to owners. 1947: Owned by Lord Line of Hull.

LORD AUSTIN   1939/44   Displacement: 473TG 193TN
Engines: 120HP = 10K
Complement: 30
Port Reg: H. 483

1937: Launched. Built at Selby by Cochrane. Owned by Pickering & Haldane of Hull. 1939: Requisitioned in September and converted to A/S. Joined the Northern Patrol. 1941: Transferred to the Iceland Command in August for Russian convoys. 1942: Escort unit for PQ.14 in April. Escort unit for the ill-fated PQ17 in June/July. 1943: Completed her last Russian convoy in December. Paid Off at Birkenhead and TIH for refitting. 1944: Completed refitting in May and re-Commissioned. Towed a barge from Clyde to Falmouth and then on to Southampton for the D-Day Landings. TPI Operation Neptune, the D-Day Landings in June, as an A/S escort. Escorted a convoy of TLSs to Juno Beach. Sustained damage when a bomb blew a hole in the ship's side but remained at sea. LOST. Triggered an acoustic mine in the Seine Bay on 24th June. Sank in 10 minutes with the loss of 7 lives.

LORD BEACONSFIELD   1939/45   Displacement: 303TG 158TN
                                    Engines: 84HP
                                    Armament: 1 x 12pdr
                                    Port Reg: GY .583
1915: Launched. Built at Selby by Cochrane. Owned by Consolidated Fisheries of Grimsby. 1939: Requisitioned in April and converted to an APV. Based at Grimsby for Fishery Protection. 1941: Converted to a M/S. 1945: Paid Off. Reduced to the Reserve. LOST. Awaiting disposal when she was wrecked in June.

LORD CECIL   1916/19 1939/40 Displacement: 228TG 88TN
                                    Engines: 72HP
                                    Armament: 1 x 12pdr
                                    Port Reg: GY. 768
1916: Launched. Built at Southbank-on-Tees by Smith's Dock. Owned by Trawlers (White Sea & Grimsby) Ltd. Requisitioned in July and converted to a M/S. 1919: Returned to owners. 1939: Requisitioned in November and designated as an APV. 1940: Returned to owners in January.

LORD DARLING   1940/44   See under PRINCE PALATINE

LORD DENMAN   1915/15   Displacement: 309TG
                                    Armament: 1 x 12pdr
                                    Admty No: 1525
                                    Port Reg: H. 118
1914: Launched. 1915: Requisitioned in June and converted to a M/S. LOST. Sunk in a collision in the White Sea on 22nd October.

LORD De RAMSAY   1916/19   Displacement: 215TG 84TN
                                    Engines: 75HP
                                    Armament: 1 x 6pdr
                                    Admty No: 1144
                                    Port Reg: GY. 911
1911: Launched. Built at Middlesborough by Smith's Dock. Owned by Consolidated Fisheries of Grimsby. 1915: Requisitioned in February and converted to a M/S. 1919: Returned to owners. *Notes*: See under LORD AIREDALE.

LORD DURHAM   1915/19   Displacement: 215TG 84TN
                                      Engines: 76HP
                                      Armament: 1 x 6pdrAA
                                      Admty No: 460
                                      Port Reg: GY. 879
1911: Launched. Built at Middlesborough by Smith's Dock. Owned by Consolidated
Fisheries of Grimsby. 1915: Requisitioned in February and converted to a M/S. 1919:
Returned to owners. *Notes*: See under LORD AIREDALE.

LORD ESSENDEN   1939/45   Displacement: 464TG 202TN
                                      Engines: 114HP
                                      Port Reg: H. 312
1936: Launched. Built at Selby by Cochrane. Owned by Pickering & Haldane of Hull.
1939: Requisitioned in September and converted to A/S. 1944: TPI Operation Neptune,
the D-Day Landings in June, as an A/S escort. 1945: Returned to owners.

LORD GAINFORD   1939/46   Displacement: 324TG 131TN
                                      Engines: 87HP
                                      Port Reg: FD. 74
1918: Launched. Built at Selby by Cochrane. Owned by Marr of Fleetwood. 1939:
Requisitioned in December and converted to a BDV. 1942: Commissioned with a Free
French crew in July. 1943: Purchased into the RN on 23rd November. 1945: RN
manned. 1946: Sold at Freetown on 8th August.

LORD GEORGE   1916/19 1939/44 Displacement: 229TG 120TN
                                      Engines: 63HP
                                      Armament: 1 x 6pdrAA
                                      Admty No: 688
                                      Port Reg: WWI: GY. 83; WWII: GY. 420
                                      P.No: WWII: FY. 996
1905: Launched. Built at Selby by Cochrane. 1915: Requisitioned in February and
converted to a M/S. 1919: Returned to owners. 1920: Acquired by E. Taylor & N.
Ashworth of Fleetwood. PR: FD. 329. Acquired by United SF Co. Ltd. of Grimsby
and renamed *Cedric*. 1939: Requisitioned in November as CEDRIC and converted
to an APV. 1940: Converted to a BBV in May. 1944: Returned to owners in October.

LORD GREY   1916/17   Displacement: 215TG
                                      Armament: 1 x 6pdrAA
                                      Admty No: 1605
                                      Port Reg: GY. 904
1911: Launched. 1915: Requisitioned in March and converted to a M/S. 1917: LOST.
Wrecked on La Barrier Shoal, Cap Gris Nez, on 2nd December.

LORD GREY   1939/46   Displacement: 346TG 135TN
Engines: 96HP
Dimensions: 140ft x 24ft
Armament: 1 x 12pdr; 1 x 20mmAA;
2 x LG (2 x 1)
Port Reg: H. 500

1928: Launched. Built at Selby by Cochrane. Owned by Pickering & Haldane of Hull. 1939: Requisitioned in December and converted to a M/S. Joined the 130th M/S Group based at Falmouth. 1941: TIH at Greenock for conversion for tropical service. Sailed from Greenock in November to join the EIF. 1942: Joined the EIF at Colombo on 25th May having taken nearly 6 months to arrive due to bad weather enroute having been TIH fro repairs at Gibraltar, Freetown, Capetown and Durban all due to damage by severe weather. 1945 Sailed from Colombo in December for return to the UK. 1945: Arrived at Devonport in February. Paid off at Hull. 1946: Returned to owners in May. 1948: Acquired by J. Bennet and renamed *Rapier*. 1956: BU.

LORD HAILSHAM   1939/43   Displacement: 445TG 179TN
Engines: 99HP
Port Reg: H. 82

1934: Launched. Built at Selby by Cochrane. Owned by Pickering & Haldanes of Hull. 1939: Purchased into the RN in August and converted to A/S. 1943: LOST. Torpedoed by German E-Boat whilst escorting Convoy WP. 300 in the Channel.

LORD HAILSHAM   **(Dave Scoble Collection)**

LORD HARDINGE   1917/18   Displacement: 212TG
Armament: 1 x 6pdrAA
Admty No: 2993
Port Reg: GY. 1013

1917: Launched. Requisitioned in January and converted to a M/S. 1918: LOST. Sunk in a collision off the Daunt LV. on 9th April.

LORD HENEAGE   1915/19   Displacement: 324TG 138TN
Engines: 93NHP = 11K
Armament: 1 x 12pdr; 1 x 7.5-inch
Bomb Thrower (A/S Howitzer)
Admty No: 1140
Port Reg: H. 27

1909: Launched. Built at Beverley by CWG. Owned by Yorkshire SFC of Hull. 1915: Requisitioned in February and converted to a M/S. 1919: Returned to owners. 1924: Sold to Portugal and renamed *Golfinho*. 1935: Mercantile Loss in the river Tagus, Portugal.

LORD HOTHAM   1939/45   Displacement: 464TG 189TN
Engines: 114HP
Port Reg: H. 309

1936: Launched. Built at Selby by Cochrane. Owned by Pickering & Haldanes of Hull. 1939: Requisitioned in August and converted to A/S. 1945: Returned to owners in September.

LORD INCHCAPE   1939/40   Displacement: 338TG 137TN
Engines: 96HP
Port Reg: H. 102

1924: Launched. Built at Selby by Cochrane. Owned by Pickering & Haldanes of Hull. 1939: Requisitioned in August and converted to a M/S. 1940: LOST. Mined off Plymouth on 25th October. Wreck subsequently raised and purchased into the RN. 1946: Sold to mercantile in August.

LORD IRWIN   1939/46   Displacement: 346TG 135TN
Engines: 96HP
Port Reg: H. 501

1928: Launched. Built at Selby by Cochrane. Owned by Pickering & Haldanes of Hull. 1939: Requisitioned in September and converted to a M/S. Fitted out at Grimsby. Based at Grimsby (ungrouped). Transferred to the Med. The first LL Sweeper to join the MF. 1944: Converted to a Calibrating Vessel. 1946: Returned to owners in January.

LORD KNOLLYS   1916/19   Displacement: 285TG 114TN
Engines: 75HP
Armament: 1 x 12pdr
Admty No: 1177

Port Reg: H. 327
1911: Launched. Built at Selby by Cochrane. 1915: Requisitioned in March and converted to a M/S. Fitted with Listening Hydrophones. 1919: Returned to owners.

LORD LANSDOWNE 1916/19 Displacement: 289TG 116TN
Engines: 79HP
Armament: 1 x 12pdr; 1 x 7.5-inch
Bomb Thrower (A/S Howitzer)
Admty No: 3020
Port Reg: H. 1004

1913: Launched. Built at Selby by Cochrane. Owned by Jutland STC of Hull. 1917: Requisitioned in February and converted to a M/S. 1919: Returned to owners.

LORD LISTER 1915/19 Displacement: 285TG 114TN
Engines: 64HP
Armament: 1 x 12pdr; 1 x 7.5-inch
Bomb Thrower (A/S Howitzer)
Admty No: 1568
Port Reg: H. 484

1912: Launched. Built at Selby by Cochrane. Owned by F. Langley of Hull. 1915: Requisitioned in May and converted to a M/S. 1919: Returned to owners.

LORD LLOYD 1939/45 Displacement: 396TG 153TN
Engines: 99HP
Armament: 1 x 12pdr; 2 x 40mm (2x1);
2 x 0.5-inch MGs (1x2); DCs
Port Reg: H. 508
P. No: FY. 157

1933: Launched. Built at Selby by Cochrane. Owned by Pickering & Haldanes of Hull. 1939: Purchased into the RN in August and converted to A/S. 1943: Based at Scapa Flow for A/S patrols in the Pentland Firth area. Employed as a tanker escort from Scotland to the Faroes and on ferry service Scotland - Orkneys. Escorted one-man Wellman S/Ms from Aberdeen to Shetland, and after they were deemed unsuccessful she was involved in dumping their warheads at sea. 1945: Sold to mercantile and retained the same name. Acquired by Lord Line of Hull. PR: H. 263.

LORD MELCHETT 1939/46 Displacement: 347TG 135TN
Engines: 96HP
Armament: 1 x 12pdr
Port Reg: H. 1

1928: Launched. Built at Selby by Cochrane. Owned by Pickering & Haldane of Hull. 1939: Requisitioned in August and converted to a M/S. Joined the Harwich M/S Groups. 1944: Converted to a D/L in April. 1946: Returned to owners in May.

LORD MERSEY   1916/19   Displacement: 326TG 134TN
                                            Engines: 93HP
                                            Armament: 1 x 12pdr; 1 x 7.5-inch
                                            Bomb Thrower (A/S Howitzer)
                                            Admty No: 1991
                                            Port Reg: H. 427
1916: Launched.   Built at Selby.   Owned by Pickering & Haldane STC of Hull.
Requisitioned in April and converted to a M/S. 1919: Returned to owners. *Notes*: The
prototype for the Admiralty 'Mersey' Class.

LORD MIDDLETON   1939/46   Displacement: 464TG 188TN
                                            Engines: 112HP
                                            Armament: 1 x 4-inch
                                            Port Reg: H. 282
1936: Launched. Built at Selby by Cochrane. Owned by Pickering & Haldane of Hull.
1939: Requisitioned in September and converted to A/S. 1941: Joined the Iceland
Command in August for Russian convoys. 1942: Convoy PQ.14 in April. Ill-fated PQ.17
in Jun/July. 1946: Returned to owners in March.

I ORD MINTO   1916/19   Displacement: 295TG 123TN
                                            Engines: 93HP
                                            Armament: 1 x 12pdr
                                            Admty No: 1516
                                            Port Reg: FD. 51
1914: Launched. Built at Selby by Cochrane. Requisitioned in May and converted
to a M/S. 1919: Returned to owners. 1938: Owned by Active Fishing Co. of
Fleetwood. Subsequently owned by Jutland Amalgamated Trs. of Hull. PR: H.105.

LORD NORTHCLIFFE   1916/19 1939/45 Displacement: 228TG 88TN
                                            Engines: 72HP
                                            Armament: 1 x 6pdr
                                            Admty No: 3260
                                            Port Reg: GY. 759
                                            P. No: WWII: FY. 780
1916: Launched. Built at Southbank-on-Tees by Smith's Dock. Owned by Trawlers
(White Sea & Grimsby) of Grimsby. Requisitioned in March and converted to a M/S.
Converted to an escort vessel. 1919: Returned to owners. 1920: Acquired by HC.
Smethurst of Grimsby. Same PR. Acquired by Trawlers (White Sea & Grimsby) Ltd.
Same PR. 1939: Requisitioned in November and converted to a BBV. 1945: Returned
to owners in November.

LORD NUFFIELD   1939/45   Displacement: 466TG 188TN
                                            Dimensions: 160ft. x 26ft.
                                            Engines: 112HP = 12K

Armament: 1 x 4-inch; 1 x 20mmAA;
2 x MG; DCs
Port Reg: H. 473

1937: Launched. Built at Selby by Cochrane. Owned by Pickering & Haldane of Hull. 1939: Requisitioned in September and converted to A/S. 1940: ICW STELLA CARINA, LADY HOGARTH and KINGSTON AMBER formed an escort Group employed on Atlantic/Med. convoys. The Group remained together throughout the War. 1942: Transferred to the MF and based at Gibraltar for N. African convoys. Sank the Italian S/M EMO off Algiers on 10th November, rescuing 49 Italian survivors. 1943: Based at Malta. Transferred to Alexandria. 1944: Group TPI Operation Husky, the Sicily Landing son July/August. TPI the Salerno Landings in September/October. Based at Tripoli for convoy escorts Corsica – Salerno. 1945: Returned to the UK and Paid Off. Returned to owners in December.

LORD PERCY   1916/20   Displacement: 215TG 84TN
                                     Engines: 75HP
                                     Armament: 1 x 6pdr
                                     Admty No: 1609
                                     Port Reg: GY. 898

1911: Launched. Built at Middlesborough by Smith's Dock. Owned by Consolidated Fisheries of Grimsby. 1915: Requisitioned in March and converted to a M/S. 1920: Returned to owners. *Notes*: See under LORD AIREDALE.

LORD PLENDER   1939/46   Displacement: 396TG 153TN
                                     Engines: 101HP
                                     Port Reg: H. 517

1933: Launched. Built at Selby by Cochrane. Owned by Pickering & Haldane of Hull. 1939: Purchased into the RN in August and converted to A/S. Joined the 19th A/S Group based at Harwich. Employed on E. Coast convoys. 1946: Sold to mercantile and retained the same name. Acquired by Lord Line of Hull. PR: H. 473.

LORD READING   1916/19   Displacement: 326TG 134TN
                                     Engines: 93HP
                                     Armament: 1 x 12pdr; 1 x 7.5-inch
                                     Bomb Thrower (A/S Howitzer)
                                     Port Reg: H. 429

1916: Launched. Built at Selby by Cochrane. Owned by Pickering & Haldane SFC of Hull. Requisitioned in April and converted to a M/S. 1919: Returned to owners.

LORD RIDLEY   1915/17   Displacement: 326TG
                                     Admty No: 850
                                     Port Reg: GY. 900

1911: Launched. Owned by Consolidated Fisheries of Grimsby. 1915: Requisitioned in February and converted to a M/S. 1917: LOST. Mined off Whitby on 10th May. *Notes*: See under LORD AIREDALE.

LORD ROBERTS   1914/16   Displacement: 293TG 117TN
Engines: 86TN
Armament: 1 x 12pdr; 1 x 3pdr
Admty No: 545
Port Reg: H. 955

1907: Launched. Built at Hull. Owned by Yorkshire SFC of Hull. 1914: Requisitioned in November. 1916: LOST. Mined off the Shipwash on 26th October.

LORD ROTHSCHILD   1917/19   Displacement: 174TG 69TN
Engines: 54HP
Admty No: Not issued
Port Reg: GY. 718

1906: Launched. Built at Govan. Owned by W. Butt AO of Grimsby. 1917: Requisitioned into the Fishery Reserve. 1919: Returned to owners.

LORD SALISBURY   1915/17   Displacement: 285TG 114TN
Engines: 75HP
Armament: 1 x 12pdr
Admty No: 1212
Port Reg: H. 323

1911: Launched. Bullt at Selby by Cochrane. Owned by Yorkshire SFC of Hull. 1915: Requisitioned in January and converted to a M/S. 1917: LOST. Mined off Eros Island, Salonika, on 4th May.

LORD SELBORNE   1917/19   Displacement: 167TG
Admty No: Not issued
Port Reg: GY. 392

1897: Launched. 1917: Requisitioned into the Fishery Reserve. 1919: Returned to owners.

LORD SELBORNE   1917/19 1940/41 Displacement: 247TG 97TN
Engines: 75HP = 10K
Armament : 1 x 12pdr
Admty No: 1652
Port Reg: WWI: GY. 1058;
WWII: GY. 509
P. No: WWII: FY. 2964

1917: Launched. Built at Beverley by CWG. Owned by Pelham SFC of Grimsby. Acquired by Beacon SFC of Grimsby. Requisitioned in October and converted to a M/S. Subsequently converted for escort duties. 1919: Returned to owners. 1928: Acquired by Earl SF Co. of Grimsby. 1940: Requisitioned in June and converted to an APV. 1941: LOST. Mined in the Humber estuary, 3 miles off Spurn Head on 31st March.

LORDSHIP   1916/19   Ex-*Lord Fisher*
Displacement: 351TG 165TN

Engines: 100HP = 11K
Armament: 1 x 12pdr; 1 x 6pdr; 1 x 7.5-
inch Bomb Thrower (A/S Howitzer)
Admty No: 1519
Port Reg: H. 264

1914: Launched. Built at Beverley by CWG. Owned by Imperial SFC of Hull. 1915: Requisitioned in May, converted to a M/S and renamed. 1916: Fitted to carry 1 x a/c. 1917: Based at Killingholme. 1919: Returned to owners and reverted to original name. 1930: Mercantile Loss. Wrecked on reefs off the N of Iceland. No loss of life.

LORD SHREWSBURY   1917/19   Ex-*Sarpedon*
Displacement: 167TG 71TN
Engines: 45HP = 9.5K
Armament: None
Admty No: Not Issued
Port Reg: GY. 395

1898: Launched. Built at Hull by CWG as Sarpedon. Owned by Standard SFC of Grimsby. PR: GY. 686. 1912: Acquired by Port of Blyth SF & Ice Co of Blyth and renamed *Lord Shrewsbury* PR: BH. 94. 1914: Acquired by Beacon SFC of Grimsby. PR: GY. 395. 1917: Requisitioned into the Fishery Reserve. 1919: Returned to owners. 1941: Mercantile War Loss. Posted missing in December. Thought to have been mined off the Humber. No survivors.

LORD SNOWDEN   1939/42   Displacement: 444TG 176TN
Engines: 101HP
Port Reg: H. 95

1934: Launched. Built at Selby by Cochrane. Owned by Pickering & Haldane of Hull. 1939: Requisitioned in August and converted to A/S. 1942: LOST. Sunk in a collision off Falmouth on 13th April.

LORD STAMP   1939/40   Displacement: 448TG 178TN
Engines: 99HP
Port Reg: H. 200

1935: Launched. Built at Selby by Cochrane. Owned by Pickering & Haldane SFC of Hull. 1939: Requisitioned in August and converted to A/S. 1940: LOST. Mined in the Channel on 14th October.

LORD STANHOPE   1916/19   Displacement: 212TG 82TN
Engines: 78HP
Armament: 1 x 12pdr
Admty No: 2961
Port Reg: GY. 931

1916: Launched. Built at Aberdeen. Requisitioned in September and converted to a M/S. 1919: Returned to owners. Acquired by W. Barton of Whitby. PR: WY. 285.

LORD STANHOPE   1939/45   Displacement: 448TG 179TN
                                        Engines: 101HP
                                        Port Reg: H. 199

1935: Launched. Built at Selby by Cochrane. Owned by Pickering & Haldane of Hull.
1939: Requisitioned in August and converted to A/S. 1944: TPI Operation Neptune, the
D-Day Landings in June, as an A/S escort. 1945: Returned to owners in November.

LORD STONEHAVEN   1939/42   Displacement: 444TG 176TN
                                        Engines: 101HP
                                        Port Reg: H. 103

1934: Launched. Built at Selby by Cochrane. Owned by Pickering & Haldane of Hull.
1939: Requisitioned in August and converted to A/S. 1942: LOST. Torpedoed by
German E-Boat off the Eddystone Light, Plymouth, on 2nd October.

LORD WAKEFIELD   1939/44   Displacement: 418TG 99TN
                                        Engines: 99HP
                                        Port Reg: H. 535

1933: Launched. Built at Selby by Cochrane. Owned by Pickering & Haldane of Hull.
1939: Purchased into the RN in August and converted to A/S. Joined the 17th A/S Group
based at Swansea. 1940: Transferred to Portsmouth as Group Leader. 1944: TPI
Operation Neptune, the D-Day Landings in June, as an A/S escort. LOST. Sunk by a/c
off Normandy on 29th July with the loss of 26 lives.

LORD WIMBORNE   1914/19   Displacement: 215TG 84TN
                                        Engines: 76HP
                                        Armament: 1 x 12pdr
                                        Admty No: 703
                                        Port Reg: GY. 916

1911: Launched. Built at Middlesborough. Owned by Consolidated Fisheries of
Grimsby. 1914: Requisitioned in February and converted to a M/S. 1919: Returned to
owners. *Notes*: See under LORD AIREDALE.

LORD WOLMER   1915/19   Displacement: 215TG 84TN
                                        Engines: 76HP
                                        Armament: 1 x 3pdr
                                        Admty No: 1235
                                        Port Reg: GY. 917

1911: Launched. Built at Middlesborough by Smith's Dock. Owned by Consolidated
Fisheries of Grimsby. 1915: Requisitioned in March and converted to a M/S. 1919:
Returned to owners. *Notes*: See under LORD AIREDALE.

LORENZO   1914/14   Displacement: 173TG
                                        Admty No: 603
                                        Port Reg: H. 865

1906: Launched. 1914: Requisitioned in September and converted to an APV. LOST. Wrecked in the Hoy Sound on 17th December.

LORINDA	1939/41	Displacement: 348TG 165TN
		Engines: 96HP = 10.8K
		Port Reg: GY. 220

1928: Launched. Built at Beverley by CWG. Owned by Fleetwood SFC of Fleetwood. PR: FD.182. 1939: Acquired by Shire Trawlers of Grimsby. PR: GY. 220. Requisitioned in September and converted to a M/S. 1941: LOST. Caught fire and foundered after an engine breakdown off Freetown W. Africa on 20th August.

LOROONE	1916/19 1939/40	Displacement: 214TG 88TN
		Engines: 58HP = 10K
		Armament: 1 x 6pdrAA
		Admty No: 1588
		Port Reg: GY. 830
		P. No: WWII: FY. 775

1913: Launched. Built at Beverley by CWG. Owned by Pelham SFC of Grimsby . 1915: Acquired by Rushworth SFC of Grimsby. Requisitioned in June and converted to a M/S. 1919: Returned to owners. 1926: Acquired by TC & F Moss of Grimsby and renamed *Claverton*. 1939: Requisitioned in November as CLAVERTON and converted to a M/S. Joined the 110th M/S Group based at Grimsby. 1940: LOST. Mined in the entrance to the Humber on 29th November.

LORRAINE	1940/46	See under THOMAS CHAMBERS
		(Vol 1 p.75)

LOTHIAN	1917/19	Displacement: 131TG 50TN
		Engines: 58HP
		Admty No: Not issued
		Port Reg: GN. 5

1904: Launched. Built at Leith. Owned by the General SFC of Edinburgh. 1917: Requisitioned into the Fishery Reserve. 1919: Returned to owners.

LOTOS	1914/19	Displacement: 216TG 83TN
		Engines: 70HP
		Armament: 1 x 12pdr
		Admty No: 471
		Port Reg: A. 112

1914: Launched. Built at Aberdeen. Owned by the National SFC of Aberdeen. Requisitioned in November and converted to a M/S. 1919: Returned to owners. 1938: Owned by L. Carnie AO of Glasgow. PR: GN.92.

LOUIS BOTHA   1916/19   1940/44   Displacement: 226TG   109TN
                                              Engines: 74HP = 9.5K
                                              Armament: 1 x 6pdr
                                              Admty No: 3289
                                              Port Reg: WWI: GY. 896
                                              WWII: GY. 305
                                              P.No: WWII: 4. 207

1916: Launched. Built at Beverley by CWG. Owned by Pelham SFC of Grimsby. Requisitioned in June and converted to an APV. 1917: Acquired by Aldersyde SFC of Grimsby. 1918: Acquired by Great Northern FCL of Hull. PR: H. 601. 1919: Returned to owners. Acquired by JW Smethurst of Grimsby. 1928: Acquired by Earl SFC of Grimsby. PR: GY. 305. 1940: Acquired by A. Black of Grimsby. Requisitioned in June and converted to an APV. Based at Grimsby for Fishery Protection. 1944: LOST. Wrecked whilst on fishery protection after stranding in fog off the S. Coast of Iceland on 7th March.

LOUISE   1914/19   Displacement: 270TG   105TN
                                                Engines: 75HP
                                              Armament: 1 x 6pdr
                                              Admty Nos: 144 & 965
                                              Port Reg: SA. 50

1907: Launched. Built at North Shields. 1914: Requisitioned in August and converted to a M/S. 1919: Returned to owners. Acquired by Taylor & Tomlinson of Fleetwood. PR: FD.120.

LOUISE - MARIE   1940/46   Displacement: 165TG
                                                Port Reg: French
                                                P.No: FY. 1917

1899: Launched. 1940: French M/S seized at Plymouth in Operation Grab on 3rd July. Commissioned as a M/S in October with a Free-French crew. Based at Lowestoft for sweeping in the North Sea. 1943: Temporarily employed towing converted London barges to the S. Coast in preparation for D-Day. 1946: Returned to the French Navy.

LOUISE et MARIE   1940/46   See under GARNET

LOVANIA   1940/46   See under NINUS

LOWTHER   1940/46   See under MILETUS

LOYAL   1939/46   Ex-*Matabele*
                                                Displacement: 440TG   168TN
                                                Engines: 99HP
                                                Port Reg: H. 159
                                                P. No: FY. 177

1935: Launched. Built at Southbank-on-Tees by Smith's Dock. Owned by Hellyer Bros. of Hull. 1939: Purchased into the RN in June and converted. Renamed LYDIARD in September. 1946: Sold to mercantile in February.

LOYAL PRINCE   1914/19   Displacement: 208TG 81TN
                                       Engines: 82HP
                                       Armament: 1 x 6pdrAA
                                       Admty No: 51
                                       Port Reg: SN. 244

1913: Launched. Built at South Shields. Owned by W. Raynor & R. Boyle. 1914: Requisitioned in August. 1919: Returned to owners.

LUCERNE   1918/19   Displacement: 198TG 83TN
                                       Engines: 55HP
                                       Port Reg: GY. 1202

1900: Launched. Built at Selby. Iron construction. Owned by Brent SFC of Grimsby. 1918: Requisitioned into the Fishery Reserve. 1919: Returned to owners.

LUCIDA   1914/19   Displacement: 251TG 97TN
                                       Engines: 82HP
                                       Armament: 1 x 12pdr; 1 x 7.5-inch
                                       Bomb Thrower (A/S Howitzer)
                                       Admty No: 925
                                       Port Reg: FD. 20

1914: Launched. Built at Dundee. Owned by Active SFC of Fleetwood. Requisitioned in November and converted to a M/S. 1919: Returned to owners. 1938: Owned by Robb of Aberdeen. PR: A. 175

LUCIENNE-JEANNE   1917/19   Displacement: 223TG
                                       Port Reg: O. 153

1907: Launched. Belgian fishing vessel. 1917: Requisitioned into the Fishery Reserve with the permission of her Belgian owners. 1919: Returned to owners.

LUCIENNE-JEANNE   1940/41   See under DANIEL HARRINGTON
                                       (Vol 1 p.50)

LUCKNOW   1914/17   Displacement: 171TG 57TN
                                       Engines: 45HP = 10K
                                       Armament: 1 x 3pdr
                                       Admty No: 649
                                       Port Reg: H. 739

1903: Launched. Built at Beverley by CWG. Owned by Hull SF & Ice Co. 1914: Requisitioned in October and converted to a M/S. 1917: LOST. Mined off Portsmouth on 18th May having struck one of the mines laid by the German UC-36 on the same day.

LUDA LADY	1939/41	See under MENA

LUDA LORD	1939/45	See under MARGARET DUNCAN

LUMINARY　　　　　1940/46　　　　Ex-*Kingfisher*
Displacement: 414T
Port Reg: American
P. No: Z. 189

1919: Launched. American fishing vessel. 1940: Purchased into the RN in September and converted to a BDV. 1946: Sold to mercantile in December.

LUNAN BAY　　　　1915/19　　　　Ex-*Maggie Walker*
Displacement: 126TG 52HP
Engines: 50HP
Armament: 1 x 3pdr
Port Reg: A. 259

1888: Launched. Built at Aberdeen. Iron construction. 1915: Requisitioned in June and converted to a BDV. 1919: Returned to owners

LUNDY　　　　　　1915/15　　　　Displacement: 188TG 73TN
Engines: 49NHP = 10K
Armament: 1 x 3pdr
Admty No: 1791
Port Reg: H. 993

1908: Launched. Built at Beverley by CWG. Owned by Hull SF & Ice Co. 1915: Requisitioned in May and converted to a M/S. Deployed to the Med. for the Dardenelles Campaign. LOST. Sunk in a collision in Suvla Bay, Turkey, on 16th August.

LUNE　　　　　　　1915/19　　　　Displacement: 197TG 78TN
Engines: 55HP
Port Reg: GY. 1143

1900: Launched. Built at Montrose. Owned by JL Green AO of Grimsby. 1915: Requisitioned in January and converted to a BDV. 1919: Returned to owners.

LUNE　　　　　　　1939/46　　　　Displacement: 310TG 119TN
Engines: 99HP
Port Reg: FD. 59
P. No: FY. 588

1930: Launched. Built at Southbank-on-Tees by Smith's Dock. Owned by Wyre STC of Fleetwood. 1939: Requisitioned in September and converted to a M/S. 1944: Converted to a WDV in May and purchased into the RN. 1946: Sold to mercantile in July. Acquired by Malcolm Smith Ltd of Aberdeen. PR: A. 299.

LUNEDA   1914/19   Displacement: 288TG 116TN
                                       Engines: 65HP
                                       Armament: 1 x 12pdr; 1 x 7.5-inch
                                       Bomb Thrower (A/S Howitzer)
                                       Admty No: 926
                                       Port Reg: FD. 230
1912: Launched. Built at Selby by Cochrane. Owned by Lancashire SFC of Fleetwood.
1914: Requisitioned in November and converted to a M/S. 1919: Returned to owners.
Acquired by Marr of Fleetwood.

LYDDITE   1918/19   Ex-*Lyd*
                                       Displacement: 111TG
1881: Launched. 1918: Requisitioned. Employed on Harbour Service. 1919: Returned
to owners.

LYDIAN   1915/15   Displacement: 244TG
                                       Admty No: 162
1908: Launched. 1915: Requisitioned in August and converted to an APV. LOST. Mined
off the South Foreland on 18th September.

LYDIARD   1939/46   See under LOYAL

LYNMOUTH   1915/19   Displacement: 140TG 59TN
                                       Engines: 46HP
                                       Armament: 1 x 12pdr
                                       Admty No: 964
                                       Port Reg: BL. 5
1892: Launched. Built at Middlesborough by Smith's Dock. Owned by ST & Shipping
Agency of Hull. 1915: Requisitioned in January. 1919: Returned to owners.

LYNX II   1914/19   Displacement: 250TG 103TN
                                       Engines: 76HP
                                       Armament: 1 x 6pdrAA
                                       Admty No: 31
                                       Port Reg: GY. 133
1906: Launched. Built at Selby by Cochrane. Owned by Grimsby & N. E. Trawling Co.
of Grimsby. 1914: Requisitioned in September and converted to a M/S. 1919: Returned
to owners. Acquired by Sir Thomas Robinson of Grimsby. Port Reg: GY. 401. 1939:
Mercantile Loss. Sunk by German U-59 to the N. of Scotland on 28th October. The
U-Boat sent over a boarding party which turned the crew into the boats and the vessel
was then sunk by gunfire. No loss of life.

LYRIC   1917/19   Displacement: 126TG
                                       Port Reg: GY. 434

1891: Launched.　1917: Requisitioned into the Fishery Reserve.　1919: Returned to owners.

LYSANDER II	1914/19	Displacement: 264TG 107TN
		Engines: 78HP = 10.5K
		Armament: 2 x 6pdr
		Admty No: 255
		Port Reg: H. 800

1903: Launched.　Built at Beverley by CWG.　Owned by Hellyer SFC of Hull.　1914: Requisitioned in August and converted to a M/S.　1917: Acquired by Mersey STL of Fleetwood.　PR: FD. 352.　1915: Renamed LYSANDER II in February.　1919: Returned to owners.　1926: Renamed *Sydnelsie*.　1935: Mercantile Loss.　Struck off the W. Coast of Ireland in June.

LYSANDER III	1916/18	Displacement: 174TG 68TN
		Engines: 52HP
		Armament: 1 x 6pdr
		Port Reg: GY. 473

1898: Launched.　Built at North Shields.　Owned by Orient SFC of Grimsby.　1916: Requisitioned.　1918: Returned to owners.

MACAW 1914/19 Displacement: 187TG 69TN
Engines: 64HP
Armament: 1 x 6pdr
Admty No: 145
Port Reg: M. 18

1909: Launched. Built at N. Shields. Owned by CC. Morley & SM Price of Milford Haven. 1914: Requisitioned in August and converted to a M/S. 1919: Returned to owners. 1938: Owned by William Gove of Aberdeen AO. Port Reg: A. 388.

MACBETH 1914/19 Displacement: 311TG 125TN
Engines: 100HP
Armament: 1 x 12pdr
Admty No: 169
Port Reg: H. 869

1906: Launched. Built at Govan. Owned by Hellyers SFC of Hull. 1914: Requisitioned in October and converted to a M/S. 1919: Returned to owners.

MACDUFF 1915/19 Displacement: 179TG 70TN
Engines: 45HP
Armament: 1 x 3pdr
Admty No: 2577
Port Reg: GY. 177

1906: Launched. Built at Glasgow. Owned by Macduff SF Co. of Grimsby. 1915: Requisitioned in January and converted to a M/S. 1917: Renamed MACDUFF II in September. 1919: Returned to owners.

MACDUFF II 1917/19 See under MACDUFF above

MACFARLANE 1915/19 Displacement: 284TG 116TN
Engines. 86HP = 11K
Armament: 1 x 6pdrAA
Admty No: 1220
Port Reg: H. 997

1908: Launched. Built at Beverley by CWG. Owned by Neptune SFC of Hull. 1915: Requisitioned in February and converted to a M/S. 1919: Returned to owners. 1933: Mercantile Loss. Stranded in the Pentland Firth in November.

MACKENZIE 1914/19 Displacement: 335TG 136TN
Engines: 86HP = 10.5K
Armament: 1 x 6pdrAA
Admty No: 336

Port Reg: H. 349

1911: Launched. Built at Beverley by CWG. Owned by Neptune SFC of Hull. 1914: Requisitioned in August and converted to a M/S. 1919: Returned to owners. 1920: Acquired by Icelandic owners and renamed *Austri*. PR: RE. 238. 1927: Mercantile Loss. Wrecked at Vatnsnes, Iceland, in September.

MACKLEAY	1917/19	Displacement: 317TG
		Armament: 1 x 12pdr; 1 x 7.5-inch
		Bomb Thrower (A/S Howitzer)
		Admty No: 3327
		Port Reg: H. 1022

1913: Launched. 1917: Requisitioned in February. 1919: Returned to owners.

MADDEN	1940/46	See under WILLIAM BROWNING
		(Vol 1 p.191)

M.A.DODDS	1915/18	Displacement: 150TG 54TN
		Engines: 50HP
		Port Reg: SN. 152

1892: Launched. Built at Aberdeen. Owned by F. Parkes of Boston. 1915: Requisitioned in June and converted to a M/S. 1918: Returned to owners in August. 1938: Owned by Rotunda Fishing Co of Aberdeen. Port Reg: DE.1.

MAFEKING	1915/19	Displacement: 181TG 65TN
		Engines: 45NHP = 10K
		Armament: 1 x 12pdr; 1 x 7.5-inch
		Bomb Thrower (A/S Howitzer)
		Admty No: 637
		Port Reg: H. 716

1903: Launched. Built at Beverley by CWG. Owned by Hull SF & Ice Co of Hull. 1914: Requisitioned in October and converted to a M/S. 1919: Returned to owners. 1922: Mercantile Loss. Wrecked on The Bunks, off Spurn Point in October.

MAGNETA	1915/19	Displacement: 322TG 130TN
		Engines: 87HP
		Armament: 1 x 12pdr; 1 x 7.5-inch
		Bomb Thrower (A/S Howitzer)
		Admty No: 1970
		Port Reg: H. 354

1915: Launched. Built at Selby by Cochrane. Owned by F & T Ross of Hull. Requisitioned in September and converted to a M/S. 1919: Returned to owners.

MAGNOLIA	1916/19	Displacement: 213TG 109TN
		Engines: 60HP

MAGNOLIA (NMM Neg No: FON1)

Armament: 1 x 6pdrAA; 1 x 2pdr
Admty No: 1741
Port Reg: GY. 226

1897: Launched. Built at Beverley. Iron construction. Owned by North Eastern SFC of Grimsby. 1915: Requisitioned in January. Renamed MAGNOLIA II in July. 1919: Returned to owners.

MAGNOLIA II   1915/19   See under MAGNOLIA

MAGNOLIA III   1915/19   Displacement: 184TG 73TN
                                                 Engines: 61HP
                                                 Armament: 1 x 6pdr
                                                 Admty No: 790
                                                 Port Reg: M. 146

1898: Launched. Built at Aberdeen. Owned by JW Knight AO of Milford Haven. 1915: Requisitioned in July and converted to a M/S. 1919: Returned to owners.

MAGPIE II   1915/19   Displacement: 278TG 114TN
                                              Engines: 75HP
                                              Armament: 1 x 6pdrAA
                                              Admty No: 680
                                              Port Reg: H. 802

1904: Launched. Built at Goole. Owned by Kelsall Bros. & Beeching of Hull. 1915: Requisitioned and converted to a M/S. 1919: Returned to owners.

MAGPIE III   1917/19   Displacement: 156TG 64TN
Engines: 50HP = 10K
Port Reg: GY. 1010

1896: Launched. Built at Hull by CWG. Owned by Pickering & Haldane STC of Hull. PR: H. 311. 1904: Sustained damage when she came under fire from Russian warships in the infamous Dogger Bank Incident. 1916: Acquired by Sleight of Grimsby. PR: GY. 1010. 1917: Requisitioned into the Fishery Reserve. 1919: Returned to owners. 1936: BU.

MAJESTIC II   1917/19   Ex-*Majestic*
Displacement: 159TG
Admty No: Not issued
Port Reg: GY. 682

1894: Launched. 1917: Requisitioned into the Fishery Reserve. 1919: Returned to owners.

MALACOLITE   1939/45   See under RICHARD BAGLEY
(V ol 1 p.71)

MALTA   1914/15   Displacement: 138TG
Admty No: 700
Port Reg: GY. 325

1897: Launched. 1914: Requisitioned in November and converted to an APV. 1915: LOST. Mined off the N. Shipwash Buoy on 1st September.

MANDA   1917/19   Displacement: 150TG
Port Reg: FD. 178

1898: Launched. 1917: Requisitioned into the Fishery Reserve. 1919: Returned to owners.

MANLY   1939/40   See under KIMBERLEY

MANNOFIELD   1917/19   Displacement: 206TG 81TN
Engines: 54HP
Port Reg: A. 526

1905: Launched. Built at North Shields. Owned by Armitage STC of Kingston-upon-Hull. 1917: Requisitioned into the Fishery Reserve. 1919: Returned to owners.

MANOR   1914/19 1939/42 Displacement: 314TG 128TN
Engines: 69HP
Armament: 1 x 12pdr
Admty No: 299
Port Reg: FD. 174
P. No: WWII: FY. 333

1913: Launched. Built at Aberdeen. Owned by Clifton STL of Fleetwood. 1914: Requisitioned in August and converted to a M/S. 1919: Returned to owners. 1939: Requisitioned in August and converted to A/S. 1942: LOST. Torpedoed by German

E-Boat whilst escorting convoy WP.183 in the Channel on 9th February. There was only 1 survivor who was picked up by the Tr. RUBY.

MANORBIER CASTLE 1915/20 Displacement: 153TG 58TN
Engines: 56HP
Port Reg: A. 439
1898: Launched. Built at North Shields. Owned by C. Dobson of Grimsby. 1915: Requisitioned in June and converted to a BBV. Employed as an Accommodation Ship. 1920: Returned to owners.

MAN o' WAR 1939/45 Displacement: 517TG 216TN
Engines: 156HP
Armament: 1 x 4-inch
Port Reg: GY. 394
P.No: FY. 104
1937: Launched. Built at Selby by Cochrane. Owned by Earl SFC of Grimsby. 1939: Requisitioned in September and converted to A/S. Joined the 21st A/S Strike Force. 1940: TPI the Norwegian Campaign in April/May. 1945: Returned to owners in July. Acquired by Hellyer Bros. of Hull. Port Reg: H. 181. *Notes*: Named after a famous American racehorse.

MANSFIELD 1917/19 Displacement: 165TG 64TN
Engines: 45HP
Port Reg: GY. 460
1897: Launched. Built at Govan. Owned by Consolidated Fisheries of Grimsby. 1917: Requisitioned into the Fishery Reserve. 1919: Returned to owners.

MANX ADMIRAL 1915/19 Displacement: 219TG 107TN
Engines: 65HP
Armament: 1 x 6pdr
Port Reg: GY. 665
1911: Launched. Built at Selby by Cochrane. Owned by WH. Beeley of Grimsby. 1914: Requisitioned in December and converted to a BDV. 1919: Returned to owners.

MANX HERO 1914/15 Displacement: 221TG
Admty No: 339
Port Reg: GY. 585
1910: Launched. 1914: Requisitioned in August and converted to a M/S. Deployed to the Med. 1915: LOST. Mined in the Kephiez minefields, Dardenelles, on 1st March.

MANX HERO 1916/19 1940/46 Displacement: 236TG 90TN
Engines: 74HP
Armament: 1 x 6pdrAA
Admty No: 3291

Port Reg: GY. 883
P. No: WWII: FY. 1741
1916: Launched. Built at Southbank-on-Tees by Smith's Dock. Requisitioned in July and converted to a M/S. 1919: Returned to owners. Acquired by P. Belman of Birmingham. 1940: Requisitioned in June and converted to a M/S. Commissioned with a Dutch Crew. 1943: Re-Commissioned with RN crew in June. 1946: Returned to owners in May.

MANX KING   1916/19   Displacement: 235TG 90TN
Engines: 74HP
Armament: 1 x 6pdrAA
Admty No: 3274
Port Reg: GY. 881
1916: Launched. Built at Southbank-on-Tees by Smith's Dock. Requisitioned in April and converted to a M/S. 1919: Returned to owners. Acquired by JW. Smethurst of Grimsby. PR: GY. 387. Acquired by AGL Meff & RF Robb of Aberdeen. PR: A. 390.

MANX PRINCE   1914/19 1939/40 Displacement: 220TG 109TN
Engines: 67HP
Armament: 1 x 6pdr
Admty No: 311
Port Reg: GY. 542
1910: Launched. Built at Selby by Cochrane. Owned by WH. Beeley of Grimsby. 1914: Requisitioned in August and converted to a M/S. 1919: Returned to owners. 1930: Owned by Bowerings SF Co. of Grimsby. 1939: Requisitioned in December and converted to an APV. 1940: Converted to a M/S in June. LOST. Mined in the entrance to the Humber on 28th November.

MANX QUEEN   1915/16   Displacement: 234TG
Armament: 1 x 6pdr
Admty No: 1529
Port Reg: GY. 491
1915: Launched. Requisitioned in June and converted to a M/S. 1916: LOST. Wrecked on File Brigg on 1st March.

MARANO   1939/45   See under PRINCESS VICTORIA

MARCONI   1916/19 1940/41 Displacement: 322TG 131TN
Engines: 86HP
Armament: 1 x 12pdr
Admty No: 3304
Port Reg: H. 488
1916: Launched. Built at Selby by Cochrane. Owned by F & T Ross of Hull. Requisitioned in August and converted to a M/S. Involved in a U-Boat action in the Channel on 14th November. ICW Tr. PELICAN and Yt. LORNA chased off a U-Boat

which was about to attack a merchantman. 1919: Returned to owners. 1938: Owned by P & T. Ross of Hull. 1940: Requisitioned in March and converted to a M/S. 1941: LOST. Sunk in a collision whilst anchored off Harwich on 20th September. Rammed by a Harwich patrol vessel. Whilst the crew were abandoning ship they were attacked by enemy a/c, but there was no loss of life.

MARETTA   1939/45   Displacement: 350TG 136TN
                                              Engines: 97HP
                                              Port Reg: FD. 45
                                              P. No: FY. 665
1929: Launched. Built at Selby by Cochrane. Owned by Marr of Fleetwood. 1939: Requisitioned in September and converted to a M/S. 1945: Returned to owners in November.

MARGARET DUNCAN   1915/19 1939/44 Displacement: 224TG 87TN
                                              Engines: 68HP
                                              Armament: 1 x 6pdr
                                              Admty No: 593
                                              Port Reg: WWI: LL. 123; WWII: GY. 50
                                              P. No: WWII: FY. 776 (M/S);
                                              Y7. 34 (Esso)
1913: Launched. Built at Selby by Cochrane. Owned by J & WA Duncan of Liverpool. 1914: Requisitioned in December. 1919: Returned to owners. Acquired by Dobson Ship Repair of Grimsby and renamed *Luda Lord*. 1939: Requisitioned in November as LUDA LORD and converted to an APV. 1940: Converted to a M/S in May. 1944: Converted to an Esso in January. Returned to owners in November.

MARGARET ROSE   1940/46   See under PAVLOVA

MARGARET WEATHERLEY   1915/19 Displacement: 211TG 79TN
                                              Engines: 66HP
                                              Port Reg: A. 344
1911: Launched. Built at Aberdeen. Owned by Wetherley's SFC of Aberdeen. 1915: Requisitioned in June and converted to a BDV. 1917: Employed as an Accommodation vessel. 1920: Returned to owners. Acquired by James Johnson of Leith. Port Reg: GN. 32. Notes: Entered in mercantile lists as *Margaret Wetherley*.

MARGATE   1914/17   Displacement: 161TG
                                              Armament: 1 x 6pdrAA
                                              Admty No: 818
                                              Port Reg: GY. 218
1897: Launched. 1914: Requisitioned in February. 1917: LOST. Sunk by German S/M off Spurn Point on 24th April.

MARIA   **(WSPL)**

MARGUERITE   1917/19   Displacement: 151TG
                                                       Port Reg: A. 594
1895: Launched. 1917: Requisitioned into the Fishery Reserve. 1919: Returned to owners.

MARIA   1941/51   Displacement: 855TG
                                                        Dimensions: 166ft. x 27ft
                                                        Port Reg: German
                                                        P. No: 4. 67
1929: Launched. German fishing vessel. 1941: German AUGUST WREIDT captured on 29th May. 1942: Converted to a WDV and commissioned into the RN on 29th May. 1951: BU.

MARIA R. OMMERING   1940/46   See under IRENE WRAY

MARIE JOSE ROSETTE   1943/45   Displacement: 139TG
                                                        Port Reg: Belgian
1936: Launched. Belgian fishing vessel. 1943: Hired from Belgian owners in December and employed on Harbour Service. 1944: Converted to an Esso. 1945: Returned to Belgium in February.

MARIE LOUISE   1917/19   Displacement: 140TG
                                                       Port Reg: O. 97
1908: Launched. Belgian fishing vessel. 1917: Requisitioned into the Fishery Reserve with the permission of her Belgian owners. 1919: Returned to Belgium.

MARIE LOUISE   1940/46   Displacement: 258TG
Port Reg: Belgian
1918: Launched. Belgian fishing vessel. 1940: Hired from Belgian owners and converted to a BDV. 1946: Returned to Belgium in January.

MARIGNAM   1940/46   Ex-*Teal*
Ex-*Marignam*
Displacement: 408TG
Armament: 1 x 12pdr
Port Reg: American
P. No: Z. 229
1919: Launched. American fishing vessel. 1940: Purchased into the RN in September and converted to a BDV. Renamed TEAL in October. 1946: Sold to mercantile and renamed *Wulkan*.

MARION   1914/18   Displacement: 128TG 51TN
Engines: 50HP
Armament: 1 x 3pdr
Admty No: 20
Port Reg: DE. 14
1891: Launched. Built at South Shields. Owned by W. High of Dundee. 1914: Requisitioned in August and converted to a M/S. 1918: LOST. Mined off Malta on 23rd February.

MARION II   1917/19   Displacement: 256TG
Port Reg: LO. 235
1906: Launched. 1917: Requisitioned into the Fishery Reserve. 1919: Returned to owners.

MARIS STELLA   1940/45   Displacement: 285TG
Port Reg: French
P. No: Z. 233
1907: Launched. French fishing vessel. 1940: French M/S seized at Southampton in Operation Grab on 3rd July. Converted to a BGV and Commissioned into the RN. 1945: Returned to France.

MARISTO   1916/19   Displacement: 287TG 1145TN
Engines: 97HP
Armament: 1 x 12pdr
Admty No: 1978
Port Reg: M. 14
1914: Launched. Built at Middlesborough by Smith's Dock. Owned by J. Thomas of Milford Haven. 1915: Requisitioned in December and converted to a M/S. 1917: Based at Portland. ICW Tr. CALIPH in the Channel, claimed an unconfirmed 'kill' when they attacked a German S/M. 1919: Returned to owners.

MARJORIE M. HASTIE   1940/45   Hastie Group
                                        Displacement: 244TG   105TN
                                        Engines: 67HP
                                        Port Reg: SN. 107
                                        P. No: FY. 1777

1930: Launched. Built at Aberdeen. Owned by R. Hastie & Sons Ltd. of N. Shields. 1940: Requisitioned in June and converted to a M/S. 1945: Returned to owners in November.

MARLBOROUGH 1916/19 1939/40 1945/46   Displacement: 213TG   102TN
                                         Engines: 66HP
                                         Port Reg: GY. 306

1907: Launched. Built at Selby by Cochrane. Owned by Queen SF Co. of Grimsby. 1914: Requisitioned in December and converted to a M/S. 1919: Returned to owners. 1939: Requisitioned in November and designated as an APV. 1940: Returned to owners on 3rd January. 1945: Requisitioned. 1946: Returned to owners in June.

MARLOES   1914/19   Displacement: 220TG   85TN
                                           Engines: 71HP
                                         Armament: 1 x 6pdrAA
                                         Admty No: 15
                                         Port Reg: M. 76

1911: Launched. Built at Middlesborough by Smith's Dock. Owned by Hesketh STL of Fleetwood. 1914: Requisitioned in August and converted to a M/S. 1919: Returned to owners.

MARNE   1915/19   Displacement: 257TG   103TN
                                           Engines: 79HP
                                         Armament: 1 x 6pdrAA
                                         Admty No: 1365
                                         Port Reg: H. 231

1915: Launched. Built at Hessle. Requisitioned in April and converted to a M/S. 1916: Renamed MARNE II in January. 1919: Returned to owners. Acquired by W. Richmond of Scartho.

MARNE II   1916/19   See under MARNE above

MARSONA   1939/40   See under JAMES CHRISTOPHER
                                           (Vol 1 p.57)

MARTHE   1917/19 1939/46 Displacement: 234TG   123TN
                                         Engines: 71NHP = 10.5K
                                         Armament: WWII: 1 x 6pdr
                                         Admty No: 1075

Port Reg: WWI: O. 43; WWII: LH. 17
P. No: WWII: Z. 157
1913: Launched. Built at Beverley by CWG. Owned by AT Golder & Co of Ostend, Belgium. 1915: Hired from Belgian owners in January and converted to a M/S. 1917: Reduced to the Fishery Reserve. 1919: Returned to owners. 1934: Acquired by TH Scales of Leith and renamed *Craig Island* PR: LH. 141. 1939: Requisitioned in November as CRAIG ISLAND and converted to a BDV. 1942: Acquired by Marr of Hull. 1946: Returned in owners in February. BU at Peterhead in May.

MARTIN   1914/19   Displacement: 242TG
                                   Armament: 1 x 12pdr
                                   Admty No: 414
                                   Port Reg: H. 187
1897: Launched. 1914: Requisitioned in November and converted to a M/S. 1915: Renamed MARTIN II in February. 1918: Returned to owners in November.

MARTIN II   1915/18   See under MARTIN above

MARTINETA   1916/20   Displacement: 279TG 115TN
                                   Engines: 70NHP = 10.5K
                                   Port Reg: GY. 505
1909: Launched. Built at Beverley by CWG. Owned by T. Baskcomb of Grimsby. 1916: Requisitioned in October and converted to a BDV. 1920: Returned to owners. Sold to Spanish owners and renamed *Tito*. 1936: Requisitioned into the Spanish Nationalist Navy. 1939: Returned to owners. 1967: BU in Spain.

MARTON   1916/19   Displacement: 232TG 95TN
                                   Engines: 54HP
                                   Armament: 1 x 6pdrAA
                                   Admty No: 1590
                                   Port Reg: FD. 38
1905: Launched. Built at Aberdeen. 1915: Requisitioned in June and converted to a M/S. 1919: Returned to owners. Acquired by JM Knight & MW Howell of Milford Haven. PR: M. 11.

MARY   1914/14   Displacement: 256TG
                                   Admty No: 361
                                   Port Reg: FD. 84
1906: Launched. 1914: Requisitioned in August and converted to a M/S. LOST. Mined off Yarmouth on 5th November.

MARY A. HASTIE   1939/45   Hastie Group
                                   Displacement: 244TG 105TN
                                   Engines: 67HP

Armament: 1 x 12pdr
Port Reg: SN. 96
P. No: FY. 1935

1930: Launched. Built at Aberdeen. Owned by R. Hastie & Son of N. Shields. 1939: Requisitioned in December and converted to an APV. 1941: Converted to a M/S and joined the Harwich M/S Group. 1945: Returned to owners.

MARY A. PURDY	1940/44	See under THOMAS HAGGERTY (Vol 1 p.189)
MARY CAM	1942/48	RAN. See under JOHN FISSER (Vol 1 p.179)
MARY WETHERLEY	1915/19	Displacement: 221TG 81TN Engines: 76HP Armament: 1 x 6pdr Admty No: 1345 Port Reg: A. 159

1907: Launched. Built at Aberdeen. Owned by Wetherley's SFC of Aberdeen. 1915: Requisitioned in April and converted to a M/S. 1919: Returned to owners. Acquired by J. Johnson of Newhaven. PR: GN. 3.

MARY WHITE	1940/46	Displacement: 271TG 118TN Engines: 470HP Port Reg: GY. 465 P. No: Z. 147

1935: Launched. Built at Aberdeen. Owned by White Trs. Ltd of Hebburn, Durham. 1940: Requisitioned in January and converted to a BDV. 1946: Returned to owners in February. 1947: Owned by Shire Trs. of Grimsby.

MASONA	1939/46	See under ST.DENIS
MASTER	1915/19	See under QUICKLY
MASTWING	1914/19	Displacement: 199TG 73TN Engines: 55HP Armament: 1 x 6pdr Admty No: 684 Port Reg: H. 981

1908: Launched. Built at Goole by Goole SB. Owned by Kelsall Bros. & Beeching of Hull. 1914: Requisitioned in November and converted to a M/S. 1919: Returned to owners.

MAUN	1914/19	Displacement: 271TG 151TN Engines: 85HP

Armament: 1 x 6pdr
Admty No: 122
Port Reg: FD. 81

1906: Launched. Built at North Shields. Owned by N. Ashworth AO of Fleetwood. 1914: Requisitioned in August and converted to a M/S. 1919: Returned to owners.

MAXIMUS	1914/19	Ex-*Ulleswater*
		Displacement: 236TG
		Armament: 1 x 6pdr
		Admty No: 997
		Port Reg: GY. 973

1898: Launched. 1914: Requisitioned in December. 1919: Returned to owners.

MAX PEMBERTON	1917/19	Displacement: 334TG 134TN
		Engines: 94HP
		Armament: 1 x 12pdr
		Admty No: 3049
		Port Reg: H. 563

1917: Launched. Built at Selby. Owned by Newington STC of Hull. Requisitioned in June and converted to a M/S. Employed on Hydrophone experiments. 1919: Returned to owners. 1928: Mercantile Loss. Took the ground off Iceland and declared a loss. Subsequently salvaged by the Icelanders.

MEDIAN	1939/40	Displacement: 217TG 96TN
		Engines: 67HP = 10K
		Armament: None
		Port Reg: GY.430

1919: Launched. Built at Beverley by CWG. Owned by Onward SF Co. of Grimsby. 1939: Requisitioned in November and designated as an APV. 1940: Returned to owners in February. 1960: BU in Belgium.

MEDIATOR	1914/16	Displacement: 178TG
		Admty No: 509 & 447
		Port Reg: A. 483

1912: Launched. 1914: Requisitioned in September and converted to an APV. 1916: LOST. Mined off Hornsea on 2nd January.

MELBOURNE	1939/40	Displacement: 466TG 169TN
		Engines: 99HP
		Port Reg: GY. 125

1936: Launched. Built at Southbank-on-Tees by Smith's Dock. Owned by Croft Baker of Grimsby. 1939: Purchased into the RN in October and converted to A/S. Joined the 23rd A/S Group. 1940: TPI the Norwegian Campaign in April/May. LOST. Sunk by enemy a/c off Norway on 22nd May.

MENA   1915/19 1939/41 Displacement: 234TG 110TN
                                            Engines: 72HP
                                            Admty No: 453
                                            Port Reg: WWI: GY. 210
                                            WWII: GY. 238.

1914: Launched. Built at Selby By Cochrane. Owned by Roberts & Ruthven of Grimsby. 1915: Requisitioned in February. 1920: Returned to owners. 1922: Sold to Hull owners and renamed *St.Elmo*. 1936: Acquired by Dobson Ship Repair Co of Grimsby and renamed *Luda Lady*. 1939: Requisitioned in November as LUDA LADY and converted to a M/S. 1941: LOST. Mined off the Humber on 22nd January.

MERISIA   1914/19   Displacement: 291TG 114TN
                                            Engines: 90HP
                                            Armament: 1 x 6pdr
                                            Admty No: 127
                                            Port Reg: FD. 153

1912: Launched. Built at Selby by Cochrane. Owned by Fleetwood SF Co. of Fleetwood. 1914: Requisitioned in September and converted to a M/S. 1919: Returned to owners.

MERLIN   1914/20   Displacement: 172TG 65TN
                                            Engines: 61HP
                                            Armament: 1 x 6pdrAA
                                            Admty No: 374
                                            Port Reg: H. 924

1906: Launched. Built at Goole by Goole SB. 1914: Requisitioned in October and converted to a M/S. 1920: Returned to owners. 1938: Owned by Kelsall Bros. & Beeching of Hull.

MERLIN   1915/19   Displacement: 186TG 75TN
                                            Engines: 50HP
                                            Armament: 1 x 3pdr
                                            Admty No: 1794
                                            Port Reg: GY. 190

1899: Launched. Built at Selby by Cochrane. Owned by Filey United ST Co. of Scarborough. 1915: Requisitioned in May and converted to a M/S. Renamed MERLIN II in August. 1919: Returned to owners.

MERLIN II   1915/19   See under MERLIN above

MEROR 1915/20   1940/43   Ex-*Emperor*
                                            Displacement: 250TG 105TN
                                            Engines: 70HP
                                            Armament: 1 x 3pdr; 1 x 2pdr

Admty No: 685
Port Reg: WWI: GY. 94; WWII: GY. 316
P. No: WWII: FY. 1836

1905: Launched. Built at Selby by Cochrane. 1914: Requisitioned in November and converted to a M/S. 1920: Returned to owners. 1938: Owned by A. Grant & Sons of Grimsby. 1940: Requisitioned in September and converted to a M/S. 1941: 72nd M/S Group based at Grimsby. 1943: LOST. Mined off the Humber on 3rd October.

MERRYDALE	1915/19	Displacement: 225TG 191TN
		Engines: 54HP
		Armament: 1 x 6pdr
		Admty No: 1759
		Port Reg: A. 334

1906: Launched. Built at Aberdeen. Owned by North Star SF Co. of Aberdeen. 1915: Requisitioned in May and converted to a M/S. 1919: Returned to owners.

MERSE	1915/17	Displacement: 296TG
		Armament: 1 x 12pdr
		Admty No: 980
		Port Reg: FD. 62

1914: Launched. 1915: Requisitioned in February and converted to a M/S. 1917: LOST. Mined off Garroch, Bute, on 22nd May.

MEUSE	1917/19	Ex-*Cariama*
		Displacement: 217TG 95TN
		Engines: 60HP = 10.5K
		Port Reg: FD. 107

1904: Launched. Built at Beverley by CWG. Owned by T. Bascomb of Grimsby. PR: GY. 4. 1907: Acquired by Reading & Dickinson of Swansea. PR: SA. 41. 1915: Acquired by Mersey STC of Fleetwood and renamed *Meuse* PR: FD. 107. 1917: Requisitioned into the Fishery Reserve. 1919: Returned to owners. 1935: BU.

MEWSLADE	1916/19 1940/46	Displacement: 275TG 108TN
		Engines: 87HP
		Armament: 1 x 6pdr
		Admty No: 1993
		Port Reg: SA. 34
		P.No: FY. 816

1916: Launched. Built at Southbank-on-Tees by Smith's Dock. Owned by Rhondda Fishing Co. of Swansea. Requisitioned in April and converted to a M/S. 1946: Returned to owners in April.

MICHAEL ANGELO	1916/19	Displacement: 285TG 114TN
		Engines: 75HP

Armament: 1 x 12pdr
Admty No: 1510
Port Reg: H. 324

1911: Launched. Built at Selby by Cochrane. Owned by Jutland STC of Hull. 1915: Requisitioned in May and converted to a M/S. 1919: Returned to owners.

MIKADO   1916/19   Displacement: 265TG 102TN
Engines: 79HP = 10.5K
Armament: 1 x 6pdr
Admty No: 1222
Port Reg: H. 823

1905: Launched. Built at Beverley by CWG. Owned by Pickering & Haldane STC of Hull. 1915: Requisitioned in February and converted to a M/S. 1918: Acquired by W. Baker & W. Jagger of Grimsby. PR: GY. 1238. 1919: Returned to owners. 1922: Sold to Canadian mercantile. 1924: Mercantile Loss. Wrecked in May to the W. of Louisbourg, Nova Scotia.

MIKASA   1916/19 1939/40 1944/44   Displacement: 274TG 107TN
Engines: 87HP
Armament: 1 x 6pdr
Port Reg: LO. 4
P. No: WWII: 4. 431

1915: Launched. Built at Middlesborough by Smith's Dock. Owned by Jenkerson & Jones of Milford Haven. 1916: Requisitioned. 1919: Returned to owners. 1939: Requisitioned in December and designated as an APV. 1940: Returned to owners in February. 1944: Requisitioned in April. Returned to owners in October.

MIKASO   1915/19   Displacement: 255TG
Armament: 1 x 6pdr; 1 x 7.5-inch Bomb
Thrower (A/S Howitzer)
Admty No: 1771
Port Reg: CF. 41

1913: Launched. 1915: Requisitioned in May. 1919: Returned to owners.

MILDENHALL   1939/39   Displacement: 466TG 169TN
Engines: 99HP
Armament: 1 x 4-inch
Port Reg: GY. 124
P. No: FY. 129

1936: Launched. Built at Southbank-on-Tees by Smith's Dock. Owned by H. Croft Baker & Sons of Grimsby. 1939: Requisitioned in July and converted to A/S. Subsequently purchased into the RN. Transferred to the French Navy in November and renamed L'AJACCIENNE.

MILETUS   1916/19 1940/46 Displacement: 313TG 126TN
                                          Engines: 84HP
                                          Armament: 1 x 12pdr
                                          Admty No: 1886
                                          Port Reg: FD. 48
                                          P. No: WWII: FY. 972

1915: Launched. Built at Hessle. Owned by Wyre STC of Fleetwood. Requisitioned in September. 1919: Returned to owners. Renamed *Lowther*. 1940: Requisitioned in February as LOWTHER and converted to a M/S. Based at Lowestoft for sweeping in the North Sea. 1946: Returned to owners in January.

MILFORD COUNTESS   1939/46   See under CHARLES LEGG
                                             (Vol 1 p.49)

MILFORD DUCHESS   1939/44   See under JAMES GILL (Vol 1 p.57)

MILFORD DUKE   1939/46   See under JAMES DITTON
                                             (Vol 1 p.57)

MILFORD EARL   1939/41   See under ANDREW APSLEY
                                             (Vol 1 p.47)

MILFORD KING   1939/45   See under VALENTINE BOWER
                                             (Vol 1 p.84)

MILFORD PRINCE   1939/45   See under THOMAS ALLEN
                                             (Vol 1 p.74)

MILFORD PRINCESS   1939/45   Displacement: 278TG 113TN
                                             Engines: 99HP
                                             Port Reg: M. 228
                                             P. No: FY. 616

1924: Launched. Built at Southbank-on-Tees by Smith's Dock. Owned by Milford ST Co. of Milford Haven. 1939: Requisitioned in September and converted to a M/S. 1940: TPI Operations Quentin/Quidnunt/Quixote on 18/19th May, the cutting of the telephone cables between Germany and UK in the North Sea. 1945: Returned to owners in September.

MILFORD QUEEN   1939/45   See under WILLIAM BROWIS
                                             (Vol 1 p.85)

MINERVA III   1917/19   Displacement: 232TG
                                             Port Reg: H.

1900: Launched. 1917: Requisitioned into the Fishery Reserve. 1919: Returned to owners.

MINERVA IV   1917/19   Displacement: 142TG 56TN
                                     Engines: 46HP
                                     Port Reg: GY. 732
1900: Launched. Built at S. Shields. Owned by Wear SF Co. of Sunderland. 1917: Requisitioned into the Fishery Reserve. 1919: Returned to owners.

MININGSBY   1914/18   Displacement: 245TG 95TN
                                     Engines: 88HP
                                     Armament: 1 x 3pdr
                                     Admty No: 33
                                     Port Reg: BN. 148
1908: Launched. Built at North Shields. Owned by Boston DS & Ice Co. of Boston, Lincs. 1914: Requisitioned in September and converted to a M/S. 1919: Returned to owners.

MINO   1915/19   Displacement: 168TG 63TN
                                     Engines: 45HP
                                     Armament: 1 x 6pdr
                                     Admty No: 416
                                     Port Reg: H. 799
1903: Launched. Built at Goole by Goole SB. Owned by Kelsall Bros. & Beeching of Hull. 1914: Requisitioned in November and converted to a M/S. 1919: Returned to owners.

MINORU   1914/20   Displacement: 260TG 106TN
                                     Engines: 76NHP = 10.5K
                                     Armament: 1 x 12pdr
                                     Admty No: 348
                                     Port Reg: GY. 484
1909: Launched. Built at Beverley by CWG. Owned by Orient SFC of Grimsby. 1914: Requisitioned in August and converted to a M/S. 1917: Renamed MINORU II in November. 1920: Returned to owners and reverted to *Minoru*. 1937: BU

MINORU II   1917/20   See under MINORU above

MIRABELLE   1939/44   See under EDWARD BARKER
                                     (Vol 1 p.170)

MIRANDA   1914/18   Displacement: 173TG 55TN
                                     Engines: 45NHP = 9.5K
                                     Armament: 1 x 6pdr
                                     Admty No: 601
                                     Port Reg: H. 875
1906: Launched. Built at Beverley by CWG. Owned by Hellyer SFC of Hull. 1916:

Requisitioned in September and converted to a M/S. 1917: Renamed MIRANDA III in February. 1918: Returned to owners. Acquired by Curzon of Milford Haven. Mercantile Loss. Wrecked in Pelwick Bay on 14th January.

MIRANDA III   1917/18   See under MIRANDA above

MIRIAM STEWART 1914/19   Displacement: 197TG 77HP
               Engines: 78HP
               Armament: 1 x 3pdr
               Admty No: 461
               Port Reg: HL. 10
1914: Launched. Built at Aberdeen. Owned by R & MJ. Stewart of Hartlepool. Requisitioned in September and converted to a M/S. 1919: Returned to owners.

MITRES   1917/19 1941/45 Displacement: 261TG 102TN
               Engines: 75HP = 9.5K
               Armament: 1 x 6pdr
               Admty No: 3078
               Port Reg: GY. 1105
               P. No: WWII: 4. 04
1917: Launched. Built at Beverley by CWG. Owned by the Loyal SF Co. of Grimsby. Requisitioned in December and converted to an APV. 1919: Returned to owners. 1940: Acquired by Black of Grimsby. Requisitioned in June and converted to an APV. 1941: Converted to a Salvage Vessel. 1943: Acquired by JE. Harrison of Grimsby. Acquired by Grimsby Motor Trs. Ltd. 1945: Returned to owners in November. 1959: BU at Antwerp, Belgium.

MIURA   1914/15   Displacement: 257TG
               Armament: 1 x 3pdr
               Admty No: 979
               Port Reg: CF. 36
1911: Launched. 1915: Requisitioned in February. LOST. Mined off Yarmouth on 23rd August.

MIURA   1916/19   Displacement: 275TG 107TN
               Engines: 87HP
               Armament: 1 x 12pdr; 1 x 6pdr
               Admty No: 3302
               Port Reg: CF. 45
1916: Launched. Built at Southbank-on-Tees by Smith's Dock. Owned by Neale & West of Cardiff. Requisitioned in August and converted to a M/S. Fitted with Listening Hydrophones. 1919: Returned to owners.

MOLLYMAWK   1917/19 1941/46 Displacement: 242TG 96TN
Engines: 80HP
Port Reg: GY. 654

1899: Launched. Built at Dundee. Owned by GF Sleight of Grimsby. 1917: Requisitioned into the Fishery Reserve. 1919: Returned to owners. 1938: Owned by J.E. Lawie AO of Aberdeen. 1941: Requisitioned in February and employed on Harbour Service. 1946: Returned to owners.

MONARCH   1915/19   Displacement: 234TG 108TN
Engines: 60HP
Armament: 1 x 12pdr; 1 x 7.5-inch
Bomb Thrower (A/S Howitzer)
Admty No: 1599
Port Reg: GY .29

1904: Launched. Built at Selby by Cochrane. Owned by Brent SFC of Grimsby. 1915: Requisitioned in July and converted to a M/S. Renamed MONARCH III in August. 1919: Returned to owners and retained the name *Monarch III.*

MONARCH III   1916/19   See under MONARCH above

MONARCH IV   1917/19   Displacement: 130TG 54TN
Engines: 40HP
Port Reg: A. 35

1895: Launched. 1917: Requisitioned into the Fishery Reserve. 1919: Returned to owners. 1938: Owned by L & GA. Breach of Lowestoft.

MONIMA   1939/45   Displacement: 374TG 156TN
Engines: 96HP = 10.9K
Armament: 1 x 12pdr
Port Reg: H. 43
P. No: FY. 677

1929: Launched. Built at Beverley by CWG. Owned by Henrikson & Co of Hull. 1939: Requisitioned in August and converted to a M/S. 1940: Senior Officer of the19th M/S Group based at Grimsby. 1945: Returned to owners in November. 1956: BU at Antwerp, Belgium.

MONIQUE-ANDREE   1940/46   Displacement: 221TG
Armament: 1 x 65mm (French)
Port Reg: French
P. No: FY. 1728

1919: Launched. French fishing vessel. 1940: French M/S seized at Plymouth in Operation Grab on 3rd July. Commissioned into the RN as an APV in September. 1946: Returned to French in March.

MONIQUE-CAMILLE   1940/46   Displacement: 277TG
                                       Port Reg: French
                                       P. No: FY. 1803
1935: Launched. French fishing vessel. 1940: French M/S seized at Southampton in
Operation Grab on 3rd July. Converted to an APV in September. Based at Grimsby for
Convoy duties. 1946: Returned to France.

MONS   1917/19   Ex-*Monarch*
                                       Displacement: 163TG 65TN
                                       Engines: 45NHP = 10K
                                       Armament: None
                                       Port Reg: GY. 806
1896: Launched. Built at Hull by CWG.   Iron construction. Owned by R. Simpson &
Co. of Hull. PR: H. 331. 1915: Acquired by H. Robinson & W. Grant of Grimsby and
renamed *Mons*. 1917: Requisitioned into the Fishery Reserve. 1919: Returned to
owners. 1924: BU.

MONTANO   1940/46   See under JAMES BERRY
                                       (Vol 1 p.174)

MOOIVLEI   1939/45   SAN
                                       Displacement: 252TG
                                       Port Reg: S. African
                                       P. No: T. 16
1935: Launched. S. African fishing vessel. 1939: Requisitioned and converted to a M/S.
Commissioned into the SAN in November. 1945: Returned to owners.

MOONRISE   1940/46   Ex-*Marioute*
                                       Displacement: 318TG
1918: Launched.   1940: Purchased into the RN and converted to a M/S.   1943:
Converted to a BGV. 1946: Sold to mercantile.

MOONSHINE   1942/46   See under POLO NORTE

MOPSA   1916/19   Displacement: 206TG 64TN
                                       Engines: 50NHP = 10K
                                       Armament: 1 x 6pdrAA
                                       Admty No: 1606
                                       Port Reg: H. 966
1907: Launched. Built at Beverley by CWG. Owned by Hellyer SFC of Hull. 1915:
Requisitioned in March and converted to a M/S. 1918: Acquired by Iago STC of Hull.
1919: Returned to owners.   1928: Renamed *Stromness*.   1939: Mercantile Loss.
Wrecked near Aberdeen.

MORAVIA   1917/19 1940/43 Displacement: 307TG 121TN
                                          Engines: 89HP = 10K
                                          Armament: WWI: 1 x 12pdr; WWII: 1 x 6pdr
                                          Admty No: 1272
                                          Port Reg: GY. 1018
                                          P. No: WWII: FY. 1819
1917: Launched. Built at Beverley by CWG. Owned by Gt. Grimsby & E. Coast SFC of
Grimsby. Requisitioned in June and converted to a M/S. 1919: Returned to owners.
1932: Sustained serious damage in heavy seas off Iceland on 9th January. The Skipper
and one crewman were lost overboard and the funnel and mizzen were washed away.
Towed back to Grimsby by *Cape Grisnez*. 1940: Requisitioned in August and
converted to an APV. 1940: Converted to a M/S. 1942: Acquired by Boston DSF & Ice
Co. of Grimsby. 1943: LOST. Mined off Sheerness on 14th March.

MORAY   1915/19   Displacement: 201TG 86TN
                                          Engines: 78HP
                                          Armament: 1 x 6pdrAA
                                          Admty No: 1630
                                          Port Reg: GN. 55
1915: Launched. Built at Leith. Owned by General SFC of Edinburgh. Requisitioned in
May and converted to a M/S. 1919: Returned to owners.

MORAY   1940/43   See under HENRY JENNINGS
                                          (Vol 1 p.173)

MORNING STAR   1915/19   Displacement: 145TG 60TN
                                          Engines: 45HP
                                          Port Reg: SH. 61
1900: Launched. Built at Aberdeen. Owned by Scarborough, Hartlepool & North Sea
FC of Scarborough. 1916: Requisitioned in June and converted to a Boom Tender.
1919: Returned to owners.

MORNING STAR VI   1917/19   Displacement: 120TG 47TN
                                          Engines: 40HP
                                          Port Reg: A. 773
1895: Launched. Built at Aberdeen. Owned by J. Baxter of Aberdeen. 1917:
Requisitioned into the Fishery Reserve. 1919: Returned to owners.

MOROCOCALA   1916/17   Displacement: 265TG
                                          Armament: 1 x 6pdr
                                          Admty No: 2656
                                          Port Reg: A. 238
1915: Launched. Requisitioned in April. 1917: LOST. Mined on 19th November off the
Daunt Light.

MORVEN   1915/19   Displacement: 198TG 80TN
                                       Engines: 50HP
                                       Armament: 1 x 6pdr
                                       Admty No: 2769
                                       Port Reg: A. 567
1902: Launched. Built at Aberdeen. Owned by Grampian FCL of Aberdeen. 1915:
Requisitioned in June and converted to a M/S. 1919: Returned to owners. 1938: Owned
by J. Graham of Aberdeen.

MORVINA   1915/19   Displacement: 226TG 113TN
                                       Engines: 75HP = 10K
                                       Armament: 1 x 6pdr
                                       Admty No: 1439
                                       Port Reg: GY. 300
1914: Launched. Built at Beverley by CWG. Owned by JL. Green of Grimsby. 1915:
Requisitioned in April and converted to a M/S. 1919: Returned to owners. 1936:
Mercantile Loss. Stranded and sank in the Orkneys.

MOUNT ARD   1939/46   Displacement: 255TG 111TN
                                       Engines: 68HP
                                       Port Reg: A. 156
                                       P. No: Z. 126
1931: Launched. Built at Aberdeen. Owned by The Dodds SF Co. of Aberdeen. 1939:
Requisitioned in September and converted to a BDV. 1946: Returned to owners in June.

MOUNT KEEN   1939/46   Displacement: 258TG 113TN
                                       Engines: 70HP
                                       Port Reg: A. 411
                                       P. No: FY. 684
1936: Launched. Built at Aberdeen. Owned by The Dodds SF Co of Aberdeen. 1939:
Requisitioned in August and converted to a M/S. 51st M/S Group based at Grimsby.
1946: Returned to owners in January.

MOY   1920/46   See under ALEXANDER HILLS
                                       (Vol 1 p.15 & 130)

MURMANSK   1939/40   Ex-*Night Watch*
                                       Displacement: 348TG 160TN
                                       Engines: 91NHP = 10.5K
                                       Armament: 1 x 12pdr
                                       Port Reg: GY. 45
1929: Launched. Built at Beverley by CWG as *Night Watch*. Owned by Nocturne SFC
of Grimsby. PR: GY. 26. 1937: Stranded at Stem Island, Norway and abandoned.
1938: Salvaged and taken back to Grimsby. TIH for repairs. 1939: Acquired by

309

Markham Cook of Grimsby and renamed *Murmansk*. Acquired by Shire Trs. of Grimsby. Requisitioned in August and converted to an APV. 1940: LOST. Took the ground off Brest on 17th June and had to be abandoned. 1942: Salvaged by the German Navy and Commissioned as Patrol Boat PB. 06. 1944: German Loss.

MUROTO   1939/44   Displacement: 340TG 124TN
                                          Engines: 99HP
                                          Port Reg: CF. 28
                                          P. No: FY. 611

1931: Launched. Built at Stockton-on-Tees by Smith's Dock. Owned by Neale & West of Cardiff. 1939: Requisitioned in August and converted to a M/S. 1940: Deployed to the Med. and joined the 91st M/S Group sweeping off Tobruk, Port Said and Suez. 1944: Returned to the UK and Paid Off. Returned to owners in November.

MYNA   1915/19 1940/46 Displacement: 333TG 134TN
                                          Engines: 86NHP = 10.5K
                                          Armament: WWI: 1 x 6pdr; 1 x 7.5-inch Bomb Thrower (A/S Howitzer)
                                          Admty No: 1174
                                          Port Reg: H. 379
                                          P. No: WWII: J. 394

1912: Launched. Built at Beverley by CWG. Owned by St. Andrew's SFC of Hull. 1915: Requisitioned in February and converted to a M/S. 1919: Returned to owners. 1932: Acquired by Haldane & Pickering of Hull. 1934: Acquired by J. McCann of Hull and renamed *Merok*. 1935: Acquired by Charleson FCL of Hull and renamed *Cape Royds*. 1935: Sold to Norwegian mercantile and renamed *Bortind*. 1940: Escaped from Norway to the Faroe Islands. Hired as BORTIND and converted to a M/S. Commissioned with a Norwegian Crew. 1946: Returned to owners. 1977: Deleted.

MYRLAND   1941/46   Displacement: 324TG
                                            Port Reg: Norwegian
                                          P. No: FY. 1784

1918: Launched. 1940: Norwegian fishing vessel taken over by the Germans at the fall of Norway. Captured by the RN at Lofoton on 6th March. 1941: Converted to a M/S and Commissioned into the RN in May. 1944: Converted to a Fire-float. 1946: Returned to Norway.

NAB WYKE   1939/46   Displacement: 348TG 138TN
                                                 Engines: 96HP
                                                 Armament: 1 x 12pdr; 1 x 20mmAA;
                                                 2 x 0.5-inch VMG (1x2); 2 x LMG (2x1)
                                                 Port Reg: H. 252
                                                 P. No: FY. 654

1930: Launched. Built at Selby by Cochrane. Owned by West Dock SF Co. of Hull. 1939: Requisitioned in August and converted to a M/S. Fitted with Oropesa Gear. Commissioned in October and based in the Firth of Forth for sweeping off the E. Coast of Scotland. 1940: TIH at Barrow-in-Furness for refitting. Fitted for LL and Acoustic sweeping and mounted an additional 1 x 20mmAA and 2 x VMG. Completed refitting in February and joined the Aberdeen Flotilla. Transferred to Invergordon in March. TIH at Barrow-in-Furness for another 6 week refit. Completed refitting in July and deployed to Wallesy for sweeping operations in the Mersey and approaches. Returned to the Firth of Forth in December. 1941: Transferred to Reykjavik, Iceland, in April. Returned to the UK in October and based at Grimsby. TIH for refitting. 1942: Completed refitting and returned to Grimsby. Joined the 134th M/S Group for sweeping in the Flamborough Head - Cromer area. 1945: Employed on barge-towing duties in the Thames. 1946: Paid Off and reduced to the Reserve. Returned to owners in March.

NADINE   1914/15   Ex-*Niobe*
                                                 Displacement: 150TG
                                                 Admty No: 693
                                                 Port Reg: GY. 138

1895: Launched. 1914: Requisitioned in November and converted to an APV. 1915: LOST. Mined off the Shipwash Buoy on 1st September.

NADINE   1917/19   Displacement: 198TG
                                                 Port Reg: O. 151

1910: Launched. Belgian fishing vessel. 1917: Requisitioned into the Fishery Reserve with the permission of her Belgian owners. 1919: Returned to owners.

NADINE   1940/46   Displacement: 247TG
                                                 Port Reg: French
                                                 P. No: FY. 1882

1919: Launched. French fishing vessel. 1940: French M/S seized at Falmouth in Operation Grab on 3rd July. Commissioned into the RN as a M/S in December. 1946: Returned to France in April.

NAIADE   1917/19   Displacement: 240TG
                                                 Armament: 1 x 6pdrAA

Admty No: 3269
Port Reg: O. 144
1907: Launched. 1916: Requisitioned in March and converted to a M/S. 1919: Returned to owners.

NAIRANA   1916/19 1939/40 Displacement: 225TG 87TN
                                      Engines: 76HP
                                      Armament: 1 x 6pdr
                                      Admty No: 2513
                                      Port Reg: WWI: M. 238
                                      WWII: GY. 630
1913: Launched. Built at Aberdeen. Owned by H. Smethurst AO of Grimsby. 1915: Requisitioned in November and converted to a M/S. 1917: Renamed NAIRANA II in March. 1919: Returned to owners. Acquired by Trawlers, White Sea & Grimsby. 1939: Requisitioned in November and designated as an APV. 1940: Returned to owners in February.

NAIRANA II   1917/19   See under NAIRANA above

NAIRN   1919/20   See under DRIVER

NAMUR   1940/46   See under BENJAMIN COOKE
                                      (Vol 1 p.48)

NANCY HAGUE   1916/19 1940/46 Displacement: 299TG 121TN
                                      Engines: 91HP
                                      Armament: 1 x 6pdr
                                      Admty No: 1360
                                      Port Reg: FD. 133
                                      P. No: WWII: Z. 166
1911: Launched. Built at Middlesborough by Smith's Dock. Owned by New Docks ST Co. of Fleetwood. 1915: Requisitioned in March and converted to a M/S. 1919: Returned to owners. 1940: Requisitioned in April and converted to a BDV. 1943: Purchased into the RN in November. 1946: Laid Up in June. Placed on the Disposal List.

NANOOSE   1944/47   RCN See under NOOTKA

NARVAL   1916/16   Displacement: 211TG 98TN
                                      Engines: 60NHP = 10K
                                      Armament: 1 x 12pdr
                                      Admty No: 3268
                                      Port Reg: O. 141
1910: Launched. Built at Beverley by CWG. Owned by AP. Aspeslagh of Ostend, Belgium. 1916: Hired in March and converted to a M/S. LOST. Disappeared on passage from Grimsby to Harwich on 26th November. Lost with all hands.

NATAL	1914/19 1940/46	Displacement: 206TG 79TN

Engines: 60HP
Armament: 1 x 3pdr
Admty No: 305
Port Reg: GY. 1277
P. No: WWII: Z. 244

1903: Launched. Built at Selby by Cochrane. Owned by HL Taylor & R Staff of Grimsby. 1914: Requisitioned in August. 1915: Renamed NATAL II in February. 1919: Returned to owners. Acquired by Diamonds SFC of Grimsby. Same PR. 1939: Requisitioned in November as NATAL II and converted to an APV. 1940: Converted to a BDV in September. Based at Grimsby. 1946: Returned to owners in September.

NATAL II	1915/18 1940/46	See under NATAL above

NAUTILUS	1916/19	Displacement: 257TG

Armament: 1 x 6pdrAA
Admty No: 3267
Port Reg: O. 128

1905: Launched. 1916: Requisitioned in March and converted to a M/S. Renamed NAUTILUS II in July. 1919: Returned to owners.

NAUTILUS	1941/46	RIN

Displacement: 290TG
P. No: FY. 092

1913: Launched. 1941: Requisitioned and converted to a M/S. Commissioned into the RIN. 1943: Converted to a RDF Calibrating Vessel. 1946: Returned to owners.

NAUTILUS II	1916/19	See under NAUTILUS 1905 above

NAVENBY	1917/19	Ex-*North Sea*

Ex-*Ottoman Empire*
Displacement: 145TG 55TN
Engines: 45HP = 10K
Port Reg: GY.1094

1891: Launched. Built at Hull by CWG as North Sea. Owned by Cargill of Hull. PR: H. 147. 1899: Renamed *Ottoman Empire*. 1913: Acquired by Cleveden STC of Fleetwood. PR: FD.180. 1917: Acquired by W. Grant of Grimsby and renamed *Navenby* PR: GY.1094. Requisitioned into the Fishery Reserve. 1919: Returned to owners. 1924: BU.

NAZARETH	1940/45	See under WILLIAM CARR

(Vol 1 p.86)

NEATH CASTLE	1916/16	Displacement: 225TG

Armament: 1 x 3pdr

Admty No: 1763
Port Reg: SA. 6

1913: Launched. 1916: Requisitioned in May. LOST. Sunk in a collision off the Orkneys on 14th August.

NEATH CASTLE   1916/19   Displacement: 275TG 107TN
                                       Engines: 87HP
                                       Armament: 1 x 12pdr
                                       Admty No: 2981
                                       Port Reg: SA. 65

1916: Launched. Built at Southbank-on-Tees by Smith's Dock. Owned by Consolidated Fisheries of Grimsby. Requisitioned in November and converted to a M/S. 1919: Returned to owners.

NEGRO   1939/45   Displacement: 402TG 151TN
                               Engines: 101HP
                               Armament: 1 x 12pdr
                               Port Reg: H. 406
                               P. No: FY. 717

1932: Launched. Built at Beverley by CWG. Owned by Hellyer Bros. of Hull. 1939: Requisitioned in September and converted to a M/S. M/S Group 31 based at Grimsby. 1945: Returned to owners in February.

NEIL GOW   1914/19   Displacement: 255TG 107TN
                                  Engines: 80HP
                                  Armament: 1 x 12pdr; 1 x 3pdr; 1 x 7.5-inch Bomb Thrower (A/S Howitzer)
                                  Admty No: 161
                                  Port Reg: GY. 624

1911: Launched. Built at Selby by Cochrane. Owned by Orient SFC of Grimsby. 1914: Requisitioned in August and converted to a M/S. 1920: Returned to owners.

NEIL MACKAY   1939/45   Displacement: 266TG 113TN
                                     Engines: 525HP
                                     Port Reg: A. 316
                                     P. No: FY. 259

1935: Launched. Built at Bremerhaven, Germany. Owned by the Aberdeen ST&F Co. of Aberdeen. 1939: Requisitioned in November and converted to A/S. 1945: Returned to owners in October.

NELLIE BRADDOCK   1914/19   Displacement: 314TG 128TN
                                         Engines: 69HP
                                         Armament: 1 x 12pdr
                                         Admty No: 521

Port Reg: FD. 175
1913: Launched. Built at Aberdeen. Owned by Clifton ST Co. of Fleetwood. 1914: Requisitioned in November and converted to a M/S. 1919: Returned to owners.

NELLIE DODDS   1914/19 1940/46 Displacement: 220TG 85TN
Engines: 66HP
Armament: 1 x 12pdr
Admty No: 426
Port Reg: WWI: SN. 159; WII: A. 937
P. No: WWII: 4. 157

1911: Launched. Built at Aberdeen. Owned by CW Robinson of Middlesborough. 1914: Requisitioned in November and converted to a M/S. 1919: Returned to owners. Acquired by North Star SF Co. of Aberdeen and renamed *Ebor Wyke*. 1940: Requisitioned in January as EBOR WYKE and converted to an APV. 1946: Returned to owners in September.

NELLIE NUTTEN   1914/16   Displacement: 184TG
Armament: 1 x 3pdr
Admty No: 81
Port Reg: GN. 89

1901: Launched. 1914: Requisitioned in August and converted to a M/S. 1916: LOST. Sunk by gunfire from U-46, U-49, U-52 and U-69 100 miles to the E. of Aberdeen on 11th July whilst escorting a fishing fleet ICW ERA and ONWARD which were also sunk.

NEPTUNIAN   1915/18   Displacement: 315TG
Armament: 1 x 6pdr
Admty No: 1523
Port Reg: H. 626

1913: Launched. 1915: Requisitioned in May and converted to a M/S. 1918: LOST. Sunk in a collision near the Albacarry Lighthouse on 27th October.

NEREE   1916/19   Ex-*Athalia*
Displacement: 230TG
Armament: 1 x 6pdrAA
Admty No: 3266
Port Reg: O. 143

1909: Launched. 1916: Hired from Belgian owners in March and converted to a M/S. Employed on Special Service. 1919: Returned to owners.

NERINE   1939/44   SAN
Displacement: 197TG
Port Reg: South African
P. No: T. 11

1925: Launched. South African fishing vessel. 1939: Requisitioned in December and converted to a M/S. Commissioned into the SAN. 1944: Returned to owners in October.

NERISSA   1915/18   Displacement: 173TG 53TN
Engines: 45NHP = 9.5K
Armament: 1 x 6pdr
Admty No: 1793
Port Reg: H. 879

1906: Launched. Built at Beverley by CWG. Owned by Hellyer SFC of Hull. 1915: Requisitioned in August. Renamed NERISSA II in December. Deployed to the Med. 1917: Acquired by WA. Massey & Sons of Hull. 1918: LOST. Wrecked off Lemnos of 28th February.

NERISSA II   1915/18   See under NERISSA above

NESS   1920/22   See under ALEXANDER PALMER
(Vol 1 p.47)

NEWBRIDGE   1915/17   Displacement: 228TG
Armament: 1 x 3pdr
Admty No: 963
Port Reg: FD. 55

1906: Launched. 1915: Requisitioned in May and converted to a M/S. 1917: LOST. Sunk in a collision off Prawle Point on 19th November.

NEW COMET   1915/17   Displacement: 177TG
Admty No: 1496
Port Reg: GN. 75

1910: Launched. 1915: Requisitioned in May and converted to a M/S. 1917: LOST. Mined off Orford Ness on 20th January.

NEW COMET   1939/45   Displacement: 244TG 93TN
Engines: 91HP
Port Reg: GN. 38
P. No: FY. 760

1915: Launched. 1938: Owned by J. Johnston of Edinburgh. 1939: Requisitioned in November and converted to an APV. 1940: Converted to a M/S in May. 1943: Converted to an Esso in December. 1945: Returned to owners in December.

NEWHAVEN II   1917/19   Displacement: 162TG 63TN
Engines: 45HP
Port Reg: GY. 232

1897: Launched. Built at Govan. Owned by Consolidated Fisheries of Grimsby. 1917: Requisitioned into the Fishery Reserve. 1919: Returned to owners.

NEWHAVEN NB   1914/19 1940/45 Displacement: 182TG 69TN
Engines: 67HP

Armament: 1 x 6pdr
Admty No: 82
Port Reg: WWI: GN. 72; WWII: A. 231
P. No: WWII: FY. 820

1909: Launched. Built at Aberdeen. Owned by D Dow & W Carnie of Newhaven. 1914: Requisitioned in August and converted to a M/S. 1919: Returned to owners. Acquired by J Walker of Aberdeen. 1940: Requisitioned in February and converted to a M/S. 1945: Returned to owners.

NEWINGTON   1915/19   Displacement: 193TG 61TN
                                    Engines: 58HP = 10.5K
                                    Port Reg: Canadian

1899: Launched. Built at Hull by CWG. Owned by City SFC of Hull. PR: H. 33. 1907: Acquired by the Canadian Government and based at Vancouver. 1915: Requisitioned and converted to an APV. Served in Canadian waters throughout WWI. 1919: Returned to the Canadian Government. 1920: Acquired by Pacific Coyle Navigation Co. of Vancouver and converted to a tug. 1959: Mercantile Loss. Foundered whilst laid up in Vancouver harbour and subsequently declared a CTL.

NEWLAND   1916/19 1940/40 Displacement: 245TG 95TN
                                 Engines: 63HP
                                 Armament: 1 x 12pdr; 1 x 7.5-inch
                                 Bomb Thrower (A/S Howitzer)
                                 Admty No: 942
                                 Port Reg: WWI: H. 713; WWII: LO. 95

1903: Launched. Built at Selby by Cochrane. Owned by City SFC of Hull. 1915: Requisitioned in January and converted to a M/S. Fitted with Listening Hydrophones. 1919: Returned to owners. Acquired by Hewett Fishing Co. of London. 1940: Requisitioned in May and designated as a M/S. Returned to owners in June.

NEW ZEALAND   1915/19   Displacement: 290TG 116TN
                                      Engines: 65HP = 11K
                                      Port Reg: H. 413

1898: Launched. Built at Hull by CWG. Owned by Hull SF & Ice Co. of Hull. 1916: Requisitioned in August and converted to a BDV. 1918: Renamed HOKIANGA in April. 1920: Returned to owners and reverted to original name. 1937: BU in Holland.

NIBLICK   1917/19   Displacement: 154TG 63TN
                                 Engines: 50HP
                                 Port Reg: GY. 520

1891: Launched. Built at Beverley. Iron construction. Owned by H. Wood AO of Grimsby. 1917: Requisitioned into the Fishery Reserve. 1919: Returned to owners.

NIBLICK 1940/45 See under WILLIAM CUMMINS
(Vol 1 p.87)

NIGHT-HAWK 1914/14 Displacement: 287TG 112TN
Engines: 67HP = 10.5K
Admty No: 57
Port Reg: GY. 643
1911: Launched. Built at Beverley by CWG. Owned by Pioneer SFC of Grimsby. 1914: Requisitioned in August and converted to a M/S. LOST. Mined in the North Sea off Scarborough on Xmas Day with the loss of six lives. Seven of her company were rescued.

NIGHT HAWK 1916/19 1940/46 Displacement: 307TG 150TN
Engines: 89HP
Armament: 1 x 6pdrAA
Admty No: 1936
Port Reg: GY. 822
P. No: WWII: FY. 1858
1915: Launched. Built at Selby by Cochrane. Owned by Grimsby SF Co. of Grimsby. Requisitioned in March and converted to a M/S. Employed on escort duties. 1919: Returned to owners. 1940: Requisitioned in June and converted to an APV. 1941: Converted to a M/S. 1946. Returned to owners in August.

NIGHTJAR 1914/19 Ex-*Cuckoo*
Displacement: 156TG 55TN
Engines: 50HP = 10K
Admty No: 388
Port Reg: H. 309
1896: Launched. Built at Hull by CWG as *Cuckoo*. Owned by J. McCann of Hull. 1914: Requisitioned. Converted to a M/S and renamed NIGHTJAR. 1919: Returned to owner and reverted to original name. 1923: Acquired by Spanish owners and renamed *Punta Azamor*. 1946: Mercantile Loss. Wrecked off Spain on 3rd July.

NIGHT RIDER 1940/47 Displacement: 327TG 171TN
Engines: 90HP
Port Reg: GY. 683
P. No: Z. 113
1915: Launched. Built at Selby by Cochrane. Owned by Nocturne Fishing Co. of Grimsby. 1940: Purchased into the RN in January and converted to a BDV. 1946: Laid Up. 1947: Sold to mercantile in February.

NILE 1915/19 Displacement: 196TG 78TN
Engines: 52HP
Port Reg: FD. 11
1898: Launched. Built at North Shields. 1915: Requisitioned in June and converted to

a BDV. 1919: Returned to owners. Acquired by TG Hancock of Milford Haven. PR: M.186.

NINUS	1915/19 1940/46	Displacement: 292TG 124TN
		Engines: 80HP = 10K
		Armament: 1 x 12pdr; 1 x 7.5-inch
		Bomb Thrower (A/S Howitzer)
		Admty No: 1536
		Port Reg: GY. 700
		P. No: WWII: FY. 942

1912: Launched. Built at Beverley by CWG. Owned by Roberts & Ruthven of Grimsby. 1915: Requisitioned in June and converted to a M/S. Fitted with Listening Hydrophones. 1919: Returned to owners. 1927: Acquired by The Earls SF Co. of Grimsby and renamed *Lovania*. 1940: Requisitioned in June as LOVANIA and converted to an APV. 1941: Converted to a M/S. 1945: Employed on Target-towing. 1946: Returned to owners in February and retained the same name. 1947: Acquired by the Inch Fishing Co. of Edinburgh and renamed *Inchgarvie*. PR: GN. 30. 1953: BU at Spezia, Italy.

| NITH | 1920/22 | See under ANDREW JEWER |
| | | (Vol 1 p.131) |

NODZU	1916/19 1939/46	Displacement: 257TG
		Armament: 1 x 12pdr
		Admty No: 1356
		Port Reg: CF. 37

1911: Launched. Owned by Neale and West of Cardiff. 1915: Requisitioned in March. 1919: LOST. Wrecked off Nash Point in the Bristol Channel when she collided with a wreck on 1st January. Subsequently salvaged.

NODZU	1939/45	Displacement: 303TG 113TN
		Engines: 99HP
		Port Reg: CF. 22
		P. No: FY. 659

1929: Launched. Built by Southbank-on-Tees by Smith's Dock. Owned by Neale & West of Cardiff. 1939: Requisitioned in September and converted to a M/S. 1945: Returned to owners in November.

NOGI	1915/19	Displacement: 257TG 100TN
		Engines: 82HP
		Armament: 1 x 6pdr
		Admty No: 192
		Port Reg: CF. 24

1908: Launched. Built at North Shields. Owned by Neale & West of Cardiff. 1914: Requisitioned in November and converted to a M/S. 1919: Returned to owners.

NOGI   1939/41   Displacement: 299TG 114TN
Engines: 99HP
Port Reg: LO. 49

1923: Launched. Built at Southbank-on-Tees by Smith's Dock. Owned by T. Jenkerson of Milford Haven. 1939: Requisitioned in August and converted to a M/S. 1941: LOST. Sunk by enemy a/c off the Norfolk coast on 23rd June.

NOOGANA   1915/19 1940/45 Displacement: 237TG 90TN
Engines: 85HP
Armament: 1 x 3pdr
Admty No: 2663
Port Reg: WWI: M. 9; WWII: SN. 47
P. No: WWII: FY. 1599

1914: Launched. Built at Aberdeen. Owned by Port St. Mary F & C of London. 1915: Requisitioned in May. 1919: Returned to owners. Acquired by R. Hastie & Sons of N. Shields and renamed *St. Olive*. 1940: Requisitioned in March as ST. OLIVE and converted to a M/S. 1945: Returned to owners in November.

NORA NIVEN   1942/44   RNZN
Displacement: 163TG

1907: Launched. 1942: Purchased into the RNZN in October and converted to a D/I. 1944: Sold to mercantile.

NORBRECK   1916/19 1939/45 Displacement: 201TG
Armament: 1 x 3pdr
Admty No: 1374
Port Reg: FD. 30
P. No: WWII: FY. 1669

1905: Launched. Built at Aberdeen. 1915: Requisitioned in April. 1919: Returned to owners. Acquired by JM. Knight & MW. Howell of Milford Haven. PR: M. 7. 1939: Requisitioned and converted to a M/S. 1945: Returned to owners

NORDHAV I   1940/40   Displacement: 644TG
Armament: 1 x 14pdr (Japanese)
1 x 6pdr
Complement: 32
Port Reg: Norwegian
P.No: 4. 375

1915: Launched. Norwegian fishing vessel. 1940: Hired from Norwegian owners in June after the fall of Norway and converted to an APV. Renamed AVALON in September. 1941: Renamed ADONIS in June and fitted with RDF. Based at Ipswich. 1943: TIH for refitting at Immingham in March. Completed refitting on 13th April and returned to Ipswich. LOST. Torpedoed by German E-Boat off Lowestoft on 15th April. Eleven survivors.

NORDHAV II   1940/45   Displacement: 425TG
                                     Port Reg: Norwegian
                                     P. No: FY. 1906
1913: Launched. Norwegian fishing vessel. 1940: Hired from Norwegian owners at the
fall of Norway and converted to a M/S. 1945: LOST. Sunk by U-Boat off Dundee on 10th
March.

NORDKAPP   1940/45   Displacement: 243TG
                                     Port Reg: Norwegian
1937: Launched. 1940: Hired from Norwegian owners after the fall of Norway and
converted to an APV. Commissioned with a Norwegian crew and remained Norwegian
manned throughout the war. 1945: Returned to Norway.

NORDLAND   1940/46   Displacement: 393TG
                                    Port Reg: German
                                    P. No: Z. 180
1922: Launched. German fishing vessel. 1940: Taken as a Prize in the N. Sea and
converted to a BDV. 1946: Laid up in January. Sold to mercantile.

NORINA   1940/45   See under KUNISHI of 1939

NORLAND   1940/45   See under PREFECT

NORMAN   1915/19   Displacement: 119TG 38TN
                                    Engines: 45NHP = 10K
                                    Armament: 1 x 6pdr
                                    Admty No: 1314
                                    Port Reg: PD. 502
1894: Launched. Built at Hull by CWG. Owned by T. Robinson of Grimsby. PR: GY.
579. 1907: Acquired by J. Mitchell & Sons of Peterhead. 1915: Requisitioned in June
and converted to a Net Layer. 1916: Renamed NORMAN III in July. 1919: Returned to
owners. Reverted to original name.

NORMAN   1915/19 1940/40 Displacement: 346TG 135TN
                                    Engines: 87HP = 11K
                                    Armament: WWI: 1 x 6pdr; 1 x 7.5-inch
                                    Bomb Thrower (A/S Howitzer)
                                    WWII: 1 x 6pdr
                                    Admty No: 1575
                                    Port Reg: H. 249
1911: Launched. Built at Beverley by CWG. Owned by Hellyer of Hull. 1915:
Requisitioned in May and converted to a M/S. Renamed NORMAN II in December.
Employed on escort duties. 1919: Returned to owners and reverted to original name.
Acquired by Hellyer Bros. of Hull and renamed *Dervish*. 1940: Requisitioned in June as

DERVISH and converted to an APV. LOST. Mined off the Humber on 9th September with the loss of 3 lives.

NORMAN II	1915/19	See under NORMAN

NORMAN III	1916/19	See under NORMAN

NORSE   1915/19   Displacement: 279TG 125TN
Engines: 85HP
Armament: 1 x 12pdr; 1 x 7.5-inch
Bomb Thrower (A/S Howitzer)
Admty No: 1352
Port Reg: FD. 72

1914: Launched. Built at Aberdeen. Owned by Mersey STL of Fleetwood. 1915: Requisitioned in March and converted to a M/S. 1919: Returned to owners.

NORSE   1939/44   Displacement: 351TG 138TN
Engines: 96HP = 10.6K
Port Reg: GY. 197
P. No: FY. 1628

1930: Launched. Built at Beverley by CWG. Owned by Hellyer Bros. of Hull. PR: H. 348. 1939: Acquired by Shire Trs. of Grimsby. Requisitioned in September and converted to a M/S. Joined the MF. 1944: Returned to owners in November. 1946: Sold to Faroese owners and renamed *Kross-Steinur*. 1955: BU in Denmark.

NORTH CAPE   1917/19   Displacement: 122TG 46TN
Engines: 50HP
Port Reg: FR. 239

1889: Launched. Built at Aberdeen. Owned by CM. Woods of Larne Harbour AO. 1917: Requisitioned into the Fishery Reserve. 1919: Returned to owners.

NORTHCOATES   1939/44   See under GEORGE CORTON
(Vol 1 p.54)

NORTHERN CHIEF   1939/45   Displacement: 655TG 243TN
Dimensions: 188ft x 28ft
Engines: Triple Expansion
1,000HP = 16K
Armament: 1 x 4-inch; 1 x 0.303-in;
LMG 2 x 0.5-in VMG (1x2)
Port Reg: LO
P. No: 4. 34

1936: Launched. Built at Bremmerhaven as part of the German WWI Reparation Programme. Owned by Mac Line of London. 1939: Requisitioned in August and converted to A/S. 1941: TPI the operation to rescue U-570 which had been captured off Ireland on 27th August by an RAF a/c. This U-Boat rendered up her Cypher m/c intact and later became HMS/M GRAPH. 1942: Temporary Loan to the USN from February to assist in their operations against U-Boats on the E. Coast of the USA. Sailed from Londonderry with a flotilla of 24 Trs. at the end of February. Returned to the RN in October and transferred to the S. African Station. 1945: Returned to owners in July. Acquired by Northern Trawlers of London and based at Grimsby. 1947: Sold to Icelandic owners.

NORTHERN DAWN   1939/46   Displacement: 655TG 265TN
Dimensions: 188ft x 28ft
Engines: Triple Expansion
1,000HP = 16K
Armament: 1 x 4-inch; 1 x 0.303-in
LMG; 2 x 0.5-in VMG (1x2)
Port Reg: LO. 136
P. No: FY. 146

1936: Launched. Built at Bremmerhaven as part of the German WWI Reparation Programme. Acquired by Mac Line of London. 1939: Requisitioned in August and converted to A/S. 1940: TPI the Norwegian Campaign in April/May. TIH at Harland & Wolff, Belfast for refitting. The first Trawler to be fitted with RDF. On completion of refitting joined the 45th Escort Group based at Londonderry. Employed on convoy escorts Scotland – Iceland. 1942: Temporary Loan to the USN, together with crew, for A/S duties. Returned to the RN in September and transferred to the S. African Station. 1946: Returned to owners in February. Acquired by Northern Trawlers of London and based at Grimsby. Port Reg: GY. 289. 1964: BU.

NORTHERN DUKE   **(MPL)**

NORTHERN DUKE   1939/46   Displacement: 655TG 233TN
Dimensions: 88ft x 28ft
Engines: Triple Expansion
1,000HP = 16K
Armament: 1 x 4-in; 1 x 0.303-in LMG;
2 x 0.5-inch VMG (1x2)
Port Reg: LO. 169
P. No: 4. 11

1936: Launched. Built at Bremmerhaven as part of the German WWI Reparation Programme. Acquired by Mac Line of London. 1939: Requisitioned in August and converted to an ABV. Based at Kirkwall for Contraband Control. 1940: Escorting a neutral ship, SS Pajola, to Lerwick on 18th January for inspection when the ship was torpedoed by the German U-25. She attacked the U-Boat which was on the surface, claiming two hits and then rammed her as she crash-dived. Being an APV she was not equipped with ASDIC and so the U-Boat escaped. Rescued the crew of the stricken vessel and landed them at Kirkwall. 1942: Converted to A/S and was one of the fleet of Trawlers loaned to the USN from February. Returned to the RN in October and transferred to the S. African Station. 1946: Returned to owners in January. Acquired by Northern Trawlers of London and based at Grimsby. Port Reg: GY.442.

NORTHERN FOAM   1939/45   Displacement: 655TG 243TN
Dimensions: 188ft x 28ft
Engines: Triple Expansion
1,000HP = 16K
Armament: 1 x 4-inch; 3 x 20mmAA;
1 x 0.303-in LMG; 2 x 0.5-in VMG (1x2)
Port Reg: LO. 153
P. No: 4. 76

1936: Launched. Built at Bremmerhaven as part of the German WWI Reparation Programme. Acquired by Mac Line of London. 1939: Requisitioned in September and converted to an ABV. 1940: Based at Kirkwall ICW NORTHERN GIFT, KINGSTON AGATE and VASCAMA, for northern Contraband patrols. 1942: Converted to A/S and was one of the fleet of Trawlers loaned to the USN. Returned to the RN in October. 1943: Employed on Atlantic convoys. 1944: TPI Operation Neptune, the D-Day Landings in June as an A/S escort. 1946: Returned to owners in February. Acquired by Northern Trawlers of London and based at Grimsby. Port Reg: GY.490.

NORTHERN GEM   1939/45   Displacement: 655TG 243TN
Dimensions: 188ft x 28ft
Engines: Triple Expansion
1,000HP = 16K
Armament: 1 x 4-in; 2 x 0.303-in
LMG(2x1); 2 x 0.5-in VMG (1x2)
Port Reg: LO. 109

1936: Launched. Built at Bremmerhaven as part of the German WWI Reparation Programme. Acquired by Mac Line of London. 1939: Requisitioned in August and converted to A/S. Employed on escort duties. 1940: Transferred to the Northern Patrol and based at Kirkwall as an ABV. TPI the Norwegian Campaign in April/May. The last RN ship to leave the area when Narvik was evacuated. 1941: Transferred to the Iceland Command in August for Russian convoys. 1942: TPI the ill-fated Russian convoy PQ17. Escort unit for convoy JW51B to Murmansk in December. Rescued over 80 survivors from the destroyer ACHATES which had been attacked by the German ADMIRAL HIPPER on 31st December in the Barents Sea. Despite the enormous danger of the sinking destroyer's depth-charges which were exploding under her stern, she went alongside to take off the survivors. 1944: TPI Operation Neptune, the D-Day Landings in June, as an A/S escort. 1945: Employed on Iceland - UK convoys. Returned to owners in November. Acquired by Northern Trawlers of London and based at Grimsby. PR: GY. 204.

NORTHERN GIFT   1939/45   Displacement: 655TG 243TN
                                        Dimensions: 188ft x 28ft
                                        Engines: Triple Expansion
                                        1,000HP = 16K
                                        Armament: 1 x 4-inch HA; 2 x 20mmAA
                                        (2x1); 1 x 0.303-in VMG; 2 x 0.5-inch
                                        VMG (1x2)
                                        Port Reg: LO. 166
                                        P. No: 4. 50

1936: Launched. Built at Bremmerhaven as part of the German WWI Reparation Programme. Acquired by Mac Line of London. 1939: Requisitioned in August and converted to an ABV. 1940: Based at Kirkwall ICW NORTHERN GEM, KINGSTONE AGATE and VASCAMA for Contraband patrols. 1942: Converted to A/S. Escorted a convoy to Gibraltar and then remained there for A/S patrols in the Straits and convoy escort to and from Algiers. Returned to the UK. 1943: Based at Belfast. Employed on Icelandic convoys and on Atlantic convoys to and from St. Johns, Newfoundland. TIH at Belfast in June for refitting when she was fitted with the 2 x 20mmAA. Completed refitting and employed on S/M exercises and on Iceland convoys. 1944: Transferred to Portland and subsequently transferred to Portsmouth. TPI Operation Neptune, the D-Day Landings in June, as an A/S escort and then towing motorised pontoons to Sword Beach. Damaged when she took the ground off the Needles in October and TIH at Birkenhead for repairs. 1945: Returned to owners in October. Acquired by Northern Trawlers of London and based at Grimsby (H. Markham). 1947: Sold to Iceland.

NORTHERN ISLES   1939/45   Displacement: 655TG 243TN
                                         Dimensions: 188ft x 28ft
                                         Engines: Triple Expansion
                                         1,000HP = 16K
                                         Armament: 1 x 4-inch; 1 x 0.303-inch

LMG; 2 x 0.5-inch VMG (1x2)
Port Reg: LO
P. No: 4. 25

1936: Launched. Built at Bremerhaven as part of the German WWI Reparation Programme. Acquired by Mac Line of London. 1939: Requisitioned in August and converted to an ABV. 1942: Converted to A/S. One of the fleet of Trawlers loaned to the USN. Returned to the RN in October and transferred to the S. African Station. 1945: LOST. Stranded near Durban on 19th January. TCL but no loss of life.

NORTHERN PRIDE   1939/45   Displacement: 655TG 243TN
                                     Dimensions: 188ft x 28ft
                                     Engines: Triple Expansion
                                     1,000HP = 16K
                                     Armament: 1 x 4-inch; 2 x 0.303-inch
                                     LMG (2x1); 2 x 0.5-in VMG (1x2)
                                     Port Reg: LO. 104
                                     P. No: FY. 105

1936: Launched. Built at Bremenhaven as part of the German WWI Reparation Programme. Owned by Mac Line of London. 1939: Requisitioned in August and converted to A/S. Based at Milford Haven. 1940: Transferred to the Northern Patrol based at Kirkwall and joined the 11th A/S Striking Force. TPI the Norwegian Campaign in April/May. 1941: Patrolling to the W. of Ireland on 1st January when she was attacked with torpedoes from the Italian S/M BAGNOLINI. All torpedoes missed. Transferred to the Iceland Command in August for Russian convoys. 1944: TPI Operation Neptune, the D-Day Landings in June, as an A/S Escort. 1945: Returned to owners in November. Acquired by Northern Trawlers of London and based at Grimsby (H. Markham) PR: GY.169.

NORTHERN PRINCE   1914/19   Displacement: 208TG 81TN
                                     Engines: 82HP
                                     Armament: 1 x 6pdr
                                     Admty No: 257
                                     Port Reg: WY. 40

1913: Launched. Built at South Shields. Owned by R. Thompson (Staithes) Ltd. of North Shields. 1914: Requisitioned in August and converted to a M/S. 1919: Returned to owners.

NORTHERN PRINCESS   1939/42   Displacement: 655TG 243TN
                                     Dimensions: 188ft x 28ft
                                     Engines: Triple Expansion
                                     1,000HP = 16K
                                     Armament: 1 x 4-in; 1 x 0.303-inch
                                     LMG; 2 x 0.5-inch VMG (1x2)
                                     Port Reg: LO
                                     P. No: 4. 06

1936: Launched. Built at Bremerhaven as part of the German WWI Reparation Programme. Acquired by Mac Lines of London. 1939: Requisitioned in August and converted to an ABV. Based at Kirkwall for Contraband patrols. 1942: Converted to A/S. One of the fleet of Trawlers that sailed from Londonderry in February for loan to the USN. LOST. Off the Grand Banks on 7th March the fleet of Trawlers on passage to the USA ran into thick fog. She disappeared overnight and her loss was attributed to the action of the German U-94, but no explosion was heard and no wreckage was found and an alternative theory was that she had run foul of an iceberg. It was not until post-war captured German records confirmed that she had been sunk by the U-94.

NORTHERN REWARD   1939/46   Displacement: 655TG 243TN
Dimensions: 188ft x 28ft
Engines: Triple Expansion
1,000HP = 16K
Armament: 1 x 4-inch; 1 x 0.303-inch
LMG; 2 x 0.5-in VMG (1x2)
Port Reg: LO
P. No: 4. 85

1936: Launched. Built at Bremerhaven as part of the German WWI Reparation Programme. Acquired by Mac Lines of London. 1939: Requisitioned in August and converted to an ABV. Based at Kirkwall on Contraband patrols. 1942: Converted to A/S. Part of the fleet of Trawlers which were loaned to the USN in February. Returned to the RN in October and transferred to the S. African Station. 1944: Returned to the UK. TPI Operation Neptune, the D-Day Landings in June, as an A/S escort. 1945: SO of A/S Group employed on Iceland - UK convoys. 1946: Returned to owners in January. Acquired by Northern Trawlers of London and based at Grimsby (H. Markham). 1947: Sold to Icelandic owners.

NORTHERN ROVER   1939/45   Displacement: 655TG 243TN
Dimensions: 188ft x 28ft
Engines: Triple Expansion
1,000HP = 16K
Armament: 1 x 4-inch; 1 x 0.303-inch
LMG; 2 x 0.5-inch VMG (1x2)
Port Reg: LO. 164
P. No: 4. 58

1936: Launched. Built at Bremerhaven as part of the German Reparation Programme. Acquired by Mac Line of London. 1939: Requisitioned in August and converted to an ABV. Based at Kirkwall for Contraband patrols. LOST. Overdue on 5th November between Iceland and Faroes whilst on passage to Kirkwall. Post-war captured German records confirmed that she had been sunk by U-59.

NORTHERN SKY   1939/45   Displacement: 655TG 243TN
Dimensions: 188ft x 28ft

Engines: Triple Expansion
1,000HP = 16K
Armament: 1 x 4-inch; 1 x 0.303-inch
LMG; 2 x 0.5-inch VMG (1x2)
Port Reg: LO
P. No: 4. 18

1936: Launched. Built at Bremerhaven as part of German WWI Reparation Programme. Acquired by Mac Line of London. 1939: Requisitioned in September and converted to an ABV. 1942: Converted to A/S. 1943: Employed on convoy rescue duties. 1944: TPI Operation Neptune, the D-Day Landings in June, as an A/S escort. Transferred to 'met' reporting duties in the mid-Atlantic. 1945: Based at Reykjavik, Iceland. Escorted and towed AFD-17 from Iceland to Gibraltar and then returned to Iceland. Carried out what has been recorded as the last attack on a U-Boat in WWII when, on the penultimate day of the war in Europe, she attacked a U-Boat off Garosskagi. Iceland. Returned to owners in December. Acquired by Northern Trawlers of London and based at Grimsby (H. Markham) PR: GY. 440. 1966: BU.

NORTHERN SPRAY   1939/45   Displacement: 655TG 243TN
                                         Dimensions: 188ft x 28ft
                                         Engines: Triple Expansion
                                         1,000HP = 16K
                                         Armament: 1 x 4-inch; 1 x 0.303-inch
                                         LMG; 2 x 0.5-inch VMG (1x2)
                                         Port Reg: LO. 140
                                         P. No: FY. 129

1936: Launched. Built at Bremerhaven as part of the German WWI Reparation Programme. Acquired by Mac Line of London. 1939: Requisitioned in September and converted to A/S. 1940: TPI the Norwegian Campaign as Group Leader. 1941: Transferred to the Iceland Command in August. 1942: Employed on Russian convoys. Whilst escorting convoy PQ.16 from Iceland to Russia on 21st May she was ordered to tow a damaged 5,000T US merchantman back to Iceland for repair. Attacked by torpedo from the German U-383 to the S. of Iceland on 24th October. The torpedo missed and the S/M broke off the attack. 1943: Employed on Icelandic and Atlantic convoys. At the end of one convoy she arrived at Newfoundland with approximately 150 survivors aboard. 1944: Escort Group B3 on the Africa - UK run. 1945: Employed in northern waters on convoy escort duties. Escorting Convoy RU.161 from Iceland to the UK in June when they were attacked by the German U-979. She saw the periscope and attacked dropping Depth-charges and then rammed the S/M. The enemy escaped but when the trawler arrived in harbour she found that her ASDIC dome had been ripped off in the ramming attack. Returned to owners in September. Acquired by Northern Trawlers of London and based at Grimsby (H. Markham) PR: GY. 190. 1964: Mercantile Loss. Wrecked off Iceland. *Notes:* Reputed to have achieved 17K upon one occasion when chasing a U-Boat.

NORTHERN WAVE   1939/45   Displacement: 655TG 243TN
Dimensions: 188ft x 28ft
Engines: Triple Expansion
1,000HP = 16K
Armament: 1 x 4-inch; 1 x 0.303-inch
LMG; 2 x 0.5-inch VMG (1x2)
Port Reg; LO. 120
P. No: FY. 153

1936: Launched. Built at Bremerhaven as part of the German WWI Reparation Programme. Acquired by Mac Line of London. 1939: Requisitioned in September and converted to A/S. 1941: Transferred to the Iceland Command in August for Russian convoys. 1942: Transferred to Belfast but remained on Russian convoys. 1943: Paid Off at Belfast. There had been 'unrest' onboard for some time and it was decided to split up the crew. Re-commissioned with a new crew. 1944: TPI Operation Neptune, the D-Day Landings in June, as an A/S escort. 1945: Returned to owners. Acquired by Northern Trawlers of London and based at Grimsby. (H. Markham) PR: GY.184. *Notes:* She was one of only 10 RN ships which served in the Atlantic in every year of the war and thus qualified for the Battle Honour: Atlantic 1939-45.

NORTH KING   1914/19   Displacement: 194TG 75TN
Engines: 73HP
Armament: 1 x 12pdr
Admty No: 512
Port Reg: A. 86

1906: Launched. Built at Aberdeen. Owned by E. Walker of Newhaven, Edinburgh. 1914: Requisitioned in September and converted to a M/S. 1919: Returned to owners. 1938: Owned by W.H. Gore and others of Aberdeen. PR: PD.487.

NORTH KING   1914/19   Displacement: 271TG
Armament: 1 x 6pdr
Admty No: 304
Port Reg: H. 882

1906: Launched. 1914: Requisitioned in August and converted to a M/S. Renamed NORTH KING II in December. 1919: Returned to owners.

NORTH KING II   1914/19   See under NORTH KING above

NORTHLYN   1939/47   See under ROBERT MURRAY
(Vol 1 p.147)

NORTHMAN   1914/19 1940/45 Displacement: 197TG 75TN
Engines: 74HP
Armament: 1 x 6pdr
Admty No: 327

Port Reg: A. 414
P. No: WWII: FY. 338

1911: Launched. Built at Aberdeen. Owned by Standard FC of Aberdeen. 1914: Requisitioned in August and converted to a M/S. 1919: Returned to owners. Acquired by IB. Wood of Aberdeen AO. Same PR. 1940: Requisitioned in July and converted to an APV. 1942: Converted to a Base Ship in January. 1945: Re-employed from June. 1946: Returned to owners in March.

NORTH NESS   1939/46   See under ANDREW SACK
                                     (Vol 1 p.47)

NORTH QUEEN   1914/19 1940/45 Displacement: 195TG 75TN
                                   Engines: 73HP
                                   Armament: 1 x 3pdr; 1 x 2pdr
                                   Admty No: 681
                                   Port Reg: A. 78
                                   P. No: WWII: FY. 253

1906: Launched. Built at Aberdeen. Owned by North Line SFC of Aberdeen. 1914: Requisitioned in November. 1919: Returned to owners. 1940: Requisitioned in February and converted to a D/L. Converted to a M/S in August. 1945: Returned to owners in June.

NORTH STAR   1914/19   Displacement: 188TG 73TN
                                     Engines: 73HP
                                     Armament: 1 x 6pdr
                                     Admty No: 267
                                     Port Reg: A. 172

1907: Launched. Built at Aberdeen. Owned by Star SFC of Aberdeen. 1914: Requisitioned in August and converted to a M/S. 1915: Renamed NORTH STAR III in December. 1919: Returned to owners.

NORTH STAR III   1915/19   See under NORTH STAR above

NORTHUMBRIA   1914/17   Displacement: 211TG 76TN
                                     Engines: 60HP = 10K
                                     Armament: 1 x 12pdr
                                     Admty No: 623
                                     Port Reg: GY. 169

1906: Launched. Built at Beverley by CWG. Owned by East Anglia FCL of Grimsby. 1914: Requisitioned in September and converted to a M/S. 1917: LOST. Mined near May Island on 3rd March by a mine which had been laid the same day by UC-29.

NORTHWARD   1914/19 1939/40 Displacement: 204TG 77TN
                                      Engines: 60HP
                                      Armament: 1 x 6pdr

Admty No: 807
Port Reg: GY. 110

1906: Launched. Built at Selby by Cochrane. Owned by the Forward SF Co. of Grimsby. 1914: Requisitioned in November and converted to a M/S. 1919: Returned to owners. 1939: Requisitioned in November and designated as an APV. 1940: Returned to owners on 25th January.

| NORTHWARD HO | 1939/46 | See under JAMES HINES (Vol 1 p.175) |

| NORTH WEST | 1917/19 | Displacement: 123TG |
| | | Port Reg: A. 479. |

1890: Launched. 1917: Requisitioned into the Fishery Reserve. 1919: Returned to owners.

NORWICH CITY	1939/46	Football Group
		Displacement: 541TG 195TN
		Dimensions: 190ft
		Engines: 99HP
		Armament: 1 x 4-inch
		Port Reg: GY. 503
		P. No: FY. 229

1937: Launched. Built at Southbank-on-Tees by Smith's Dock. Owned by Consolidated Fisheries of Grimsby. 1939: Requisitioned in September and converted to A/S. 1942: Temporary Loan to the USN, together with crew, for A/S duties. Returned to the RN in October and transferred to the S. African Station. Based at Durban for convoy duties. 1946: Returned to owners. 1964: BU.

NOTRE DAME de FRANCE	1940/45	Displacement: 433TG
		Port Reg: French
		P. No: FY. 363

1931: Launched. French fishing vessel. 1940: French APV seized at Plymouth in Operation Grab on 3rd July and converted to A/S. 1941: Commissioned with a Dutch crew. 1942: Commissioned with RN crew. 1945: Returned to France in December.

NOTRE DAME de MONT LIGEON	1940/45	Displacement: 234TG
		Port Reg: French
		P. No: Z. 227

1899: Launched. French fishing vessel. 1940: Seized in operation Grab on 3rd July and converted to a BGV. Operational from October. 1945: Returned to France in October.

NOTTS COUNTY	1939/42	Football Group
		Displacement: 541TG 195TN
		Dimensions: 190ft oa
		Engines: 99HP
		Armament: 1 x 4-inch

Port Reg: GY. 487
P. No: FY. 250

1938: Launched. Built at Southbank-on-Tees by Smith's Dock. Owned by Consolidated Fisheries of Grimsby. 1939: Requisitioned in September and converted to A/S. 1942: LOST. Torpedoed by the German U-701 to the S. of Iceland on 8th March.

NOVELLI	1916/19	Displacement: 226TG 109TN
		Engines: 94HP = 9.5K
		Armament: 1 x 12pdr; 1 x 7.5-inch
		Bomb Thrower (A/S Howitzer)
		Admty No: 3279
		Port Reg: GY. 889

1916: Launched. Built at Beverley by CWG. Owned by North Western SFC of Grimsby. Requisitioned in May and converted to a M/S. 1918: Acquired by Great Northern SFC of Hull. PR: H. 592. 1919: Returned to owners. 1959: BU at Boom, Belgium. Game to the last, she was being sailed to Belgium when her engines broke down and she had to be towed into Yarmouth for repairs. Eventually she arrived at the breakers.

NUBIA	1917/19 1939/40	Displacement: 196TG 62TN
		Engines: 59HP = 10K
		Port Reg: GY. 1275

1903: Launched. Built at Hull by CWG. Owned by Gt. Grimsby & E. Coast SF Co. of Grimsby. 1917: Requisitioned into the Fishery Reserve. 1919: Returned to owners. 1937: Acquired by Japan FCL of Grimsby. 1939: Requisitioned in November and renamed WEAZEL. Designated as an APV. 1940: Returned to owners in February. 1941: Mercantile Loss. Sunk in a collision off the River Tyne on 17th October with the loss of 6 lives.

NUMITOR	1916/18	Displacement: 242TG
		Armament: 1 x 12pdr; 1 x 6pdrAA
		Admty No: 3270
		Port Reg: O. 127

1903: Launched. 1916: Requisitioned in March and converted to a M/S. 1918: LOST. Mined off Orford Ness on 20th April.

NUNTHORPE HALL	1919/20	See under SEAMEW

NYLGHAN	1915/19	Displacement: 261TG 112TN
		Engines: 70HP
		Armament: 1 x 12pdr
		Admty No: 1488
		Port Reg: GY. 363

1908: Launched. Built at Oulton Broad. Owned by Morris & Fisher of Grimsby. 1915: Requisitioned in May and converted to a M/S. 1919: Returned to owners.

OAKWOLD   1915/15   Displacement: 129TG 52TN
Engines: 35HP
Admty No: 959
Port Reg: GY. 948

1895: Launched. Built at Beverley. Owned by Northwold SFC of Grimsby. 1915: Requisitioned in January and converted to an APV. Returned to owners in November. 1938: Owned by J.C. Wilson of Plymouth.

OASIS   1940/46   Ex-*Al Suez*
Displacement: 207TG
Speed: See notes below
Complement: 14 (1 x PO, 1 x LSM,
12 x LE West Africans)
Port Reg: Egyptian

1898: Launched. Egyptian fishing vessel. 1940: Purchased into the RN in March and converted to an APV. 1944: Based at Freetown, W. Africa. Employed on carrying stores up-river and dumping obsolete ammunition at sea. 1946: Sold to mercantile. *Notes*: Iron built. The engines were so poor that she could barely make 2K against a flood tide. The steering gear, an arrangement of chains and rods, was badly rusted and took tremendous effort with the huge 6ft. ship's wheel. There was no power-assisted steering. It was unwise to employ the steam whistle as this invariably drenched anyone on deck with scalding steam.

OCEAN BRINE   1939/44   See under LINN o' DEE

OCEAN COMRADE   1914/18   Ex-*Melbourne*
Displacement: 133TG 57TN
Engines: 35HP = 9.5K
Admty No: 160
Port Reg: YH. 405

1892: Launched. Built at Hull by CWG as *Melbourne*. Iron construction. Owned by Hull SF & Ice Co. of Hull. PR: H. 200. 1913: Acquired by Bloomfields of Gt. Yarmouth and renamed *Ocean Comrade* PR: YH. 405. 1914: Requisitioned in August and converted to a M/S. Subsequently converted to a Net Layer. 1918: Reduced to the Fishery Reserve in March. 1919: Returned to owners. 1929: Acquired by Dutch owners and renamed *Beka*. 1931: Acquired by W. Barnard of Lowestoft and renamed *Ocean Comrade* PR: LT. 244. 1937: BU in Germany.

OCEAN EDDY   1940/46   Displacement: 231TG 99TN
Engines: 63HP
Port Reg: LH .62

P. No: Z. 143

1929: Launched. Built at Aberdeen. Owned by A. Flockhart AO of Edinburgh. 1940: Requisitioned in January and converted to a BDV. 1946: Returned to owners in February.

OCEAN FISHER	1940/45	See under DANIEL HILLIER (Vol 1 p.169)

OCEANIC	1914/19	Displacement: 168TG 69TN Engines: 53HP Armament: 1 x 12pdr Admty No: 391 Port Reg: H. 449

1896: Launched. Built at Grimsby. Owned by Kelsall Bros. & Beeching of Hull. 1914: Requisitioned in November and converted to a 'Q' Ship. 1915: Renamed OCEANIC IV in February. 1919: Returned to owners.

OCEANIC II	1917/19	Displacement: 235TG 109TN Engines: 55HP Armament: 2 x 3pdr Port Reg: GY. 863

1898: Launched. Built at Hull. Owned by TA Marper & H Rachkend of Cleethorpes. 1917: Requisitioned into the Fishery Reserve. 1919: Returned to owners.

OCEANIC IV	1915/19	See under OCEANIC above

OCEAN PRINCE	1914/19	Displacement: 203TG 70TN Engines: 50HP Port Reg: A. 576

1902: Launched. Built at Govan. Owned by Aberdeen Fishing Supply Assoc. of Aberdeen. 1914: Requisitioned in September and converted to a BDV. 1920: Returned to owners.

OCEAN PRINCESS	1914/19	Displacement: 203TG 78TN Engines: 50HP Armament: 1 x 6pdrAA; 1 x 7.5-inch Bomb Thrower (A/S Howitzer) Admty No: 111 Port Reg: A .580

1902: Launched. Built at Govan. Owned by Aberdeen Fishing Supply Assoc. of Aberdeen. 1914: Requisitioned in November and converted to a M/S. 1919: Returned to owners. 1938: Owned by A.G.L. Meff of Aberdeen.

OCEAN QUEEN	1914/19	Displacement: 284TG 113TN Engines: 78HP

Armament: 1 x 6pdrAA
Admty No: 546
Port Reg: GY. 1115

1906: Launched. Built at Hull. Owned by H Buras of Grimsby. 1914: Requisitioned in November and converted to a M/S. 1919: Returned to owners.

OCEAN SCOUT	1915/17	Displacement: 200TG
		Armament: 1 x 6pdrAA
		Admty No: 1555

1915: Launched. Requisitioned in July. 1917: LOST. Sunk in a collision off W. Ireland on 21st December.

OCEAN VICTOR	1939/40	See under JOHN FAIRMAN
		(Vol 1 p.178)

OCEAN VIEW	1940/45	Displacement: 248TG 106TN
		Engines: 64HP
		Port Reg: LH. 63
		P. No: FY. 863

1930: Launched. Built at Aberdeen. Owned by A. Flockhart AO of Edinburgh. 1940: Requisitioned in February and converted to a M/S. 1945: Returned to owners in December.

OCTAVIA	1917/19	Displacement: 173TG 68TN
		Engines: 45HP = 9.5K
		Port Reg: H. 876

1906: Launched. Built at Beverley by CWG. Owned by Hellyer SFC of Hull. 1917: Requisitioned into the Fishery Reserve. 1919: Returned to owners. 1926: Acquired by WC Farrow of Hull. PR: H. 274. 1937: Mercantile Loss. Sunk in a collision with *George Cousins* off Ramsay, IOM, on 13th February. No loss of life.

OCTOROON	1915/19	Displacement: 195TG 85TN
		Engines: 78HP
		Armament: 1 x 6pdrAA
		Admty No: 1431
		Port Reg: HL .68

1914: Launched. Built at Aberdeen. Owned by Sutton STC of Hartlepool. 1915: Requisitioned in April and converted to a M/S. 1919: Returned to owners.

OFFA	1915/19	Displacement: 313TG 135TN
		Engines: 79HP
		Armament: 1 x 12pdr 1 x 7.5-inch
		Bomb Thrower (A/S Howitzer)
		Admty No: 1406
		Port Reg: GY. 975

1913: Launched. Built at Selby by Cochrane. Owned by A. Bannister of Grimsby. 1915: Requisitioned in March. Renamed OFFA II in December. 1919: Returned to owners. 1938: Owned by MA Olesen of Grimsby and AA Winter of Cleethorpes. PR: GY. 827.

OFFA II   1915/19   See under OFFA above

OGANO   1940/44   See under HUGH BLACK (Vol 1 p.55)

OHM   1939/45   See under WELBECK of 1915

OKINO   1914/15   Displacement: 241TG
                                     Admty No: 285
                                     Port Reg: GY. 4
1914: Launched. Requisitioned in August and converted to a M/S. Deployed to the Med. 1915: LOST. Mined near Yeni Cale in the Dardenelles on 8th March.

OKINO   1917/19 1940/46 Displacement: 241TG 123TN
                                     Engines: 98HP
                                     Armament: 1 x 12pdr; 1 x 7.5-inch
                                     Bomb Thrower (A/S Howitzer)
                                     Admty No: 3051
                                     Port Reg: GY. 1060
                                     P. No: WWII: Z. 146
1917: Launched. Built at Selby by Cochrane. Owned by HL Taylor & HG Hopwood of Grimsby. Requisitioned in July and converted to a M/S. 1919: Returned to owners. Acquired by Diamonds SFC of Grimsby. 1940: Requisitioned in January and converted to a BDV. Based at Grimsby. 1945: Returned to owners in January.

OKU   1916/19   Displacement: 248TG 95TN
                                     Engines: 81HP
                                     Armament: 1 x 12pdr; 1 x 6pdr
                                     Admty No: 1355
                                     Port Reg: CF. 25
1909: Launched. Built at South Shields. Owned by Neale & West of Cardiff. 1915: Requisitioned in March and converted to a M/S. 1919: Returned to owners.

OKU   1939/45   Displacement: 303TG 113TN
                                     Engines: 99HP
                                     Port Reg: CF. 3
                                     P. No: FY. 660
1929: Launched. Built at Southbank-on-Tees by Smith's Dock. Owned by Neale & West of Cardiff. 1939: Requisitioned in August and converted to a M/S. Based at Grimsby. 1945: Returned to owners.

| OLDEN TIMES | 1939/40 | See under JOSHUA BUDGET (Vol 1 p.182) |

OLDHAM   1915/19   Displacement: 165TG 64TN
                                Engines: 45HP
                                Armament: 1 x 12pdr
                                Admty No: 825
                                Port Reg: GY. 538
1898: Launched. Built at Govan. Owned by Consolidated Fisheries of Grimsby. 1914: Requisitioned in December. 1919: Returned to owners.

OLININA   1939/45   Displacement: 425TG 160TN
                                Engines: 99HP
                                Port Reg: H .89
                                P. No: FY. 154
1934: Launched. Built at Southbank-on-Tees by Smith's Dock. Owned by Victoria Fishing Co. of Hull. 1939: Requisitioned in August and converted to A/S. 1940: Based at Portland. TPI Operation Dynamo, the evacuation of Dunkirk. 1944: TPI Operation Neptune, the D-Day Landings in June, as an A/S escort. 1945: Returned to owners in December.

OLIVE IV   1916/19   Displacement: 328TG
1907: Launched. 1916: Requisitioned. 1919: Returned to owners.

OLIVE CAM   1939/46   RAN
                                Ex-*Nodzu*
                                Displacement: 281TG 110TN
                                Engines: 85HP = 10.5K
                                Port Reg: Australian
                                P. No: FY. 76
1920: Launched. Built at Beverley by CWG as *Nodzu*. Owned by Neale & West of Cardiff. PR: CF. 1. 1928: Acquired by Cam & Sons of Sydney, Australia and renamed *Olive Cam*. 1939: Requisitioned into the RAN in October and converted to a M/S. 1946: Returned to owners in May. 1954: Mercantile Loss. Wrecked after striking a submerged rock off New South Wales on 2nd November.

OLIVINE   1915/19   Displacement: 289TG 115TN
                                Engines: 67HP
                                Armament: 1 x 12pdrAA
                                Admty No: 1211
                                Port Reg: H. 849
1905: Launched. Built at Govan. Owned by The British Tr. Co. of Bootle. 1915: Requisitioned in January and converted to a M/S. 1919: Returned to owners.

OLYMPIA   1917/19 1939/45 Displacement: 261TG 216TN
Engines: 75HP
Armament: 1 x 12pdr; 1 x 3.5-inch
Bomb Thrower (A/S Howitzer)
Admty No: 3064
Port Reg: WWII: GY. 1080
P. No: WWII: FY. 1586

1917: Launched. Built at Beverley by CWG. Owned by The Gt. Grimsby & E. Coast SF Co. Requisitioned in September and converted to a M/S. Fitted with Listening Hydrophones. 1919: Returned to owners. 1939: Requisitioned in December and converted to a M/S. Based at Grimsby. 1945: Returned to owners in August.

ONETOS   1914/19 1939/46 Displacement: 217TG 79TN
Engines: 70HP
Armament: 1 x 6pdr
Admty No: 283
Port Reg: WWI: A. 592; WWII: GN. 1
P. No: WWII: FY. 761

1913: Launched. Built at Aberdeen. Owned by AR Tucker & JC Tippett of Cardiff. 1914: Requisitioned in August and converted to a M/S. 1919: Returned to owners. Acquired by L Carnie AO of Glasgow. 1939: Requisitioned in November and converted to an APV. 1940: Converted to a M/S in June. 1944: Converted to a WDV. 1946: Returned to owners in January. Acquired by Stephen Fishing Co. of Aberdeen.

ONTARIO   1914/19   Displacement: 208TG 100TN
Engines: 65HP
Armament: 1 x 6pdrAA
Admty No: 274
Port Reg: GY. 213

1907: Launched. Built at N. Shields. Owned by the Dominion SF Co of Grimsby. 1914: Requisitioned in August and converted to a M/S. 1919: Returned to owners.

ONWARD   1915/16   Displacement: 266TG 112TN
Engines: 98HP
Armament: 1 x 12pdr
Admty No: 399
Port Reg: H. 980

1908: Launched. Built at Selby by Cochrane. Owned by Great Northern SFC of Hull. 1914: Requisitioned in December and converted to a M/S. 1916: LOST. Sunk by gunfire from U-46, U-49, U-52 and U-69 off Aberdeen on 11th July.

ONWARD II   1915/19 1939/40 Displacement: 209TG 79TN
Engines: 60HP
Port Reg: GY. 87

P. No: WWII: FY. 887

1905: Launched. Built at Selby by Cochrane. Owned by the Forward SF Co. of Grimsby. 1915: Requisitioned. 1919: Returned to owners. 1939: Requisitioned in November as ONWARD and converted to a M/S. 1944: Returned to owners in November.

ONYX   1915/19   Displacement: 248TG 98TN
                                        Engines: 76HP
                                        Armament: 1 x 6pdr; 1 x 7.5-inch Bomb
                                        Thrower (A/S Howitzer)
                                        Admty No: 1186
                                        Port Reg: H. 1029

1913: Launched. Built at Selby by Cochrane. Owned by Kingston STC of Hull. 1915: Requisitioned in April and converted to an Escort Vessel. Renamed ONYX II in May. 1919: Returned to owners.

ONYX II   1915/19   See under ONYX above

OPHIR II   1914/19 1939/40 Displacement: 213TG 105TN
                                          Engines: 68HP
                                        Armament: 1 x 6pdrAA
                                        Admty No: 351
                                        Port Reg: GY. 171
                                        P. No: WWII: Z. 235

1906: Launched. Built at Selby by Cochrane. Owned by the Forward SF Co. of Grimsby. 1914: Requisitioned in August and converted to a M/S. 1915: Renamed OPHIR II in February. 1919: Returned to owners. 1939: Requisitioned in November and designated as an APV. 1940: Returned to owners in February.

OPHIR III   1915/19   Displacement: 230TG 84TN
                                          Engines: 70NHP = 10.5K
                                        Armament: 1 x 12pdr; 1 x 7.5-inch
                                        Bomb Thrower (A/S Howitzer)
                                        Admty No: 1204
                                        Port Reg: H. 725

1903: Launched. Built at Hull by CWG. Owned by Pickering & Haldane STC of Hull. 1915: Requisitioned in January and converted to a M/S. Renamed OPHIR III in February. 1918: Acquired by Crampin SFC of Grimsby. PR: GY. 1220. 1919: Returned to owners. 1933: Acquired by Walker STC of Aberdeen and renamed *Star of Moray*. PR: A. 232. 1934: Acquired by Hewett FCL of London and renamed *Ladylove*. PR: LO. 167. 1940: Requisitioned in July as LADYLOVE and designated as M/S. Returned to owners in October. 1941: Mercantile Loss. Possibly torpedoed off Iceland. Lost with all hands.

ORANAISE   1940/46   Displacement: 738TG
                                          Port Reg: French

1919: Launched. French fishing vessel. 1940: French APV seized at Portsmouth in Operation Grab on 3rd July. Commissioned with a Free French crew. Converted to a BDV in December and manned with a RN crew. 1946: Returned to France in January.

ORCADES	1914/16	Displacement: 270TG
		Admty No: 40
		Port Reg: GY. 640

1911: Launched. 1914: Requisitioned in August and converted to a M/S. 1916: LOST. Mined off Grimsby on 14th April.

ORIANDA	1914/14	Displacement: 273TG
		Admty No: 99
		Port Reg: GY. 291

1914: Launched. Requisitioned in September and converted to a M/S. LOST. Mined off Scarborough on 19th December.

ORIENTAL STAR	1939/39	Displacement: 427TG 162TN
		Engines: 99HP
		Armament: 1 x 4-inch
		Port Reg: H. 98
		P. No: FY. 178

1934: Launched. Built at Southbank-on-Tees by Smith's Dock. Owned by Gresham Trs. Ltd. of Hull. 1939: Purchased into the RN in August and converted to A/S. Transferred to the French Navy on 28th November and renamed La SETOISE.

ORIFLAMME	1918/19	See under WALLINGTON

ORIOLE	1914/19	Displacement: 172TG 65TN
		Engines: 60HP
		Armament: 1 x 6pdr
		Admty No: 636
		Port Reg: H. 926

1907: Launched. Built at Goole by Goole SB. Owned by Kelsall Bros. & Beeching of Hull. 1914: Requisitioned in October and converted to a M/S. 1915: Renamed ORIOLE II in December. 1919: Returned to owners.

ORIOLE II	1915/19	See under ORIOLE above

ORIZABA	1915/19 1940/45	Displacement: 233TG 91TN
		Engines: 70HP = 10.5K
		Armament: 1 x 6pdr
		Port Reg: GY. 356
		P. No: WWII: FY. 1897 (M/S)
		Y7. 23 (Esso)

1908: Launched. Built at Beverley by CWG. Owned by A. Bannister of Grimsby. 1914: Requisitioned in December and converted to a BDV. 1918: Returned to owners. 1919: Acquired by Forward of SFC of Grimsby. 1940: Requisitioned in August and converted to a M/S. 1944: Converted to an Esso in March. Returned to owners in December. 1946: Laid up at Grimsby. 1949: BU at Gateshead.

ORLANDO	1914/15	Displacement: 276TG
		Admty No: 365
		Port Reg: DY. 248

1907: Launched. 1914: Requisitioned in August and converted to a M/S. 1915: LOST. Wrecked at Stornaway on 14th March.

ORMONDE	1914/19 1940/41	Displacement: 250TG 201TN
		Engines: 69HP
		Armament: 1 x 6pdrAA
		Port Reg: GY. 162
		P. No: WWII: FY. 782

1906: Launched. Built at Selby by Cochrane. Owned by the Arctic SF Co. of Grimsby. 1914: Requisitioned in August and converted to a M/S. 1917: Renamed ORMONDE II in November. 1919: Returned to owners. 1939: Requisitioned in November and converted to an APV. 1940: Converted to a M/S in November. 1941: LOST. Sunk by enemy a/c off E. Scotland on 16th February.

| ORMONDE II | 1917/19 | See under ORMONDE above |

OROPESA	1915/19 1940/46	Displacement: 324TG 171TN
		Engines: 84HP
		Armament: WWI: 1 x 6pdr;
		WWII: 1 x 12pdr
		Admty No: 711
		Port Reg: GY. 358
		P. No: WWII: FY. 1916

1914: Launched. Built at Selby by Cochrane. Owned by A. Bannister AO of Grimsby. Requisitioned in November and converted to a M/S. 1915: Renamed OROPESA II in June. 1919: Returned to owners. Acquired by Portuguese owners and renamed *Estrella do Mar*. 1940: Purchased into the RN as ESTRELLO do MAR. 1942: Converted to a M/S and renamed DUSK. 1946: Sold to mercantile and renamed *Akbari*.

| OROPESA II | 1915/19 | See under OROPESA above |

ORPHEUS	1914/19 1940/46	Displacement: 228TG 91TN
		Engines: 69HP
		Armament: 1 x 6pdrAA
		Admty No: 41

Port Reg: GY. 74
P. No: WWII: FY. 1700
1905: Launched. Built at Selby by Cochrane. Owned by the Arctic SFC of Grimsby.
1914: Requisitioned in August and converted to a M/S. 1915: Renamed ORPHEUS II
in December. 1919: Returned to owners. 1940: Requisitioned in June and converted to
a M/S. 1946: Returned to owners in January.

ORPHEUS II	1915/19	See under ORPHEUS above

ORSINO	1914/16	Displacement: 172TG
		Armament: 1 x 3pdr
		Admty No: 602
		Port Reg: H. 864

1906: Launched. 1914: Requisitioned in September. 1916: LOST. Torpedoed by a
German S/M between Loch Eribol and Stromness on 28th September.

ORTHOS	1914/17	Displacement: 218TG
		Admty No: 282
		Port Reg: A. 591

1913: Launched. 1914: Requisitioned in August and converted to a M/S. 1917: LOST.
Mined off Lowestoft on 9th April.

ORVICTO	1916/19 1940/45	Displacement: 226TG 109TN
		Engines: 74HP = 9.5K
		Armament: WWI: 1 x 6pdr; 1 x 7.5-inch
		Bomb Thrower (A/S Howitzer).
		WWII: 1 x 3pdr
		Admty No: 2962
		Port Reg: GY. 897
		P. No: WWII: FY. 909

1916: Launched. Built at Beverley by CWG. Owned by South Western SFC of Grimsby.
Requisitioned in September and converted to a M/S. 1919: Returned to owners. 1933:
Acquired by Sir Thomas Robinson & Son of Grimsby. Port Reg: GY. 1179. 1940:
Requisitioned in April and converted to a D/L. Converted to an APV in November and
employed on Examination Service. Based at Grimsby. 1943: Convoy escort based at
Grimsby. 1945: Returned to owners in October. 1961: BU in Holland.

OSAKO	1940/45	See under JOHN BRENNAN
		(Vol 1 p.60)

OSBORNE STROUD	1914/20 1939/40	Displacement: 209TG 79TN
		Engines: 66HP
		Armament: 1 x 6pdr
		Admty No: 3

Port Reg: A

1912: Launched. Built at Aberdeen by Hall. Owned by Stroud SFC of Aberdeen. 1914: Purchased into the RN in July and converted to a M/S. 1920: Sold to mercantile and retained the same name. Acquired by Isaac B. Wood of Aberdeen AO and renamed *Beathwood*. Same PR. 1939: Requisitioned in December as BEATHWOOD and designated as an APV. 1940: Returned to owners.

OSIRIS III	1917/19	Displacement: 173TG 62TN
		Engines: 50HP = 10K
		Port Reg: GY. 986

1898: Launched. Built at Hull by CWG. Owned by Roberts & Ruthven of Grimsby. 1917: Requisitioned into the Fishery Reserve. 1919: Returned to owners. 1933: BU.

OSPREY II	1915/19	Displacement: 295TG 114TN
		Engines: 85HP
		Armament: 1 x 12pdr
		Admty No: 1354
		Port Reg: FD. 129

1911: Launched. Built at Middlesborough by Smith's Dock. Owned by Cygnet SFC of Fleetwood. 1915: Requisitioned in March and converted to a M/S. 1919: Returned to owners.

OSPREY III	1915/19	Displacement: 332TG

1905: Launched. 1915: Requisitioned. 1919: Returned to owners.

OSTA	1917/19 1939/44	Displacement: 230TG 90TN
		Engines: 75HP
		Armament: WWI: 1 x 6pdrAA; 24 Mines
		(M/L)
		WWII: 1 x 6pdrAA
		Admty No: 1591
		Port Reg: FD. 106
		P. No: WWII: FY. 737

1915: Launched. Built at Aberdeen. Owned by The New Docks STC of Fleetwood. Requisitioned in May and converted to a M/L. 1917: Converted to a M/S. 1920: Returned to owners. 1939: Requisitioned in November and converted to an APV. 1940: Converted to a M/S in May. 1944: Converted to a BDV in January. Returned to owners in November.

OSTERO	1917/19	Displacement: 138TG
		Port Reg: GY. 200

1897: Launched. 1917: Requisitioned into the Fishery Reserve. 1919: Returned to owners.

OSTRICH   1915/19   Displacement: 244TG 89TN
                                            Engines: 63NHP = 10.25K
                                            Armament: 1 x 6pdrAA; 24 Mines (M/L)
                                            Admty No: 1750
                                            Port Reg: H. 729
1903: Launched. Built at Hull by CWG. Owned by St. Andrews SFC of Hull. 1915:
Requisitioned in September and converted to a M/L. Renamed OSTRICH II in October.
1916: Converted to a M/S. 1919: Returned to owners. 1926: Sold to Swedish owners
and renamed *Titania*. 1959: BU.

OSTRICH   1917/19   Displacement: 148TG 69TN
                                            Engines: 45HP
                                            Port Reg: GY.311
1891: Launched. Built at Beverley. Iron construction. Owned by HL Taylor of Grimsby.
1917: Requisitioned into the Fishery Reserve. 1919: Returned to owners.

OSTRICH II   1915/19   See under OSTRICH above

OSTRICH III   1917/19   Displacement: 148TG
                                            Port Reg: HL. 61
1898: Launched. 1917: Requisitioned into the Fishery Reserve. 1919: Returned to
owners.

OSWALDIAN   1917/19 1940/40 Displacement: 261TG 102TN
                                            Engines: 75HP = 9.5K
                                            Armament: 1 x 12pdr
                                            Admty No: 1651
                                            Port Reg: GY. 1104
1917: Launched. Built at Beverley by CWG. Owned by the Loyal SF Co of Grimsby.
Requisitioned in September and converted to a M/S. 1919: Returned to owners. 1940:
Acquired by Sir A. Black of Grimsby. Requisitioned in May and converted to an APV. Based
at Milford Haven. LOST. Mined in the Bristol Channel on 4th August. Seven survivors.

OTHELLO   1914/19 1939/41 Displacement: 201TG 94TN
                                            Engines: 67HP
                                            Armament: 1 x 6pdr
                                            Admty No: 619
                                            Port Reg: GY. 333
                                            P. No: FY. 783
1907: Launched. Built at Selby by Cochrane. Owned by the Forward SF Co. of Grimsby.
1914: Requisitioned in September. 1919: Returned to owners. 1939: Requisitioned in
November and converted to an APV. 1940: Converted to a BGV in August. 1941: LOST.
Mined in the Humber on 11th April.

OTHELLO II   1915/15   Displacement: 206TG   64TN
Engines: 50HP = 10K
Armament: 1 x 6pdr
Admty No: 1193
Port Reg: H. 956
1907: Launched. Built at Beverley by CWG. Owned by Hellyer SFC of Hull. 1915: Requisitioned in March. LOST. Mined off Leathercoat on 31st October. Only 1 survivor.

OTHONNA   1915/17   Displacement: 180TG
Armament: 1 x 6pdr
Admty No: 940
Port Reg: M. 24
1899: Launched. 1915: Requisitioned in January and converted to a M/S. 1917: LOST. Mined off Fifeness on 20th April.

OTTILIE   1915/19   Displacement: 226TG   113TN
Engines: 68HP = 9.5K
Armament: 1 x 6pdrAA
Admty No: 1757
Port Reg: GY. 144
1914: Launched. Built at Beverley by CWG. Owned by Marshall Line SFC of Grimsby. 1915: Requisitioned in May and converted to a M/S. 1916: Acquired by AW. Baxter of Grimsby. 1919: Returned to owners. Acquired by N. Green of Grimsby. 1955: BU in Belgium.

OTTOMAN EMPIRE   1917/19   Displacement: 162TG
Port Reg: FD. 180
1891: Launched. 1917: Requisitioned into the Fishery Reserve. 1919: Returned to owners.

OUR BAIRNS   1939/46   See under JAMES SIBBALD
(Vol 1 p.59)

OUSE   1916/19   Displacement: 167TG   66TN
Engines: 45HP
Port Reg: GW. 15
1900: Launched. Built at Govan. 1916: Requisitioned in February and converted to a BDV. 1919: Returned to owners. 1938: Owned by A. Gouldby of Kessingland AO. PR: LT. 572.

OUSE   1920/41   See under ANDREW KING
(Vol 1 p.131)

OUTPOST   1943/45   See under VIDETTE

OVERDALE WYKE   1939/46   Displacement: 338TG 137TN
                                    Engines: 96HP
                                    Armament: 1 x 12pdr
                                    Port Reg: H. 42
1924: Launched. Built at Selby by Cochrane. Owned by West Dock SF Co. of Hull.
1939: Purchased into the RN in July and converted to a M/S. 1940: Transferred to the
Ceylon Govt. 1946: Deleted.

OWL   1914/19   Displacement: 169TG 64TN
                                    Engines: 45HP
                                    Armament: 1 x 6pdr
                                    Admty No: 373
                                    Port Reg: H. 801
1903: Launched. Built at Goole by Goole SB. Owned by Kelsall Bros. & Beeching of
Hull. 1914: Requisitioned in October and converted to a M/S. 1915: Renamed OWL II
in February. 1919: Returned to owners.

OWL II   1915/19   See under OWL above

OWL III   1917/19   Displacement: 117TG 41TN
                                    Engines: 30HP
                                    Port Reg: A. 618
1896: Launched. Built at North Shields. Owned by T. Davidson of Aberdeen. 1917:
Requisitioned into the Fishery Reserve. 1919: Returned to owners.

OXWICH CASTLE   1915/19   Displacement: 252TG
                                    Armament: 1 x 6pdrAA
                                    Admty No: 144
                                    Port Reg: SA. 46
1907: Launched. Built at North Shields. Owned by Consolidated Fisheries of Grimsby.
1915: Requisitioned in January and converted to a M/S. 1919: Returned to owners.

OYAMA   1914/19   Displacement: 257TG 100TN
                                    Engines: 68HP
                                    Armament: 1 x 12pdr; 1 x 7.5-inch
                                    Bomb Thrower (A/S Howitzer)
                                    Admty No: 628
                                    Port Reg: CF. 23
1908: Launched. Built at North Shields. Owned by Neale & West of Cardiff. 1914:
Requisitioned in October and converted to a M/S. 1919: Returned to owners.

OYAMA   1939/39   Displacement: 340TG 123TN
                                    Engines: 99HP
                                    Port Reg: CF. 29

1931: Launched. Built at Stockton-on-Tees. Owned by Neale & West of Cardiff. 1939: Requisitioned in August and designated as a M/S. Returned to owners in November.

OYSTERMOUTH CASTLE 1917/19 1940/46 Displacement: 283TG 112TN
Engines: 85HP
Armament: 1 x 6pdr
Admty No: 3060
Port Reg: SA. 4
P. No: WWII: 4. 101

1914: Launched. Built at Middlesborough by Smith's Dock. Owned by Castle STC of Swansea. 1917: Requisitioned in August. 1919: Returned to owners. 1938: Owned by Consolidated Fisheries of Grimsby. 1940: Requisitioned in May and converted to an APV. Based at Grimsby for Fishery Protection. 1941: Converted to a M/S. 1946: Returned to owners in January.

PALISADE   1944/46   See under NAMUR

PAMELA   1915/19   Displacement: 331TG
1911: Launched. 1915: Requisitioned. 1919: Returned to owners.

PANORAMA   1940/46   Ex-*Rocro*
                                           Displacement: 408TG
                                           Port Reg: American
1919: Launched. American fishing vessel. 1940: Purchased in to the RN in June and
converted to a BDV. 1942: Stranded in the Saloum River, W. Africa on 30th October and was
consequently in French hands until 23rd November. 1946: Sold to mercantile in March.

PARKMORE   1915/19 1939/46 Displacement: 199TG 86TN
                                           Engines: 80HP
                                           Armament: 1 x 6pdrAA
                                           Admty No: 164
                                           Port Reg: HL. 76
                                           P. No: WWII: FY. 807
1915: Launched. Built at Aberdeen. Owned by RH Davidson AO of Hartlepool.
Requisitioned in October and converted to a M/S. 1919: Returned to owners. 1939:
Requisitioned and converted to a M/S. 1946: Returned to owners.

PARRAMATTA   1914/14 1917/19 Displacement: 168TG 63TG
                                           Engines: 60HP
                                           Armament: 1 x 6pdr
                                           Admty No: 678 & 814
                                           Port Reg: H. 445
1891: Launched. Built at North Shields. Owned by Kelsall Bros. & Beeching of Hull. 1914:
Requisitioned in December and designated as a M/S. 1915: Returned to the Fishing Fleet.
1917: Requisitioned into the Fishery Reserve. 1919: Returned to owners.

PARTHIAN   1914/16   Displacement: 202TG 90TN
                                           Engines: 67HP
                                           Armament: 1 x 6pdr
                                           Admty No: 328
                                           Port Reg: GY. 646
1911: Launched. Built at Beverley by CWG. Owned by Onward SF Co. of Grimsby.
1914: Requisitioned in August and converted to a M/S. 1915: Renamed PARTHIAN II
in December. 1919: Returned to owners.

PARTHIAN II   1916/19   See under PARTHIAN above

PASSEREAU 1940/45 Ex-*Dale Castle*
Ex-*St.Pierre*
Ex-*Mamelina No.10*
Displacement: 148TG 57TN
Engines: 50HP = 10K
Port Reg: French
1892: Launched. Built at Hull by CWG as *Dale Castle*. Owned by GHD Birt of Hull. PR: H. 195. 1904: Acquired by French owners and renamed *St. Pierre*. 1908: Acquired by Spanish owners and renamed *Mamelina No. 10*. 1917: Acquired by the French Navy (Marine Nationale Francaise) and renamed PASSERAU. 1919: Sold to French mercantile. 1940: Requisitioned by the French Navy and converted to a M/S. Escaped to England at the fall of France. Seized at Southampton in Operation Grab on 3rd July and Commissioned into the RN as a M/S. 1945: Returned to France. Subsequently registered as a War Loss.

PASSING 1914/19 Displacement: 459TG 291TN
Engines: 68HP = 10K
Armament: 1 x 12pdr
Admty No: 58 & 1542
Port Reg: GY. 877
1913: Launched. Built at Beverley by CWG. Owned by South Western SFC of Grimsby. 1914: Requisitioned and converted to a M/S. Mined off Bridlington in December and towed into Scarborough by the BRIGHTON QUEEN. TIH for repairs. 1917: Acquired by the North Western SFC of Grimsby. 1919: Returned to owners. 1920: Acquired by Belgian owners and renamed *Boula Matari*. 1925: Acquired by French owners and renamed *Pacifique*. 1928: Mercantile Loss. Went missing whilst fishing off Newfoundland. Lost with all hands.

PATRICIA CAM 1942/43 RAN
?: Launched. 1942: Requisitioned and converted to a M/S. Commissioned into the RAN. 1943: LOST. Sunk by Japanese a/c off Wessel Island in the Pacific in January.

PATRIE 1940/46 Displacement: 745TG
Port Reg: French
1920: Launched. French fishing vessel. 1940: French APV seized at Southampton in Operation Grab on 3rd July. Commissioned into the RN as an APV. 1944: Converted to a BDV in February. 1946: Returned to France in January.

PATTI 1939/46 Displacement: 339TG 146TN
Engines: 91HP
Armament: 1 x 12pdr
Port Reg: GY. 63
P. No: 4. 102
1928: Launched. Built at Selby by Cochrane. Owned by Premier SF Co. of Grimsby.

1939: Requisitioned in November and converted to an APV. Based at Grimsby for Fishery Protection. 1941: Converted to a M/S. 1946: Returned to owners in January.

PAULINE   1917/19   Displacement: 133TG 52TN
                                             Engines: 47HP
                                             Port Reg: SD. 6
1899: Launched. Built at South Shields. Owned by Wear SFC of Sunderland. 1917: Requisitioned into the Fishery Reserve. 1919: Returned to owners.

PAUL RYKENS   1939/45   Displacement: 266TG 113TN
                                               Engines: 525HP
                                             Armament: 1 x 4-inch
                                             Port Reg: A. 313
                                             P. No: FY. 257
1935: Launched. Built at Bremerhaven. Owned by The Aberdeen ST & F Co. of Aberdeen. 1939: Requisitioned in November and converted to A/S. 1945: Returned to owners in December. Acquired by Northern Trs. Ltd of London.

PAVLOVA   1914/19 1940/46 Displacement: 342TG 190TN
                                               Engines: 68NHP = 10.5K
                                             Armament: 1 x 6pdr
                                             Admty No: 56
                                             Port Reg: GY. 716
                                             P. No: WWII: FY. 802
1912: Launched. Built at Beverley by CWG. Owned by South Western SFC of Grimsby. 1914: Requisitioned in August and converted to a M/S. 1915: Acquired by T. Baskcombe of Grimsby and renamed *Euthamia*. 1919: Returned to owners. 1936: Acquired by Mar Rose of Fleetwood and renamed *Margaret Rose*. 1940: Acquired by Loch FCL of Hull. Purchased into the RN March as MARGARET ROSE and converted to a BDV. 1946: Paid Off and Laid Up in July. Sold to mercantile. Acquired by Norwegian owners and renamed *Morna*. 1951: BU in Belgium.

PAYNTER   1939/45   Cricketer Group
                                               Displacement: 472TG 201TN
                                               Engines: 133HP
                                               Port Reg: GY. 480
                                               P. No: FY. 242
1937: Launched. Built at Selby by Cochrane. Owned by Crampins of Grimsby. 1939: Requisitioned in September and converted to A/S. 1942: Employed on Arctic convoys. 1945: Returned to owners in September. 1946: Acquired by Perihelion SF Co. of Grimsby. 1960: BU.

PEARL   1914/19   Displacement: 198TG 79TG
                                               Engines: 60HP
                                               Armament: 1 x 6pdr

                              Admty No: 830
                              Port Reg: GY. 1121
1899: Launched. Built at Beverley. Owned by TC Moss of Grimsby. 1914: Requisitioned
in November and converted to a M/S. 1919: Returned to owners.

PEARL   1914/19   Displacement: 289TG
                                    Armament: 1 x 12pdr
                                    Admty No: 306
                                    Port Reg: WWI: H. 883; WWII: A. 364
                                    P. No: WWII: Z. 121
1913: Launched. 1914: Requisitioned in August and converted to a M/S. Fitted with
Listening Hydrophones. 1915: Renamed PEARL II in February. 1919: Returned to owners.
Acquired by Trs. (White Sea & Grimsby) and renamed *Cadella*. PR: GY. 221. Acquired by
Boston DSF & Ice Co. of Boston, Lincs. PR: A. 364. 1939: Requisitioned in October as
CADELLA and converted to a BDV. Based at Grimsby. 1946: Returned to owners.

PEARL II   1915/19   See under PEARL 1913

PEARY   1915/19   Displacement: 289TG 115TN
                                    Engines: 79HP
                                    Armament: 1 x 12pdrAA
                                    Admty No: 1350
                                    Port Reg: H. 1016
1913: Launched. Built at Selby. Owned by Jutland STC of Hull. 1915: Requisitioned in
May and converted to a M/S. 1919: Returned to owners.

PEGASUS   1917/19   Displacement: 219TG 98TN
                                    Engines: 86HP
                                    Armament: 1 x 12pdr
                                    Admty No: 3068
                                    Port Reg: GY. 1101
1917: Launched. Built at Goole by Goole SB. Owned by Lindsay SFC of Grimsby.
Requisitioned in December and converted to a M/S. 1920: Returned to owners.

PEGGY NUTTEN   1916/19 1940/44 Displacement: 193TG 75TN
                                    Engines: 67HP
                                    Armament: 1 x 6pdrAA
                                    Admty No: 1171
                                    Port Reg: A. 170
                                    P. No: WWII: 4. 450
1907: Launched. Built at Aberdeen. Owned by P. Belman of Southport. 1915:
Requisitioned in April and converted to a M/S. 1919: Returned to owners. 1938: Owned
by Geo. Wood AO of Aberdeen. 1940: Requisitioned in February and converted to a
BDV. 1944: Converted to a Fuel Carrier in March. Returned to owners in November.

PEKEN	1914/19 1940/45	Displacement: 228TG 119TN
		Engines: 66HP
		Armament: 1 x 6pdr
		Admty No: 24
		Port Reg: GY. 354
		P. No: WWII: FY. 1821

1908: Launched. Built at Selby by Cochrane. Owned by HL Taylor AO of Grimsby. 1914: Requisitioned in August and converted to a M/S. 1919: Returned to owners. Acquired by Diamond SFC of Grimsby. 1940: Requisitioned in July and converted to a M/S. 1945: Returned to owners in August. Notes: aka PEKIN in WWI.

| PEKIN | 1914/19 | See under PEKEN above |

| PEKIN | 1919/19 | See under JOHN DUNKIN |
| | | (Vol 1 p.178) |

| PEKIN | 1919/20 | See under FESTING GRINDALL |
| | | (Vol 1 p.53) |

PELAGOS	1916/19	Displacement: 231TG 89TN
		Engines: 71HP
		Armament: 1 x 6pdrAA; 1 x 7.5-inch
		Bomb Thrower (A/S Howitzer)
		Admty No: 3295
		Port Reg: A. 623

1916: Launched. Built at Aberdeen. Requisitioned. 1919: Returned to owners. 1924: Owned by W. Carnie of Edinburgh. PR: GN. 93.

| PELAGOS | 1940/45 | See under CHARLES DONNELLY |
| | | (Vol 1 p.49) |

PELICAN	1914/19 1943/44	Displacement: 248TG 94TN
		Engines: 71HP
		Armament: 1 x 12pdr
		Admty No: 527
		Port Reg: WWI: PH. 98; WII: FD. 7
		P. No: WWII: Y7. 16

1908: Launched. Built at Aberdeen. Owned by the Red Rose STL of Fleetwood. 1914: Requisitioned in November and converted to a M/S. 1919: Returned to owners. Acquired by Cevic SF Co. of Fleetwood and renamed *Cevic*. 1943: Requisitioned in January as CEVIC and converted to an Esso. Deployed to the Med. 1944: Returned to the UK in March and converted to a Water Carrier. TPI Operation Neptune, the D-Day Landings in June. Returned to owners in August.

PELICAN II   1916/19 1944/44 Displacement: 205TG 78TN
             Engines: 60HP
             Armament: 1 x 12pdr
             Admty No: 3265
             Port Reg: GY. 91
             P. No: WWII: 4. 427
1905: Launched. Built at Selby by Cochrane. Owned by Sleights SF Co. of Grimsby.
1916: Requisitioned in July and converted to a M/S. Based at Portland. ICW Tr.
MARCONI and Yt. LORNA in the Channel on 14th September, sighted a German U-Boat
about to attack a Mercantile and drove it off. 1920: Returned to owners. 1944:
Requisitioned in April and converted to an Esso. Returned to owners in November.

PELTON   1939/40   Displacement: 357TG 141TN
             Engines: 96HP
             Port Reg: H. 288
1925: Launched. Built at Beverley by CWG. Owned by F & T Ross of Hull. 1939:
Requisitioned in August and converted to a M/S. 1940: TPI Operations
Quentin/Quidnunc/Quixote, the cutting of the telephone cables between Germany and
UK, in the North Sea. LOST. Torpedoed by E-Boat off Yarmouth on 24th December.

PEMBROKE   1922/39   See under DANIEL FEARALL
             (Vol 1 p.133)

PEMBROKE CASTLE 1917/19   Displacement: 153TG 58TN
             Engines: 56HP
             Port Reg: A. 531
1898: Launched. Built at North Shields. Owned by Port St. Mary Fishing & Curing Co.
of London. 1917: Requisitioned into the Fishery Reserve. 1919: Returned to owners.

PENELOPE   ?   Displacement: 149TG
Reported as Requisitioned in WWI. NFI

PENGUIN   1914/19   Displacement: 190TG 74TN
             Engines: 63HP
             Armament: 1 x 6pdr
             Port Reg: PH. 178
1902: Launched. Built at Aberdeen. Owned by H. Ford of Birmingham. 1914:
Requisitioned in November and converted to as M/S. 1919: Returned to owners.
Acquired by Hewitt Fishing Co. of London. Port Reg: LO. 97.

PENGUIN   1915/19   Displacement: 151TG 65TN
             Engines: 45HP = 10K
             Port Reg: SH. 223
1895: Launched. Built at Hull by CWG. Owned by Pickering & Haldane STC of Hull. 1915:

Requisitioned and employed on Harbour Service. 1916: Acquired by J. Johnson of Scarborough. 1919: Returned to owner. Acquired by HW. Barker of Scarborough. PR: SH. 223. 1926: Sold to Spanish owners and renamed *Punta Acazar*. 1969: BU in Spain.

PENGUIN II   1917/19   Displacement: 123TG
                                                Port Reg: LT.
1891: Launched. 1917: Requisitioned into the Fishery Reserve. 1919: Returned to owners.

PENNARD CASTLE   1914/19   Displacement: 259TG   100TN
                                                Engines: 57HP
                                                Armament: 1 x 6pdr
                                                Admty No: 138
                                                Port Reg: SA. 38
1907: Launched. Built at Maryport. Owned by Consolidated Fisheries of Grimsby. 1914: Requisitioned in September and converted to a M/S. 1919: Returned to owners.

PENRICE CASTLE   1915/19   Displacement: 255TG   100TN
                                                Engines: 85HP
                                                Armament: 1 x 3pdr
                                                Admty No: 1799
                                                Port Reg: SA. 7
1913: Launched. Built at Middlesborough by Smith's Dock. Owned by Consolidated Fisheries of Grimsby. 1915: Requisitioned in June. 1919: Returned to owners.

PENTLAND FIRTH   1939/42   Displacement: 458TG   189TN
                                                Engines: 154HP = 12.3K
                                                Armament: 1 x 4-inch
                                                Port Reg: H. 123
                                                P. No: FY. 108
1934: Launched. Built at Beverley by CWG. Owned by Firth ST Co. of Hull. 1939: Purchased into the RN in August and converted to A/S. 1942: Loaned to the USN from February. LOST. Sunk in a collision with the US. M/S CHAFFINCH off New York on 19th September.

PERDRANT   1940/45   Displacement: 311TG
                                                Port Reg: French
                                                P. No: FY.1714
1919: Launched. French fishing vessel. 1940: French M/S NOTRE DAME d' ESPER-ANCE seized at Plymouth in Operation Grab on 3rd July. Renamed and Commissioned into the RN. 1945: Returned to France.

PERICLES   1917/19   Displacement: 208TG   82TN
                                                Engines: 45HP = 10K
                                                Admty No: Not issued

Port Reg: H. 131

1910: Launched. Built at Beverley by CWG. Owned by Hellyer SFC of Hull. 1917: Requisitioned into the Fishery Reserve. 1919: Returned to owners. 1935: Acquired by AR Butheley of Aberdeen and renamed *Mary Bruce* PR: A. 393. 1953: BU at Gateshead.

PERIDOT	1914/15	Displacement: 214TG
		Admty No: 733
		Port Reg: H. 234

1894: Launched. 1914: Requisitioned in December and converted to an APV. 1915: Returned to owners in January. 1917: Mercantile Loss. Captured by German S/M and blown up 60 miles S x E from Sydero on 10th July.

PERIDOT	1939/40	Ex-*Manchester City*
		Ex-*Barry Castle*
		Displacement: 398TG 151TN
		Engines: 99HP
		Port Reg: GY .53

1933: Launched. Built at Southbank-on-Tees by Smith's Dock as *Barry Castle*. South Wales owners. 1934: Acquired by Consolidated Fisheries of Grimsby and renamed *Manchester City*. 1939: Purchased into the RN in August. Renamed PERIDOT and converted to A/S. 1940: LOST. Mined off Dover on 15th March.

PERIHELION	1914/20 1939/42	Displacement: 215TG 98TN
		Engines: 76HP
		Armament: 1 x 6pdr
		Admty No: 608
		Port Reg: WWI: GY. 197; WWII: GN. 3

1914: Launched. Built at Goole. Owned by Perihelion SFC of Grimsby. Requisitioned in September and converted to a M/S. 1920: Returned to owners. Acquired by D. Dryburgh of Edinburgh AO. Re-registered and renamed *Inverclyde*. 1939: Requisitioned in August as INVERCLYDE and converted to a Water Carrier. 1942: LOST. Foundered in tow off Beachy Head on 16th October.

PERSIAN EMPIRE	1915/19	Displacement: 195TG 76TN
		Engines: 63HP = 10.5K
		Armament: 1 x 6pdr; 1 x 7.5-inch Bomb
		Thrower (A/S Howitzer)
		Admty No: 799
		Port Reg: H. 476

1899: Launched. Built at Hull by CWG. Owned by Cargill STC of Hull. 1914: Requisitioned in December and converted to a M/S. 1919: Returned to owners. 1921: Acquired by Cook & Ireland of Fleetwood. PR: FD. 83. 1948: Acquired by Standard SFC of Grimsby. PR: GY. 49. 1953: BU at Grimsby.

PERSIMMON   1914/15   Displacement: 255TG
                                          Admty No: 302
                                          Port Reg: GY. 126
1911: Launched. 1914: Requisitioned in August and converted to an APV. 1915: Returned to the Fishing Fleet in January. Mercantile Loss. Captured by German S/M 50 miles NE from Buchaness on 5th June and sunk by gunfire.

PETERBOROUGH   1914/19   Displacement: 161TG 63TN
                                          Engines: 45HP
                                          Armament: 1 x 6pdrAA
                                          Admty No: 631
                                          Port Reg: GY. 244
1897: Launched. Built at Govan. 1914: Requisitioned in October and converted to a M/S. 1919: Returned to owners. Acquired by G. Whamond of Hartlepool & J. Storr of Whitby. PR: HL. 41.

PETER HENDRICKS   1939/46   Displacement: 266TG 113TN
                                          Engines: 525HP
                                          Port Reg: A. 315
                                          P. No: FY. 260
1935: Launched. Built at Bremerhaven, Germany. Owned by Aberdeen ST & Fishing Co. of Aberdeen. 1939: Requisitioned in November and converted to A/S. 1941: Escorting a convoy from Chatham to the Clyde when she was in collision with HMS/M UMPIRE which was surfaced with engine trouble. The S/M sank with the loss of all but 4 of her company. 1946: Returned to owners in February.

PETREL   1914/14   Displacement: 151TG 64TN
                                          Engines: 45NHP = 10K
                                          Admty No: 363
                                          Port Reg: SD. 5
1893: Launched. Built at Hull by CWG. Owned by Pickering & Haldane STC of Hull. PR: H. 222. 1912: Acquired by J. Hall of Sunderland. PR: SD. 5. 1914: Requisitioned in August and designated as a M/S. Returned to owners in November. 1915: Acquired by H. Wood of Grimsby. PR: GY. 609. 1917: Mercantile Loss. Captured by a German S/M 120 miles off Aberdeen on 30th March and sunk by gunfire.

PETUNIA   1915/19   Displacement: 151TG 85TN
                                          Engines: 60HP
                                          Armament: 1 x 6pdr AA; 1 x 7.5-inch
                                          Bomb Thrower (A/S Howitzer)
                                          Admty No: 941
                                          Port Reg: GY. 710
1899: Launched. Built at Selby. 1915: Requisitioned in January and converted to a M/S.

Renamed PETUNIA II in December. 1919: Returned to owners. Acquired by North Eastern STC of Grimsby.

PETUNIA II	1915/19	See under PETUNIA above

PETUNIA III   1917/19   Displacement: 209TG 71TN
Engines: 60HP
Port Reg: GY. 710

1899: Launched. Built at Aberdeen. Owned by Southern STC of Waterford. 1917: Requisitioned into the Fishery Reserve. 1919: Returned to owners.

P. FANNON   1915/19   Displacement: 211TG 78TN
Engines: 69HP
Armament: 1 x 6pdr
Admty No: 1816
Port Reg: A. 349

1915: Launched. Built at Aberdeen. Owned by The Aberdeen Pioneer SFC. Requisitioned in July and converted to a M/S. Based at Scapa Flow for convoy escort duties. 1919: Returned to owners.

PHALAROPE   1917/19   Displacement: 124TG
Port Reg: SH. 274

1907: Launched. 1917: Requisitioned into the Fishery Reserve. 1919: Returned to owners.

PHILLIPE   1940/41   See under PETER DOBBIN
(Vol 1 p.184)

PHOEBE   1914/19   Displacement: 278TG 109TN
Engines: 76HP
Armament: 1 x 6pdr AA ;1 x 7.5-inch
Bomb Thrower (A/S Howitzer)
Admty No: 44
Port Reg: H. 881

1907: Launched. Built at Goole. Owned by Sun STC of Hull. 1914: Requisitioned in September and converted to a M/S. 1915: Renamed PHOEBE II in December. 1919: Returned to owners.

PHOEBE II   1914/19   See under PHOEBE above

PHOEBE III   1917/19   Displacement: 278TG 53TN
Engines: 45HP = 9.5K
Armament: 1 x 12pdr; 1 x 7.5-inch
Bomb Thrower (A/S Howitzer)

Port Reg: FD. 121

1906: Launched. Built at Beverley by CWG. Owned by Hellyer SFC of Hull. 1917: Requisitioned into the Fishery Reserve. 1919: Returned to owners and reverted to original name. Acquired by Dobson SFC of Grimsby. PR: GY. 665. 1923: Acquired by Hull SF & Ice Co. PR: H. 901. 1952: BU at Milford Haven.

PHRONTIS   1914/19 1940/46 Displacement: 288TG 114TN
                                          Engines: 90HP
                                          Armament: 1 x 12pdr
                                          Admty No: 520
                                          Port Reg: WWII: FD. 42
                                          P. No: WWII: 4. 141

1911:Launched. Built at Selby by Cochrane. Owned by The Mount SF Co. of Fleetwood. 1914: Requisitioned in September and converted to a M/S. 1919: Returned to owners. 1940: Requisitioned in May and converted to A/S. 1942: Manned with a Belgian crew. 1943: Converted to a M/S and RN manned. 1946: Returned to owners in January.

PHYLLIS   1942/44   RNZN
                                          Displacement: 158TG

1912: Launched. 1942: Purchased in October and converted to a D/L. Commissioned into the RNZN. 1944: Paid Off in February and Laid Up. Placed on the Sale List.

PHYLLIS BELMAN   1915/19   Displacement: 211TG 78TN
                                          Engines: 69HP
                                          Armament: 1 x 6pdrAA
                                          Admty No: 1545
                                          Port Reg: A. 298

1915:Launched. Built at Aberdeen. Owned by P. Belman of Liverpool. Requisitioned in June and converted to a M/S. 1919: Returned to owners.

PHYLLISIA   1939/46   See under SAMUEL JAMESON
                                          (Vol 1 p.147)

PICT   1939/46   Displacement: 462TG 166TN
                                          Engines: 99HP
                                          Armament: 1 x 4-inch
                                          Port Reg: H. 298
                                          P. No: FY. 132

1936: Launched. Built at Southbank-on-Tees by Smith's Dock. Owned by Hull Northern Fishing Co. 1939: Purchased into the RN in August and converted to A/S. 1946: Sold to mercantile and retained the same name. Acquired by Hellyer Bros. of Hull. PR: H. 162.

PICTON CASTLE   1915/17   Displacement: 245TG
                                          Armament: 1 x 3pdr

Admty No: 2672
Port Reg: SA. 107
1911: Launched. 1915: Requisitioned in May and converted to a M/S. 1917: LOST.
Mined off Dartmouth on 19th February.

PICTON CASTLE   1939/45   Displacement: 560T 307TG 116TN
                                        Engines: 91HP
                                        Armament: 1 x 12pdr; 2 x LGs (2x1);
                                        2 x 0.5-inch MGs (1x2); DCs
                                        Port Reg: SA. 82
                                        P. No: FY. 628

1928: Launched. Built at Selby by Cochrane. Owned by Consolidated Fisheries of
Grimsby. 1939: Requisitioned in August and converted to a M/S. Operated on the East
Coast between Shields and the Thames. 1940: TPI Operation Dynamo, the evacuation
of Dunkirk in May/June. Returned to East Coast operations. 1945: TPI mine-clearing
operations off the Norwegian coast. Returned to owners in December. 1955: Sold to
Norwegian owners and renamed Tetys. 1960: Renamed *Utstraum*. 1970: Renamed
Steinfrost. Converted to a diesel driven cargo vessel. Subsequently renamed *Dolmar*.
1994: Acquired by the Windward Isles Sailing Ship Co. of America for conversion to a
sailing vessel. 1995: TIH at Lunengurg, NS for conversion to a three-masted sailing
barque and reverted to her original name *Picton Castle*. 1997: Sailed from Lunenburg
in December on a round-the-world cruise under sail. 1999: Arrived at Lunenburg having
sailed 37,000 miles on her cruise. Still in service (2004).

PICTON CASTLE   **(Tom Gamble)**

PICTON CASTLE following conversion to fully rigged barque. (Tom Gamble)

| PIERRE-ANDRE | 1940/46 | See under ROBERT CAHILL (Vol 1 p.146) |

PIERRE-ANDRE   1940/46   See under ROBERT CAHILL
(Vol 1 p.146)

PIERRE-GUSTAV   1940/46   Displacement: 218TG
Fuel: Diesel
Port Reg: French
P. No: FY. 1805

1923: Launched. French fishing vessel. 1940: French M/S seized at Southampton in Operation Grab on 3rd July. Commissioned into the RN as a M/S in November. Fitted with an Acoustic Hammer. Based at Portland for sweeping in the Channel. 1946: Returned to France in March.

PIGEON   1914/19   Displacement: 166TG 44TN
Engines: 41HP
Armament: 1 x 6pdrAA
Port Reg: H. 155

1897: Launched. Built at North Shields. Owned by Kelsall Bros. & Beeching of Hull. 1914: Requisitioned in November and converted to a M/S. 1915: Renamed PIGEON II in December. 1919: Returned to owners.

PIGEON II   1915/19   See under PIGEON above

PINEWOLD   1917/19   Displacement: 141TG 55TN
Engines: 40HP
Port Reg: GY. 177

1898: Launched. Built at Beverley. Owned by Northwold SFC of Grimsby. 1917: Requisitioned into the Fishery Reserve. 1919: Returned to owners.

PINTAIL   1914/19   Displacement: 199TG 73TN
Engines: 55HP
Armament: 1 x 12pdr; 1 x 6pdr
Admty No: 382
Port Reg: H. 982

1908: Launched. Built at Goole by Goole SB. Owned by Kelsall Bros. & Beeching of Hull. 1914: Requisitioned in October and converted to a M/S. 1919: Returned to owners.

PIONEER   WWI   Displacement: 121TG

1901: Launched. Reported as Requisitioned in WWI. NFI.

PITFOUR   1917/19   Displacement: 227TG 98TN
Engines: 82HP
Armament: 1 x 6pdrAA; 24 mines (as M/L); 1 x 6pdr AA; 1 x 7.5-in Bomb

Thrower (A/S Howitzer) (M/S)
Admty No: 2976
Port Reg: PD. 241

1916: Launched. Built at Leith. Owned by Peterhead TCL. Requisitioned in October and converted to a M/L. 1917: Converted to a M/S and rearmed. 1919: Returned to owners.

PITSTRUAN   1914/17   Displacement: 206TG
                                          Armament: 1 x 3pdr
                                          Admty No: 89
                                          Port Reg: A. 585

1913: Launched. 1914: Requisitioned in August and converted to a M/S. 1917: LOST. Mined off Noss Head Lighthouse on 13th April.

PITSTRUAN   1940/44   Displacement: 211TG 91TN
                                          Engines: 63HP
                                          Port Reg: A. 86
                                          P. No: FY. 1791

1930: Launched. Built at Aberdeen. Owned by Gt. Western Fishing Co. of Aberdeen. 1940: Requisitioned in May and converted to a M/S. 1944: Converted to an Esso. Returned to owners in November.

PLETHOS   1914/18   Displacement: 210TG
                                          Armament: 1 x 12pdr; 1 x 6pdr
                                          Admty No: 468
                                          Port Reg: A. 545

1913: Requisitioned in September and converted to a M/S. 1918: LOST. Mined off Montrose on 23rd April.

PLYM   1917/19   Displacement: 193TG 75TN
                                          Engines: 45HP
                                          Armament: 1 x 6pdrAA
                                          Admty No: 1273
                                          Port Reg: H. 254

1904: Launched. Built at Govan. Owned by Quebec SFC of Scarborough. 1917: Requisitioned in March and converted to a M/S. 1919: Returned to owners.

POCHARD   1917/18   Displacement: 146TG
                                          Port Reg: A. 250

1889: Launched. 1917: Requisitioned into the Fishery Reserve. 1918: LOST. Mined in the North Sea on 28th June. No loss of life.

POINTER   1915/19 1940/45 Displacement: 198TG 77TN
                                          Engines: 67HP
                                          Armament: 1 x 6pdrAA; 1 x 7.5-inch

Bomb Thrower (A/S Howitzer)
Admty No: 1196
Port Reg: WWI: A. 57; WWII: A. 943
P. No: WWII: FY. 1896

1906: Launched. Built at Aberdeen. Owned by WH. Burn of St. Andrews. 1915: Requisitioned in May and converted to a M/S. 1919: Returned to owners. Acquired by P & J Johnston Ltd. & J. Taylor of Aberdeen. Re-registered. 1940: Requisitioned in January and converted to a M/S. 1945: Returned to owners in December.

POINTZ CASTLE   1915/19 1939/45 Displacement: 283TG 112TN
                                Engines: 85HP
                                Armament: 1 x 12pdr
                                Admty No: 2666
                                Port Reg: SA. 5
                                P. No: WWII: FY. 630

1914: Launched. Built at Middlesborough by Smith's Dock. Owned by Consolidated Fisheries of Grimsby. 1915: Requisitioned in May and fitted with Listening Hydrophones. 1919: Returned to owners. 1939: Requisitioned in August and converted to a M/S. 1945: Returned to owners in April.

POLAR PRINCE   1915/19   Displacement: 194TG 86TN
                                Engines: 80HP
                                Admty No: 95
                                Port Reg: SN. 171

1915: Launched. Built at Wilmington Quay. Owned by R. Irvin & Sons of N. Shields. Requisitioned in September and converted to a M/S. 1919: Returned to owners.

POLLY JOHNSON   1939/40   See under JOHN AIKENHEAD
                                (Vol 1 p.59)

POLO NORTE   1941/46   Displacement: 344TG
                                Armament: 1 x 12pdr
                                Port Reg: Portuguese
                                P. No: FY. 1922

1917: Launched. Portuguese Fishing vessel. 1941: Purchased into the RN and converted to a M/S. 1942: Renamed MOONSHINE. 1946: Sold to mercantile in January.

POMONA   1914/19   Displacement: 161TG 65TN
                                Engines: 45HP
                                Armament: 1 x 12pdr
                                Admty No: 401
                                Port Reg: H. 462

1899: Launched. Built at Beverley. Owned by Hull SF & Ice Co. 1914: Requisitioned in

October. 1918: Returned to owners in December. 1938: Owned by WH East of Milford Haven. Port Reg: M. 212.

POONAH	1914/15	Displacement: 171TG 57TN
		Engines: 45HP = 10K
		Admty No: 530
		Port Reg: H. 737

1903: Launched. Built at Beverley by CWG. Owned by Hull SF & Ice Co. of Hull. 1914: Requisitioned in November and converted to a M/S. 1915: Deployed to the Med. for the Dardenelles Campaign. LOST. Sank after a collision in Suva Bay, Turkey.

| PORTADOWN | 1942/43 | See under PROCTOR (Vol 1 p.160) |

| PORTAFERRY | 1942/43 | See under PROBE (Vol 1 p.159) |

| PORTHLEVEN | 1942/43 | See under PRODIGAL (Vol 1 p.160) |

| PORTIA | 1941/46 | See under UNITIA |

PORTIA III	1917/19	Ex-*Portia*
		Displacement: 178TG 76TN
		Engines: 55NHP = 10K
		Port Reg: GY. 828

1895: Launched. Built at Hull by CWG. Owned by Hellyer of Hull. PR: H. 280. 1915: Acquired by South Western FCL of Grimsby. 1917: Requisitioned into the Fishery Reserve and renamed PORTIA III. 1919: Returned to owners and reverted to original name. 1931: BU by Ward at Preston.

| PORTISHAM | 1942/43 | See under PROCTOR (Vol 1 p.160) |

PORT JACKSON	1917/19	Displacement: 197TG 76TN
		Engines: 52HP
		Port Reg: FD. 6

1904: Launched. Built at Aberdeen. Owned by A. Black of Grimsby. 1917: Requisitioned into the Fishery Reserve. 1919: Returned to owners.

| PORT JACKSON | 1942/43 | See under PRODUCT (Vol 1 p.160) |

| PORTMADOC | 1942/43 | See under PROFESSOR (Vol 1 p.160) |

| PORT NATAL | 1942/43 | See under PROMISE (Vol 1 p.160) |

| PORTOBELLO | 1942/43 | See under PROPHET (Vol 1 p.160) |

PORTPATRICK   1942/43   See under PROTEST (Vol 1 p.159)

PORTREATH   1942/43   See under PROWESS (Vol 1 p.159)

PORT ROYAL   1942/43   See under PROOF (Vol 1 p.159)

PORTRUSH   1942/43   See under PROPERTY (Vol 1 p.159)

PORTSMOUTH   1915/19   Displacement: 178TG 68TN
                                     Engines: 51HP
                                     Armament: 1 x 12pdr
                                     Admty No: 800
                                     Port Reg: M. 61
1903: Launched. Built at North Shields. Owned by O. Curphy AO of Milford Haven.
1915: Requisitioned in January and converted to a M/S. 1919: Returned to owners.

PORT STANLEY   1942/43   See under PRONG (Vol 1 p.159)

POSTBOY   1940/46   Ex-*Le Royal*
                                   Displacement: 316TG
                                   P. No: FY. 1750
1941: Launched. 1940: Requisitioned in October and converted to a M/S. 1946:
Returned to owners in July.

POWIS CASTLE   1916/19 1940/45 Displacement: 175TG 107TN
                                      Engines: 87HP
                                      Armament: 1 x 6pdr
                                      Admty No: 3318
                                      Port Reg: SA. 68
                                      P. No: WWII: FY. 874
1916: Launched. Built at Southbank-on-Tees by Smith's Dock. Owned by Consolidated
Fisheries of Grimsby. Requisitioned in December and converted to a M/S. 1919:
Returned to owners. 1940: Requisitioned in February and converted to a M/S. 1943:
Converted to an A/S Training Ship. 1945: Employed on Target-towing. Returned to
owners in December.

PREFECT   1916/19 1940/45 Displacement: 302TG 159TN
                                 Engines: 84HP
                                 Armament: WWI: 1 x 12pdr; 1 x 7.5-in
                                 Bomb Thrower (A/S Howitzer).
                                 WWII: 1 x 4-inch
                                 Admty No: 1984
                                 P. No: WWII: 4. 106 (APV)
                                 FY. 1561 (M/S)

1916: Launched. Built at Selby by Cochrane. Owned by the Earl SFC of Grimsby. Requisitioned in March and converted to a M/S. 1919: Returned to owners. 1940: Requisitioned in May as NORLAND and converted to an APV. 1943: Converted to a M/S. Joined the 22nd M/S Group based at Grimsby. 1945: Returned to owners in October.

PREMIER	1915/19	Displacement: 253TG 98TN
		Engines: 50HP
		Armament: 1 x 6pdr AA
		Admty No: 514 & 848
		Port Reg: GY. 385

1908: Launched. Built at Selby by Cochrane. Owned by Anchor SFC of Grimsby. 1914: Requisitioned in September and converted to a M/S. 1919: Returned to owners.

PRESIDENCY	1915/19	See under PRESIDENT

PRESIDENT	1914/19	Displacement: 257TG 109TN
		Engines: 75HP
		Armament: 1 x 12pdr
		Admty No: 72
		Port Reg: GY. 262

1907: Launched. Built at Selby by Cochrane. Owned by J. Methven of Grimsby. 1914: Requisitioned in December. 1915: Renamed PRESIDENCY in February. 1919: Returned to owners.

PRESIDENT BRIAND	1940/41	Displacement: 227TG
		Port Reg: French

1932: Launched. French fishing vessel. 1940: French M/S seized at Southampton in Operation Grab on 3rd July. Commissioned into the RN as a M/S in September. 1941: Transferred to the MWT.

PRESIDENT STEVENS	1917/19	Displacement: 212TG
		Port Reg: O. 85

1905: Launched. Belgian fishing vessel. 1917: Requisitioned into the Fishery Reserve with the permission of her Belgian owners. 1919: Returned to owners.

PRESTON NORTH END	1939/45	Football Group.
		Details: See under Groups
		Displacement: 419TG 159TN
		Engines: 99HP
		Armament: 1 x 12pdr
		Port Reg: GY. 82
		P. No: FY. 230

1934: Launched. Built at Southbank-on-Tees by Smith's Dock. Owned by Consolidated

Fisheries of Grimsby. 1939: Requisitioned in September and converted to A/S. 1945: Returned to owners in November.

PRETORIA   1915/20   Displacement: 180TG 70TN
                                        Engines: 45HP = 10K
                                        Armament: 1 x 6pdr
                                        Admty No: 368
                                        Port Reg: H. 701
1902: Launched. Built at Beverley by CWG. Owned by Hull SF & Ice Co. 1914: Requisitioned in October and converted to a M/S. 1920: Returned to owners. 1924: Mercantile Loss. Sank in a collision with the trawler *Ellesmere* in the North Sea on 18th January. No loss of life.

PRETORIA   1915/15   Displacement: 283TG
                                        Admty No: 32
                                        Port Reg: GY. 180
1906: Launched. 1915: Requisitioned in March and designated as a M/S. Renamed PRETORIA II in May. Returned to owners in September. 1917: Mercantile Loss. Captured by a German S/M 60 miles S x E from Sydero on 10th July and sunk by gunfire.

PRETORIA   1917/19   Displacement: 159TG
                                        Port Reg: SN. 245
1900: Launched. 1917: Requisitioned into the Fishery Reserve. 1919: Returned to owners.

PRETORIA II   1915/15   See under PRETORIA above

PRIMROSE   1916/19
1916: Requisitioned and converted to a BDV. 1919: Returned to owners.

PRINCE CHARLES   1917/19   Displacement: 226TG
                                        Port Reg: O. 36
1904: Launched. Belgian Fishing vessel. 1917: Requisitioned into the Fishery Reserve with the permission of her Belgian owners. 1919: Returned to owners.

PRINCE CONSORT   1917/19   Displacement: 155TG 55TN
                                        Engines: 50NHP = 10K
                                        Port Reg: GY. 1036
1890: Launched. Built at Hull by CWG. Iron construction. Owned by Pickering & Haldane SFC of Hull. 1911: Acquired by T. Davidson of Aberdeen. PR: A.358. 1917: Acquired by JR. Mordant of Grimsby. PR: GY. 1036. Requisitioned into the Fishery Reserve. 1919: Returned to owners. 1924: BU.

PRINCE de LEIGE   1940/45   Displacement: 324TG
                                          Port Reg: Belgian
                                          P. No: Z. 172
1926: Launched. 1940: Hired from Belgian owners in September and converted to a
BDV. 1944: Transferred to the FE and joined the BPF. 1945: Returned to the UK and
Paid Off. Returned to Belgium.

PRINCE LEO   1915/19 1940/44   Displacement: 218TG 86TN
                                      Engines: 58HP
                                      Armament: 1 x 6pdrAA
                                      Admty No: 1634
                                      Port Reg: GY. 920
                                      P. No: WWII: FY. 998
1913: Launched. Built at Selby by Cochrane. Owned by Trawlers (White Sea &
Grimsby) of Grimsby. 1915: Requisitioned in May and converted to a M/S. 1919:
Returned to owners. 1939: Requisitioned in November and converted to a M/S. 1940:
Converted to a BDV in June. 1944: Returned to owners in August.

PRINCE PALATINE   1914/19 1940/44   Displacement: 256TG 100TN
                                           Engines: 70HP
                                           Armament: 1 x 12pdr
                                           P. No: WWII: FY.1774
                                           Admty No: 341
                                           Port Reg: H. 95
1914: Launched. Built at Selby by Cochrane. Requisitioned in August and converted to
a M/S. Fitted with Listening Hydrophones. 1919: Returned to owners. Acquired by
J. Kay & M. Isaacs of Grimsby. PR: GY. 1186. 1940: Requisitioned in August as LORD
DARLING and converted to a M/S. 1941: Converted for the Examination Service. 1944:
Returned to owners in November.

PRINCEPS   1916/19   Displacement: 264TG 106TN
                                   Engines: 73HP
                                   Armament: 1 x 6pdr
                                   Admty No: 1504
                                   Port Reg: GY. 636
1911: Launched. Built at Selby Cochrane. Owned by Anchor SFC of Grimsby. 1914:
Requisitioned in August. 1919: Returned to owners.

PRINCE VICTOR   1915/19 1944/44   Displacement: 207TG 94TN
                                         Engines: 65HP
                                         Armament: 1 x 6pdr
                                         Admty No: 1442
                                         Port Reg: GY. 569
1910: Launched. Built at Selby by Cochrane. Owned by Zaree SFC of Grimsby. 1915:

Requisitioned in April and converted to a M/S. 1919: Returned to owners. Acquired by Trs. (White Sea & Grimsby). 1944: Requisitioned in February and converted to an Esso. Returned to owners in November.

PRINCESS ALICE   1915/18   Displacement: 225TG 84TN
                                         Engines: 57HP
                                         Armament: 1 x 6pdr
                                         Admty No: 2655
                                         Port Reg: SN. 15
1914: Launched. Built at Aberdeen. Owned by Dodds SFC of Aberdeen. 1915: Requisitioned in April. Deployed to the Med. 1918: LOST. Sunk in a collision off Alexandria on 6th March.

PRINCESS BEATRICE   1914/14   Displacement: 214TG
                                         Admty No: 287
                                         Port Reg: SN. 202
1912: Launched. 1914: Requisitioned in August and converted to a M/S. LOST. Mined off the Belgian Coast on 5th October.

PRINCESS JULIANA   1914/19   Displacement: 266TG 107TN
                                         Engines: 78HP
                                         Armament: 1 x 6pdr
                                         Admty No: 199
                                         Port Reg: H. 824
1905: Launched. Built at Hull. Owned by Croston SFC of Fleetwood. 1914: Requisitioned in November and converted to a M/S. 1919: Returned to owners.

PRINCESS LOUISE   1914/19   Displacement: 106TG 39TN
                                         Engines: 30HP
                                         Port Reg: GW. 29
1898: Launched. Built at Whiteinch. Owned by A. Paterson of Oban. 1914: Requisitioned and employed on Harbour Service throughout the War. 1919: Returned to owners.

PRINCESS LOUISE   1915/19   Displacement: 289TG 113TN
                                         Engines: 70NHP = 10.5K
                                         Armament: 1 x 6pdr
                                         Admty No: 1176
                                         Port Reg: H. 140
1905: Launched. Built at Beverley by CWG. Owned by Armitage STC of Hull. PR: H. 825. 1913: Stranded and taken out of service. 1914: Re-registered H.140 and returned to service. 1915: Requisitioned in February and converted to a M/S. Renamed PRINCESS LOUISE II in March. 1919: Returned to owners and reverted to original name. 1927: Sold to Belgian owners and renamed *Pastoor Pype*. 1930: Acquired by

Dewsland Trs. of Fleetwood and renamed *Daneland.* PR: FD. 58. 1941: Mercantile Loss. Sunk by German a/c 30 mile N. 1/2 W. of Rathin O'Birne Island on 6th April. All 12 crew rescued.

PRINCESS LOUISE II   1915/19   See under PRINCESS LOUISE above

PRINCESS MARIE JOSE   1915/19 1939/45 Displacement: 274TG 109TN
                                          Engines: 80HP = 10.5K
                                          Armament: 1 x 12pdr; 1 x 7.5-inch
                                          Bomb Thrower (A/S Howitzer)
                                          Admty No: 1770
                                          Port Reg: WWI: H. 242; WWII: H. 220
                                          P.No: WWII: 4. 97

1915: Launched. Built at Beverley by CWG. Owned by Armitage STC of Hull. Requisitioned in May and converted to a M/S. Towing S/M C-27 off Fair Island in the Atlantic on 20th July when the German S/M U-23 surfaced and began to shell the Trawler. C-27 successfully stalked the German and sank her. 1919: Returned to owners. 1920: Acquired by Sun STC of Fleetwood. PR: FD. 12. 1934: Acquired by Robertson & Wood of Aberdeen and renamed *Feughside.* PR: A. 114. 1939: Acquired by Loch FCL of Hull and renamed *Loch Hope* PR: H. 220. Requisitioned in December as LOCH HOPE and converted to an APV. 1945: Acquired by A & M Smith of Hull. Returned to owners in December. 1947: Mercantile Loss. Mined off the E. Coast of Iceland by a mine trawled up in the net. One crew member was killed.

PRINCESS MARIE JOSE   1917/19   Displacement: 222TG
                                          Port Reg: O. 38

1913: Launched. Belgian fishing vessel. 1917: Requisitioned into the Fishery Reserve with the permission of her Belgian owners. 1919: Returned to owners.

PRINCESS MARY   1915/19 1940/45 Displacement: 225TG 84TN
                                            Engines: 57HP
                                          Armament: 1 x 12pdr
                                          Admty No: 1181
                                          Port Reg: WWI: SN. 27; WWII: SN. 11
                                          P. No: WWII: FY. 876

1914: Launched. Built at Aberdeen. Owned by Dodds SFC of Aberdeen. 1915: Requisitioned in March. Fitted with Listening Hydrophones. 1919: Returned to owners. 1940: Requisitioned in February and converted to a M/S. 1945: Returned to owners in September.

PRINCESS MELTON   1914/19   Displacement: 224TG 91TN
                                            Engines: 50HP
                                          Armament: 1 x 6pdr
                                          Admty No: 322

Port Reg: A. 440
1901: Launched. Built at Hull. 1914: Requisitioned in August and converted to a M/S. 1919: Returned to owners. 1920: Acquired by E. Taylor AO of Fleetwood. PR: FD. 326.

PRINCESS OLGA   1916/18   Displacement: 245TG 93TN
                                         Engines: 82HP
                                         Armament: 1 x 6pdrAA
                                         Admty No: 3031
                                         Port Reg: SN. 326
1916: Launched. Built at Selby by Cochrane. Owned by Dodds SFC of Aberdeen. Requisitioned in April and converted to a M/S. 1918: LOST. Mined off Le Havre on 14th June.

PRINCESS ROYAL   1914/19   Displacement: 213TG 79TN
                                         Engines: 56HP
                                         Armament: 1 x 6pdrAA
                                         Admty No: 518
                                         Port Reg: SN. 209
1913: Launched. Built at Aberdeen. Owned by Dodds SF Co. of Aberdeen. 1914: Requisitioned in September and converted to a M/S. 1915: Renamed PRINCESS ROYAL II in February. 1919: Returned to owners.

PRINCESS ROYAL II   1914/19   See under PRINCESS ROYAL above

PRINCESS VICTORIA   1915/15   Displacement: 272TG 84TN
                                         Engines: 75HP = 10.5K
                                         Armament: 1 x 3pdr
                                         Admty No: 1971
                                         Port Reg: H. 766
1903: Launched. Built at Hull by CWG. Owned by Armitage STC of Hull. 1915: Requisitioned in September. LOST. Sunk in a collision off Ushant on 7th November.

PRINCESS VICTORIA   1916/19 1939/45 Displacement: 245TG 93TN
                                         Engines: 82HP
                                         Armament: 1 x 6pdr
                                         Admty No: 3320
                                         Port Reg: WWI: SN. 321
                                         WWII: GY. 166
                                         P. No: WWII: FY. 777
1916: Launched. Built at Selby by Cochrane. 1917: Requisitioned in January and converted to a M/S. 1919: Returned to owners. Acquired by Sir Thomas Robinson & Son of Grimsby and renamed *Marano*. 1939: Requisitioned in November as MARANO and converted to an APV. 1940: Converted to a M/S in June. 1945: Returned to owners in January.

PROCYON   1917/19   Ex-*Strathmartin*
                                          Displacement: 195TG 76TN
                                          Engines: 64HP
                                          Armament: 1 x 3pdr
                                          Port Reg: A. 899
1903: Launched. Built at Aberdeen. 1915: Requisitioned in June and converted to a
BDV. 1919: Returned to owners. Acquired by T. Davidson AO of Aberdeen.

PROTECTOR   1915/18   Displacement: 161TG
1904: Launched. 1915: Requisitioned. 1918: Returned to owners.

PUFFIN   1914/19   Displacement: 199TG 73TN
                                          Engines: 55HP
                                          Armament: 1 x 12pdr
                                          Admty No: 659
                                          Port Reg: H. 974
1907: Launched. Built at Goole by Goole SB. Owned by Kelsall Bros. & Beeching of Hull.
1914: Requisitioned in October and converted to a M/S. 1919: Returned to owners.

PUNNET   1939/46   Ex-*Cape Matapan*
                                          Displacement: 556T 320TG
                                          Measurements: 120ft x 24ft
                                          Engines: 96HP
                                          Armament: 1 x 12pdr
                                          Port Reg: H. 239
                                          P. No: Z. 04
1925: Launched. Built at Selby by Cochrane. Owned by Hudson SFC of Hull. 1939:
Purchased into the RN in April, renamed and converted to a BDV. 1946: Sold to
mercantile in January. Acquired by Woodburn (Fishing) of Aberdeen and reverted to
Cape Matapan PR: A. 80.

PYROPE   1939/40   Displacement: 295TG 135TN
                                          Engines: 89HP = 11.3K
                                          Armament: 1 x 12pdr
                                          Port Reg: H. 424
1932: Launched. Built at Beverley by CWG. Owned by Kingston STC of Hull. 1939:
Requisitioned in August and converted to a M/S. Joined 2nd M/S Group based at
Sheerness. 1940: LOST. Sunk by enemy a/c in the Thames Estuary on 12th August

QUAIL   1914/15   Displacement: 162TG
                                          Armament: 2 x 3pdr
                                          Admty No: 645
                                          Port Reg: H. 236
1897: Launched. Owned by Baskcombe of Grimsby. 1914: Requisitioned in November

and converted to a M/S. 1915: Renamed QUAIL III in February. LOST. Sunk in a collision off Portland on 23rd June.

QUAIL II   1917/19   Displacement: 265TG 108TN
                                         Engines: 70NHP = 11K
                                         Port Reg: GY. 219
1906: Launched. Built at Beverley by CWG. Owned by T. Baskcomb of Grimsby. 1917: Requisitioned into the Fishery Reserve. 1919: Returned to owners. 1933: Acquired by Amalgamated SFC of Grimsby. 1935: BU in Holland.

QUAIL III   1914/15   See under QUAIL above.

QUANNET   1939/46   Ex-*Dairycoates*
                                         Displacement: 350TG 141TN
                                         Engines: 95HP
                                       Port Reg: H. 270
                                       P. No: Z .44
1926: Launched. Built at Selby by Cochrane. Owned by The City SF Co. of Hull. 1939: Purchased into the RN in May, renamed and converted to a BDV. 1946: Sold to mercantile in January and reverted to *Dairycoates*. Acquired by Northern Fishing Co. of Aberdeen. PR: A. 88.

QUASSIA   1917/19   Displacement: 207TG 98TN
                                           Engines: 58HP
                                         Port Reg: GY. 1141
1899: Launched. Built at Grimsby. Iron construction. Owned by TW. Baskcombe of Grimsby. 1917: Requisitioned into the Fishery Reserve. 1919: Returned to owners. 1938: Owned by Charles Dobson of Grimsby.

QUEEN   1914/20   Displacement: 161TG 62TN
                                           Engines: 50HP = 9.5K
                                         Armament: 1 x 6pdr
                                         Admty No: 691
                                         Port Reg: GY.1197
1900: Launched. Built at Hull by CWG. Iron construction. Owned by Queen SF Co. of Grimsby. 1914: Requisitioned in November and converted to a M/S. 1915: Renamed QUEEN II on February. 1917: Renamed QUEST in June. 1920: Returned to owners and reverted to original name. 1951: BU at Gateshead.

QUEEN II   1914/19   See under QUEEN above

QUEEN ALEXANDRA   1917/19 1940/40 Displacement: 231TG 93TN
                                           Engines: 63HP = 10.5K
                                         Port Reg: H. 530

1901: Launched. Built at Hull by CWG. Iron construction. Owned by Armitage STC of Hull. 1917: Requisitioned into the Fishery Reserve. 1919: Returned to owners. 1927: Acquired by Mason Trs. of Fleetwood. 1940: Requisitioned in September and designated as a M/S. Returned to owners in October. 1952: BU at Barrow by Ward.

QUERCIA	1915/19 1942/46	Displacement: 288TG 144TN
		Engines: 89HP = 10.5K
		Armament: 1 x 12pdr
		Admty No: 446
		Port Reg: GY. 680
		P. No: WWII: Y7. 43 (Esso)
		4. 336 (Water Carrier).

1912: Launched. Built at Beverley by CWG. Owned by Great Grimsby & East Coast SFC of Grimsby. 1914: Requisitioned in December and converted to a M/S. Employed as an Escort. 1919: Returned to owners. 1941: Acquired by J. Bennet of Grimsby. 1942: Requisitioned in August and converted to an Esso. 1942: Converted to a Water Carrier in March. Transferred to the MF. 1943: Part of the supply group known colloquially as "Walt Disney's Navy" ferrying supplies to the invasion forces throughout the Med. 1945: Returned to owners in December. 1950: BU at Hessle.

QUEST   1917/19   See under QUEEN

QUICKLY	1915/18	Displacement: 242TG 94TN
		Engines: 70HP
		Armament: 2 x 12pdrs; 1 x 6pdrAA
		Admty No: 675
		Port Reg: H. 99

1897: Launched. Built at Howden-on-Tees. Owned by Kelsall Bros. & Beeching of Hull. 1914: Requisitioned in October and converted to a M/S. 1915: Converted to a 'Q' Ship in July. 1918: Returned to owners in November. Notes: Operated as a 'Q' Ship under the names of *Carolina*, *Master*, Q.32, *Sinton* and *Swift*.

QUIXOTIC	1917/19	Displacement: 197TG
		Port Reg: GY. 982

1898: Launched. 1917: Requisitioned into the Fishery Reserve. 1919: Returned to owners.

CHAPTER 17 - RADNOR CASTLE to RUTLANDSHIRE

RADNOR CASTLE   1939/47   See under WILLIAM CHASEMAN
(Vol 1 p.86)

RAETIA   1915/19 1939/46 Displacement: 295TG 121TN
Engines: 89HP = 10.5K
Armament: 1 x 12pdr
WWII: 2 x MG (2x1) (APV)
Admty No: 1232
Port Reg: GY. 707
P. No: WWII: 4. 142 (APV)
Y7. .26 (Esso)

1912: Launched. Built at Beverley by CWG. Owned by Gt. Grimsby & E. Coast SFC of Grimsby. 1915: Requisitioned in March and converted to a M/S. 1919: Returned to owners. 1939: Requisitioned in August and converted to an APV. 1942: Acquired by Boston DS & Ice Co. of Grimsby. 1944: Converted to an Esso. 1946: Returned to owners in February. Sold to BU.

RAGLAN CASTLE   1915/19   Displacement: 274TG 108TN
Engines: 87HP
Armament: 1 x 12pdr
Admty No: 1957
Port Reg: SA. 30

1915: Launched. Built at Middlesborough by Smith's Dock. Owned by Consolidated Fisheries of Grimsby. Requisitioned in November and converted to a M/S. Employed on N/L experiments. 1919: Returned to owners.

RAGLAN CASTLE   1939/47   See under GEORGE GREEVES
(Vol 1 p.54)

RAINBOW   1915/19 1940/46 Displacement: 176TG 68TN
Engines: 67HP
Armament: 1 x 3pdr
Admty No: 1547
Port Reg: A. 69

1906: Launched. Built at Aberdeen. 1915: Requisitioned in April. 1919: Returned to owners. Acquired by T. Davidson and I. Wood of Aberdeen. 1940: Purchased into the RN in January as DOLORES and converted to a D/L. 1946: Sold.

RAINDROP   1914/19   Displacement: 167TG 65TN
Engines: 67HP
Armament: 1 x 6pdr

Admty No: 117
Port Reg: A. 434
1912: Launched. Built at Aberdeen. Owned by T. Davidson AO of Aberdeen. 1914: Requisitioned in September and converted to a M/S. 1919: Returned to owners.

RAJAH   1914/18   Displacement: 172TG 70TN
                                      Engines: 50HP
                                      Armament: 1 x 6pdrAA
                                      Admty No: 694
                                      Port Reg: GY. 3
1899: Launched. Built at Beverley. Iron Construction. Owned by Sleights SF of Grimsby. 1914: Requisitioned in November and converted to a M/S. 1918: Returned to owners in September.

RALCO   1914/1   1939/40 R-o Group
                                      Displacement: 228TG 108TN
                                      Engines: 70HP
                                      Armament: 1 x 6pdrAA
                                      Admty No: 672
                                      Port Reg: GY. 663
1911: Launched. Built at Beverley by CWG. Owned by Sleight of Grimsby. 1914: Requisitioned in November and converted to a M/S. 1918: Returned to owners in December. 1939: Requisitioned in November and designated as an APV. 1940: Returned to owners on 22nd January. 1955: BU in Belgium.

RAMBLER   1915/20   Displacement: 162TG 65TN
                                      Engines: 50HP = 10K
                                      Armament: 1 x 6pdrAA
                                      Port Reg: LL. 10
1898: Launched. Built at Hull by CWG. Owned by J. Duncan & Sons of Liverpool. 1915: Requisitioned in November and converted to a BDV. 1919: Acquired by A. Walker of Aberdeen. PR: A. 150. 1920: Returned to owners. 1929: Acquired by Walker STFC of Aberdeen. 1937: BU.

RANEE   1917/19   Displacement: 194TG 78TN
                                      Engines: 52HP
                                      Port Reg: GY. 1157
1900: Launched. Built at Hull. Owned by Bowerings SFC of Grimsby. 1917: Requisitioned into the Fishery Reserve. 1919: Returned to owners.

RATAPIKO   1914/19 1940/45 Displacement: 247TG 90TN
                                      Engines: 79HP
                                      Armament: 1 x 12pdr
                                      Port Reg: WWI: A. 446; WWII: LH. 86

1912: Launched. Built at Aberdeen. Owned by JG Smith of Fleetwood. 1914: Requisitioned in August and converted to a M/S. 1919: Returned to owners in December. 1938: Owned by TH Scales & Son of Newhaven, Edinburgh. 1940: Requisitioned in July and converted to a M/S. 1945: Returned to owners in December.

RATTLER 1917/19 Displacement: 149TG 55TN
Engines: 45HP
Port Reg: FD. 199

1891: Launched. Built at Govan. Iron Construction. Owned by J. Marr & Son of Fleetwood. 1917: Requisitioned into the Fishery Reserve. 1919: Returned to owners.

RATTRAY 1914/15 1917/19 Displacement: 182TG 71TN
Engines: 59HP
Admty No: 357
Port Reg: WWI: GY. 720; WWII: A. 872

1900: Launched. Built at Aberdeen. 1914: Requisitioned in August and converted to a M/S. 1915: Returned to the Fishing Fleet in August. 1917: Requisitioned into the Fishery Reserve. 1919: Returned to owners. Acquired by L. Bloom AO of Grimsby.

RAVEN 1914/19 Displacement: 172TG 65TN
Engines: 51HP
Armament: 1 x 12pdr
Admty No: 407
Port Reg: H. 858

1906: Launched. Built at Goole by Goole SB. Owned by Kelsall Bros. & Beeching of Hull. 1914: Requisitioned in October and converted to a M/S. 1915: Renamed RAVEN II in February. Renamed RAVEN III in August. 1919: Returned to owners.

RAVEN II 1915/19 See under RAVEN above

RAVEN III 1915/19 See under RAVEN above

RAYMOND 1917/19 Displacement: 221TG
Port Reg: O. 130

1910: Launched. Belgian fishing vessel. 1917: Requisitioned into the Fishery Reserve with the permission of her Belgian owners. 1919: Returned to owners.

RAYMOND 1940/45 Displacement: 131TG
Port Reg: Belgian
P. No: 4. 99

1930: Launched. Belgian fishing vessel. 1940: Hired from Belgian owners in August and converted to a BDV. 1942: Employed on Target-towing from November. 1945: Returned to Belgium in November.

RAYMONT   1916/19 1939/46 Displacement: 226TG 109TN
                Engines: 74HP = 9.5K
                Armament: 1 x 6pdr
                Admty No: 2967
                Port Reg: WWI: GY. 895; WII: GY. 304
                P. No: WWII: FY. 785

1916: Launched. Built at Beverley by CWG. Owned by South Western SFC of Grimsby. Requisitioned in September and converted to a M/S. 1918: Acquired by Great Northern SFC of Hull. PR: H. 599. 1919: Returned to owners. 1926: Acquired by Trawlers (White Sea & Grimsby). 1939: Requisitioned in November and converted to an APV. Based at Grimsby. 1940: Converted to a M/S in August. 1942: Acquired by Trawlers, Grimsby Ltd. 1944: Converted to a Store Carrier in August. 1946: Returned to owners in March and Laid Up. 1949: BU at Gateshead.

RAYON d' OR   1939/45   RCN
                Displacement: 342TG 190TN
                Engines: 68HP = 10.5K
                Port Reg: Canadian

1912: Launched. Built at Beverley by CWG. Owned by South West SFC of Grimsby. PR: GY. 719. 1914: Acquired by Olsesen & Jenson 0f Grimsby. 1916: Acquired by Golden Ray FC of Halifax, Nova Scotia. 1939: Requisitioned and converted to a M/S. Commissioned into the RCN. 1945: Returned to owners. Acquired by E. Pawlite of Halifax. 1954: BU in Canada.

REBOUNDO   1939/45   See under WILLIAM BURTE
                (Vol 1 p.85)

RECEPTO   1914/17   R-o Group
                Displacement: 245TG 107TN
                Engines: 80NHP = 10.5K
                Admty No: 47
                Port Reg: GY. 245

1914: Launched. Built at Beverley by CWG. Owned by Sleights of Grimsby. Requisitioned in November and converted to a M/S. 1917: LOST. Mined in Tees Bay on 16th February.

RECOIL   1940/40   Ex-German *Blankenburg*
                Displacement: 344TG

1938: Launched as German fishing vessel *Blankenburg*. Subsequently purchased by British owners and renamed Recoil. 1940: Requisitioned in June and converted to A/S. Based at Portland. LOST. Disappeared with all hands on 28th September whilst on anti-invasion patrol in the Channel. Probably mined. Only one body was recovered, that of a S/Lt found in the sea the following month.

RECONO   1916/20 1939/45 R-o Group
                                       Displacement: 248TG 108TN
                                         Engines: 80HP = 10.5K
                                         Armament: 1 x 6pdrAA
                                         Admty No: 1988
                                         Port Reg: GY. 625
                                         P. No: WWII: FY. 786

1915: Launched. Built at Beverley by CWG. Owned by Sleight of Grimsby. Requisitioned in March and converted to a M/S. Employed as an escort. 1920: Returned to owners. 1933: Acquired by Sleight & Humphrey of Grimsby. 1939: Requisitioned in November and converted to an APV. Based at Grimsby. 1940: Converted to a M/S in June. Joined the 111th M/S Group based at Grimsby. 1943: Joined the 110th M/S Group based at Grimsby. 1945: Converted to a BBV in January. Returned to owners in July. 1962: BU at Ghent, Belgium.

RECORDO   1915/20 1939/40 R-o Group
                                          Displacement: 230TG 105TN
                                         Engines: 63HP = 10K
                                         Armament: 1 x 3pdr
                                         Admty No: 1128
                                         Port Reg: GY .507

1910: Launched. Built at Beverley by CWG. Owned by Sleight of Grimsby. 1915: Requisitioned in February and converted to a M/S. 1920: Returned to owners. 1933: Acquired by Sleight & Humphrey of Grimsby. 1939: Requisitioned in November and designated as an APV. 1940: Returned to owners on 8th February. 1955: BU at Bruges, Belgium.

REDCAP   1914/17   Displacement: 199TG
                                           Armament: 1 x 3pdr
                                         Admty No: 411
                                         Port Reg: H. 692

1907: Launched. 1914: Requisitioned in November and converted to a M/S. 1915: Returned to owners in December. 1917: Mercantile Loss. Captured by a German S/M 97 miles E. from Longstone on 1st March and sunk by gunfire.

RED GAUNTLET   1939/43   Displacement: 338TG 128TN
                                           Engines: 99HP
                                         Armament: 1 x 12pdr
                                         Port Reg: LO. 33
                                         P. No: FY. 900

1930: Launched. Built at Stockton. Owned by The Iago ST Co. of Fleetwood. 1939: Requisitioned in August and converted to a M/S. Joined the Harwich M/S Groups. 1943: LOST. Torpedoed by a German E-Boat whilst sweeping off Harwich on 5th August. Heavy casualties.

REDWING   1917/19   Displacement: 119TG
                                            Port Reg: A. 425
1896: Launched. 1917: Requisitioned into the Fishery Reserve. 1919: Returned to owners.

REEVE   1914/19   Displacement: 172TG 65TN
                                            Engines: 51HP
                                            Armament: 1 x 6pdr
                                            Admty No: 423
                                            Port Reg: H. 846
1905: Launched. Built at Goole by Goole SB. Owned by Kelsall Bros. & Beeching of Hull.
1914: Requisitioned in November and converted to a M/S. 1919: Returned to owners.

REFORMO   1941/46   See under MOLLYMAWK

REFUNDO   1917/19 1940/4   R-o Group
                                            Displacement: 258TG 113TN
                                            Engines: 80HP = 10.5K
                                            Armament: 1 x 6pdrAA; 1 x 7.5-inch
                                            Bomb Thrower (A/S Howitzer)
                                            Admty No: 3053
                                            Port Reg: GY. 1063
                                            P. No: WWII: FY. 830
1917: Launched.   Built at Beverley by CWG.   Owned by Sleight of Grimsby.
Requisitioned in July and converted to a M/S. Fitted with Listening Hydrophones. 1919:
Returned to owners. 1939: Requisitioned in November and converted to a M/S. Joined
the 117th M/S Group based at Harwich. 1940: Fitted out as a trials ship with a 'Bucket',
an electric hammer device designed to detonate acoustic mines at a range of approx. 1
mile. LOST. Testing the equipment off Harwich on 18th December she detonated a mine
under her bow killing two of her Company. She sank after being towed inshore.

REGAL   1915/19   Displacement: 212TG 77TN
                                            Engines: 63NHP = 10K
                                            Armament: 1 x 6pdrAA
                                            Admty No: 1539
                                            Port Reg: GY. 158
1906: Launched.   Built at Beverley.   Owned by Loyal SFC of Grimsby.   1915:
Requisitioned in June and converted to a M/S.   1919: Returned to owners.   1933:
Mercantile Loss. Took the ground off NE Iceland and abandoned. No loss of life.

REGAL   1939/45   Ex-*Lorenzo*
                                            Displacement: 409TG 163TN
                                            Engines: 111HP = 11.4K
                                            Port Reg: GY .28
                                            P. No: FY. 180

1933: Launched. Built at Beverley by CWG. PR: H. 518. Owned by Hull Northern FC of Hull. 1939: Acquired by Loyal SFC of Grimsby in January and renamed *Regal*. PR: GY. 28. Requisitioned in August and converted to A/S. 1945: Returned to owners in July. 1946: Acquired by Great Grimsby & East Coast SFC of Grimsby and renamed *Nubia*. PR: GY. 208. 1948: Acquired by Henriksen of Hull and renamed *Tervani*. PR: H. 530. 1959: BU in Belgium.

REGARDO	1915/19	1939/45	R-o Group
			Displacement: 248TG 108TN
			Engines: 80HP = 10.5K
			Armament: 1 x 12pdrAA
			Admty No: 1963
			Port Reg: GY. 623
			P. No: WWII: FY. 831 (M/S);
			Y7. 33 (Esso)

1915: Launched. Built at Beverley by CWG. Owned by Sleights of Grimsby. Requisitioned in December and converted to an APV. 1919: Returned to owner. 1933: Acquired by Sleight & Humphrey of Grimsby. 1939: Requisitioned in November and converted to an APV. 1940: Converted to a M/S in May. Based at Grimsby. Ungrouped. 1943: Based at Dover for sweeping duties around 'Hellfire Corner'. Sustained damage from a near-miss shell in July. 1944: Converted to an Esso in January. 1945: Returned to owners in December. 1962: BU at Bruges, Belgium.

REGINA	1917/19	Displacement: 125TG 51TN
		Engines: 44HP
		Port Reg: A. 202

1891: Launched. Built at Hull. Owned by F. Ballard of Aberdeen. 1917: Requisitioned into the Fishery Reserve. 1919: Returned to owners.

| REHEARO | 1940/46 | See under JOHN BURLINGHAM |
| | | (Vol 1 p.61) |

REIGHTON WYKE	1939/45	Displacement: 465TG 173TN
		Engines: 120HP
		Port Reg: H. 425
		P. No: FY. 134

1937: Launched. Built at Selby by Cochrane. Owned by West Dock SF Co of Hull. 1939: Requisitioned in August and converted to A/S. 1943: TPI Operation Avalanche, the Salerno Landings in Sep/Oct sweeping in the approaches. 1945: Returned to owners in December.

REINDEER	1914/20	Displacement: 192TG 76TN
		Engines: 62HP = 10K
		Armament: 1 x 6pdrAA

Admty No: 816
Port Reg: GY. 1236

1902: Launched. Built at Beverley by CWG. Iron construction. Owned by Morris & Fisher of Grimsby. 1914: Requisitioned in November and converted to a M/S. 1915: Renamed REINDEER II in January. 1920: Returned to owners and reverted to original name. 1937: BU at Thornaby.

REINDEER II	1915/20	See under REINDEER above

REINE des FLOTS   1940/46   Displacement: 608TG
Port Reg: French
P. No: FY. 343

1923: Launched. French fishing vessel. 1940: French APV seized at Portsmouth in Operation Grab on 3rd July. Converted to A/S and commissioned into the RN in August with a Free French crew. 1946: Transferred to the French Navy.

RELEVO   1915/16   R-o Group
Displacement: 176TG
Armament: 1 x 12pdr
Admty No: 1615
Port Reg: GY. 670

1912: Launched. Owned by Sleight of Grimsby. 1915: Requisitioned in April. 1916: LOST. Wrecked off El Arijh on 30th December.

RELIANCE II   1914/19   Displacement: 203TG 84TN
Engines: 58HP
Armament: 1 x 6pdr
Admty No: 999
Port Reg: GY. 30

1904: Launched. Built at Selby by Cochrane. Owned by HC. Baker AO of Grimsby. 1914: Requisitioned in December and converted to a M/S. 1919: Returned to owners.

RELONZO   1915/20 1939/41 R-o Group
Displacement: 245TG 107TN
Engines: 80HP = 10.5K
Armament: 1 x 12pdr
Admty No: 1614
Port Reg: GY. 229
P. No: WWII: FY. 843

1914: Launched. Built at Beverley by CWG. Owned by Sleight of Grimsby. 1915: Requisitioned in April. Fitted with Listening Hydrophones. 1920: Returned to owners. 1933: Acquired by Sleight & Humphrey of Grimsby. 1939: Requisitioned in April and converted to an APV. 1940: Converted to a M/S in May. Joined the 136th M/S Group based at Birkenhead. 1941: LOST. Mined in the Crosby Channel, Liverpool, on 20th January.

RELONZO   **(IWM Neg No: SP1479)**

REMAGIO   1915/18   R-o Group
                                          Displacement: 174TG   76TN
                                          Engines: 62HP = 10K
                                          Armament: 1 x 3pdr
                                          Admty No: 1487
                                          Port Reg: GY. 843
1913: Launched. Built at Beverley by CWG. Owned by Sleight of Grimsby. 1915:
Requisitioned in May and converted to a M/S. 1919: Returned to owners. 1933:
Acquired by Sleight & Humphrey of Grimsby. 1956: BU at Bruges, Belgium.

REMARGO   1917/19   R-o Group
                                          Port Reg: GY
? Launched. Owned by Sleight of Grimsby. 1917: Requisitioned into the Fishery
Reserve. 1919: Returned to owners.

REMARKO   1917/16   R-o Group
                                          Displacement: 245TG 107TN
                                          Engines: 80HP = 10.5K
                                          Admty No: 1489
                                          Port Reg: GY. 228
1914: Launched. Built at Beverley by CWG. Owned by Sleight of Grimsby. 1915:
Requisitioned in May and converted to a M/S. 1916: LOST. Mined off Lowestoft on 3rd
December by a mine laid on 7th November by UC. 4. The CO was the only loss of life.

REMEXO   1915/19 1939/45 R-o Group
Displacement: 231TG 108TN
Engines: 63HP = 10K
Armament: 1 x 4-inch; 1 x 7.5-inch
Bomb Thrower (A/S Howitzer)
Admty No: 1136
Port Reg: GY. 721
P. No: WWII: FY. 893

1912: Launched. Built at Beverley by CWG. Owned by Sleight of Grimsby. 1915: Requisitioned in February and converted to a M/S. 1920: Returned to owners. 1933: Acquired by Sleight & Humphrey of Grimsby. 1939: Requisitioned in November and converted to an APV. Based at Grimsby. 1940: Converted to a M/S in June. Joined the 110th M/S Group at Grimsby. 1944: Converted to a BBV. 1945: Returned to owners in December. 1959: BU at Hemixen, Belgium.

REMILLO   1940/41   See under ROBERT BETSON
(Vol 1 p.72)

REMINDO   1917/18   R-o Group
Displacement: 258TG 113TN
Engines: 80HP = 10.5K
Armament: 1 x 12pdr
Admty No: 3065
Port Reg: GY. 1098

1917: Launched. Built at Beverley by CWG. Owned by Sleight of Grimsby. Requisitioned in September. Fitted with Listening Hydrophones. 1918: LOST. Disappeared off Portland on 2nd February. Cause unknown until subsequently confirmed that she had been sunk by UC-79.

REMO   1915/21   R-o Group
Displacement: 169TG 69TN
Engines: 55HP
Armament: 1 x 6pdr
Admty No: 948
Port Reg: GY. 1206

1900: Launched. Built at Selby by Cochrane. Owned by Sleight of Grimsby. 1915: Requisitioned in January and converted to a M/S. 1920: Returned to owners.

RENARRO   1915/19   R-o Group
Displacement: 230TG 107TN
Engines: 70HP = 10.5K
Armament: 1 x 3pdr
Admty No: 1043
Port Reg: GY. 868

1913: Launched. Built at Beverley by CWG. Owned to Sleight of Grimsby. 1915: Requisitioned in February and converted to a M/S. Deployed to the Med. for operations in the Dardenelles. 1918: LOST. Mined in the Dardenelles on 10th November.

RENCO   1915/19   R-o Group
                                          Displacement: 230TG 105TN
                                          Engines: 63HP = 10K
                                          Armament: 1 x 6pdr
                                          Admty No: 1130
                                          Port Reg: GY. 512
1910: Launched. Built at Beverley by CWG. Owned by Sleight of Grimsby. 1915: Requisitioned in February and converted to a M/S. 1919: Returned to owners. 1956: BU at Gateshead.

RENNET   1939/46   Ex-*Deepdale Wyke*
                                          Displacement: 567T 335TN
                                          Engines: 96HP
                                          Armament: 2 x MG
                                          Port Reg: H. 459
                                          P. No: Z. 99
1928: Launched. Built at Selby by Cochrane. Owned by West Dock SF Co. of Hull. 1939: Purchased into the RN in May and converted to a BDV. Based at Rosyth. 1941: Transferred to the MF. 1944: Transferred to Aden. 1946: Sold to mercantile in January and renamed *Red Archer*. Acquired by Iago STC of Fleetwood. PR: LO. 430.

RENOVO   1917/19   R-o Group
                                          Displacement: 170TG 59TN
                                          Engines: 55HP = 9.5K
                                          Port Reg: GY .23
1904: Launched. Built at Beverley by CWG. Owned by Sleight of Grimsby. 1917: Requisitioned into the Fishery Reserve. 1919: Returned to owners. 1938: Acquired by Consolidated Fisheries of Lowestoft and renamed *Walsingham*. PR: LT. 279. 1940: Mercantile Loss. Sunk in a collision in the North Sea.

RENZO   1914/19 1940/45 R-o Group
                                          Displacement: 230TG 108TN
                                          Engines: 70HP = 10K
                                          Armament: 1 x 6pdr
                                          Admty No: 198
                                          Port Reg: GY. 826
                                          P. No: WWII: FY. 893
1913: Launched. Built at Beverley by CWG. Owned by Sleight of Grimsby. 1914: Requisitioned in November and converted to a M/S. 1919: Returned to owners. 1933: Acquired by Sleight & Humphrey of Grimsby. 1939: Requisitioned in November and

converted to an APV. 1940: Converted to a M/S in May. 1945: Returned to owners in October. 1955: BU at Bruges, Belgium.

REPERIO   1915/19   R-o Group
Displacement: 230TG 91TN
Engines: 63HP = 10.5K
Port Reg: GY. 298

1907: Launched. Built at Beverley by CWG. Owned by Sleight of Grimsby. 1915: Requisitioned in January and converted to a BDV. 1918: Returned to owners in December. 1962: BU at Ghent, Belgium.

REPORTO   1915/19 1939/40 R-o Group
Displacement: 230TG 107TN
Engines: 63HP = 10.5K
Armament: 1 x 6pdr
Admty No: 455
Port Reg: GY. 380

1908: Launched. Built at Beverley by CWG. Owned by Sleight of Grimsby. 1915: Requisitioned in February and converted to a M/S. 1919: Returned to owners. Acquired by Sleight & Humphrey of Grimsby. 1939: Requisitioned in November and designated as an APV. 1940: Returned to owners in January. 1956: BU at Bruges, Belgium.

REPRO   1915/17   R-o Group
Displacement: 230TG 105TN
Engines: 63HP = 10K
Armament: 1 x 12pdr
Admty No: 1138
Port Reg: GY. 510

1910: Launched. Built at Beverley by CWG. Owned by Sleight of Grimsby. 1915: Requisitioned in February and converted to a M/S. 1917: LOST. Mined off Tod Head in the Tees estuary on 26th April. The mine had been laid on 19th April by UC-41.

RESERCHO   1917/19   R-o Group
Displacement: 258TG 113TN
Engines: 80HP = 10.5K
Armament: 1 x 12pdr
Admty No: 3081
Port Reg: GY. 1103

1917: Launched. Built at Beverley by CWG. Owned by Sleight of Grimsby. 1918: Requisitioned in January and converted to a M/S. 1919: Returned to owners. 1933: Acquired by Sleight & Humphrey of Grimsby. 1939: Mercantile Loss. Struck a mine on 28th December which had been laid by the German U-15 off Flamborough Head. No loss of life.

RESMILO   1917/19 1940/41 R-o Group
                                   Displacement: 258TG 113TN
                                   Engines: 80HP = 10.5K
                                   Armament: 1 x 12pdr 1 x 3.5-inch
                                   Bomb Thrower (A/S Howitzer)
                                   Admty No: 3021
                                   Port Reg: GY. 1029
1917: Launched.   Built at Beverley by CWG.   Owned by Sleight of Grimsby.
Requisitioned in March and converted to a M/S. Fitted with Listening Hydrophones.
1920: Returned to owners. 1933: Acquired by Sleight & Humphrey of Grimsby. 1940:
Requisitioned in September and converted to a M/S. Joined the 70th M/S Group based
at Aberdeen. 1941: LOST. Sunk by enemy a/c at Peterhead, Scotland on 20th June.
No loss of life.

RESOLVO   1915/20 1939/40 R-o Group
                                   Displacement: 231TG 108TN
                                   Engines: 70HP = 10.5K
                                   Armament: 1 x 6pdrAA
                                   Admty No: 459
                                   Port Reg: GY. 942
                                   P. No: WWII: FY. 821
1913: Launched. Built at Beverley by CWG. Owned by Sleight of Grimsby. 1915:
Requisitioned in February and converted to a M/S. 1920: Returned to owners. 1933:
Acquired by Sleight & Humphrey of Grimsby. 1939: Requisitioned in November and
converted to a M/S. 1940: LOST. Mined in the Thames Estuary on 12th October.
Beached near Sheerness but became a CTL and sold to BU.

RESONO   1915/15   R-o Group
                                   Displacement: 230TG 105TN
                                   Engines: 63HP = 10K
                                   Admty No: 1042
                                   Port Reg: GY. 508
1910: Launched. Built at Beverley by CWG. Owned by Sleight of Grimsby. 1915:
Requisitioned in January and converted to a M/S. LOST. Mined near the Sunk LV. on
Boxing Day.

RESPARKO   1916/19 1939/40 R-o Group
                                   Displacement: 248TG 108TN
                                   Engines: 80HP = 10.5K
                                   Armament: 1 x 12pdr
                                   Admty No: 2958
                                   Port Reg: GY. 926
                                   P. No: WWII: FY. 822
1916: Launched.   Built at Beverley by CWG.   Owned by Sleight of Grimsby.

Requisitioned in September and converted to a M/S. 1919: Returned to owners. 1933: Acquired by Sleight & Humphrey of Grimsby. 1939: Requisitioned in November and converted to an APV. 1940: Converted to a M/S in April. Based at Portsmouth. LOST. Sunk by enemy a/c at Falmouth on 20th August. No loss of life.

RESPONDO   1917/19   R-o Group
                 Displacement: 209TG 82TN
                 Engines: 60HP
                 Port Reg: GY. 1019
1905: Launched. Built at Selby by Cochrane. Owned by Sleight of Grimsby. 1917: Requisitioned into the Fishery Reserve. 1919: Returned to owners. 1938: Owned by Burton ST Co of Hartlepool. PR: HL. 63.

RESPONSO   1914/15   R-o Group
                 Displacement: 228TG 107TN
                 Engines: 70HP = 10K
                 Armament: 1 x 3pdr
                 Admty No: 196
                 Port Reg: GY. 666
1911: Launched. Built at Beverley by CWG. Owned by Sleight of Grimsby. 1914: Requisitioned in January. 1915: LOST. Wrecked near Sanday Island on 31st December.

RESTLESS   1915/15   Displacement: 125TG
                 Admty No: 1041
                 Port Reg: GY. 379
1891: Launched. 1915: Requisitioned in January and designated as an APV. Returned to owners in December. 1916: Mercantile Loss. Captured by a German S/M 40 miles SE x E from Spurn LV. and sunk by gunfire.

RESTRIVO   1914/19 1939/45 R-o Group
                 Displacement: 245TG
                 Engines: 80HP = 10.5K
                 Armament: 1 x 3pdr
                 Admty No: 48
                 Port Reg: GY. 265
                 P. No: WWII: FY. 834
1914: Launched. Built at Beverley by CWG. Owned by Sleight of Grimsby. Requisitioned in November and converted to a M/S. 1919: Returned to owners. 1933: Acquired by Sleight & Humphreys of Grimsby. 1939: Requisitioned in November and converted to an APV. 1940: Converted to a M/S in April. 1945: Returned to owners in January. 1962: BU at Ghent, Belgium.

RETAKO   1915/19 1939/45 R-o Group
                 Displacement: 245TG 107TN

Engines: 80HP = 10.5K
Armament: 1 x 12pdr
Admty No: 1608
Port Reg: GY. 253
P. No: WWII: FY. 834

1914: Launched. Built at Beverley by CWG. Owned by Sleight of Grimsby. 1915: Requisitioned in April. 1919: Returned to owners. 1933: Acquired by Sleight & Humphrey of Grimsby. 1939: Requisitioned in November and converted to an APV. 1940: Converted to a M/S in June. 1945: Returned to owners in January. 1962: BU at Ghent, Belgium.

RETRIEVER	1941/46	See under URANIA of 1941

RETRUDO   1915/19   R-o Group
                                          Displacement: 178TG 68TN
                                          Engines: 61K = 10K
                                          Armament: 1 x 6pdr
                                          Admty No: 1623
                                          Port Reg: GY. 952

1914: Launched. Built at Beverley by CWG. Owned by Sleight of Grimsby. 1915: Requisitioned in April and converted to a M/S. 1920: Returned to owners. 1933: Acquired by Sleight & Humphrey of Grimsby. 1956: BU at Boom, Belgium.

RETURNO   1915/19 1939/45 R-o Group
                                          Displacement: 245TG 107TN
                                          Engines: 80HP = 10.5K
                                          Armament: 1 x 6pdr
                                          Admty No: 1602
                                          Port Reg: GY. 264
                                          P. No: WWII: FY. 839 (M/S);
                                          Y7. 27 (Esso)

1914: Launched. Built at Beverley by CWG. Owned by Sleight of Grimsby. 1915: Requisitioned in March and converted to a M/S. 1919: Returned to owners. 1933: Acquired by Sleight & Humphrey of Grimsby. 1939: Requisitioned in December and converted to an APV. 1940: Converted to a M/S in June. 1944: Converted to an Esso in March. 1945: Returned to owners. 1962: BU at Ghent, Belgium.

REVELLO   1915/19 1939/43 R-o Group
                                          Displacement: 230TG 107TN
                                          Engines: 63HP = 10.5K
                                          Armament: WWI: 1 x 3pdr;
                                          WWII: 1 x 6pdr
                                          Admty No: 673
                                          Port Reg: GY. 373

P. No: WWII: FY. 778

1908: Launched. Built at Beverley by CWG. Owned by Sleight of Grimsby. 1914: Requisitioned in November. 1919: Returned to owners. 1933: Acquired by Sleight & Humphrey of Grimsby. 1939: Requisitioned in November and converted to an APV. 1940: Converted to a M/S. 1941: Vessel sank in August and subsequently salvaged and returned to owners. 1943: Re-requisitioned by the MAFF. 1946: Returned to owners. 1959: Mercantile Loss. Foundered near the Spurn LV. on 7th December. No loss of life.

REVESBY	1916/19	Displacement: 194TG 79TN
		Engines: 80HP
		Port Reg: BN. 50

1898: Launched. Built at Liverpool. Owned by FW. Simpson & T. Shone of Scarborough. 1916: Requisitioned in November and converted to a BDV. 1919: Returned to owners.

R.H.DAVIDSON	1916/19	Displacement: 210TG 91TN
		Engines: 78HP
		Armament: 1 x 6pdr
		Admty No: 3296
		Port Reg: HL. 79

1916: Launched. Built at Aberdeen. Owned by Hartlepool STC. Requisitioned in July and converted to an APV. 1945: Returned to owners in July.

RHODESIA	1915/15	Displacement: 153TG 55TN
		Engines: 40HP = 9K
		Admty No: 1215
		Port Reg: H. 443

1899: Launched. Built at Hull by CWG. Owned by Hull SF & Ice Co. 1915: Requisitioned in January and converted to an APV. LOST. Wrecked near Stornaway on 19th April.

RHONE	1914/19	Displacement: 117TG 47TN
		Engines: 44HP
		Armament: 1 x 6pdrAA
		Admty No: 1045
		Port Reg: GY. 521

1893: Launched. Built at Beverley. Iron construction. Owned by Sleight of Grimsby. 1914: Requisitioned in December. 1918: Returned to owners in July.

RIALTO	1915/19	R-o Group
		Displacement: 139TG 53TN
		Engines: 40HP
		Armament: 1 x 6pdrAA
		Admty No: 1045

Port Reg: GY. 360

1897: Launched. Built at Beverley. Iron construction. Owned by Sleight of Grimsby. 1915: Requisitioned in January. 1919: Returned to owners.

RIANO   1915/19 1944/44 R-o Group
                         Displacement: 212TG 79TN
                         Engines: 63HP = 10.5K
                         Armament: 1 x 6pdrAA
                         Admty No: 671
                         Port Reg: GY. 181
                         P. No: WWII: 4. 429

1906: Launched. Built at Beverley by CWG. Owned by Sleight of Grimsby. 1914: Requisitioned in November and converted to a M/S. 1919: Returned to owners. 1933: Acquired by Sleight & Humphrey of Grimsby. 1944: Requisitioned and designated as an APV. Returned to owners in October. 1960: BU at Bruges, Belgium.

RIBBLE   1917/19   Displacement: 193TG 75TN
                                      Engines: 45HP
                                      Armament: 1 x 6pdrAA
                                      Admty No: 1274
                                      Port Reg: H. 255

1904: Launched. Built at Govan. Owned by Great Northern SFC of Hull. 1918: Requisitioned in January and converted to a M/S. 1919: Returned to owners.

RIBBLE II   1915/19   Displacement: 197TG 79TN
                                      Engines: 45HP
                                      Armament: 1 x 6pdr
                                      Admty No: 957
                                      Port Reg: GY. 1159

1900: Launched. Built at Montrose. Owned by JL. Green AO of Grimsby. 1915: Requisitioned in February and converted to a M/S. 1919: Returned to owners.

RIBY   1915/19   Displacement: 214TG 98TN
                                      Engines: 67HP
                                      Armament: 1 x 12pdr
                                      Port Reg: GY. 594

1910: Launched. Built at Beverley by CWG. 1915: Requisitioned in June and converted to a BDV. 1919: Returned to owners. 1938: Owned by The Connie ST Co. of Scarborough.

RICHARD IRVIN   1914/19   Displacement: 197TG
                                      Armament: 1 x 6pdr

1909: Launched. 1914: Requisitioned in August and converted to a M/S. 1919: Returned to owners.

RICHMOND 1917/19 Displacement: 162TG 63TN
Engines: 45HP
Port Reg: GY. 255
1897: Launched. Built at Govan. Owned by Consolidated Fisheries of Grimsby. 1917: Requisitioned into the Fishery Reserve. 1919: Returned to owners.

RICHMOND CASTLE 1914/19 Ex-*Loch Leven*
Displacement: 178TG 68TN
Engines: 62HP
Armament: 1 x 6pdrAA
Admty No: 258
Port Reg: SN. 60
1901: Launched. Built at Aberdeen. Owned by A. Walker of Aberdeen. 1914: Requisitioned in August and converted to a M/S. 1919: Returned to owners. Acquired by Dundee SF Co. of Dundee. PR: DE. 29.

RIFSNES 1939/40 Displacement: 431TG 163TN
Engines: 99HP = 11K
Armament: 1 x 12pdr
Port Reg: H. 451
1932: Launched. Built at Beverely by CWG. Owned by Oddsson & Co. of Hull. 1939: Requisitioned in August and converted to a M/S. Based at Yarmouth. 1940: LOST. Sunk by enemy a/c off Ostend on 20th May with the loss of three lives.

RIGHTO 1939/44 See under MATTHEW BERRYMAN
(Vol 1 p.68)

RIGOLETTO 1915/19 1940/45 R-o Group
Displacement: 212TG 79TN
Engines: 63HP = 10.5K
Armament: 1 x 12pdr
Admty No: 726
Port Reg: GY. 185
P. No: WWII: 4. 451
1906: Launched. Built at Beverley by CWG. Owned by Sleight of Grimsby. 1914: Requisitioned in December and converted to a M/S. 1919: Returned to owners. 1933: Acquired by Sleight & Humphrey of Grimsby. 1940: Requisitioned in April and converted to a BDV. 1944: Converted to an Esso in April. 1945: Returned to owners in July. 1956: BU at Gateshead.

RILETTE 1917/19 Displacement: 212TG 82TN
Engines: 78HP
Armament: 1 x 12pdr; 1 x 7.5-inch
Bomb Thrower (A/S Howitzer)

Admty No: 334
Port Reg: GY. 1046

1917: Launched. Built at Aberdeen. Owned by EE. Cox of Grimsby. Requisitioned in May and converted to a M/S. Fitted with Listening Hydrophones. 1919: Returned to owners. 1938: Owned by TH Scales & Sons of Edinburgh. PR: LH.35.

RINALDO	1914/209	R-o Group
		Displacement: 166TG 68TN
		Engines: 55HP
		Armament: 1 x 6pdr
		Admty No: 686
		Port Reg: GY. 1199

1900: Launched. Built at Beverley. Iron construction. Owned by Sleight of Grimsby. 1914: Requisitioned in November and converted to a M/S. 1915: Renamed RINALDO II in February. Converted to a BDV. 1920: Returned to owners.

| RINALDO II | 1915/20 | See under RINALDO above |

RINOVIA	1939/40	Ex-*Blakkur*
		Displacement: 403TG 166TN
		Engines: 99HP = 11K
		Port Reg: GY. 378

1931: Launched. Built at Beverley by CWG. Owned by Rinovia SFC of Grimsby. 1938: Renamed *Rinovia*. Same owner. 1939: Requisitioned in August and converted to a M/S. 1940: Took the ground at Dartmouth in September and re-floated. LOST. Mined off Falmouth on 2nd November approximately 2 miles from St. Anthony Light.

RINTO	1914/19	R-o Group
		Displacement: 169TG 66TN
		Armament: 1 x 6pdrAA
		Port Reg: GY. 1146

1900: Launched. Built at Selby by Cochrane. Iron Construction. Owned by Sleight of Grimsby. 1914: Requisitioned in November and converted to a M/S. 1919: Returned to owners.

RIPARVO	1915/18	R-o Group
		Displacement: 230TG 107TN
		Engines: 70HP = 10.5K
		Armament: 1 x 3pdr
		Admty No: 1236
		Port Reg: GY. 870

1913: Launched. Built at Beverley by CWG. Owned by Sleight of Grimsby. 1915: Requisitioned in March. Deployed to the Med. 1918: LOST. Sunk in a collision to the N. of Benghazi.

RIPPLE   1940/40   Displacement: 301TG
                                               Port Reg: American
1918: Launched.   American fishing vessel.   1940: Earmarked for Lend/Lease but
subsequently cancelled.

R. IRVIN   1914/19   Displacement: 208TG
                                               Armament: 1 x 6pdrAA
                                               Admty No: 52
                                               Port Reg: SN. 246
1913: Launched.   1914: Requisitioned in August and converted to a M/S.   1919:
Returned to owners.

RISKATO   1916/19 1940/46 R-o Group
                                               Displacement: 248TG 108TN
                                               Engines: 80HP = 10.5K
                                               Armament: WWI: 1 x 6pdrAA ;
                                               WWII: 1 x 12pdr
                                               Admty No: 3281
                                               Port Reg: GY. 914
                                               P. No: WWII: 4. 302
1916: Launched.   Built at Beverley by CWG.   Owned by Sleight of Grimsby.
Requisitioned in May and converted to a M/S.   1919: Returned to owners.   1933:
Acquired by Sleight & Humphrey of Grimsby.   1940: Requisitioned in June and
converted to an APV. 1946: Returned to owners in May. 1956: BU at Gateshead.

RISTANGO   1915/19 1940/40 R-o Group
                                               Displacement: 178TG 68TN
                                               Engines: 61HP = 10K
                                               Armament: 1 x 6pdrAA
                                               Admty No: 819
                                               Port Reg: GY. 946
1913: Launched.   Built at Beverley by CWG.   Owned by Sleight of Grimsby.   1914:
Requisitioned in November and converted to a M/S.   1919: Returned to owners.   1933:
Acquired by Sleight & Humphrey of Grimsby.   1940: Requisitioned in June for conversion
to a BGV. LOST. Sank after fouling the Medway Boom at Sheerness 14th November.

RIVER ANNAN   1939/45   See under GEORGE CASTLE
                                               (Vol 1 p.171)

RIVER CLYDE   1939/40   See under RICHARD CUNDY
                                               (Vol 1 p.72)

RIVER ESK   1940/45   See under WILLIAM BOND
                                               (Vol 1 p.190)

RIVER GARRY	1939/45	See under JOHN COPE (Vol 1 p.177)
RIVER LEVEN	1939/45	See under JOHN EDSWORTH (Vol 1 p.178)
RIVER LOSSIE	1940/45	See under ARTHUR HEWIN (Vol 1 p.168)
RIVER NESS	1939/40	See under DAVID BUCHAN (Vol 1 p.170)
RIVER SPEY	1940/44	See under DAVID CONN (Vol 1 p.170)

RIVER YTHAN   1940/40   Displacement: 61TN
Engines: 66HP
Port Reg: A. 188

1905: Launched. Built at Aberdeen. 1938: Owned by A. King and B. Allenby of Aberdeen. 1940: Earmarked for Requisitioning but not taken up.

RIVIERE   1916/19 1940/44   Displacement: 226TG 109TN
Engines: 74HP = 9.5K
Armament: 1 x 6pdrAA
Admty No: 1261
Port Reg: WWI: GY. 893; WWII: GY. 14

1916: Launched. Built at Beverley by CWG. Owned by A. Black of Grimsby. Requisitioned in May and converted to a M/S. 1919: Returned to owners. 1926: Acquired by The Earl SF Co. of Grimsby. 1940: Requisitioned in April and converted to a BBV. 1944: Returned to owners in April. 1953: Mercantile Loss. Sank in a collision with SS *Firelight* . Only 3 survivors of the 13 crew.

ROBERT HASTIE   1915/19 1939/46   Hastie Group
Displacement: 210TG 81TN
Engines: 80HP
Armament: WWI: 1 x 6pdr;
WWII: 1 x 3pdr
Port Reg: SN.189
P. No: WWII: FY. 771

1912: Launched. Built at S. Shields by Rennoldson. Owned by Hastie of N. Shields. 1915: Requisitioned. 1919: Returned to owners. 1939: Requisitioned in November and converted to an APV. Based at Grimsby. 1941: Converted for Air/Sea Rescue. 1946: Returned to owners in January.

ROBERT SMITH   1915/17   Displacement: 211TG
1915: Launched. Requisitioned. 1917: LOST. Sunk by unknown cause in the Atlantic
on 20th July.

ROBERT STROUD   1939/46   Displacement: 219TG 96TN
                                        Engines: 63HP
                                        Port Reg: A. 123
                                        P. No: FY. 687
1930: Launched. Built at Aberdeen. Owned by HE Stroud of Aberdeen. 1939:
Requisitioned in August and converted to a M/S. 1946: Returned to owner in April.

ROBIN   1914/19   Displacement: 169TG 64TN
                                Engines: 45HP
                                Armament: 1 x 6pdrAA
                                Admty No: 376
                                Port Reg: H. 4
1904: Launched. Built at Goole. Owned by Kelsall Bros. & Beeching of Hull. 1914:
Requisitioned in October and converted to a M/S. 1915: Renamed ROBIN II. 1919:
Returned to owners.

ROBIN II   1915/19   See under ROBIN above

ROBINA   1917/19   Displacement: 168TG
                                 Port Reg: GY. 1003
1903: Launched. 1917: Requisitioned into the Fishery Reserve. 1919: Returned to
owners.

ROBINIA   1917/19   Displacement: 208TG 97TN
                                  Engines: 58HP
                                  Port Reg: GY. 1147
1900: Launched. Built at Grimsby. Iron construction. Owned by North Eastern SFC of
Grimsby. 1917: Requisitioned into the Fishery Reserve. 1919: Returned to owners.
1938: Owned by TC & F Moss of Grimsby.

ROB ROY   1914/15   Displacement: 153TG
1898: Launched. 1914: Requisitioned. 1919: Returned to owners.

ROCHE BONNE   1940/41   Displacement: 258TG 110TN
                                      Engines: 85HP
                                      Port Reg: A. 433
1913: Launched. Built at Middlesborough by Smith's Dock. 1940: Owned by J. Mackie
& A. Robertson Jr. of Aberdeen. Requisitioned in February and converted to a M/S.
1941: LOST. Sunk by enemy a/c off the Lizard on 7th April.

ROCHE CASTLE   1915/19   Displacement: 241TG 117TN
Engines: 91HP
Armament: 1 x 12pdr
Admty No: 1353
Port Reg: SA. 88

1910: Launched. Built at Selby by Cochrane. Owned by Consolidated Fisheries of Grimsby. 1919: Returned to owners.

ROCHESTER   1914/19   Displacement: 165TG 64TN
Engines: 45HP
Armament: 1 x 3pdr
Admty No: 642
Port Reg: GY. 671

1898: Launched. Built at Govan. Owned by Consolidated Fisheries of Grimsby. 1914: Requisitioned in October and converted to a M/S. 1919: Returned to owners.

ROCHE VELEN   1940/45   See under WILLIAM HUTCHINSON
(Vol 1 p.193)

RODINO   1915/19 1939/40 R-o Group
Displacement: 230TG 108TN
Engines: 70HP
Armament: 1 x 12pdr
Admty No: 1230
Port Reg: GY. 836
P. No: WWII: FY. 840

1913: Launched. Built at Beverley by CWG. Owned by Sleight of Grimsby. 1915: Requisitioned in June and converted to a M/S. 1920: Returned to owners. 1939: Requisitioned in November and converted to a M/S. Based at Grimsby (Ungrouped). 1940: LOST. Sunk by enemy a/c off Dover on 24th July. *Notes*: aka RODINA.

RODNEY   1915/17   Displacement: 246TG 100TN
Engines: 70HP = 10.5K
Armament: 1 x 12pdr; 1 x 7.5-inch
Bomb Thrower (A/S Howitzer)
Admty No: 953
Port Reg: GY. 195

1906: Launched. Built at Beverley by CWG. Owned by W. Grant of Grimsby. 1915: Requisitioned in May and converted to a M/S. 1917: Renamed RODNEY III in March. 1919: Returned to owners and reverted to original name. 1941: Mercantile Loss. Sank on 3rd March following a collision with the trawler *Carieda*.

RODNEY III   1917/19   See under RODNEY above

RODOSTO   1915/19   R-o Group
                                           Displacement: 174TG 76TN
                                           Engines: 62HP = 10K
                                           Armament: 1 x 12pdr
                                           Admty No: 1490
                                           Port Reg: GY. 839
1913: Launched. Built at Beverley by CWG. Owned by Sleight of Grimsby. 1915:
Requisitioned in May. 1920: Returned to owners. 1956: BU at Bruges, Belgium.

RODRIGO   1917/19   R-o Group
                                           Displacement: 169TG 69TN
                                           Engines: 55HP
                                           Port Reg: GY. 1208
1900: Launched. Built at Selby by Cochrane. Owned by Sleight of Grimsby. 1917:
Requisitioned into the Fishery Reserve. 1919: Returned to owners.

ROLAND   1917/19   Displacement: 159TG 59TN
                                           Engines: 58HP
                                           Port Reg: A. 876
1899: Launched. Built at South Shields. Owned by GF. Paul of Aberdeen. 1917:
Requisitioned into the Fishery Reserve. 1919: Returned to owners.

ROLANDO   1914/19   R-o Group
                                           Displacement: 120TG 48TN
                                           Engines: 40HP
                                           Armament: 1 x 6pdrAA
                                           Admty No: 1046
                                           Port Reg: GY. 65

ROLLS-ROYCE   **(Courtesy of Mr Murray)**

1896: Launched. Built at Beverley. Iron construction. Owned by Sleight of Grimsby.
1915: Requisitioned in January. 1919: Returned to owners.

ROLLO   1917/19   Displacement: 167TG
                                              Port Reg: GY. 647
1899: Launched. 1917: Requisitioned into the Fishery Reserve. 1919: Returned to owners.

ROLLS ROYCE   1940/46   See under HERCULES III

ROLULO   1915/15   R-o Group
                                              Displacement:170TG 69TN
                                              Engines: 59HP = 9K
                                              Admty No: 1468
                                              Port Reg: GY. 399
1909: Launched. Built at Beverley by CWG. Owned by Sleight of Grimsby. 1915:
Requisitioned in April and converted to an APV. LOST. Wrecked on Obb Rock, Isle of
Lewis, on 27th May.

ROMAN EMPIRE   1916/19   Displacement: 182TG 63TN
                                              Engines: 60NHP = 10.5K
                                              Armament: 1 x 6pdr
                                              Admty No: 832
                                              Port Reg: H. 431
1898: Launched. Built at Hull by CWG. Owned by Cargill STC of Hull. 1915:
Requisitioned in April and converted to a M/S. 1919: Returned to owners. 1920:
Acquired by Jutland Amalgamated Trs. of Hull. 1923: Mercantile Loss. Sank after
springing a leak off Flamborough on 27th December.

ROMANOFF   1917/19   Ex-*Romanoff*
                                              Ex-*Cecelie*
                                              Displacement: 178TG 63TN
                                              Engines: 55HP = 10K
                                              Port Reg: GY. 639
1900: Launched. Built at Hull by CWG. Owned by A. Black of Grimsby. PR: GY. 1204.
1909: Acquired by Faroese owners and renamed *Cecelie*. 1911: Acquired by Earl SFC of
Grimsby and renamed *Romanoff*. PR: GY. 639. 1917: Acquired by Baynton & Jagger of
Grimsby. Requisitioned into the Fishery Reserve. 1919: Returned to owners. 1937: BU.

ROMILLY   1916/19   Displacement: 214TG 83TN
                                              Engines: 60HP
                                              Port Reg: GY .437
1905: Launched. Built at Selby by Cochrane. Owned by Kottingham TC of Grimsby.
1915: Requisitioned in March and converted to a M/S. 1919: Returned to owners.

ROMULUS   1915/19   Displacement: 159TG 76TN
                                          Engines: 45HP
                                          Port Reg: GY .146

1885: Launched. Built at Beverley. Owned by N. Blow of Grimsby. 1915: Requisitioned in October and converted to a BGV. 1919: Returned to owners.

RONDO   1915/15   R-o Group
                                          Displacement: 117TG
                                          Admty No: 666
                                          Port Reg: GY .528

1893: Launched. Owned by Sleight of Grimsby. 1915: Requisitioned and converted to an APV. LOST. Wrecked in the Shetlands on 3rd March.

RONONIA   1915/19   Displacement: 213TG 89TN
                                          Engines: 66HP = 10K
                                          Dimensions: 117ft x 21ft 6ins x 12ft
                                          Armament: 1 x 6pdr
                                          Admty No: 1594
                                          Port Reg: GY. 865

1913: Launched. Built at Beverley by CWG. Owned by Pelham SFC of Grimsby. 1915: Requisitioned in January and converted to a M/S. Acquired by Neva SIC of Fleetwood. 1919: Returned to owners. 1942: Mercantile Loss. Lost with all hands off Iceland in March.

RONSO   1915/20 1939/46 R-o Group
                                          Displacement: 248TG 108TN
                                          Engines: 80HP = 10.5K
                                          Armament: 1 x 6pdr
                                          Admty No: 862
                                          Port Reg: GY. 605
                                          P. No: WWII: FY. 841 (M/S)
                                          Y7. 29 (Esso)

1915: Launched. Built at Beverley by CWG. Owned by Sleight of Grimsby. 1916: Requisitioned in January and converted to a M/S. 1920: Returned to owners. 1933: Acquired by Sleight & Humphrey of Grimsby. 1939: Requisitioned in November and converted to an APV. 1940: Converted to a M/S in April. Based at Grimsby (Ungrouped). 1944: Converted to an Esso in March. 1946: Returned to owners in March. 1962: BU at Ghent, Belgium.

ROSA   1915/19   Displacement: 242TG 93TN
                                          Engines: 58HP
                                          Armament: 1 x 3pdr
                                          Admty No: 973
                                          Port Reg: M. 16

1904: Launched. Built at N. Shields. Owned by MW. Howell & JM. Knight of Milford

Haven. 1915: Requisitioned in January and converted to a M/S. 1919: Returned to owners. 1938: Owned by Dobson of Grimsby.

ROSALIND   1915/19   Displacement: 174TG 68TN
                                              Engines: 45HP
                                              Armament: 1 x 3pdr
                                              Admty No: 1780
                                              Port Reg: H. 839

1905: Launched. Built at Beverley. 1915: Requisitioned in October and converted to a M/S. Renamed ROSALIND II in December. 1919: Returned to owners in December. Acquired by E. Catchpole AO of Lowestoft. PR: LT. 977. 1947: Owned by Rosalind Fishing Co. of Fleetwood.

ROSALIND II   1915/19   See under ROSALIND

ROSARENO   1917/19   R-o Group
                                              Displacement: 166TG 49TN
                                              Engines: 55HP = 9.5K
                                              Port Reg: GY. 1233

1902: Launched. Built at Beverley by CWG. Owned by GF Sleight of Grimsby. 1917: Requisitioned into the Fishery Reserve. 1919: Returned to owners. 1938: Acquired by Consolidated Fisheries of Grimsby and renamed *Rendlesham*. 1940: Mercantile Loss. Wrecked on a submerged rock off Cape Clear on 5th November.

ROSCO   1917/19   Displacement: 166TG 50TN
                                              Engines: 55HP = 9.5K
                                              Port Reg: GY. 1232

1902: Launched. Built at Beverley by CWG. Owned by GF Sleight of Grimsby. 1917: Requisitioned into the Fishery Reserve. 1919: Returned to owners. 1938: Acquired by Consolidated Fisheries of Grimsby and renamed *Lavenham*. PR: LT. 274. 1951: BU at Milford Haven.

ROSE   1910/21   Ex-*Nizam*
                                              Displacement: 243TG
                                              Armament: 1 x 6pdrAA
                                              Admty No: 53

1907: Launched. Built by Smith's Dock. 1910: Purchased into the RN for M/S trials and experiments at Portland. 1914: Based at Devonport as a M/S Training ship for Trawler Reserve crews. 1921: Sold to mercantile and renamed *Aby*.

ROSE   1914/17   Displacement: 213TG
                                                  Armament: 1 x 6pdr
                                              Admty No: 592
                                              Port Reg: GY. 312

1907: Launched. 1914: Requisitioned in December and converted to a M/S. 1915: Renamed ROSE II in February. 1917: LOST. Mined in Belfast Lough on 23rd April.

ROSE   1915/19 1940/45   Displacement: 218TG 86TN
                                            Engines: 66HP
                                            Armament: 1 x 12pdr
                                            Admty No: 1183
                                            Port Reg: GW. 26
                                            P. No: WWII: FY. 1577

1911: Launched. Built at Aberdeen. Owned by JS. Boyle of Glasgow. 1915: Requisitioned in April and converted to a M/S. Fitted with Listening Hydrophones. Renamed ROSE IV in May. 1919: Returned to owners. 1938: Owned by Mrs. Boyle of Glasgow. 1940: Requisitioned in March and converted to a D/L. Converted to a M/S and renamed ROSETTE. 1945: Returned to owners in November.

ROSE II   1915/17   See under ROSE of 1907

ROSE IV   1915/19 1940/40   See under ROSE of 1911

ROSEBERY   1917/19   Displacement: 103TG
                                            Port Reg: GN. 8

1897: Launched. 1917: Requisitioned into the Fishery Reserve, 1919: Returned to owners.

ROSEMONDE   1940/42   Displacement: 364TG
                                            Port Reg: French

1910: Launched. French fishing vessel. 1940: French M/S seized at Southampton in Operation Grab on 3rd July. Commissioned into the RN as a M/S. 1942: LOST. Sunk by U-203 in the Atlantic on 22nd January.

ROSE of ENGLAND   1915/19 1939/40 1940/46
                                            Displacement: 223TG 86TN
                                            Engines: 68HP
                                            Armament: 1 x 6pdrAA
                                            Admty No: 507
                                            Port Reg: WWI: LL. 6; WWII: GY. 236
                                            P. No: WWII: FY. 562

1909: Launched. Built at Selby by Cochrane. Owned by J. Duncan of Liverpool. 1915: Requisitioned in January and converted to a M/S. 1919: Returned to owners. 1939: Requisitioned in November and designated as an APV. 1940: Returned to owners in January. Re-Requisitioned in September and converted to a M/S. Joined M/S Group 110 based at Grimsby. 1941: Joined the 72nd M/S Group based at Grimsby. 1946: Returned in January.

ROSETTA	1915/19	Displacement: 236TG 95TN
		Engines: 69HP
		Armament: 1 x 3pdr
		Admty No: 2340
		Port Reg: FD. 100

1907: Launched. Built at Aberdeen. Owned by G. Kelton of Dunsfold, Surrey. 1915: Requisitioned in April and converted to a N/L. 1919: Returned to owners.

| ROSETTE | 1940/45 | See under ROSE of 1911 |

ROSSKEEN	1914/19	Displacement: 196TG 77TN
		Engines: 70HP
		Armament: 1 x 4-inch; 1 x 12pdr;
		1 x 6pdr (As a 'Q' Ship)
		Admty No: 633
		Port Reg: GN. 14

1906: Launched. Built at Aberdeen. Owned by J. Lyle of Leith. 1914: Requisitioned in October and converted to a M/S. 1917: Converted to a 'Q' Ship in March and re-armed. 1918: Reverted to M/S in November. 1919: Returned to owners. Notes: 'Q' Ship Names: *Aldabaran*, *Bendigo II*, *Ethulwulf General*, *Hunter* and *New Comet*.

ROSY MORN	1915/16	Displacement: 181TG
		Armament: 1 x 6pdr
		Admty No: 2770
		Port Reg: SH. 59

1914: Launched. 1915: Requisitioned in May. 1916: LOST. Mined near the Dogger Bank on 13th January.

| ROTHER | 1920/22 | See under ANTHONY ASLETT |
| | | (Vol 1 p.131) |

| ROTHERSLADE | 1940/46 | See under JOHN KIDD (Vol 1 p.64) |

ROTO	1915/19	R-o Group
		Displacement: 170TG 59TN
		Engines: 55HP = 9.5K
		Armament: 1 x 6pdr; 1 x 7.5-inch Bomb
		Thrower (A/S Howitzer)
		Admty No: 947
		Port Reg: GY. 22

1904: Launched. Built at Beverley by CWG. Owned by Sleight of Grimsby. 1915: Requisitioned in January and converted to a M/S. 1920: Returned to owners. 1933: Acquired by Sleight & Humphrey of Grimsby. 1952: BU at Dunston.

ROTTERDAM 1940/46 Displacement: 231 TG
Armament: 1 x 2pdr
P No: FY1741

1916: Launched. Dutch Fishing Vessel. Hired from Dutch owners in June and converted to a M/S. Commissioned with a Dutch crew. 1943: Recommissioned with RN crew in June. 1946: Returned to Holland in July.

ROWSAY 1917/19 Displacement: 207TG 81TN
Engines: 50HP = 9.5K
Admty No: 1665
Port Reg: H. 410

1912: Launched. Built at Beverley by CWG. 1917: Requisitioned in February. Fitted with Listening Hydrophones and converted to a Hydrophone Tender. 1919: Returned to owners. 1932: Mercantile Loss. Sunk in a collision with SS *Vargo* in the North Sea on 12 June.

ROWSLEY 1915/19 Displacement: 213TG 89TN
Engines: 68HP
Armament: 1 x 6pdr
Admty No: 1610
Port Reg: GY. 751

1912: Launched. Built at Beverley by CWG. Owned by WH. Beeley of Grimsby. 1915: Requisitioned in August and converted to a M/S. 1919: Returned to owners.

ROXANO 1915/19 1939/45 R-o Group
Displacement: 228TG 113TN
Engines: 70HP
Armament: WWI: 1 x 3pdr;
WWII: 1 x 6pdr
Admty No: 718
Port Reg: GY. 320
P. No: WWII: 4. 456

1907: Launched. Built at Grimsby. Owned by Sleight of Grimsby. 1914: Requisitioned in December. 1919: Returned to owners. 1939: Requisitioned in November and converted to an APV. 1940: Converted to a BBV in October. 1944: Converted to an Esso in April. 1945: Returned to owners in May.

ROYALIST 1917/19 Displacement: 183TG 66TN
Engines: 58HP = 10K
Port Reg: GY.1090

1898: Launched. Built at Hull by CWG. Owned by G. Walton of Hull. PR: H. 428. 1901: Acquired by Dublin STC of Dublin. PR: D. 206. 1917: Acquired by GF Sleight of Grimsby. PR: GY. 1090. Requisitioned into the Fishery Reserve. 1919: Returned to owners. 1935: BU.

ROYALLIEU   1915/19 1939/45 Displacement: 211TG 76TN
                                           Engines: 70HP = 10.5K
                                           Armament: 1 x 12pdr; 1 x 6pdr
                                           Admty No: 1145
                                           Port Reg: GY. 313
                                           P. No: WWII: FY. 838
1907: Launched. Built at Beverley by CWG. Owned by A Black of Grimsby. 1910: Acquired
by TW. Baskcombe of Grimsby. 1915: Requisitioned in February and converted to a M/S.
1919: Returned to owners. Acquired by Overseas SFC of Grimsby. 1939: Requisitioned in
November and converted to an APV. 1940: Converted to a M/S in April. 1945: Returned to
owners in November. 1953: Renamed *Rizzio*. 1961: BU at Bruges, Belgium.

ROYALO   1916/19 1939/40 R-o Group
                                           Displacement: 248TG 108TN
                                           Engines: 80HP = 10.5K
                                           Armament: 1 x 6pdrAA
                                           Admty No: 2955
                                           Port Reg: GY. 941
                                           P. No: WWII: FY. 825
1916: Launched. Built at Beverley by CWG. Owned by Sleight of Grimsby.
Requisitioned in August and converted to a M/S. 1919: Returned to owners. 1933:
Acquired by Sleight & Humphrey of Grimsby. 1939: Requisitioned in November and
converted to an APV. 1940: Converted to a M/S in January. LOST. Mined whilst
sweeping in Mounts Bay, Cornwall on 1st September.

R.R.S.   1914/19   Displacement: 159TG 73TN
                                           Armament: 1 x 6pdrAA
                                           Admty No: 241
                                           Port Reg: YH. 245
1913: Launched. Built at Selby by Cochrane. Owned by Richard Sutton of Gt.
Yarmouth. 1914: Requisitioned in September. 1919: Returned to owner.

RUBENS   1940/41   Displacement: 320TG
                                           Port Reg: Belgian
1937: Launched. Belgian fishing vessel. 1940: Hired from Belgian owners in August and
converted to A/S. 1941: LOST. Sunk by enemy a/c in the Western Approaches on 13th
February.

RUBY   1915/15   Displacement: 198TG
                                           Armament: 1 x 3pdr
                                           Admty No: 1742
                                           Port Reg: GY. 1136
1899: Launched. 1915: Requisitioned in July and converted to a M/S. Deployed to the
Med. LOST. Wrecked in Grandes Bay, Crete, on 24th November.

RUBY   1916/17   Displacement: 251TG
                Armament: 1 x 12pdr
                Admty No: 2970
                Port Reg: H. 494

1916: Launched. Requisitioned in September and converted to a M/S. 1917: LOST.
Torpedoed by U-Boat off Ushant on 17th October.

RUDILAIS   1939/46   See under RICHARD BANE
                (Vol 1 p.71)

RUFF   1914/19   Displacement: 169TG 64TN
                Engines: 45HP
                Armament: 1 x 6pdr
                Admty No: 676
                Port Reg: H. 34

1904: Launched. Built at Goole by Goole SB. Owned by Kelsall Bros. & Beeching of Hull.
1914: Requisitioned in November and converted to a M/S. 1919: Returned to owners.

RUGBY   1916/19 1940/46 Displacement: 274TG 123TN
                Engines: 79HP = 10.5K
                Armament: WWI: 1 x 6pdrAA; 1 x 7.5-
                inch Bomb Thrower (A/S Howitzer)
                WWII: 1 x 12pdr
                Admty No: 2979
                Port Reg: GY. 994
                P. No: WWII: 4. 162 (APV)
                Y7. 30 (Esso)

1916: Launched. Built at Beverley by CWG. Owned by W. Grant of Grimsby.
Requisitioned in November and converted to a M/S. 1917: Renamed RUGBY II in
November. 1919: Returned to owners and reverted to original name. 1938: Acquired by
H. & FD Robinson of Grimsby. 1939: Acquired by Earl SFC of Grimsby. 1940:
Requisitioned in May and converted to an APV. Based at Grimsby for Fishery Protection.
1942: Converted to a M/S in March. 1943: Converted to an Esso in December. 1946:
Returned to owners in May. 1955: BU by Ward at Inverkeithing.

RUGBY II   1917/19   See under RUGBY above

RUNSWICK BAY 1939/46   Ex-*Gambri*
                Displacement: 349TG 52TN
                Engines: 96HP = 11.1K
                Port Reg: H. 33
                P. No: FY. 750

1929: Launched. Built at Beverley by CWG. Owned by Grant & Baker SFC of Grimsby.
1932: Acquired by Howe SFC of Grimsby. 1934: Acquired by Marine SFC of Hull and

renamed *Runswick Bay*. 1939: Requisitioned in August and converted to a M/S. Deployed to the S. Atlantic. 1942: Transferred to the W. African Command. 1946: Returned to owners in July. 1947: Renamed *Hassett*. 1953: Mercantile Loss. Wrecked to the N. of Wick on 18th September. In a rescue operation in very heavy weather involving the Wick Lifeboat and the destroyer HMS SCORPION, 15 men were rescued by Breeches Buoy whilst 5 others were swept overboard and lost.

RUPERT   1914/16   Displacement: 114TG
                                                Armament: 1 x 6pdr
                                                Admty No: 433
                                                Port Reg: GY. 463

1892: Launched. 1914: Requisitioned in November and converted to a M/S. 1915: Returned to owners in June. 1917: Mercantile Loss. Captured by German S/M 42 miles ENE from the Tyne on 6th February and subsequently blown up.

RUSHCOE   1915/19 1939/45 Displacement: 338TG 189TN
                                                Engines: 88HP = 10K.
                                                Armament: WWI: 1 x 12pdr
                                                Admty No: 1546.
                                                Port Reg: WWI: GY. 522; WWII: H. 447
                                                P. No: FY. 524

1915: Launched as *Jellicoe*. Built at Beverley by CWG. Owned by Earl SFC of Grimsby. Requisitioned in July converted to a M/S and renamed RUSHCOE. 1917: Acquired by Neal Green of Grimsby and renamed *Cerisio*. 1919: Returned to owners. 1922: Acquired by Hellyer Bros. of Hull. PR: H. 447. 1939: Requisitioned in September as CERISIO and converted to a M/S. 1940: 41st M/S Flot. based on Aberdeen. 1945: Returned to owners. 1947: Acquired by Lord Line of Hull. 1948: Acquired by Danish owners and converted to a cargo vessel. 1976: Acquired by owners in St. Vincent, WI and renamed *Kelvin & Clyde*. 1983: Reduced to a Storage Hulk at Port of Spain, Trinidad.

RUSSELL II   1915/20   Displacement: 246TG 100TN
                                                Engines: 63HP = 10.5K
                                                Armament: 1 x 6pdr; 24 mines
                                                Port Reg: GY.192
                                                P. Nos: N. 3A & N. 87

1906: Launched. Built at Beverley by CWG. Owned by W. Garrett of Grimsby. 1915: Requisitioned in May and converted to a M/L. 1920: Returned to owners. Retained name *Russell II*. 1930: Acquired by Rugby SFC of Grimsby and reverted to *Russell*. 1957: BU at Gateshead.

RUTHIN CASTLE   1916/17   Displacement: 275TG
                                                Armament: 1 x 6pdr
                                                Admty No: 3317
                                                Port Reg: SA. 67

1916: Launched. Requisitioned in December and converted to a M/S. 1917: LOST. Mined off Skinningrove, Yorkshire, on 21st May.

RUTLANDSHIRE 1939/40 Shire Group
Displacement: 458TG 164TN
Engines: 99HP
Armament: 1 x 4-inch
Port Reg: GY. 335

1936: Launched in September. Built at Southbank-on-Tees by Smith's Dock. Owned by Rutland SF (H. Markham) of Grimsby. 1939: Requisitioned in October and converted to A/S. Joined the 23rd A/S Group. 1940: TPI the Norwegian Campaign in April. LOST. Took the ground at Namsos, Norway, on 20th April after being bombed by German a/c. 1941: Salvaged by the Germans in August. Renamed UBIER and commissioned into the German Navy. 1942: German Loss. Mined on 6th December.

SABINA   1940/45   See under CHARLES DOYLE
                                      (Vol 1 p.169)

SABINE   1917/19   Displacement: 111TG 46TN
                                      Engines: 40HP
                                      Port Reg: A. 865
1888: Launched. Built at Birkenhead. 1917: Requisitioned into the Fishery Reserve.
1919: Returned to owners. Owned by GA. Cooper of Aberdeen.

SABREUR   1916/19 1939/40 Displacement: 188TG 82TN
                                      Engines: 69HP = 10K
                                      Armament: 1 x 6pdrAA
                                      Admty No: 2964
                                      Port Reg: GY. 932
                                      P. No: WWII: FY. 824
1916: Launched.   Built at Beverely by CWG.   Owned by A Black of Grimsby.
Requisitioned in September and converted to a M/S. 1918: Acquired by Strand SFC of
Grimsby. 1919: Returned to owners. 1937: Acquired by T. Robinson & Sons of Grimsby.
1939: Requisitioned in December and converted to an APV. 1940: Converted to a M/S.
1941: Renamed BADINAGE.   1944: Paid Off and reduced to the Reserve.   1945:
Returned to owners in March and reverted to original name. 1960: BU at Gateshead.

ST. ACHILLEUS   1939/40   Displacement: 484TG 189TN
                                      Engines: 154HP = 12.3K
                                      Armament: 1 x 4-inch
                                      Port Reg: H. 127
                                      P. No: FY. 152
1934: Launched. Built at Beverely by CWG. Owned by Thomas Hamling of Hull. 1939:
Requisitioned in August and converted to A/S. Joined the 12th A/S Group based at
Grimsby. 1940: Joined the 11th A/S Group based at Harwich. TPI Operation Dynamo
in May. LOST. Mined off Dunkirk on 31st May.

ST. AGNES   1914/19   Displacement: 205TG 79TN
                                      Engines: 80HP
                                      Armament: 1 x 6pdr
                                      Admty No: 296
                                      Port Reg: SN. 88
1908: Launched. Built at South Shields. Owned by Hastie of North Shields. 1914:
Requisitioned in August and converted to a M/S. 1919: Returned to owners. *Notes*:
Mercantile Lists as *St. Agnes No.1.*

ST. AMANDUS   1939/39   Displacement: 400TG 152TN
                                      Engines: 102NHP = 11.3K
                                      Port Reg: H. 505
                                      P. No: FY. 176
1933: Launched. Built at Beverley by CWG. Owned by T. Hamling of Hull. 1939:
Purchased into the RN in July and converted to A/S. Transferred to the French Navy in
October as APV P.132 and renamed CANCALAIS. 1940: French Loss. Mined off the
Dyke LV. off Calais on 30th April.

ST. ANDRONICUS   1939/39   Displacement: 398TG 151TN
                                      Engines: 102HP = 11.4K
                                      Port Reg: H. 536
                                      P. No: FY. 111
1933: Launched. Built at Beverley by CWG. Owned by T. Hamling of Hull. 1939:
Purchased into the RN in August and converted to A/S. Transferred to the French Navy in
October as APV P.134 and renamed LORIENTAISE. 1940: TIH at Boulogne for repair and
scuttled by the French in the face of the German advance. Salvaged and repaired by the
Germans. Commissioned into the German Navy as PA2. 1944: Damaged in a RAF
bombing raid on Nantes on 14th June and scuttled. 1946: Salvaged. 1947: Acquired by
French mercantile and renamed *Colbert*. 1955: Mercantile Loss. Sank in a collision with
another French trawler off Cap Gris Nez on 26th June with the loss of 9 lives.

ST. APOLLO   1940/41   Displacement: 608TG 207TG
                                      Engines: 165NHP = 12K
                                      Armament: 1 x 4-inch
                                      Port Reg: H. 351
1940: Launched. Built at Beverley by CWG. Owned by Firth STC of Hull. Purchased
into the RN in February and converted to A/S. 1941: Joined the 3rd Escort Group based
at Greenock. Employed on Atlantic convoy escort. LOST. Sunk in a collision with HMS
SARDONYX off the Hebrides on 22nd November.

ST. ARCADIUS   1940/45   Displacement: 403TG 156TN
                                      Engines: 102HP = 11.5K
                                      Port Reg: H. 482
                                      P. No: 1939: FY. 135; 1940: FY .360
1934: Launched. Built at Beverley by CWG. Owned by T. Hamling of Hull. 1939:
Purchased into the RN in August and converted to A/S. Transferred to the French Navy
as APV P.135 and renamed La NANTAISE. 1940: Seized at Portsmouth in Operation
Grab on 3rd July and reverted to her original name. 1945: Due to be returned to the
French Navy in June. LOST. Sunk in collision with the *SS Helencrest* in the Downs on
8th July.

ST. ATTALUS   1939/39   Displacement: 399TG 154TN
                                      Engines: 102HP = 11.5K

Port Reg:H.48

P. No: FY.183

1934: Launched. Built at Beverely by CWG. Owned by T. Hamling of Hull. 1939: Purchased into the RN in July and converted to A/S. Transferred to the French Navy in September as APV P.133 and renamed La HAVRAISE. 1942: Scuttled at Toulon on 27th November. 1943: Salvaged and repaired by the Germans. Commissioned into the German Navy as VJ. 6078. 1944: German Loss. Torpedoed by the French S/M CASABIANCA off La Coitat on 9th June.

ST. CATHAN	1939/42	Displacement: 565TG 210TN
		Engines: 157NHP = 12.3K
		Armament: 1 x 4-inch
		Port Reg: H. 353
		P.No: FY. 234

1936: Launched. Built at Beverley by CWG. Owned by T. Hamling of Hull. 1939: Requisitioned in September and converted to A/S. 1940: TPI the Norwegian Campaign in Aprill/May where she survived 29 attacks by enemy a/c. 1942: Temporary Loan to the USN from February. LOST. Sunk in a collision with the Dutch merchantman *SS Hebe* off Georgetown, S. Carolina on 11th April. The *Hebe* also sank.

ST. CELESTIN	1939/48	Displacement: 352TG 149TN
		Engines: 96HP = 10.8K
		Port Reg: H. 192
		P. No: Z. 104

1925: Launched. Built at Beverley by CWG. Owned by T. Hamling of Hull. 1937: Acquired by H. Franklin of Hull. 1939: Requisitioned in September and converted to a BDV. 1945: Returned to owners. 1946: Acquired by Lord Line of Hull and renamed *Lord Portal*. 1954: BU at Ghent, Belgium.

ST. CLAIR	1915/19 1940/47	Displacement: 255TG 102TN
		Engines: 70HP = 10.5K
		Armament: 1 x 6pdr; 1 x 3pdr
		Admty No: 1844
		Port Reg: WWI: H. 803; WWII: FD. 15
		P. No: WWII: FY. 1876

1903: Launched. Built at Hull by CWG. Owned by T. Hamling of Hull. 1915: Requisitioned in August and converted to a M/S. 1919: Returned to owners. 1924: Acquired by Dinas ST Co. of Fleetwood. 1940: Requisitioned in June and converted to a M/S. Renamed SUNSPOT and purchased into the RN on 15th September. 1947: Sold to mercantile in May. Acquired by Northern Trs. of Grimsby. PR: GY. 387. 1949: Mercantile Loss. Having taken the ground on Stroma in the Pentland Firth, she was refloated but was swept across the Firth and took the ground again on rocks off Swona. All crew taken off by lifeboat. BU in situ.

ST. CLOUD   1917/19   Displacement: 189TG 93TN
Engines: 50HP
Port Reg: GY. 856

1899: Launched. Built at Birkenhead. Owned by J. Coombes of Grimsby. 1917: Requisitioned into the Fishery Reserve. 1919: Returned to owners.

ST. CUTHBERT   1916/19   Displacement: 311TG 162TN
Engines: 80HP
Armament: 1 x 12pdr; 1 x 7.5-inch
Bomb Thrower (A/S Howitzer)
Admty No: 1992
Port Reg: GY. 824

1916: Launched. Built at Selby by Cochrane. Requisitioned in April and converted to a M/S. 1919: Returned to owners. Acquired by New Docks STC of Fleetwood. PR: FD.137.

ST. CYR   1915/19   Displacement: 315TG 126TN
Engines: 84HP
Armament: 1 x 12pdr
Admty No: 1527
Port Req: H. 257

1915: Launched. Built at Selby by Cochrane. Requisitioned in June and converted to a M/S. 1919: Returned to owners. Acquired by AV. Cole of Cheltenham.

ST. DENIS   1916/19 1939/46 Displacement: 294TG 126TN
Engines: 78HP
Armament: 1 x 12pdr
Admty No: 3326
Port Reg: WWI: H. 228; WWII: FD. 113
P. No: WWII: Z. 138

1915: Launched. Built at Selby by Cochrane. Owned by JF Storr of Hull. 1916: Requisitioned in February. 1919: Returned to owners. 1938: Owned by Mason Trs. of Fleetwood having been renamed *Masona*. 1939: Requisitioned in December as MASONA and converted to a BDV. 1943: Purchased into the RN in November. 1946: Sold to mercantile. 1947: BU

ST. DONATS   1939/41   Displacement: 349TG 146TN
Engines: 96HP = 10.8K
Port Reg: H. 35

1924: Launched. Built at Beverley by CWG. Owned by T. Hamling of Hull. 1939: Requisitioned in August and converted to a M/S. Based at Grimsby (Ungrouped). 1941: Joined the 17th M/S Group based at Grimsby. LOST. Sunk in a collision with HMS COTSWOLD in the Humber on 1st March.

ST. ELMO   1915/19   Displacement: 314TG 125TN
Engines: 86HP = 11K
Armament: 1 x 12pdr; 1 x 7.5-inch
Bomb Thrower (A/S Howitzer)
Admty No: 1583
Port Reg: H. 3

1914: Launched. Built at Beverley by CWG. Owned by St. Andrew's SFC of Hull. 1915: Requisitioned in May and converted to a M/S. 1919: Returned to owners. 1921: Mercantile Loss. Wrecked off the S. Coast of Iceland on 6th March. No loss of life.

ST. ELSTAN   1939/45   Displacement: 564TG 209TN
Engines: 157HP = 12.4K
Armament: 1 x 4-inch
Port Reg: H. 484
P. No: FY. 240

1937: Launched. Built at Beverley by CWG. Owned by T. Hamling of Hull. 1939: Requisitioned in August and converted to A/S. 1941: Joined the Iceland Command for Russian Convoys. 1942: TPI convoy PQ.16. 1945: Returned to owners in December. 1966: BU at Ghent, Belgium.

ST. GERMAIN   1916/19   Ex-*Golden City*
Displacement: 307TG
Armament: 1 x 6pdr
Admty No: 552
Port Reg: H. 929

1907: Launched. 1915: Requisitioned in February and converted to a M/S. 1916: Fitted to carry 1 x a/c. 1919: Returned to owners.

ST. GORAN   1939/40   Displacement: 565TG 210TN
Engines: 157HP = 12.3K
Port Reg: H. 356

1936: Launched. Built at Beverley by CWG. Owned by T. Hamling of Hull. 1939: Requisitioned in September and converted to A/S. Joined the 15th A/S Strike Force based at Aberdeen for operations around the N. of Scotland. 1940: TPI the Norwegian Campaign in April/May. LOST. Damaged by enemy a/c at Namsos on 3rd May during the Allied troop evacuation and scuttled.

ST. GOTHARD   1917/19   Displacement: 156TG
Port Reg: GN. 46

1894: Launched. 1917: Requisitioned into the Fishery Reserve. 1919: Returned to owners.

ST. HUBERT   1916/19   Displacement: 349TG 140TN
Engines: 86HP = 10.5HP

Armament: 1 x 6pdr
Admty No: 3306
Port Reg: H. 493

1916: Launched. Built at Beverley by CWG. Owned by The St. Andrews SFC of Hull. Requisitioned in September and converted to a M/S. 1919: Returned to owners. 1922: Seized by the USSR Navy off the Russian coast in March. Crew returned to the UK in a Russian Icebreaker. 1923: Vessel returned in October. 1939: Acquired by Faroese mercantile and renamed *Nyggjaberg*. 1942: Faroese Mercantile Loss. Left the Faroes on 15th February bound for the Icelandic fishing grounds and was not seen again.

ST. IVES   1915/16   Displacement: 325TG 145TN
                                   Engines: 86HP = 11K
                                   Admty No: 1192
                                   Port Reg: H. 11

1909: Launched. Built at Beverley by CWG. Owned by T. Hamling of Hull. 1915: Requisitioned in May and converted to an APV. 1916: LOST. Mined off St. Anthony Head, Falmouth, on 21st December with the loss of 12 lives.

ST. JAN BERCHMANS   1940/46   Displacement: 114TG
                                       Port Reg: Belgian

1935: Launched. Belgian fishing vessel. 1940: Hired from Belgian owners in September and converted to an APV. 1942: Reduced to Harbour Service in July. 1946: Returned to owners in April.

ST. JOHNS   1915/18   Displacement: 208TG 80TN
                                    Engines: 50HP = 10K
                                    Armament: 1 x 3pdr
                                    Admty No: 1906
                                    Port Reg: H. 81

1910: Launched. Built at Beverley by CWG. Owned by Hull SF & Ice Co. 1915: Requisitioned in October and converted to a M/S. 1918: LOST. Sunk by gunfire from the German S/M U-105 45 miles N. of Tory Island on 3rd June. *Notes*: One of the first trawlers to be completed with electric lighting.

ST. KATHERINE   1939/46   Displacement: 337TG

1927: Launched. 1939: Requisitioned in October and converted for the Examination Service. 1944: Converted to an Accommodation Ship in January. 1946: Returned to owners in January.

ST. KENAN   1939/46   Displacement: 565TG 210TN
                                    Engines: 157HP = 12.3K
                                    Port Reg: H. 360
                                    P. No: FY. 264

1936: Launched. Built at Beverley by CWG. Owned by T. Hamling of Hull. 1939:

Requisitioned in September and converted to A/S. Joined the 15th A/S Strike Force based at Aberdeen for operations around the N. of Scotland. 1940: TPI the Norwegian Campaign in April/May. 1941: Transferred to the Iceland Command in August for Russian Convoys. 1942: TPI Convoy PQ.18 in September. 1946: Returned to owners in February. 1951: Acquired by Boyd Line of Hull and renamed *Arctic Invader*. 1966: BU at Antwerp.

ST. KILDA	1917/19	Displacement: 187TG 68TN
		Engines: 45HP = 10K
		Port Reg: H. 355

1904: Launched. Built at Beverley by CWG. Owned by Hull SF & Ice Co. 1917: Requisitioned into the Fishery Reserve. 1919: Returned to owners. 1936: BU by Metal Industries at Charlestown, Fife.

ST. LAWRENCE	1914/15	Displacement: 196TG
		Admty No: 291
		Port Reg: GY. 1131

1899: Launched. 1914: Requisitioned in October and designated as an APV. Returned to owners in November. 1915: Mercantile Loss. Captured by a German S/M 88 miles E. a half N. from the Spurn LV. on 22nd April and sunk by gunfire with the loss of two crew members.

ST. LAWRENCE No.1	1917/19	Displacement: 211TG
		Port Reg: SN. 102

1909: Launched. 1917: Requisitioned into the Fishery Reserve. 1919: Returned to owners.

ST. LEONARD	1914/19 1940/46	Displacement: 296TG 124TN
		Engines: 79HP
		Armament: WWI: 1 x 6pdr;
		WWII: 1 x 12pdr
		Admty No: 454
		Port Reg: WWI: FD. 333
		WWII: GY. 799

1912: Launched. Built at Selby by Cochrane. Owned by Port St. Mary Fishing & Curing Co of London. 1915: Requisitioned in February and converted to a M/S. 1919: Returned to owners. Acquired by Portuguese Mercantile. 1940: Purchased into the RN from Portuguese owners as TREVO TERCEIRO and converted to a M/S. 1942: Renamed FINESSE. 1946: Sold to mercantile and retained the name *Finesse*. Acquired by Easton TC of Swansea. PR: SA. 16.

ST. LEONARD II	1914/19	Displacement: 210TG 81TN
		Engines: 80HP
		Admty No: 462

Port Reg: SN. 217

1913: Launched. Built at S. Shields by Rennoldson. Owned by Hastie of N. Shields. 1914: Requisitioned in August and converted to a M/S. 1919: Returned to owners. *Notes*: Mercantile Lists as *St. Leonard No.1.*

ST. LOMAN   1939/46   Displacement: 565TG 210TN
                                              Engines: 157HP = 12.3K
                                              Armament: 1 x 4-inch; 3 x LG (3x1);
                                              48 DCs
                                              Port Reg: H .381
                                              P. No: FY. 276

1936: Launched. Built at Beverley by CWG. Owned by T. Hamling of Hull. 1939: Requisitioned in September and converted to A/S. Joined the 15th A/S Strike Force based at Aberdeen for operations around the N. of Scotland. 1940: TIH for rearming prior to the Norwegian Campaign. The LG mounted aft was replaced with 1 x 20mmAA. TPI the Norwegian Campaign in April/May which resulted in the award of 3 x DSCs and 6 x DSMs to her Company. TIH at Aberdeen for refitting. Shetland Islands Guardship June/July. Transferred to the Western Approaches Command based at Belfast. Credited with sinking a U-Boat on 28th July. Temporary transfer to Portsmouth for Channel patrols and then returned to Belfast. Employed as convoy escort. Credited with another U-Boat sinking on 11th September. CO awarded bar to DSC. Ship's Company received 1 x MID and 2 x DSMs. Sustained damage in a collision with a merchantman in December and TIH at Aberdeen for repair. 1941: Transferred to the Clyde in January for Atlantic convoys. Credited with the destruction of yet another U-Boat on 8/9th May. Rescued a RAF pilot from the sea on 9th July which resulted in the award of 2 x Bronze Medals of the Royal Humane Society. 1942: Temporary Loan to the USN from March as SO of the Group. Sank her fourth U-Boat on 26th April. Sank her fifth U-Boat on 10/11th May. Escorted the damaged AMC QUEEN OF BERMUDA from Halifax to New York . TIH at New York for refitting and then returned to the RN in October. Sank her sixth U-Boat on 12th November. Awarded a further DSM and 2 x MiD. Transferred to the S. Africa Station. 1945: Returned to the UK and Paid Off. 1946: Returned to owners in July. 1951: Acquired by Boyd Line of Hull and renamed *Arctic Adventurer.* 1964: Suffered a boiler explosion 90 miles off the Scottish coast on 8th December. Three engine-room men killed. Towed back to Hull but repair was not considered economic. 1965: BU at Ghent, Belgium.

ST. LOUIS   1917/19   Displacement: 233TG 92TN
                                              Engines: 70HP
                                              Armament: 1 x 6pdr
                                              Admty No: 1202
                                              Port Reg: H. 503

1900: Launched. Built at Beverley. Owned by T. Hamling of Hull. 1917: Requisitioned in December and converted to a M/S. 1919: Returned to owners.

ST. LUCIA 1917/19 Displacement: 186TG 73TN
Engines: 50HP = 10K
Port Reg: H. 937
1907: Launched. Built at Beverley by CWG. Owned by The Hull SF & Ice Co. of Hull.
1917: Requisitioned into the Fishery Reserve. 1919: Returned to owners. 1952: BU by
Ward at Preston.

ST. MALO 1915/19 1939/46 Displacement: 335TG 136TN
Engines: 86HP = 10.5K
Armament: WWI: 1 x 12pdr
WWII: 1 x 12pdr; 2 x 0.5-inchAA (1x2);
2 x MG (2x1)
Admty No: 1375
Port Reg: H. 371
P. No: WWII: FY. 581
1911: Launched. Built at Beverley by CWG. Owned by T. Hamling of Hull. 1915:
Requisitioned in April. 1918: Acquired by St. Malo SFC of Grimsby. PR: GY.523. 1919:
Returned to owners. 1932: Acquired by EC Grant of Grimsby and renamed *Wardour*.
1935: Acquired by Clan SFC of Grimsby. 1939: Requisitioned in August as WARDOUR
and converted to a M/S. 1946: Returned to owners in April. 1954: BU in Southern
Ireland.

ST. MAURICE 1914/20 Displacement: 251TG 101TN
Engines: 65HP
Armament: 1 x 6pdrAA; 24 mines
(M/L); 1 x 6pdrAA; 1 x 7.5-inch Bomb
Thrower (A/S Howitzer)
Admty No: 551
Port Reg: H. 715
1903: Launched. Built at Govan. Owned by T. Hamling of Hull. 1914: Requisitioned in
September and converted to a M/S. 1918: Purchased into the RN in May and
converted to a M/L. 1921: Sold to mercantile.

ST. MELANTE 1939/46 Displacement: 358TG 155TN
Engines: 96HP = 10.8K
Armament: 1 x 12pdr
Port Reg: H. 367
P. No: FY. 753
1927: Launched. Built at Beverley by CWG. Owned by T. Hamling of Hull. 1939:
Requisitioned in September and converted to a M/S. 1945: Returned to owners in
August. Acquired by Amalgamated Trs. of Grimsby. PR: GY. 80. 1950: Renamed
Womersley. 1953: Acquired by Sleight of Grimsby and renamed *Rapallo*. 1956: BU at
Bruges, Belgium.

ST. MINVER	1939/46	See under JONATHAN COLLINS (Vol 1 p.144)

ST. NECTAN	1940/46	Displacement: 565TG 210TN
		Engines: 157HP = 12.3K
		Port Reg: H. 411
		P. No: 4. 139

1937: Launched. Built at Beverley by CWG. Owned by T. Hamling of Hull. 1940: Requisitioned in May and converted to an APV. Based at Harwich. TIH for conversion to A/S at S. Shields. 1941: Completed conversion in January and deployed to Gibraltar. 1946: Returned to owners in April. 1967: BU at Antwerp.

ST. OLIVE	1940/45	See under NOOGANA

ST. VINCENT	1914/19	Displacement: 186TG 67TN
		Engines: 50HP = 10K
		Armament: 1 x 12pdr
		Admty No: 369
		Port Reg: H. 933

1907: Launched. Built at Beverley by CWG. Owned by Hull SF & Ice Co. 1914: Requisitioned in October and converted to a M/S. 1915: Renamed ST. VINCENT II in February. 1919: Returned to owners and reverted to original name. 1951: BU by Ward at Milford Haven.

ST. VINCENT II	1915/19	See under ST. VINCENT above

ST. WISTAN	1940/46	Displacement: 564TG 209TN
		Engines: 157HP = 12.4K
		Port Reg: H. 486
		P. No: 4. 105

1937: Launched. Built at Beverley by CWG. Owned by T. Hamling of Hull. 1940: Requisitioned in May and converted to an APV. 1941: Converted to A/S in January. Deployed to the S. Atlantic. 1942: Transferred to the Western Atlantic Command. 1946: Returned to owners in May. 1966: BU at Ghent, Belgium.

ST. ZENO	1940/46	Displacement: 608TG 207TN
		Engines: 165HP = 12K
		Port Reg: H. 255
		P. No: FY. 280

1940: Launched. Built at Beverley by CWG. Owned by T. Hamling of Hull. Purchased into the RN in March and converted to A/S. 1942: Temporary Loan to the USN in February. Returned to the RN in October and transferred to the S. Africa Station. 1946: Sold to mercantile in May and retained the same name. Acquired by Firth ST Co. of Hull. 1952: Renamed *Banyers*. 1966: BU at Antwerp.

SAINT-PIERRE II   1940/40   Displacement: 265TG
                                          Port Reg: French
1904: Launched. French fishing vessel. 1940: French M/S seized at Plymouth in
Operation Grab on 3rd July. LOST. Sunk on 29th July.

SALACON   1917/19   Displacement: 211TG 83TN
                                          Engines: 65HP = 10.5K
                                          Port Reg: GY. 55
1905: Launched. Built at Beverley by CWG. Owned by the Standard SFC of Grimsby.
1917: Requisitioned into the Fishery Reserve. 1919: Returned to owners. 1940:
Mercantile Loss. Mined in the North Sea near the Spurn LV. on 7th September with the
loss of 8 of the 12 crew.

SALOME   1915/19   Displacement: 252TG 96TN
                                          Engines: 73HP
                                          Armament: 1 x 12pdr
                                          Admty No: 2670
                                          Port Reg: M. 230
1908: Launched. Built at Dundee. 1915: Requisitioned in May. 1919: Returned to
owners. Acquired by J. Johnson of Scarborough. PR: SH. 306.

SALVINI   1916/19 1940/44 Displacement: 226TG 109TN
                                          Engines: 74HP = 9.5K
                                          Armament: 1 x 6pdrAA
                                          Admty No: 3283
                                          Port Reg: WWI: GY. 892
                                          WWII: GY. 70
                                          P. No: WWII: 4. 457
1916: Launched. Built at Beverley by CWG. Owned by A Black of Grimsby.
Requisitioned in June and converted to a M/S. 1917: Acquired by R Hill of Grimsby.
1919: Returned to owner. 1918: Acquired by Great Northern SFC of Hull. PR: H. 593.
1925: Acquired by The Earl SFC of Grimsby. 1940: Requisitioned in April and
converted to a BBV. Acquired by A Black of Grimsby, the original owner. 1943: Acquired
by Shire Trs. of Grimsby. 1944: Converted to an Esso in April. Returned to owners in
November. 1959: BU at Wormer, Holland.

SAMURAI   1915/19   Displacement: 221TG 86TN
                                          Engines: 73HP
                                          Armament: 1 x 6pdrAA
                                          Admty No: 1443
                                          Port Reg: GY. 175
1914: Launched. Built at Middlesborough by Smith's Dock. Owned by Sleight of
Grimsby. 1915: Requisitioned in August and converted to a M/S. 1920: Returned to
owners.

SANDMARTIN   1944/46   See under JAY of 1926

SANDRINGHAM   1914/19   Displacement: 179TG 61TN
                                        Engines: 55HP = 9.5K
                                        Armament: 1 x 12pdr
                                        Port Reg: GY. 59
1905: Launched. Built at Beverley by CWG. Owned by the Queen SFC of Grimsby.
1914: Requisitioned in December and converted to a BDV. 1919: Returned to owners.
1930: Acquired by Grant & Son of Grimsby and renamed *Penn*. 1940: Mercantile Loss.
Sailed from Grimsby on 7th April to fish in the North Sea. Her lifeboat was recovered at
Cley in Norfolk. Presumed mined in April and lost with all nine hands.

SANDRINGHAM   1939/46   Displacement: 254TG 99TN
                                        Engines: 83HP
                                        Port Reg: GY. 303
                                        P. No: FY. 589
1930: Launched. Built at Selby by Cochrane. Owned by the Queen SF Co of Grimsby.
1939: Requisitioned in August and converted to a M/S. 1940: Joined the 40th M/S Group
based at Grimsby. 1945: Joined the 72nd M/S Group based at Grimsby. 1946: Returned
to owners in July.

SANGARIUS   1939/41   Displacement: 211TG 78TN
                                        Engines: 69HP
                                        Armament: 1 x 3pdr
                                        Port Reg: A .863
                                        P. No: 4. 160
1915: Launched. Built at Aberdeen. 1939: Owned by Alexander & Bruce AO of
Aberdeen. Requisitioned in December and converted to an APV. Based at Grimsby.
1941: Returned to owners in December

SANSERIT   1917/19   Displacement: 212TG 82TN
                                        Engines: 78HP
                                        Armament: 1 x 6pdr
                                        Admty No: 2997
                                        Port Reg: GY. 996
1915: Launched. Built at Aberdeen. Owned by CH. George of Caistor-on-Sea. 1917:
Requisitioned in February and converted to a M/S. 1919: Returned to owners.

SANSON   1915/19 1939/46 Displacement: 231TG 90TN
                                        Engines: 69HP = 10K
                                        Armament: 1 x 6pdr; 1 x 7.5-inch Bomb
                                        Thrower (A/S Howitzer)
                                        Admty No: 1863
                                        Port Reg: GY. 295

P. No: WWII: FY. 901(M/S)

Y7. 31(Esso)

1907: Launched. Built at Beverley by CWG. Owned by the Standard SFC of Grimsby. 1915: Requisitioned in September and converted to a M/S. 1919: Returned to owners. 1937: Acquired by Japan FCL of Grimsby. 1939: Requisitioned in November and converted to an APV. 1940: Converted to a M/S in June. 1944: Converted to an Esso in June. 1946: Returned to owners in September. 1951: BU.

SANSONNET	1939/40	Engines: 78HP
		Port Reg: A. 862

1916: Launched. Built at Aberdeen. Owned by Alexander Bruce AO of Aberdeen. 1939: Requisitioned in November and designated as an APV. 1940: Returned to owners in February.

SAON	1939/45	Ex-*Bayflower*
		Displacement: 386TG 155TN
		Engines: 99HP
		Measurements: 150ft
		Port Reg: H. 487
		P. No: FY. 159

1933: Launched. Built at Selby by Cochrane. Owned by the Yorkshire SFC of Hull. 1939: Acquired by the Standard SFC of Grimsby. Requisitioned in September and converted to A/S. Based at Dover ICW CAYTON WYKE. Attacked the German S/M U-16 on 23rd October and drove her onto the Goodwin Sands where she was subsequently destroyed. 1940: Purchased into the RN in January. ICW BLACKBURN ROVERS and WESTELLA on 2nd June detected a U-Boat by ASDIC. During the subsequent attack BLACKBURN ROVERS entered a British minefield, struck a mine and sank. WESTELLA went to the rescue but also struck a mine and sank. It was left to SAON to rescue over 30 survivors from the two ships. 1945: Sold to mercantile. Acquired by the Hull Ice Co. and then re-acquired by the Standard SFC. PR: GY. 139. 1958: BU in August. *Notes*: Built with an unusual cruiser stern.

SAPLER	1917/19 1940/45	Displacement: 262TG 104TN
		Engines: 76HP
		Armament: WWI: 1 x 12pdr;
		WWII: 1 x 6pdr
		Admty No: 3077
		Port Reg: WWI: H. 580; WWII: GN. 47
		P. No: WWII: FY. 1938

1917: Launched. .Built at Selby by Cochrane. Requisitioned in December and converted to a M/S. 1919: Returned to owners. Acquired by Dryburgh of Edinburgh and renamed *Invercauld*. 1940: Requisitioned in December as INVERCAULD and converted to a M/S. 1945: Returned to owners in November.

SAPPHIRE   1914/18   Displacement: 156TG
                                      Armament: 1 x 6pdr
                                      Admty No: 277
                                      Port Reg: A. 889
1903: Launched.   1914: Requisitioned in August and converted to a M/S.   1915:
Renamed SAPPHIRE III in February.   1918: Returned to owners in November.

SAPPHIRE III   1916/19   See under SAPPHIRE

SARAH   1917/19   Displacement: 135TG 52TN
                                      Engines: 38HP
                                      Port Reg: SN. 40
1899: Launched.   Built at Montrose.   Owned by J. Smart of N. Shields.   1917:
Requisitioned into the Fishery Reserve.   1919: Returned to owners.

SARAH ALICE   1914/19   Displacement: 299TG
                                      Armament: 1 x 3pdr
                                      Admty No: 329
                                      Port Reg: FD. 140
1911: Launched.   1914: Requisitioned in August and converted to a M/S.   1916: LOST.
Sunk by German S/M to the N. of Fairisle on 26th September.

SARAH A. PURDY   1940/46   See under JOHN HUNS (Vol 1 p.180)

SARAH HIDE   1939/46   Displacement: 162TG 68TN
                                      Engines: 56HP
                                      Armament: 1 x MG
                                      Port Reg: LT. 1157
                                      P. No: FY. 968
1921: Launched.   Built at Aberdeen.   Owned by Kittiwake Ltd. of Lowestoft.   1939:
Requisitioned in November and converted to a M/S.   1946: Returned to owners in
January. *Notes*: Aka SARAH HYDE.

SARBA   1915/19 1939/46 Displacement: 315TG 129TN
                                      Engines: 69HP
                                      Armament: 1 x 12pdr; 1 x 7.5-inch
                                      Bomb Thrower (A/S Howitzer)
                                      Admty No: 928
                                      Port Reg: FD. 177
                                      P. No: Z. 139
1913: Launched.   Built at Aberdeen.   Owned by Clifton Trs. of Fleetwood.   1914:
Requisitioned in November and converted to a M/S.   1919: Returned to owners.   1939:
Requisitioned in November and converted to a BDV.   Subsequently purchased into the
RN.   1946: Sold to mercantile on 27th September.

SARDIUS	1915/18	Displacement: 213TG 93TN
		Engines: 55HP
		Armament: 1 x 12pdr
		Admty No: 727
		Port Reg: H. 197

1892: Launched. Built at Hull. Iron construction. Owned by Kingston STC. 1914: Requisitioned in December. 1918: Returned to owners.

SARDIUS	1915/18	Displacement: 206TG
		Armament: 1 x 3pdr
		Admty No: 3357
		Port Reg: GY. 1140

1900: Launched. 1915: Requisitioned in June and converted to a M/S. Renamed SARDIUS II in August. 1918: LOST. Wrecked in Pendower Cove, near Tolpedon, Penwith, Cornwall, on 13th February.

SARDIUS II	1915/18	See under SARDIUS above

SARGON	1914/19 1939/45	Displacement: 297TG 121TN
		Engines: 68HP = 10.5K
		Armament: 1 x 6pdr
		Admty No: 297
		Port Reg: GY. 858
		P. No: WWII: FY. 572

1913: Launched. Built at Beverley by CWG. Owned by Standard SFC of Grimsby. 1914: Requisitioned in December and converted to a M/S. 1919: Returned to owners. 1939: Requisitioned in August and converted to a M/S. 1945: Returned to owners in July. 1948: Mercantile Loss. Wrecked off Iceland in a blizzard in December. Eleven lives lost and 6 rescued.

SARK	1917/19	Displacement: 145TG 57TN
		Engines: 45HP
		Port Reg: GW. 25

1895: Launched. Built at Govan. Iron construction. Owned by N Ashworth AO of Fleetwood. 1917: Requisitioned into the Fishery Reserve. 1919: Returned to owners.

SARONTA	1940/45	See under VAMBERY

SARPEDON	1917/19 194045	Displacement: 344TG 138TN
		Engines: 89HP = 10K
		Armament: 1 x 12pdr
		Admty No: 2998
		Port Reg: GY. 984
		P. No: WWII: 4. 05

1916: Launched. Built at Beverley by CWG. Owned by Standard SFC of Grimsby. 1917: Requisitioned in January and converted to a M/S. Renamed SARPEDON II in March. 1919: Returned to owners and reverted to original name. 1940: Requisitioned in June as SARPEDON and converted to an APV. Based at Grimsby for Fishery Protection. 1942: Converted to a M/S in January. Acquired by St. Andrews FCL of Hull. 1945: Returned to owners in July. Acquired by K. Persival of Hull. PR: H. 142. 1947: Acquired by Anglo SFC of Grimsby. PR: GY. 466. 1952: BU at Thornaby-on-Tees.

SARPEDON II	1916/19	See under SARPEDON above

SARRAIL	1917/19 1940/45	Displacement: 255TG 95TN
		Engines: 82HP
		Armament: 1 x 12pdr
		Admty No: 3050
		Port Reg: WWI: GY. 1071
		WWII: GN. 15
		P. No: WWII: FY. 503

1917: Launched. Built at Aberdeen. Owned by E. Taylor & N. Ashworth of Fleetwood. Requisitioned in July and converted to a M/S. 1919: Returned to owners. Acquired by A.G. Brown of Granton and renamed *Bilsdean*. 1940: Requisitioned in February as BILSDEAN and converted to a M/S. 1945: Returned to owner in November.

SASEBO	1915/19 1939/46	Displacement: 255TG 99TN
		Engines: 85HP
		Armament: 1 x 12pdr
		Admty No: 1773
		Port Reg: WWI: CF. 42; WWII: H. 382
		P. No: WWII: FY. 1730

1913: Launched. Built at Middlesborough by Smith's Dock. Owned by Neale & West of Cardiff. 1915: Requisitioned in June and converted to a M/S. 1919: Returned to owners. Acquired by the Lord Line of Hull and renamed *Avola*. 1939: Requisitioned in August as AVOLA and converted to a M/S. 1946: Returned to owners in April.

SASEBO	1939/46	Displacement: 308TG 116TN
		Engines: 99HP
		Armament: 1 x 12pdr
		Port Reg: CF. 27
		P. No: FY. 828

1928: Launched. Built at Southbank-on-Tees by Smith's Dock. Owned by Neale & West of Cardiff. 1939: Requisitioned in August and converted to a M/S. 1946: Returned to owners in February.

SATA	1939/45	Displacement: 340TG 123TN
		Engines: 99HP

Port Reg: CF. 30

1931: Launched. Built at Stockton-on-Tees. Owned by Neale & West of Cardiff. 1939: Requisitioned in August and converted to a M/S. 1945: Returned to owners.

SATURN   1916/19 1939/45 Displacement: 230TG 107TN
                                  Engines: 76HP
                                  Armament: 1 x 6pdrAA
                                  Admty No: 2971
                                  Port Reg: GY. 976
                                  P. No: WWII: FY. 823 (M/S)
                                  Y7. 37 (Esso)

1916: Launched. Built at Goole by Goole SB. Owned by Trawlers (White Sea & Grimsby) of Grimsby. Requisitioned in September and converted to a M/S. 1919: Returned to owners. 1939: Requisitioned in November and converted to an APV. 1940: Converted to a M/S in June. 1944: Converted to an Esso in March. 1945: Returned to owners in December.

SAURIAN   1916/19 1940/45 Displacement: 219TG 102TN
                                  Engines: 67HP
                                  Armament: 1 x 12pdr
                                  Admty No: 3293
                                  Port Reg: GY. 901
                                  P. No: WWII: FY. 1726

1916: Launched. Built at Selby by Cochrane. Owned by HC Baker of Grimsby. Requisitioned in July and converted to a M/S. 1919: Returned to owners. 1940: Requisitioned in June and converted to an APV. 1945: Returned to owners.

SAVITIRI   1917/19   Displacement: 212TG 102TN
                                  Engines: 67HP
                                  Armament: 1 x 6pdrAA; 1 x 7.5-inch
                                  Bomb Thrower (A/S Howitzer); 24
                                  Mines
                                  Admty No: 1271
                                  Port Reg: GY. 1028

1917: Launched. Built at Aberdeen. Owned by RW Milburn of Whitby. Requisitioned in June and converted to a M/L. 1919: Returned to owners.

SAWFLY   1939/45   Ex-*Tenby Castle*
                                  Displacement: 307TG 117TN
                                  Engines: 91HP
                                  Port Reg: SA. 89
                                  P. No: FY. 629

1928: Launched. Built at Selby by Cochrane. Owned by Consolidated Fisheries of Grimsby. 1939: Requisitioned in August and converted to a M/S. 1940: Based at Portland. 1945: Returned to owners in October.

SAXON   1914/19   Displacement: 239TG 93TN
                                          Engines: 57HP
                                          Armament: 1 x 12pdr; 1 x 7.5-inch
                                          Bomb Thrower (A/S Howitzer)
                                          Admty No: 627
                                          Port Reg: FD. 159

1907: Launched. Built at North Shields. Owned by Saxon STL of Fleetwood. 1914: Requisitioned in September and converted to a M/S. 1919: Returned to owners.

SAXON II   1915/18   Displacement: 119TG 37TN
                                          Engines: 43NHP = 10K
                                          Armament: 1 x 6pdr
                                          Admty No: 732
                                          Port Reg: GY. 722

1894: Launched. Built at Hull by CWG. Owned by A Bannister of Grimsby. 1915: Requisitioned in January. 1918: Returned to owners. 1931: Mercantile Loss. Foundered off the Tyne in April.

SAXONIA   1939/40   See under IRWELL

SAXON PRINCE   1915/16   Displacement: 237TG
                                          Armament: 1 x 3pdr
                                          Admty No: 262
                                          Port Reg: SN. 58

1907: Launched. Owned by Bannister of Grimsby. 1914: Requisitioned in August and converted to a M/S. 1916: LOST. Disappeared in very heavy weather off Dover on 28th March.

SCALBY WYKE   1939/45   Displacement: 443TG 170TN
                                          Engines: 114HP
                                          Port Reg: H. 185
                                          P. No: FY. 258

1935: Launched. Built at Selby by Cochrane. Owned by West Dock SF of Hull. 1939: Requisitioned in October and converted to A/S. 1945: Returned to owners in October.

SCARBOROUGH   1915/19   Displacement: 161TG 63TN
                                          Engines: 45HP
                                          Armament: 1 x 6pdr
                                          Admty No: 632
                                          Port Reg: GY. 266

1897: Launched. Built at Govan. Owned by Consolidated Fisheries of Grimsby. 1914: Requisitioned in October and converted to a M/S. 1919: Returned to owners. 1938: Owned by Consolidated of Grimsby. PR: LT.136.

SCARRON 1915/19 1940/45 Displacement: 296TG 122TN
Engines: 69HP = 10K
Armament: WWI: 1 x 12pdr;
1 x 6pdrAA; 1 x 3.5-inch Bomb
Thrower; WWII: 2 x MG
Admty No: 1864
Port Reg: GY. 935
P. No: WWII: FY. 1913

1913: Launched. Built at Beverley by CWG. Owned by the Standard SFC of Grimsby.
1915: Requisitioned in September and converted to a M/S. 1919: Returned to owners.
1940: Requisitioned in June and converted to an APV. 1942: Acquired by St Andrews
SFC of Hull. 1941: Converted to a M/S. 1945: Returned to owners in December. 1946:
BU at Llanelly.

SCHIEHALLION 1914/15 Displacement: 198TG
Admty No: 352
Port Reg: A. 905

1903: Launched. 1914: Requisitioned in August and converted to a M/S. Deployed to
the Med. 1915: LOST. Mined in the Med. on 9th June.

SCHIEHALLION 1916/19 Displacement: 225TG 84TN
Engines: 70HP
Armament: 1 x 6pdrAA
Admty No: 2990
Port Reg: A. 727

1916: Launched. Built at Aberdeen. Owned by Grampian FCL of Aberdeen.
Requisitioned in December and converted to a M/S. 1919: Returned to owners.

SCHIPPERKE 1916/19 Displacement: 331TG 142TN
Engines: 84HP = 10.5K
Armament: 1 x 12pdr; 1 x 7.5-inch
Bomb Thrower (A/S Howitzer)
Admty No: 1749
Port Reg: H. 308

1911: Launched. Built at Beverley by CWG. Owned by Humber STC of Hull. 1915:
Requisitioned in September. 1919: Returned to owners. 1923: Acquired by Spanish
owners and renamed *Pedro*. 1936: Requisitioned by the Spanish Navy. 1942: Spanish
Navy Loss. Sank whilst in tow on 15th April having stranded the previous month off
Morocco.

SCOMBER 1915/19 1940/47 Displacement: 321TG 139TN
Engines: 89HP
Armament: 1 x 6pdrAA
Admty No: 445

Port Reg: FD. 98

P. No: WWII: Z. 183

1914: Launched. Built at Selby by Cochrane. Owned by Mount SFC of Fleetwood. Requisitioned in December and converted to a M/S. 1919: Returned to owners. 1940: Purchased into the RN in May and converted to a BDV. 1947: Sold to mercantile in February.

SCOOPER	1915/19	Ex-*Kastoria*
		Displacement: 195TG 77TN
		Engines: 55HP = 10K
		Armament: 1 x 6pdr
		Admty No: 1745
		Port Reg: GY. 1155

1900: Launched. Built at Hull by CWG. Owned by Great Grimsby & East Coast SFC of Grimsby. 1913: Acquired by E. Bacon of Grimsby in November. Acquired by Spartan SFC of Grimsby in December and renamed *Scooper*. 1915: Requisitioned in July and converted to a BDV. 1919: Returned to owners. Acquired by Lindsey SFC of Grimsby. 1961: BU at Den Helder, Holland.

SCORPIO	191719	Displacement: 145TG 77TN
		Engines: 45HP
		Port Reg: GY. 467

1888: Launched. Built at Hull. Iron construction. Owned by Scorpio SFC of Scarborough. 1917: Requisitioned into the Fishery Reserve. 1919: Returned to owners.

| SCORPION | 1917/19 | Displacement: 155TG |
| | | Port Reg: SH. 182 |

1891: Launched. 1917: Requisitioned into the Fishery Reserve. 1919: Returned to owners.

SCOT	1915/19	Displacement: 202TG 79TN
		Engines: 75
		Armament: 1 x 6pdr; 1 x 7.5-inch Bomb Thrower (A/S Howitzer)
		Admty No: 1580
		Port Reg: A. 179

1907: Launched. Built at Aberdeen. Owned by Standard SFC of Aberdeen. 1915: Requisitioned in May and converted to a M/S. 1919: Returned to owners. 1938: Owned by W Wood AO of Aberdeen.

| SCOTIA | 1917/19 | Displacement: 149TG |
| | | Port Reg: LH. 68 |

1891: Launched. 1918: Requisitioned into the Fishery Reserve. 1919: Returned to owners.

SCOTLAND   1917/19   Displacement: 152TG 63TN
      Engines: 35HP = 10K
      Port Reg: H. 348

1897: Launched. Built at Hull by CWG. Owned by Hull SFC. 1917: Requisitioned into the Fishery Reserve. 1919: Returned to owners. Mercantile Loss. Presumed mined off Flamborough Head in March.

SCOTT   1915/15   Displacement: 288TG 115TN
      Engines: 70HP
      Armament: 1 x 6pdr; 24 Mines
      Admty No: 3218
      Port Reg: H. 968
      P. No: N. 2A

1913: Launched. Built at Selby Cochrane. Owned by Pickering & Haldane SFC of Hull. 1915: Requisitioned in April and converted to a M/L. LOST. Mined off the Tongue LV on 22nd October.

SCOTTISH   1939/45   Displacement: 558T 222TN
      Engines: 99HP
      Armament: 1 x 4-inch
      Port Reg: GY. 397
      P. No: FY. 245

1937: Launched. Built at Southbank-on-Tees by Smith's Dock. Owned by Vinur SFC of Grimsby. 1939: Requisitioned in October and converted to A/S. 1940: Converted to an ABV in December. 1945: Returned to owners in March.

SCOTTISH BELLE   1915/19   Displacement: 145TG 60TN
      Engines: 50HP
      Port Reg: A. 512

1890: Launched. Built at Kinghorn. Owned by R Brown of Aberdeen. 1915: Requisitioned in June and converted to a BDV. 1919: Returned to owners.

SCOUTER   1915/19   Ex-*Moravia*
      Displacement: 195TG 77TN
      Engines: 55HP = 10K
      Armament: 1 x 6pdr
      Admty No: 1600
      Port Reg: GY. 1180

1900: Launched. Built at Hull by CWG. Owned by Great Grimsby & East Coast SFC of Grimsby. 1915: Requisitioned in July and converted to a M/S and renamed. Acquired by Lindsey SFC of Grimsby in September. 1919: Returned to owners. 1956: BU in Holland.

SEAFLOWER   1909/19   Ex-*Osprey II*
      Displacement: 560T 275TG

Armament: 1 x 12pdrAA
Admty No: 1

1908: Launched. Built at Goole by Goole SB. 1909: Purchased into the RN in April and converted to a Trials M/S. 1914: Based at Chatham/Sheerness ICW SEAMEW as M/S Training Ship for Trawler Reserve crews. 1920: Renamed SEA ROVER in January. Sold to mercantile and renamed *Heinrich Beerman.*

SEAFLOWER   **(NMM Neg No: FFC1)**

SEAHAWK   1917/19   Displacement: 169TG 64TN
                                                   Engines: 52HP
                                                   Port Reg: GN. 37

1898: Launched. Built at Aberdeen. Owned by J. Coombes of Grimsby. 1917: Requisitioned into the Fishery Reserve. 1919: Returned to owners. 1938: Owned by Plymouth Trs. of Plymouth.

SEAHORSE III   1917/19   Displacement: 229TG 92TN
                                                   Engines: 70HP = 10K
                                                   Port Reg: GY. 1011

1901: Launched. Built at Hull by CWG. Owned by Pickering & Haldane STC of Hull. PR: H. 533. 1916: Acquired by Sleight of Grimsby. PR: GY. 1011. 1917: Requisitioned into the Fishery Reserve. 1919: Returned to owners. 1925: Acquired by Spanish owners and renamed *Santa Teolinda.* 1933: Mercantile Loss. Sank in a collision with a Spanish merchantman on 29th June.

SEA KING   1917/20 1939/40 Displacement: 321TG 130TN
                                                   Engines: 94HP
                                                   Armament: 1 x 12pdr
                                                   Admty No: 3321

Port Reg: GY. 1251

1916: Launched. Built at Selby by Cochrane. Owned by Grant & Baker SFC of Grimsby. 1917: Requisitioned in January and converted to a M/S. Reported to be subsequently converted to a 'Q' Ship. 1919: Returned to owners. Acquired by Boston DSF & Ice Co. of Fleetwood. 1939: Requisitioned in August and converted to a M/S. Joined the 40th M/S Group based at Grimsby. 1940: LOST. Sunk by an underwater explosion in the Grimsby Roads on 9th October. Believed mined.

SEALARK   1915/18   Displacement: 182TG
                                        Armament: 1 x 6pdrAA
                                        Admty No: 1213
                                        Port Reg: H. 407

1893: Launched. 1915: Requisitioned in January and converted to a M/S. Renamed SEALARK II in February. 1918: LOST. Sunk in a collision off St. John's Point on 30th September.

SEALARK II   1915/18   See under SEALARK above

SEALION   1914/19   Displacement: 231TG 93TN
                                        Engines: 70HP = 10K
                                        Armament: 2 x 6pdrs
                                        Admty No: 259
                                        Port Reg: H. 542

1902: Launched. Built at Hull by CWG. Owned by Pickering & Haldane STC of Hull. 1914: Requisitioned in August and converted to a M/S. 1918: Acquired by WW. Crampin SFC of Grimsby. PR: GY.1221. 1919: Returned to owners. 1934: BU.

SEAMEW   1909/19   Ex-*Nunthorpe Hall*
                                        Displacement: 240TG
                                        Armament: 1 x 12pdr
                                        Admty No: 2

1909: Launched. Built at Southbank-on-Tees by Smith's Dock. Purchased into the RN in April. Based at Portland and employed on M/S trials. 1914: Based at Chatham/Sheerness ICW SEAFLOWER as M/S Training Ship for Trawler Reserve personnel. 1920: Renamed NUNTHORPE HALL (original commercial name) in January. Sold to mercantile in May and retained the same name. Acquired by Kelsall Bros. & Beeching of Hull. PR: LO. 393.

SEA MIST   1940/45   See under SAMUEL DOWDEN
                                        (Vol 1 p.147)

SEA MONARCH   1916/19 1940/47 Displacement: 329TG 138TN
                                        Engines: 100HP = 11K
                                        Armament: 1 x 12pdr; 1 x 7.5-inch

Bomb Thrower (A/S Howitzer)
Admty No: 1983
Port Reg: WWI: H. 411; WWII: FD. 169
P. No: WWII: Z. 115

1915: Launched. Built at Beverley by CWG. 1916: Requisitioned in February and converted to a M/S. 1919: Returned to owners. 1928: Acquired by the Dinas STC of Fleetwood. 1940: Requisitioned in January. 1943: Purchased into the RN on 23rd November. 1946: Paid Off. Laid Up in July and placed on the Sale List. 1947: Sold to JN Connell in January and BU at Glasgow.

SEA RANGER   1915/19 1940/40 Displacement: 263TG 103TN
                                     Engines: 78HP
                                     Armament: 1 x 12pdr; 1 x 6pdrAA
                                     Admty No: 1219
                                     Port Reg: WWI: H. 188; WWII: H. 418

1914: Launched. Built at Selby by Cochrane. Owned by Pickering & Haldane of Hull. 1915: Requisitioned in February and converted to a M/S. 1919: Returned to owners. Acquired by Trident SF Co. of Hull and renamed *Dungeness*. 1940: Requisitioned in May as DUNGENESS and converted to an APV. LOST. Bombed into a TCL by enemy a/c off Haisborough, Norfolk on 15th November.

SEA ROVER   1919/20   See under SEAFLOWER

SEA SEARCHER   1915/19   Displacement: 263TG 103TN
                                     Engines: 78HP
                                     Armament: 1 x 6pdr
                                     Admty No: 1187
                                     Port Reg: H. 148

1914: Launched. Built at Beverley. Owned by Humber STC of Hull. 1915: Requisitioned in March and converted to a M/S. 1917: Employed as an Escort. 1919: Returned to owners.

SEA SWEEPER   1915/19   Displacement: 329TG 138TN
                                     Engines: 99HP = 11K
                                     Armament: 1 x 12pdr
                                     Admty No: 1979
                                     Port Reg: H. 409

1915: Launched. Built at Beverley by CWG. Owned by Humber STC of Hull. 1916: Requisitioned in January and converted to a M/S. Fitted with Listening Hydrophones. 1919: Returned to owners. 1928: Acquired by Dinas ST Co. of Fleetwood. PR: FD. 171. 1939: Mercantile Loss. Captured by U-33 off Tory Island on 20th November and sunk by gunfire.

SEAWARD HO   1915/19   Displacement: 331TG 138TN
                                     Engines: 84HP = 10.5K
                                     Armament: 1 x 12pdr; 1 x 7.5-inch

Bomb Thrower (A/S Howitzer)
Admty No: 1512
Port Reg: H. 312

1915: Launched. Built at Beverley by CWG. Owned by ST White of Hull. Requisitioned in May and converted to a M/S. 1918: Renamed ATTENTIVE III in May. 1919: Returned to owners and reverted to original name. 1920: Acquired by Newington STC of Hull and renamed *Guy Thorne*. 1933: Acquired by JE Rushworth of Grimsby and renamed *Winooka*. 1936: Mercantile Loss. Sank in a collision with another trawler off the W. Coast of Scotland on 15th March.

SEDDON   1916/19 1940/46   Displacement: 296TG 115TN
                                         Engines: 89HP = 9.5K
                                         Armament: 1 x 6pdrAA
                                         Admty No: 3313
                                         Port Reg: GY. 991
                                         P. No: WWII: 4. 166 (APV)
                                         FY. 1993 (M/S)

1916: Launched. Built at Beverley by CWG. Owned by Standard SFC of Grimsby. Requisitioned in November and converted to a M/S. 1919: Returned to owners. 1940: Requisitioned in June and converted to an APV. 1941: Converted to a M/S. 1946: Returned to owners in February. 1960: BU.

SEDGEFLY   1939/39   Displacement: 590TG
                                           Armament: 1 x 4-inch
                                           P. No: FY. 122

1939: Launched. Requisitioned in September and converted to A/S. LOST. Mined off the Tyne on 16th December.

SEDOCK   1939/40   See under PATRICK DEVINE
                                           (Vol 1 p.183)

SEMIRAMIS   1914/19   Displacement: 246TG 126TN
                                           Engines: 70HP = 10.5
                                           Armament: 1 x 12pdr; 1 x 7.5-inch
                                           Bomb Thrower (A/S Howitzer)
                                           Admty No: 358
                                           Port Reg: GY. 324

1907: Launched. Built at Beverley by CWG. Owned by Roberts & Ruthven of Grimsby. 1914: Requisitioned in August and converted to a M/S. 1919: Returned to owners. 1925: Acquired by Swedish owners and renamed *Goran*. 1953: Acquired by Honduras owners. 1964: BU.

SEMNOS   1915/19 1939/45   Displacement: 216TG 80TN
                                         Engines: 70HP

Armament: 1 x 3pdr
Admty No: 1195
Port Reg: WWI: HL. 91 WWII: A. 423
P. No: WWII: FY. 726

1914: Launched. Built at Aberdeen. Owned by Friarage SFC of Hartlepool. 1915: Requisitioned in March and converted to a M/S. 1919: Returned to owners. Acquired by Silver Star FCL of Aberdeen. 1939: Requisitioned in November and converted to a D/L. Subsequently converted to an APV. 1945: Returned to owners in October.

SENATEUR DUHAMEL   1940/42   Displacement: 913T
Armament: 1 x 4-inch
Port Reg: French
P. No: FY. 327

1927: Launched. French Fishing vessel. 1940: Seized in the Atlantic on 28th December. 1941: Converted to A/S in January and commissioned into the RN. 1942: Temporary Loan to the USN. LOST. Sunk in a collision off Wilmington, N. Carolina, on 6th May.

SENATOR   1915/17   Displacement: 211TG 76TN
Engines: 60HP = 10K
Armament: 1 x 3pdr
Admty No: 295
Port Reg: GY. 61

1905: Launched. Built at Beverley by CWG. Owned by Pelham SFC of Grimsby. 1910: Acquired by Earl SFC of Grimsby. 1912: Acquired by Marshall Line SF of Grimsby. 1913: Acquired by JL. Green of Grimsby. 1914: Acquired by Reunion SFC of Grimsby. 1915: Requisitioned in August and converted to a M/S. Acquired by Crampin of Grimsby in December. 1917: LOST. Mined off Tory Island on 21st May.

SERAPION   1917/19 1939/40   Displacement: 195TG 64TN
Engines: 55HP = 10K
Port Reg: GY. 1154

1900: Launched. Built at Hull by CWG. Owned by Standard SFC of Grimsby. 1915: Acquired by HG Hopwood & HL. Taylor of Grimsby. 1917: Requisitioned into the Fishery Reserve. 1919: Returned to owners. 1922: Acquired by Diamonds SFC of Grimsby. 1939: Requisitioned in November and designated as an APV. 1940: Returned to owners in January. 1946: Mercantile Loss. Sank following a collision with another trawler in the North Sea on 5th November. No loss of life.

SERFIB   1917/19   Displacement: 210TG 82TN
Engines: 1HP
Armament: 1 x 6pdr
Admty No: 3034
Port Reg: H. 536

1917: Launched. Built at Selby by Cochrane. Owned by East Riding SFC of Hull.

Requisitioned in April and converted to a M/S. 1919: Returned to owners. *Notes*: Some mercantile lists as *Serfile*.

SERIEMA   1916/19   Displacement: 279TG 115TN
                                            Engines: 70HP = 10.5K
                                            Armament: 1 x 6pdr
                                            Port Reg: GY. 504
1909: Launched. Built at Beverley by CWG. Owned by T. Bascombe of Grimsby. 1916: Requisitioned in June and converted to a BDV. 1919: Returned to owners. 1935: Acquired by Mayfair FC of Grimsby and renamed *Mayfair*. 1939: BU in March.

SESOSTRIS   1916/19   Displacement: 293TG 123TN
                                            Engines: 89HP
                                            Armament: 1 x 12pdr; 1 x 3.5-inch
                                            Bomb Thrower (A/S Howitzer)
                                            Admty No: 1998
                                            Port Reg: GY. 894
1916: Launched. Built at Whiteinch. Owned by Roberts & Ruthven of Grimsby. Requisitioned in May and converted to a M/S. Fitted with Listening Hydrophones. 1919: Returned to owners.

SETHON   1916/19 1940/45 Displacement: 295TG 114TN
                                            Engines: 89HP = 9.5K
                                            Armament: 1 x 6pdrAA; 1 x 7.5-inch
                                            Bomb Thrower (A/S Howitzer)
                                            Admty No: 3310
                                            Port Reg: GY. 928
                                            P. No: WWII: FY. 883
1916: Launched. Built at Beverely by CWG. Owned by the Standard SFC of Grimsby. Requisitioned in October and converted to a M/S. 1919: Returned to owners. 1940: Requisitioned in June and converted to an APV. 1941: Converted to a M/S. 1945: Returned to owners in October. 1959: BU at Boom, Belgium.

SETTER   1916/19   Displacement: 171TG 66TN
                                            Engines: 58HP
                                            Armament: 1 x 6pdr
                                            Admty No: 729
                                            Port Reg: A. 129
1899: Launched. Built at Aberdeen. Owned by J & R Moon of Aberdeen. 1914: Requisitioned in December. 1917: Renamed SETTER II. 1918: Reduced to the Fishery Reserve. 1919: Returned to owners. Reverted to original name.

SETTER II   1917/19   See under SETTER

SETTSU   1914/19   Displacement: 231TG 66TN
                                           Engines: 58HP
                                           Armament: 1 x 6pdr; 1 x 7.50-inch
                                           Bomb Thrower (A/S Howitzer)
                                           Admty No: 650
                                           Port Reg: CF. 38
1912: Launched. Built at Selby by Cochrane. Owned by Neale & West of Cardiff. 1914:
Requisitioned in October and converted to a M/S. 1919: Returned to owners.

SETTSU   1939/45   Displacement: 301TG 113TN
                                           Engines: 99HP
                                           Port Reg: LO. 75
                                           P. No: Z. 140
1924: Launched. Built at Southbank-on-Tees by Smith's Dock. Owned by Jenkerson of
Milford Haven AO. 1939: Requisitioned in December and converted to a BDV. 1945:
Returned to owners.

SHACKLETON   1915/20   Displacement: 288TG 115TN
                                           Engines: 79HP
                                           Armament: 1 x 3pdr; 24 mines
                                           Admty No: 3219
                                           Port Reg: H. 1003
                                           P. Nos: N. 0A N. 93
1913: Launched. Built at Selby by Cochrane. Owned by Pickering & Haldane STC of
Hull. 1915: Requisitioned in May and converted to a M/L. 1920: Returned to owners.

SHACKLETON   **(IWM Neg No: SP2992)**

436

SHAMA   1918/19 1941/42 Displacement: 191TG 72TN
                                       Engines: 55HP
                                       Armament: 1 x 12pdr
                                       Admty No: 3083
                                       Port Reg: H. 641
1918: Launched. Built at Goole by Goole SB. Owned by Kelsall Bros. & Beeching of
Hull. Requisitioned in April and converted to a M/S. 1919: Returned to owners. 1941:
Requisitioned in January. 1942: Returned to owners in January.

SHAMROCK   1917/19 1939/45 Displacement: 184TG 73TN
                                       Engines: 50HP = 10K
                                       Port Reg: WWI: H. 483
                                       WWII: LT. 406
                                       P. No: WWII: FY. 768
1899: Launched. Built at Hull by CWG. Owned by J. Duncan of Liverpool. 1917:
Requisitioned into the Fishery Reserve. 1919: Returned to owners. 1928: Acquired by
Consolidated Fisheries of Grimsby. 1939: Requisitioned in November and converted to
an APV. 1940: Converted to a BDV in May. 1945: Stricken from the lists. Possibly
expended as a target.

SHANDWICK   1914/19 1940/46 Displacement: 166TG 65TN
                                       Engines: 67HP
                                       Armament: 1 x 6pdrAA
                                       Admty No: 509
                                       Port Reg: A. 448
                                       P. No: WWII: FY. 1587
1912: Launched. Built at Aberdeen. Owned by W. Wood & T Davidson of Aberdeen.
1914: Requisitioned in September and converted to a M/S. 1919: Returned to owners.
1940: Requisitioned in January and converted to a D/L. Converted to a M/S in
September. 1946: Returned to owners in January.

SHELDON   1915/19 1940/45 Displacement: 288TG 144TN
                                       Engines: 89HP = 10.5K
                                       Armament: WWI: 1 x 6pdr; 1 x 7.5-inch
                                       Bomb Thrower (A/S Howitzer)
                                       WWII: 2 x MG
                                       Admty No: 1407
                                       Port Reg: GY. 696
                                       P. No: WWII: 4. 143 (APV)
                                       Y7. 38 (Esso)
1912: Launched. Built at Beverley by CWG. Owned by The Standard SFC of Grimsby.
1915: Requisitioned in March and converted to a M/S. 1919: Returned to owners. 1940:
Acquired by T. Robinson of Grimsby. Requisitioned in May and converted to an APV.
1942: Converted to a M/S in March. 1944: Converted to an Esso in March. 1945:

Returned to owners in January. 1953: Mercantile Loss. Assumed to have been lost with all hands in heavy weather on the way to the Faroes in January.

SHELOMI   1915/19   Displacement: 175TG 68TN

Engines: 66HP

Armament: 1 x 6pdr

Admty No: 804

Port Reg: A. 406

1912: Launched. Built at Aberdeen. Owned by T. Davidson AO of Aberdeen. 1914: Requisitioned in November and converted to a M/S. Fitted with Listening Hydrophones. 1919: Returned to owners. 1938: Owned by AA Davidson of Aberdeen.

SHERATON   1915/19 1940/45 Displacement: 283TG 120TN

Engines: 94HP = 10.5K

Armament: 1 x 6pdr

Admty No: 1659

Port Reg: GY. 230

P. No: WWII: FY. 1788

1907: Launched. Built at Beverley by CWG. Owned by the Standard SFC of Grimsby. 1915: Requisitioned and converted to a BDV. 1919: Returned to owners. 1940: Requisitioned in June and converted to an APV. Based at Grimsby for convoy duties. 1944: Returned to owners in September. 1946: Acquired by the RAF as a target vessel. 1947: RAF Loss. Wrecked near Hunstanton LH, Norfolk.

SHIELBURN   1944/44   See under ANN FORD MELVILLE

SHIKARI   1915/19   Displacement: 221TG 86TN

Engines: 78HP

Armament: 1 x 12pdr

Admty No: 1617

Port Reg: GY. 179

1914: Launched. Built at Middlesborough by Smith's Dock. Owned by Staples SFC of Grimsby. 1915: Requisitioned in April and converted to a M/S. 1917: Employed as a Base Ship. 1918: Renamed SHAKARI II in February. 1919: Returned to owners.

SIALKOT   1914/19   Displacement: 308TG 138TN

Engines: 84HP = 10.5K

Armament: BDV: 1 x 6pdrAA

M/S: 1 x 12pdr; 1 x 6pdrAA

Admty No: 1660

Port Reg: GY. 780

1912: Launched. Built at Beverley by CWG. Owned by EC Grant & JW Little of Grimsby. 1914: Requisitioned in December and converted to a BDV. 1918: Converted to a M/S and rearmed. 1919: Returned to owners. 1924: Sold to Icelandic owners and renamed *Geir.* 1946: Acquired by Faroese owners and renamed *Vitin.* 1952: BU at Rosyth.

SICYON   1914/19   Displacement: 283TG   120TN
                                           Engines: 92HP = 10.5K
                                           Armament: 1 x 6pdrAA
                                           Admty No: 30
                                           Port Reg: GY. 163

1906: Launched. Built at Beverley by CWG. Owned by Standard SFC of Grimsby. 1914: Requisitioned in September and converted to a M/S. 1919: Returned to owners. 1933: Mercantile Loss. Took the ground in a blizzard off North East Iceland on 15th January. No loss of life.

SICYON   1939/46   Ex- *Lady Margot*
                                           Displacement: 344TG   155TN
                                           Engines: 96HP = 11K
                                           Port Reg: GY. 376
                                           P. No: FY. 669

1930: Launched. Built at Beverley by CWG. Owned by Jutland Amalgamated Trs. of Hull. PR: H. 188. 1937: Acquired by Standard SFC of Grimsby and renamed *Sicyon* PR: GY. 376. 1939: Requisitioned in September and converted to a M/S. 1946: Returned to owners in July. 1953: Acquired by Marr of Hull. 1954: BU at Grimsby.

SIDMOUTH   1914/19   Displacement: 220TG   105TN
                                             Engines: 54HP
                                           Armament: 1 x 6pdr
                                           Admty No: 123
                                           Port Reg: BL.1

1906: Launched. Built at N. Shields. Owned by W. Davies & HG Bisknell of Milford Haven. 1914: Requisitioned in August and converted to a M/S. 1919: Returned to owners. 1938: Owned by AA Davidson of Aberdeen. PR: A.103.

SIESTA   1940/44   See under A. ROSE

SILANION   1916/19   Displacement: 199TG   79TN
                                             Engines: 59HP
                                           Armament: 1 x 6pdr
                                           Admty No: 949
                                           Port Reg: GY. 128

1903: Launched. Built at North Shields. Owned by Standard SFC of Grimsby. 1915: Requisitioned in February and converted to a M/S. 1917: Returned to owners.

SILANION   1940/45   Displacement: 366TG   166TN
                                             Engines: 97HP

Port Reg: GY. 541
P. No: Z. 116

1930: Launched. Built at Selby by Cochrane. Owned by The Standard SFC of Grimsby. 1940: Requisitioned in January and converted to a BDV. 1945: Returned to owners.

SILICIA   1914/19 1939/41 Displacement: 250TG 99TN
Engines: 62HP = 10K
Armament: 1 x 6pdrAA
Admty No: 60
Port Reg: GY. 809

1912: Launched. Built at Beverley by CWG. Owned by the Gt. Grimsby & E. Coast SFC of Grimsby. 1914: Requisitioned in September and converted to a M/S. 1919: Returned to owners. 1937: Acquired by Japan FCL of Grimsby. 1939: Requisitioned in August and converted to a M/S. Joined the 72nd M/S Group based at Grimsby. 1941: LOST. Mined off the Humber on 8th May

SILURIA   1917/19 1944/45 Displacement: 207TG 81TN
Engines: 60HP
Port Reg: GY. 801

1907: Launched. Built at Goole by Goole SB. Owned by Sleight of Grimsby. 1917: Requisitioned into the Fishery Reserve. 1919: Returned to owners. 1944: Requisitioned in April, renamed CORYPHENE and converted to an Esso. 1945: Returned to owners in January. Reverted to mercantile name.

SILVERDYKE   1939/40   See under JAMES ALDRIDGE
(Vol 1 p.173)

SIMERSON   1915/19 1940/46 Displacement: 248TG 99TN
Engines: 62HP = 10K
Armament: WWI: 1 x 12pdr
WWII: 1 x 6pdr
Admty No: 1447
Port Reg: GY. 960
P. No: 4. 278

1913: Launched. Built at Beverley by CWG. Owned by the Standard SFC of Grimsby. 1915: Requisitioned in May and converted to a M/S. 1919: Returned to owners. 1937: Acquired by Japan FCL of Grimsby. 1940: Requisitioned in July and converted to an APV. 1946: Returned to owners in June. 1956: BU at Antwerp.

SIMPSON   1917/19 1940/45 Displacement: 260TG 102TN
Engines: 75HP = 9.5K
Armament: 1 x 6pdr
Admty No: 1269
Port Reg: GY. 1024

P. No: WWII: 4. 278 (APV)

FY. 545 (M/S)

1916: Launched. Built at Beverley by CWG. Owned by the Standard SFC of Grimsby. Requisitioned in May and converted to a M/S. 1919: Returned to owners. 1940: Acquired by A Black of Grimsby. Requisitioned in June and converted to an APV. 1942: Converted to a M/S in May. 1945: Returned to owners in December. 1956: BU at Gateshead.

SINDONIS	1939/41	Ex-*Soudanese*
		Displacement: 440TG 164TN
		Engines: 99HP
		Armament: 1 x 4-inch
		Port Reg: GY. 92
		P. No: FY. 120

1934: Launched. Built at Southbank-on-Tees by Smith's Dock. Owned by Loyal SFC of Grimsby. 1939: Requisitioned in August and converted to A/S. 1941: Deployed to the Med. and joined the Inshore Squadron off Tobruk. LOST. Sunk by enemy a/c at Tobruk on 29th May.

SINGAPORE	1917/19	Displacement: 159TG 63TN
		Engines: 45HP = 10K
		Port Reg: H. 505

1900: Launched. Built at Hull by CWG. Owned by Hull SF & Ice Co. 1917: Requisitioned into the Fishing Reserve. 1919: Returned to owners. 1920: Mercantile Loss. Sank in a collision with HMS ADVENTURE which was anchored in the River Humber on 12th January. Six lives lost.

SIR JAMES RECKITT	1915/19 1940/46	Displacement: 324TG 125TN
		Engines: 93HP = 11K
		Armament: WWI: 1 x 12pdr; 1 x 3.5-inch Bomb Thrower (A/S Howitzer);
		WWII: 1 x 12pdr
		Admty No: 1887
		Port Reg:WWI: H. 32
		WWII: Portuguese
		P.No: WWII: FY. 1927

1909: Launched. Built at Beverley by CWG. Owned by Pickering & Haldane STC of Hull. 1915: Requisitioned in September and converted to a M/S. Fitted with Listening Hydrophones. 1918: Acquired by A Bannister of Grimsby. PR: GY. 1203. 1919: Returned to owners. 1922: Acquired by Portuguese owners and renamed *Estrella d'Alva*. 1940: Purchased into the RN from Portuguese owners as ESTRELLA d' ALVA. 1942: Converted to a M/S and renamed SUNBURST. 1946: Sold to mercantile at Kilindini in January. Re-acquired by original Portuguese owners and reverted to *Estrella D'Alva*. 1956: BU.

SIR JOHN FRENCH   1916/19   Displacement: 351TG 152TN
Engines: 100HP = 11K
Armament: 1 x 12pdr
Admty No: 1501
Port Reg: H. 262

1914: Launched. Built at Beverley by CWG. Owned by Imperial SFC of Hull. 1915: Requisitioned in May and converted to a M/S. Fitted with Listening Hydrophones. 1916: Fitted to carry 1 x Schnieder a/c. Employed on North Sea anti-Zeppelin patrols. 1918: Acquired by J. Willows of Grimsby PR: GY.1152. 1919: Returned to owners. 1920: Acquired by Sir John French SFC of Halifax, Nova Scotia. 1923: Mercantile Loss. Wrecked in Fortune Bay, Newfoundland on 23rd July.

SIR JOHN LISTER   1939/45   See under PETER KILLIN (Vol 1 p.70)

SIR MARK SYKES   1915/19   Displacement: 307TG 124TN
Engines: 93HP
Armament: 1 x 12pdr; 1 x 3.5-inch
Bomb Thrower (A/S Howitzer)
Admty No: 1513
Port Reg: H. 43

1914: Launched. Built at Selby by Cochrane. Owned by Pickering & Haldane of Hull. 1915: Requisitioned in May and converted to a M/S. Fitted with Listening Hydrophones. 1919: Returned to owners.

SISAPON   1939/40   Displacement: 326TG 133TN
Engines: 92HP = 10.5K
Port Reg: GY .483

1928: Launched. Built at Beverley by CWG. Owned by the Standard SFC of Grimsby. 1939: Requisitioned in September and converted to a M/S. Fitted out at Grimsby. 1940: Based at Grimsby (Ungrouped). LOST. Mined off Harwich on 12th June.

SISTERS MELVILLE   1915/17   Displacement: 260TG
Admty No: 1951
Port Reg: A. 459

1915: Launched. Requisitioned in November and converted to a M/S. 1917: LOST. Mined near Aldeburgh on 13th February.

SITVEL   1914/19 1939/40   Displacement: 290TG 116TN
Engines: 84HP
Armament: WWI: 1 x 12pdr; 1 x 7.5-inch Bomb Thrower (A/S Howitzer);
WWII: 1 x 12pdr
Admty No: 197
Port Reg: FD. 49

1914: Launched. Built at Selby by Cochrane. Owned by Marr of Fleetwood. Requisitioned in December and converted to a M/S. 1919: Returned to owners. Renamed *Velia*. 1939: Requisitioned in December as VELIA and converted to an APV. 1940: LOST. Sunk in the Harwich area on 19th October. Presumed mined.

SKERNE   1917/19   Displacement: 150TG 54TN
                                            Engines: 45HP
                                            Port Reg: H. 453
1891: Launched. Built at Glasgow. Iron construction. Owned by HW Barker of Billingsgate. 1917: Requisitioned into the Fishery Reserve. 1919: Returned to owners.

SKILPAD   1951/58   SAN. See under SPINDRIFT

SLASHER   1916/19   Ex-*Sethon*
                                              Displacement: 195TG 77TN
                                            Engines: 55HP = 10K
                                            Armament: 1 x 6pdr
                                            Admty No: 1744
                                            Port Reg: GY. 1167
1900: Launched. Built at Hull by CWG. Owned by Standard SFC of Grimsby. 1913: Acquired by Spartan STC of Grimsby and renamed *Slasher*. 1915: Requisitioned in July as SLASHER and converted to a M/S. Acquired by Lindsey SFC of Grimsby in September. 1919: Returned to owners. 1940: Mercantile War Loss. Sunk by German a/c in the North Sea on 1st June.

SLEBECH   1915/19 1939/46 Displacement: 222TG 85TN
                                              Engines: 68HP
                                            Armament: 1 x 6pdrAA
                                            Admty No: 1758
                                            Port Reg: WWI: FD. 74; WWII: M. 199
                                            P. No: WWII: Y7. .28
1908: Launched. Built at N. Shields. Owned by J. Uttley of Fleetwood. 1915: Requisitioned in May and converted to a M/S. 1919: Returned to owners. 1938: Owned by Huddlestone of Milford Haven. 1939: Requisitioned in December and converted to a M/S. 1943: Converted to an Esso in March. 1944: Converted to a Water Carrier in January. 1946: Returned to owners in January.

SMEW   1916/19   Displacement: 223TG 86TN
                                              Engines: 54HP
                                            Armament: 1 x 6pdr
                                            Admty No: 1201
                                            Port Reg: H .75
1907: Launched. Built at Tonning. Owned by Jordan & Wheeldon of Hull. 1915: Requisitioned in January and converted to a M/S. 1919: Returned to owners.

SNAKEFLY   1939/45   See under FANE of 1939

SNIPE   1915/19   Displacement: 166TG 66TN
                                              Engines: 41HP
                                              Armament: 1 x 3pdr
                                              Admty No: 384
                                              Port Reg: H. 133
1897: Launched. Built at North Shields. Owned by Kelsall Bros. & Beeching of Hull.
1914: Requisitioned in November and converted to a BDV. 1920: Returned to owners.

SOAR   1916/19   Displacement: 219TG 85TN
                                              Engines: 77HP
                                              Armament: 1 x 12pdr
                                              Admty No: 1620
                                              Port Reg: FD. 155
1915: Launched. Built at Middlesborough by Smith's Dock. Owned by Ward & Son of
Fleetwood. Requisitioned in April and converted to a M/S. 1919: Returned to owners.
1938: Owned by Kelman & Robertson of Aberdeen. Port Reg: A. 284. 1940: Mercantile
Loss. Wrecked.

SOLDIER PRINCE   1914/19   Displacement: 156TG 61TN
                                              Engines: 46HP
                                              Armament: 1 x 3pdr
                                              Admty No: 284
                                              Port Reg: SN. 277
1900: Launched. Built at South Shields. Owned by A Walker of Aberdeen. 1914:
Requisitioned in August and converted to a M/S. 1920: Returned to owners.

SOLOMON   1939/42   Ex-*Lady Rachael*
                                              Displacement: 357TG 153TN
                                              Engines: 96HP = 10.6K
                                              Port Reg: GY. 372
1928: Launched. Built at Beverley by CWG. Owned by Jutland Amalgamated Trs. of
Hull. PR: H. 457. 1937: Acquired by Standard SFC of Grimsby and renamed *Solomon*
PR: GY. 372. 1939: Requisitioned in August and converted to a M/S. Based at Grimsby
(Ungrouped). 1940: Joined the 17th M/S Group based at Grimsby. 1942: LOST. Mined
to the N. of Cromer on 1st April.

SOLON   1914/19   Displacement: 295TG 120TN
                                              Engines: 96HP = 10.5K
                                              Armament: 1 x 6pdrAA
                                              Admty No: 55
                                              Port Reg: GY. 714
1913: Launched. Built at Beverley by CWG. Owned by The Standard SFC of Grimsby.

1914: Requisitioned in August and converted to a M/S. 1919: Returned to owners. 1928: Mercantile Loss. Took the ground off Iceland in October. One crewman died of exposure once they had managed to get ashore.

SOLON   1939/46   Displacement: 348TG 148TN
Measurements:140ft x 24ft 6ins
Engines: 96HP = 10.5K
Armament: 1 x 12pdr; 1 x LG
Port Reg: GY. 337
P. No: FY. 601

1931: Launched. Built at Beverley by CWG. Owned by The Standard SFC of Grimsby. 1939: Requisitioned in November and converted to a M/S. Fitted with Oropesa gear. Joined the M/S Group based at Lowestoft for sweeping from Lowestoft to Sheringham Shoal. 1940: Patrolling a swept channel off Gt. Yarmouth in February when she was attacked by two Heinkel IIIs. She was on the receiving end of over 20 bombs only one of which was a direct hit and that failed to explode and bounced over the side. There were also thousands of bullets and incendiaries aimed at her but she survived with only medium damage and two killed. 1946: Returned to owners in June. 1948: Acquired Devon FCL of Hull and renamed *Orsino* PR: H. 579. 1955: BU at Gateshead.

SOMERVILLE   1917/19   Displacement: 149TG 55TN
Engines: 45HP
Port Reg: GY. 301

1891: Launched. Built at Govan. Owned by W Would of Grimsby. 1917: Requisitioned into the Fishery Reserve. 1919: Returned to owners.

SONNEBLOM   1921/34   See under JOHN EDMUND (Vol 1 p.141)

SOPHOS   1915/19   Displacement: 217TG 80TN
Engines: 70HP
Armament: 1 x 3pdr
Admty No: 1185
Port Reg: A. 22

1914: Launched. Built at Aberdeen. Owned by National SFC (Aberdeen). 1915: Requisitioned in March and converted to a M/S. 1919: Returned to owners.

SOPHRON   1916/17   Displacement: 195TG 62TN
Engines: 59HP = 10K
Armament: 1 x 6pdrAA
Admty No: 725
Port Reg: GY. 1270

1903: Launched. Built at Hull by CWG. Owned by Standard SFC of Grimsby. 1914: Requisitioned in December and converted to a M/S. 1917: LOST. Mined off the Firth of Tay on 22nd August.

SORANUS	1940/45	See under ARIES

SOUBRETTE	1940/45	See under SAMUEL GASBY
		(Vol 1 p.186)

SOUTHCOATES	1940/45	See under SAMUEL DRAKE
		(Vol 1 p.73)

SOUTH SEA	1940/42	RNZN
		Displacement: 322TG
		Port Reg: NZ

1913: Launched. New Zealand fishing vessel. 1940: Requisitioned and converted to a M/S. Commissioned into the RNZN on 12th August. 1942: LOST. Sunk in a collision with the *Wahine* on 19th December.

SOUTHWARD	1917/19	Displacement: 225TG
		Port Reg: GY. 288

1907: Launched. 1917: Requisitioned into the Fishery Reserve. 1919: Returned to owners.

SOUTHWARD HO	1944/45	See under THOMAS COWELL
		(See Addenda p.531)

SPANIARD	1939/42	Displacement: 455TG
		Armament: 1 x 4-inch
		P. No: FY. 144

1937: Launched. 1939: Purchased into the RN in August and converted to an A/S. Employed on convoy escorts. 1942: LOST. Destroyed in an explosion at Lagos on 5th December. *Notes*: See Notes under KELT.

SPARROW	1909/20	Ex-*Josephine I*
		Displacement: 550T 266TG
		Armament: 1 x 12pdr
		Admty No: 58

1908: Launched. Built at Goole by Goole SB. 1909: Purchased into the RN in April for M/S experiments at Portland. 1914: Based at Portsmouth as M/S Training Ship for Trawler Reserve Crews. 1920: Renamed JOSEPHINE I, her original mercantile name, in January. Sold to mercantile in May and renamed *Orion*.

SPARTAN	1917/19	Trawler/Drifter/Trawler
		Displacement: 120TG 40TN
		Engines: 45HP = 10K
		Port Reg: GN. 63

1893: Launched. Built at Hull by CWG as a trawler. Owned by T. Robinson of Grimsby.

1907: Acquired by CR Seller of Peterhead and converted to a drifter. PR: PD.206. 1915: Acquired by TL Devlin of Granton. PR: GN. 63. 1917: Requisitioned into the Fishery Reserve. 1919: Returned to owner. 1926: BU.

SPEEDWELL	1914/18	Displacement: 273TG
		Armament: 1 x 12pdr; 1 x 6pdr
		Admty No: 392
		Port Reg: H. 481

1899: Launched. 1914: Requisitioned in November and converted to a M/S. 1915: Renamed SPEEDWELL II in February. 1916: Converted to a 'Q' Ship. 1918: LOST. Took the ground in Mounts Bay on 15th July and broke up. *Notes*: Operated under the names of Q.33, *Glendale*, *Roger*, and *Vanda* as a 'Q' Ship.

SPEETON	1915/15	Displacement: 205TG
		Armament: 1 x 3pdr
		Admty No: 1908
		Port Reg: H.104

1913: Launched. 1915: Requisitioned in October. LOST. Mined off Lowestoft on 31st December.

SPHENE	1940/45	See under AVANTURINE

SPIDER	1909/14	Ex-*Assyrian*
		Displacement: 256TG
		Armament: 1 x 6pdr
		Admty No: 54

1908: Launched. Built at Selby by Cochrane. 1909: Purchased into the RN in April and converted to a M/S. Employed on M/S experiments at Portland. 1914: Based at Portsmouth as M/S Training Ship for Fishery Reserve Crews. LOST. Wrecked off Lowestoft on 24th November.

SPIDER	1915/19	Displacement: 271TG 107TN
		Engines: 78HP
		Armament: 1 x 12pdr
		Admty No: 1378
		Port Reg: H. 914

1906: Launched. Built at Hull. 1915: Requisitioned in April and converted to a M/S. 1919: Returned to owners. 1920: Acquired by Grant & Baker SFC of Grimsby. PR: GY. 1254.

SPINDRIFT	1940/58	Displacement: 926T
		Measurements: 160ft. x 26ft.
		Port Reg: German
		P. No: FY. 1654

1940: German Armed Trawler POLARIS captured in April. Renamed and commissioned

SPINDRIFT **(Republic of South Africa)**

into the RN as an A/S Training Ship from June. 1942: Converted to a M/L in January. 1946: Transferred to the SAN. 1951: Renamed SKILPAD. 1958: Sold to BU.

SPINET   1939/46   Ex-*St. Merryn*
                                        Displacement: 352TG 148TN
                                        Engines: 96HP = 10.8K
                                        Port Reg: H. 40
1924: Launched. Built at Beverley by CWG. Owned by T Hamling of Hull. 1939: Requisitioned in September, renamed SPINET and converted to a BDV. Based at Lyness. 1946: Returned to owners in June and reverted to original name. 1953: Acquired by Sleight of Grimsby and renamed *Rubato*. PR: GY. 84. 1956: BU at Bruges, Belgium.

SPRAY   1940/40   Displacement: 305TG
1940: American fishing vessel nominated for transfer under Lend/Lease. Transfer cancelled.

SPRINGWELL   1917/19   Displacement: 286TG 113TN
                                          Engines: 80HP
                                        Armament: 1 x 12pdr
                                          Admty No: 3341
                                          Port Reg: FD
1917: Launched. Built at Goole by Goole SB. Owned by the Sun STC of Hull. Requisitioned in May and converted to a M/S. 1919: Returned to owners.

SPURS   1939/45   Football Group
Displacement: 399TG 150TN
Engines: 99HP
Port Reg: GY. 515
P.No: FY. 168

1933: Launched. Built at Southbank-on-Tees by Smith's Dock. Owned by Consolidated Fisheries of Grimsby. 1939: Purchased into the RN in August and converted to A/S. 1945: Sold to mercantile and retained the same name. Re-acquired by Consolidated Fisheries. PR: GY.148.

STAFNES   1939/45   Displacement: 456TG 244TN
Engines: 132HP
Port Reg: GY. 297
P. No: FY. 192

1936: Launched. Built at Selby by Cochrane. Owned by Rinovia SF Co. of Grimsby. 1939: Purchased into the RN in September and converted to A/S. 1945: Sold to mercantile and retained the same name. Re-acquired by the Rinovia SFC. PR: GY. 172.

STALBERG   1940/45   Displacement: 358TG 153TN
Engines:103HP
Port Reg: GY. 145
P. No: Z. 108

1929: Launched. Built at Selby by Cochrane. Owned by Consolidated Fisheries of Grimsby. 1940: Requisitioned in January and converted to a BDV. 1945: Returned to owners in November. 1957: BU.

SPURS   **(MPL)**

STALKER	1915/19 1944/44	Ex-*Jeria*

STALKER   1915/19 1944/44   Ex-*Jeria*
Displacement: 197TG 61TN
Engines: 50HP = 10K
Armament: 1 x 6pdr; 1 x 7.5-inch Bomb
Thrower (A/S Howitzer)
Admty No: 1838
Port Reg: GY. 496
P. No: WWII: 4. 428

1899: Launched. Built at Hull by CWG as Jeria. Iron construction. Owned by Great Grimsby & East Coast SFC of Grimsby. 1913: Acquired by Spartan SFC of Grimsby and renamed *Stalker*. 1915: Requisitioned in July and converted to a M/S. Acquired by Lindsey SFC of Grimsby in September. 1919: Returned to owners. 1941: Sustained damage when she was bombed by German a/c whilst in the River Humber on 1st April. 1944: Requisitioned in April as CHOICE and converted to an Esso. LOST. Sank in a collision with the Tug EMPIRE SAMSON off Arrowmanches, Normandy on 25th August.

STALWART   1917/19   Displacement: 333TG 136TN
Engines: 82HP = 10.5K
Armament: 1 x 12pdr; 1 x 7.5-inch
Bomb Thrower (A/S Howitzer)
Admty No: 2999
Port Reg: H .213

1914: Launched. Built at Beverley by CWG. Owned by J Hollingworth of Hull. 1917: Requisitioned in March and converted to a M/S. 1918: Renamed STALWART II in February. Acquired by H Burns of Grimsby. PR: GY. 1116. 1919: Returned to owners and reverted to original name. 1921: Acquired by Spanish owners. 1927: Renamed *Santa Rosa*. 1936: Commissioned into the Basque Navy and renamed GAZ TIEZ. 1937: Captured by the Nationalist Navy and renamed VIRGEN DEL CARMEN. 1985: BU.

STALWART II   1918/19   See under STALWART above

STANDARD   1917/19   Displacement: 162TG 63TN
Engines: 52HP
Port Reg: H. 460

1899: Launched. Built at North Shields. Owned by H. Smethurst AO of Grimsby. 1917: Requisitioned into the Fishery Reserve. 1919: Returned to owners.

STANLEY WEYMAN   1915/19   Displacement: 288TG 115TN
Engines: 79HP
Armament: 1 x 12pdr; 1 x 7.5-inch
Bomb Thrower (A/S Howitzer)
Admty No: 1210
Port Reg: H. 1005

1913: Launched. Built at Selby by Cochrane. Owned by Newington STC of Hull. 1915: Requisitioned in January and converted to a M/S. 1919: Returned to owners.

STAR of BRITAIN	1914/19 1940/45	Displacement: 228TG 89TN
		Engines: 58HP
		Admty No: 465
		Port Reg: A. 239
		P. No :WWII: FY. 1678 (M/S)
		Y7. 39 (Esso)

1908: Launched. Built at Aberdeen. Owned by the Walker SFC of Aberdeen. 1914: Requisitioned in September and converted to a M/S. 1919: Returned to owners. 1940: Requisitioned in June and converted to a M/S. 1944: Converted to an Esso in March. 1945: Returned to owners in November.

| STAR of DEVORAN | 1939/41 | See under STAR OF PEACE |

STAR of FREEDOM	1915/17	Displacement: 258TG
		Armament: 1 x 12pdr
		Admty No: 955
		Port Reg: FD. 200

1911: Launched. 1915: Requisitioned in January and converted to a M/S. 1917: LOST. Mined off Trevose Head, Cornwall, on 19th April

| STAR of FREEDOM | 1939/46 | See under INCHGARTH |

| STAR of HOPE | 1917/19 | Displacement: 124TG |
| | | Port Reg: A. 411 |

1896: Launched. 1917: Requisitioned into the Fishery Reserve. 1919: Returned to owners.

| STAR of LIBERTY | 1940/46 | See under JOHN CALLAGHAN |
| | | (Vol 1 p.177) |

STAR of ORKNEY	1939/46	Displacement: 273TG 117TN
		Engines: 73HP
		Port Reg: A. 421
		P. No: FY .683

1936: Launched. Built at Aberdeen by Hall Russell. Owned by Walker SF Co. of Aberdeen. 1939: Requisitioned in August and converted to a M/S. 1946: Returned to owners in September. *Notes*: This vessel was used as the basis for the design of the Round Table Class.

STAR of PEACE	1915/19 1939/41	Displacement: 239TG 91TN
		Engines: 78HP
		Armament: 1 x 6pdr

Admty No: 1952
Port Reg: WWI: A. 481; WWII: A. 304

1915: Launched. Built at Aberdeen. Owned by Walker SFC of Aberdeen. Requisitioned in November and converted to a M/S. 1919: Returned to owners. 1939: Requisitioned and converted to a M/S. 1941: LOST. Sunk by enemy a/c off N. Shields on 30th September.

STAR of PENTLAND   1940/46   Displacement: 239TG 93TN
                                           Engines: 70HP
                                           Port Reg: A. 245

1915: Launched. Built at Aberdeen. Owned by Walker SFC of Aberdeen. 1940: Requisitioned in January and converted to a M/S. 1946: Returned to owners in May.

STAR OF PENTLAND   **(MPL)**

STAR of the EAST   1914/19   Displacement: 218TG 86TN
Engines: 82HP
Armament: 1 x 6pdr
Admty No: 331
Port Reg: A. 464

1912: Launched. Built at Aberdeen. Owned by Walker SFC of Aberdeen. 1914: Requisitioned in August and converted to a M/S. 1919: Returned to owners. 1938: Owned by Scales & Son of Edinburgh. PR: LH. 36.

STAR of the EMPIRE   1914/19   Displacement: 210TG 86TN
Engines: 82HP
Armament: 1 x 3pdr
Admty No: 318
Port Reg: A. 508

1912: Launched. Built at Aberdeen. Owned by Walker SFC of Aberdeen. 1914: Requisitioned in August and converted to a M/S. 1919: Returned to owners.

STAR of the ISLES   1914/19   Displacement: 217TG 86TN
Engines: 82HP
Armament: 1 x 6pdrAA
Admty No: 319
Port Reg: A. 452

1912: Launched. Built at Aberdeen. Owned by Walker SFC of Aberdeen. 1914: Requisitioned in August and converted to a M/S. 1919: Returned to owners. 1938: Owned by Scales & Son of Edinburgh. Port Reg: LH. 45.

STAR of the NORTH   1914/19   Displacement: 192TG 74TN
Engines: 67HP
Armament: 1 x 6pdrAA
Admty No: 118
Port Reg: A. 633

1903: Launched. Built at Aberdeen. Owned by Walker SFC of Aberdeen. 1914: Requisitioned in August and converted to a M/S. 1919: Returned to owners. 1938: Owned by Craig AO of Aberdeen PR: A. 116.

STAR of the OCEAN   1914/19   Displacement: 203TG 80TN
Engines: 70HP
Port Reg: A. 901

1903: Launched. Built at Aberdeen. Owned by Walker SFC of Aberdeen. 1915: Requisitioned in June and converted to a BDV. 1919: Returned to owners. 1938: Owned by McKenzie Ltd. of Aberdeen.

STAR of the REALM   1940/46   See under WILLIAM WESTENBURGH
(Vol 1 p.151)

STAR of the SOUTH   1917/19   Displacement: 182TG   69TN
Engines: 67HP
Port Reg: GY. 676

1903: Launched. Built at Aberdeen. Owned by Walker SFC of Aberdeen. 1917: Requisitioned into the Fishery Reserve. 1919: Returned to owners. Acquired by J Coombes of Harrogate. PR: GY. 676.

STAR of the WAVE   1916/19   Displacement: 205TG   79TN
Engines: 61HP
Armament: 1 x 6pdrAA; 1 x 7.5-inch
Bomb Thrower (A/S Howitzer)
Admty No: (i) 67   (ii) 510   (iii) 1956
Port Reg: A. 913

1904: Launched. Built at Aberdeen. Owned by Walker SFC of Aberdeen. 1914: Requisitioned in September and converted to a M/S. 1919: Returned to owners.

STAR of the WAVE   1940/45   See under W.S. BURTON

STAUNCH   1940/44   See under BENGAL of 1915

STAUNTON   1914/20   1940/40   Displacement: 283TG   120TN
Engines: 90HP = 10.75K
Armament: 1 x 6pdr
Admty No: 710
Port Reg: GY. 350

1907: Launched. Built at Beverley by CWG. Owned by Standard SFC of Grimsby. 1914: Requisitioned in November and converted to an APV. 1920: Returned to owners. 1940: Requisitioned in June for conversion to an APV. Returned to owners in July. Mercantile Loss. Presumed sunk by a magnetic mine in the Thames Estuary off the Knoll Buoy on 28th July. She was being returned to her owners and all 13 crew were lost.

STELLA CONOPUS   1939/45   Displacement: 418TG   162TN
Engines: 105TN
Port Reg: H. 273
P. No: FY. 248

1936: Launched. Built at Selby by Cochrane. Owned by Charleson & Smith of Hull. 1939: Requisitioned in August and converted to A/S. 1945: Took the surrender of a U-Boat off Loch Eriboll, N. Scotland, on the last day of the war. Returned to owners in November.

STELLA CAPELLA   1939/42   Ex-*Admiral Hawke*
Displacement: 507TG   195TN
Engines: 132HP = 12.5K
Armament: 1 x 4-inch

Port Reg: H. 476
P. No: FY. 107

1937: Launched. Built at Beverley by CWG as *Admiral Hawke*. Owned by CH Smith of Hull. 1938: Acquired by Charleson & Smith of Hull and renamed *Stella Capella*. 1939: Purchased into the RN in August and converted to A/S. Joined the 12th A/S Strike Force at Belfast. 1940: TPI the Norwegian Campaign in April/May. 1941: Joined the 41st A/S Group based at Iceland. 1942: LOST. Torpedoed by U-701 off Iceland on 11th March.

STELLA CARINA   1939/45   Displacement: 440TG 168TN
                                        Engines: 114HP = 9K
                                        Armament: 1 x 12pdr
                                        Port Reg: H. 327
                                        P. No: FY. 352

1936: Launched. Built at Selby by Cochrane. Owned by Charleson & Smith of Hull. 1939: Requisitioned in November and converted to an APV. 1941: Converted to A/S in March. ICW LORD NUFFIELD, LADY HOGARTH and KINGSTON AMBER formed an escort Group employed on Atlantic/Med convoys. 1942: TIH at Milford Haven for refitting. Re-Commissioned and employed on Atlantic Convoys after work-up at Tobermory. 1943: Transferred to the MF and based at Gibraltar for convoy work to N. Africa. Transferred firstly to Malta and then to Alexandria. TPI Operation Avalanche, the Salerno Landings in Sept/Oct patrolling the approaches. 1944: TPI Operation Husky, the Sicily Landings in July/August. TPI the landings at Salerno in Sept/Oct. Transferred to Tripoli for convoy escorts Corsica – Salerno. 1945: Returned to the UK and Paid Off. Returned to owners in May.

STELLA CARINA

STELLA DORADO   1939/40   Displacement: 416TG
Port Reg: H.
P. No: FY. 131

1935: Launched. Owned by Charleson & Smith of Hull. 1939: Purchased into the RN in August and converted to A/S. 1940: TPI Operation Dynamo, the evacuation of Dunkirk on May/June. LOST. Torpedoed by U-Boat off Dunkirk on 1st June.

STELLA LEONIS   1939/46   Displacement: 345TG   136TN
Engines: 96HP
Port Reg: H. 423
P. No: FY. 706

1928: Launched. Built at Selby by Cochrane. Owned by Charleson & Smith of Hull. 1939: Requisitioned in September and converted to a M/S. 1944: Converted to a D/L. TPI Operation Neptune, the D-Day Landings in June, as a D/L attached to the 7th M/S Flot. in Force J. 1946: Returned to owners in July.

STELLA ORION   1939/40   Displacement: 417TG   159TN
Engines: 105HP
Port Reg: H. 215

1935: Launched. Built at Selby by Cochrane. Owned by Charleson & Smith of Hull. 1939: Requisitioned in September and converted to a M/S. 1940: LOST. Mined in the Thames Estuary on 11th November.

STELLA PEGASI   1939/45   Displacement: 441TG   191TN
Engines: 133HP
Armament: 1 x 12pdr; 2 x 0.5-inchAA
(1x2); 2 x VMG (2x1)
Port Reg: H. 90
P. No: FY. 155

1935: Launched. Built at Selby by Cochrane. Owned by Charleson & Smith of Hull. 1939: Requisitioned in September and converted to A/S. 1945: Returned to owners in June. *Notes*: Entered in mercantile lists as *Stella Pegasis*.

STELLA POLARIS   1940/45   Displacement: 498TG   190TN
Engines: 132HP
Port Reg: H. 383
P.No: 4. 258 (APV)

1936: Launched. Built at Selby by Cochrane. Owned by Charleson & Smith Trs. of Hull. 1940: Requisitioned in May and converted to an APV. 1941: Converted to A/S. 1942: Temporary Loan to the USN from February. Returned to the RN on October and transferred to the S. Africa Station. 1945: Returned to the UK and Paid Off. Returned to owners in October.

STELLA RIGEL   1939/45   Ex-*Lady Beryl*
                                       Ex-*Ocean Duke*
                                       Displacement: 358TG 153TN
                                       Engines: 96HP = 11K
                                       Armament: 1 x 12pdr
                                       Port Reg: H. 283
                                       P. No: FY. 657

1926: Launched. Built at Beverley by CWG as *Lady Beryl*. Owned by Jutland Amalgamated Trs. of Hull. 1935: Acquired by Ocean SFC of Hull and renamed *Ocean Duke*. 1938: Acquired by Charleson & Smith of Hull and renamed *Stella Rigel*. 1939: Requisitioned in September and converted to a M/S. 1943: In collision with the Tr. DONNA NOOK off Harwich on 25th September. Whilst sweeping they were attacked by E-Boats and both Trs. took evading action. Unfortunately they were too close in company and DONNA NOOK was rammed amidships, rolled onto her beam ends and sank. 1945: Returned to owners in July. Renamed *Alamein*. 1949: Renamed *Lady Olwen*. 1955: Renamed *Remindo* PR: GY. 252. Mercantile Loss. Driven ashore in a gale when her cable parted in the Faroes with the loss of four lives.

STELLA SIRIUS   1939/40   Displacement: 404TG 156TN
                                        Engines: 99HP
                                        Port Reg: H.22

1934: Launched. Built at Southbank-on-Tees by Smiths Dock. Owned by Charleson & Smith Trs. of Hull. 1939: Requisitioned in September and converted to A/S. 1940: LOST. Sunk by air attack when French a/c attacked Gibraltar on 25th September. 1919: Cancelled.

STEWART BOYLE   1914/19   Displacement: 197TG 77TN
                                        Engines: 66HP
                                        Armament: 1 x 6pdrAA
                                        Admty No: 517
                                        Port Reg: GW .27

1911: Launched. Built at Aberdeen. Owned by JS Boyle of Glasgow. 1914: Requisitioned in October and converted to a M/S. 1920: Returned to owner.

STOCKADE   19 44/46   See under ANSON of 1915

STOKE CITY   1939/46   Football Group
                                     Displacement: 422TG 161TN
                                     Engines: 99HP
                                     Armament: 1 x 4-inch; 3 x 20mmAA
                                     (3x1)
                                     Port Reg: GY. 114
                                     P. No: FY. 232

1935: Launched on 7th December. Built at Southbank-on-Tees by Smith's Dock.

Owned by Consolidated Fisheries of Grimsby. 1939: Requisitioned in September and converted to A/S. 1941: Deployed to the Med. Joined the Inshore Squadron off Tobruk. Sustained damage by enemy a/c. 1946: Returned to owners in February.

STONEFLY	1939/45	Ex-*Malayan*
		Displacement: 238TG 93TN
		Engines: 77HP = 10.2K
		Port Reg: GY. 322
		P. No: FY. 596

1930: Launched. Built at Beverley by CWG. Owned by Robinson of Grimsby. 1939: Requisitioned in August, renamed and converted to a M/S. 1945: Returned to owners in September and reverted to her original name. 1961: Sold to Greek interests and renamed *Ritsa*. 1965: Renamed *Lindos*. 1985: BU in Greece.

STORMCENTRE	1942/46	See under DANIEL MUNRO
		(Vol 1 p.133)

STORMCOCK	1917/19	Displacement: 151TG 63TN
		Engines: 50HP = 10K
		Port Reg: H. 405

1892. Launched. Built at Hull by CWG. Owned by Pickering & Haldane of Hull. PR: H. 207. 1913: Acquired by Sunrise FCL of Fleetwood. 1917: Requisitioned into the Fishery Reserve. 1918: Acquired by Armitage STC of Hull. PR: H. 405. 1919: Returned to owners. Acquired by EW. Hall of Lowestoft. PR: LT. 393. 1924: Acquired by Plymouth owners. 1937: BU.

STORMCOCK	1939/40	See under CAPETOWN II

STORNOWAY	1915/19	Displacement: 208TG 80TN
		Engines: 50HP = 10K
		Armament: 1 x 6pdr
		Admty No: 1792
		Port Reg: H. 83

1910: Launched. Built at Beverley by CWG. Owned by Hull SF & Ice Co. 1915: Requisitioned in January and converted to a M/S. 1919: Returned to owners. 1936: BU. *Notes*: One of the first Trawlers to be fitted with electric lighting.

STOUR	1920/22 1939/46	See under DANIEL FEARALL
		(Vol 1 p.133)

STRATHAFTON	1914/19	Displacement: 209TG 81TN
		Engines: 74HP
		Armament: 1 x 12pdr
		Port Reg: A. 551

STORNOWAY (MPL)

1913: Launched. Built at Aberdeen. Owned by Aberdeen ST & FCL of Aberdeen. 1914: Requisitioned in August and converted to a M/S. 1919: Returned to owners.

STRATHAIRLIE   1915/19   Displacement: 193TG 75TN
                                                   Engines: 67HP
                                                   Armament: 1 x 6pdrAA
                                                   Admty No: 1168
                                                   Port Reg: A. 39

1905: Launched.   Built at Aberdeen.   Owned by R Main of Aberdeen.   1915: Requisitioned in February and converted to a M/S. 1919: Returned to owners.

STRATHALLADALE   1915/19 1944/44 Displacement: 199TG 77TN
                                  Engines: 67HP
                                  Armament: 1 x 12pdr
                                  Admty No: 950
                                  Port Reg: WWI: A. 189; WWII: A. 285
1908: Launched. Built at Aberdeen. Iron construction. Owned by J Inglis of Peebles.
1915: Requisitioned in February and converted to a M/S. 1919: Returned to owners. 1938:
Owned by J & C Brown of Aberdeen. 1944: Requisitioned in April and converted to an
Esso. Returned to owners in October.

STRATHALLAN   1915/19   Displacement: 175TG 67TN
                                  Engines: 55HP
                                  Port Reg: GN. 76
1900: Launched. Built at Aberdeen. Owned by W Lyle of Leith. 1915: Requisitioned in
May and converted to a Decoy. 1916: Re-employed. 1917: Reduced to the Fishery
Reserve. 1919: Returned to owners.

STRATHALVA   1917/19   Displacement: 215TG 93TN
                                  Engines: 74HP
                                  Armament: 2 x 6pdrAA
                                  Admty No: 3005
                                  Port Reg: A. 757
1917: Launched. Built at Aberdeen. Owned by Aberdeen ST & FC of Aberdeen.
Requisitioned in February. 1919: Returned to owners.

STRATHATHOL   1914/19   Displacement: 209TG 81TN
                                  Engines: 74HP
                                  Armament: 1 x 12pdr
                                  Admty No: 100
                                  Port Reg: A. 477
1912: Launched. Built at Aberdeen. Owned by Aberdeen ST & FC of Aberdeen. 1914:
Requisitioned in August and converted to a M/S. 1919: Returned to owners.

STRATHAVON   1914/19 1940/44 Displacement: 202TG 79TN
                                  Engines: 67HP
                                  Armament: 1 x 6pdr
                                  Admty No: 333
                                  Port Reg: WWI: A. 96; WWII: SH. 147
1906: Launched. Built at Aberdeen. 1914: Requisitioned in August and converted to a
M/S. 1919: Returned to owners. Acquired by Gamecock STC of Scarborough. 1938:
Owned by McKenzie Ltd. of Aberdeen. 1940: Requisitioned in December and converted
to a BBV. 1945: Returned to owners in November.

STRATHBLANE   1915/19   Displacement: 186TG 73TN
                                         Engines: 56HP
                                         Port Reg: A. 431
1901: Launched. Built at Aberdeen. 1915: Requisitioned in June and converted to a BDV.
Subsequently converted to Accommodation Ship. 1919: Returned to owners. Acquired by
Dundee SFC. PR: DE. 11.

STRATHBORVE   1940/41   Displacement: 216TG 94TN
                                         Engines: 60HP
                                         Port Reg: A. 139
1930: Launched. Built at Aberdeen. Owned by Aberdeen SF Co. 1940: Requisitioned
in August and converted to a M/S. Joined the 152nd M/S Group based at Grimsby.
1941: LOST. Mined off the Humber on 6th September. *Notes*: Mercantile listing:
Strathborne.

STRATHBRAN   1916/19   Displacement: 212TG 91TN
                                         Engines: 74HP
                                         Armament: 1 x 6pdrAA
                                         Admty No: 3259
                                         Port Reg: A .536
1915: Launched. Built at Aberdeen. Owned by Aberdeen ST & FC of Aberdeen. 1916:
Requisitioned in February and converted to a M/S. 1919: Returned to owners.

STRATHCARRON   1914/19   Displacement: 209TG 81TN
                                         Engines: 74HP
                                         Armament: 1 x 12pdr
                                         Admty No: 98
                                         Port Reg: A. 552
1913: Launched. Built at Aberdeen. Owned by Aberdeen ST & FC of Aberdeen. 1914:
Requisitioned in August and converted to a M/S. 1919: Returned to owners.

STRATHCLOVA   1914/19   Displacement: 210TG 82TN
                                         Engines: 74HP
                                         Armament: 1 x 6pdr
                                         Admty No: 66
                                         Port Reg: A. 552
1913: Launched. Built at Aberdeen. Owned by the Aberdeen ST & FC of Aberdeen.
1914: Requisitioned in August and converted to a M/S. 1919: Returned to owners.

STRATHCLUNIE   1915/19   Displacement: 211TG 82TN
                                         Engines: 74HP
                                         Armament: 1 x 6pdrAA
                                         Admty No: 1199
                                         Port Reg: A. 583

1913: Launched. Built at Aberdeen. Owned by Aberdeen ST & FC of Aberdeen. 1915: Requisitioned in April and converted to a M/S. 1919: Returned to owners.

STRATHCOE   1916/48   Displacement: 215TG 93TN
Engines: 74HP
Armament: WWI: 1 x 6pdrAA; 24 mines
Admty No: 2991
Port Reg: A. 751
P. No: WWII: FY. 1594

1916: Launched in December. Built at Aberdeen by Hall Russell. Owned by Aberdeen ST & SF of Aberdeen. 1917: Requisitioned in January and converted to a M/S. 1918: Purchased into the RN and converted to a M/L. 1924: Converted to a Base Ship in January, renamed VERNON and attached as a tender to HMS VERNON, Portsmouth, for M/L trials. 1933: MF based at Malta. 1938: Reverted to STRATHCOE. Paid Off and reduced to the Reserve. 1939: Placed on the Sale List. 1942: Brought forward and employed on Harbour Service. 1943: Converted to an Esso. 1946: Sold to mercantile and retained the same name. Acquired by The Granton TC of Edinburgh. PR: GN. 21. 1959: Mercantile Loss on 4th February.

STRATHDEE   1915/19   Displacement: 193TG 74TN
Engines: 67HP
Armament: 1 x 6pdrAA
Admty No: 1179
Port Reg: A. 60

1906: Launched. Built at Aberdeen. Owned by Aberdeen ST & FC of Aberdeen. 1915: Requisitioned in March and converted to a M/S. 1919: Returned to owners. Acquired by AF McConkey of Scarborough. Acquired by Sutton of E. Hartlepool. PR: SH. 136.

STRATHDERRY   1914/19 1940/41 Displacement: 193TG 74TN
Engines: 67HP
Armament: 1 x 3pdr
Admty No: 95
Port Reg: WWI: A. 401; WWII: A. 226
P. No: WWII: FY. 1810

1911: Launched. Built at Aberdeen. 1914: Requisitioned in August and converted to a M/S. 1917: Converted to a BDV. 1919: Returned to owners. Acquired by F Spashett of Lowestoft. PR: LT. 532. Acquired by County FC of Lowestoft. PR: LT. 532. Acquired by Stephen FC of Aberdeen. 1940: Requisitioned in February and converted to a D/L. Converted to an APV in September. 1941: Returned to owners in November.

STRATHDEVON   1915/19 1940/42 Displacement: 212TG 91TN
Engines: 74HP
Armament: 1 x 3pdr
Admty No: 1960

Port Reg: A. 539
P. No: WWII: FY. 1810

1915: Launched. Built at Aberdeen. Owned by the Aberdeen ST & FC of Aberdeen. Requisitioned in November and converted to a M/S. 1919: Returned to owners. 1940: Requisitioned in January and converted to a M/S. Converted to an APV in September. 1942: Returned to owners in February.

STRATHDON   1917/19   Displacement: 155TG 57TN
                                     Engines: 60HP
                                     Port Reg: GY. 997

1891: Launched. Built at Aberdeen. 1917: Requisitioned into the Fishery Reserve. 1919: Returned to owners. Acquired by Sleight of Grimsby. PR: GY. 997.

STRATHEARN   1915/19   Displacement: 152TG 56TN
                                     Engines: 49HP
                                     Port Reg: GN. 40

1898: Launched. Built at Aberdeen. 1915: Requisitioned in May and converted to a Decoy. 1917: Reduced to the Fishery Reserve. 1919: Returned to owners. Acquired by J Inglis of Peebles. Acquired by G Devlin & A Stuart of Edinburgh. PR: GN. 40.

STRATHEBRIE   1915/19   Displacement: 210TG 90TN
                                     Engines: 74HP
                                     Armament: 1 x 6pdr
                                     Port Reg: A .59

1914: Launched. Built at Aberdeen. Owned by the Aberdeen ST & FC of Aberdeen. 1915: Requisitioned in June and converted to a BDV. 1917: Converted to a Base Ship. 1919: Returned to owners.

STRATHEDEN   1915/19   Displacement: 201TG 77TN
                                     Engines: 67HP
                                     Armament: 1 x 6pdr
                                     Admty No: 1189
                                     Port Reg: A. 308

1906: Launched. Built at Aberdeen. 1915: Requisitioned in March. 1919: Returned to owners. Acquired by North Sea STC of Scarborough. Acquired by Peter & J Johnstone of Aberdeen.

STRATHELLA   1915/19 1940/44 Displacement: 210TG 82TN
                                     Measurements: 115ft. x 22ft.
                                     Engines: 74HP
                                     Armament: WWI: 2 x 6pdr; WWII: 2 x
                                     6pdr; 2 x Browning MGs (2x1)
                                     Admty No: 101
                                     Port Reg: A. 586

1913: Launched. Built at Aberdeen. Owned by the Aberdeen ST & FC of Aberdeen. 1914: Requisitioned in August and converted to a M/S. 1919: Returned to owners. 1940: Requisitioned in July and converted to an APV. Based at Akureyn, Iceland, for Harbour Defence. 1943: TIH at the end of the year at N. Shields for refitting. 1944: Completed refitting. On her way back to Iceland she was detailed as part of the escort for Convoy UR.105 from Loch Ewe to Iceland, sailing on 11th January. Enroute the convoy encountered very severe weather and was obliged to heave to and in doing so she lost contact with the convoy. Shortly afterwards she suffered an engine breakdown and when this was finally rectified she ran out of fuel. Adrift and with her wireless destroyed by the severe weather the Admiralty posted her missing and relatives of her company were informed accordingly. She was finally rescued off Greenland on 13th February over a month after sailing from Loch Ewe. LOST. Foundered off Iceland on 1st July. 1946: Wreck raised in August and returned to owners. Acquired by David Wood AO of Aberdeen.

STRATHELLIOT   1915/19 1940/46   Displacement: 211TG 93TN
                                                 Engines: 74HP
                                                 Armament: 1 x 6pdr
                                                 Admty No: 1182
                                                 Port Reg: A. 46
                                                 P. No: WWII: 4. 379

1915: Launched. Built at Aberdeen. Owned by the Aberdeen ST & FC of Aberdeen. Requisitioned in March and converted to a M/S. 1919: Returned to owners. 1940: Requisitioned in January and converted to a D/L. Converted to an APV in September. 1942: Converted to a Store Carrier. 1946: Returned to owners.

STRATHERRICK   1914/19   Displacement: 201TG 77TN
                                                   Engines: 67HP
                                                 Armament: 1 x 6pdrAA; 1 x 7.5-inch
                                                 Bomb Thrower (A/S Howitzer)
                                                 Admty No: 417
                                                 Port Reg: A. 105

1906: Launched. Built at Aberdeen. 1914: Requisitioned in September and converted to a M/S. 1919: Returned to owners. Acquired by Clarence STC of Scarborough. Acquired by John W Johnstone of Aberdeen.

STRATHFINELLA   1914/19 1944/44   Displacement: 192TG 74TN
                                                   Engines: 67HP
                                                 Armament: 1 x 12pdr
                                                 Admty No: 466
                                                 Port Reg: WWI: A. 341; WWII: A. 63

1911: Launched. Built at Aberdeen. 1914: Requisitioned in September and converted to a M/S. 1919: Returned to owners. Acquired by J Breach of Lowestoft. Acquired by

P & J Johnstone Ltd. of Aberdeen. 1944: Requisitioned in April and converted to an Esso. Returned to owners in October.

STRATHGAIRN 1916/19 Displacement: 211TG 93TN
Engines: 74HP
Armament: 1 x 6pdrAA
Admty No: 1366
Port Reg: A. 251
1915: Launched. Built at Aberdeen. Owned by the Aberdeen ST & FC of Aberdeen. Requisitioned in March and converted to a M/S. 1919: Returned to owners.

STRATHGARRY 1915/15 Displacement: 202TG
Port Reg: A. 97
1906: Launched. 1915: Requisitioned in June and converted to a BDV. LOST. Sunk in a collision at Scapa Flow on 6th June.

STRATHGARRY 1940/45 Displacement: 202TG 87TN
Engines: 75HP
Armament: 1 x 3pdr
Port Reg: A. 45
P. No: FY. 1632
1924: Launched. Built at Aberdeen. Owned by the Aberdeen ST & SF of Aberdeen. 1940: Requisitioned in April and converted to a D/L. Converted to an APV in September. 1942: Converted to a Mooring Vessel in August. 1945: Returned to owners in December.

STRATHGELDIE 1914/19 Displacement: 192TG 74TN
Engines: 67HP
Armament: 1 x 3pdr
Admty No: 87
Port Reg: A. 399
1911: Launched. Built at Aberdeen. 1914: Requisitioned in August and converted to a M/S. 1919: Returned to owners. Acquired by F Spashett of Lowestoft. Acquired by J Walker AO of Aberdeen.

STRATHISLA 1915/19 Displacement: 193TG 76TN
Engines: 67HP
Armament: 1 x 6pdr
Admty No: 130
1905: Launched. Built at Aberdeen. 1915: Requisitioned and converted to a Mooring Vessel. 1919: Returned to owners. Acquired by JL Green of Grimsby. PR: GY. 987.

STRATHISLA II 1917/19 Displacement: 154TG
Port Reg: GN. 11
1894: Launched. 1917: Requisitioned into the Fishery Reserve. 1919: Returned to owners.

STRATHLEE   1917/19   Displacement: 215TG 93TN
                                      Engines: 74HP
                                      Armament: 1 x 6pdrAA
                                      Port Reg: A. 756

1917: Launched. Built at Aberdeen. Owned by the Aberdeen SF & T Co. Requisitioned in May and converted to a M/S. 1919: Returned to owners.

STRATHLETHEN   1915/19   Displacement: 192TG 74TN
                                        Engines: 67HP
                                      Armament: 1 x 3pdr
                                      Port Reg: A. 493

1910: Launched. Built at Aberdeen. 1915: Requisitioned in June and converted to a BDV. 1919: Returned to owners. 1938: Owned by Craig of Aberdeen. PR: A. 948.

STRATHLOCHY   1916/19   Displacement: 221TG 91TN
                                        Engines: 74HP
                                      Armament: 1 x 6pdrAA
                                      Admty No: 3249
                                      Port Reg: A. 596

1915: Launched. Built at Aberdeen. Owned by the Aberdeen ST & FC of Aberdeen. 1916: Requisitioned in January and converted to a M/S. 1919: Returned to owners.

STRATHLOSSIE   1914/19   Displacement: 193TG 74TN
                                        Engines: 67HP
                                      Armament: 1 x 6pdr
                                      Admty No: 92
                                      Port Reg: A. 316

1910: Launched. Built at Aberdeen. 1914: Requisitioned in August and converted to a M/S. 1919: Returned to owners. Acquired by Resolute FCL of Lowestoft.

STRATHLUI   1916/19   Displacement: 199TG 77TN
                                        Engines: 67HP
                                      Armament: 1 x 12pdr; 1 x 7.5-inch
                                      Bomb Thrower (A/S Howitzer)
                                      Admty No: 1578
                                      Port Reg: A. 191

1908: Launched. 1914: Requisitioned in August and converted to a M/S. 1919: Returned to owners. Acquired by J Inglis of Peebles. PR: GN. 2.

STRATHMAREE   1915/19 1939/45 Displacement: 210TG 90TN
                                        Engines: 74HP
                                      Armament: WWII: 1 x 3pdr
                                      Port Reg: A.72
                                      P. No: WWII: FY. 1638

1914: Launched. Built at Aberdeen. Owned by the Aberdeen SF & T Co. 1915: Requisitioned in June and converted to a BDV. 1919: Returned to owners. 1939: Requisitioned in November and converted to an APV. 1942: Converted to a Store Carrier. 1945: Returned to owners in November.

STRATHMARTIN   1915/19 1944/44 Displacement: 210TG 90TN
                                           Engines: 74HP
                                           Armament: 1 x 6pdrAA
                                           Admty No: 1573
                                           Port Reg: A. 79
1914: Launched. Built at Aberdeen. Owned by the Aberdeen ST & FC of Aberdeen. 1915: Requisitioned in April and converted to M/S. 1919: Returned to owners. 1944: Requisitioned in March and converted to an Esso. 1945: Returned to owners in November.

STRATHMORAY   1914/19   Displacement: 209TG 81TN
                                           Engines: 74HP
                                           Armament: 1 x 6pdr
                                           Admty No: 335
                                           Port Reg: A. 480
1912: Launched. Built at Aberdeen. Owned by Aberdeen ST & FC of Aberdeen. 1914: Requisitioned in August and converted to a M/S. 1919: Returned to owners.

STRATHNETHY   1914/19   Displacement: 211TG 82TN
                                           Engines: 74HP
                                           Armament: 1 x 6pdrAA
                                           Admty No: 112
                                           Port Reg: A. 582
1913: Launched. Built at Aberdeen. Owned by Aberdeen ST & FC of Aberdeen. 1914: Requisitioned in August and converted to a M/S. 1919: Returned to owners.

STRATHORD   1914/19   Displacement: 195TG 76TN
                                           Engines: 67HP
                                           Armament: 1 x 3pdr
                                           Admty No: 102
                                           Port Reg: A. 54
1906: Launched. Built at Aberdeen. 1914: Requisitioned in August and converted to a M/S. 1919: Returned to owners. Acquired by AFG McConkey of Scarborough.

STRATHRANNOCH   1917/17   Displacement: 215TG
                                           Armament: 1 x 6pdrAA
                                           Admty No: 2994
                                           Port Reg: A. 752
1917: Launched. Requisitioned in January and converted to a M/S. LOST. Mined off St. Alban's Head on 6th April.

STRATHRANNON   1940/46   See under JAMES BASHFORD
(Vol 1 p.174)

STRATHRYE   1916/19   Displacement: 212TG 91TN
Engines: 74HP
Armament: 1 x 12pdr
Admty No: 3253
Port Reg: A. 599

1915: Launched. Built at Aberdeen. Owned by the Aberdeen ST & FC of Aberdeen.
1916: Requisitioned in January and converted to a M/S. 1919: Returned to owners.

STRATHSPEY   1915/19 1939/42 Displacement: 202TG 79TN
Engines: 67HP
Armament: 1 x 6pdrAA
Admty No: 1169
Port Reg: A. 92
P. No: WWII: Z. 161

1906: Launched. Built at Aberdeen. 1915: Requisitioned in February and converted to
a M/S. 1919: Returned to owners. Acquired by North Sea STC of Scarborough. 1938:
Owned by Scales & Sons of Edinburgh. 1939: Requisitioned in November and
converted to a DDV. 1942: Returned to owners in May.

STRATHTUMMEL   1914/19   Displacement: 210TG 83TN
Engines: 74HP
Armament: 1 x 6pdrAA
Admty No: 511
Port Reg: A. 402

1911: Launched. Built at Aberdeen. Owned by Aberdeen ST & FC of Aberdeen. 1914:
Requisitioned in September and converted to a M/S. 1919: Returned to owners. 1938:
Owned by Craig of Aberdeen.

STRATHUGIE   1914/19 1940/45 Displacement: 210TG 90TN
Engines: 74HP
Armament: 1 x 3pdr
Admty No: 1570
Port Reg: A. 61
P. No: WWII: FY. 1941

1914: Launched. Built at Aberdeen. Owned by the Aberdeen ST & FC of Aberdeen.
Requisitioned in April and converted to a M/S. 1919: Returned to owners. 1940:
Requisitioned in January and converted to a D/L. Converted to a M/S in September.
1945: Returned to owners in September.

STRATHURIE   1914/19   Displacement: 210TG 83TN
Engines: 74HP

Armament: 1 x 3pdr
Admty No: 115
Port Reg: A. 403

1911: Launched. Built at Aberdeen. Owned by Aberdeen ST & FC of Aberdeen. 1914: Requisitioned in August and converted to a M/S. 1919: Returned to owners.

STRATON   1917/18   Displacement: 197TG
                                            Port Reg: GY. 694

1899: Launched. 1917: Requisitioned into the Fishery Reserve. 1918: LOST. Mined 26 miles E from the Humber LV. on 8th February. No loss of life

STRENUOUS   1915/19   Displacement: 166TG

1904: Launched. 1915: Requisitioned and converted to a BDV. 1919: Returned to owners.

STREPHON   1915/19 1940/46 Displacement: 249TG 98TN
                                            Engines: 62HP = 10K
                                            Admty No: 1233
                                            Port Reg: GY. 810
                                            P. No: WWII: FY. 1829

1912: Launched. Built at Beverley by CWG. Owned by Standard SFC of Grimsby. 1915: Requisitioned in March and converted to a M/S. Fitted with Listening Hydrophones. 1919: Returned to owners. 1937: Acquired in February by Hopwood & Taylor of Grimsby. Acquired in June by Japan FC of Grimsby. 1940: Requisitioned in August and converted to a M/S. 1946: Returned to owners in February. 1961: BU in Holland.

STROMO   1917/19   Displacement: 142TG
                                            Port Reg: GY. 546

1892: Launched. 1917: Requisitioned into the Fishery Reserve. 1919: Returned to owners.

STRONSAY   1915/19   Displacement: 207TG 81TN
                                            Engines: 49HP = 9.5K
                                            Armament: 1 x 6pdr
                                            Admty No: 1969
                                            Port Reg: H. 387

1911: Launched. Built at Beverley by CWG. Owned by Hull SF & Ice Co. of Hull. 1915: Requisitioned in September and converted to a M/S. 1919: Returned to owners. 1938: BU.

STRYMON   1915/17   Displacement: 198TG 62TN
                                            Engines: 55HP = 10K
                                            Armament: 1 x 12pdr
                                            Admty No: 1842
                                            Port Reg: GY. 912

1899: Launched. Built at Hull by CWG. Owned by Standard SFC of Grimsby. 1914: Acquired in January by Green & Baker of Grimsby. Acquired in April by Strand SFC of Grimsby. 1915: Requisitioned and converted to a M/S. 1917: LOST. Mined off the Shipwash LV. on 27th October.

STURDEE	1939/40	See under MICHAEL BRION (Vol 1 p.183)

STURTON	1939/44	Displacement: 251TG 124TN Engines: 74HP = 10.5K Armament: 1 x 12pdr Port Reg: GY.1241 P. No: FY. 1595

1920: Launched. Built at Beverley by CWG. Owned by Victoria SFC of Grimsby. 1929: Acquired by Lindsey SFC of Grimsby. 1939: Requisitioned in August and converted to a M/S. 1944: Converted to an Esso in April for the D-Day Landings. Returned to owners in November. 1961: BU in Holland.

SUCCESSFUL	1916/19	

Reported as serving. NFI.

SUCCESSION	1916/19	Displacement: 212TG 82TN Engines: 78HP Armament: 1 x 6pdrAA Admty No: 2972 Port Reg: GY. 979

1916: Launched. Built at Lowestoft. Requisitioned in September and converted to a M/S. 1919: Returned to owners.

SULBY	1914/19	Displacement: 287TG 111TN Engines: 92HP Armament: 1 x 6pdrAA Admty No: 131 Port Reg: FD. 87

1909: Launched. Built at N. Shields. Owned by Wyre STC of Fleetwood. 1914: Requisitioned in August and converted to a M/S. 1919: Returned to owners. 1938: Owned by Keay of Fleetwood.

SUMA	1917/19	Displacement: 284TG 112TN Engines: 87HP Port Reg: CF. 2

1914: Launched. Built at Middlesborough by Smith's Dock. Owned by Neale & West of Cardiff. 1917: Requisitioned into the Fishery Reserve. 1919: Returned to owners.

SUMA	1939/46	Displacement: 302TG 114TN
		Engines: 99HP
		Armament: 1 x 12pdr; 1 x 20mmAA
		Port Reg: CF. 19
		P.No: FY. 618

1927: Launched. Built at Southbank-on-Tees by Smith's Dock. Owned by Neale & West of Cardiff. 1939: Purchased into the RN in August and converted to a M/S. 1946: Sold to mercantile in March.

SUNBEAM IV	1917/19	Displacement: 133TG 49TN
		Engines: 48HP
		Port Reg: DE. 13

1891: Launched. Built at Leith. Iron construction. Owned by DJ McKinnon of Dundee. 1917: Requisitioned into the Fishery Reserve. 1919: Returned to owners.

SUNBURST	1942/46	See under ESTRELLA d' ALVA

SUN CLOUD	1914/19	Displacement: 213TG 89TN
		Engines: 67HP = 10K
		Armament: 1 x 6pdrAA
		Admty No: 611
		Port Reg: GY. 753

1912: Launched. Built at Beverley by CWG. Owned by Pelham SFC of Grimsby. 1913: Acquired by North Western SFC of Grimsby. 1914: Acquired by Grimsby & North Sea SFC of Grimsby. Requisitioned in September and converted to a M/S. 1919: Returned to owners. Mercantile Loss. Posted missing with all hands in the North Sea in July.

SUNLIGHT	1917/19	Displacement: 168TG 68TN
		Engines: 50HP
		Port Reg: A. 766

1894: Launched. Built at Aberdeen. 1917: Requisitioned into the Fishery Reserve. 1919: Returned to owners.

SUNLIGHT	1939/44	See under THOMAS GRAHAM
		(Vol 1 p.188)

SUNRISE	1917/19	Displacement: 167TG 64TN
		Engines: 50HP
		Port Reg: A. 648

1891: Launched. Built at Aberdeen. Owned by Red Rose STL of Fleetwood. 1918: Requisitioned into the Fishery Reserve. 1919: Returned to owners.

SUNRISE	1940/46	See under EMILIA PRIMEIRO

SUNSHINE   1915/19   Displacement: 167TG
1900: Launched. 1915: Requisitioned and converted to a M/S. 1919: Returned to owners.

SUNSPOT   1940/47   See under ST. CLAIR

SUSARION   1917/19 1940/41 Displacement: 260TG 102TN
                                        Engines: 75HP = 9.5K
                                        Armament: 1 x 12pdr
                                        Admty No: 3002
                                        Port Reg: GY. 1012
1917: Launched. Built at Beverley by CWG. Owned by the Standard SFC of Grimsby. Requisitioned in February and converted to a M/S. 1919: Returned to owners. 1940: Acquired by A Black of Grimsby. Requisitioned in June and converted to an APV. Based at Grimsby. 1941: LOST. Sunk by enemy a/c off the Humber on 7th May.

SUTHERNES   1940/45   Displacement: 269TG 107TN
                                        Engines: 78HP
                                        Armament: 1 x 6pdr
                                        Port Reg: H. 331
                                        P No: 4, 174
1915: Launched. Built at Beverley by CWG. Owned by the Trident SF Co. of Hull. 1940: Requisitioned in June and converted to an APV. 1942: Converted to a M/S in February. 1945: Returned to owners in September.

SUZETTE   1939/40   See under EDWARD GREY
                                        (Vol 1 p.170)

SWALLOW   1914/18   Displacement: 243TG
                                        Armament: 1 x 3pdr
                                        Admty No: 654
                                        Port Reg: H. 97
1897: Launched. 1914: Requisitioned in October and converted to a M/S. 1918: LOST. Sunk in a collision off Whitby on 29th March.

SWALLOW   1914/19   Displacement: 204TG 81TN
                                        Engines: 60HP
                                        Armament: 1 x 6pdrAA
                                        Admty No: 261
                                        Port Reg: A. 76
1906: Launched. Built at Aberdeen. Owned by J Lewis of Aberdeen. 1914: Requisitioned in August and converted to a M/S. Renamed SWALLOW II in December. 1919: Returned to owners.

SWALLOW   1917/19   Displacement: 200TG
Port Reg: GN. 1144
1900: Launched. 1917: Requisitioned into the Fishery Reserve. 1919: Returned to owners.

SWALLOW II   1914/19   See under SWALLOW 1914

SWAN   1914/19 1940/45 Displacement: 239TG 84TN
Engines: 70HP = 10.5K
Armament: 1 x 6pdr
Admty No: 811
Port Reg: WWI: H. 700; WWII: LO. 47
P. No: WWII: FY. 1880
1902: Launched. Built at Hull by CWG. Owned by Pickering & Haldane of Hull. 1914: Requisitioned in December and converted to a M/S. 1915: Renamed SWAN II in February. 1919: Returned to owners. 1930: Acquired by Hewett FCL of London. PR: LO. 47. 1940: Requisitioned in March as SWAN III and converted to a M/S. 1941: Converted to a Boiler Cleaning Tender. 1945: Returned to owners in April. 1949: BU.

SWAN III   1915/19 1940/45 See under SWAN above

SWANSEA CASTLE   1917/19 1940/46 Displacement: 256TG 100TN
Engines: 82HP
Port Reg: SA. 108
P. No: WWII: FY. 1817
1912: Launched. Built at Middlesborough by Smith's Dock. Owned by Consolidated Fisheries of Grimsby. 1917: Requisitioned into the Fishery Reserve. 1919: Returned to owners. 1938: Owned by Consolidated Fisheries of Grimsby. 1940: Requisitioned in July and converted to a M/S. 1946: Returned to owners in February.

SWANSEA CASTLE   **(Steve Bush Collection)**

SWEEPER   1914/19   Displacement: 395TG 235TN
                                         Engines: 68HP = 10K
                                         Armament: 1 x 6pdr; 1 x 6pdrAA;
                                         1 x 7.5-inch Bomb Thrower (A/S
                                         Howitzer)
                                         Admty Nos: 54 & 1224
                                         Port Reg: GY. 853
                                         P. No: WWII: FY. 1906

1913: Launched. Built at Beverley by CWG. Owned by South Western SFC of
Grimsby. 1914: Requisitioned in August and converted to a M/S. 1915: Acquired by
T. Bascombe of Grimsby. 1919: Returned to owners. 1936: Acquired by Norwegian
owners. 1939: Requisitioned by the Norwegian Navy and renamed NORDHAV II.
1940: Arrived in the Faroes Islands in June. Commissioned into the RN and
converted to a M/S. Joined the 71st M/S Group based at Dundee 1945: LOST. Sunk
by a U-714 off Dundee on 10th March.

SYLVIA   1915/18   Displacement: 213TG 85TN
                                         Engines: 60HP
                                         Port Reg: GY. 1112

1898: Launched. Built at Beverley. Owned by the Forward SF Co of Grimsby. 1915:
Requisitioned in June and converted to a DDV. 1918: Returned to owners. 1941:
Mercantile Loss. Sunk by enemy a/c off the Faroes on 7th April.

SYRIAN   1939/40   See under WILLIAM FORBES
                                         (Vol 1 p.149)

SYRIAN   1940/46   See under THOMAS THRESHER
                                         (See Addenda)

SYRINGA   1914/17   Displacement: 243TG 93TN
                                         Engines: 58HP
                                         Armament: 1 x 3pdr
                                         Port Reg: M. 21

1905: Launched. Built at N. Shields. 1914: Requisitioned in August and converted to a
M/S. 1917: Renamed SYRINGA II in March. 1919: Returned to owners. Acquired by
RJ Williams AO of Milford Haven. Acquired by C. Dobson of Grimsby. PR: GY.1309.

SYRINGA II   1917/19   See under SYRINGA of 1914

TACSONIA 1917/19 Displacement: 243TG 93TN
              Engines: 58HP
              Armament: 1 x 6pdrAA
              Admty No: 783
              Port Reg: M. 36
1905: Launched. Built at N. Shields. Owned by JM Knight & M Howell of Milford Haven.
1915: Requisitioned in January and converted to a M/S. 1919: Returned to owners.
Acquired by C. Dobson of Grimsby. PR: GY.1308. 1938: BU.

TAGALIE 1914/19 Displacement: 210TG 81TN
              Engines: 78HP
              Armament: 1 x 6pdrAA
              Admty No: 451
              Port Reg: GY. 744
1912: Launched. Built at Middlesborough by Smiths Dock. Owned by Sleight of
Grimsby. 1914: Requisitioned in September and converted to a M/S. 1919: Returned
to owners.

TAIPO 1915/17 Displacement: 247TG
              Armament: 1 x 12pdr
              Admty No: 1627
              Port Reg: GY. 415
1914: Launched. 1915: Requisitioned in May and converted to a M/S. 1917: LOST.
Mined off the Royal Sovereign LV. on 24th June.

TAIPO 1939/44 See under FLINTSHIRE

TALLY HO 1915/19 Displacement: 216TG 85TN
              Engines: 60HP
              Armament: 1 x 6pdr
              Admty No: 1973
              Port Reg: H. 522
1900: Launched. Built at Hessel. Owned by ST White of Hull. 1915: Requisitioned in
October and converted to a M/S. Employed as a M/S Training Vessel. 1919: Returned
to owners.

TAMORA 1939/46 See under WILLIAM LOFT (Vol 1 p.88)

TAMURA 1915/17 Displacement: 268TG 111TN
              Engines: 85HP
              Armament: 1 x 6pdrAA

Admty No: 3046
Port Reg: CF. 47

1917: Launched. Built at Selby by Cochrane. Owned by Neale & West of Cardiff. Requisitioned in June and converted to a M/S. 1919: Returned to owners.

TANAGER	1915/19	Displacement: 192TG 71TN
		Engines: 55HP
		Armament: 1 x 3pdr
		Admty No: 386
		Port Reg: H. 134

1910: Launched. Built at Goole by Goole SB. Owned by Kelsall Bros. & Beeching of Hull. 1914: Requisitioned in November and converted to a M/S. 1919: Returned to owners.

TANJORE	1914/19	Displacement: 168TG 168TN
		Engines: 45HP = 10K
		Armament: 1 x 6pdr
		Admty No: 634
		Port Reg: H. 759

1903: Launched. Built at Beverley by CWG. Owned by Hull SF & Ice Co. of Hull. 1914: Requisitioned in October and converted to a M/S. 1919: Returned to owners. 1924: Mercantile Loss. Sunk in the North Sea by an explosion caused by firing a signal rocket. No loss of life.

TANJORE	1941/42	RIM. See under MADRAS (Vol 1 p.67)

TARANA	1940/46	Displacement: 347TG
		Port Reg: French
		P. No: 4. 263

1932: Launched. French fishing vessel. 1940: French M/S seized at Southampton in Operation Grab on 3rd July. Converted to an APV and added to the Navy List. 1945: Paid Off and Laid Up in October. 1946: Returned to the French in May.

TARANAKI	1914/19	Displacement: 247TG 91TN
		Engines: 79HP
		Armament: 1 x 12pdr; 1 x 6pdrAA
		Admty No: 337
		Port Reg: A. 445

1912: Launched. Built at Aberdeen. 1914: Requisitioned in August and converted to a M/S. 1915: Converted to a 'Q' Ship. Reverted to a M/S. 1919: Returned to owners. Acquired by JG Smith of Fleetwood.

TARTAN	1915/19	1939/46	Displacement: 202TG 89TN
			Engines: 67HP = 10K

Armament: WWI: 1 x 6pdrAA;
WWII: 1 x 3pdr
Admty No: 1607
Port Reg: GY. 723
P. No: WWII: 4. 45 (APV) FY. 915 (M/S)

1912: Launched. Built at Beverley by CWG. Owned by T. Robinson of Grimsby. 1915: Requisitioned in April and converted to a M/S. 1919: Returned to owners. 1939: Requisitioned in November and converted to an APV. 1942: Converted to a M/S in March. 1946: Returned to owners in March. 1963: BU at Sunderland.

TARTARIN	1940/45	Displacement: 288TG
		Port Reg: French
		P. No: FY. 1799

1931: Launched. French fishing vessel. 1940: French M/S seized at Southampton in Operation Grab on 3rd July. Converted to an APV in October and added to the Navy List. Based at Grimsby. 1942: Re-converted to a M/S in June. 1945: Returned to the French in October.

TASMANIA	1917/19	Displacement: 146TG 50TN
		Engines: 45HP = 10K
		Port Reg: FD. 171

1891: Launched. Built at Hull by CWG. Iron construction. Owned by Hull SF & Ice Co. PR: H. 122. 1912: Acquired by Active FCL of Fleetwood. 1917: Requisitioned into the Fishery Reserve. Acquired by HE Stroud of Aberdeen. PR: A. 737. 1919: Returned to owners. 1924: BU.

TAURUS	1917/19	Displacement: 128TG
		Port Reg: A. 655

1883: Launched. 1917: Requisitioned into the Fishery Reserve. 1919: Returned to owners.

TAYMOUTH	1917/19	Displacement: 137TG 54TN
		Engines: 57HP
		Port Reg: A .54

1899: Launched. Built at Dundee. Owned by WW Crampin of Grimsby. 1917: Requisitioned into the Fishery Reserve. 1919: Returned to owners.

TAYSIDE	1917/19	Displacement: 137TG 54TN
		Engines: 57HP
		Port Reg: A. 156

1899: Launched. Built at Dundee. Owned by Croston STC of Fleetwood. 1917: Requisitioned into the Fishery Reserve. 1919: Returned to owners.

TEAL	1914/17	Displacement: 165TG 64TN
		Engines: 41HP

Armament: 1 x 6pdr
Admty No: 418
Port Reg: H. 90

1897: Launched. Built at North Shields. Owned by Kelsall Bros. & Beeching of Hull. 1914: Requisitioned in November and converted to a M/S. 1917: LOST. Wrecked off Buckie on 2nd January.

TEAL	1940/46	See under MARIGNAM

TEAZER	1940/40	See under CLEOPATRA II

TEHANA	1939/46	Displacement: 333TG 128TN
		Engines: 99HP
		Port Reg: LO. 132
		P. No: FY. 525

1929: Launched. Built at Selby by Cochrane. Owned by Brand & Curzon of Milford Haven. 1939: Requisitioned in August and converted to a M/S. 1944: Converted to a WDV. 1946: Returned to owners in March.

TEKOURA	1939/45	Displacement: 368TG 130TN
		Measurements: 135ft
		Engines: 99HP
		Armament: 1 x 4-inch; 1 x 20mmAA;
		2 x LG (2x1); DCT & DCRs
		Port Reg: LO. 14
		P. No: FY. 247

1930: Launched. Built at Selby by Cochrane. Owned by Brand & Curzon of Milford Haven. 1939: Requisitioned in October and converted to A/S. Based at Scapa Flow for escorts and A/S patrols off Scotland. 1945: Paid Off in April and reduced to the Reserve. Returned to owners in August. 1947: Acquired by Heward Trs. Ltd. of London. 1954: BU.

TENBY	1915/19 1940/45	Displacement: 215TG 84TN
		Engines: 74HP
		Armament: 1 x 12pdr
		Admty No: 2579
		Port Reg: WWI: GY. 353; WWII: Dutch
		P. No: WWII: FY. 1733

1913: Launched. Built at Middlesborough by Smiths Dock. Owned by WH Johnson AO of Grimsby. 1915: Requisitioned in June and converted to a M/S. Fitted with Listening Hydrophones. 1919: Returned to owners. Acquired by Dutch owners. 1940: Hired from Dutch owners in June and converted to a M/S. Manned with a Dutch Crew. 1945: Returned to Holland.

TENBY CASTLE   1915/19   Displacement: 256TG 101TN
                                       Engines: 80HP
                                       Armament: 1 x 12pdr; 1 x 7.5-inch
                                       Bomb Thrower (A/S Howitzer)
                                       Admty No: 977
                                       Port Reg: SA. 53

1908: Launched. Built at North Shields. Owned by Consolidated Fisheries of Grimsby.
1915: Requisitioned in February and converted to a M/S. Converted to a 'Q' Ship in
June. 1917: Re-converted to a M/S. 1919: Returned to owners.

TERN   1914/15   Displacement: 199TG
                                       Admty No: 548
                                       Port Reg: H. 961

1907: Launched. 1914: Requisitioned in October and converted to an APV. 1915: LOST.
Wrecked in Loch Eriball on 23rd February.

TEROMA   1939/45   See under ISAAC HEATH (Vol 1 p.56)

TERRIER   1914/19   Displacement: 179TG 68TN
                                       Engines: 62HP
                                       Armament: 1 x 12pdr
                                       Admty No: 356
                                       Port Reg: A. 34

1905: Launched. Built at Aberdeen. Owned by H.H. Girdlestone of Aberdeen. 1914:
Requisitioned in August and converted to a M/S. 1919: Returned to owners. 1938:
Owned by I Wood AO of Aberdeen. PR: LT. 339.

TERVANI   1914/16   Displacement: 457TG 301TN
                                       Engines: 89HP = 11K
                                       Armament: 2 x 12pdrs; 1 x 2pdr
                                       Admty No: 3204
                                       Port Reg: GY. 10

1914: Launched. Built at Beverley by CWG. Owned by A. Black of Grimsby. 1914:
Acquired by South Western SFC of Grimsby. 1915: Acquired by T. Baskcomb of
Grimsby. Requisitioned in May and converted to a M/S. 1916: LOST. Mined off Orford
Ness on 5th December.

TERVANI   1939/43   Ex-*Rylston*
                                       Displacement: 409TG 154TN
                                       Engines: 104HP = 10.9K
                                       Armament: 1 x 12pdr
                                       Port Reg: H. 343
                                       P. No: 4. 110

1930: Launched. Built at Beverley by CWG. Owned by Henrikson of Hull. 1939:

Renamed Tervani. Requisitioned in October and converted to an APV. 1941: Converted to a M/S. 1943: LOST. Sunk by the Italian S/M ACCIAIO off Algiers on 7th February.

TEST	1920/22	See under PATRICK BOWE (Vol 1 p.69)

TETTENHALL 1916/17 Displacement: 227TG
Admty No: 1538
Port Reg: FD. 43

1905: Launched. 1915: Requisitioned in June and converted to a M/S. 1917: LOST. Mined off Lowestoft on 23rd May.

TEUTON 1915/20 Displacement: 141TG 31TN
Engines: 45HP = 10K
Armament: 1 x 6pdr
Admty No: 780
Port Reg: GY. 795

1898: Launched. Built at Hull by CWG. Owned by A Bannister of Grimsby. 1901: Acquired by Onward SFC of Grimsby. 1915: Requisitioned in January and converted to a M/S. 1918: Reduced to the Fishery Reserve. Renamed ANGOLIAN in June. 1920: Returned to owners. 1934: Renamed *Hazeldene*. PR: BCK. 47. 1953: BU at Barrow.

TEVIOT 1920/23 See under GEORGE IRELAND
(Vol 1 p.172)

TEWERA 1939/46 Displacement: 335TG 130TN
Engines: 99HP
Armament: 1 x 12pdr
Port Reg: LO. 9

1930: Launched. Built at Selby by Cochrane. Owned by Brand & Curzon of Milford Haven. 1939: Requisitioned in August and converted to a M/S. 1946: Returned to owners.

TEXAS 1940/44 See under TR. 57 (Vol 1 p.83)

THANET 1916/19 Displacement: 172TG 67TN
Engines: 45HP = 10K
Port Reg: H .549

1902: Launched. Built at Beverley by CWG. Iron construction. Owned by the Hull SF & Ice Co. 1915: Requisitioned in September and converted to a Water Carrier. 1919: Returned to owners. 1936: BU at Charlestown.

THEBAN 1914/19 Displacement: 202TG 90TN
Engines: 67HP = 10K

Armament: 1 x 6pdr
Admty No: 617
Port Reg: GY. 937

1913: Launched. Built at Beverley by CWG. Owned by T. Robinson of Grimsby. 1914: Requisitioned in September and converted to an APV. 1918: Returned to owners in December. 1919: Mercantile Loss. Lost with all hands in November.

THE BANYERS   1914/15   Displacement: 448TG 281TN
                                      Engines: 89HP = 11K
                                      Admty No: 450
                                      Port Reg: GY. 128

1914: Launched. Built at Beverley by CWG. Owned by South Western SFC of Grimsby. Requisitioned in December and converted to a M/S. 1915: LOST. Mined off Scarborough whilst sweeping on 6th January.

THEIR MERIT   1939/45   See under TR. 37 (Vol 1 p.81)

THE NORMAN   1916/19   Displacement: 225TG 86TN
                                      Engines: 57HP
                                      Armament: 1 x 6pdrAA; 24 Mines (As
                                      M/L) 1 x 6pdrAA; 1 x 7.5-inch Bomb
                                      Thrower (A/S Howitzer) (As M/S)
                                      Admty No: 1762
                                      Port Reg: CF. 30

1908: Launched. Built at North Shields. 1915: Requisitioned in May and converted to a M/L. 1917: Converted to a M/S and rearmed. 1919: Returned to owners. Acquired by Hesketh STL of Fleetwood. PR: FD.145. *Notes*: Possible sister-ship to THE ROMAN.

THE ROMAN   1914/19 1939/46 Displacement: 224TG 86TN
                                      Engines: 57HP
                                      Armament: 1 x 6pdr
                                      Admty No: 195
                                      Port Reg: WWI: CF. 29 WWII: FD. 151
                                      P. No: WWII: FY. 1530 (M/S)
                                      Y7. 5 (Esso)

1909: Launched. Built at N. Shields. 1914: Requisitioned in November and converted to a M/S. 1919: Returned to owners. Acquired by The Saxon ST Co. of Fleetwood. 1939: Requisitioned in December and converted to an APV. 1940: Converted to a M/S in July. 1944: Converted to an Esso in March. 1946: Returned to owners in August. *Notes*: Possible sister-ship to THE NORMAN.

THE TETRARCH   1914/19   Displacement: 225TG 112TN
                                      Engines: 58HP = 10K
                                      Armament: 1 x 3pdr

Admty No: 254
Port Reg: GY. 945

1913: Launched. Built at Beverley by CWG. Owned by North Western FCL of Grimsby. 1914: Requisitioned in August and converted to a M/S. 1919: Returned to owners. 1940: Mercantile Loss. Sunk in a collision with a merchantman of Coquet Island with the loss of nine lives.

THE TOWER	1939/45	See under THOMAS DENNISON (Vol 1 p.188)

THERESA BOYLE	1915/19	Displacement: 224TG 99TN
		Engines: 83HP
		Armament: 1 x 3pdr
		Admty No: 1311
		Port Reg: FD. 26

1915: Launched. Built at Aberdeen. Owned by Port St. Mary F & C of London. Requisitioned in September and converted to a M/S. 1919: Returned to owners. 1938: Owned by Lyle of Edinburgh. PR: GN. 4.

THEWAY	1939/46	Displacement: 263TG 115TN
		Engines: 69HP
		Port Reg: A. 336
		P. No: Z. 127

1931: Launched. Built at Aberdeen. Owned by J. Craig AO of Aberdeen. 1939: Requisitioned in September and converted to a BDV. Based at Scapa Flow for BD duties. 1946: Returned to owners.

THISTLE	1914/14 1916/19	Displacement: 158TG 61TN
		Engines: 50HP
		Armament: 1 x 3pdr
		Admty No: 517
		Port Reg: SN. 311

1901: Launched. Built at South Shields. Owned by Purdy SFC of North Shields. 1914: Requisitioned in March and designated as a M/S. Returned to owners in December. 1916: Requisitioned in March and converted to a BDV. 1919: Returned to owners.

THISTLE	1915/19	Displacement: 178TG 73TN
		Engines: 55HP
		Armament: 1 x 3pdr
		Port Reg: FD. 226

1904: Launched. Built at Aberdeen. Owned by E. Taylor AO of Fleetwood. 1915: Requisitioned in October and converted to a BDV. 1919: Returned to owners.

THISTLE	1915/19	Displacement: 228TG 91TN
		Engines: 67HP

Armament: 1 x 3pdr
Admty No: 909
Port Reg: LL. 64

1906: Launched. Built at Sandhaven. Owned by J Henry & WA Duncan of Liverpool. 1915: Requisitioned in February and converted to a M/S. 1916: Renamed THISTLE IV in April. 1919: Returned to owners.

THISTLE IV	1915/19	See under THISTLE above
THOMAS BOMKWORTH	1919/21	See under JOHN BOMKWORTH (Vol 1 p.60)
THOMAS DEAS	1917/21	See under JAMES JOHNSON (Vol 1 p.58)

THOMAS STRATTEN   1917/17   Displacement: 309TG
Armament: 1 x 12pdr
Admty No: 3000
Port Reg: H. 116

1914: Launched. 1917: Requisitioned in March. LOST. Mined off the Butt of Lewis on 20th October.

THOMAS SUTTON   1916/19   Displacement: 211TG 80TN
Engines: 78HP
Armament: 1 x 6pdrAA
Admty No: 3276
Port Reg: HL. 80

1916: Launched. Built at Aberdeen. Owned by Sutton STC of Hartlepool. Requisitioned in May and converted to a M/S. 1919: Returned to owners.

THOMAS W. IRVIN   1916/19   Displacement: 209TG 90TN
Engines: 78HP
Armament: 1 x 6pdr
Admty No: 3257
Port Reg: SN. 265

1915: Launched. Built at Aberdeen. Owned by Irvin & Sons of N. Shields. 1916: Requisitioned in February and converted to a M/S. 1919: Returned to owners.

THOMAS YOUNG   1915/19   Displacement: 194TG
Armament: 1 x 12pdr; 1 x 6pdr
Admty No: 1143
Port Reg: SN. 67

1914: Launched. 1915: Requisitioned in February and converted to a M/S. 1919: Returned to owners.

THORNEY   1942/42   See under DABCHICK (Vol 1 p.42)

THRIFTY   1939/46   Displacement: 139TG

1916: Launched. 1939: Requisitioned in December and converted to a M/S. 1940: Based at Portland for sweeping in the Channel. TPI Operation Dynamo, the evacuation of Dunkirk, in May-June. 1946: Returned to owners in April.

THRUSH IV   1917/19   Displacement: 134TG
                                                      Port Reg: GY. 1055

1893: Launched. 1917: Requisitioned into the Fishery Reserve. 1919: Returned to owners.

TILBURYNESS   1939/40   See under JOSEPH BARRETT
                                                     (Vol 1 p.65)

TINA NUTTEN   1915/19   Displacement: 187TG 72TN
                                                     Engines: 67HP
                                                     Armament: 1 x 6pdrAA
                                                     Admty No: 1200
                                                     Port Reg: A. 333

1911: Launched. Built at Aberdeen. 1915: Requisitioned in April and converted to a M/S. 1919: Returned to owners. 1920: Acquired by Vetis SFC of Lowestoft. PR: LT. 521. 1938: Owned by John Walker of Aberdeen. PR: A. 181.

TIRADE   1942/46   Ex-*Transportador*
                                                     Displacement: 209TG
                                                     Port Reg: Portuguese
                                                     P. No: 4. 294

1899: Launched. Portuguese fishing vessel. 1942: Purchased from Portuguese owners in May and converted to an APV. Renamed TIRADE. 1944: Damaged in collision with HMS TEDWORTH in the Firth of Clyde in January. TIH for repair. 1946: Sold to mercantile in March.

TOBAGO   1917/19   Displacement: 160TG 63TN
                                                     Engines: 45HP = 10K
                                                   Port Reg: H. 482

1899: Launched. Built at Hull by CWG. Owned by Hull SF & Ice Co. 1917: Requisitioned into the Fishery Reserve. 1920: Returned to owners. 1923: Acquired by GD Utting of Lowestoft. PR: LT.1293. 1930: Renamed *Tresco*. 1951: BU at Milford Haven.

TOCSIN   1940/45   See under LIBRA

TOKIO   1914/17   Displacement: 295TG
                                                     Armament: 1 x 3pdr
                                                   Admty No: 313

1907: Launched. 1914: Requisitioned in August and converted to a M/S. 1917: LOST. Sunk by SMS EMDEN and Destroyers of the German Third Half-Flotilla on 12th December whilst escorting a Scandinavian Convoy ICW Destroyers PELLEW and PARTRIDGE and the Trawlers COMMANDER FULLERTON, LIVINGSTONE and LORD ALVERSTONE. All the ships in the convoy were sunk as were all the escorts with the exception of PELLEW.

TOKIO II	1914/19 1939/46	Displacement: 221TG 113TN
		Engines: 66HP
		Armament: 1 x 6pdr
		Admty No: 25
		Port Reg: GY. 157
		P. No: WWII: FY. 788 (M/S)
		Y7. 40 (Esso)

1906: Launched. Built at Selby by Cochrane. Owned by HL Taylor of Grimsby. 1914: Requisitioned in August and converted to a M/S. 1917: Temporary Loan to the Japanese Navy from June. 1918: Returned to the RN in December. 1919: Returned to owners. Acquired by Diamonds SFC of Grimsby. Same PR. 1939: Requisitioned in December and converted to an APV. 1940: Converted to a M/S in July. 1944: Converted to an Esso in March. 1946: Returned to owners in January. Notes: Listed as TOKYO II in WWII Lists.

TOM MOORE	1915/19	Ex-*Clan Grant*
		Displacement: 194TG 76TN
		Engines: 54HP
		Armament: 1 x 3pdr
		Port Reg: D. 216

1903: Launched. Built at N. Shields. Owned by Dublin ST Ice & Cold FC of Dublin. 1915: Requisitioned in June and converted to a BDV. 1919: Returned to owners.

TOM TIT	1914/14	Displacement: 169TG
		Admty No: 424
		Port Reg: H. 35

1904: Launched. 1914: Requisitioned in November and converted to an APV. LOST. Wrecked off Peterhead on 26th December.

TONGKOL	1939/44	RAN
		Displacement: 292TG
		P. No: J. 137

1926: Launched. 1939: Requisitioned and converted to a M/S. Commissioned into the RAN in October. 1944: Sold to mercantile in September.

| TOPAZ | 1916/19 1939/40 | Displacement: 251TG 98TN |
| | | Engines: 76HP |

Armament: 1 x 6pdrAA
Admty No: 1262
Port Reg: WWI: H. 511; WWII: H. 830
P. No: WWII: FY. 905

1916: Launched. Built at Selby by Cochrane. Owned by the Yarborough SFC of Grimsby. Requisitioned in November and converted to a M/S. 1919: Returned to owners. Acquired by Beeley & Sleight of Grimsby and renamed *Valdora*. 1939: Requisitioned in November as VALDORA and converted to an APV. 1940: LOST. Sunk by enemy a/c off Cromer on 12th January.

TOPAZ   1916/16   Displacement: 142TG 57TN
                                       Engines: 45HP = 10K
                                       Port Reg: H. 307

1895: Launched. Built at Hull by CWG. Owned by Kingston STC of Hull. 1908: Sunk in a collision with another trawler in the Humber and subsequently salvaged. 1910: Sold to Swedish owners. 1916: Reported as requisitioned for a short period and returned. 1931: Acquired by Norwegian owners. 1941: Mercantile Loss. Sunk by enemy a/c off Norway on 15th December.

TORFRIDA   1917/19   Displacement: 115TG 56TN
                                       Engines: 50HP
                                       Port Reg: A. 866

1881: Launched. Built at Govan. Owned by G Craig of Aberdeen. 1917: Requisitioned into the Fishery Reserve. 1919: Returned to owners.

TORNADO   1940/43   See under EL MENZALA

TORNADO II   1943/46   See under EL MENZALA

TORONTO   1916/19   Displacement: 204TG 77TN
                                         Engines: 55HP
                                       Armament: 1 x 6pdrAA
                                       Admty No: 3335
                                       Port Reg: H. 218

1915: Launched. Built at Selby by Cochrane. Owned by Hull SF & Ice Co. 1917: Requisitioned in March and converted to a M/S. 1919: Returned to owners.

TOUCHSTONE   1914/18 1940/41 Displacement: 173TG 68TN
                                       Engines: 45HP = 9.5K
                                       Armament: 1 x 6pdr
                                       Admty No: 46
                                       Port Reg: WWI: H. 934; WWII: A. 229
                                       P. No: WWII: FY. 1610

1907: Launched. Built at Beverley by CWG. Owned by Hellyer SFC of Hull. 1914:

Requisitioned in September and converted to a M/S. 1918: Returned to owners in November. 1938: Acquired by D Wood AO of Aberdeen. 1940: Requisitioned in March and converted to a M/S. 1941: Returned to owners in December. 1956: BU at Granton.

TOURACO   1914/19   Ex-*Penguin*
Displacement: 245TG 113TN
Engines: 76HP = 10.5K
Armament: 1 x 6pdrAA; 1 x 7.5-inch
Bomb Thrower (A/S Howitzer)
Admty No: 609
Port Reg: GY. 347

1908: Launched. Built at Beverley by CWG. Renamed whilst building. Owned by Cleethorpes STC of Grimsby. 1914: Requisitioned in September and converted to a M/S. 1918: Acquired by WH Beeley of Grimsby. 1919: Acquired by Talbot STC of Grimsby. 1920: Returned to owners. 1926: Acquired by RW Lewis of Aberdeen and renamed *Jean Hay*. 1937: BU.

TOURMALINE   1916/19   Displacement: 289TG 115TN
Engines: 67HP
Armament: 1 x 6pdr
Admty No: 1231
Port Reg: H. 850

1905: Launched. Built at Govan. Owned by Kingston STC of Hull. 1915: Requisitioned in March and converted to a M/S. 1919: Returned to owners.

TOWHEE   1914/17   Displacement: 199TG
Armament: 1 x 3pdr
Admty No: 370
Port Reg: H. 907

1900: Launched. 1914: Requisitioned in October and converted to a M/S. 1917: LOST. Disappeared whilst on escort duty in the Channel on 15th June.

TRANIO   1939/41   Displacement: 275TG 109TN
Engines: 61HP
Port Reg: M. 196

1918: Launched. Built at South Shields. Owned by HG Rees of Milford Haven. 1939: Requisitioned in November and converted to a M/S. 1941: LOST. Sunk by enemy a/c whilst in tow in the North Sea on 26th June.

TRANSVAAL   1917/19 1939/44 Displacement: 250TG 119TN
Engines: 88HP
Armament: 1 x 12pdr; 1 x 6pdrAA
Port Reg: FD. 381
P. No: WWII: Y7. 45 (Esso)

1916: Launched. Built at Selby by Cochrane. Owned by the Transvaal STC of Fleetwood. Requisitioned in September and converted to a M/S. 1919: Returned to owners. 1939: Requisitioned in December and converted to an APV. 1942: Converted to an Esso and joined the MF. 1943: Part of the Supply Group known colloquially as 'Walt Disney's Navy' ferrying supplies to the invasion forces throughout the Med. 1944: Left the MF to return to the UK. LOST. On her way home from the Med. foundered in a gale in the Channel on 18th November.

TRENT   1914/19   Displacement: 218TG 84TN
                                      Engines: 65HP
                                      Armament: 1 x 6pdr
                                      Admty No: 120
                                      Port Reg: FD. 12

1904: Launched. Built at North Shields. Owned by R & J. Moon of Aberdeen. 1914: Requisitioned in August and converted to a M/S. 1917: Renamed TRENT II in March. 1919: Returned to owners.

TRENT II   1917/19   See under TRENT

TREVO TERCEIRO   1940/42   Displacement: 296TG
                                      Armament: 1 x 12pdr
                                      Port Reg: Portuguese
                                      P. No: FY. 1683.

1912: Launched. Portuguese fishing vessel. 1940: Purchased into the RN and converted to a M/S. 1942: Renamed FINESSE. 1946: Sold to mercantile.

T.R. FERANS   1915/19   Displacement: 307TG 124TN
                                      Engines: 93HP
                                      Armament: 1 x 12pdr; 1 x 7.5-inch
                                      Bomb Thrower (A/S Howitzer)
                                      Admty No: 1518
                                      Port Reg: H. 1027

1913: Launched. Built at Selby by Cochrane. Owned by Pickering & Haldane STC of Hull. 1915: Requisitioned in May and converted to a M/S. 1919: Returned to owners.

T.R. FERANS   1939/45   See under EDWARD COLLINGWOOD
                                      (Vol 1 p.52)

TRIBUNE   1916/19   Displacement: 302TG 158TN
                                      Engines: 84HP
                                      Armament: 1 x 6pdrAA; 1 x 7.5-inch
                                      Bomb Thrower (A/S Howitzer)
                                      Admty No: 1847
                                      Port Reg: GY. 563

1915: Launched. Built at Selby by Cochrane. Owned by Anchor SFC of Grimsby. Requisitioned in September and converted to a M/S. 1918: Renamed TRIBUNE II in February. 1920: Returned to owners.

TRIBUNE II	1918/20	See under TRIBUNE above

TRIER	1915/19	Displacement: 324TG 141TN
		Engines: 82HP = 10.5K
		Armament: 1 x 12pdr
		Admty No: 1377
		Port Reg: H. 153

1910: Launched. Built at Beverley by CWG. Owned by J. Hollingsworth of Hull. 1915: Requisitioned in April and converted to a M/S. 1918: Acquired by H Burns of Grimsby. PR: GY. 1117. 1919: Returned to owners. 1921: Acquired by Spanish owners and renamed *Santa Cristina*. 1935: Mercantile Loss. Wrecked near Conil.

TRITELIA	1939/45	See under R.H.DAVIDSON

TRITON	1915/19 1939/45	Displacement: 230TG 87TN
		Engines: 71HP
		Armament: 1 x 6pdr
		Admty No: 1769
		Port Reg: WWI: SA. 61; WWII: GY. 384
		P. No: WWII: Y7. 42 (Esso)

1907: Launched. Built at Dundee. Owned by W. Sutherland of Aberdeen. 1915: Requisitioned in May and converted to a M/S. 1919: Returned to owners. Acquired by C. Dobson of Grimsby. 1939: Requisitioned in December and converted to an APV. 1940: Renamed WRANGLER. 1944: Converted to an Esso in February. 1945: Returned to owners.

TROGON	1914/19	Displacement: 182TG 65TN
		Engines: 55HP
		Armament: 1 x 12pdr; 1 x 6pdrAA
		Admty No: 677
		Port Reg: H. 949

1907: Launched. Built at Goole by Goole SB. Owned by Kelsall Bros. & Beeching of Hull. 1914: Requisitioned in November and converted to a M/S. 1919: Returned to owners.

TROJAN	1915/19 1940/45	Displacement: 140TG 54TN
		Engines: 45HP = 10K
		Armament: 1 x 6pdr
		Admty No: 782
		Port Reg: GY. 848
		P. No: WWII: Z. 218

1898: Launched. Built at Hull by CWG. Owned by T. Robinson of Grimsby. 1914: Requisitioned in December and converted to a M/S. 1918: Renamed TROJAN II. 1919: Returned to owners and reverted to original name. 1932: Acquired by JC Wilson of Plymouth. 1940: Requisitioned and converted to a BGV. 1945: Returned to owners. 1952: Mercantile Loss. Sunk in a collision with a Liberian tanker off the Eddystone Light on 17th May. No loss of life.

TROJAN II   1918/19   See under TROJAN above

TROMOY   1944/44   See under EDAY (Vol 1 p.21 & 110)

TROMOY   1944/46   See under MINCARLO (Vol 1 p.118)

TRUMPETER   1914/19   Displacement: 192TG 73TN
                                     Engines: 55HP
                                     Armament: 1 x 6pdrAA
                                     Port Reg: H. 1020
1913: Launched. Built at Goole by Goole SB. Owned by Kelsall Bros. & Beeching of Hull. 1914: Requisitioned in October and converted to a M/S. 1919: Returned to owners.

TRYGON   1915/15   Displacement: 289TG 112TN
                                     Engines: 88HP = 11K
                                     Armament: 1 x 3pdr
                                     Admty No: 978
                                     Port Reg: FD .221
1908: Launched. Built at Beverley by CWG. Owned by Mount SFC of Fleetwood. 1915: Requisitioned in February and converted to an APV. LOST. Sunk in a collision in the Clyde on 30th March.

TUGELA   1915/16   Displacement: 233TG 85TN
                                     Engines: 70HP = 11K
                                     Armament: 1 x 3pdr
                                     Admty No; 1817
                                     Port Reg: H. 521
1900: Launched. Built at Hull by CWG. Owned by Neptune SFC of Hull. 1913: Acquired by East Riding SFC of Hull. 1915: Requisitioned in July and converted to an APV. 1916: LOST. Mined off Lowestoft on 26th June.

TUMBY   1939/45   See under JOHN HAILE (Vol 1 p.180)

TUNISIAN   1939/42   Displacement: 238TG 99TN
                                     Engines: 77HP = 10.3K
                                     Port Reg: GY. 319
                                     P. No: Z. 128

1930: Launched. Built at Beverley by CWG. Owned by Robinson of Grimsby. 1939: Requisitioned in October and converted to a BDV. 1942: LOST. Mined off Harwich on 9th July.

TURBOT	1942/42	See under REDSHANK (Vol 1 p.42)

TURCOMAN	1939/45	Displacement: 455TG 165TN
		Engines: 99HP
		Armament: 1 x 4-inch
		P. No: FY. 130

1937: Launched. Built at Southbank-on-Tees by Smith's Dock. Owned by Hellyer Bros. of Hull. 1939: Purchased into the RN in August and converted to A/S. Employed on Atlantic Convoy escorts. 1943: W. Africa Escort Force based at Freetown. 1945: Sold to mercantile in December. Re-acquired by Hellyer Bros. of Hull. Port Reg: H. 163.

TURQUOISE	1917/19	Displacement: 164TG 69TN
		Engines: 50HP = 10.5K
		Port Reg: H. 335

1896: Launched. Built at Hull by CWG. Owned by Kingston STC of Hull. 1918: Requisitioned into the Fishery Reserve. 1919: Returned to owners. 1923: Acquired by W Mitchell of Aberdeen. PR: A. 951. 1927: Acquired by Dutch owners and renamed *De Dree*. 1935: BU.

TUSCAN	1917/19	Displacement: 178TG 58TN
		Engines: 55HP = 9.5K
		Port Reg: GY. 82

1905: Launched. Built at Beverley by CWG. Owned by Onward SFC of Grimsby. 1917: Requisitioned into the Fishery Reserve. 1919: Returned to owners. 1925: Acquired by Spanish owners and renamed *Gure Ametza*. 1968: BU in Spain

TWOSTEP	1943/46	See under TARANTELLA (Vol 1 p.97)

TYNDRUM	1917/19	Displacement: 192TG
		Port Reg: LL. 375

1902: Launched. 1917: Requisitioned into the Fishery Reserve. 1919: Returned to owners.

TYNE PRINCE	1914/19	Displacement: 206TG 77TN
		Engines: 76HP
		Armament: 1 x 12pdr; 1 x 6pdrAA
		Admty No: 93
		Port Reg: SN. 97

1909: Launched. Built at N. Shields. Owned by W. Raynor & R. Boyle of N. Shields. 1914: Requisitioned in August and converted to a M/S. 1919: Returned to owners.

TYNE WAVE   1917/18   Displacement: 121TG
Port Reg: A.

1891: Launched. 1917: Requisitioned into the Fishery Reserve. 1918: LOST. Captured by a U-Boat off the Shetlands on 23rd April and sunk by gunfire. No loss of life.

TYPHOON   1940/45   See under SYRIAN 1939

CHAPTER 20 - UGIE BANK to UVULARIA

UGIE BANK 1914/19 1939/40 1944/44 Displacement: 205TG 79TN
Engines: 82HP
Port Reg: PD. 85
P. No: WWII: 4. 430
1913: Launched. Built at Aberdeen by Hall Russell. Owned by PD Tr. Co. 1915: Requisitioned in June and converted to a BDV. 1919: Returned to owners. Acquired by Associated Trs. of Yarmouth. 1938: Owned by R Irvin of N. Shields. 1939: Requisitioned in December and converted to an APV. 1940: Returned to owners in March. 1944: Requisitioned in March and converted to an Esso. Returned to owners in October.

UHDEA 1914/19 Displacement: 191TG
Admty No: 124
Port Reg: M. 200
1906: Launched. 1914: Requisitioned in August and converted to a M/S. 1915: Converted to a BDV in September. 1919: Returned to owners.

UIVER 1940/45 Displacement: 200TG
Port Reg: Dutch
P. No: FY. 1720
1920: Launched. Dutch fishing vessel. 1940: Hired from Dutch owners in August and converted to a M/S. Commissioned with a Dutch crew. 1942: Commissioned in November with RN crew. 1945: Returned to owners in November.

ULSTER 1915/19 Displacement: 185TG
Port Reg: A. 337
1897: Launched. 1915: Requisitioned in September and converted to a BDV. 1919: Returned to owners.

ULYSSES 1916/17 Displacement: 165TG
Armament: 1 x 6pdr
Admty No: 1047
Port Reg: GY. 198
1889: Launched. 1915: Requisitioned in January and converted to a M/S. 1917: Renamed ULYSSES II in July. 1918: Returned to owners in November.

ULYSSES II 1917/18 See under ULYSSES above

UNDAUNTED 1917/19 Displacement: 141TG
Port Reg: A. 49
1895: Launched. 1917: Requisitioned into the Fishery Reserve. 1919: Returned to owners.

UNICORN   1915/19   Displacement: 134TG
                Armament: 1 x 3pdr
                Admty No: 2196
                Port Reg: INS. 249

1895: Launched. 1915: Requisitioned in June and converted to a N/L. 1920: Returned to owners. *Notes*: aka Tr/Dr

UNITIA   1914/19 1940/46 Displacement: 296TG 122TN
                Engines: 69HP
                Armament: WWI: 1 x 6pdrAA;
                WWII: 2 x MG
                Admty No: 699
                Port Reg: GY. 924
                P. No: WWII: FY. 1852 (M/S)

1913: Launched. Built at Beverley by CWG. Owned by Gt. Grimsby & E. Coast SF Co. 1914: Requisitioned in December and converted to a M/S. 1919: Returned to owners. 1940: Requisitioned in May and converted to an APV. 1941: Converted to a M/S in May. Renamed PORTIA. 1946: Returned to owners in January.

URANA   1914/19   Displacement: 308TG
                Armament: 1 x 6pdrAA
                Admty No: 425
                Port Reg: FD. 73

1914: Launched. Requisitioned in November and converted to a M/S. Employed on escort duties. 1919: Returned to owners.

URANIA   1914/19   Displacement: 226TG
                Armament: 1 x 6pdr
                Admty No: 960
                Port Reg: AR. 1

1907: Launched. 1914: Requisitioned in December and converted to a M/S. 1919: Returned to owners.

URANIA   1941/46   Displacement: 869TG
                Port Reg: French
                P. No: FY. 261

1930: Launched. 1941: French fishing trawler seized off Gibraltar on 9th January. Renamed RETREIVER and converted to A/S. Completed in November. 1946: Returned to France in July.

URE   1920/22   See under HENRY JENNINGS
                (Vol 1 p.173)

URIE 1917/19 1940/44 Displacement: 226TG 87TN
Engines: 71HP
Armament: 1 x 6pdr
Admty No: 1267
Port Reg: WWI: A. 754; WWII: GN. 40
P. No: WWII: FY. 1948

1917: Launched. Built at Aberdeen. Requisitioned in May. 1919: Returned to owners.
1938: Owned by Devlin of Granton. 1940: Requisitioned in August as CORIOLANUS
and converted to a M/S. Renamed CRAFTSMAN in December. 1944: Returned to
owners in October.

URKA 1917/19 Displacement: 249TG 96TN
Engines: 82HP
Armament: 1 x 12pdr
Admty No: 3328
Port Reg: FD. 289

1917: Launched. Built at Goole by Goole SB. Owned by The Clifton STC of Fleetwood.
Requisitioned in March and converted to a M/S. 1919: Returned to owners.

UVULARIA 1917/19 Displacement: 207TG
Port Reg: GY. 1190

1900: Launched. 1917: Requisitioned into the Fishery Reserve. 1919: Returned to owners.

VAILLANT   1940/46   Displacement: 916TG
                                          Port Reg: French

1921: Launched. French fishing vessel. 1940: French Patrol Vessel seized at Sheerness in Operation Grab on 3rd July. Converted to an APV and Commissioned in August with a Free French crew. 1941: Commissioned with RN crew in May. 1942: Renamed BALISE in March and converted to a BGV. 1946: Returned to France.

VALDORA   1939/40   See under TOPAZ

VALENTIA   1917/19   Displacement: 164TG 64TN
                                          Engines: 45HP
                                          Port Reg: GY. 568

1898: Launched. Built at Irvine. Owned by Consolidated Fisheries of Grimsby. 1917: Requisitioned into the Fishery Reserve. 1919: Returned to owners.

VALE OF CLYDE   1914/19   Displacement: 226TG 83TN
                                          Engines: 76HP
                                          Armament: 1 x 12pdr; 1 x 6pdrAA
                                          Admty No: 515
                                          Port Reg: A. 192

1908: Launched. Built at Aberdeen. Owned by M Wilkins & G Moreland of Manchester. 1914: Requisitioned in September and converted to a M/S. 1919: Returned to owners.

VALE OF FORTH   1916/19 1940/44 Displacement: 226TG 88TN
                                          Engines: 71HP
                                          Armament: 1 x 6pdrAA
                                          Admty No: 3257
                                          Port Reg: A. 542
                                          P. No: WWII: FY. 252

1916: Launched. Built at Aberdeen. Owned by Bon Accord SFC of Aberdeen. Requisitioned in April and converted to a M/S. 1919: Returned to owners. Acquired by G Robb & Sons of Aberdeen and renamed *Viking Deeps*. 1940: Requisitioned in June as VIKING DEEPS and converted to an APV. 1943: Transferred to the Examination Service. 1944: Returned to owners in November.

VALE OF FRUIN   1915/19   Displacement: 211TG
                                          Armament: 1 x 6pdr
                                          Admty No: 3250
                                          Port Reg: A .546

1915: Launched. 1916: Requisitioned in December and converted to a M/S. 1919: Returned to owners.

VALE OF LENNOX   1916/19   Ex-*Gardar Landnemi*
                                     Displacement: 233TG 88TN
                                     Engines: 81HP
                                     Armament: 1 x 12pdr; 1 x 7.5-inch
                                     Bomb Thrower (A/S Howitzer)
                                     Admty No: 991
                                     Port Reg: LH. 264
1909: Launched. Built at Aberdeen. Owned by Harvey & Miller of Liverpool. 1914: Requisitioned in December and converted to a M/S. 1919: Returned to owners.

VALE OF LEVEN   1915/17   Displacement: 223TG
                                     Armament: 1 x 6pdr
                                     Admty No: 1188
                                     Port Reg: A. 177
1907: Launched. 1915: Requisitioned in March and converted to a M/S. 1917: LOST. Sunk in a collision off Worthing on 10th July.

VALERIA   1917/19   Displacement: 189TG 76TN
                                     Engines: 55HP
                                     Port Reg: GY. 818
1898: Launched. Built at Selby by Cochrane & Cooper. Owned by Arctic SF of Grimsby. 1916: Acquired by Consolidated Fisheries of Grimsby. 1917: Requisitioned into the Fishery Reserve. 1919: Returned to owners. 1925: Acquired by Lowestoft owners. 1940: Mercantile Loss. Bombed by enemy a/c near The Smalls in August.

VALESCA   1916/19 1939/45 Displacement: 188TG 82TN
                                     Engines: 69HP = 10K
                                     Armament: 1 x 6pdrAA; 1 x 7.5-inch
                                     Bomb Thrower (A/S Howitzer)
                                     Admty No: 2963
                                     Port Reg: GY. 915
                                     P. No: WWII: FY. 814
1916: Launched. Built at Beverley by CWG. Owned by the South Western SFC of Grimsby. Requisitioned in September and converted to a M/S. 1919: Returned to owners. 1928: Acquired by Earl SFC of Grimsby. 1939: Requisitioned in November and converted to an APV. 1940: Converted to a M/S in July. 1941: Converted to a Wreck Location Vessel in December. 1945: Returned to owners in December. 1950: Acquired by Belgian owners and renamed *Charvic*. 1972: Renamed *Java IV*. 1991: Deleted.

VALMONT   1916/19 1939/45 Displacement: 245TG 108TN
                                     Engines: 92HP = 11K
                                     Armament: 1 x 6pdr
                                     Admty No: 864
                                     Port Reg: GY. 885

1916: Launched. Built at Beverley by CWG. Owned by South Western SFC of Grimsby. Requisitioned in May and converted to a M/S. 1918: Returned to owners. 1929: Acquired by the Lindsay SFC of Grimsby. 1939: Requisitioned in November and converted to a M/S. Based at Grimsby. 1945: Returned to owners in December. 1961: BU in Holland in October.

VALPA	1915/16	Displacement: 230TG
		Armament: 1 x 12pdr
		Admty No: 1543
		Port Reg: FD. 160

1915: Launched. Requisitioned in June. 1916: LOST. Mined off Spurn Head on 19th March.

VAMBERY	1917/19 1940/45	Displacement: 316TG 127TN
		Engines: 84HP
		Armament: 1 x 6pdr; 1 x 7.5-inch Bomb Thrower (A/S Howitzer)
		Admty No: 1280
		Port Reg: GY. 1082
		P. No: WWII: FY. 1849

1917: Launched. Built at Selby by Cochrane. Owned by Atlas SFC of Grimsby. Requisitioned in July and converted to a M/S. Employed on Escort Duties. 1920: Returned to owners. Acquired by Earl SFC of Grimsby and renamed *Saronta*. Same PR. 1940: Requisitioned in June as SARONTA and converted to an APV. 1941: Converted to a M/S in January. 1945: Returned to owners in December.

VAN DYCK	1941/45	Ex-*Kingston Diamond*
		Displacement: 352TG 147TN
		Engines: 96HP = 11K
		Port Reg: O. 298 (Belgian)
		P. No: FY. 106

1926: Launched. Built at Beverley by CWG as *Kingston Diamond*. Owned by Kingston STC of Hull. PR: H. 294. 1939: Acquired by Belgian owners and renamed *Van Dyck*. 1940: Fled to Britain at the fall of Belgium and arrived at Fleetwood in May. 1941: Hired in February and converted to A/S. 1945: Returned to owners in November. 1948: Acquired by Faroese owners and renamed *Eideskollur*. 1952: Renamed *Venus*. 1960: BU in Holland. *Notes*: The first of the famous 'Kingston' fleet of trawlers.

VAN OOST	1940/45	Ex-*Tourmaline*
		Displacement: 352TG 147TN
		Engines: 96HP = 11K
		Port Reg: O. 296 (Belgian)
		P. No: FY. 330

1926: Launched. Built at Beverley by CWG as *Tourmaline*. Owned by Kingston STC of Hull. PR: H. 290. 1939: Acquired by Belgian owners and renamed *Van Oost*. 1940: Fled to Britain at the fall of Belgium and arrived at Milford Haven in May. Hired in July and converted to an APV. 1945: Returned to owners in November. 1948: Acquired by the Polish Government Fishing Fleet and renamed *Merkury*. 1961: BU.

VAN ORLEY   1941/41   Ex-*Kingston Garnet*
                                           Displacement: 352TG 146TN
                                           Engines: 96HP = 10.9K
                                           Port Reg: O. 299 (Belgian)

1927: Launched. Built at Beverley by CWG as *Kingston Garnet*. Owned by Kingston STC of Hull. PR: H. 323. Subsequently purchased into the Belgian fishing fleet. 1940: Fled to Britain at the fall of Belgium and arrived at Fleetwood in May. 1941: Hired in June and converted to an APV. Deployed to the Western Approaches Command at Liverpool. LOST. Sunk by enemy a/c at Liverpool on 4th May. Wreck raised in November and BU.

VARANGA   1939/45   Displacement: 361TG 171TN
                                           Engines: 96HP = 10.8K
                                           Port Reg: GY .61
                                           P. No: FY. 1625

1929: Launched. Built at Beverley by CWG. Owned by Letten Bros. of Grimsby. 1930: Acquired by Atlas SFC of Grimsby. 1939: Requisitioned in August and converted to a M/S. Served at Iceland throughout WWII. 1945: Returned to owners in November. Acquired by Iago STL of London and renamed *Red Crusader*. PR: LO. 462. 1955: BU in Belgium.

VARANIS   1914/19 1939/45 Displacement: 258TG 107TN
                                           Engines: 69HP
                                           Armament: 1 x 6pdrAA
                                           Admty No: 5
                                           Port Reg: GY. 511
                                           P. No: WWII: FY. 1613

1909: Launched. Built at Selby by Cochrane. Owned by Arctic SF Co. of Grimsby. 1914: Requisitioned in August and converted to a M/S. 1919: Returned to owners. 1939: Requisitioned in December and converted to an APV. Based at Grimsby. 1940: Converted to a M/S in July. Joined the 112th M/S Group based at Grimsby. 1943: Joined the 110th M/S Group based at Grimsby. 1944: Converted to a BBV in October. 1945: Returned to owners in November.

VASCAMA   1939/45   Displacement: 447TG 200TN
                                           Engines: 114HP
                                           Armament: 1 x 4-inch; 2 x 20mmAA
                                           (2x1); DCs
                                           Port Reg: GY. 164
                                           P. No: FY. 185

1935: Launched. Built at Selby by Cochrane and completed in April. Owned by Atlas SFC of Grimsby. 1939: Purchased into the RN in September and converted to A/S. 1940: Based at Kirkwall ICW NORTHERN FOAM, NORTHERN GIFT and KINGSTONE AGATE employed on contraband control and A/S patrols between Norway and Greenland. 1941: Sank the German U-551 in the N. Atlantic on 23rd March. Shelled by U-564 in the Atlantic in June. A shell hit the bridge, killing her Captain, but the ship survived. ICW RAF Catalina a/c sank the U-452 in the Atlantic on 23rd August. 1943: Temporary Loan to the Portuguese Navy from October and renamed P.6 for the duration of the Loan. 1944: Returned to the RN in August, reverted to original name and employed on Iceland convoys. 1945: Placed on the Sale List in July. Acquired by her original owners and re-registered GY. 147. 1962: BU in Belgium.

VASCO DA GAMA	1915/19	Displacement: 265TG 101TN
		Engines: 58HP
		Armament: 1 x 6pdr
		Admty No: 1584
		Port Reg: A. 260

1910: Launched. Built at Aberdeen. Owned by WH Dodds of Aberdeen. 1915: Requisitioned in May and converted to a M/S. 1919: Returned to owners.

| VELIA | 1939/40 | See under SITVEL |

VENATOR	1916/19	Displacement: 293TG 135TN
		Engines: 79HP
		Armament: 1 x 6pdrAA
		Admty No: 1520
		Port Reg: GY. 827

1913: Launched. Built at Selby by Cochrane. Owned by Atlas SFC of Grimsby. 1915: Requisitioned in May. 1919: Returned to owners.

| VENETIA III | 1917/19 | Displacement: 201TG |
| | | Port Reg: GY.1127 |

1899: Launched. 1917: Requisitioned into the Fishery Reserve. 1919: Returned to owners.

VENOSTA	1917/19 1939/45	Displacement: 516TG 126TN
		Engines: 84HP
		Armament: 1 x 12pdr; 1 x 7.5-inch
		Bomb Thrower (A/S Howitzer)
		Admty No: 1654
		Port Reg: GY.1098

1917: Launched. Built at Selby by Cochrane. Owned by the Atlas SFC of Grimsby. Requisitioned in October and converted to a M/S. Fitted with Listening Hydrophones. 1919: Returned to owners. Acquired by Venosta Ltd. of Halifax, Nova Scotia. 1939:

Requisitioned in December for service with the RCN and converted to a M/S. 1941: Converted to a BGV. 1945: Returned to owners.

VENTOSE	1940/44	Displacement: 185TG
		Port Reg: French
		P. No: FY. 1754

1936: Launched. French fishing vessel. 1940: French M/S Seized at Southampton in Operation Grab on 3rd July and converted to an APV. Based at Grimsby. 1941: Employed on the Examination Service. 1943: Converted for Air/Sea rescue. 1944: Returned to France in July.

VENTURE	1914/19 1939/40 1944/44	Displacement: 193TG 73TN
		Engines: 60HP
		Armament: 1 x 12pdr
		Admty No: 692
		Port Reg: GY. 66
		P. No: WWII: FY. 815

1905: Launched. Built at Selby by Cochrane. 1914: Requisitioned in November and converted to a M/S. 1919: Returned to owners. 1938: Owned by W Barton & F Bacon of Grimsby. 1939: Requisitioned in November and converted to an APV. 1940: Renamed DASHER in January. Returned to owners in February. 1944: Requisitioned in April as BUCEPHALUS and converted to an Esso. Employed ferrying fuel to the D-Day landing beaches. Returned to owners in November.

VERA	1915/19	Displacement: 333TG 149TN
		Engines: 87HP = 10.5K
		Armament: 1 x 12pdr; 1 x 7.5-inch
		Bomb Thrower (A/S Howitzer)
		Admty No: 1569
		Port Reg: H. 960

1907: Launched. Built at Beverley by CWG. Owned by Humber STC of Hull. 1915: Requisitioned in May and converted to a M/S. 1919: Returned to owners. 1925: Mercantile Loss. Wrecked at Myrdalssandur, S. Iceland on 5th March.

VERA GRACE	1914/19	Displacement: 232TG 89TN
		Engines: 68HP
		Armament: 1 x 6pdrAA
		Admty No: 135
		Port Reg: FD .211

1908: Launched. Built at Dundee. Owned by Marr & Sons of Fleetwood. 1914: Requisitioned in August and converted to a M/S. 1919: Returned to owners.

| VERBENA | 1915/19 | Displacement: 152TG 67TN |
| | | Engines: 45HP |

Armament: 1 x 3pdr
Admty No: 827
Port Reg: GY. 176

1897: Launched. Built at Beverley. Owned by the Atlas SF Co. of Grimsby. 1915: Requisitioned in April. Renamed VERBENA II in December. 1918: Returned to owners. Acquired by H. Wood AO of Grimsby. Same PR.

VERBENA II	1915/18	See under VERBENA above

VERCHERES	1943/43	RCN
		Displacement: 157TG

1901: Launched. 1943: Requisitioned for service in the RCN. LOST. Destroyed by fire at Sorel, Quebec, on 9th May.

VERESIS	1915/20 1939/44	Displacement: 302TG 157TN
		Engines: 84HP
		Armament: WWI: 1 x 6pdr
		WWII: 1 x 12pdr
		Port Reg: GY. 483
		P. No: WWII: FY. 1862

1915: Launched. Built at Selby by Cochrane. Owned by Atlas SFC of Grimsby. Requisitioned in April. 1920: Returned to owners. Acquired by The Earl SFC of Grimsby.

VERNON   (IWM Neg No: Q65760)

Renamed *Wyoming*. 1939: Requisitioned in November as WYOMING and converted to an APV. Based at Grimsby for Fishery Protection. 1941: Converted to a M/S. 1944: LOST. Mined off Harwich on 20th May.

VERNON	1938/38	See under STRATHCOE

VESPER	1914/19	Displacement: 264TG
		Armament: 1 x 12pdr
		Admty No: 1340
		Port Reg: GY.156

1906: Launched. Built at Selby. Owned by G White & J Willows of Grimsby. 1914: Requisitioned in August and converted to a M/S. 1917: Renamed VESPER II in February. 1918: Returned to owners.

VESPER II	1917/18	See under VESPER above.

VESTA	1916/19	Displacement: 240TG 100TN
		Engines: 63HP
		Armament: 1 x 6pdr
		Admty No: 828
		Port Reg: GY. 57

1905: Launched. Built at Selby by Cochrane. Owned by Atlas SFC of Grimsby. 1914: Requisitioned in November and converted to a M/S. 1919: Returned to owners.

VICTOR	1914/19	Displacement: 193TG 92TN
		Engines: 55HP
		Port Reg: A.511

1897: Launched. Built at Beverley. 1914: Requisitioned in June and converted to a BDV. 1919: Returned to owners. Acquired by AC Mitchell of Milford Haven AO. PR: M. 76.

VICTOR	1914/19	Displacement: 201TG 79TN
		Engines: 60HP
		Armament: 1 x 6pdr
		Admty No: 110
		Port Reg: PD. 75

1906: Launched. Built at Torry. Owned by Peterhead TCL of Peterhead. 1914: Requisitioned in August and converted to a M/S. 1915: Renamed VICTOR II in February. 1919: Returned to owners. Acquired by R Irvin & Sons of N. Shields. PR: M. 97.

VICTOR II	1915/19	See under VICTOR above

VICTORIA	1915/19 1940/45	Displacement: 221TG 87TN
		Engines: 57HP
		Armament: 1 x 6pdr

Admty No: 1752

Port Reg: WWI: M. 117; WWII: SH. 268

1912: Launched. Built at Middlesborough by Smith's Dock. 1915: Requisitioned in April and converted to a M/S. Renamed VICTORIA II in June. 1920: Returned to owners. Acquired by the Co-operative Fishing Soc. of Scarborough. PR: SH. 268. 1940: Requisitioned in March and converted to a M/S. 1945: Returned to owners in January.

VICTORIA II   1915/20   See under VICTORIA above

VICTORIAN   1939/46   Displacement: 447TG 168TN

Engines: 99HP

Port Reg: GY. 94

P. No: FY. 114

1935: Launched. Built at Southbank-on-Tees by Smith's Dock. Owned by Loyal SFC of Grimsby. 1939: Purchased into the RN in August and converted to A/S. 1946: Placed on the Sale List in January. Re-acquired by the Loyal SFC. PR: GY. 151.

VICTORIAN II   1915/19   Ex-*Victorian*

Displacement: 195TG 62TN

Engines: 55HP = 10K

Armament: 1 x 6pdrAA

Admty No: 1841

Port Reg: GY. 1189

1900: Launched. Built at Hull by CWG. Owned by W Butt & W Hill of Grimsby. 1912: Acquired by Loyal SFC of Grimsby. 1913: Acquired by W Ellis of Grimsby. 1915: Requisitioned in August and converted to a M/S. Renamed VICTORIAN II. 1919: Returned to owners and reverted to original name. 1928: Acquired by TC & F Moss of Grimsby and renamed *Croxton*. 1940: Mercantile Loss. Sunk by enemy a/c in the North Sea on 11th January.

VICTORIAN PRINCE   1915/19   Displacement: 126TG 48TN

Engines: 47HP

Port Reg: SN. 242

1897: Launched. Built at South Shields. Owned by R Irvin of North Shields. 1915: Requisitioned in June and converted to a BDV. 1917: Reduced to the Fishery Reserve. 1919: Returned to owners.

VICTORIA REGINA   1915/19   Displacement: 146TG 55TN

Engines: 52HP

Armament: 1 x 6pdr

Admty No: 320

Port Reg: A. 590

1897: Launched. Built at Aberdeen. Owned by T Davidson AO of Aberdeen. 1914: Requisitioned in August and converted to a M/S. 1918: Returned to owners in November.

VICTRIX   1915/17   Ex-*Victory*
Displacement: 164TG 60TN
Engines: 45HP
Armament: 1 x 3pdr
Admty No: 972
Port Reg: LT. 499

1898: Launched. Built at Hull. Owned by GF Mullender of Lowestoft AO. 1915: Requisitioned in February and employed on Harbour Service. Returned to owners in November.

VICTRIX   1939/45   Displacement: 472TG 176TN
Engines: 120HP = 12.4K
Armament: 1 x 4-inch
Port Reg: H. 428
P. No: FY. 244

1937: Launched. Built at Beverley by CWG. Owned by Henricksen & Co. of Hull. 1939: Requisitioned in September and converted to A/S. 1944: TPI Operation Neptune, the D-Day Landings in June as an A/S escort. 1945: Returned to owners in December. 1966: BU at Ghent, Belgium.

VIDETTE   1916/19 1943/45   Displacement: 240TG 100TN
Engines: 63HP
Armament: 1 x 12pdr
Admty No: 834
Port Reg: GY. 54
P. No: WWII: Y7. 25

1905: Launched. Built at Selby by Cochrane. Owned by Trs. (White Sea & Grimsby) of Grimsby. 1914: Requisitioned in November and converted to a M/S. 1917: Renamed VIDETTE II in February. 1919: Returned to owners. 1943: Requisitioned in March as OUTPOST and converted to an Esso. 1945: Returned to owners in April.

VIDETTE II   1917/19   See under VIDETTE above

VIDONIA   1914/19 1940/44   Displacement: 276TG 124TN
Engines: 70HP
Armament: WWI: 1 x 12pdr.
WWII: 1 x 6pdr
Admty No: 10
Port Reg: GY. 257
P. No: WWII: 4. 33 (APV) Y7. 12 (Esso)

1907: Launched. Built at Selby by Cochrane. Owned by Arctic SFC of Grimsby. 1914: Requisitioned in December and converted to a M/S. 1919: Returned to owners. Acquired by Lindsey SFC of Grimsby. 1940: Requisitioned in June and converted to an APV. 1943: Converted to an Esso in April. 1944: LOST. Sunk in a collision in the Channel on 6th October.

VIERNOE   1915/19 1939/45 Displacement: 273TG 145TN
                  Engines: 79TN
                  Armament: 1 x 6pdr; 1 x 7.5-inch Bomb
                  Thrower (A/S Howitzer)
                  Admty No: 1503
                  Port Reg: GY. 297

1914: Launched. Built at Selby by Cochrane. Owned by AW Green of Grimsby AO. 1915: Requisitioned in May and converted to a M/S. 1919: Returned to owners. 1939: Requisitioned for service in the RCN and converted to a M/S. 1941: Converted to a BGV. 1945: Returned to owners.

VIGILANT   1914/19   Displacement: 279TG 114TN
                  Engines: 67HP
                  Armament: 1 x 12pdr
                  Admty No: 396
                  Port Reg: H. 232

1904: Launched. Built at Govan. Owned by Great Northern SFC of Hull. 1914: Requisitioned in November. 1915: Renamed VIGILANT II in February. 1919: Returned to owners and retained the name *Vigilant II* in commercial use.

VIGILANT   1917/19   Displacement: 139TG
                  Port Reg: A. 534

1902: Launched. 1917: Requisitioned into the Fishery Reserve. 1919: Returned to owners.

VIGRA   1940/46   Displacement: 184TG
                  Port Reg: Norwegian
                  P. No: 4. 01

1899: Launched. Norwegian fishing vessel. 1940: Fled to Britain at the fall of Norway. Hired from Norwegian owners and employed as a ferry. 1946: Returned to owners.

VIKING BANK   1940/45   Displacement: 335TG
                  Port Reg: Dutch
                  P. No: FY. 1781

1927: Launched. Dutch fishing vessel. 1940: Hired from Dutch owners in July and converted to a M/S. Commissioned with a Dutch crew. 1945: Returned to owners.

VIKING DEEPS   1940/44   See under VALE OF FORTH

VIKINGS   1940/42   Displacement: 1159TG
                  Port Reg: French
                  P. No: U. 78

1935: Launched. French fishing vessel. 1940: French Patrol Vessel seized in Operation Grab on 3rd July. Commissioned as an APV in August with a Free French crew. 1942: LOST. Sunk by U-542 off the Syrian coast on 30th April.

VILDA   1940/46   Ex-*Westray Firth*
Displacement: 358TG 154TN
Engines: 96HP = 10.8K
Port Reg: GY 4
P. No: Z. 118

1929: Launched. Built at Beverley by CWG. Owned by J Stewart (Hull) TCL. PR: H. 125. 1939: Acquired by Premier SFC of Grimsby. PR: GY. 4. 1940: Requisitioned in January and converted to a BDV. 1946: Returned to owners in September. 1955: BU at Gateshead.

VINDELICIA   1914/19 1940/45 Displacement: 248TG 99TN
Engines: 62HP = 10K
Armament: WWI: 1 x 6pdrAA;
WWII: 1 x 6pdr
Admty No: 452
Port Reg: GY. 954
P. No: WWII: FY. 1711 (APV);
Y7. 5 (Esso)

1913: Launched. Built at Beverley by CWG. Owned by Gt. Grimsby & E. Coast SFC. 1914: Requisitioned in September and converted to a M/S. 1919: Returned to owners. 1937: Acquired by the Japan FC of Grimsby. 1940: Requisitioned in June and converted to an APV. 1942: Returned to owners. 1943: Re-requisitioned in March and converted to an Esso in April. 1944: TPI in the Normandy Operations in the 35th Landing Barge/Supply/Repair Flot. Employed on Target-towing. 1945: Returned to owners in December. 1960: Mercantile Loss. Sank in heavy weather 90 miles off the Humber.

VIOLA   1914/19   Displacement: 173TG 174TN
Engines: 45HP= 9.5K
Armament: 1 x 12pdr
Admty No: 614
Port Reg: H. 868

1906: Launched. Built at Beverley by CWG. Owned by Hellyer SFC of Hull. 1914: Requisitioned in September and converted to a M/S. 1915: Renamed VIOLA III in November. 1919: Returned to owners. Acquired by Norwegian owners and renamed *Kapsduen*. 1926: Acquired by Argentinian owners and renamed *Dias*. Converted to a whaler. 1974: Mercantile Loss. Scuttled at Grytuiken in the Falklands.

VIOLA   1914/20 1939/40 Displacement: 228TG 91TN
Engines: 69HP
Armament: 1 x 12pdr
Admty No: 6
Port Reg: GY. 67
P. No: WWII: FY. 573

1905: Launched. Built at Selby by Cochrane. Owned by Arctic SFC of Grimsby. 1914:

Requisitioned in August and converted to a M/S. 1916: Renamed VIOLA II in December. 1920: Returned to owners. 1939: Requisitioned in November and converted to an APV. 1940: Converted to a M/S. Renamed ELENA. 1945: Returned to owners in January.

VIOLA II	1916/20	See under VIOLA

VIOLA III	1915/19	See under VIOLA

VIOLET CAIE   1917/19   Ex-*Graphic*
Displacement: 141TG 68TN
Engines: 45HP = 10K
Port Reg: GY. 1051

1889: Launched. Built at Beverley by CWG as *Graphic*. Owned by C Hellyer & J Chant of Hull. PR: H. 78. 1890: Acquired by Portuguese owners and renamed *Chire*. 1917: Acquired by GF Sleight of Grimsby and renamed V*iolet Caie*. Requisitioned into the Fishery Reserve. 1919: Returned to owners. 1925: Acquired by French owners and renamed *Jacqueline-Louise*. 1937: BU.

VIREO   1914/19 1939/41 Displacement: 192TG 73TN
Engines: 55HP
Armament: WWI: 1 x 6pdrAA;
WWII: 1 x 6pdr
Admty No: 383
Port Reg: H. 446
P. No: WWII: FY. 1531

1912: Launched. Built at Goole by Goole SB. Owned by Kelsall Bros. & Beeching of Hull. 1914: Requisitioned in October and converted to a M/S. 1919: Returned to owners. 1939: Requisitioned in December and converted to an APV. 1941: Returned to owners in December.

VIRGINIAN   1914/19   Displacement: 211TG 83TN
Engines: 67HP = 10K
Armament: 1 x 3pdr
Admty No: 618
Port Reg: GY. 211

1906: Launched. Built at Beverley by CWG. Owned by the Onward SFC of Grimsby. 1914: Requisitioned in September and converted to a M/S. 1915: Renamed VIRGINIAN II in February. 1919: Returned to owners and reverted to original name. 1946: Mercantile Loss. Sank in a collision with the troopship *Empire Rapier* off the Humber on 5th November. No loss of life.

VIRGINIAN II	1915/19	See under VIRGINIAN above

VISENDA   1939/46   Displacement: 455TG 185TN
Engines: 120HP = 12K
Armament: 1 x 4-inch
Port Reg: GY. 377
P. No: FY. 138

1937: Launched. Built at Beverley by CWG and completed in April. Owned by the Atlas SF Co. of Grimsby. 1939: Requisitioned in August and converted to A/S. Based at Kirkwall for contraband control and A/S patrols. 1941: Depth-charged and sank the German U-551 in the N. Atlantic on 23rd March. Attacked by the surfaced German U-564 in the Shetlands/Faroes Gap on 22nd June. She received several hits one of which struck the bridge and killed the CO, Lt. Winder. When she returned fire with her 4-inch the S/M submerged and escaped as the trawler's ASDIC was out of action. Paid Off into dockyard hands for repair. Re-commissioned on completion. 1943: TPI Operation Avalanche, the Salerno Landings in Sep/Oct, patrolling the approaches. 1946: Returned to owners in February. 1959: BU at Bruges, Belgium.

VITALITY   1915/17   Displacement: 202TG
Admty No: 1481
Port Reg: SH. 63

1914: Launched. 1915: Requisitioned in May and converted to a M/S. 1917: LOST. Mined off Orford Ness on 20th October.

VIVANTI   1916/17   Displacement: 226TG 109TN
Engines: 75HP = 9K
Armament: 1 x 12pdr
Admty No: 3264
Port Reg: GY. 878

1915: Launched. Built at Beverley by CWG. Owned by North Western SFC of Grimsby. 1916: Requisitioned in March and converted to a M/S. 1917: LOST. Foundered off Fairlight, Hastings, on 17th March.

VIVIANA   1939/46   Displacement: 452TG 310TN
Engines: 114HP
Port Reg: GY. .233
P. No: FY. 238

1936: Launched. Built at Selby by Cochrane. Owned by the Atlas SF Co. of Grimsby. 1939: Requisitioned in October and converted to A/S. Based at Grimsby (Ungrouped). 1943: Transferred to the S. African Station and based at Durban for convoy escorts. 1946: Returned to owners in May.

VIZALMA   1940/45   Displacement: 672TG 205TN
Engines: 165HP = 12K
Port Reg: GY. 101
P. No: FY. 286

1940: Launched. Built at Beverley by CWG. Owned by the Atlas SFC of Grimsby. Requisitioned in June whilst building and completed as A/S. 1941: Transferred to the Iceland Command in August for Russian Convoys. 1945: Returned to owners in December. 1964: BU at Dunston.

VOLANTE   1914/19   Displacement: 255TG 107TN
                                              Engines: 75HP
                                              Armament: 1 x 6pdr
                                              Admty No: 713
                                              Port Reg: GY. 235
1907: Launched. Built at Selby by Cochrane. Owned by H Wood AO of Grimsby. 1915: Requisitioned in January and converted to a M/S. 1919: Returned to owners.

VOLESUS   1915/19   Displacement: 293TG 132TN
                                              Engines: 79HP
                                              Armament: 1 x 6pdrAA
                                              Admty No: 713
                                              Port Reg: GY. 851
1913: Launched. Built at Selby by Cochrane. Owned by G. Craig AO of Aberdeen. 1915: Requisitioned in April and converted to a M/S. Employed as convoy escort. 1919: Returned to owners. 1938: Owned by Dobson Ship Repairing Co of Grimsby.

VOLTA   1917/19   Displacement: 156TG 60TN
                                              Engines: 45HP
                                              Port Reg: H. 111
1890: Launched. Built at Beverley. Iron construction. Owned by F & T Ross of Hull. 1917: Requisitioned into the Fishery Reserve. 1919: Returned to owners. 1938: Owned by Consolidated Fisheries of Grimsby.

VOLUNTEER   1917/19   Displacement: 112TG 44TN
                                              Engines: 43HP
                                              Port Reg: SSS. 8
1891: Launched. Built at North Shields. Owned by G Craig of Aberdeen. 1917: Requisitioned into the Fishery Reserve. 1919: Returned to owners.

VONOLEL   1915/19   Displacement: 264TG 106TN
                                              Engines: 73HP
                                              Armament: 1 x 6pdr
                                              Port Reg: GY. 628
1911: Launched. Built at Selby by Cochrane. Owned by Atlas SFC of Grimsby. 1915: Requisitioned and converted to a M/S. 1919: Returned to owners.

VULCAN   1936/47   Ex-*Mascot*
                                              Ex-*Aston Villa*

Details: See under Groups (Vol 1)
Displacement: 623TG.
Measurements: 153ft x 2ft 6-inch
Port Reg: GY
P. No: T. 51

1933: Launched. Owned by Consolidated Fisheries of Grimsby. 1936: Purchased into the RN on 11th July and converted to a DS for MTBs. 1939: Joined the MF. 1941: Returned to the UK and TIH for refitting. Completed refitting and returned to the MF. 1945: Returned to the UK. 1947: Sold to mercantile in February and renamed *Fotherby*. 1950: Renamed *Miriam*. 1953: Renamed *Pollux*.

VULTURE   1914/18   Displacement: 190TG 57TN
                                                Engines: 58HP = 10K
                                                Armament: 1 x 3pdr
                                                Admty No: 310
                                                Port Reg: H. 470

1899: Launched. Built at Hull by CWG. Owned by St. Andrews SFC of Hull. 1914: Requisitioned in August and converted to a M/S. 1915: Renamed VULTURE II in February. 1918: LOST. Sunk after striking a wreck in Loch Eriboll on 16th March. No loss of life.

VULTURE II   1915/18   See under VULTURE above

WALDORF   1915/19   Displacement: 293TG 132TN
Engines: 79HP
Armament: WWI: 1 x 6pdrAA;
WWII: 1 x 12pdr
Admty No: 854
Port Reg: WWI: GY. 927
WWII: GY. 202
P. No: WWII: 4. 45

1913: Launched. Built at Selby by Cochrane. 1915: Requisitioned in May and converted to a M/S. 1919: Returned to owners. Acquired by the Loyal SF Co. of Grimsby and renamed *Alfredian*. 1939: Requisitioned in November as ALFREDIAN and converted to an APV. 1946: Returned to owners in September.

WALLACE   1917/19   Displacement: 100TG
Port Reg: GN. 12

1883: Launched. 1917: Requisitioned into the Fishery Reserve. 1919: Returned to owners.

WALLENA   1914/19 1939/46 Displacement: 225TG 112TN
Engines: 67HP
Armament: 1 x 3pdr
Admty No: 907
Port Reg: WWI: GY. 12; WWII: GY. 132
P. No: WWII: FY. 832

1914: Launched. Built at Beverley by CWG. 1915: Requisitioned in November and con-verted to a M/S. 1919: Returned to owners. 1938: Owned by Kottingham TC of Grimsby. 1939: Requisitioned in November and converted to an APV. 1940: Converted to a M/S in June. 1945: Converted to a BGV in April. 1946: Returned to owners in September.

WALLINGTON   1915/19   Displacement: 259TG
Admty No: Not Issued

1911: Launched.   1915: Requisitioned and converted to a BDV.   1918: Renamed ORIFLAMME. 1919: Returned to owners.

WALPOLE   1914/19   Displacement: 302TG
Armament: 1 x 6pdr; 1 x 7.5-inch Bomb
Thrower (A/S Howitzer)
Admty No: 1625
Port Reg: GY. 269

1914: Launched.   1915: Requisitioned in May.   1918: Renamed WALPOLE II in February. 1919: Returned to owners.

WALPOLE II   1918/19   See under WALPOLE above

WALTER S. BAILEY   1916/19   Displacement: 224TG
     Armament: M/S: 1 x 6pdrAA;
     Q. Ship: 1 x 4-inch; 1 x 12pdr;
     1 x 3.5-inch Bomb Thrower
     Admty No: 265
     Port Reg: H. 546

1902: Launched. 1914: Requisitioned in August and converted to a M/S. 1917: Converted to a 'Q' Ship in October and rearmed. 1918: Reverted to M/S in November. 1919: Returned to owners. Notes: As a 'Q' Ship operated under the names of *Mayflower* and *W.S. Bailey.*

WALTHAM   1914/17   Displacement: 162TG
     Armament: 1 x 6pdr
     Admty No; 689
     Port Reg: GY. 303

1897: Launched. 1914: Requisitioned in December and converted to a M/S. 1917: LOST. Disappeared off the Isle of Man on 10th October. Assumed to have been sunk by a S/M.

WALWYNS CASTLE   1915/19 1940/46   Displacement: 255TG 100TN
     Engines: 85HP
     Armament: WWI: 1 x 12pdr;
     1 x 7.5-inch Bomb Thrower (A/S
     Howitzer); WWII: 1 x 6pdr
     Admty No: 1774
     Port Reg: SA. 9
     P. No: WWII: FY. 866

1913: Launched. Built at Middlesborough by Smith's Dock. 1915: Requisitioned in June and converted to a M/S. 1919: Returned to owners. 1938: Owned by Consolidated Fisheries of Grimsby. 1940: Requisitioned in March and converted to a M/S. 1946: Returned to owners in March.

WARBLER   1914/19   Displacement: 192TG
     Armament: 1 x 3pdr
     Admty No: 412
     Port Reg: H. 507

1912: Launched. 1914: Requisitioned in November and converted to a M/S. 1919: Returned to owners.

WARDOUR   1939/46   See under ST. MALO

WAR DUKE   1917/19 1939/46 Displacement: 247TG 97TN
                                          Engines: 75HP
                                          Armament: WWI: 1 x 12pdr
                                          WWII: 1 x 6pdr
                                          Admty No: 1268
                                          Port Reg: GY. 1037
                                          P. No: WWII: FY. 582

1917: Launched. Built at Beverley by CWG. Owned by Kottingham TC of Grimsby. Requisitioned in May and converted to a M/S. 1919: Returned to owners. 1939: Requisitioned in November and converted to an APV. 1940: Converted to a M/S in June. Based at Grimsby for sweeping in the North Sea. 1944: Reverted to an APV. 1946: Returned to owners in April.

WAR GREY   1917/19   Displacement: 246TG 97TN
                                          Engines: 74HP = 9.5K
                                          Armament: 1 x 12pdr
                                          Admty No: 3342
                                          Port Reg: GY. 1033

1917: Launched. Built at Beverely by CWG. Owned by South Western SFC of Grimsby. Requisitioned in July and converted to a M/S. Fitted with Listening Hydrophones. 1918: Acquired by Great Northern Steam Ship Fishing Co. of Hull. PR: H. 612. 1919: Returned to owners. 1944: Stranded off Iceland in March. Re-floated and TIH at Hull for repair. 1945: Acquired by Hull Merchants Amalgamated Trs. of Hull and renamed Tobruk. PR: H. 14. 1950: Acquired by A. Hay of Aberdeen and renamed *G.D. Taylor*. PR: A. 644. 1955: BU at Granton.

WARLAND   1916/19 1940/42 Displacement: 214TG 88TN
                                          Engines: 58HP
                                          Armament: WWI: 1 x 6pdrAA;
                                          1 x 7.5-inch Bomb Thrower (A/S
                                          Howitzer); WWII: 1 x 12pdr
                                          Admty No: 1626
                                          Port Reg: GY. 819

1912: Launched. Built at Beverley by CWG. Owned by Earl SF Co. of Grimsby. 1916: Requisitioned in May and converted to a M/S. 1919: Returned to owners. 1940: Purchased into the RN on 24th May and converted to A/S. 1942: LOST. Sunk by enemy a/c in the North Sea on 18th February.

WAR LORD   1915/19   Displacement: 226TG 109TN
                                          Engines: 75HP
                                          Armament: 1 x 6pdr
                                          Admty No: 1444
                                          Port Reg: GY. 341

1914: Launched. Built at Beverley by CWG. 1915: Requisitioned in April and converted to a M/S. 1919: Returned to owners. 1938: Owned by JE Harrison & JC Store of Grimsby.

WARRIOR II	1915/19	Displacement: 236TG
		Armament: 1 x 12pdr
		Admty No: 1048
		Port Reg: GY. 944

1890: Launched. 1915: Requisitioned in February. 1919: Returned to owners.

WAR STAR	1915/19 1940/46	Displacement: 225TG 112TN
		Engines: 68HP
		Armament: 1 x 6pdrAA
		Admty No: 1633
		Port Reg: GY. 73
		P. No: WWII: FY. 292

1914: Launched. Built at Beverely by CWG. Owned by Earl SF of Grimsby. 1915: Requisitioned in August and converted to a M/S. 1919: Returned to owners. 1940: Requisitioned in May and converted to an APV. 1942: Converted to a M/S in July. 1944: Converted to an Esso in May. 1946: Returned to owners in February.

WARTER PRIORY	1914/19	Displacement: 299TG 121TN
		Engines: 75HP
		Armament: 1 x 12pdr; 1 x 6pdr;
		1 x 7.5-inch Bomb Thrower (A/S
		Howitzer)
		Admty No: 653
		Port Reg: H. 811

1906: Launched. Built at Hull. Owned by Hull SF & Ice Co. 1914: Requisitioned in October and converted to a M/S. 1919: Returned to owners.

WARWICK DEEPING	1939/40	Displacement: 445TG 182TN
		Engines: 111HP
		Port Reg: H. 136
		P. No: FY. 182

1934: Launched. Built at Selby by Cochrane. Owned by Newington STC of Hull. 1939: Requisitioned in August and converted to A/S. 1940: LOST. Sunk by German destroyers in the Channel 25 miles SW of St. Catherines Point on 12th October.

WARWICKSHIRE	1939/42	Displacement: 465TG 168TN
		Engines: 99HP
		Port Reg: GY. 290
		P. No: FY. 113

1936: Launched in March. Built at Southbank-on-Tees by Smith's Dock. Owned by Warwickshire SF (H. Markham) of Grimsby. 1939: Requisitioned in August and converted to A/S. Joined the 22nd A/S Group. 1940: TPI the Norwegian Campaign in April/May. LOST. Sunk off Trondhiem by enemy a/c on 30th April. 1942: Salvaged by the Germans and Commissioned on April as ALANE. 1943: German Loss. Sunk by the Russian S/M S-51 on 19th July.

WAR WING	1916/19 1936/46	Displacement: 226TG 109TN	
		Engines: 75HP	
		Armament: 1 x 6pdrAA	
		Admty No: 3286	
		Port Reg: GY. 857	
		P. No: WWII: FY. 906	

1914: Launched. Built at Beverley by CWG. 1916: Requisitioned in June and converted to a M/S. 1919: Returned to owners. 1938: Owned by the Dobson Ship Repair Co. of Grimsby. 1939: Requisitioned in December and converted to an APV. 1940: Converted to a M/S in June. 1946: Returned to owners in January.

WASHINGTON	1914/19 1939/39	Displacement: 209TG 81TN	
		Measurements: 117ft.	
		Engines: 65HP	
		Armament: 1 x 12pdr	
		Admty No: 833	
		Port Reg: GY. 468	

1909: Launched. Built at Selby by Cochrane. Owned by the Premier SFC of Grimsby. 1914: Requisitioned in December and converted to a M/S. 1919: Returned to owners. 1938: Owned by the Overseas SF Co. of Grimsby. 1939: Requisitioned in November and designated as a M/S. LOST. Whilst on passage to Gt. Yarmouth to fit out she was sunk with all hands on 6th December by a mine which had been laid the previous night by the German U-59.

WATERFLY	1939/42	Ex-*Walpole*	
		Displacement: 387TG 185TN	
		Engines: 105HP = 11K	
		Port Reg: GY. 385	
		P. No: FY. 681	

1931: Launched. Built at Beverley by CWG as *Walpole*. Owned by EC Grant of Grimsby. 1939: Requisitioned in September and converted to a M/S and renamed. Based at Kirkwall for sweeping at Scapa Flow. 1941: Transferred to the Dover Patrol and joined the 46th M/S Group. 1942: LOST. Sunk by enemy a/c off Dungeness on 17th September. She received a direct hit in the magazine. Only 1 survivor.

WAVEFLOWER	1939/40	Displacement: 368TG 142TN	
		Engines: 96HP	
		Port Reg: H. 58	
		P. No: FY. 703	

1929: Launched. Built at Selby by Cochrane. Owned by the Yorkshire SF Co. of Hull. 1939: Purchased into the RN and converted to a M/S by Doigs of Grimsby. 1940: LOST. Mined off Aldeburgh on 21st October.

WAVENEY	1920/22	See under JAMES CONNOR (Vol 1 p.57)

WAYNEFLETE	1917/19	Displacement: 157TG Port Reg: GY. 746

1901: Launched. 1917: Requisitioned into the Fishery Reserve. 1919: Returned to owners.

WEAR	1920/22	See under JOHN BOMKWORTH (Vol 1 p.60)

WEAZEL	1939/40	See under NUBIA

WEIGELIA	1914/16	Displacement: 262TG Armament: 1 x 3pdr Admty No: 153 Port Reg: M. 96

1911: Launched. 1914: Requisitioned in August and converted to a M/S. 1916: LOST. Mined off Dover on 18th February.

WELBECK	1915/19 1939/45	Displacement: 302TG 128TN Engines: 84HP Armament: WWI 1 x 6pdr; 24 Mines Port Reg: WWI: GY. 455; WWII: H. 128 P. Nos: WWI: (i) N. 4A (ii) N. 8A. WWII: FY. 561 (M/S)

1915: Launched. Built at Selby by Cochrane. Requisitioned in May and converted to a M/L. 1920: Returned to owners. Acquired by F & T Ross of Hull and renamed *Ohm*. 1939: Requisitioned in August as OHM and converted to a M/S. Formed the 41st M/S Group ICW FORT ROYAL, ROBERT BOWEN and THOMAS ALTOFT and based at Aberdeen for sweeping off the N.E. Coast of Scotland. 1940: Group sweeping 20 miles NE of Aberdeen on 9th February when they were attacked by 2 x Heinkel 111s. FORT ROYAL and ROBERT BOWEN were sunk, but the other two survived. 1941: Transferred to Ardrossan. 1945: Returned to owners in December.

WELBECK	1940/46	See under WILLIAM RAM (Vol 1 p.7151)

WELLARD	1939/45	Ex-*El Capitan* Displacement: 514TG 280TN

Engines: 156HP = 12.8K
Port Reg: GY. 450
P. No: FY. 137

1937: Launched in July as *El Capitan*. Built at Beverley by CWG. Owned by Earl SF Co. of Grimsby. 1938: Acquired by Crampin SF of Grimsby and renamed *Wellard*. 1939: Purchased into the RN in August and converted to A/S. Joined the 21st A/S Strike Group. 1940: TPI the Norwegian Campaign in April/May. 1942: Temporary Loan to the USN from February. Returned to RN in October and transferred to the S. African Station. 1946: Sold to mercantile and retained the same name. Re-acquired by Crampins of Grimsby. PR: GY. 300. 1961: BU in September.

WELLSBACH   1939/45   Displacement: 369TG 149TN
                                        Engines: 96HP = 10.4K
                                        Port Reg: H. 277
                                        P. No: FY. 652

1930: Launched. Built at Beverley by CWG. Owned by F & T Ross of Hull. 1939: Requisitioned in August and converted to a M/S. 1945: Returned to owners in September. 1946: Acquired by Wyre Trs. of Fleetwood and renamed *Wyre Warrior*. PR: FD. 178. 1955: BU in Belgium. Notes: Mercantile Lists as *Welsbach*.

WEMYSS   1914/19   Displacement: 167TG
                                        Armament: 1 x 12pdr;1 x 6pdrAA
                                        Admty No: 475
                                        Port Reg: GN. 28

1905: Launched. 1914: Requisitioned in November and converted to a M/S. 1919: Returned to owners.

WESTELLA   1939/40   Displacement: 413TG 160TN
                                        Engines: 106HP
                                        Port Reg: H.124
                                        P. No: FY.161

1934: Launched. Built at Selby by Cochrane. Owned by Marr of Fleetwood. 1939: Purchased into the RN in August and converted to A/S. 1940: TPI Operation Dynamo, the evacuation of Dunkirk, in May/June. LOST. Sunk off Dunkirk on 2nd June. Believed mined or torpedoed.

WESTERN EXPLORER   1940/45   Displacement: 113TG

1938: Launched. 1940: Requisitioned in October and converted for the Examination Service. 1945: Returned to owners.

WESTHOLME   1939/46   Displacement: 152TG 67TN
                                        Engines: 35HP
                                        Port Reg: LT. 216

1918: Launched. Built at Rotterdam. 1938: Owned by Waveney SDF of Lowestoft.

1939: Requisitioned in September and employed on harbour service throughout the war.
1946: Returned to owners.

WESTLYN   1940/47   Displacement: 284TG 112TN
                                          Engines: 85HP
                                          Port Reg: FD. 8
                                          P. No: Z. 154

1914: Launched. Built at Middlesborough by Smith's Dock. 1938: Owned by T Cardwell
& RH Bagshaw of Fleetwood. 1940: Purchased into the RN in February and converted
to a BDV. 1945: Sold to mercantile in May.

WESTRAY   1917/19   Displacement: 207TG 81TN
                                          Engines: 50HP = 9.5K
                                          Armament: 1 x 6pdrAA
                                          Admty No: 1277
                                          Port Reg: H. 390

1911: Launched. Built at Beverley by CWG. Owned by the Hull SF & Ice Co. 1917:
Requisitioned in February and converted to a M/S. 1919: Returned to owners.
1938: BU.

WESTWARD HO   1914/19   Displacement: 146TG
                                          Armament: 1 x 6pdr
                                          Admty No: 394
                                          Port Reg: H. 347

1897: Launched. 1914: Requisitioned in December and converted to a M/S. 1915:
Renamed WESTWARD HO II in May. 1919: Returned to owners.

WESTWARD HO II   1915/19   See under WESTWARD HO above

WEYMOUTH II   1915/19   Displacement: 178TG
                                          Armament: 1 x 6pdr
                                          Admty No: 939
                                          Port Reg: BL. 11

1903: Launched. 1915: Requisitioned in February and converted to a M/S. 1919:
Returned to owners.

W.H. HASTIE   1916/19   Hastie Group
                                          Armament: 1 x 12pdr

?: Launched. Owned by Hastie of N. Shields. 1916: Requisitioned. 1919: Returned to
owners.

WHITBY   1917/19   Displacement: 164TG 64TN
                                          Engines: 45HP
                                          Port Reg: GY. 524

1898: Launched. Built at Irvine by Irvine SB. 1917: Requisitioned into the Fishery Reserve. 1919: Returned to owners. 1938: Owned by Youds of Milford Haven.

WHITECAP   1941/45   Displacement: 303TG
Port Reg: American
1916: Launched. American fishing vessel. 1941: Purchased from American owners. 1945: Sold to mercantile in November.

WHITE EAR   1914/19   Displacement: 191TG 73TN
Engines: 55HP
Armament: 1 x 6pdr
Admty No: 542
Port Reg: H. 129
1914: Launched. Built at Goole by Goole SB. Owned by Kelsall Bros. & Beeching of Hull. Requisitioned in October and converted to a M/S. 1919: Returned to owners.

WHITE FRIAR   1916/19   Displacement: 286TG
Armament: 1 x 12pdr
Admty No: 1191
Port Reg: H . 886
1906: Launched. 1915: Requisitioned in March and converted to a M/S. 1919: Returned to owners.

WHITE QUEEN   1915/16   Displacement: 108TG
1897: Launched. 1915: Requisitioned for Harbour Service. 1916: Returned to owners in April.

WHITETHROAT   1918/19   See under WREN

WHOOPER   1914/16   Displacement: 302TG
Admty No: 668
Port Reg: FD. 15
1914: Launched. Requisitioned in December and converted to a M/S. 1916: LOST. Mined off Lowestoft on 30th June.

W.H. PODD   1915/19   Displacement: 225TG 87TN
Engines: 76HP
Armament: 1 x 6pdrAA
Admty No: 154
Port Reg: M. 1
1914: Launched. Built at Aberdeen. 1915: Requisitioned in February and converted to a M/S. 1919: Returned to owners. 1938: Owned by Mrs. I.S. Boyle of Glasgow. PR: GW. 34.

WIGAN   1916/19 1940/46 Displacement: 275TG 108TN
                                     Engines: 88HP
                                     Armament: 1 x 12pdr
                                     Admty No: 1997
                                     Port Reg: FD. 241
                                     P. No: WWII: FY. 1583
1916: Launched. Built at Southbank-on-Tees by Smith's Dock. Owned by the Palantine
STC of Fleetwood. Requisitioned in May and converted to a M/S. 1919: Returned to
owners. 1940: Requisitioned in February and converted to a M/S. Based at Dover for
sweeping in the Channel. 1946: Returned to owners.

WILD ROSE   1914/18   Displacement: 156TG
                                     Armament: 1 x 6pdr
                                     Admty No: 314
                                     Port Reg: SN. 325
1902: Launched.   1914: Requisitioned in August and converted to a M/S.   1918:
Returned to owners.

WILLET   1914/19   Displacement: 199TG 73TN
                                     Engines: 50HP
                                     Armament: 1 x 6pdrAA
                                     Admty No: 646
                                     Port Reg: H. 976
1908: Launched. Built at Goole by Goole SB. Owned by Kelsall Bros. & Beeching of Hull.
1914: Requisitioned in October and converted to a M/S. 1919: Returned to owners.

WILLIAM ALLEN   1915/19   Displacement: 203TG 87TN
                                     Engines: 76HP
                                     Armament: 1 x 3pdr; 1 x 7.5-inch Bomb
                                     Thrower (A/S Howitzer)
                                     Admty No: 719
                                     Port Reg: A. 165
1914: Launched. Built at Aberdeen. 1915: Requisitioned in January and converted to a
M/S. 1919: Returned to owners. 1938: Owned by P & J Johnstone of Aberdeen.

WILLIAM H. HASTIE   1916/19 1940/43 Hastie Group.
                                     Displacement: 229TG 89TN
                                     Engines: 83HP
                                     Armament: 1 x 12pdr
                                     Admty No: 1999
                                     Port Reg: SN. 283
1916: Launched. Built at Aberdeen. Owned by R. Hastie & Sons of N. Shields.
Requisitioned in July and converted to a M/S. Fitted with Listening Hydrophones.
1919: Returned to owners. 1940: Requisitioned in August and converted for the

Examination Service. 1941: Converted to a Salvage Vessel. 1945: Returned to owners in March.

WILLIAM MORRISON 1915/15 Displacement: 211TG
Armament: 1 x 3pdr
Admty No: 3217
Port Reg: A. 355

1915: Requisitioned in September and converted to a M/S. LOST. Mined near the Sunk Head Buoy on 28th November.

WILLIAM PURDY 1914/19 1940/45 Displacement: 194TG 86TN
Engines: 83HP
Armament: 1 x 3pdr
Admty No: 801
Port Reg: SN. 92

1914: Launched. Built at Willington Quay. Owned by GR Purdy Trs. Ltd. of North Shields. Requisitioned in November and converted to a M/S. 1919: Returned to owners. 1940: Requisitioned in February and converted to a BBV. 1945: Returned to owners in October.

WILLIAM STEPHEN 1939/43 See under JOSEPH ANNISON
(Vol 1 p.182)

WILLIAM STROUD 1915/19 1944/45 Displacement: 214TG 80TN
Engines: 57HP
Port Reg: A.107
P. No: WWII: 4. 460

1914: Launched. Built at Aberdeen. Owned by Strouds SF of Aberdeen. 1915: Requisitioned in June and converted to a BGV. 1919: Returned to owners. 1944: Requisitioned in March and converted to an Esso. 1945: Returned to owners in March.

WILLIAM WESNEY 1939/40 Displacement: 364TG 171TN
Engines: 91HP
Armament: 1 x 12pdr
Port Reg: GY.168

1930: Launched. Built at Beverley by CWG. Owned by Crampin SF of Grimsby. 1939: Requisitioned in September and converted to a M/S. 1940: LOST. Mined off Orford Ness on 7th November.

WILLONYX 1915/19 Displacement: 327TG
Armament: 1 x 6pdr; 1 x 3.5-inch Bomb
Thrower (A/S Howitzer)
Admty No: 1747
Port Reg: GY. 544

1915: Launched. Requisitioned in August and converted to a M/S. 1919: Returned to owners.

WIMPOLE	1916/19 1940/45	Displacement: 320TG 163TN
		Engines: 88HP
		Armament: 1 x 12pdr
		Admty No: 2956
		Port Reg: GY. 923

1916: Launched. Built at Selby by Cochrane. Requisitioned in August and converted to a M/S. Also employed on escort duties. 1919: Returned to owners. Acquired by Kopanes SF Co of Grimsby and renamed *Andanes*. 1940: Requisitioned in May as ANDANES and converted to an APV. 1941: Converted to a BDV in January. 1945: Returned to owners.

WINDSHIFT   1916/19

1916: Requisitioned. 1919: Returned to owners.

WINDSOR	1916/19	Displacement: 222TG 97TN
		Engines: 66HP
		Armament: 1 x 6pdrAA
		Admty No: 2988
		Port Reg: GY. 998

1916: Launched. Built at Selby by Cochrane. Owned by Queen SFC of Grimsby. Requisitioned in December and converted to a M/S. 1918: Renamed WINDSOR II in February. 1919: Returned to owners.

WINDSOR II   1918/19   See under WINDSOR above

WINDWARD HO	1939/46	Displacement: 263TG 105TN
		Engines: 78HP
		Port Reg: GY. 158
		P. No: FY. 574

1920: Launched. Built at Beverley by CWG. Owned by H Croft Baker of Grimsby. 1939: Requisitioned in August and converted to a M/S. 1946: Returned to owners.

WISTARIA	1915/16	Displacement: 143TG 53TN
		Engines: 44HP
		Armament: 1 x 6pdr
		Admty No: 735
		Port Reg: GY. 302

1891: Launched. Built at Canning Town. 1915: Requisitioned in January and converted to a M/S. Renamed WISTARIA II in December. 1919: Returned to owners. 1938: Owned by Consolidated Fisheries of Grimsby. PR: LT. 97.

WISTARIA II   1916/19   See under WISTARIA 1915

| WITHAM | 1939/44 | See under STEPHEN KENNEY (Vol 1 p.186) |

WITHAM   1939/44   See under STEPHEN KENNEY
                             (Vol 1 p.186)

WITHERNSEA   1939/46   Ex-German *Lawica*
                             Displacement: 257TG 97TN
                             Engines: 70HP
                             Port Reg: H. 263
                             P. No: FY. 1637

1918: Launched. Built at Flensburg. 1938: Owned by Pearson of Hull. 1939: Requisitioned in December and converted to an APV. 1940: Converted to a M/S in July. 1946: Returned to owner.

WOLBOROUGH   1939/46   Displacement: 459TG
1937: Launched. 1939: Purchased into the RN in September and converted to an A/S. 1946: Sold to mercantile in May.

WOLSELEY   1917/19   Displacement: 159TG 61TN
                             Engines: 55HP
                             Port Reg: SN. 345
1903: Launched. Built at S. Shields. 1917: Requisitioned into the Fishery Reserve. 1919: Returned to owners. 1938: Owned by Brackenbury AO of Grimsby.

WOLVES   1939/45   Football Group
                             Displacement: 422TG
                             P. No: FY.158
1934: Launched. Owned by Consolidated Fisheries of Grimsby. 1939: Purchased into the RN in August and converted to an A/S. 1945: Sold to mercantile in October.

WOODS   1939/40   See under JAMES BRODIGAN
                             (Vol 1 p.175)

WORSLEY   1914/15   Displacement: 309TG 138TN
                             Engines: 84HP = 10.5K
                             Armament: 1 x 3pdr
                             Port Reg: GY. 814
1912: Launched. Built at Beverley by CWG. Owned by EC Grant of Grimsby. 1915: Requisitioned in July and converted to a M/S. LOST. Mined off Aldeburgh on 14th August.

WRANGLER   1940/45   See under TRITON 1939

WREN   1914/19   Displacement: 166TG
                             Armament: 1 x 6pdrAA
                             Admty No: 682
                             Port Reg: H. 215

1897: Launched. 1914: Requisitioned in November and converted to a M/S. 1918: Renamed WHITETHROAT in June. 1919: Returned to owners.

WRENTHORPE   1915/19   Displacement: 225TG 91TN
                                     Engines: 54HP
                                     Armament: 1 x 6pdrAA
                                     Admty No: 1534
                                     Port Reg: FD. 80
1906: Launched. Built at Aberdeen. 1915: Requisitioned in June and converted to a M/S. 1919: Returned to owners. 1938: Owned by Baxter of Aberdeen. PR: A. 351.

W.S. BURTON   1917/19 1940/46 Displacement: 234TG
                                     Armament: 1 x 6pdrAA
                                     Admty No: 3036
                                     Port Reg: HL. 86
                                     P. No: WWII: FY. 1590
1917: Launched. Requisitioned in April and converted to a M/S. 1919: Returned to owners. 1940: Requisitioned in March and converted to a M/S. 1946: Returned to owners.

WYNDHAM   1916/19   Displacement: 303TG 157TN
                                     Engines: 84HP
                                     Armament: 1 x 12pdr; 1 x 5-inch Bomb
                                     Thrower (A/S Howitzer)
                                     Admty No: 3033
                                     Port Reg: GY. 930
1916: Launched. Built at Selby by Cochrane. Owned by Consolidated Fisheries of Grimsby. Requisitioned in August and converted to a M/S. 1919: Returned to owners.

WYOMING   1939/44   See under VERESIS

WYRE   1915/19 1940/45 Displacement: 295TG 115TN
                                     Engines: 92HP
                                     Armament: 1 x 12pdr
                                     Admty No: 962
                                     Port Reg: FD.132
                                     P. No: WWII: Z. 198
1911: Launched. Built at Middlesborough by Smith's Dock. Owned by Wyre ST Co. of Fleetwood. 1915: Requisitioned in April and converted to a M/S. Fitted with Listening Hydrophones. 1919: Returned to owners. 1940: Requisitioned in June and converted to a BDV. 1945: Returned to owners in August.

XANIA   1914/19   Displacement: 161TG 63TN
                                           Engines: 45HP
                                           Armament: 1 x 6pdrAA
                                           Admty No: 641
                                           Port Reg: GY. 330

1897: Launched. Built at Govan. 1914: Requisitioned in October and converted to a
M/S. 1919: Returned to owners. 1938: Owned by Consolidated Fisheries of Grimsby.
PR: LT. 765.

XERXES   1914/15   Displacement: 243TG
                                           Armament: 1 x 6pdr
                                           Admty No: 835
                                           Port Reg: SA. 55

1908: Launched. 1914: Requisitioned in December and converted to a M/S. 1915:
LOST. Sunk in a collision off Girdle Ness on 16th November.

XYLOPIA   1914/19   Displacement: 262TG 103TN
                                           Engines: 76HP
                                           Armament: 1 x 12pdrAA
                                           Admty No: 17

1911: Launched. Built at Selby by Cochrane. 1914: Purchased into the RN in July and
converted to a M/S. 1919: Sold to mercantile and retained the same name. 1938:
Owned by C Dobson of Grimsby. PR: GY.1306.

YASHIMA   1939/46   Displacement: 303TG 113TN
                                           Engines: 99HP
                                           Port Reg: CF. 6
                                           P. No: FY. 1894

1929: Launched. Built at Southbank-on-Tees by Smith's Dock. Owned by Neale & West
of Cardiff. 1939: Requisitioned in August and converted to a M/S. 1940: Based at Dover.
1946: Returned to owners on in April.

YESSO   1914/17   Displacement: 229TG
                                           Armament: 1 x 6pdr
                                           Admty No: 166
                                           Port Reg: GY. 600

1911: Launched. 1914: Requisitioned in August and converted to a M/S. 1917: LOST.
Mined off Aberdeen on 9th February.

YESSO   1939/41   See under HENRY FLIGHT
                                           (Vol 1 p.172)

YEZO	1939/46	Displacement: 301TG 113TN
		Engines: 99HP
		Armament: 1 x 12pdr
		Port Reg: LO. 74
		P. No: FY. 829

1924: Launched. Built at Southbank-on-Tees by Smith's Dock. Owned by Jenkerson of Milford Haven AO. 1939: Requisitioned in November and converted to a M/S. 1944: Disarmed and converted to a WDV. 1946: Returned to owners.

| YMUIDEN | 1941/46 | See under ZWARTE ZEE |

YOKOHAMA	1915/19	Displacement: 291TG
		Armament: 1 x 12pdr
		Admty No: 1227
		Port Reg: H. 20

1909: Launched. 1915: Requisitioned in February and converted to a M/S. 1919: Returned to owners.

YORICK	1917/19	Displacement: 213TG 78TN
		Engines: 45HP = 10K
		Port Reg: H. 49

1909: Launched. Built at Beverley by CWG. Owned by Hellyer SFC of Hull. 1917: Requisitioned into the Fishery Reserve. 1919: Returned to owners. 1955: BU at Charlestown.

YORK CITY	1939/45	Football Group
		Displacement: 398TG 153TN
		Engines: 99HP
		Port Reg: GY. 193
		P. No: FY. 110

1933: Launched. Built at Southbank-on-Tees by Smith's Dock. Owned by Consolidated Fisheries of Grimsby. 1939: Requisitioned in September and converted to an A/S. Joined the 17th A/S Group based at Swansea. 1943: A/S Group ICW Sister-ships DERBY CITY, GRIMSBY TOWN, HUDDERSFIELD TOWN and LEEDS UNITED. Remained with this Group for the remainder of the war. Based at Milford Haven for operations in the Western Approaches. Escorted a convoy of Landing Craft to Gibraltar and then joined the MF. Employed on Med. Convoys. Returned to Milford Haven and the Western Approaches at the end of the year. 1945: Returned to owners in November.

YTHAN BRAES	1942/46	Displacement: 268TG 108TN
		Engines: 80HP
		Port Reg: A. 744
		P. No: 4. 339

1917: Launched. Built at Aberdeen. Owned by A.W. King of Aberdeen. 1942:

Requisitioned in August and converted to an Esso. Converted to a Water Carrier in November. 1946: Returned to owners.

YUCCA   1914/18   Displacement: 198TG
                                              Admty No: 307
                                              Port Reg: M. 159

1912: Launched. 1914: Requisitioned in August and converted to a M/S. 1918: LOST. Mined off Lowestoft on 24th May.

YULAN   1917/19   Displacement: 144TG 54TN
                                              Engines: 45HP
                                              Port Reg: GY. 348

1891: Launched. Built at Canning Town. 1917: Requisitioned into the Fishery Reserve. 1919: Returned to owners.

ZAREBA   1940/45   Ex-*Ellena*
                                              Displacement: 257TG 100TN
                                              Engines: 93HP
                                              Port Reg: FD. 394
                                              P. No: FY. 1814

1921: Launched as *Ellena*. Built at Aberdeen. Owned by Clifton ST Ltd. of Fleetwood. 1940: Requisitioned in August, converted to a M/S and renamed. 1944: Converted to a BBV. 1945: Returned to owners.

ZENA DARE   1914/19   Displacement: 242TG
                                              Armament: 1 x 3pdr
                                              Admty No: 540
                                              Port Reg: SA. 112

1909: Launched. 1914: Requisitioned in December and converted to a M/S. 1919: Returned to owners.

ZENNOR   1917/19   Displacement: 166TG
                                              Port Reg: GY. 337

1897: Launched. 1918: Requisitioned into the Fishery Reserve. 1919: Returned to owners.

ZETLAND   1917/19   Displacement: 165TG
                                              Port Reg: GY. 760

1898: Launched. 1917: Requisitioned into the Fishery Reserve. 1919: Returned to owners.

ZODIAC II   1917/19   Displacement: 149TG
                                              Port Reg: GY. 151

1890: Launched. 1917: Requisitioned into the Fishery Reserve. 1919: Returned to owners.

ZONIA   1914/19   Ex-*Apollo*
                  Displacement: 150TG 58TN
                  Engines: 41HP
                  Armament: 1 x 6pdrAA
                  Admty No: 707
                  Port Reg: GY. 227

1898: Launched. Built at Govan. 1914: Requisitioned in November and converted to a M/S. 1919: Returned to owners. Acquired by Consolidated Fisheries of Grimsby. PR: LT. 118.

ZWARTE ZEE   1940/46   Displacement: 194TG
                  Port Reg: Dutch
                  P. No: FY. 1937

1899: Launched. 1940: Hired from Dutch owners in July and converted to a M/S. Commissioned with a Dutch crew. 1941: Renamed YMUIDEN. 1942: Re-Commissioned with a RN crew in October. 1946: Returned to Holland in April.

BOWELL   1942/42   See under CAMPENIA

CAMPENIA   1942/46   Isles Class
Details: See under Classes.
1942: Launched on 1st June. Built in Canada by the Collingwood SY. Renamed
BOWELL in September. Renamed MISCOU in November. 1946: Sold to mercantile and
renamed *Cleveland*.

ST. KILDA   1942/46   Isles Class
Details: See under Classes
Armament: 1 x 12pdr DP;
3 x 20mmAA (3x1)
P.No: T.209
1941: Ordered on 21st February. 1942: Launched on 29th May. Built at Aberdeen by
Alex Hall. 1946: Sold to mercantile in October and renamed *Glaes Compaen*. 1952:
Renamed *Professor Hensen*.

TIMOTI IY CRAWLEY   1917/20 1940/46 Castle Class
Details: See under Classes
Displacement: 121TN
Engines: 61HP
Armament: 1 x 12pdr
Admty No: 3710
Port Reg: WWII: A.461
P.No: WWII: Z.165
1917: Launched on 4th October. Built at Troon by Ailsa SB and completed as an Escort.
1920: Sold to mercantile and renamed Loch Long. Acquired by Loch Line ST & F Co of
Aberdeen. 1940: Requisitioned in February as LOCH LONG and converted to a BDV.
Subsequently purchased into the RN. 1946: Sold to mercantile.

THOMAS ATKINSON   1917/22 1940/45 Mersey Class
Details: See under Classes.
Displacement 130TN.
Engines: 69HP
Armament: 1 x 12pdr
Admty No: 3546
Port Reg: WWII: FD.93
P.No: WWII: FY.578
1917: Launched on 8th May. Built at Selby by Cochrane and completed as a M/S.
1923: Sold to mercantile and renamed *Cavendish*. Acquired by Hudson SFC of Hull.
PR: 909 Acquired by Adam SFC of Fleetwood. 1940: Requisitioned in February as

ERITH and converted to a M/S. Based at Grimsby (Ungrouped). 1943: Joined the 21st M/S Group based at Grimsby. 1945: Returned to owners in June.

THOMAS BAILEY	1917/22	Mersey Class
		Details: See under Classes
		Armament: 1 x 12pdr
		Admty No: 3558

1917: Launched on 4th August. Built at Selby by Cochrane and completed as a M/S. 1922: Sold to mercantile and renamed *Pamxon*.

THOMAS CORNWALL	1918/18	Mersey Class
		Details: See under Classes
		Armament: 1 x 12pdr; 1 x 3.5-inch
		Bomb Thrower (A/S Howitzer)
		Admty No: 3702

1918: Launched. Built at Renfrew by Lobnitz and delivered on 10th June. LOST. Sunk in a collision off Flamborough Head on 29th October.

THOMAS COWELL	1919/20	1944/45 Strath Class
		Details: See under Classes
		Admty No: 4475
		Port Reg: WWII: A.16

1917: Launched on 18th June. Built at Leith by Bow McLachlan. Fitted with Listening Hydrophones. 1920: Sold to mercantile, acquired by Hollinwood STFC of Hull and renamed *Dudley*. Port Reg: H.162. Acquired by G. Leiper AO of Aberdeen and renamed *Southward Ho*. 1944: Requisitioned in March as SOUTHWARD HO and converted to an Esso. 1945: Returned to owners in February.

THOMAS CRUIZE	1918/19	Mersey Class
		Details: See under Classes
		Admty No: 3706

1918: Launched. Built at Renfrew by Lobnitz. 1919: Completed as a fishing vessel and delivered on 30th January. Sold to mercantile and renamed *Celerina*. 1922: Mercantile Loss on 11th December.

THOMAS JAGO	1918/22 1940/47 Mersey Class
	Details: See under Classes
	Admty No: 3835
	P.No: WWII: Z.226

1918: Launched. Built at Selby by Cochrane. And completed as an escort. 1922: Sold to mercantile and renamed *St. Valery*. Acquired by Jutland Amalgamated Trs. Of Hull and renamed *Lady Eleanor*. 1940: Requisitioned as LADY ELEANOR and converted to a BDV. Purchased into the RN in November. 1947: Sold to mercantile.

THOMAS JARVIS   1918/28   Mersey Class
                                        Details: See under Classes
                                        Armament: 1 x 12pdr
                                        Admty No: 3840
1918: Launched. Built at Selby by Cochrane. Employed on Special Service. 1920: Renamed AXE.

THOMAS JOHNS   1918/45   Mersey Class
                                        Details: See under Classes
                                        Armament: 1 x 12pdr
                                        Admty No: 3837
                                        P.No: WWII: T.49
1918: Launched. Built at Selby by Cochrane and delivered on 3rd September. 1920: Renamed EDEN. 1921: Transferred on loan to the SAN and renamed IMMORTELLE. 1934: Returned to the RN and reverted to EDEN. 1939: Laid Up and placed on the Disposal List. 1941: Brought Forward for harbour service. 1942: Reduced to a hulk. 1945: Sold to BU.

THOMAS MALONEY   1919/20 1940/45 Mersey Class
                                        Details: See under Classes
                                        Admty No: 4247
                                        Port Reg: WWII: H.112
                                        P.No: WWII: FY.1618
1919: Launched on 14th June. Built at Selby by Cochrane and completed as a fishing vessel. Sold to mercantile, acquired by the Boston DSF & Ice Co of Fleetwood and renamed *St. Neots*. 1940: Requisitioned in February as ADAM and converted to a M/S. Based at Dover for Channel sweeping. 1945: Returned to owners.

THOMAS MATTHEWS   1919/19   Mersey Class
                                        Details: See under Classes
                                        Admty No: 4246
1919: Launched. Built at Selby by Cochrane and completed as a fishing vessel. Sold to mercantile and renamed *Earl Beatty*.

THOMAS THRESHER   1918/22   1940/46 Mersey Class
                                        Details: See under Classes
                                        Armament: 1 x 12pdr
                                        Admty No: 3572
                                        Port Reg: WWII: Norwegian
                                        P.No: WWII: FY.1732
1918: Launched. Built at Selby by Cochranne and completed as a M/S. 1922: Sold to mercantile, acquired by the Grimsby SFC and retained the same name. Acquired by Norwegian owners and renamed *Syrian*. 1940: Hired from Norwegian owners in April as SYRIAN and converted to a M/S. 1946: Returned to Norway in January.

THOMAS WHIPPLE 1918/22 Mersey Class
Details: See under Classes
Armament: 1 x 12pdr

1918: Launched. Built at Selby by Cochrane. 1922: Sold to mercantile and renamed *Lord Lascelles*.

MASTIFF **(MPL)**

**Parts I and II
COMBINED INDEX**

COMBINED INDEX

Name	Ref	Name	Ref	Name	Ref
AMOS	2.13	ANTIOCH II	2.19	ARLIEUX	1.28
AMPERE	2.14	Antonella	1.125	ARMAGEDDON	2.26
AMPLIFY	2.14	ANTONIO	2.19	ARMANA	2.26
AMRITSAR	1.35	ANWOTH	2.19	ARMENTIERS	1.28
AMROTH CASTLE	2.14	ANZAC	2.19	ARNOLD BENNETT	2.26
AMSTERDAM	2.14	ANZAC II	2.19	Aro	1.215
AMY	2.14	APLEY	2.19	AROHA	1.91
Andalusite	2.102	Apollo	2.529	A. ROSE	2.26
Andanes	2.523	AQUAMARINE (1915)	2.19	Arrabida	1.160
ANDANES (1917)	2.14	AQUAMARINE (1939)	2.20	ARRAN	1.105
ANDANES (1940)	2.14	AQUARIUS	2.20	ARRAS	1.28
Anderby	1.60	ARAB	1.iv, 2.20	ARREST	2.27
ANDES	1.3, 2.15	Arab	1.218	ARSENAL	2.27
ANDRADITE	2.15	ARABESQUE	2.20	ARTEGAL	2.27
ANDRE-LOUIS	2.15	ARABIAN	2.21	ARTHUR CAVANAGH	1.48
ANDRE MONIQUE	2.15	ARACARI	2.21	ARTHUR HERWIN	1.168
ANDREW ANDERSON	1.47	Aragonite	1.58	ARTHUR LESSIMORE	1.48
ANDREW APSLEY	1.47	ARAGONITE	2.21	ARTHUR ROSE	2.27
ANDREW JEWER	1.131	ARALIA	2.21	ARUM	2.27
ANDREW KING	1.131	Arcila	1.148	Asama	2.9
Andrew Marvel	1.64	Arctic Adventurer	2.416	ASAMA (1917)	2.27
ANDREW MARVEL	2.15	ARCTIC EXPLORER	1.17, 2.21	ASAMA (1939)	2.27
ANDREW McWILLIAMS	1.131	ARCTIC HUNTER	2.22	ASH	1.195
ANDREW SACK	1.47	Arctic Hunter	2.22	Ashare	1.113
ANDROMEDA	2.15	Arctic Invader	2.415	ASHLYN	2.27
ANDYK	2.14, 2.16	ARCTIC PIONEER	2.22	ASHTON	2.28
Anemono	2.10	ARCTIC PRINCE	2.22	ASIA	2.28
ANGELE-MARIE	2.16	ARCTIC RANGER	2.22	ASIE	2.28
ANGELUS	2.16	Arctic Rover	1.28, 2.235	ASPASIA	2.29
ANGERTON	2.16	ARCTIC TRAPPER	2.23	A. SPENCE MACDONALD	2.29
ANGLE (1915)	2.16	Arctic Venturer	2.22	Assan Reis	1.105
ANGLE (1939)	2.16	ARCTURUS	1.208	Assyrian	2.447
ANGLIA	2.16	ARCTURUS II	1.208	Asterby	1.87
ANGOLIAN	2.17	ARDENT	2.23	ASTON VILLA	2.29
ANGUS	2.17	ARDENT II	2.23	Aston Villa	2.510
ANGUS McDONALD	1.131	ARFON	2.23	Astros	1.89
ANIDA	2.17	Argo	1.112	ASTROS	2.29
ANN FORD MELVILLE	2.17	ARGO	2.23	Athalia	2.315
ANN LEWIS	2.17	ARGON	2.23	ATHELSTAN	2.29
ANN MELVILLE	2.17	ARGON II	2.23	ATHENIAN	2.30
Annabelle	1.171	ARGYLLSHIRE	2.24	ATLANTIC	2.30
ANNABELLE	2.18	ARIADNE II	2.24	Atlas	1.111
Anne	1.125	ARIAN	2.24	ATTENTIVE II	2.30
Anne T. Williams	1.125	ARIANA	2.24	AUCKLAND	2.30
ANNET	1.105	ARIEL	2.24	AUCUBA	2.30
Annie Melling	1.64	ARIEL II	2.24	AUDREY	2.30
ANNIE MELLING	2.18	Ariemis	1.122	Augustine Isabelle	1.73
ANNIE WALKER	2.18	ARIES	2.24	AUGUST WREIDT (German)	2.294
ANSON	2.18, 2.93	ARIES II	2.25	AUK (1914)	2.31
ANSON II	2.18	ARIES II	2.25	AUK (1915)	2.31
Antares	1.62	ARIES III	2.25	AUREA	2.31
ANT	2.18	Arinbjorn Hersir	1.143	AURORA	2.31
ANTARES	1.208	Aris	1.111	AURORA II	2.31
ANTARES II	1.208	ARISTEA	2.25	AUSTRALIA	2.31
ANTHONY ASLETT	1.131	ARKWRIGHT	2.25	Austri	2.288
ANTHONY HOPE	2.18	Arlette	1.171	Authorpe	1.80
ANTIC	2.19	ARLETTE	2.25	AVACANORA	2.32
ANTICOSTI	1.105	ARLEY	2.25	AVALANCHE	2.32

AVALON	2.32
Avanturina	1.48
AVANTURINE (1939)	2.32
AVANTURINE (1940)	2.32
Avola	2.424
AVOLA	2.32
AVON	2.32
AVON II	2.33
Avondale	1.191
Avondee	1.188
AVONDEE	2.33
Avonglen	2.76
AVONGLEN	2.33
AVONMOUTH	2.33
AVON STREAM	2.33
AVON WATER	2.33
AWATERE	1.91
AXIOS (Greek)	1.133
Axum	1.109
AYACANORA	2.33
AYRESHIRE	2.33
B.1 (Portuguese)	1.147
BABIANA	2.35
BABS	2.35
Bacip	1.79
BADEN POWELL II	2.35
BADINAGE	2.35
BAFFIN	1.106
BAHAWALPUR	1.36, 1.38
BALDAQUE da SILVA (Portuguese)	
	1.120
BALFOUR	2.35
BALGOWNIE	2.35
BALISE	2.35
BALMEDIE	2.35
BALMORAL	2.35
BALTA	1.106
Balthasar	1.199
Balthazar	1.102
BALTIC	2.36
BANDELERO	2.36
Banks o' Dee	1.213
BANNU	1.35
Banyers	2.418
BANYERS	2.36
BARBADOS	2.36
BARBARA ROBB	2.36
Barbara Robertson	1.138
BARBARA ROBERTSON	2.37
Barbro	1.105
Bardolf	2.90
BARDSEY	1.106
BAREILLY	1.36
BARETO de MENEZES (Brazilian)	
	1.43
BARISAL	1.36, 1.39
BARLE	2.37

BARNARD BOYLE	1.168
BARNET	1.142, 2.37
Barnett	1.101, 2.52
BARNSLEY	2.37
BARNSNESS	2.37
Barnsness	2.88
BORGIA	1.154
BARODA	1.36, 1.38
Baron Ruzette	1.208
BARON RUZETTE	2.37
Barry Castle (1946)	1.99
Barry Castle (1939)	2.355
BASSET	1.18, 1.36
BASSANIO	2.37
BASS ROCK	2.37
BASTION	2.38
BASUTO	2.38
BATTLEAXE	1.31
BAY	1.195
BAYARD	2.38
Bayflower	2.421
BAY INNAUNG	1.36
Beachflower	1.220
Beathwood	2.343
BEATHWOOD	2.38
BEATRICE	2.38
BEATRICE II	2.38
Beauline Verneil	1.61
BEAULNE VERNEUIL	2.38
Beaumaris Castle	1.56
BEAUMARIS CASTLE	2.38
BEDFORDSHIRE	1.17, 2.39
BEDOUIN	2.39
BEECH	1.217
BEECHWOLD	2.39
BEGA	2.39
BEGAUM	2.39
Beka	2.333
BELLDOCK	2.40
BELLEROPHON	2.40
BELLEROPHON II	2.40
Bellona	2.138
BELLONA	2.40
BELLONA III	2.40
BELLWORT	2.40
BELMONT	2.40
BELTON	2.40
BEMPTON	2.40
BEN AGDALE	2.41
BEN ALDER	2.41
Benalloigan	1.208
Ben Ardna (ex-JOHN BRADFORD)	
	1.176
Ben Ardna (ex-WILLIAM BARLOW)	
	1.190
BEN ARDNA (1914)	2.41
BEN ARDNA (1939)	2.41
BENARES	1.36

BEN ATTOW	2.41
BEN BARVAS	2.41
BENBECULA	1.106
Ben Bheula	1.76
BEN BEULAH	2.41
Bengali	1.74
BEN BHRACHIE	2.42
BEN BREAC	2.42
BEN CHOURN	2.42
BEN DEARG	2.43
BENDIGO	2.32, 2.47
Bendigo II	2.403
BEN DORAN	2.43
BEN EARN	2.43
BEN GAIRN	2.43
BENGAL	2.47
BENGAL II	2.48
BENGALI	2.48
BEN GLAMAIR	2.43
BEN GLAS	2.43
BEN GULVAIN	2.44
BEN HEILEM (1914)	2.44
BEN HEILEM (1939)	2.44
BEN HOLDEN	2.44
BEN HOPE	2.44
BEN IDRIS	2.45
BEN IVER	2.45
BENJAMIN COLEMAN	1.168
BENJAMIN COOKE	1.48
Benjamin Gelcer	1.99
BENJAMIN HAWKINS	1.131
BENJAMIN STEVENSON	1.48
BEN LAWYERS	2.45
BEN LEDI	2.45
BEN LORA	2.45
BEN LOYAL	2.45
BEN LUI	2.46
BEN MEIDIE	2.46
Ben Nevis	2.31
BEN RINNES	2.43, 2.46
BEN ROSSAL	2.46
BEN ROY	2.46
BEN SCREEL	2.47
BENSTROME	2.48
Ben Strom	2.48
BEN TARBERT	2.47
BENTON CASTLE	2.48
BEN TORC	2.47
BENVOLIO	2.49
BEN VURIE	2.47
BEN ZINNES	2.47
BERAR	1.36
BERBERIS	1.217
Berenga	2.166
BERENGA	2.49
Bergen	1.217
BERGEN	2.49
Berkshire	1.201

CADELLA	2.66	CANTABRICO (Spanish)	1.60	CAREW CASTLE	2.77
Cadella	2.351	CANTATRICE	2.71	*Cariama*	2.301
CADET	2.66	CAP d' ANTIFER	2.71	CARIEDA	2.77
CADORNA	2.66	CAPE ARGONA	1.24, 2.71	CARILON	2.77
Caerphilly Castle	1.76	*Cape Barfleur*	2.118	CARISBROOKE	2.78
CAERPHILLY CASTLE	2.66	CAPE BARRACOUTA	2.72	CARLTON	2.78
CAERSIN	1.211	*Cape Barracouta*	2.72	CARMANIA II	2.78
CAESAR	2.66	CAPE CHELYUSKIN	2.72	*Carnarvon Castle*	1.87
CAESAR II	2.66	CAPE COMORIN	2.72	*Carolina*	2.374
CAIRNWELL	2.66	*Cape Cleveland*	1.103	CAROLINE	2.78
CAILIFF	1.108	*Cape Duner*	1.203	*Cartagena*	1.77
Cairnrigh	1.210	*Cape Finesterre (1949)*	1.103	CARYSFORT II	2.78
CAIRO	2.67	*Cape Finesterre (1935)*	1.218	*Casimar*	2.113
Caithnesshire	1.207	CAPE FINESTERRE	2.72	CASORIA	2.79
CALCUTTA (1918)	1.48	*Cape Gloucester*	1.157	CASPIAN	2.79
CALCUTTA (1939)	1.36	*Cape Grisnez*	2.308	CASSANDRA	2.79
CALDY (1943)	1.108	*Cape Guardafui*	1.218	CASSANDRA II	2.79
CALDY (1915/19, 1939/40)	2.67	*Cape Hatteras*	1.87	CASSOWARY	2.79
CALEDONIA	2.67	*Cape Kanin*	1.222	*Castelnau*	1.142
CALEDONIA II	2.67	CAPE MARIATO	2.73	CASTELNAU	2.79
Caliama II	1.184	*Cape Matapan*	2.372	CASTLEROCK	2.79
Caliban	1.55	CAPE MELVILLE	2.73	CASTLETON	2.80
CALIBAN	2.67	CAPE NYEMETSKI	2.73	*Castleton*	2.134
Calicut	1.31	*Cape Otway*	1.135	CASTOR	2.80
CALIPH	2.67	CAPE PALLISER	2.73	CASTOR II	2.80
Callancroft	1.47	CAPE PASSARO	2.73	CASWELL	2.80
CALLIOPE	2.68	*Cape Pembroke*	2.188	*Catherine*	1.110
CALLIOPE II	2.68	CAPE PORTLAND	2.74	*Catulus*	2.149
CALLSIN	1.211	*Cape Rpyds*	2.310	CAULONIA	2.80
CALUMSIN	1.211	*Cape St. Vincent*	1.134	CAVALCADE	2.80
CALVAY	1.108	CAPE SIRETOKO	2.74	CAVE	2.80
CALVI	2.68	CAPE SPARTEL	2.74	*Cavendish*	1.88
Calvi	2.68	*Cape Spartivento*	1.222	*Cawdor*	1.53
CALVIA	2.68	*Capetown*	2.74	CAWNPORE	1.36
CALVINIA	2.68	CAPETOWN II	2.74	CAYRIAN	2.81
Calyclavia	1.49	*Cape Trafalgar*	1.134	CAYTON WYKE	2.81
CALYPSO	2.69	CAPE TRAFALGAR	2.75	CECIL COOMBES	2.81
CAMBODIA	2.69	CAPE WARWICK	1.17, 2.75	*Cecelie*	2.399
CAMBRIA	2.69	*Cape Warwick*	1.199	CECIL RHODES	2.81
CAMBRIAN	2.69	CAPRICORNUS	2.75	CEDAR (1935)	1.218
CAMBRIAN II	2.69	*Capstone*	1.59	CEDAR (1915)	2.81
CAMBRIDGESHIRE	2.69	CAPSTONE	2.75	CEDAR LEAF	2.81
CAMBRISIN	1.211	CAPTAIN	2.76	*Cedric*	2.272
Cameron	2.261	*Captain Arsene Blonde*	1.121	CEDRIC	2.82
CAMEO	2.70	CAPTAIN POLLEN	2.76	*Celerina*	2.531
Camilla	2.229	CARBILL	2.76	*Celeste Aida*	1.115
CAMPANIA II	2.70	CARBINEER	1.152	CELIA	1.163
CAMPENIA	2.530	CARBINEER II	1.153	CELTIA	2.82
CAMPOBELLO	1.109	CARBOSIN	1.212	CENSIN	1.212
CAMPSIN	1.211	*Cardiff Castle*		CENTURION	2.82
CANADA	2.70	(ex-EDWARD GALLAGHER)	1.52	CEPHEUS	2.82
CANADA II	2.70	*Cardiff Castle* (ex-GRILSE)	1.99	CERBERUS	2.82
CANADIAN PRINCE	2.70	CARDIFF CASTLE (1914)	2.76	CEREALIA	2.82
CANCALAIS (French)	2.410	CARDIFF CASTLE (1939)	2.76	CERESIA	2.82
CANCER	2.70	*Cardigan Castle*	1.51	CERISIO	2.83, 2.407
CANDIDATE	2.71	CARDINAL	2.77	*Cerisio*	2.407
CANNA	1.109	CARENCY	2.77	*Ceriesio*	2.223
CANNOSIN	1.211	*Caretta*	1.201	CETUS	2.83

CEVIC (1918)	2.83
CEVIC (1943)	2.83
Cevic	2.352
CEYLONITE	2.83
Ceylonite	1.187
Cesar de Paepe	1.63
CHALCEDONY (1914)	2.83
CHALCEDONY (1939)	2.83
CHALLENGER	2.84
CHAMBERLAIN	2.84
Champion	2.97
CHAMPION	2.84
CHANCELLOR (1915)	2.84
CHANCELLOR (1917)	2.84
Chandbali	1.81
CHANDBALI	2.85
Chandos	1.188
CHANDOS	2.85
CHANTICLEER	2.85
CHARLES ADAIR	1.132
CHARLES ANTRAM	1.49
CHARLES ASTIE	1.132
CHARLES BARBER	1.168
CHARLES BLIGHT	1.169
CHARLES BOYES	1.49
CHARLES CARROLL	1.169
CHARLES CHAPPELL	1.49
CHARLES COUCHER	1.169
CHARLES DONELLY	1.49
CHARLES DOYLE	1.169
CHARLES HAMMOND	1.132
CHARLES LAWRENCE	1.169
CHARLES LEGG	1.49
CHARLES VAILLANT	2.85
CHARLSIN	1.212
CHARMOUTH	2.85
Charvic	2.497
CHASSE MARIE	2.85
CHASSIRON	2.86
CHECKSIN	1.212
Chemomoretz	1.109
Cheriton	1.77
CHERSIN	2.212
CHERUSKER. (German)	2.221
CHERWELL	1.132, 2.86
CHESTER	2.86
CHESTER II	2.86
CHESTNUT	1.196
CHIEFTAN	2.86
CHIEFTAN II	2.86
CHIKARA	2.86
CHILTERN	2.87
CHINA	2.87
Ching Hai	1.106
Chiltern	1.140
Chire (1908)	1.207
Chire (1890)	2.508
CHITTAGONG	1.36

CHOICE (1914)	2.87
CHOICE (1944)	2.87
Chokai Maru	1.206
CHORLEY	2.83, 2.87
Christabelle	1.176
Christina	1.115
Christina T. Purdy	1.176
CHRISTINA T. PURDY	2.87
CHRISTOPHER	2.87
CHRISTOPHER DIXON	1.132
CHRYSEA	2.87
CHRYSOLITE	2.88
CHURCHSIN	1.212
CICERO	2.88
CICERO II	2.88
Cicely Blanche	1.70
CINCERIA	1.214, 2.88
Cinzia	1.117
Cisnell	1.71
Cissie Scratchard	1.184
CITY OF ABERDEEN	2.88
CITY OF CARLISLE	2.88
CITY OF DUNDEE	2.89
CITY OF EDINBURGH	2.89
CITY OF HULL	2.89
City of Hull	2.118
CITY OF LIVERPOOL	2.89
CITY OF LONDON	2.80
CITY OF MANCHESTER	2.89
CITY OF PERTH	1.169, 2.89
CITY OF SELBY	2.89
CITY OF YORK	2.90
Clacton	2.135
CLAESJE	2.90
CLAIRE	2.90
Clan Grant	2.485
Claribelle	1.190
CLARIBELLE	2.90
CLARINET	2.91
CLAROSIN	1.213
CLASSIN	1.213
CLAVERTON	2.90
Claverton	2.281
Claymore	2.31
CLEARSIN	1.213
CLEMENTINA II	2.91
CLEON	2.91
CLEOPATRA (II)	2.91
CLEOPATRA (III)	2.92
CLEOPATRA II	2.91
Cleopatra II	2.91
CLEOPATRA III	2.91
CLEVELA	2.91
CLEVELLA	2.91
Cleveland	2.530
Clifton	2.22
CLIFTON	2.92
CLIO	2.92

Clixby	1.56
CLONSIN	1.213
CLOTILDE	2.92
CLOUGHSTONE	2.92
Cloughton Wyke	1.142
CLOUGHTON WYKE	2.92
CLYDE	2.92
CLYNE CASTLE (1914)	2.93
CLYNE CASTLE (1939)	2.93
Clyro	1.77
CLYTHNESS	2.93
COADJUTOR	2.93
COALAXE	1.31
COALSIN	1.213
COBBERS	2.93
COCHIN	1.36, 1.39
COCHIN (ex-MULTAN)	1.37
COCHRANE	1.37
COCKADE	2.18, 2.93
COCKATRICE	2.93
COCKATRICE II	2.93
Coimbra	1.114
Colbert	2.410
COLDSTREAMER	1.156
COLIN CRAIG	1.49
COLL	1.109
COLLEAGUE	2.93
COLLFNA	2.94
COLLINGWOOD	2.94
COLNE	1.132, 2.94
COLOMBO (1919)	1.50
Colonel Rockwell	1.82
Colonel Roosevelt	1.83
COLSAY	1.109
COLTMAN	2.94
COLUMBA	2.94
COLUMBIA	2.95
Colwyn Bay	1.102
COMBER	2.95
COMET	2.95
Comitatus	1.64
COMITATUS	2.95
COMMANDANT	2.95
Commandant Gamas	1.178
COMMANDANTE LORETTI	
(Brazilian)	1.77
COMMANDER EVANS	2.95
COMMANDER FULLERTON	2.95
COMMANDER HOLBROOK	2.96
COMMANDER HORTON	2.96
COMMANDER NASMITH	2.96
Commiles	1.68
COMMILES	2.96
COMMISSIONER	2.96
Commodator	1.71
COMMODORE	2.97
COMMODORE	2.97
COMOX	1.37

COMPANION	2.97	CORNELIUS CARROLL	1.169	CROWLIN	1.109
Compass	2.71	CORNET	2.103	CROWSIN	1.215
COMPT HORACE Van der BURGH		CORONA	2.103	CROXBY	2.109
	2.97	CORONATIA	2.103	Croxton	2.504
Compton	2.75	CORONET	1.73, 2.104	CRUCIS	1.208
Computator	1.52	Corrie Roy	2.104	CRYSTAL	2.110
COMPUTATOR	2.97	CORRY ROY	2.104	CT.51, USN	1.83
COMRADE	2.97	CORTASIN	1.214	CT.53, USN	1.83
Conan Doyle	2.49	CORTINA	2.104	CT.58, USN	1.83
CONAN DOYLE	2.98	CORVI	1.208	CT.59, USN	1.83
Concertator	1.65	CORVUS	2.104	Cuatro	1.312
CONCERTATOR	2.98	CORYPHENE	2.104	CUCKOO (1917)	2.110
CONCORD	2.98	CORYTHAIX	2.104	CUCKOO (1940)	2.110
CONCORD III	2.98	COTILLION	1.94	CUDWOSIN	1.215
CONDOR II	2.98	Cotsmuir	1.76	CUIRASS	2.110
CONDUCTOR	2.98	COTSMUIR (1915)	2.105	CULBASIN	1.215
CONFEDERATE	2.98	COTSMUIR (1940)	2.105	CULBLEAN	2.110
CONGO	2.98	COUNCILLOR	2.105	CUMBRAE	1.110, 1.115
Congre	1.63	COUNT	2.105	Cunningham	2.241
CONGRE	2.99	COUNTY OF FIFE	2.105	Curlew	2.188
CONINGSBY	2.99	COURSER	2.105	CURLEW	2.110
CONISTON	2.99	COURTIER (1915)	2.106	Curtana	2.110
CONNIE	2.99	COURTIER (1939)	2.106	CURTANA	2.110
Conovium	1.214	Courtland	2.134	CUTTACK	1.37
CONQUEROR II	2.99	COVENTRY CITY	1.17, 2.106	CYELSE	2.111
CONQUISTADOR	2.99	COVERLEY	1.94	CYGNET	2.111
CONSBRO	2.99	Cradock	1.191	CYGNET II	2.111
CONSORT	2.99	CRADOSIN	1.214	CYGNET III	2.111
CONSTANCE	2.100	CRAFTSMAN	2.102, 2.106	CYGNI	1.209
CONTENDER	2.100	CRAIG COILLEACH	2.106	Cynthia	2.111
CONTROLLER	2.100	CRAIGELLACHIE	2.106	CYNTHIA	2.111
CONWAY	2.100	CRAIGENDARROCH	2.107	Cymrea	1.55
CONWAY CASTLE	2.100	CRAIG EWAN	2.107	CYPRESS	1.218
COOKSIN	1.213	CRAIG GOWAN	2.107	CYRANO	2.112
COOMASIN	1.214	CRAIGIEVAR	2.107		
COOT	2.101	CRAIG ISLAND	2.107	DABCHICK	1.42
COPINSAY	1.109	Craig Island	2.297	DACCA	1.37
COQUET	2.101	CRAIG MILLAR	2.107	DAGNY	2.113
CORAL	1.203	CRAIGMORE	2.107	Dagon	2.113
Coral Island	1.130	CRAIGSIN	1.214	DAGON (1915)	2.113
CORCYRA	2.101	CRAIK	2.107	DAGON (1939)	2.113
CORDELA	2.101	CRAITHIE (1914)	2.108	DAHLIA	2.113
CORELLA	2.101	CRAITHIE (1916)	2.108	Dahlia II	2.113
Corella	2.102	Crammond Island	1.141	DAHLIA II	2.113
CORENA	2.102	CRAMMOND ISLAND	2.108	Diadem	2.200
Corena	2.102	CRANEFLY	2.108	Daily Chronicle	1.71
CORIENTES	2.102	Craonne Beauriex	1.70	Daily Express	1.74
CORINSIN	1.214	CRASSULA	2.108	Daily Mirror	1.52
CORIOLANUS		CRATER	2.108	DAIMLER	2.113
(Shakespearian Class)	1.163	CRESCENT II	2.109	Dairycoates	2.373
CORIOLANUS (1940)	2.102	Cresswell	1.84	DAISY II	2.114
CORMORANT II	2.102	CRESTFLOWER	2.109	DALE	2.114
CORMORANT IV	2.102	Crevette	1.189	Dale Castle	2.349
CORNCRAKE	1.41, 1.99, 2.103	CREVETTE	2.109	DALE CASTLE	2.114
Cornelia	1.112	CROMSIN	1.214	DALMATIA	2.114
CORNELIAN (1935)	1.199	CROTON	2.109	Dalmatia	2.114
CORNELIAN (1917)	2.103	CROUPIER	2.109	DALMATIAN	2.114
CORNELIUS BUCKLEY	1.132	Crowlin	1.109	Damito	1.69

DAMITO	2.114	DELILA	2.119	DONSIDE		2.125
DAMSAY	1.110	DELPHIN II	2.119	*Donesse*		1.134
Dana	1.143	DELPHINE	2.119	DOON (1917)		2.125
DANDINI	2.115	DELPHINUS	2.119	DOON (1920)	1.133, 2.125	
DANDOLO	2.115	DELTA	2.119	*Doonie Braes*		1.171
DANE	2.115	*Denis*	1.62	DOONIE BRAES		2.125
DANE II	2.115	DENIS CASEY	1.51	*Dora*		1.211
DANEMAN	2.115	DENTARIA	2.120	*Dora* (Q Ship)		2.101
DANESTON	2.116	DEODAR	1.196	DORA		2.125
DANIA	2.116	DERBY	2.120	DORANDO		2.126
DANIEL CLOWDEN	1.50	DERBY COUNTY	2.120	*Dorbie*		1.32
Daniel Clowden	1.50	*Dervish*	1.200	DORCAS		2.126
DANIEL DICK	1.50	DERVISH	2.120	DOREEN		2.126
DANIEL DIZMONT	1.169	DERWENT (1917)	2.120	*Dorileen* (ex-JOHN BRADFORD)		
DANIEL FEARALL	1.133	DERWENT (1920)	2.120			1.176
DANIEL HARRINGTON	1.50	*Derwent*	2.259	*Dorileen* (ex-WILLIAM BARLOW)		
DANIEL HENLEY	1.50	DESIREE	2.121			1.190
DANIEL HILLIER	1.169	DESTINN	2.121	DORILEEN		2.126
DANIEL LEARY	1.50	DEVANHA	2.121	DORINDA		2.126
DANIEL McPHERSON	1.133	DEVERON	2.121	DORIS (1917)		2.126
DANIEL MUNRO	1.133	DEWSLAND	2.121	DORIS (1918)		2.127
DANIEL STROUD	2.116	DHOON (1916)	2.122	DOROTHY F.		2.127
Dan Layers	1.21	DHOON (1940)	2.122	DOROTHY GRAY		2.127
Danurie II	2.89	DHOON GLEN	2.122	DOROTHY LAMBERT		2.127
Dargle	2.224	DIADEM	2.122	*Douglas H. Smith*		1.144
DARGLE	2.116	DIAMOND	2.122	DOURO		2.127
Darmstadt	1.212	DIAMOND II	2.122	DOVE		2.127
Darnett Ness	1.75	DIAMOND III	2.122	DOVE II		2.127
DARNET NESS	2.116	*Diana*	2.235	DOVER		2.128
DAROGAH	2.116	DIANA	2.122	DOWNIEHILLS		2.128
DARRACQ	2.116	DIANA II	2.123	DRACO		2.128
DARTHEMA	2.117	*Dias* (Argentinian)	2.507	*Dragaberg*		1.219
DARTMOUTH	2.117	DIGIT	2.123	DRAGON		2.128
DARWEN	2.117	*Diksmuide 7*	1.120	DRAGON II		2.128
Darwen	2.251	DINAPORE	1.37	*Dragon Vert*		1.82
DASHER	2.117	DINAS	2.123	*Dragoon*		1.103
DAVARA	2.117	DINORAH	2.123	DRAGOON		1.153
Davarr Island	1.222	*Dire Dewa*	1.109	DRAKE		2.128
DAVID BLAKE	1.170	DIRK	2.123	DRAKE II		2.128
DAVID BUCHAN	1.170	DIRKJE	2.123	DRANGEY		2.129
DAVID CONN	1.170	DISA	2.123	*Drattur*		1.222
DAVID DILLON	1.51	DIVER	2.123	DREADAXE		1.31
David Haigh	1.84	DIXON	2.124	DREADNOUGHT II		2.129
DAVID HAIGH	2.117	DOCHET	1.110	DRIVER		2.129
DAVID MIFFON	1.133	DOCTOR LEE	2.124	DROMIO		2.129
DAVID OGILVIE	1.51	DOGGER BANK	2.124	DRUMBLADE		2.129
DAVY	2.117	*Doktor Krugler*	1.210	DRUMBLAIR		2.129
DEAN SWIFT	2.118	DOLFJIN	2.124	DRUMMER		1.153
Dean Swift	2.118	*Dolmar*	2.359	DRUMMER BOY		2.130
DEBENEY	2.118	DOLORES	2.124	DRUMOAK		2.130
DEE (1920)	1.31	DOMINICK ADDISON	1.51	*Drumskeugh*		2.115
DEE (1917)	2.118	DOMINICK DUBINE	1.51	DRUMTOCHTY		2.130
DEFENDER	2.118	DOMQUE GENTILE	1.51	DRUSILLA		2.130
Deepdale Wyke	2.385	DON	2.124	DRYPOOL		2.130
DEGARA LEROSA	1.133	DONALDA	2.124	DUCHESSE de BRABANT		2.130
De la Pole	1.67	DONALD & DORIS	2.125	*Dudley*		2.531
De La POLE	2.118	DONNA NOOK	2.125	*Dulcibelle*		1.168
DELHI	2.119	*Donostia*	2.126	DULCIBELLE		2.131

EPHRIAM BRIGHT	1.53	ETOILE POLAIRE	2.155	FANE (1914)	2.163
EPINE	2.148	ETON	2.155	FANE (1939)	2.163
Epiros, SS	1.31	ETRURIA	2.155	FARA	1.111
EPWORTH	2.149	ETRURIAN	2.156	FARADAY	2.164
EQUATOR	2.149	ETRUSCAN	2.156	FARNE	1.111
EQUERRY	2.149	ETTRICK	1.134, 2.156	FASTNET	1.134, 2.164
Equerry	2.149	EUCLASE	2.156	*Fatima*	1.40
EQUINOX	2.149	EUDOCIA	2.156	FAVORITA	2.164
EQUITY	2.150	EUREKA	2.157	FAWN	2.164
ERA	2.150	EURIPEDES	2.157	FELICIA	2.164
ERIC STROUD	2.150	*Euryalus*	2.205	FELIPE CAMARO Brazilian	1.43
ERIDANUS	2.150	EUSTON	2.157	*Fenia*	1.122
Erik Jall	2.123	EUTHAMIA	2.157	FENTONIAN	2.164
ERILLUS	2.150	*Euthamia*	2.350	*Fermo*	1.59
ERIMO	2.150	EVADNE	2.157	FERMO	2.165
ERIN (1914)	2.151	EVANGEL	2.158	FERNANDES VIERA (Brazilian)	
ERIN (1940)	2.151	EVA WALES	2.158		1.43
ERIN II	2.151	*Evelina*	1.180	*Fernando De C.*	1.809
ERISKAY	1.110	EVELINA	2.158	FERRIBY	2.165
ERITH	2.151	EVELINE	2.158	*Ferrol*	1.81
ERMINE	2.151	EVELINE NUTTEN	2.158	FESTING GRINDALL	1.53
ERNA	1.8, 2.151	EVELYN	2.158	*Festing Grindall*	1.53
ERNE(1920)	1.62	*Evelyn Rose*	1.149	FESTUBERT	1.29
ERNE (1914)	2.152	EVELYN ROSE	2.159	FETLAR	1.111
Ernest Solvay	1.87	EVEREST	2.159	FEUGH	2.165
EROICAN	2.152	EVERGREEN	2.159	*Feughside*	2.370
EROS (1914)	2.152	EVERTON	2.159	FEZENTA	2.166
EROS (1917)	2.152	EVESHAM	2.159	FIARAY	1.111
Erik Jall	2.	EWALD	2.159	FIAT	2.166
ESCALLONIA	2.153	EXCEL II	2.160	FIDELIA	2.166
ESCORT	2.153	EXCELLENT (1915)	2.160	FIELDGATE	2.94, 2.166
ESHER	2.153	EXCELLENT (1919)	1.134	*Field Marshal Plumer*	1.147
ESKE	2.153	EXCELLENT (1922)	1.134	*Field Marshal Robertson*	1.139
Eskimo	1.108	EXCELLENT, French	1.150	FIFESHIRE	2.166
ESMERALDA	2.154	EXE	2.160	FIFENELLA	2.167
Esquimaux (1939)	2.11	EXETER	2.160	*Fighter*	2.75
Esquimaux (1946)	1.156	EXMOUTH	2.160	*Filiep Coenen*	1.61
ESSEX (1914)	2.153	EXMOUTH II	2.160	FILEY	2.167
ESSEX (1918)	2.154	EXPERT	2.160	*Filey Bay*	2.167
ESSEX II	2.154	EXYAHNE	2.160	FILEY BAY	2.167
ESSEX III	2.154	EZEKIEL JOHNSON	1.134	FILLA	1.111
'Essos'	2.ix			*Findus I*	1.201
Esteburg	1.212	FAIAL (Portuguese)	1.196	FINESSE	2.167
Estelle Yvonne	1.136	FAIR ISLE	2.162	*Finesse*	2.415
ESTRELLA d'ALVA	2.154	FAIR ISLEII	2.162	FINLANDE	2.168
Estrella d'Alva	2.441	FAIRVIEW	2.162	*Finmark*	1.32
Estrella do Mar	2.341	*Fairway*	1.146	FINTRAY	2.168
ESTRELLA do MAR	2.154	FAIRWAY	2.162	FIR	1.196
ESTRELLA do NORTE	2.154	FAITH	2.162	FIREFLY	2.168
Estrella Do Norte	1.133	FALCON	2.162	*Firsby*	1.172
ETHEL	2.154	FALMOUTH (1909)	2.162	FISHERGATE	2.168
Ethel Crawford	1.181	FALMOUTH (1897)	2.163	FISHTOFT	2.168
ETHEL NUTTEN	2.154	FALMOUTH II	2.163	FIRMAXE	1.31
ETHEL TAYLOR	2.155	FALMOUTH III	2.163	*Fjellberg*	1.110
ETHELWULF	2.155	FALSTAFF	2.163	*Flanders*	1.49
Ethulwulf General	2.403	Famous Personnel	1.24	FLANDERS	2.168
ETNA	2.155	FANCY	2.163	FLANDRE	2.169
Etoile Lolaire III	1.74	FANDANGO	1.94	*Flash*	1.73

FLATHOLM	1.111	FOXTROT	1.94	GAROLA	2.179
Flavia	1.193	FOYLE	1.134, 2.173	GARRY	1.31, 2.179
FLEETWING II	2.169	*Frai*	1.125	*Garry*	1.31
FLEETWOOD	2.169	FRANCIS CONLIN	1.53	GARU	2.179
FLEMING	2.169	FRANCIS FRENCH	1.134	GASPE	1.37
FLICKER	2.169	FRANCOLIN	2.174	GATESHEAD	1.112
FLINT	1.112	*Frank*	1.195	GAUL (1915)	2.179
FLINT CASTLE	2.169	*Frankfurt-Main*	1.107	GAUL (1939)	2.179
FLINTSHIRE	2.170	FRANC TIREUR	2.174	GAVA	2.179
Flixton	1.193	FRASCATI	2.174	GAVINA	2.180
FLIXTON	2.170	FRASER	2.174	GAVOTTE	1.94
Florence Brierley	1.140	FRASER EAVES	1.134	GAYA	1.37
FLORENCE BRIERLEY	2.170	*Fravaria*	1.38	GAZ TIEZ	2.450
FLORENCE DOMBEY	2.170	FREDERICK BUSH	1.53	*G.D. Taylor*	2.514
Florence Johnson	1.144	FREDERICK BOYCE	1.170	*Geir*	2.439
Florencia	1.82	*Frederico Bartoli*	1.122	GELSINA	2.180
Floribelle	1.187	FRESSIA	2.174	GEMMA	2.180
Floric	1.214	*Fregate II*	1.153	GEMUNU	1.38
FLORIO	2.170	FREISE	2.58	GENERAL	2.180
FLOTTA	1.112	*Freiston*	1.172	*General Birdwood*	1.139
FLUELLEN	1.164	FREYA	2.174	GENERAL BIRDWOOD	2.180
FLY	2.170	FRIARAGE	2.175	GENERAL BOTHA	2.180
Flying Angel	1.61	FRIGATE BIRD II	2.175	GENERAL FOCH	2.181
FLYING ADMIRAL	2.171	FRIESLAND (1915)	2.175	GENERAL GORDON	2.181
FLYING WING	2.171	FRIESLAND (1940)	2.175	GENERAL JOFFRE	2.181
FOAMCREST	2.171	*Fritha*	1.35	*General Rawlinson*	1.147
Fontenay	1.80	*Frobisher*	1.131	GENEVIEVE, French	1.174
FONTENOY	2.171	FROSTAXE	1.31	GEORGE ADGELL	1.53
Forbes	1.130	FUDAY	1.112	GEORGE AIKEN	1.53
Force	1.136	Fuel Carriers	1.21	GEORGE ANDREW	1.134
FORCE	2.171	FUJI	2.175	GEORGE AUNGER	1.53
FORFEIT	2.103, 2.171	FULMAR	2.176	GEORGE BLIGH	1.135
Forma	1.40	FUNDY	1.37	GEORGE BORTHWICK	1.170
FORT ALBERT	2.171	*Furka*	1.114	GEORGE BROWN	1.135
FORT EDWARD	2.171	FUSILIER (1915)	1.153	GEORGE BURTON	1.171
FORT GEORGE	2.171	FUSILIER (1942)	1.156	GEORGE CASTLE	1.171
Fotherby	2.	FUTURIST	2.176	GEORGE CLARKE	1.53
Fort Lamalgue	1.164	FYLDEA	2.176	GEORGE CLINES	1.171
Fort Malbousquet	1.113			GEORGE COCHRANE	1.54
Fort Robert	1.174	GABIR	2.177	GEORGE CORTON	1.54
FORT ROBERT	2.172	GABY	2.177	GEORGE COULSTON	1.171
Fort Rona	1.179	GADFLY	2.177	GEORGE COUSINS	1.54
Forthvale	1.184	GADRA	2.177	*George Cousins*	2.335
Fortrose	1.182	GAELIC	2.177	GEORGE DARBY	1.54
FORT ROSE	2.172	GAIRSAY	1.112	GEORGE D. IRVIN	2.181
FORT ROYAL	2.172	*Galleon*	2.68	GEORGE DIXON	1.62, 2.181
FORT RYAN	2.172	GALLINULE	2.177	GEORGE FENWICK	1.135
FORTUNA	2.172	*Galopin*	1.80	GEORGE FRENCH	1.171
FORT WILLIAM	2.172	GALVANI	2.177	GEORGE GREENFIELD	1.54
FORWARD	2.173	GAMBRI	2.178	GEORGE GREEVES	1.54
Forward II	2.173	*Gambri*	2.406	GEORGE HARRIS	1.54
FORWARD II	2.173	GAMECOCK	2.178	GEORGE H. HASTIE	2.181
FORWARD HO	2.173	GANILLY	1.112	GEORGE HODGES	1.172
FOSDYKE	2.173	GANTON	2.178	GEORGE IRELAND	1.172
FOSS	2.173	*Gardar Landnemi*	2.497	GEORGE LANE	1.172
Fotherby	2.511	GARDENIA	2.178	GEORGE MARTIN	1.136
FOULA	1.112	GARMO	2.178	GEORGE MILBURN	2.182
FOULNESS	1.112	GARNET	2.178	GEORGE ROBB	2.182

George R. Purdy	1.173	GORREGAN	1.112	GULFOSS	2.194
GEORGE R. PURDY	2.182	GOSHAWK	2.187	GULLAND	1.113
GEORGE SCOTT	2.182	GOSHAWK II	2.187	*Guloy*	1.105
GEORGE STROUD	2.182	*Gosse*	1.80	GUNNER(1914)	1.154
George Turner	1.212	GOTE (German)	2.74	GUNNER (1939)	2.194
GEORGE WESTPHAL	1.136	GOTH	2.187	*Gure Armetza*	2.491
Georgette	1.175	GOWAN	2.187	GURTH	2.194
GEORGETTE	2.182	GOZO	2.187	*Guttaberg*	2.105
GERBERDINA JOHANNA	2.182	GRACE WETHERLEY	2.188	*Guy Thorne*	2.433
GERTRUDE CAPPLEMAN	2.182	GRACKLE	2.188	*Gwmaho*	1.76
GILDEROY	2.182	GRAEMSAY	1.113	GWEAL	1.107, 1.113, 2.194
Gillian	1.181	GRAIN	1.113	GWENLLAIN	2.194
GILLIAN	2.183	GRAMPIAN	2.188	GWMAHO	2.195
GILLSTONE	1.112	GRAND DUKE	2.188		
GILLYGATE	2.183	*Grand Fleet*	1.138	HAARLEM	2.196
Girard	1.133	GRANTON N.B.	2.188	*Haima*	1.122
GIRARD	2.183	GRANUWEAL	2.189	HALCYON II	2.196
Girolamo Cassar	1.84	*Graphic*	2.508	HALIFAX	2.196
Girdler Glen	2.31	GRASSHOLM	1.113	*H.A.L.Russell*	2.116
GIOVANNI GUINTI	1.55	GRAYLING	1.99	HAMLET (1940)	1.164
GIVENCHY	1.29	GREAT ADMIRAL	2.189	HAMLET (1914)	2.196
GLACIER	2.183	GREATAXE	1.32	HAMMOND	2.196
Gladys	1.139	GREBE	2.189	HAMPSHIRE	2.196
GLADYS	2.183	GRECIAN	2.189	*Hannah Woddbridge*	1.50
Glaes Compaen	2.530	GRECIAN EMPIRE	2.189	HANNARAY	1.113
GLAMIS CASTLE	2.183	GRECIAN PRINCE	2.189	*Hans Hummersund*	1.109
GLATIAN	2.183	GREENFLY	2.190	Harbour Service	1.23
GLEN BERVIE	2.183	GREEN HOWARD	2.190	*Hargood*	1.103
GLEN BOYNE	2.184	GREGNESS	2.190	*Hargood*	2.20
GLEN COVA	2.184	GREGORY	2.190	HARLECH CASTLE	2.197
Glendale	2.447	GRENADA	2.190	HARRIS	1.113
GLEN ESK	2.184	GRENADIER	2.191	HARRY ROSS	2.197
GLEN KIDSTONE	2.184	GRETA	2.191	*Harry Hawke*	1.66
GLENOGIL (1914)	2.184	GRETA II	2.191	*Harry Melling*	1.65
GLENOGIL (1915)	2.184	GRETA III	2.191	HASCOSAY	1.113
GLEN PROSEN	2.184	GRIFFIN	2.191	*Hassett*	2.406
GLEN PROSEEN	2.184	GRIFFITH GRIFFITH	1.55	HATANO (1916)	2.197
GLENROY	2.185	*Grigorousa*	1.122	HATANO (1939)	2.197
GLORIA (1914)	2.185	GRIMENCO	2.191	HATSUSE	2.198
GLORIA (1915)	2.185	GRILSE	1.99	*Haukanes*	1.85
GLORIA II	2.185	GRIMSBY	2.191	HAUTAPU	1.91
G.M.	2.185	GRIMSBY TOWN	2191	*Havardur Isfindingur*	1.133
GOELAND II	2.185	*Grimurkamban*	1.149	*Havborgin*	1.218
GOEREE	2.185	*Gris Nez*	1.146	HAWK	2.198
GOLDAXE	1.31	GROENLAND	2.192	*Hawkins*	2.241
Golden City	2.413	GROSBEAK	2.192	HAWTHORN	1.218
GOLDEN GLEAM	2.186	*Grosmont Castle*	1.65	HAWTHORN II	2.198
Golfinho	2.274	GROSMONT CASTLE	2.193	*Hayburn Wyke*	1.146
Gonerby (1922)	1.84	*Grotius*	2.134	HAYBURN WYKE	2.198
Gonerby (1924)	1.85	*Grouin du Cou* (French)	1.66	HAYLING	1.114
GONZALO	2.186	GROUSE	2.193	HAZEL	1.196
GOOD HOPE	2.186	GRUINARD	1.113	*Hazledene*	2.480
GOOD LUCK	2.186	GRUNA	2.193	HEATHER	2.198
GOOLGWAI	2.186	GUARDSMAN	1.157	*Hebden*	1.207
GOONAMBEE	2.186	GUAVA	2.193	*Heinrich Beeman*	2.430
GOORANGAI	2.186	GUILLEMOT	2.193	HEKLA	2.198
GOOSANDER	2.187	*Guiseppina*	1.105	HELCIA	2.199
Goran	2.433	GULL	2.194	HELGIAN	2.199

HELIOS	2.199	HOLLY	1.219	IMPERIALIST	2.210
HELLISAY	1.114	HOLYROOD	2.203	IMPERIAL PRINCE	2.210
Helm	1.196	Holman Projector	1.16	IMPERIAL QUEEN	2.211
HELVETIA	2.199	HOME GUARD	1.157	*Imprevu*	1.52
HENE CASTLE	2.199	*Hondo*	1.51	INA WILLIAMS	2.211
Henriville	2.85	HONDO	2.204	INCHCOLM	1.115
Henricus	1.88	HONJO (1917)	2.204	INCHGARTH	2.211
Henriette	1.185	HONJO (1939)	2.204	*Inchgarvie*	2.319
HENRIETTE (1939)	2.199	HONNINGSVAAG	2.204	*Inchgower*	1.181
HENRIETTE (1940)	2.200	*Hood*	1.172	INCHGOWER	2.211
HENRIQUE DIAS (Brazilian)	1.43	*Hope*	2.31	INCHKEITH (1941)	1.115
HENRY BATTERSBY	1.172	HORACE STROUD	2.204	INCHKEITH (1915)	2.212
HENRY BUTCHER	1.172	HORATIO (1940)	1.164	INCHMARNOCK	1.115
HENRY CHEVALLIER	1.55	HORATIO (1914)	2.205	INDIA (1915)	2.212
HENRY COLBY	1.172	*Hordern*	1.75	INDIA (1917)	2.212
HENRY CORY	1.55	HORNBEAM	1.219	INDIAN EMPIRE	2.212
HENRY CRAMWELL	1.136	HORNPIPE	1.94	INGOMAR	2.212
HENRY FLIGHT	1.172, 2.21	HORNSEA	2.205	*Ingouville*	1.70
HENRY FORD	1.136	HORTENSIA	2.205	INKPEN	1.102, 1.103
HENRY GRATTON	2.200	HOUBARA	2.205	INVERCAULD	2.213
HENRY HARDING	1.172	*Hourtin*	1.66	*Invercauld*	2.421
HENRY JENNINGS	1.173	HOVERFLY	2.205	INVERCLYDE	2.213
HENRY LANCASTER	1.136	HOVERLEY	2.76	*Inverclyde*	2.355
HENRY MARSH	1.136	HOWE	2.206	*Inverdon*	1.68
HEORTNESSE	2.200	HOXA	1.114	INVERFORTH	2.213
Heppens	1.214	HOY	1.114	*Inverforth*	2.218
Herbert	2.213	HUDDERSFIELD TOWN	2.206	*Inverleigh*	1.29
HERCULES	2.200	HUGH BLACK	1.55	*Invermeill*	1.185
HERCULES II	2.200	HUGH WALPOLE	2.206	*Inverspey*	1.88
HERCULES III	2.200	HULL CITY	2.206	*Invertay*	2.70
HERCULES IV	2.201	*Humphrey*	1.185	INVERTAY	2.213
Her Majesty	2.260	HUMPHREY	2.206	*Inverythan*	1.53
HERMES (Greek)	1.160	HUNDA	1.114	*Iolite*	1.60
HERMETRAY	1.114	HUNGARIAN	2.206	*Ion*	1.109
HERMIA	2.201	*Hunter*	2.403	IONA	2.213
HERO	1.8, 2.201	HUNTER	2.207	IONIC	2.213
HERO II	2.202	HUXLEY	2.207	IPSWICH	2.213
HEROINE	2.202	HYAENA	2.207	IRANIAN	2.213
Heron	1.82	HYDRA	2.207	IRAWADI	2.213
HERON	2.202	HYDRA II	2.207	IRENE WRAY	2.214
HERRING	1.99			IRONBOUND	1.115
HERTFORDSHIRE	1.17, 2.202	IAGO	2.208	*Irvana*	1.48
H. E. STROUD	2.202	IBIS (French)	1.169	IRVANA	2.214
HEUGH	2.202	IBIS	2.208	IRWELL	2.214
HIBERNIA II	2.203	IBIS V	2.208	ISA	2.214
HICKORY	1.196	ICEAXE	1.32	ISABEL	2.214
Highbridge	1.53	ICELAND	2.208	ISABELLA FOWLIE	2.215
HIGHLANDER	1.153	IDA ADAMS	2.208	*Isernia*	1.157
HILARIA	2.203	IDENA	2.208	ISERNIA	2.215
HILDASAY	1.114	*Ijuin*	1.56	ISAAC ARTHAN	1.55
Hildina	1.88	IJUIN	2.209	ISAAC CHANT	1.136
HILDINA	2.203	ILFRACOMBE	2.209	ISAAC DOBSON	1.173
HINAU	1.91	ILUSTRA	2.209	ISAAC HARRIS	1.173
HIROSE	2.203	IMBRIN (French)	1.145	ISAAC HEATH	1.56
HOBART	2.203	IMELDA	2.209	ISIS (1915)	2.215
Hochmeister	1.122	IMERSAY	1.114	ISIS (1917)	2.215
Hodari	1.125	IMMORTELLE	2.209	ISLAND PRINCE (1914)	2.215
HOLDENE	2.203	IMPERIA	2.209	ISLAND PRINCE (1919)	2.215

ISLAY	1.115	JAMES HINES	1.175	JERICHO	2.224
ISLE OF MAN	2.215	JAMES HULBERT	1.137	JESSICA	2.224
ISLE OF WIGHT	2.216	JAMES HUNNIFORD	1.58	JESSIE NUTTEN	2.224
Isly	1.115	JAMES JOHNSON	1.58	JOHANNESBURG	2.224
ISRAEL ALDCROFT	1.173	*James Johnson*	1.133	*John*	1.85
ISTRIA	2.216	JAMES JONES	1.137	JOHN	2.224
Italia Caesar	2.248	JAMES LAVENNY	1.58	JOHN ABBOT	1.176
ITALY	2.216	JAMES LAY	1.58	JOHN AIKENHEAD	1.59
ITCHEN	2.216	JAMES LENHAM	1.176	JOHN ANDERSON	1.59
ITONIAN	2.216	JAMES LONG	1.138	JOHN APPLEBY	1.139
IVANHOE	2.217	JAMES LUDFORD	1.138	JOHN ARTHUR	1.139
IZAAC WALTON	2.217	JAMES MANSELL	1.138	JOHN ASHLEY	1.60
		James Mansell	1.138	JOHN BAPTISH	1.60
JABOO II	2.218	JAMES McDONALD	1.138	JOHN BARRY	1.176
J. BAELS MAURICX	2.218	JAMES McLAUGHLIN	1.138	JOHN BATEMAN	1.60
JACAMAR	2.218	JAMES PEAKE	1.58	JOHN BELL	1.176
JACINTA	2.218	JAMES PITCHERS	2.220	JOHN BENSON	1.60
JACINTH	2.218	JAMES POND	1.59	JOHN BOMKWORTH	1.60
Jacj Johnson	1.169	JAMES ROBERTSON	1.59	JOHN BOWLER	1.176
JACKDAW	2.219	JAMES SECKAR	1.59	JOHN BRADFORD	1.176
Jacqueline	1.79	JAMES SIBBALD	1.59	JOHN BRASKET	1.177
JACQUELINE CLASINE	2.219	JAMES S. MELVILLE	2.220	JOHN BRENNAN	1.60
Jacqueline-Louise	2.508	JAMES WRIGHT	1.139	JOHN BRICE	1.61
Jacques	1.86	JAMES YOUNG	1.139	JOHN BRITTON	1.61
Jade	1.75	JAN de WAELE	2.220	JOHN BROOKER	1.61
JADE	1.204	*Janera*	1.62	JOHN BULLER	1.177
JAMAICA	2.219	JANE ROSS	2.220	JOHN BULLOCK	1.61
JAMES ADAMS	1.136	*Jannikke*	1.94	JOHN BURLINGHAM	1.61
JAMES ALDRIDGE	1.173	*Jan Ove*	1.196	JOHN CALLAGHAN	1.177
JAMES ARCHIBALD	1.173	JANUS	2.220	JOHN CAMPBELL	1.62
JAMES BAIRD	1.56	JANUS II	2.221	JOHN CASEWELL	1.62
JAMES BARRIE	2.219	*Jan Volders*	1.76	JOHN CATTLING	1.62
JAMES BASHFORD	1.174	JAPAN	2.221	JOHN CHATWAY	1.62
JAMES BEAGAN	1.174	JARDINE	2.221	JOHN CHIVERS	1.62
JAMES BENTOLE	1.174	*Jason*	1.115	JOHN CHURCH	1.62
JAMES BERRY	1.174	JASON	2.221	JOHN CLAVELL	1.62
JAMES B. GRAHAM	2.219	JASPER (1935)	1.199	*John C. Meikle*	2.107
JAMES BOYLE	1.56	JASPER (1914)	2.221	JOHN C. MEIKLE	2.225
JAMES BRODIGAN	1.175	JASPER (1917)	2.221	JOHN COLLINS	1.62
JAMES BUCHANAN	1.136	*Java IV*	2.497	JOHN CONDON	1.177
JAMES BURGESS	1.56	JAVELIN	2.222	JOHN CONNE	1.177
JAMES CATON	1.137	JAY (1914)	2.222	JOHN COOMBE	1.63
JAMES CEPELL	1.56, 2.19	JAY (1940)	2.222	JOHN COOPER	1.63
JAMES CHAPMAN	1.57	JEAN EDMUNDS	2.222	JOHN COPE	1.177
JAMES CHRISTOPHER	1.57	JEAN FREDERICK	2.222	JOHN CORBETT	1.177
JAMES COILE	1.57	*Jean Hay*	2.487	JOHN CORMACK	1.140
JAMES CONNER	1.57	JEANIE STEWART	2.222	JOHN CORWARDER	1.178
JAMES COSGROVE	1.57	*Jeanne*	1.79	JOHN COTTRELL	1.140
JAMES CURRY	1.175	*Jeannie Annette*	1.214	JOHN CREIGHTON	1.63
JAMES DINTON	1.57	*Jeannie M. Robertson*	1.188	JOHN CURRAN	1.178
JAMES EVANS	1.175	JELDY, Norwegian	1.122	JOHN DAVIES	1.63
JAMES FEAGAN	1.175	JELLICOE	2.223	JOHN DETHRIDGE	1.140
JAMES FENNEL	1.175	*Jellicoe*	2.407	JOHN DIXON	1.140
JAMES GARRICK	1.175	JENNET	1.14, 2.223	JOHN DONOVAN	2.225
JAMES GILL	1.57	JENNIFER	2.223	JOHN DORMOND	1.63
JAMES GREEN	1.58	JEREMIAH LEWIS	1.139	JOHN DOWNIE	1.140
JAMES HARTWELL	1.175	*Jeria*	2.450	JOHN DUNKIN	1.178
JAMES HAYES	1.137	JERIA	2.223	JOHN DUNN	1.140

JOHN DUPUIS	1.178	JOHN SHERBURN	2.226	*Karachi*	1.54
JOHN DUTTON	1.140	*John Smart*	1.176	*Kari Solmundarson*	1.60
JOHN EBBS	1.140	JOHN T. GRAHAM	2.226	*Kari*	1.60
JOHN EDMUND	1.141	JOHN THORLING	1.65	*Karlesefni*	1.140
JOHN EDSWORTH	1.178	JOHN WELSTEAD	1.143	*Karl Grammersdorf*	1.215
JOHN E. LEWIS	2.225	*John W. Johnson*	1.131	KASTORIA	2.228
John Elliot	1.181	JOHN YULE	1.143	KATE LEWIS	1.8, 2.229
JOHN EVANS	1.63	JONATHAN BAZINO	1.181	KATHLEEN BURTON	2.229
JOHN FAIRMAN	1.178	JONATHAN BENJAMIN	1.181	*Keelby*	1.212
JOHN FELTON	1.141	JONATHAN BRONTON	1.181	*Kelby*	1.58
JOHN FISSER	1.179	JONATHAN CLARKE	1.144	KELT	2.229
JOHN FITZGERALD	1.179	JONATHAN COLLINS	1.144	*Kelvin* (1920)	1.69
JOHN FRANCOIS	1.179	JONATHAN COLLIS	1.181	*Kelvin* (1919)	1.145
JOHN GAUNTLEY	1.63	JONATHAN GREIG	1.181	*Kelvin & Clyde*	2.407
JOHN GEOGHAN	1.63	JONATHAN HARDY	1.182	KELVIN	2.229
JOHN GILLMAN	1.63	JONQUIL	2.226	KENNERY	1.67
JOHN GRAHAM	1.63	*Jose Ignacio De C.*	1.80	KENNET (1915)	2.229
JOHN GRAY	1.179	*Joselle*	1.82	KENNET (1920)	2.230
JOHN GREGORY	1.64	*Jose Maria*	2.104	KENNEYMORE	2.230
JOHN GULIPSTER	1.64	*Joseph & Sarah Miles*	2.vii	KENSINGTON	2.230
JOHN G. WATSON (1914)	2.225	JOSEPH & SARAH MILES	2.226	KERNEVAL	2.230
JOHN G. WATSON (1916)	2.225	JOSEPH ANNISON	1.182	KERRERA	1.115
JOHN HAILE	1.180	JOSEPH BARRET	1.65	KERYADO	2.230
JOHN HEATH	1.180	JOSEPH BURGIN	1.182	*Kesteven*	1.52
JOHN HIGH	2.225	JOSEPH BUTTON	1.66	KESTREL II	2.230
JOHN HIGHLAND	1.141	JOSEPH COATES	1.182	*Keyes*	1.189
JOHN H. IRVIN	2.226	JOSEPH CONNELL	1.66	*Khedive*	2.207
JOHN HOWARD	1.180	JOSEPH CROWELL	1.66	KIAMARI	1.38
JOHN HUNS	1.180	JOSEPH DOE	1.66	*Kia Ora*	2.101
JOHN HUNTER	1.180	JOSEPH DUHAMEL	2.227	*Kib*	2.235
JOHN JACKSON	1.180	JOSEPH GIDDICE	1.66	KIDDERPORE	1.67
JOHN JACOBS	1.141	JOSEPH GORDON	1.66	KIDWELLY CASTLE	2.230
JOHN JEFFERSON	1.142	JOSEPH HODGKINS	1.66	KIELDER CASTLE	2.231
JOHN JOHNSON	1.142	JOSEPH MURRAY	1.144	*Kieth Hall*	1.212
JOHN KENNEDY	1.181	JOSEPHINE I	2.227	*Kildier*	2.231
JOHN KIDD	1.64	JOSHUA ARABIN	1.67	*Kilgerran Castle*	1.50
JOHN LANGSHAW	1.181	JOSHUA BUDGET	1.182	*Kilindini*	1.55
JOHN LEMON	1.142	JOSHUA CARRETTS	1.182	KILLDEER	2.231
JOHN LEVER	1.142	*Joule*	1.179	KILLEGRAY	1.115
JOHN LEWIS	1.65	JUBBALPORE (1919)	1.67	KILYAS (Turkish)	1.142
JOHN LYONS	1.65	JUBBALPORE (1942)	1.38, 1.40	KIMBERLEY (1914)	2.231
JOHN MANN	1.142	*Julia Brierley*	1.100	KIMBERLEY (1915)	2.231
JOHN MARSHALL	1.142	JULIET (1940)	1.164	KIMBERLEY II	2.231
JOHN MASON (1918)	1.142	JULIET (1914)	2.227	KIMBERLEY IV	2.232
JOHN MASON (1920)	1.142	JUNCO	2.227	KINALDIE	2.232
JOHN MASON (1920)	2.226	JUNIPER	1.iv, 1.196	KINCORTH	2.232
JOHN McCONNELL	1.143	*Jupiter*	2.60	KINELLAR	2.232
JOHN MELEBURY	1.143	JURA	1.115	KING ARTHUR	2.232
JOHN MINUTE	1.143	*Jutlandia*	1.214	KING CANUTE	2.232
JOHN MONDAY	1.143			KING EDWARD	2.233
John Morrice	1.186	KALMIA	2.228	KING EGBERT	2.233
JOHN MORRIS	1.143	KALMIA II	2.228	KING EMPEROR	1.8, 2.233
JOHN MOSS (1918)	1.143	KALSO	2.228	KING ERIK	2.233
JOHN MOSS (1919)	1.180	*Kanuck*	1.145	*Kingfisher*	2.284
JOHN MURPHY	1.143	KAPHREDA	2.228	KINGFISHER	2.234
JOHN PASCO	1.143	*Kapsduen*, Norwegian	2.507	KING FREDERICK	2.233
JOHN POLLARD	1.65	*Karabighi*	1.176	*King Frederick III*	2.233
JOHN QUILLIAM	1.143	KARACHI	1.38	KING GEORGE	2.234

KING HAROLD	2.234	*Kopanes*	2.224	LADYSMITH		2.250
KING HENRY	2.234	KOPANES	2.244	LADY STANLEY		2.250
KING LEAR	2.235	KORAB I	2.244	LAERTES		1.165
KING RICHARD	2.235	KOROWA	2.244	*Laforey*		2.83
Kingscourt	1.190	*Korso*	1.115	La HAVRAISE		2.411
KINGSCOURT	2.235	KOSMOS	2.244	LAHORE (1941)		1.38
KINGS GREY	2.235	*Kristianborg*	1.118	LAHORE (1948)		1.38
KING SOL	2.235	*Kross-Steinur*	2.322	LAKSHMI		1.205
KING STEPHEN	2.236	KUDOS	2.244	L'AJACCIENNE		2,302
KINGSTON	2.236	KUMARIHAMI	1.205	La NANTAISE (French)		2.410
KINGSTON AGATE	2.236	KUMU	2.244	La NANTISE		2.250
KINGSTON ALALITE	2.237	KUNISHI (1917)	2.245	LANCER (1914)		1.153
KINGSTON AMBER	2.237	KUNISHI (1939)	2.245	LANCER (1942)		1.157
KINGSTON ANDALUSITE	2.238	KURD	2.245	LANCER II	1.153,	2.251
KINGSTON BERYL	2.238	KUROKI	2.245	LANERCOST		2.251
KINGSTON CAIRNGORM	2.238	*Kuvera*	1.180	*Lanka*		1.205
KINGSTON CEYLONITE	2.238	KUVERA	2.245	LANDKYS		1.205
KINGSTON CHRYSOBERYL	2.239	KYMERIC	2.245	LANGDON McKENNON		1.144
KINGSTON CHRYSOLITE	2.239	*Kyoto*	1.71	*Langland Bay*		2.240
Kingston Coral	1.219	*Kyriaki*	1.125	LAPAGERIA		2.251
KINGSTON CORAL	2.239			LAPWING		2.251
KINGSTON CORNELIAN	2.239	La BLANCHE II (French)	1.58	LAPWING II		2.251
KINGSTON CRYSTAL	2.239	LABORE ET HONORE	2.247	LAPWING III		2.251
Kingston Cyanite	1.220	*Labrador*	1.82	LAPWING V		2.251
KINGSTON CYANITE	2.240	*Laceby*	1.213	LARCH		1.219
Kingston Diamond	2.498	LACENNIA	2.247	LARCHWOLD		2.252
Kingston Emerald	2.249	LACERTA	2.247	LARK		2.252
KINGSTON GALENA	2.240	LADAS	2.247	LARK II		2.252
Kingston Garnet	2.499	*Lady Adelaide*	1.203	*Larwood*		2.117
KINGSTON JACINTH	2.240	LADY BERYL	2.247	LARWOOD		2.252
KINGSTON OLIVINE	2.240	*Lady Beryl*	2.457	La SETOISE (French)		2.340
KINGSTON ONYX	2.240	*Lady Eleanor*	2.149	L'ATLANTIQUE		2.252
Kingston Pearl	2.222	LADY ELEANOR	2.248	*Latimer*		1.122
KINGSTON PERIDOT	2.241	*Lady Elsa*	2.248	La TOULONNAISE (French)		2.196
Kingston Ruby	2.250	LADY ELSA	1.18, 2.248	LAURA		2.253
KINGSTON SAPPHIRE	2.241	*Lady Enid*	1.142, 2.110	LAUREATE		2.253
KINGSTON TOPAZ	2.241	LADY ENID	2.248	LAUREL		1.220
KINGSTON TURQUOISE	2.241	*Lady Estelle*	2.66	LAUREL II		2.253
KINGSWAY	2.242	LADY ESTELLE	2.248	*Laurette*		1.146
KINTYRE	1.116	LADY HOGARTH	2.248	LAVEROCK		2.253
KIRKELLA	2.242	*Lady June*	1.221	LAVINIA		2.253
Kirkland	1.59	*Lady Lillian*	1.204	*Lawica* (German)		2.524
KIRKLAND	2.242	LADY LILLIAN	2.249	LAWRENCE HUGHSON		1.182
KIRKLINTON	2.242	*Ladylove*	2.339	LAWRENNY CASTLE		2.253
KIRTON	2.242	LADY LOVE	2.249	*Laxmi*		1.54
KITE	2.242	*Lady Madeleine* (MOONSTONE)		LAXMI		2.253
KITE II	2.242		1.204	LEAM		2.254
KITTERN	1.116	*Lady Madeleine* (LOCH ALSH)		LEANDER		2.254
KITTIWAKE	2.242		2.261	LEANDROS		2.254
KITTY	2.242	LADY MADELEINE	2.249	*Ledger No.778*		2.236
KIWI	1.128	*Lady Margot*	2.439	LEEDS		2.254
Klan	1.196	*Lady Olwen*	2.457	*Leeds United*		2.206
KLONDIKE	2.242	LADY PHILOMENA	2.249	LEEDS UNITED		2.254
K.M. Hardy	1.145	*Lady Rachael*	2.444	LEICESTER CITY		2.254
KNOT	2.242	LADY ROSEMARY	1.18	LEITH N.B.		2.255
KODAMA	2.242	*Lady Rosemary*	2.114	LEMBERG		2.255
KOLABA	1.36, 1.38	LADY ROSEMARY	2.250	*Lena Melling*		1.67
KOORAH	2.244	LADY SHIRLEY	2.250	LENA MELLING		2.255

552

Lenato	1.76	LOCH AWE	2.262	LONGSET	2.269
LEO	2.255	Loch Blair	1.174	LOON	2.269
LEONATO	2.255	LOCH BLAIR	2.262	LOOS	1.29
Leonidas	2.72	LOCH BROOM	2.262	L'ORAGE	2.269
LEONORA	2.256	Loch Buie	1.55	LORD AIREDALE	2.269
Lephreto	1.89	LOCH BUIE	2.262	Lord Allenby	1.180
LEPHRETO	2.256	LOCH DOON (1914)	2.262	LORD ALLENDALE	2.269
Le Royal	2.365	LOCH DOON (1939)	2.263	LORD ALVERSTONE	2.270
Le TIGER	1.17, 2.256	Loch Earn	2.182	LORD ASHBY	2.270
LEUKOS	2.256	LOCH ERIBOL	2.263	LORD ASHFIELD	2.270
LEVEN	2.256	Loch Eriboll	2.263	Lord Astor	1.135
LEWIS McKENZIE	1.144	Loch Esk	2.116	LORD AUSTIN	2.270
LEWIS REEVES	1.144	LOCH ESK (1914)	2.263	Lord Bann	2.223
LEWIS ROATLEY	1.144	LOCH ESK (1939)	2.263	LORD BEACONSFIELD	2.271
LEYLAND (1917)	2.257	LOCH EYE	2.2643	Lord Beaverbrook	1.221
LEYLAND (1939)	2.257	LOCH GARRY	2.263	Lord Birkenhead	1.149
LEYS	2.257	LOCH HOPE	2.263, 2.370	Lord Brentford	1.220
LIBERATOR	2.257	Loch Hope	2.370	Lord Byng	1.149
LIBERIA	2.257	LOCH HOURNE	2.264	LORD CECIL	2.271
LIBRA (1914)	2.257	LOCHIEL	2.264	LORD DARLING	2.271
LIBRA (1940)	2.258	LOCH INVER	2.264	Lord Davidson	1.217
LIBYAN	2.258	LOCH KILDONIAN	2.264	Lord Dawson	1.217
LIDDOCH	2.258	Loch Kinnord	1.66	LORD DENMAN	2.271
Liddock	1.173	Loch Laggan	1.209	LORD De RAMSAY	2.271
Lieth Hall	1.215	LOCH LAGGAN	2.264	LORD DURHAM	2.271
LIFFEY	1.33, 2.258	LOCH LEE	2.264	Lord Ernle	1.145
Lightship No.3 (Canadian)	1.29	LOCH LEVEN	2.265	LORD ESSENDEN	2.272
Lightship No.5 (Canadian)	1.29	Loch Leven	2.392	Lord Fisher	2.278
Lightship No.20 (Canadian)	1.29	LOCH LOMOND	2.265	Lord Foyle	2.22
Lightship No.22 (Canadian)	1.29	LOCH LONG	2.265	Lord Gainford	1.132
Ligny	1.55	LOCH LOYAL	2.265	LORD GAINFORD	2.272
LIGNY	2.258	LOCH LYON	2.265	LORD GEORGE	2.272
LILAC	1.220	LOCH MAREE	2.265	Lord Gort	2.139
Lillen	1.117	LOCH MELFORT	2.266	LORD GREY (1916)	2.272
LILY MELLING	2.258	Loch Moidart	1.139	LORD GREY (1939)	2.273
Limeslade	1.60	LOCH MOIDART	2.266	LORD HAILSHAM	2.273
LIMEWOLD	2.259	LOCH MONTIETH	2.266	LORD HARDINGE	2.274
Lincoln City	1.199	Loch Morar	1.66	Lord Harewood	1.143
LINCOLN CITY	2.259	LOCH MORAR	2.266	Lord Hawke	1.144
LINCOLNIA	2.259	Loch Naver	1.52	LORD HENEAGE	2.274
LINCOLNSHIRE	2.259	LOCH NAVER (1915)	2.266	Lord Hewart	1.217
LINDISFARNE	1.116	LOCH NAVER (1939)	2.266	LORD HOTHAM	2.274
Lindos	2.458	LOCH OSKAIG	2.267	LORD INCHCAPE	2.274
Lindsay	1.74	Loch Park	1.61	LORD IRWIN	2.274
LINGAY	1.116	LOCH RANNOCH	2.267	Lord Knaresborough	1.146
LINNET (1914)	2.259	LOCH SHIEL	2.267	LORD KNOLLYS	2.274
LINNET (1917)	2.260	LOCH SHIN	2.267	Lord Lancaster	1.139
LINN o' DEE	2.260	LOCH STROM	2.267	LORD LANSDOWNE	2.275
LITTLE EMMA	2.260	LOCH TULLA	2.267	Lord Lascalles	2.532
LIVINGSTONE	2.260	LOCH TUMMEL	2.268	LORD LISTER	2.275
LIZZIE	2.260	LOCH WASDALE	2.268	LORD LLOYD	2.275
LIZZIE MELLING	2.261	Lois	1.139	LORD MELCHETT	2.275
Lobelia	2.72	LOIS (1915)	2.268	LORD MERSEY	2.276
LOBELIA	2.261	LOIS (1940)	2.268	LORD MIDDLETON	2.276
LOBELIA II	2.261	LOLIST	2.268	LORD MINTO	2.276
LOCH ALSH	2.261	LOMBARD	2.268	Lord Montgomery	2.38
LOCH ARD	2.261	LONGA	1.117	LORD NORTHCLIFFE	2.276
LOCH ASSATER	2.261	LONGSCAR	2.269	LORD NUFFIELD	2.276

LORD PERCY	2.277	LUDA LORD	2.284	*Malcolite*	1.71
LORD PLENDER	2.277	*Luda Lord*	2.293	MALCOLITE	2.290
Lord Portal	2.411	LUMINARY	2.284	*Maldonna*	1.92
LORD READING	2.277	LUNAN BAY	2.284	MALTA	2.290
LORD RIDLEY	2.277	LUNDY (1942)	1.117	*Malvern*	1.131
LORD ROBERTS	2.278	LUNDY (1915)	2.284	*Malvolio*	1.84
LORD ROTHSCHILD	2.278	LUNE (1915)	2.284	*Malmata*	2.190
LORD SALISBURY	2.278	LUNE (1939)	2.284	*Mamelina No.10*	2.349
Lord Selborne (GY.392)	2.111, 2.278	LUNEDA	2.285	*Manchester City*	2.355
LORD SELBORNE (GY.1058)	2.278	*Lushby*	1.62	MANDA	2.290
LORDSHIP	2.278	*Lyd*	2.285	MANGROVE	1.196
LORD SHREWSBURY	2.279	LYDDITE	2.285	MANITOULIN	1.117
LORD SNOWDEN	2.279	LYDIAN	2.285	MANLY	2.290
LORD STAMP	2.279	LYDIARD	2.285	MANNOFIELD	2.290
LORD STANHOPE (1916)	2.279	*Lynandi*	1.71	MANOR	2.290
LORD STANHOPE (1939)	2.280	*Lyngas*	1.113	MANORBIER CASTLE	2.291
LORD STONEHAVEN	2.280	LYNMOUTH	2.285	MAN o' WAR	2.291
Lord Talbot	1.151	LYNX II	2.285	MANSFIELD	2.291
Lord Tay	2.248	LYRIC	2.285	MANUKA	1.91
Lord Tennyson	1.171	LYSANDER II	2.286	MANX ADMIRAL	2.291
Lord Trent	1.219	LYSANDER III	2.286	MANX HERO (1914)	2.291
LORD WAKEFIELD	2.280			MANX HERO (1916)	2.291
LORD WIMBORNE	2.280	MACAW	2.287	MANX KING	2.292
LORD WOLMER	2.280	*Macbeth*	1.55	MANX PRINCE	2.292
Lorenzo	2.380	MACBETH (1940)	1.165	MANX QUEEN	2.292
LORENZO	2.280	MACBETH (1914)	2.287	MAPLE	1.220
LORIENTAISE (French)	2.410	MACDUFF	2.287	*Marano*	2.371
LORINDA	2.281	MACDUFF II	2.287	MARANO	2.292
Lorne	2.101	MACFARLANE	2.287	MARCONI	2.292
Lorne	2.31	MACKENZIE	2.287	*Mardep*	1.82
LOROONE	2.281	MACKEREL	1.99	MARETTA	2.293
Lorraine	1.75	MACKLEAY	2.288	MARGARET DUNCAN	2.293
LORRAINE	2.281	*Madden*	1.191	*Margaret Rose*	2.350
LOTHIAN	2.281	MADDEN	2.288	MARGARET ROSE	2.293
LOTOS	2.281	M.A. DODDS	2.288	MARGARET WEATHERLEY	2.293
Loughrigg	1.147	MADRAS	1.67	*Margaret Wetherley*	2.293
LOUIS BOTHA	2.282	MADURA	1.39	MARGATE	2.293
LOUISE	2.282	MAFEKING	2.288	MARGUERITE	2.294
LOUISE-MARIE	2.282	MAGDALEN	1.117	MARIA	2.294
LOUISE et MARIE	2.282	*Maggie Walker*	2.284	*Maria Amalia*	1.207
LOVANIA	2.282	MAGNETA	2.288	MARIA R. OMMERING	2.294
Lovania	2.319	*Magnolia* (1955)	1.195	*Marie Anne*	1.82
Lowhar	1.214	*Magnolia*	2.183	*Marie Caroline*	1.83
LOWTHER	2.282	MAGNOLIA (1935)	1.220	*Marie Gilbert*	1.82
Lowther	2.303	MAGNOLIA (1916)	2.288	*Marie Jacqueline*	1.83
Loyal	1.157	MAGNOLIA II	2.289	MARIE JOSE ROSETTE	2.294
LOYAL	2.282	MAGNOLIA III	2.289	MARIE LOUISE (1917)	2.294
LOYAL PRINCE	2.283	MAGPIE II	2.289	MARIE LOUISE (1940)	2.295
Lucia Venturi	1.109	MAGPIE III	2.290	*Marie Mad*	1.83
Lucerne	2.10	*Magul*	1.196	*Marie Simone*	1.81
LUCERNE	2.283	*Mai*	1.53	*Marie Therese III*	1.83
LUCIDA	2.283	*Maiken*	1.197	*Marie Yette*	1.81
Lucienne-Jeanne	1.50	MAIMAI	1.91	MARIGNAM	2.295
LUCIENNE-JEANNE	2.283	*Majestic*	2.290	*Marignam*	2.295
LUCKNOW (1942)	1.38	MAJESTIC II	2.290	MARION	2.295
LUCKNOW (1914)	2.283	MALANGEN (German)	2.204	MARION II	2.295
LUDA LADY	2.284	*Malaga*	1.79	*Marioute*	2.307
Luda Lady	2.300	*Malayan*	2.458	MARIS STELLA	2.295

554

Name	Ref	Name	Ref	Name	Ref
MARISTO	2.295	MESSINES	1.29	Mirabelle	1.170
MARJORIE M. HASTIE	2.296	Meissonier SS	1.89	MIRABELLE	2.304
MARLBOROUGH	2.296	Melbourne (1935)	1.201	MIRANDA	2.304
MARLOES	2.296	Melbourne (1914)	2.333	MIRANDA III	2.305
Maroy	1.117	MERISIA	2.300	Miriam	2.511
MARNE	2.296	Merkury (Polish)	2.498	MIRIAM STEWART	2.305
MARNE II	2.296	MERLIN (1914)	2.300	MISCOU	1.118
Marsona	1.57	MERLIN (1915)	2.300	MITRES	2.305
MARSONA	2.296	MERLIN II	2.300	MIURA (1914)	2.305
MARTHE	2.296	Merok	2.310	MIURA (1916)	2.305
MARTIN	2.297	MEROR	2.300	M.J. Reid	1.137
MARTIN II	2.297	MERRYDALE	2.301	MOA	1.128
MARTINETA	2.297	MERSE	2.301	Mollux VI	1.196
MARTON	2.297	MEUSE	2.301	MOLLYMAWK	2.306
Mary	1.221	MEWSLADE	2.301	MONARCH	2.306
MARY	2.297	MEWSTONE	1.117	Monarch III	2.306
MARY A. HASTIE	2.297	Micaela de C	1.86	MONARCH III	2.306
Mary A. Johnson	1.145	MICHAEL ANGELO	2.301	MONARCH IV	2.306
Mary A. Purdy	1.189	MICHAEL BRION	1.183	Monchique	1.209
MARY A. PURDY	2.298	MICHAEL CLEMENTS	1.144	Mond	1.211
Mary Bruce	2.354	MICHAEL GING	1.68	MONGHYR	1.39
MARY CAM	2.298	MICHAEL GRIFFITHS	1.68	MONIMA	2.306
Mary Croan	2.251	MICHAEL MALONEY	1.68	MONIQUE-ANDREE	2.306
Mary Crowther	1.182	MICHAEL McDONALD	1.145	MONIQUE-CAMILLE	2.307
MARY WETHERLEY	2.298	MIKADO	2.302	Mons	2.307
MARY WHITE	2.298	MIKASA	2.302	MONS	2.307
MASCOT (1935)	1.13	MIKASO	2.302	Montano	1.174
Mascot	2.510	Mildenhall	1.201	MONTANO	2.307
Masona	2.412	MILDENHALL	2.302	Mont Cassel	1.151
MASONA	2.298	MILETUS	2.303	MOOIVLEI	2.307
Masona	2.240	Milford Countess	1.49	Moona	1.91
Master	2.374	MILFORD COUNTESS	2.303	MOONRISE	2.307
MASTER	2.298	Milford Duchess	1.57	MOONSHINE	2.307
MASTIFF	1.18, 1.39	MILFORD DUCHESS	2.303	MOONSTONE	1.204
MASTWING	2.298	Milford Duke	1.57	Moorsom	2.241
Matabele	2.282	MILFORD DUKE	2.303	MOPSA	2.307
MATIAS de ALBUQUERQUE		Milford Earl	1.47	Moravia	2.429
(Brazilian)	1.43	MILFORD EARL	2.303	MORAVIA	2.308
Matong	1.91	Milford King	1.84	Moray	1.173
MATTHEW BERRYMAN	1.68	MILFORD KING	2.303	MORAY (1915)	2.308
MATTHEW CASSADY	1.68	Milford Prince	1.74	MORAY (1940)	2.308
MATTHEW CROOKE	1.182	MILFORD PRINCE	2.303	MORGAN JONES	1.68
MATTHEW FLYNN	1.68	MILFORD PRINCESS	2.303	Morna	2.350
MATTHEW HARTLEY	1.183	Milford Queen	1.85	MORNING STAR	2.308
MAUN	2.298	MILFORD QUEEN	2.303	MORNING STAR VI	2.308
Mavis Rose	1.198	Millimumul	1.154	MOROCOCALA	2.308
MAXIMUS	2.299	Milyna	2.238	MORRIS DANCE	1.95, 1.96
MAX PEMBERTON	2.299	MINALTO	1.117	MORVEN	2.309
Mayfair	2.435	Minato Maru No. 3	1.205	MORVINA	2.309
Mayflower	2.513	MINCARLO	1.118	MOUNT ARD	2.309
Maythorne	1.196	Mindello II	1.208	MOUNT KEEN	2.309
MAZURKA	1.94	MINERVA III	2.303	MOUSA	1.118
MEDIAN	2.299	MINERVA IV	2.304	MOY	1.130, 2.309
MEDIATOR	2.299	MININGSBY	2.304	MULL	1.118
MELBOURNE	2.299	MINO	2.304	MULLETT	1.99
MENA	2.300	MINORU	2.304	Mulloka	1.92
Mendip	2.32	MINORU II	2.304	MULTAN	1.37, 1.39
MENTOR, Destroyer	1.213	MINUET	1.95	Mumby	1.52

Name	Ref.	Name	Ref.	Name	Ref.
Murmansk	2.309	NESS	1.47, 2.316	*Normanby*	
MURMANSK	2.309	NEWBRIDGE	2.316	(ex-WILLIAM SPENCER)	1.89
MUROTO	2.310	*New Comet*	2.403	NORSE (1915)	2.322
Murten	1.95	NEW COMET (1915)	2.316	NORSE (1939)	2.322
MYNA	2.310	NEW COMET (1939)	2.316	NORTH CAPE	2.322
Myrland	1.143	NEWHAVEN II	2.316	NORTHCOATES	2.322
MYRLAND	1.143, 2.310	NEWHAVEN NB	2.316	*Northern Barrage*	1.11
MYRTLE	1.220	NEWINGTON	2.317	NORTHERN CHIEF	1.18, 2.322
		NEWLAND	2.317	NORTHERN DAWN	1.18, 2.323
NAB WYKE	2.311	*New Prince*	2.72	NORTHERN DUKE	1.18, 2.324
NADINE (1914)	2.311	NEW ZEALAND	2.317	NORTHERN FOAM	1.18, 2.324
NADINE (1917)	2.311	*Niblick*	1.87	NORTHERN GEM	2.324
NADINE (1940)	2.311	NIBLICK (1917)	2.317	*Northern Gift*	2.202
Nador	1.115	NIBLICK (1940)	2.318	NORTHERN GIFT	2.325
NAGPUR	1.39, 1.40	NICHOLAS COUTEUR	1.145	NORTHERN ISLES	1.18, 2.325
NAIADE	2.311	NICHOLAS DEAN	1.145	NORTHERN PRIDE	2.326
NAIRANA	2.312	*Nicholas K*	1.164	NORTHERN PRINCE	2.326
NAIRANA II	2.312	*Nicola Jacovitti*	1.125	NORTHERN PRINCESS	1.18, 2.326
NAIRN	2.312	*Niedermehenen*	1.106	NORTHERN REWARD	1.18, 2.327
NAMUR	2.312	NIGHT-HAWK (1914)	2.318	NORTHERN ROVER	2.327
Nam Viet	1.126	NIGHT HAWK (1916)	2.318	NOERTHERN SKY	2.327
NANCY HAGUE	2.312	NIGHTJAR	2.318	NORTHERN SPRAY	2.328
Nando	1.125	NIGHT RIDER	2.318	NORTHERN WAVE	2.329
Naniwo Maru	1.205	*Night Watch*	2.309	NORTH KING (A.86)	2.329
NANOOSE	2.312	NILE	2.318	NORTH KING (H.882)	2.329
Napier	2.69	*Ninette*	1.188	NORTH KING II	2.329
NARVAL	2.312	NINUS	2.319	NORTHLYN	2.329
NASIK	1.39	*Niobe*	2.311	NORTHMAN	2.329
NATAL	2.313	*Nishiso Maru No. 1*	1.205	*Northmoor*	1.212
NATAL II	2.313	*Nishiiso Maru No. 2*	1.205	*North Ness*	1.48
NATHANIEL COLE	1.69	NITH	1.145, 2.319	NORTH NESS	2.330
Nautilus	2.222	*Nizam*	2.401	*Northlyn*	1.147
NAUTILUS (1916)	2.313	*Njordur*	1.85	NORTH QUEEN	2.330
NAUTILUS (1941)	2.313	NODZU (1916)	2.319	*North Sea*	2.313
NAUTILUS II	2.313	NODZU (1939)	2.319	NORTH STAR	2.330
NAVENBY	2.313	*Nodzu*	2.337	NORTH STAR III	2.330
Navenby	2.313	NOGI (1915)	2.319	NORTHUMBRIA	2.330
NAZARETH	1.86, 2.313	NOGI (1939)	2.320	NORTHWARD	2.330
Neath Castle	1.99	NONOOSE	1.39	*Northward Ho*	1.176
NEATH CASTLE	2.313	NOOGANA	2.320	NORTHWARD HO	2.331
NEATH CASTLE	2.314	NOOTKA	1.39	NORTH WEST	2.331
NEAVE	1.119	NORA NIVEN	2.320	NORWICH CITY	1.18, 2.331
NEGRO	2.314	NORBRECK	2.320	NOTRE DAME d'ESPERANCE	
NEIL GOW	2.314	*Nordale*	2.224		2.354
NEIL MACKAY	2.314	NORDHAV I	2.320	*Notre Dame de France*	1.145
NEIL SMITH	1.69	NORDHAV II	2.321	NOTRE DAME de FRANCE	2.331
NELLIE BRADDOCK	2.314	NORDKAPP	2.321	*Notre Dame de Lorette*	1.143
Nellie Crawford	1.88	NORDLAND	2.321	NOTRE DAME de MONT LIGEON	
NELLIE DODDS	2.315	*Nordzeel*	1.192		2.331
NELLIE NUTTEN	2.315	NORINA	2.245	NOTTS COUNTY	2.331
Neptuna	1.207	NORLAND	2.321	NOVELLI	2.332
NEPTUNIAN	2.315	*Norman*	1.156	*Nubia*	2.381
NEREE	2.315	NORMAN (1894)	2.321	NUBIA	2.332
Nere Fedea	2.81	NORMAN (1911)	2.321	NUMITOR	2.332
Nereus	1.215	NORMAN II	2.322	*Nunthorpe Hall*	2.431
NERINE	2.315	NORMAN III	2.322	NUNTHORPE HALL	2.332
NERISSA	2.316	*Normanby*		NYLGHAN	2.332
NERISSA II	2.316	(ex-ANDREW ANDERSON)	1.47	*Nyggjaberg*	2.413

Nypuberg	1.149	ONYX	2.339	OUSE (1916)	2.345
		ONYX II	2.339	OUSE (1920)	2.345
OAK	1.221	OPHIR II	2.339	OUTPOST	2.345
OAKWOLD	2.333	OPHIR III	2.339	OVERDALE WYKE	2.346
OASIS	2.333	*Ophelia*	2.138	OWEN McMANNERS	1.145
Obsidian	1.61	OPHELIA	1.165	OWL	2.346
Ocean Brine	2.260	ORANAISE	2.339	OWL II	2.346
OCEAN BRINE	2.333	*Oranjezicht*	1.220	OWL III	2.346
Ocean Clipper	1.172	ORCADES	2.340	OXANA	1.119
OCEAN COMRADE	2.333	ORFASY	1.119	OXWICH CASTLE	2.346
Ocean Duke	2.457	ORIANDA	2.340	OYAMA (1914)	2.346
OCEAN EDDY	2.333	ORIENTAL STAR	2.340	OYAMA (1939)	2.346
Ocean Ensign	1.141	ORIFLAMME	2.340	OYSTERMOUTH CASTLE	2.347
Ocean Fisher	1.169	ORIOLE	2.340		
OCEAN FISHER	2.334	ORIOLE II	2.340	P.5 (Portuguese)	2.74
Ocean Harrier	1.55	*Orion*	1.211	P.6 (Portuguese)	2.500
OCEANIC	2.334	ORIZABA	2.340	P.7, Portuguese	1.113
OCEANIC II	2.334	ORLANDO	2.341	PA.2 (German)	2.410
OCEANIC IV	2.334	ORMONDE	2.341	P & Y	2.145
OCEAN PRINCE	2.334	ORMONDE II	2.341	PACHMARI	1.39
OCEAN PRINCESS	2.334	ORONSAY	1.119	*Pacifique*	2.349
OCEAN QUEEN	2.334	OROPESA	2.341	PAHAU	1.91
OCEAN SCOUT	2.335	OROPESA II	2.341	PALISADE	2.348
Ocean Victor	1.179	ORPHEUS	2.341	PAMELA	2.348
OCEAN VICTOR	2.335	ORPHEUS II	2.342	PAMPONA	1.43
OCEAN VIEW	2.335	ORSAY	1.119	*Pamxon*	2.530
Ocean Vinca	2.63	ORSINO	2.342	PANORAMA	2.188
OCTAVIA	2.335	*Orsino*	2.445	PAPATERA	1.43
OCTOROON	2.335	ORTHOS	2.342	PARATI	1.43
Odin	1.113	ORVICTO	2.342	PARGO	1.43
OFFA	2.335	*Osako*	1.60	PARKMORE	2.348
OFFA II	2.336	OSAKO	2.342	PARRAMATA	2.348
Ofotfjord	1.94	OSBORNE STROUD	2.38, 2.342	PARTHIAN	2.348
Ogano	1.55	*Oseby*	1.66	PARTHIAN II	2.348
OGANO	2.336	OSIRIS III	2.343	PARU	1.43
Ohm	2.517	*Osprey II*	2.429	PARVATI	1.205
OHM	2.336	OSPREY II	2.343	*Pasages*	1.79
OKINO (1914)	2.336	OSPREY III	2.343	PASSEREAU	2.349
OKINO (1917)	2.336	*Ost*	1.214	PASSING	2.349
OKSAY (Norwegian)	1.115	OSTA	1.8, 2.343	*Pastoor Pype*	2.369
OKU (1916)	2.336	OSTERO	2.343	PAT CAHERTY	1.183
OKU (1939)	2.336	OSTRICH (1915)	2.344	PAT MERRYGAN	1.145
Olden Times	1.182	OSTRICH (1917)	2.344	PATNA	1.39
OLDEN TIMES	2.337	OSTRICH II	1.8, 2.344	PATRICIA CAM	2.349
OLDHAM	2.337	OSTRICH III	2.344	*Patricia Hague*	1.220
OLININA	2.337	OSWALDIAN	2.344	*Patricia Scullion*	1.169
OLIVE	1.197	OTHELLO (1941)	1.165	PATRICK BORROW	1.183
OLIVE IV	2.337	OTHELLO (1914)	2.344	PATRICK BOWE	1.69
OLIVE CAM	2.337	OTHELLO II	2.345	PATRICK CULLEN	1.69
OLIVER PICKIN	1.69	*Othello*	2.256	PATRICK DEVINE	1.183
Olvina	2.72	OTHONNA	2.345	PATRICK DONOVAN	1.69
OLIVINE	2.337	OTTILIE	2.345	PATRICK MITCHELL	1.145
OLYMPIA	2.338	*Ottoman Empire*	2.313	PATRIE	2.349
ONETOS	2.338	OTTOMAN EMPIRE	2.345	PATTI	2.349
Onslow	2.249	*Our Bairns*	1.59	*Paul*	1.211
ONTARIO	2.338	OUR BAIRNS	2.345	*Pauline*	2.134
ONWARD	2.338	*Our Tena*	2.147	PAULINE	2.350
ONWARD II	2.338	OUSE (1920)	1.145	PAUL RYKENS	2.350

Name	Ref	Name	Ref	Name	Ref
PAVLOVA	2.350	PETUNIA	2.356	POLO NORTE	2.363
PAYNTER	2.350	PETUNIA II	2.357	*Pollux*	2.511
PEARL (1899)	2.350	PETUNIA III	2.357	POMONA	2.363
PEARL (1913)	2.351	P. FANNON	2.357	POONA	1.40
PEARL (1935)	1.200	PHALAROPE	2.357	POONAH	2.364
PEARL II	2.351	PHILLIPE	2.357	PORCHER	1.119
PEARY	2.351	*Phillippe*	1.184	POTADOWN	2.364
Pedro	2.427	PHILLIP GODBY	1.70	PORTAFERRY	1.159, 2.364
PEGASUS	2.351	*Philippian*	1.74	PORT JACKSON	1.160
PEGGY NUTTEN	2.351	PHINEAS BEARD	1.70	PORTHLEVEN	1.160, 2.364
PEKEN	2.352	PHOEBE	2.357	PORT NATAL	1.160
PEKIN (1914)	1.183, 2.352	PHOEBE II	2.357	PORTIA	2.364
PEKIN (1919)	2.352	PHOEBE III	2.357	*Portia*	2.364
Pelagos	1.49	PHRONTIS	2.358	PORTIA III	2.364
PELAGOS (1916)	2.352	PHYLLIS	2.358	PORTISHAM	1.160, 2.364
PELAGOS (1940)	2.352	PHYLLIS BELMAN	2.358	PORT JACKSON (1917)	2.364
PELEGRIME	1.43	*Phyllisia*	1.147	PORT JACKSON (1942)	2.364
PELICAN	2.83, 2.352	PHYLLISIA	2.358	PORTMADOC	2.364
PELICAN II	2.353	*Phyllis Rosalie*	1.199	PORT NATAL	2.364
PELTON	2.353	*Pict*	2.139	PORTOBELLO	1.159, 2.364
PEMBROKE (1922)	1.133, 2.353	PICT	2.358	*Porto Norte*	1.159
PEMBROKE	1.145	*Picton Castle*	2.123	PORT PATRICK	1.159, 2.365
PEMBROKE CASTLE	2.353	PICTON CASTLE (1911)	2.358	PORTREATH	1.159, 2.365
PENELOPE	2.353	PICTON CASTLE (1928)	2.359	PORT ROYAL	1.159, 2.365
Penfret	1.63	*Pierre-Andre*	1.146	PORTRUSH	1.159, 2.365
Penguin	2.487	PIERRE ANDRE	1.146, 2.361	PORTSMOUTH	2.365
PENGUIN (1914)	2.353	*Piorre Francois Deswarte*	1.57	*Portush*	1.159
PENGUIN (1915)	2.353	PIERRE-GUSTAV	2.361	PORTSDOWN	1.103
PENGUIN II	2.354	PIGEON	2.361	PORT STANLEY	1.159, 2.365
Penn	2.420	PIGEON II	2.361	POSTBOY	2.365
Pennant Numbers	1.16	*Pilote 4*	1.141	POWIS CASTLE	2.365
PENNARD CASTLE	2.354	*Pilote 5*	1.136	PREFECT	2.365
PENRICE CASTLE	2.354	*Pilote Gironde*	1.83	PREMIER	2.366
PENTLAND FIRTH	1.18, 2.354	PINE	1.197	PRESIDENCY	2.366
PERCY BRETT	1.184	PINEWOLD	2.361	PRESIDENT	2.366
PERDRANT	2.354	PINTAIL	2.361	PRESIDENT BRAND	2.366
PERICLES	2.354	PIONEER	2.361	*President F.D. Roosevelt*	1.113
PERIDOT (1914)	2.355	PIROUETTE	1.95	*President Francqui*	1.52
PERIDOT (1939)	2.355	PITFOUR	1.8, 2.361	*President Rose*	1.213
PERIHELION	2.355	*Pitstruan*	1.181	PRESIDENT STEVENS	2.366
Perna	1.117	PITSTRUAN (1914)	2.362	PRESTON NORTH END	2.366
Perseus	2.222	PITSTRUAN (1940)	2.362	PRETORIA (1902)	2.367
PERSIAN EMPIRE	2355	PLADDA	1.119	PRETORIA (1906)	2.367
PERSIMMON	2.356	PLANUDES (Q Ship)	1.154	PRETORIA II	2.367
PESHAWAR	1.39	*Plassy*	1.164	PRIMROSE	2.367
PETER BLUMBERRY	1.70	PLETHOS	2.362	PRINCE CHARLES	2.367
PERTERBOROUGH	2.356	*Plico*	1.125	PRINCE CONSORT	2.367
PETER CAREY	1.70	PLYM	2.362	PRINCE de LIEGE	2.368
PETER DOBBIN	1.184	POCHARD	2.362	PRINCE LEO	2.368
PETER HALL	1.70	PODDLE (Polish)	1.140	PRINCE PALATINE	2.368
PETER HENDRICKS	2.356	POINTER	2.362	PRINCEPS	2.368
PETER HOFFMAN	1.145	POINTZ CASTLE	2.363	PRINCE VICTOR	2.368
Peterjon	1.164	POLAR PRINCE	2.363	PRINCESS ALICE	2.369
PETER JONES	1.145	POLEAXE	1.32	PRINCESS BEATRICE	2.369
PETER KILLIN	1.70	POLKA	1.95	PRINCESS JULIANA	2.369
PETER LOVITT	1.70	POLLACK	1.99	PRINCESS LOUISE (1914)	2.369
PETER MAGEE	1.145	*Polly Johnson*	1.59	PRINCESS LOUISE (1915)	2.369
PETREL	2.356	POLLY JOHNSON	2.363	PRINCESS LOUISE II	2.370

RESPONDO	2.388	R. IRVIN	2.394	ROBIN II	2.396
RESPONSO	2.388	RISKATO	2.394	*Robina*	2.172
RESTLESS	2.388	RISTANGO	2.394	ROBINA	2.396
RESTRIVO	2.388	*Ritsa*	2.458	ROBINIA	2.396
RETAKO	2.388	RIVER ANNAN	2.394	*Robitzsch*	1.213
RETIEVER	2.389	*River Ayr*	1.169	ROB ROY	2.396
RETRUDO	2.389	*River Clyde*	1.72	ROCHE BLEUE (French)	1.182
RETURNO	2.389	RIVER CLYDE	2.394	ROCHE BONNE	2.396
REVELLO	2.389	*River Dart*	1.33	ROCHE CASTLE	2.397
REVESBY	2.390	*River Don*	1.183	ROCHE FRANCOIS (French)	1.171
R.H. DAVIDSON	2.390	*River Earn*	1.175	ROCHE GRISE (French)	1.172
RHODESIA	2.390	*River Esk*	1.191	ROCHE NOIRE (French)	1.190
Rhodolite	1.73	RIVER ESK	2.394	ROCHESTER	2.397
RHONE	2.390	*River Findhorn*	1.175	*Roche Velan*	1.193
RIALTO	2.390	*River Forth*	1.67	ROCHE VELEN	2.397
RIANO	2.391	*River Garry*	1.177	*Rocro*	2.348
RIBBLE	2.391	RIVER GARRY	2.395	*Roderigo*	1.149
RIBBLE II	2.391	*River Kelvin*	1.172	RODINA	2.397
RIBY	2.391	*River Kent*	1.65	RODINO	2.397
RICHARD BACON	1.71	*River Leven*	1.178	RODNEY	2.397
RICHARD BAGLEY	1.71	RIVER LEVEN	2.395	RODNEY III	2.397
RICHARD BAIVE	1.71	*River Lossie*	1.168	RODOSTO	2.398
RICHARD BANE	1.71	RIVER LOSSIE	2.395	RODRIGO	2.398
RICHARD BENNETT	1.184	*River Ness*	1.170	*Roger*	2.447
RICHARD BETSON	1.72	RIVER NESS	2.395	ROLAND	2.398
RICHARD BOWDEN	1.184	*River Nith*	1.178	ROLANDO	2.398
RICHARD BRISCOLL	1.184	*River Orchy*	1.103	*Rollor*	2.07
RICHARD BULKELEY	1.145	*River Spey*	1.170	ROLLO	2.399
RICHARD CROFTS	1.72	RIVER SPEY	2.395	*Rolls Royce*	2.201
RICHARD CUNDY	1.72	*River Tay*	1.172	ROLLS ROYCE	2.399
RICHARD COLLIVER	1.146	*River Tummell*	1.188	ROLULO	2.399
RICHARD DORRODALE	1.146	*River Tweed*	1.186	ROMAN EMPIRE	2.399
RICHARD HEAVER	1.184	*River Ythan*	2.83	*Romanito*	1.83
RICHARD IRVIN	2.391	RIVER YTHAN	2.395	ROMANOFF	2.399
RICHARD JEWELL	1.146	RIVIERE	2.395	ROMEO	1.165
RICHARD ROBERTS	1.72	*Rizzio*	2.405	ROMILLY	2.399
RICHMOND	2.392	ROBERT BARTON	1.146	ROMULUS	2.400
RICHMOND CASTLE	2.392	ROBERT BETSON	1.72	RONALDSAY	2.120
RIFSNES	2.392	ROBERT BOOKLESS	1.146	RONAY	1.120
Righto	1.68	ROBERT BOWEN	1.72	RONDO	2.400
RIGHTO	2.392	ROBERT CAHILL	1.146	RONONIA	2.400
RIGOLETTO	2.392	ROBERT CLOUGHTON	1.72	RONSO	2.400
RILETTE	2.392	*Robert Crohn*	1.162	*Roode Zee*	2.48
RIMU	1.91	ROBERT DARBY	1.146	ROSA	2.400
RINALDO	2.393	ROBERT DAVIDSON	1.73	ROSALIND (1941)	1.165
RINALDO II	2.393	ROBERT DOUBLE	1.146	ROSALIND (1915)	2.401
Rino	1.125	ROBERT DRUMMOND	1.146	ROSALIND II	2.401
RINOVIA	2.393	ROBERT FAIRCLOTH	1.185	ROSARENO	2.401
RINTO	2.393	ROBERT FINLAY	1.147	ROSCO	2.401
Rio Douro	1.207	ROBERT GIBSON	1.185	ROSE (1910)	1.3, 2.401
Rio Guadiana	1.207	ROBERT HARDING	1.185	ROSE (1914)	2.401
Rio Lima	1.207	ROBERT HASTIE	2.395	ROSE (1915)	2.402
Rio Mesa	1.54	*Robert Hewitt*	1.220	ROSE II	2.402
Rio Minho	1.208	*Robert Limbrick*	1.162	ROSE IV	2.402
Rio Tejo	1.208	ROBERT MURRAY	1.147	ROSEBERY	2.402
Rio Vouga	1.209	ROBERT SMITH	2.396	*Rosedale Wyke*	1.135
RIPARVO	2.393	ROBERT STROUD	2.396	ROSEMONDE	2.402
RIPPLE	2.394	ROBIN	2.396	*Rose of England*	2.234

ROSE of ENGLAND	2.402	*St. Amant*	1.142	*St.Pierre*		2.349
Roseness	2.66	ST. ANDRONICUS	2.410	ST. PIERRE D'ALCANTAR (French)		
ROSETTA	2.403	*St. Anne*	1.115			1.137
ROSETTE	2.403	ST. APOLLO	2.410	*St. Pierre —St. Paul*		1.70
ROSEVEAN	1.120	*St.Arcadius*	2.216	*St. Romanus*		1.221
ROSSKEEN	2.403	ST. ARCADIUS	2.410	*St. Rose*		1.221
ROSY MORN	2.403	*St.Attalus*	2.249	*St. Stephen*		1.221
ROTHER	1.147, 2.403	ST. ATTALUS	2.410	*St. Valery*		2.531
Rotherslade	1.65	*St. Barnaby*	1.66	ST. VINCENT		2.418
ROTHERSLADE	2.403	ST BASTILE (French)	1.102	ST. VINCENT II		2.418
ROTO	2.403	ST. CATHAN	1.18, 2.411	ST. WISTAN		2.418
ROTTERDAM	2.404	ST. CELESTIN	2.411	ST. ZENO	1.18,	2.418
ROUSAY	1.120	ST. CLAIR	2.411	SAINT BENOIT (French)		1.132
Rover	1.214	ST. CLOUD	2.412	SAINTE-PIERRE II		2.419
ROWAN	1.197	ST. CUTHBERT	2.412	*Saiph*		2.66
ROWSAY	2.404	ST. CYR	2.412	SALACON		2.419
ROWSLEY	2.404	ST. DENIS	2.412	SALOME		2.419
ROXANO	2.404	ST. DONATS	2.412	SALSETTE		1.73
ROYALIST	2.404	*St. Elmo*	2.300	*Saltaire*		1.186
ROYALLIEU	2.405	ST. ELMO	2.413	SALTARELO		1.96
Royal Marine	1.102	ST. ELOI	1.29	SALVADOR CORREIA (Portuguese)		
ROYAL MARINE	1.157	ST. ELSTAN	2.413			1.96
ROYALO	2.405	*St. Endellion*	1.140	SALVINI		2.419
Royal Regiment	1.147	*St. Georg*	1.212	*Salvo*		1.125
R.R.S.	2.405	ST. GERMAIN	2.413	*Samba*		1.197
Rubato	2.448	*St. Gerontius*	1.220	SAMUEL BAKER		1.185
RUBENS	2.405	ST. GORAN	2.413	SAMUEL BARKAS		1.185
Ruby	1.64	*St. Gothard*	2.31	SAMUEL BENBOW		1.185
RUBY (1935)	1.200	ST. GOTHARD	2.413	SAMUEL CUNNINGHAM		1.185
RUBY (1915)	2.405	ST. HUBERT	2.413	SAMUEL DAWSON		1.73
RUBY (1916)	2.406	*St. Irene*	1.220	SAMUEL DOWDEN		1.147
Rudilais	1.71	ST. IVES	2.414	SAMUEL DRAKE		1.73
RUDILAIS	2.406	ST. JAN BERCHMANS	2.414	SAMUEL GASBY		1.186
RUFF	2.406	ST. JOHNS	2.414	SAMUEL GREEN		1.73
RUGBY	2.406	ST. JULIEN	1.29	SAMUEL HAMPTON		1.186
RUGBY II	2.406	*St Just*	2.168	SAMUEL JAMESON		1.147
RUMBA	1.95	ST. KATHERINE	2.414	SAMUEL LOVITT		1.186
RUNSWICK BAY	2.406	ST. KENAN	2.414	SAMUEL MARTIN		1.147
RUPERT	2.407	*St. Keverne*	1.144	SAMUEL SPENCER		1.73
RUSHCOE	2.407	ST. KILDA (1917)	2.415	SAMURAI		2.419
RUSKHOLM	1.120	ST. KILDA (1942)	2.530	SANDA		1.121
Russell	2.407	ST. LAWRENCE	2.415	SANDMARTIN		2.420
RUSSELL II	1.8, 2.407	ST. LAWRENCE No. 1	2.415	SANDRAY		1.121
RUTHIN CASTLE	2.407	ST. LEONARD	2.415	SANDRINGHAM (1914)		2.420
RUTLANDSHIRE	2.408	ST. LEONARD II	2.415	SANDRINGHAM (1939)		2.420
Rylston	1.56, 2.479	ST. LOMAN	1.18, 2.416	SANGARIUS		2.420
RYSA	1.120	ST. LOUIS	2.416	*San Juan*		1.73
		ST. LUCIA	2.417	*San Pedro*		1.177
S-81, E-Boat (German)	1.199	ST. MALO	2.417	SANSERIT		2.420
Sabina	1.169	ST. MAURICE	1.8, 2.417	SANSON		2.420
SABINA	2.409	ST. MELANTE	2.417	SANSONNET		2.421
SABINE	2.409	*St. Merryn*	2.448	*Santa Cristina*		2.489
SABREUR	2.409	*St. Minver*	1.144	SANTA MARIA (Portuguese)		1.126
ST. ACHILLEUS	2.409	ST. MINVER	2.418	*Santa Rosa*		2.450
ST. AGNES (1943)	1.121	ST. NECTAN	2.418	*Santa Teolinda*		2.430
ST. AGNES (1914)	2.409	*St. Olive*	2.320	*Santander*		1.78
St. Alexandra	1.219	ST. OLIVE	2.418	*Santiago Rusinol*		1.51
ST. AMANDUS	2.409	*St. Oswald*	1.202	*Santini*		1.148

Sletnes	2.196	Stanfrel	1.70	STONECHAT	1.42
S.L.Haldane	2.113	STANLEY WEYMAN	2.450	Stoneferry	1.136
SLUNA	1.122	Star of England	1.212	STONEFLY	2.458
SMEW	2.443	STAR of BRITAIN	2.451	Storess	1.133
SNAKEFLY	2.444	STAR of DEVORAN	2.451	STORMCENTRE	1.133, 2.458
S. Nicola	1.49	Star of Freedom (1917)	1.207	STORMCOCK (1917)	2.458
SNIPE	2.444	Star of Freedom (1946)	1.162	STORMCOCK (1939)	2.458
Snorri Sturluson	1.138	STAR of FREEDOM (1915)	2.451	STORNAWAY	2.458
SOAR	2.444	STAR of FREEDOM (1939)	2.451	STOUR	1.133, 2.458
SOLDIER PRINCE	2.444	STAR of HOPE	2.451	STRATHAFTON	2.458
SOLOMON	2.444	Star of Liberty	1.177	STRATHAIRLIE	2.458
SOLON (1914)	2.444	STAR of LIBERTY	2.451	STRATHALLADALE	2.460
SOLON (1939)	2.445	Star of Moray	2.339	Strathallen	1.71
Sollum	1.103	STAR of ORKNEY	2.451	STRATHALLEN	2.460
Solva	2.5	STAR of PEACE	2.451	STRATHALVA	2.460
Solway Firth	2.148	STAR of PENTLAND	2.452	STRATHATHOLL	2.460
Somersby	1.77	Star of Scotland	1.190	STRATHAVON	2.460
SOMERVILLE	2.445	STAR of the EAST	2.453	STRATHBLANE	2.461
SONNEBLOM	1.141, 2.445	STAR of the EMPIRE	2.453	Strathborne	2.461
Sonntag	1.214	STAR of the ISLES	2.453	STRATHBORVE	2.461
Sophie	1.213	Star of the North	1.162	STRATHBRAN	2.461
Sophie Busse	2.144	STAR of the NORTH	2.453	STRATHCARRON	2.461
SOPHOS	2.445	STAR of the OCEAN	2.453	STRATHCLOVA	2.461
SOPHRON	2.445	Star of the Orient	1.210	STRATHCLUNIE	2.461
SORANUS	2.446	Star of the Realm	1.151	STRATHCOE	1.8, 2.462
Soubrette	1.186	STAR of the REALM	2.453	STRATHDEE	2.462
SOUBRETTE	2.446	Star of the South	1.162	STRATHDERRY	2.462
Southcoates	1.73	STAR of the SOUTH	2.454	STRATHDEVON	2.462
SOUTHCOATES	2.446	STAR of the WAVE	2.454	STRATHDON	2.463
SOUTH SEA	2.446	Start Point	1.50	STRATHEARN	2.463
SOUTHWARD	2.446	STAUNCH	2.454	STRATHEBRIE	2.463
Southward Ho	2.531	STAUNTON	2.454	STRATHEDEN	2.463
SOUTHWARD HO	2.446	Staxton Wyke	2.249	STRATHELLA	2.463
Spaniard	1.103	STEAMAXE	1.33	STRATHELLIOT	2.464
SPANIARD	2.446	STEEPHOLM	1.123	STRATHERRICK	2.464
SPARROW	1.3, 2.446	Steinfrost	2.359	STRATHFINELLA	2.464
SPARTAN	2.446	Stelios	1.122	STRATHGAIRN	2.465
SPEEDWELL	2.447	STELLA CANOPUS	2.454	STRATHGARRY (1906)	2.465
SPEETON	2.447	Stella Capella	1.103	STRATHGARRY (1924)	2.465
SPHENE	2.447	STELLA CAPELLA	2.454	STRATHGELDIE	2.465
SPIDER (1909)	1.3, 2.447	Stella Carina	1.103	Strathglass	1.181
SPIDER (1915)	2.447	STELLA CARINA	2.455	STRATHISLA	2.465
Spika	2.31	STELLA DORADO	2.456	STRATHISLA II	2.465
SPINDRIFT	2.447	STELLA LEONIS	2.456	STRATHLEE	2.466
SPINET	2.448	Stella Orion	1.157	STRATHLETHEN	2.466
Splies	1.149	STELLA ORION	2.456	STRATHLOCHY	2.466
SPRAY	2.448	STELLA PEGASI	2.456	STRATHLOSSIE	2.466
Springbok	1.136	Stella Pegasis	2.456	STRATHLUI	2.466
SPRINGWELL	2.448	STELLA POLARIS	1.18, 2.456	STRATHMAREE	2.466
SPURS	2.449	STELLA RIGEL	2.457	STRATHMARTIN	2.467
STAFFA	1.123	STELLA SIRIUS	2.457	STRATHMORAY	2.467
STAFNES	2.449	STEPHEN FOLEY	1.148	STRATHNETHY	2.467
STALBERG	2.449	STEPHEN KENNEY	1.186	STRATHORD	2.467
STALKER	2.450	STEWART BOYLE	2.457	Strathrannoch	1.174
Stalwart	1.144	STOCKADE.	2.457	STRATHRANNOCH	2.467
STALWART	2.450	Stockham	2.241	STRATHRANNON	2.468
STALWART II	2.450	STOKE CITY	2.457	STRATHRYE	2.468
STANDARD	2.450	STONEAXE	1.33	STRATHSPEY	2.468

STRATHTUMMEL	2.468	SWITHA	1.124
STRATHUGIE	2.468	SWORD DANCE	1.96
STRATHURIE	2.468	SYCAMORE	1.221
Strathyre	1.220	*Sydnelsie*	2.286
Strato	1.50	SYLPHET	1.40
STRATON	2.469	SYLVIA	2.474
STRENUOUS	2.469	*Syrian*	1.149
STREPHON	2.469	SYRIAN (1939)	2.474
STROMA	1.123	SYRIAN (1940)	2.474
STROMO	2.469	SYRINGA (1935)	1.222
Stromness	2.307	SYRINGA (1914)	2.474
STRONSAY (1942)	1.123	SYRINGA II	2.474
STRONSAY (1915)	2.469		
Struan	1.191	T. 6 (Russian)	1.32
STRYMON (Greek)	1.135	T. 12 (Russian)	1.33
STRYMON	2.469	T. 14 (Russian)	1.33
Sturdee	1.183	T. 17 (Russian)	1.32
STURDEE	2.470	T. 19 (Russian)	1.32
STURTON	2.470	T. 20 (Russian)	1.33
Stuttgart	1.214	T. 31 (Russian)	1.33
SUCCESSFUL	2.470	T. 33 (Russian)	1.32
SUCCESSION	2.470	T. 34 (Russian)	1.31
SULBY	2.470	*Table Bay*	1.83
SUMA (1917)	2.470	TACSONIA	2.475
SUMA (1939)	2.471	TAGALIE	2.475
Sumatra	1.220	TAHAY	1.124
SUNBEAM IV	2.471	*Taiaora*	1.92
SUNBURST	2.471	*Taipo*	2.170
SUNCLOUD	2.471	TAIPO (1915)	2.475
Sung Hwei	1.114	TAIPO (1939)	2.475
Sung Li	1.37	TALLY HO	2.475
Sunlight	1.189	*Tamora*	1.88
SUNLIGHT (1917)	2.471	TAMORA	2.475
SUNLIGHT (1939)	2.471	TAMURA	2.475
SUNRISE (1917)	2.471	TANAGER	2.476
SUNRISE (1940)	2.145	TANGO	1.97
SUNSHINE	2.472	TANJORE (1941)	1.67, 2.476
SUNSPOT	2.472	TANJORE (1914)	2.476
Supply Vessels	1.22	TARANA	2.476
SUREAXE	1.33	TARANAKI	2.476
Surinam	1.125	TARANTELLA	1.97
SURSAY	1.124	TARTAN	2.476
SUSARION	2.472	TARTARIN	2.477
SUTHERNES	2.472	TASMANIA	2.477
Suzette	1.170	TAURUS	2.477
SUZETTE	2.472	TAWHAI	1.91
Sverrehund	1.118	TAYMOUTH	2.477
SWALLOW (H. 97)	2.472	TAYSIDE	2.477
SWALLOW (A.76)	2.472	*Teal*	2.295
SWALLOW (1900)	2.473	TEAL (1914)	2.477
SWALLOW II	2.473	TEAL (1940)	2.477
SWAN	2.473	TEAZER	2.91
SWAN III	2.473	*Tees Bay*	1.76
Swanland	2.235	TEHANA	2.478
Swansea Castle	1.100	TEKOURA	2.478
SWANSEA CASTLE	2.473	*Temehani*	1.154
SWEEPER	2.474	TENBY	2.478
Swift	2.374	*Tenby Castle*	2.425

TENBY CASTLE		2.479
Tenedos		1.51
TERCEIRA (Portuguese)		1.114
TERN		2.479
Ternoise		1.148
Teroma		1.56
TEROMA		2.479
TERRIER		2.479
Tervani		2.381
TERVANI (1914)		2.479
TERVANI (1939)		2.479
TEST		1.69
TEST		2.480
TETTENHALL		2.480
TEUTON		2.480
TEVIOT	1.172,	2.480
Tewera		2.480
TEXADA		1.124
Texas		2.480
THEIPVAL		1.29
THANET		2.480
THEBAN		2.480
The Banyers		2.36
THE BANYERS		2.481
The Bruce		1.139
Their Merit		1.81
THEIR MERIT		2.481
THE NORMAN		1.8, 2.481
Theophile Massart		1.74
Thermo		1.109
THE ROMAN		2.481
THE TETRARCH		2.481
The Tower		1.188
THE TOWER		2.482
THERESA BOYLE		2.482
THEWAY		2.482
TIMOTHY CRAWLEY		2.530
THISTLE (1914)		2.482
THISTLE (FD. 226)		2.482
THISTLE (LL. 64)		2.482
THISTLE IV		2.483
THOMAS ADNEY		1.74
THOMAS ALEXANDER		1.74
THOMAS ALLEN		1.74
THOMAS ALTOFT		1.74
THOMAS ANSELL		1.186
THOMAS ATKINSON		2.530
THOMAS BAILEY		2.531
THOMAS BARCLAY		1.186
THOMAS BARTLETT		1.74
THOMAS BILLINGCOLE		1.186
THOMAS BIRD		1.186
THOMAS BOOTH		1.75
THOMAS BOMKWORTH		2.483
THOMAS BOUDIGE		1.75
THOMAS BRAUND		1.187
THOMAS BRYAN		1.187
THOMAS BUCKLEY		1.187

Name	Ref	Name	Ref	Name	Ref
THOMAS BURNHAM	1.187	TIREE	1.124	TRICHONOPOLY	1.40
THOMAS CALTRAFFE	1.187	*Titania*	2.344	*Tridente*	1.95
THOMAS CHAMBERS	1.75	*Tithorn*	1.115	TRIER	2.489
THOMAS CLAYTON	1.187	*Tito*	2.297	*Tristania*	1.195
THOMAS COLLARD	1.187	TOBAGO	2.484	TRITELIA	2.489
THOMAS CONNOLLY	1.75	*Tobruk*	2.	TRITON	2.489
THOMAS COPSEY	1.187	TOCOGAY	1.125	TRODDAY	1.125
THOMAS CORNWALL	2.531	TOCSIN	2.484	TROGON	2.489
THOMAS COWELL	2.531	*Togimo*	1.71	TROJAN	2.489
THOMAS CROFTON	1.75	TOKIO	2.484	TROJAN II	2.489
THOMAS CRUIZE	2.531	TOKIO II	2.485	TROMOY (Norwegian)	1.110, 1.118
THOMAS CURR	1.187	TOKYO II	2.485	TROMOY (Norwegian)	2.490
THOMAS CURRELL	1.188	TOM MOORE	2.485	TRONDRA	1.125
THOMAS DANIELS	1.76	TOM TIT	2.485	*Trondur-I-Gottu*	1.222
THOMAS DEAR	1.188	TONGKOL	2.485	TROOPER	1.154
THOMAS DEAS	2.483	*Toni*	1.213	TRUMPETER	2.490
THOMAS DENNISON	1.188	TOPAZ (H.511)	2.485	TRYGON	2.490
THOMAS DOWDING	1.76	TOPAZ (H. 307)	2.486	*Tubal Cain*	2.220
THOMAS EVISON	1.188	TOPAZE	1.201	TUGELA	2.490
THOMAS FOLEY	1.188	*Toran*	1.105	TUI	1.128
THOMAS GOBLE	1.76	TORFRIDA	2.486	*Tulipbank*	1.119
THOMAS GOODCHILD	1.188	TORNADO	2.486	*Tulipdale*	1.116
THOMAS GRAHAM	1.188	TORNADO II	2.486	*Tulipglen*	1.119
THOMAS GREEN	1.76	TORONTO	2.486	*Tumby*	1.180
THOMAS HAGGERTY	1.189	*Totton*	1.165	TUMBY	2.490
THOMAS HANKINS	1.76	TOUCHSTONE	2.486	TUNISIAN	2.490
THOMAS HENRIX	1.189	TOURACO	2.487	TURBOT	1.42, 1.100, 2.491
THOMAS JAGO	2.531	TOURMALINE (1935)	1.201	*Turcoman*	1.74
THOMAS JERVIS	2.532	TOURMALINE (1916)	2.487	TURCOMAN	1.102, 2.491
THOMAS JOHNS	2.532	*Tourmaline*	2.498	*Turoy*	1.115
THOMAS LAUNDRY	1.76	TOWHEE	2.487	TURQUOISE (1917)	2.491
THOMAS LAVERICKS	1.189	TR.1 – TR.5	1.77	TURQUOISE (1935)	1.202
THOMAS LAWRIE	1.77	TR.6 – TR.11	1.78	TUSCAN	2.491
THOMAS LEEDS	1.77	TR.12 – TR.21	1.79	TWOSTEP (1943)	1.97
THOMAS MALONEY	2.532	TR.22 – TR.33	1.80	TWOSTEP (1943)	2.491
THOMAS MATTHEWS	2.532	TR.34 – TR.41	1.81	TYNDRUM	2.491
THOMAS ROBINS	1.77	TR.42 – TR.50	1.82	*Tynemouth Castle*	1.192
THOMAS STRATTON	2.483	TR.51 – TR.60	1.83	TYNE PRINCE	2.491
THOMAS SUTTON	2.483	*Tranio*	1.53	TYNE WAVE	2.492
THOMAS THRESHER	2.532	TRANIO	2.287	TYPHOON (ex-SYRIAN))	1.149
THOMAS TWINEY	1.77	*Transportador*	2.484	TYPHOON (1940)	2.492
THOMAS WHIPPLE	2.533	*Transport Union*	1.70	*Tyrwhitt*	1.168
THOMAS W. IRVIN	2.483	TRANQUIL	2.186		
THOMAS YOUNG	2.483	TRANSVAAL	1.22	U-15	2.386
Thor	1.121	TRANSVAAL	2.487	U-16	2.421
Thora	2.135	TRAVE (W. German)	1.112	U-33	2.432
THORNEY	2.484	TRAVENCORE	1.40	U-46	2.150, 2.315, 2.338
Thracian	2.49	*Trawler Prince*	1.87	U-49	2.150, 2.315, 2.338
THRIFTY	2.484	TRENT	2.488	U-52	2.150, 2.315, 2.338
THRUSH IV	2.484	TRENT II	2.488	U-59	2.285, 2.516
Thrush	2.13	*Tres*	1.32	U-62	2.150
Thuringia	1.157	*Tresco*	2.484	U-69	2.150, 2.315,2.338
Tilbury Ness	1.66	TREVO TERCEIRO	2.488	U-94	2.326
TILBURYNESS	2.484	T.R. FERANS (1915)	2.488	U-105	2.414
Tilsitt	2.123	T.R. FERANS (1939)	2.488	U-111	2.250
TIMOTHY BRANNON	1.189	*T.R. Ferans*	1.52	U-201	1.165
TINA NUTTEN	2.484	TRIBUNE	2.488	U-203	2.402
TIRADE	2.484	TRIBUNE II	2.489	U-215	2.256

U-371	1.115	VALE of CLYDE	2.496	*Victory*	2.505
U-374	2.250	VALE of FORTH	2.496	VICTRIX (1915)	2.505
U-452	2.500	VALE of FRUIN	2.496	VICTRIX (1939)	2.505
U-521	1.102	VALE of LENNOX	2.497	VIDAL de NEGREIROS	(Brazilian)
U-542	2.506	VALE of LEVEN	2.497		1.43
U-547	1.102	VALERIA	2.497	VIDETTE	2.505
U-551	2.500	*Valerie W*	1.190	VIDETTE II	2.505
U-552	2.11	VALESCA	2.497	VIDONIA	2.505
U-558	2.39	VALLAY	1.126	VIERNOE	2.506
U-564	2.500	VALMONT	2.497	*Vigilant*	1.106
U-605	2.54	VALPA	2.498	VIGILANT (1914)	2.506
U-570	2.237	VALSE	1.97	VIGILANT (1917)	2.506
U-701	2.455	VAMBERY	2.498	VIGILANT II	2.506
U-714	2.474	*Vanda*	2.447	*Vigilant II*	2.506
U-731	2.52	VAN DYCK	2.498	VIGRA	2.506
U-732	2.210	VAN OOST	2.498	VIKING BANK	2.506
U-979	2.328	VAN ORLEY	2.499	*Viking Deeps*	2.496
U-1009	2.197	VARANGA	2.499	VIKING DEEPS	2.506
UAD LUCAS (Spanish)	1.47	VARANIS	2.499	VIKINGS	2.506
UAD MARTIN (Spanish)	1.62	*Vardberg*	1.218	VILDA	2.507
UAD MULUYA (Spanish)	1.57	*Varel*	1.215	VIMY	1.29
UAD QUER, (Spanish)	1.131	VASCAMA	2.499	*Vinca*	1.207
UAD RAS	1.60	VASCO DA GAMA	2.500	VINDELICIA	2.507
UAD TARGA (Spanish)	1.69	VATERSAY	1.126	*Vingtor*	1.117
UBIER (German)	2.408	VELETA	1.97	*Vinur*	2.61
UGIE BANK	2.493	*Velia*	2.443	VIOLA	2.507
UHDEA	2.493	VELIA	2.500	VIOLA II	2.508
UIVER	2.493	*Velox*	1.107	VIOLA III	2.508
Ulleswater	2.299	VENATOR	2.500	VIOLET CAIE	2.508
ULSTER	2.493	VENETIA III	2.500	VIREO	2.508
Ulva	1.105	VENOSTA	2.500	VIRGINIAN	2.508
ULVA	1.125	VENTOSE	2.501	VIRGINIAN II	2.508
ULYSSES	2.493	VENTURE	2.501	*Viscount Allenby*	1.147
ULYSSES II	2.493	*Venus*	2.498	*Viscount Grey*	1.137
Una	1.33	VERA	2.501	VISENDA	2.509
UNDAUNTED	2.493	VERA GRACE	2.501	VITALITY	2.509
UNICORN	2.494	VERBENA	2.501	*Vitin*	2.439
Union	1.164	VERBENA II	2.502	VIVANTI	2.509
UNITIA	2.494	VERCHERES	2.502	VIVIANA	2.509
UNST	1.126	VERESIS	2.502	VIZALMA	2.509
URANA	2.494	VIRGEN DEL CARMEN	2.450	VIZGAPATAM	1.40
URANIA (1914)	2.494	VERNON	2.462	VJ 6078 (German)	2.411
URANIA (1941)	2.494	VERNON (1938)	2.503	VOLANTE	2.510
URE	2.494	*Veslemoy*	1.105	*Volen*	1.96
URIE	2.495	VESPER	2.503	VOLESUS	2.510
URKA	2.495	VESPER III	2.503	*Vollen*	1.196
Utstraum	2.359	VESTA	2.503	VOLTA	2.510
UVULARIA	2.495	*Vesturskin*	2.196	VOLUNTEER	2.510
		VICTOR (A.511)	2.503	VONOLEL	2.510
Vaagness	1.159	VICTOR (PD.75)	2.503	*Vouri*	1.126
VACEASAY	1.126	VICTOR II	2.503	VPG 111 FRANKE (German)	2.252
VAILLANT	2.496	VICTORIA	2.503	VULCAN (1936)	2.510
Valafell	1.99	VICTORIA II	2.504	VULTURE	2.511
Valdora	2.485	*Victoria Laura*	1.207	VULTURE II	2.511
VALDORA	2.496	VICTORIAN	2.504		
Valentia	1.81	VICTORIAN II	2.504	WAIAU	1.91
VALENTIA	2.496	VICTORIAN PRINCE	2.504	WAIHO	1.91
VALENTINE BOWER	1.84	VICTORIA REGINA	2.504	WAIITI	1.92

WAIKAKA	1.92	*Westhill*	1.220	WILLIAM CASTLE	1.191
WAIKANAE	1.92	WESTHOLME	2.518	WILLIAM CHALMERS	1.191
WAIKATO	1.92	*Westhope*	2.241	WILLIAM CHASEMAN	1.86
WAIMA	1.92	*Westlyn*	2.90	WILLIAM CHATWOOD	1.148
WAIPU	1.92	WESTLYN	2.519	WILLIAM COBURNE	1.87
WAKAKURA	1.92	WESTRAY (1917)	2.519	WILLIAM COGSWELL	1.191
WALDORF	2.512	WESTRAY (1941)	1.126	WILLIAM CORAN	1.87
WALLACE	2.512	*Westray Firth*	2.507	WILLIAM COURTNEY	1.148
WALLENA	2.512	WESTWARD HO	2.519	WILLIAM COWLING	1.87
WALLASEA	1.126	WESTWARD HO II	2.519	WILLIAM CUMMINS	1.87
WALLINGTON	2.512	WEYMOUTH II	2.519	WILLIAM DARNOLD	1.87
WALNUT	1.197	WHALSAY	1.126	WILLIAM DOAK	1.148
WALPOLE	2.512	*Wheatstone*	1.181	WILLIAM DOCHERTY	1.148
Walpole	2.516	W.H. HASTIE	2.519	WILLIAM DONALDS	1.148
WALPOLE II	2.513	WHITBY	2.519	WILLIAM DOWNES	1.87
Walsingham	2.385	WHITE CAP	2.520	WILLIAM DRAKE	1.87
WALTER BURKE	1.84	WHITE EAR	2.520	WILLIAM FALL	1.191
WALTER CAVE	1.84	WHITE FRIAR	2.520	*William Fenton*	1.108
WALTER S. BAILEY	2.513	*White Nile*	2.60	WILLIAM FERRINS	1.191
WALTHAM	2.513	WHITE QUEEN	2.520	WILLIAM FLEMING	1.87
WALWYNS CASTLE	2.513	WHITETHROAT (1944)	1.126	WILLIAM FORBES	1.149
WARBLER	2.513	WHITETHROAT (1918)	2.520	WILLIAM FORD	1.49
Wardour	2.417	WHITETHORN	1.197	WILLIAM GIBBONS	1.192
WARDOUR	2.513	WHITING	1.100	WILLIAM GILLETT	1.192
WAR DUKE	2.514	WHOOPER	2.520	WILLIAM GRIFFIN	1.192
WAR GREY	2.514	W.H. PODD	2.520	WILLIAM GRIFFITHS	1.88
WARLAND	2.514	WIAY	1.127	WILLIAM HALLETT	1.192
WAR LORD	2.514	WIGAN	2.521	WILLIAM HANBURY	1.193
WARRIOR II	2.515	WILD ROSE	2.521	WILLIAM HANNAM	1.88
WAR STAR	2.515	WILLET	2.521	WILLIAM HARRISON	1.193
WATER PRIORY	2.515	WILLIAM ABRAHAMS	1.148	WILLIAM HARVEY	1.193
Warwick Deeping	2.248	WILLIAM ALLEN	2.521	WILLIAM H. HASTIE	2.521
WARWICK DEEPING	2.515	WILLIAM ASHTON	1.189	WILLIAM HONNOR	1.149
Warwickshire	1.202	*William Ashton*	1.189	WILLIAM HUMPHREYS	1.88
WARWICKSHIRE	2.515	WILLIAM BARLOW	1.189	WILLIAM HUTCHINSON	1.193
WAR WING	2.516	WILLIAM BARNETT	1.190	WILLIAM INWOOD	1.149
WASHINGTON	2.516	WILLIAM BARROW	1.190	WILLIAQM IVEY	1.193
WATERFLY	2.516	WILLIAM BEATTY	1.84	WILLIAM JACKSON	1.149
WAVEFLOWER	2.516	WILLIAM BEAUMONT	1.190	WILLIAM JOHNSON	1.149
WAVENEY	2.517	WILLIAM BEETON	1.84	WILLIAM JONES	1.149
WAYNEFLETE	2.517	WILLIAM BELL	1.84	WILLIAM KING	1.193
WEAR	2.517	WILLIAM BENNETT	1.85	WILLIAM KNIGHT	1.88
WEAZEL	2.517	WILLIAM BENTLEY	1.190	WILLIAM LAMBKIN	1.88
WEIGELIA	2.517	WILLIAM BIGGS	1.190	WILLIAM LEECH	1.150
WELBECK (1915)	1.8, 2.517	WILLIAM BODY	1.85	*William Leech*	1.150
WELBECK (1940)	2.517	WILLIAM BOND	1.190	WILLIAM LEEK	1.88
Welbeck	1.151	WILLIAM BOREHAM	1.191	WILLIAM LOFT	1.88
WELLARD	1.18, 2.517	WILLIAM BROWIS	1.85	WILLIAM MAINLAND	1.150
WELLSBACH	2.518	WILLIAM BROWNING	1.191	WILLIAM MANNELL	1.89
Wellvale	1.80	WILLIAM BUNCE	1.85	WILLIAM MARSHALL	1.150
WEMYSS	2.518	WILLIAM BURTE	1.85	WILLIAM MOIRIS	1.150
Werner Felter	1.196	WILLIAM BUTLER	1.191	WILLIAM MORRIS	1.150
West	1.215	WILLIAM CABLE	1.85	WILLIAM MORRISON	2.522
WESTELLA	2.518	WILLIAM CALDWELL	1.86	WILLIAM MORTON	1.150
WESTERN EXPLORER	2.518	WILLIAM CALE	1.86	WILLIAM MUCK	1.150
Westhawk	2.114	WILLIAM CARBERRY	1.86	WILLIAM PURDY	2.522
Westhaze	2.20	WILLIAM CARR	1.86	WILLIAM RAM	1.150
Westheron	2.223	WILLIAM CARRICK	1.86	WILLIAM RIVERS	1.151

WILLIAM SPENCER	1.89	WRANGLER	2.489	Yolanda	1.183
William Stephen	1.182	Wreck Dispersal	1.22	YORICK	2.527
WILLIAM STEPHEN	2.522	WREN	2.524	YORK CITY	2.527
WILLIAM STROUD	2.522	WRENTHORPE	2.525	Ypapandi	1.114
WILLAIM SYMONS	1.89	W.S. Bailey	2.513	YPRES	1.29
WILLIAM WESNEY	2.522	W.S. BURTON	2.525	YTHAN BRAES	2.527
WILLIAM WESTENBURGH	1.151	Wulkan	2.295	YUCCA	2.528
WILLIAM WILLMOT	1.89	Wulsdorf	1.212	YULAN	2.528
WILLONYX	2.522	Wurzburg	1.211	Yvonne Claude	1.80
WILLOW	1.222	Wyberton	1.183		
WIMPOLE	2.523	WYNDHAM	2.525	Zapad	1.33
Windshift	2.523	Wyoming	2.502	ZAREBA	2.528
Windsor	1.32	WYOMING	2.525	ZENA DARE	2.528
WINDSOR	2.523	Wyre	2.170	Zencon	1.54
WINDSOR II	2.523	WYRE	2.525	ZENNOR	2.528
WINDWARD HO	2.523	Wyre British	2.61	Zero	1.108
Winooka	2.433	Wyre Corsair	1.71	ZETLAND	2.528
WISTARIA (1915)	2.523	Wyre General	2.139	Zircon	1.54
WISTARIA (1939)	1.197	Wyre Mariner	2.83	ZODIAC II	2.528
WISTARIA II	2.523	Wyre Monitor	2.241	ZONIA	2.529
Witham	1.186	Wyre Warrior	2.518	ZWART ZEE	2.529
WITHAM	2.524	Wyre Woolton	1.202		
WITHERNSEA	2.524				
Wodan	1.113	XANIA	2.526		
WOLBOROUGH	2.524	Xaun	1.136		
WOLSELEY	2.524	XERXES	2.526		
WOLVES	2.524	XYLOPIA	2.526		
Womersley	2.417				
WOODAXE	1.33	YASHIMA	2.526		
Woodburn	1.56	YESSO (1914)	2.526		
Woodbury	2.201	YESSO (1939)	2.526		
WOODS	2.524	YESTOR	1.103		
Woolton	1.202	YEZO	2.527		
WORSLEY	2.524	YMUIDEN	2.527		
Wostock	1.32	YOKOHAMA	2.527		